Bruns Wal...

55 Greenfield Cr.

St Albert, Alta.

THE LAW AND BUSINESS ADMINISTRATION IN CANADA

Third Edition

J. E. Smyth
Department of Political Economy
University of Toronto

D. A. Soberman
Faculty of Law
Queen's University

Prentice-Hall of Canada, Ltd.
Scarborough, Ontario

Canadian Cataloguing in Publication Data

Smyth, James E., 1920-
　The law and business administration
in Canada

Bibliography: p.
Includes index.
ISBN 0-13-526319-0

1. Commercial law—Canada. I. Soberman,
D.A., 1929-　　II. Title.

346'.71'07　　C76-017004-5

Prentice-Hall, Inc., Englewood Cliffs, *New Jersey*
Prentice-Hall International, Inc., *London*
Prentice-Hall of Australia, Pty., Ltd., *Sydney*
Prentice-Hall of India Pvt., Ltd., *New Delhi*
Prentice-Hall of Japan, Inc., *Tokyo*
Prentice-Hall of Southeast Asia (PTE.) Ltd., *Singapore*

ISBN 0-13-526319-0

3　4　5　JD　80　79　78　77

PRINTED AND BOUND IN CANADA

Preface to the First Edition

The law of business administration is not a precisely defined body of law; its apparent boundaries are often determined by the special interests of those who · come to study it. On the other hand, to insist that the subject embraces *all* the law affecting the administration of business enterprises is to ask for an encyclopedia of law, for a modern business may encounter virtually every kind of legal problem at one time or another. As a result, we have had to make a value judgment about which topics are most important and about the extent of the treatment we should give to each; the contents of this book are unavoidably a reflection of these preferences.

Undoubtedly there are other topics worthy of consideration in a book on law and business administration—such topics, for example, as copyrights, patents, and trademarks, wills, estate planning, criminal law, and the operation of administrative tribunals. In addition, some might prefer a more exhaustive treatment of one or more of the areas of labour law, combines legislation, the law of negotiable instruments, and the law of tort. We have chosen to confine the contents of the book to their present scope for a number of reasons—in particular, to restrict the size of the book and to avoid a superficial treatment of subjects that are especially technical.

We have proceeded on the premise that contracts create the basic legal relationships in business. Accordingly, an important part of this book consists of a short treatise on the law of contract. In our view a study of this one subject-area in depth offers both more discipline and more practical value than can be had from devoting the same time to skimming the surface of half a dozen other topics in "survey" fashion. Moreover, an adequate treatment of contract necessarily entails an explanation of such important business concepts as tenders, options, standard form contracts, assignments, trusts, and negotiable instruments; and it sets the stage for a later study of such business transactions as the sale of goods and the formation of contracts of insurance, guarantee, bailment, employment, and agency.

We have chosen not to treat the law of negotiable instruments in separate chapters but to develop it in more modest proportions as an extension of the law governing the assignment of contractual rights. In our view a lengthier treatment is unnecessary. Modern banking practice has done much to resolve the problems that might otherwise arise in the use of negotiable instruments, and in view of the tremendous volume of business now transacted by the device, there is surprisingly little litigation over this part of the law. In any event, we are fortunate in having a short but definitive work already available on this subject: *The Law of Negotiable Instruments in Canada* by J. D. Falconbridge is an excellent reference work for those who would pursue the subject more intensively.

The law of real property forms a second important area of concern for business; the basic concepts of land law form a necessary background for important transactions where the law of contract and real property combine—the renting, mortgaging, and sale of land and buildings. Accordingly, we discuss these topics in that order.

We believe the book contains material that is at least ample for a full year's course in business law. Instructors who do not have class time equivalent to a full year's course or who prefer to cover the work more slowly may choose, for example, to omit the chapters on Capacity, Legality, and Mistake, respectively. They may choose to omit, also, the chapters on Insurance and Guarantee and on the Operation of Companies, particularly if these topics are touched on in other courses of the curriculum.

The Cases for Discussion following each chapter are designed to illustrate the application of the principles discussed in the preceding text material. After many (but not all) of these cases we have made reference to actual reported cases that have dealt with similar problems. Sometimes we have stayed fairly close to the facts of the reported case; at other times we have simplified the facts or varied them to suit the needs of the chapter. Accordingly, although the arguments in the actual reported case should be valuable, the court's decision need not always be appropriate to the hypothetical case presented for discussion.

We acknowledge with gratitude the encouragement, assistance, and indulgence of our colleagues in the Faculty of Law and School of Business at Queen's University, where this book was written. In a book covering such wide-ranging topics as contracts, land law, labour law, corporations, and creditors' rights, readers will undoubtedly discover errors and points of disagreement; for these we accept full responsibility. Nevertheless, the book has been immeasurably improved through the kindness of colleagues and students who have drawn errors and shortcomings to our attention. In particular we are grateful to Professor H. R. S. Ryan of the Faculty of Law for his careful criticisms and suggestions through many parts of the book, especially the chapters on land law, and to Professors H. J. Lawford and R. F. Gosse, who read portions of the manuscript and supplied valuable information. Professor Donald Wood of the Industrial Relations Centre made valuable suggestions for our chapter on the Contract of Employment. A number of friends in the Kingston business community were unfailingly patient in answering our questions about practice. We are also indebted to the students in the classes of Commerce '64 and '65 and M.B.A. '63 and '64 who were inescapably exposed to a large part of this book in mimeographed form and who, in good humour, helped to unmask many ambiguities. Our special thanks go to Professor Edwin Harris of the Faculty of Law at Dalhousie University, who, in reading the entire manuscript, has saved us from many embarrassments.

J.E.S.
D.A.S.

Preface to the Second Edition

A main purpose of the second edition has been to include an introductory chapter on Torts and two chapters on Negotiable Instruments, in response to the suggestions of numerous instructors.

Our explanation of the doctrine of *stare decisis* is expanded in Chapter 3 and Chapter 6 now includes a section on Promissory Estoppel. In addition, Chapter 17 on the Sale of Goods contains a brief discussion of the new consumer protection legislation. The occasion has also afforded an opportunity to bring statutory references up to date and to add some new questions for review and cases for discussion.

The authors are grateful to Professors Bonham and McDonald of the Faculty of Law at Queen's University and to Professor Huberman of the University of British Columbia for their helpful review of the new chapters.

J.E.S.
D.A.S.

Preface to the Third Edition

The eight years since the second edition have witnessed rapid change in the law. No other comparable period has seen so much legislative reform in so many areas. This process is continuing and may even accelerate through the 1970s into the 1980s. With change has come ever greater complexity in the law. We decided, therefore, that it has become much more important now to try to give readers a better overview of the law. Accordingly, under the heading of "The Law in its Social Context" we have added a new chapter and expanded the former introductory chapters. Our purpose is to give readers a better understanding of the legal system and the processes by which law changes. We hope these chapters will make the remainder of the book more easily understood.

The chapters devoted to the law of contract remain the largest single subject in this edition. Although the law of contract changes slowly through the decisions of the judges, new consumer protection legislation may have substantial effects upon it. Unfortunately, the developments in this area have been unsystematic and confusing. It remains to be seen to what extent they will increase the real protection afforded to the consuming public. We have included discussions of these changes at various points throughout the chapters on contract.

Areas in this edition where greatest change has taken place are land law (with respect to residential tenancies and condominiums), corporation law, secured transactions and creditors' rights. The chapters on corporation law have been substantially rewritten and much expanded to take into account significant statutory changes in the field. Unfortunately, changes in the chapter on creditors' rights have been limited by the fact that we must await a new bankruptcy act. A new bill was introduced in Parliament in the spring of 1975 based on the Report of the Study Committee on Bankruptcy and Insolvency Legislation (1970) with the understanding that the bill would be a basis for discussion and would not be passed by Parliament. It is expected to be reintroduced in the following session, subject to further amendment. As of January 1, 1976, no new bankruptcy legislation has been passed by Parliament. It would be impractical to rewrite the chapter on creditors' rights on a speculative basis of anticipated changes. Accordingly, the chapter on creditors' rights has been revised and brought up to date as of September 1, 1975.

We are grateful for the advice received from numerous colleagues in reading new portions of the manuscript, and in particular to Professors Gordon Simmons and Marvin Baer of the Faculty of Law at Queen's University and Professor Gail Brent of the Faculty of Law at the University of Western Ontario for their helpful review and suggestions in rewriting several chapters. We should also like to thank Professors Stuart Ryan, Kenneth Swan, William Lederman and Robert Land of the Faculty of Law at Queen's University for their advice and assistance.

The authors wish also to express their gratitude to Messrs. E. A. DuVernet, K. G. R. Gwynne-Timothy, D. Murphy, W. R. Rauenbusch and R. I. R. Winter who, as practising lawyers and part-time colleagues, have made numerous comments, criticisms and suggestions for new case material.

J.E.S.
D.A.S.
January, 1976

Contents

7   Formation of a Contract: Capacity to Contract   139

8   Formation of a Contract: Legality of Object   152

9   Grounds Upon Which a Contract May be Impeached: Mistake   172

10   Grounds Upon Which a Contract May be Impeached: Misrepresentation, Undue Influence, and Duress   190

PART THREE: SPECIAL TYPES OF CONTRACT

16   The Contract of Sale: Its Nature and Effect   320

17   The Contract of Sale: Remedies of the Parties   342

18   Insurance and Guarantee   360

19   Bailment   388

Explanation of Abbreviations

Throughout the text and footnotes, references occur to reported decisions of the courts, to statutes, and to legal periodicals. Listed below are the abbreviations for the most frequently cited source materials.

CANADA

Reports

C.C.C.	Canadian Criminal Cases	O.R.	Ontario Reports
		O.W.N.	Ontario Weekly Notes
C.P.R.	Canadian Patent Reports	S.C.R.	Supreme Court Reports
D.L.R.	Dominion Law Reports	W.L.R.	Western Law Reports
M.P.R.	Maritime Provinces Reports	W.W.R.	Western Weekly Reports
N.B.R.	New Brunswick Reports	**Statutes**	
N.S.R.	Nova Scotia Reports		Revised Statutes of
		R.S.A.	Alberta
		R.S.B.C.	British Columbia
O.L.R.	Ontario Law Reports	R.S.C.	Canada

R.S.M.	Manitoba		
R.S.N.B.	New Brunswick		
R.S.Nfld.	Newfoundland		
R.S.N.S.	Nova Scotia		
R.S.O.	Ontario		
R.S.P.E.I.	Prince Edward Island		
R.S.Q.	Quebec		
R.S.S.	Saskatchewan		

Periodicals

Can. B. Rev.	Canadian Bar Review
Can. B. Jour.	Canadian Bar Journal
U.B.C. Law Rev.	University of British Columbia Law Review
U. of T. Law Journal	University of Toronto Law Journal

UNITED KINGDOM

Reports

All E.R.	All England Reports
E.R.	English Reports (Reprint)
I.R.	Irish Reports
L.J. Ex.	Law Journal Exchequer
L.J.P.C.	Law Journal Privy Council
L.T.	Law Times Reports
T.L.R.	Times Law Reports

Law Report Series

Law Reports 1865-75

L.R.C.P.	Common Pleas
L.R.Ch.	Chancery
L.R.Eq.	Equity Cases
L.R.Ex.	Exchequer
L.R.H.L.	House of Lords
L.R.Q.B.	Queen's Bench

Law Reports 1875-80

C.P.D.	Common Pleas Division

Ex.D.	Exchequer Division

Law Reports 1875-91

App. Cas.	Appeal Cases
Ch.D.	Chancery Division
P.D.	Probate Division
Q.B.D.	Queen's Bench Division

Law Reports 1891-date

A.C.	Appeal Cases
Ch.	Chancery Division
K.B. or Q.B.	King's (Queen's) Bench Division
P.	Probate Division

Law Reports 1953-date

W.L.R.	Weekly Law Reports

Statutes

(U.K.) at end of reference

Table of Statutes

Table of Cases

PART ONE

The Law In Its Social Context

CHAPTER 1

Law, Freedom and Society

LAW AND CONSCIENCE

It would be comforting to be able to provide a concise definition of "law". Unfortunately, no one has yet devised a satisfactory definition, even within hundreds of pages of text. Consider the following illustrations:

Illustration A:

> Mary Brown was at home tending her sick 18-month-old baby. He had a high temperature caused by an undetermined virus. Suddenly Mrs. Brown realized that the child had lapsed into a coma. Fearing that he was in a state of convulsion and might die, she rushed the child to her car and drove to the nearest hospital. Within a few moments she was driving at 70 m.p.h. in a 30-m.p.h. zone. On arrival at the hospital the child was placed in emergency care, and the doctor commended Mrs. Brown for having saved the life of her child. A policeman arrived on the scene and presented Mrs. Brown with a summons for dangerous driving.

Illustration B:

> James Black was just two weeks old and suffering from a generally fatal blood deficiency that could only be cured by a complete transfusion of his blood. His parents are members of a religious sect which prohibits blood transfusions, and they refused to give permission for transfusions. The obstetrician in charge of the hospital applied to the court to make the infant a

ward of the Children's Aid Society so that permission for the transfusion could be obtained from the Society. After the court had made James Black a ward of the Society, but before the tranfusions had been administered, his parents removed him from the hospital in breach of the court order.

Mary Brown drove her car far in excess of the speed limit, a speed limit designed to promote safety. She thereby endangered the lives of other users of the streets, but she did so in order to save the life of her own child. Mrs. Brown would not argue that the 30-mile speed limit was unreasonable or unjust, but only that in the circumstances she was justified in breaking the law or, possibly, that the law should not apply to that particular situation. On the other hand, the parents of James Black broke the law because they believed it was a bad law in that it was being applied to them and their child against their religious beliefs. Mrs. Brown believed that she had the right to make every effort to *save* the life of her child; James Black's parents believed they had the right to *risk* the life of their child for their religious beliefs. In both cases, the law was apparently broken.

What is "law"? Is it the same thing as "justice"? Why should we obey the law? Is it ever right to break the law? These questions are raised in the context of the situations described above. There are no clear answers. In most respects, the difficulties have remained unchanged over the centuries. Intelligent, moderate men and women generally agree that there are times when an individual is justified in breaking the law, although they would add that, generally speaking, the law should be obeyed. They would also agree that there are unjust laws, but even these ought to be obeyed because of the chaotic consequences for society if many people failed to obey them. Even while trying to get unjust laws changed by normal, lawful means, we should nevertheless behave in compliance with them.

Law and justice, then, do not always coincide. But, one may ask, "Is an unjust law really law?" In some circumstances, rare though they may be, a law has been argued to be so atrociously unjust that it need not be obeyed by anyone. To put the argument another way, such a "law" is no law at all, and should not bind us. If this is so, how can we distinguish an invalid law from a valid law? This question is one of the most perplexing ever raised. To shed a little light on it we will briefly examine the two oldest contrasting theories of law.

NATURAL LAW

The most venerable theory is called *natural law*. There are two main streams within this philosophy. The older is based on religious belief. When a religion establishes a set of moral and ethical values it necessarily prescribes rules of conduct based on these values. In ancient societies, the religious leaders were usually the holders of power, and translated these religious rules into laws. Thus law originated within religious teachings. Since religious precepts are considered by those who formulate them to be eternal and immutable truths, so too are the fundamental principles of law — natural law — based on them, even though detailed rules and their particular applications may vary as society changes.

The second view of natural law does not depend on a theistic religious view of the world. Rather, it rests on the assumption that rational man, by applying his inherent abilities of reason and logic to his perception of the world, will arrive at basic principles of justice. This position was taken by some of the ancient Greek philosophers, and although almost forgotten for many centuries, it was reasserted in the 17th century in an extreme form. The Dutch philosopher and lawyer Grotius stated that the truths arrived at by man would exist independently of God. Indeed, if God were not in total harmony with these principles, He would not be God.

Despite their differences in belief about how we perceive the underlying principles, both views lead to the same basic view of law. Fundamental, immutable moral principles find their expression in general legal principles, and these may be further formulated in detailed rules for a particular society. One of the most eloquent expressions that combines these two views of natural law, based on the teachings of the 17th-century English philosopher John Locke, is found in the Declaration of Independence of the United States: "We hold these *truths to be self-evident:* that all men are created equal, that they are *endowed by their Creator* with certain unalienable rights, that among these are life, liberty and the pursuit of happiness." [Italics supplied.]

LAWS OF NATURE AND LAWS OF MAN

In the modern world, the word "law" has two distinct meanings. There are the physical laws, *laws of nature,* that we learn in studying the natural sciences such as physics, chemistry and biology. A primary example is the law of gravity. A second meaning of the word "law" refers to rules governing our conduct. A law prohibiting stealing does not make it physically impossible for a man to steal: it says that he should not steal, and that he will be punished if found guilty of stealing. This is a *normative* law as opposed to a *physical* law. A man may break a normative law and risk the consequences: he cannot "break" the law of gravity.

This distinction, which seems so evident to us, was not recognized until comparatively recent times. As late as the 17th century the expressions "natural law" (referring to men's conduct) and "laws of nature" (referring to the physical universe) were used interchangeably. Laws describing natural phenomena such as the movements of heavenly bodies, the seasons, biological reproduction, and the properties of various elements, were considered to be in no way different from laws governing men's conduct, and all were considered to have been laid down by the Creator — or by an unchanging system of logic.

Paradoxically, natural law can on the one hand be a vehicle for reform and revolution, or give strong support to a highly conservative view of society, supporting the *status quo,* on the other. In the French and American revolutions, the battle cry was that the great principles of natural law (as exemplified in our quotation from the American Declaration of Independence) had been offended by man-made laws. In France the revolution used Rousseau's words: "Man is born free but is everywhere in chains." The laws that placed him in chains, therefore, were invalid. Natural law thus gave legitimacy to the revolutionary cry. Yet the same natural law has also been proclaimed in aid of the divine right of kings, to support an existing monarchy. A most striking (and unsuccessful) example is the claim of divine support made by the English monarchs in the 17th century before the revolution that deposed and eventually beheaded Charles I. The idea of divine right has been used to justify the maintenance of an aristocracy and to prescribe ranks of merit, and hence privilege, down to the lowliest serf: it has even been used to justify systems of slavery.

As we shall see, this two-edged sword of legal philosophy applies to other definitions of law as well as natural law. As an abstraction, legal philosophy tends to be neutral; partisans of different views of society inject their values into the philosophical system to give it the particular political cast of reaction or radicalism desired.

NATURAL LAW UNDER ATTACK—LEGAL POSITIVISM

A harmonious and unified view of the laws of nature and of man was a satisfying system for believers. By the 17th century, however, any semblance of unity in the Christian world of Western Europe was gone, and a variety of religious beliefs dominated different regions of the continent. Nation-states with diverse and conflicting national interests had arisen, and they amended their laws to suit their own interests. There was no longer one way to God, truth, and a righteous life. With each religious group heaping critical abuse on all others, skepticism grew among many of the thinkers of 17th-century Europe. As we have noted, some thinkers rejected faith in God and substituted man's ability to reason as the greatest single power in the world. They began to construct their own rational systems of moral conduct and of laws that should be based on them. Just as in the case of religious faith, however, no single rational system appealed to all men. Some, like John Locke, propounded fundamental principles based on natural law. Others were skeptical of the existence of any unchanging, basic rules.

A particularly significant departure occurred in the philosophy of the Scottish thinker David Hume. It was Hume who first clearly distinguished between physical laws and normative laws. Hume made a further crucial distinction among the normative rules themselves. He stated that some normative rules were "law" because they created a code of behaviour complete with sanctions for failure to live by that code. In contrast, other normative rules existed without sanctions for their breach. These were moral rules: failure to observe them might create annoyance or indignation in others, and a bad conscience in the wrongdoer, but no more than that. Hume's basic distinction, then, was between ascertainable rules that are binding, the law that "is", and rules that men "ought" to observe even in the absence of legal compulsion. His distinction was between the "is" and the "ought", or between *law* and *morals*.

What Hume called "law" has since become known as *positive law*. Those who insist upon a clear distinction between the "is" and the "ought" are called *legal positivists*. Legal positivism is concerned with ascertaining the body of law that "is", with describing those criteria or tools that can be used to distinguish positive law from all other rules. Some positivists disclaim any concern for what is good or bad about law because in order to assess the goodness or badness of a legal rule they would have to refer to a standard external to the law itself. Their concern is only with legal rules as such. They would not deny the importance of assessing the value of law, but would say that is a task for the legislator, not the legal theorist.

How does one define law in a positivist system? The positivist asserts that law must come from a person or group of persons holding power over the general population. Those holding power can impose sanctions on individuals who break the law. John Austin, a 19th-century English legal philosopher, described law as "the command of a sovereign". He did not view the sovereign as merely a person called "the King". Austin described the sovereign in the England of his time as "the King in Parliament". The "command" of the sovereign was an act of Parliament duly passed by both houses and receiving royal assent from the monarch.

Austin's definition of law presents difficulties, some of which he acknowledged himself. For example, while his definition is relatively satisfactory when applied to a constitutional monarchy with a unitary system of government such as exists in England, it is much more difficult to apply to a federal country such as Canada or the United States, where as well as a national government, there are several governments at the provincial or state level. In the case of the United States, his definition faces an added difficulty: lawful authority emanates from the Constitution, and a document can hardly be personified as a sovereign.

Modern legal thinkers have refined Austin's theory into more sophisticated 20th-century models. In place of a sovereign they recognize a basic law, a constitution habitually obeyed by the citizens of a country. This basic law enjoys a minimum level of acceptance by the general population just as long as they regard the constitution as legitimate and binding.

The closed legal systems of positivists, however, do not provide a standard for measuring the minimum general level of acceptance. In order to conclude that a system of law is operating in positivist terms, an observer must base his decision on his own values, outside the logical system of the positivist. In unstable societies, the problem for the observer is sometimes very difficult to resolve. Thus, in the midst of a revolution when the old constitution has been denounced by many citizens and it may not be possible to ascertain whether anyone holds power, there might appear to be no law at all. In such a period, what happens to existing debts and obligations, or to people who commit acts normally considered to be criminal? How does the eventual victor establish himself as the lawful authority? Is it merely a nose-counting operation, so that government exists again when the victor has sufficient (whatever that word may imply) acceptance to proclaim laws and administer sanctions? Positivist theories do not explain how a system of law re-emerges.

Let us assume that the positivist approach provides us with a useful definition for ascertaining what the law is in a stable society, when it is completely clear who holds the power. Neither natural law nor positivism has answered the question: is it ever right to break the law? There is an adage that much learning in philosophy does not make a person good. In law, we have a parallel: much learning in legal philosophy does not provide easy answers to difficult moral questions about the law.

Illustration A:

"Three men and a boy were shipwrecked in a small boat 1,000 miles at sea in the South Atlantic. What little food they had was exhausted within a few days. For the next six days they had no food whatever, and subsisted only on rainwater. All three men were married, with young families. Two of the men suggested that if no relief came someone should be sacrificed to save the rest. The third man dissented and the boy was not consulted. A day later, the two men suggested to the third that they should cast lots to determine who should be put to death to save the rest, but the third refused to consent. The proposal was not put to the boy, who at that time was very much weakened and lying helpless in the bottom of the boat. The three men spoke of their families and suggested that it would be better to kill the boy so that their lives should be saved. The first man proposed that if there was no vessel in sight by next morning, the boy should be killed. In the following day, the two men offered a prayer for forgiveness for committing so rash an act, and then proceeded to kill the boy with a knife. The three men fed upon the body of the boy for four days until they were picked up by a passing ship. The first two men were charged with murder while the third was not charged with any offence."[1]

Illustration B:

In 1944 in Germany a woman, wishing to be rid of her husband, denounced him to the authorities for insulting remarks he had made about Hitler while home on leave from the German army. The wife was under no legal duty to report his act, but what he had said was apparently in violation of statutes making it illegal to make statements detrimental to the government of the Third Reich. . . . The husband was arrested and sentenced to death, apparently pursuant to these statutes, though he was not executed but sent to the front. In 1949 the wife was prosecuted in a West German court for an offence which we would describe as illegally depriving a person of his freedom. . . . This was punishable as a crime under the German Criminal

---

[1] Regina v. Dudley and Stephens (1884) 14 Q.B.D. 273.

Code of 1871 which had remained in force continuously since its enactment. The wife pleaded that her husband's imprisonment was pursuant to
the Nazi statutes and hence that she had committed no crime.[2]

One thousand miles at sea, in a small boat that could hardly be considered as
part of the "national territory" of the home country of the shipwrecked men, is
there any ascertainable positive law? (Indeed, should the law of any country
apply?) Do these men constitute a miniature community that can make its own
laws to suit its needs? Assuming the law of one country is applied to them,
should they be acquitted of any crime by reason of justification in their dire circumstances? Assuming the law of a particular country does not apply, are there
immutable principles of justice that ought to be used to judge men's conduct, no
matter where they find themselves? And if there are immutable principles, ought
they ever to be applied to override the established positive law of a country? In
the context of Illustration B, should the plea of the wife — that her act was lawful
under existing Nazi positive law — fail because principles of natural law nullify
the apparently valid positive law of an evil regime? If so, does the earlier law of
Germany apply in the circumstances? Might it be argued in both cases that no
positive law existing at the time had been broken, and that to punish either the
men at sea or the war wife is to create *retroactive law* to deal with a situation
after it has arisen? In most legal systems there is a strong aversion to retroactive
law — making something a crime when at the time the act was committed it was
not a crime.

The above illustrations show that legal systems can be confronted with extremely difficult moral questions. No solution is entirely satisfactory, and reasonable men can strongly disagree about the appropriate disposition of a difficult
case. In view of this disagreement, it would be impossible to conclude that law
and justice always coincide. There will always be disagreement in ascertaining
what the law is in a particular situation, and even greater disagreement about
whether its application has led to a just solution. Nor does legal philosophy help
us decide whether it is ever right to break the law. At best, it can make the
problem clearer and focus our minds on the central issue.

PURPOSES OF A LEGAL SYSTEM

We turn now from the examination of particular laws, and their relation to justice, to examine the broader significance of a system of law. Earlier, we stated
most reasonable men would agree that, generally speaking, law ought to be
obeyed. What purposes are served when men obey the rules of a legal system?
Most thinkers, whether looking at this question primarily as a legal matter or as a
political and social issue, believe that freedom from violent conflict and the assurance of reasonably predictable and orderly relations among men are essential

---

[2] Cited from H. L. A. Hart, "Positivism, Analytical Jurisprudence and Concept of Law," 71 *Harvard Law Review*, p. 595 (1958). Copyright 1958 by the Harvard Law Review Association.

qualities of society. Men need to feel free from fear that arbitrary force will be used against them by their neighbours or the state. They should be able to rely with reasonable certainty on normal expectations being met — for example, that they will receive the agreed wages for their work, that they will be fairly compensated for injury caused by the fault of another person, and that a system of rules will be applied fairly in striving for a settlement of serious disputes. These are but a few of the expectations considered necessary, or at least highly desirable, in a society.

A legal system provides the broad framework for the detailed rules that create the essential qualities of a stable society. If men feel free to either obey or break the rules as they wish, then the rules will not secure the minimum standards of peace and predictability. We may conclude, therefore, that citizens generally ought to obey the law because in so doing they promote a reasonably harmonious society. If a legal system is to encourage most men to accept this view, it must appear to them to be generally just, so that they are willing to make the following assumption about particular laws: that in the absence of other information a law is expected to produce just results. The assumption should be strong enough so that if an unjust result seems to follow, the first step should be a careful re-examination of the process to make sure no mistake has been made along the way, and it was not the *application* of the law rather than the law itself that was unjust. A group of citizens may finally come to the conclusion, based on their own values, that the law really is a bad law, and ought to be substantially altered or else repealed altogether.

CHALLENGING THE PURPOSES OF A LEGAL SYSTEM

In the above discussion, we have made the basic assumption that a legal system is essential for a harmonious society. Our illustrations raise issues that do not contest this assumption. Rather, they are concerned with identifying and describing law and distinguishing it from other kinds of obligations. For this purpose, the illustrations contain highly emotional dilemmas that bring positive law into conflict with personal conviction based on moral or religious beliefs.

We can also, however, look at law primarily in an economic, social and political context. From this perspective, some thinkers have attacked the very assumption that law is necessary or even desirable. Anarchists and Marxists in the 19th century were confronted with the unquestionable horrors of the Industrial Revolution that turned landless peasants into factory workers and subjected them to dreadful living and working conditions. Those critics saw law as primarily a tool designed to perpetuate inequality and preserve privilege and power for the elite: law kept the proletariat in bondage.

Long before Marx, men had considered what society would be like in a "natural state", without law and sanctions. In the 4th century St. Augustine interpreted the Judaeo-Christian account of the Fall of Man as supporting the need for law to restrain men's baser instincts. Other views of man and law were proposed from time to time, but from St. Augustine through the Middle Ages and into the 18th century, the dominant view was that the legal order was needed to protect man from himself. In the 17th century, the English philosopher Thomas Hobbes asserted that in a world with no enforced legal order, life would be "nasty, brutish and short". He argued that man's natural propensities are aggressive and violent. A society based on brute force would be the very antithesis of a community where fairness and peace reign. People would live in constant fear, and their homes would indeed be castles.

There was some historical support for Hobbes' view. Looking back from the 17th century, Hobbes viewed the Dark Ages as a period of lawlessness and fear. To protect themselves against marauding invaders from the east and north, and gangs of brigands and pirates, men would pledge their allegiance to the most powerful in their midst. He would become their liege lord: in return for supplies and services, especially military service, from his vassals, he offered protection from outsiders and settled disputes among the vassals themselves. Thus, the system of feudalism was born primarily to give life a measure of security and normality under the aegis of a feudal landlord. Eventually, in most European countries, the most powerful lord was able to obtain pledges of loyalty from lesser lords and proclaim himself king, even though his crown might be worn precariously. The prevailing theology of the Middle Ages aided these developments: St. Augustine's belief, that laws administered with a firm hand were needed to keep man's tendency to greed and violence in check, was interpreted as supporting a divine choice of those who demonstrated their God-given strength and courage — or their ruthlessness — to become rulers.

From classical Greek times, despite St. Augustine's dominant influence, another view of man survives — that of an innocent and benevolent creature, corrupted by an oppressive society with its system of laws and coercion. (Supporters of this view have never explained satisfactorily how innocent man created his corrupt society in the first place.) Although the view had been eclipsed by the doctrine of original sin in man, it persisted, and in the 18th century was reinforced by the coming of modern science. Man began to explain many of the mysteries of the physical world, and leading philosophers of the time noted that man's power of reason had apparently enabled him to arrive at truths independently of a theological base. Now if man could solve many of the mysteries of natural science, why not those of his own nature and of society? Man himself was exalted and idealized, in contradiction to the idea of original sin.

The benevolent view of man received fresh impetus from the Romantics at the beginning of the 19th century. The solution they proposed for society's ills was to abandon artificial urban societies and return to nature, to a simple rustic life where man could recapture his state of innocence and happiness. Hobbesian ideas of the state and law and order were anathema to the Romantics. Romanticism also contained the seeds of anarchism. Anarchists did not want simply to flee the city: that would not solve the problem for the poor benighted souls left under the evil oppression of the organized state. Instead they wished to destroy, stamp out entirely, this organized oppression — the state and its laws.

MARXISM

Marxism is closely related to anarchism. Marx was little concerned with man in his mythical original "state of nature"; yet he did assume that once he was freed from the corrupting influence of a class society, man would be benevolent towards his fellows. Marx spent most of his time analyzing society in terms of property, power, and economics. Even scholars who disagree strongly with his values and conclusions will concede that Marx made a great contribution to the social sciences by emphasizing the relationship between the distribution of power and wealth in a society, and that society's prevailing ideas and values.

Marx observed that ownership of property — wealth — was the most important element separating the classes in society. The upper classes, though few in number, owned most of the wealth, and in industrialized countries, wealth consisted in large measure of factories and mines, the means of production. Thus they controlled the means of livelihood and the very lives of the workers.

In the mid-19th century, the legal systems of those countries in the process of industrialization — chiefly Britain, the United States, Prussia, and France — gave great protection to the owners of property in a variety of ways. In the first place, penalties for theft were very severe, frequently even providing for capital punishment even when no violence was involved in the crime. Secondly, taxes on income and wealth were either nonexistent or negligible. Governments raised money mainly by taxes in the form of excise duties on goods, where the cost is passed on to the consumer of the goods no matter how poor he is. This form of taxation is now considered regressive by economists, because it throws a disproportionate tax burden on low-income people.

Thirdly, most forms of labour unions were prohibited as constituting criminal activity "in restraint of trade". Legislators and courts held the view that agreements among workers interfered with the freedom of each individual worker to bargain with his employer. And this "freedom" to bargain was considered sacred. As a result, workers were forbidden to organize and bargain with factory owners about rates of pay and other working conditions. Because of the unequal bargaining powers of an individual worker and the owner of a factory, freedom to bargain was a myth: either the worker accepted the terms offered or he had no work and no pay. At a time when there was no unemployment insurance or state welfare plan, refusing a job was tantamount to accepting starvation. Even the most partisan supporter of management today, although he might argue that the pendulum has swung the other way and that unions have more bargaining power than management, would recognize that 19th-century law concerning labour unions was so grossly unfair as to be barbaric. Working conditions reflected this situation: they were often unhealthy and dangerous, and the workers were paid a pittance.

Fourthly, as we shall discuss in more detail later,[3] the law of negligence made employers virtually immune from legal action by employees for injuries

---

[3] Chapter 21 under "Workmen's Compensation".

suffered by them under almost all conditions, whether in a mine, a factory, a railway yard, or an office. The employer reaped the benefits of the employee's efforts, but the employee took the risk of injury and disability without compensation.

The picture of society presented by these key elements in the legal system supported Marx's view that the legal mechanism of the state operated in large measure for the benefit of the property-owning classes. Most people today, with the benefit of the enlightened hindsight of the late 20th century, would probably agree with Marx's argument up to this point. But Marx went on to assert that the upper classes would never surrender any of their protection and privileges through persuasion or other forms of non-violent pressure. For Marx, the only way — indeed, the inevitable way — was violent overthrow of the upper classes by a workers' revolution. A belief in the general inevitability of the historical process (including, in Marx's interpretation, the destruction of the legal system that protects the wealthy classes) is called *historical determinism*. In the last two decades of the 19th century, and in the early 20th century, many of the worst abuses and inequalities were reduced or eliminated by acts of Parliament and without revolution. The process is a continuing, even accelerating, one.

The number of crimes for which capital punishment could be imposed was drastically reduced; they were limited almost entirely to crimes of violence against other persons and acts of treason. In the field of taxation, systems were introduced for taxing the incomes of individuals and corporations at progressive rates, increasing as income increases, and in many countries, including Canada, Britain and the United States, are now the principal source of revenue. Not only were labour unions made legal, but a separate system of labour law has been developed, with rules for recognition of unions, settling struggles between rival unions and promoting peaceful settlement of disputes between unions and management. The system is far from perfect, but it does represent a genuine, substantial effort to create a fair system. The law of negligence too has been drastically changed to provide compensation to workers injured on the job, and induce or even compel owners to improve safety and health standards on their premises.

Although the wealthy classes do not willingly give up their privileges, there is much evidence in many developed countries that they will not mount the barricades to defend them. Instead, in the process of bargaining with other segments of society, they will trade off many privileges in order to retain some benefits. In addition, even without being altruistic, intelligent people in a privileged position will often act out of long-term enlightened self-interest. For example, a businessman who voluntarily improves working conditions or offers a generous profit-sharing plan to his employees may well improve his own profits. In an expanding economy such as Western countries have enjoyed since Marx's day, it has been possible for everyone to have more. Whether or not Marx himself might have modified his views, modern-day Marxists will have none of soft-pedalling the evils they see in capitalist society. They point to many social injustices that still exist, and conclude by asserting that much of the benefit reaped in Western industrial countries has been at the expense of the people of the former colonial world in Asia, Africa and Latin America.

Marx also believed that when the proletariat had overthrown the upper classes a classless society would be created, and the state and its system of coercive law would simply "wither away". The reason would be that law is needed only in an oppressive society. In the new classless world there would be no oppression, since each man would have what he needed and share the goods of society with his fellow men. Even before the Bolshevik Revolution in Russia, many attempts were made to create truly communal societies run on either anarchistic or Marxist principles. In these communities, usually established on farms remote from large cities, all things were owned in common; there was no private property, no formal government, no police, no coercion — at least in theory. Invariably they collapsed within a few months or years. The explanation given by believers in the commune is that although members joined with the best of intentions, they had been so corrupted by the evil, class-ridden society that they could not escape their ingrained, dangerously selfish traits. It was their anti-communal faults that destroyed the communities.

Perhaps these idealistic little societies were precursors of the problems of the communist world. In the U.S.S.R., far from withering away, the apparatus of the state seems ever growing. There is an enormous impersonal bureaucracy from which the individual must seek permission to do many of the things we in Canada do as a matter of course, if we so choose: change educational programs, change jobs, move from one part of the country to another, publish an article or a book, or leave the country. Communist theorists claim that the Russian experiment is still in a transitional period, when, as in the communes, many people remain who were corrupted by the former regime or by insidious outside propaganda. Once these "revisionists" have died out, the state will indeed wither away. But the Bolshevik Revolution of 1917 is now well over a half-century old. There are very few people still alive who were not in their infancy at the time. And there has been no evidence of even a slight decrease in the size of the government or in its coercive powers. Skeptics may well wonder whether Marx's 19th-century idealism concerning the utopian communist state is not the equivalent of heaven or nirvana in more ancient religious beliefs.

Wide disagreement is also encountered in communists' own analysis of their societies. An interesting example is the story of an eminent Russian legal theorist named Pashikanis. Pashikanis developed an analysis of law called the *exchange theory*. He wrote a book and a number of essays in the 1920s and early '30s employing his theory to analyze Western capitalist society. He used the marketplace as a model to explain much of what happens in Western countries, concluding that law was needed in a society based on a system of bargaining, but had no place in a Marxist society.

We have noted that classical Marxist theory has always maintained that when the ultimate condition of communism is achieved, the state will wither away and no law will be needed. Pashikanis' analysis supported the classical theory: he was acclaimed as a great philosopher and attained high office in the Soviet government. However, by the mid-1930s, the Russians realized that they needed a more or less permanent legal system for the indefinite future; Pashikanis' persuasive conclusions were an embarrassment to them, especially his strong case for dismantling the legal system before Marxist society reached its culmination. Since they could not live with Pashikanis' conclusions, they declared him a revisionist and a traitor. He was removed from his office and disappeared from the scene in 1937, never to be heard from again.[4]

THE GOLDEN MEAN

The great Greek philosopher Aristotle recognized two broad categories of law which he called *retributive justice* and *distributive justice,* a classification that remains generally recognized today. Retributive justice is concerned with those rules that usually come to mind when the word law is mentioned — rules that prohibit acts considered to be injurious to others. Criminal law is the most obvious example. The government uses sanctions to enforce retributive rules and wrongdoers are punished. Our illustrations at the beginning of this chapter about the shipwrecked men and the Nazi wife were concerned with the breach of rules of retributive justice.

Distributive justice concerns the allocation of resources and wealth among the citizens of a society. The essential characteristic of these laws is that they *redistribute* wealth by taking from those who have much and giving to those who have little and cannot adequately provide for themselves. At an earlier time in history this type of redistribution was considered to be the subject of charity, although now it is part of government welfare schemes for such groups as the poor and the sick. Yet welfare, thus narrowly defined, is but a small part of distributive law. Our laws provide far more important instruments of redistribution of wealth: a public system of education; prepaid medical care; unemployment insurance; subsidies and transfer payments by the federal government for regional development; transportation systems, and various types of equalization payments. Funds to sustain these programs are raised by progressive income tax and, as in unemployment insurance and medical care insurance, by compulsory premium payments; benefits are paid, for example to those who are unemployed or who have incurred medical expenses, without regard to the source of contributions.

Marxists claim that both the retributive and distributive aspects of law in Western capitalist society are designed to maintain the privileged classes in power: the retributive rules prevent activity that would harm those in possession of wealth, and the distributive rules give as little as possible to the working classes in order to keep them relatively passive, or at least unwilling to risk the little they have in a revolution. This conspiratorial view of society, depicting an incredibly brilliant and villainous upper class, is in striking contrast to the essential purity of man that, according to Marx, will one day let him live in perfect harmony without law.

---

[4] For a fuller account of Pashikanis and the communist concept of law, see Kamenka and Erh-Soon Tay, ''Beyond the French Revolution: Communist Socialism and the Concept of Law,'' 21 *U of T Law Journal,* p. 109 (1971). See esp. p. 110, n. 1.

Aristotle believed that man was neither mainly greedy and brutish nor a wholly innocent, well-meaning creature. For Aristotle, the great danger lay in extremes. He saw man's greatest achievement as moderation in all things — the "Golden Mean". He recognized, in modern terms, that although man has a tendency towards greed and violence, he also has a conscience — a sense of right and wrong — and can be motivated by love and pity. Moreover, man has the power of reason and the ability to distinguish good from evil. Unfortunately, all men do not have these qualities in the same measure, nor are they all equal in intelligence and strength. Most important, they do not all perceive things in the same way and do not all have the same priorities. Even with an earnest will to do what is right and fair, two men will often disagree strongly about the merits of a dispute between themselves or between other men. The reason idealistic communal societies fail is not because their members are imperfect converts to anarchism or Marxism, but because men do not share the same priorities and vary greatly in their strength and influence over others.

If this middle view of man is more accurate than either extreme, how is man to live in society when there will inevitably be honestly-held, deep disagreement? He does not wish to abandon his freedom entirely to a Hobbesian absolute ruler in order to be saved from his own self, nor can he hope to live in a utopia entirely without rules. Man, then, must use his conscience, his sense of justice, and his power of reason to devise a system of rules that will resolve disputes and treat men as fairly as possible in the distribution of society's benefits. As he learns by experience, and as conditions change, he will need constantly to revise his system in striving for justice.

JEREMY BENTHAM

This moderate, rational view of law and society has a strong appeal, but it is also deceptive, for it gives no criteria by which to judge whether laws are good or bad. There have been some remarkable attempts to set standards by which we should be able to assess the value of laws. The most influential effort affecting much of the 19th-century law reform was that of the great English reformer Jeremy Bentham at the end of the 18th century. Bentham developed the *principle of utility,* which asserted that the goal of society should be to increase the sum total of human happiness. The two factors by which happiness can be measured are pleasure and pain. By decreasing the amount of pain and increasing the amount of pleasure the ends of society would be served:

> Utility therefore really meant no more than what served to increase human happiness, the sum of which was to be assessed by calculating the stock of pleasure and pain which resulted from a particular course of action. For this purpose numerical standards were adopted, each man's happiness being considered the equal in value of that of any other man, so that the test of utility was what served the happiness of the largest possible number. Bentham's principle was aimed at "maximizing" human happiness accord-

ing to the slogan "the greatest happiness of the greatest number". Although Bentham rejected natural law with scorn — for him natural rights were not just nonsense, but "nonsense upon stilts" — he was nothing if not a rationalist in the spirit of the Enlightenment. . . . Ironically, Bentham's own principle that one man's happiness was of equal worth to another's, owed much to the widely established "natural" right to equality . . .

Despite a certain naïveté in his belief that happiness could be virtually quantified in almost arithmetical terms, Bentham's work laid a solid juridical foundation for much of the reform of the law which was one of the most crying needs of the early nineteenth century . . .[5]

While Bentham's philosophy was not entirely neutral, as Professor Lloyd has noted, nevertheless his philosophy alone was not sufficient to bring about reforms. It required the insertion of Bentham's personal values, and those of other 19th-century liberal reformers, to give his theories vigour and effectiveness. Reforms can never exceed the perception of social evils and the values of the day, whatever philosophy is employed; almost one hundred years passed after Bentham put forward his utilitarian views before some of the worst abuses were ended by legislation.

SOCIAL ENGINEERING

At the end of the 19th century, the American legal philosopher Roscoe Pound was greatly influenced by the growth of the new social sciences, especially sociology. He saw a series of conflicts between constantly changing interests as a principal feature of society. As certain interests increased and grew dominant, their demands would be recognized through changes in the law. But the process was unsystematic and subject to chance events: some interests would obtain recognition too easily, while others might go unheeded for too long. Pound envisaged law as a tool of "social engineering" to be used for consciously evaluating and adjusting competing interests.

. . . As the saying is, we all want the earth. We all have a multiplicity of desires and demands which we seek to satisfy. There are very many of us but there is only one earth. The desires of each continually conflict with or overlap those of his neighbours. So there is, as one might say, a great task of social engineering. There is a task of making the goods of existence, the means of satisfying the demands and desires of men living together in a politically organized society, if they cannot satisfy all the claims that men make upon them, at least go around as far as possible. This is what we mean when we say that the end of law is justice. We do not mean justice as an individual virtue. We do not mean justice as the ideal relation among men. We mean a regime. We mean such an adjustment of relations and ordering

---

[5] Lloyd, *The Idea of Law,* pp. 98-9. Harmondsworth: Penguin Books, 1964.

of conduct as will make the goods of existence, the means of satisfying human claims to have things and do things, go round as far as possible with the least friction and waste.[6]

Pound believed that most of society's ills were the result of ignorance. By scientific study of people's needs and expectations, and of prevailing values, more rational adjustments of the rights given to competing interests could be made to improve the lot of society. In many respects Pound's philosophy is a sophisticated child of utilitarianism; it rejects the absolute values of natural law and seeks to obtain its values, its criteria for change, from scientific study of the community.

Pound's theory raised three important questions. First, does law influence the development of society (and if so, to what extent), or is it merely a reflection of changing values and other developments within society? Secondly, to what extent can scientific methods truly be used to improve the quality of lawmaking? Or are the social sciences really neutral, and used by partisan groups to bolster a view to which they are already committed? Thirdly, if scientific methods really can be effective in exposing society's ills and our own shortcomings in dealing with them, is there not the danger that they will in the process destroy important myths we need for our peace of mind? Suppose for example, as some writers claim, psychoanalysis of all judges would reveal that dispassionate judicial decisions are no more than the result of accumulated bias and other frailties of judges.

LAW AS AN INSTRUMENT OF SOCIAL CHANGE

These three questions are related: if law is nothing more than a reflection of society's values, there is no point in seeking scientific methods to improve lawmaking. (Such a search would be pointless also for a totally committed Marxist who believes in historical determinism, since law will disappear after the revolution of the proletariat succeeds.) But most of us are keenly aware that at best, the law reflects imperfectly the values of our society. Even in a totalitarian state, those holding power are unlikely to be able to make the law mirror their values completely. In a pluralistic democracy with many conflicting values, the law often reflects a contradictory mixture. Changes usually take place through a series of halting steps.

Occasionally, something approaching an "informed public will" becomes apparent and a major change does take place in accord with it. A remarkable example occurred in the history of universal medical care in Canada. Over a decade, a relatively small but eloquent group of people persuaded the federal government that Canada needed and could afford a government-sponsored universal medical-care scheme. However, implementation of the plan depended

---

[6] Pound, *Social Control Through Law,* pp. 64-5. New Haven: Yale University Press, 1942.

upon provincial co-operation and provincial legislation. Some provincial governments joined willingly, while others feared the cost to them would be overwhelming. Still others opposed the plan philosophically and politically. When
the federal government used its fiscal powers to exert strong pressure on the
recalcitrant provinces to join (through the threatened loss of substantial federal
grants for failure to do so), these provinces found themselves unable to resist for
long because their own electorates favoured the federal position. Thus, popular
support for the medical-care scheme permitted the federal government to sustain
its pressure against sometimes bitter opposition. Although a number of provincial government members may strongly resent the methods employed by the federal government, none today would speak out seriously against the principle of
universal medical care.

No doubt the conditions at the time of the main debate were ideal for the
democratic process: the issue was one affecting everyone personally; eloquent
advocates, both for and against, had outlined the problem in great detail; newspapers, radio and television gave a good deal of time to the issue; not only politicians but doctors, economists and laymen, had ample opportunity to air their
views. Fortunately too, the question had little to do with conflicts among political personalities and the country was enjoying the kind of economic prosperity
that made the plan attainable. Thus the law changed to reflect public opinion.

A cynic might say that the medical-care debate was no more than a happy
accident, the exception that tests the rule; rarely does the law reflect society's
values and real needs, because political expediency and chance dominate the
legislative process. Responsible leaders of government have long recognized
how difficult it is to prepare and carry out a program of legislative reform. Many
events at home and abroad can change a government's fortunes and plans — its
miscalculations of the public mood, political scandals, technological changes —
and often lead to an election and change of government.

One way to overcome some of these difficulties is to announce, as much as
several years in advance, that a particular problem needs intensive study, and to
appoint a special study group staffed by experts to examine the problem with a
view to making recommendations to solve, or at least alleviate, the difficulties.
Following the British tradition, major studies in Canada are usually undertaken
by royal commissions. When the Cabinet announces a royal commission, it sets
out the commission's terms of reference, appoints a chairman who is typically a
respected elder statesman — perhaps a senator, or a specialist in the field to be
studied — and several other commissioners to give political or geographic balance, depending on the nature of the problem. The commission then hires staff
and also gives contracts for independent studies of specific aspects of its area of
concern. Usually, it also holds a series of public hearings to receive the views of
interested groups and individuals in various parts of the country. When all
reports are in and the commissioners have settled on their recommendations, they
submit their report to the government for publication and debate in the hope that
statutory reform will follow.

Our cynic might well be most cynical of all towards royal commissions.

Most royal commissions, he would say, are nothing more than evasions, ways for a government to delay action on uncomfortable problems about which any decision is likely to cause it embarrassment. In two or three years, by the time the commission reports, the problem may have gone away — or become someone else's responsibility. Because of the time a royal commission takes, it frequently reports to a new government elected after it began its work, a new government that, as the former opposition, may have been against establishing the commission in the first place and have no interest in implementing any of its recommendations. Even when a government is not antipathetic, the commission itself, during its years of study, may have drifted away from political reality to the consideration of theoretical and impractical solutions, so that its recommendations are quietly filed and gather dust on library shelves.

The political process being the chancy thing it is, there is unfortunately much truth in criticisms of royal commissions. It is indeed difficult to systematically plan and implement legal and social reforms. Nevertheless, a number of such commissions have actually led to major reforms, and still others have changed our way of thinking about a problem and thus, though less directly, influenced changes in that area over a number of years. The report of the Royal Commission on Health Services chaired by Mr. Justice Hall played an important part in the eventual introduction of universal medical care in Canada.[7]

No matter what one may think of royal commissions and other specialized research and fact-finding groups employed by government, their studies will become ever more necessary and more common: as technical and environmental problems increase in complexity, laymen — members of Parliament and others — will need experts to make studies and translate them into as simple terms as possible before the necessary legislation can be passed to cope with these problems. Continuing attempts to minimize air pollution by internal-combustion engines has led to extremely complicated legislation in Canada and the United States about the manufacture and operation of motor vehicles, legislation affecting producers of cars all over the world. The question has been further complicated by belated recognition of energy conservation as a major factor in future design of all vehicles for transportation of both people and goods. Improving the purity of water resources, reducing noise levels, and protecting the ecology of the north, are examples of other areas requiring increasingly sophisticated study and advice. Like it or not, we must rely more and more on scientific study before changing laws in the immediate future.

CONCLUSION

In this chapter we have discussed the two main streams of legal philosophy: law and conscience — the relation between law and the individual's convictions; and law and society — the legal system as a basic element in organized society. We

---

[7] Canada, Royal Commission on Health Services, *Report*. Ottawa: Queen's Printer, 1964-5.

have tried to raise those questions that we believe are most important. It would be impossible to discuss all the major works in legal philosophy in less than a very large volume. For those readers interested in further readings on the subject, please refer to the bibliography at pages 739-40.

QUESTIONS FOR REVIEW

1. What basic element do different theories of natural law share?
2. Is an unjust law still law?
3. Distinguish a normative law from other kinds of laws.
4. What contradictory uses may be made of natural law?
5. Explain Hume's distinction between the "is" and the "ought".
6. What difficulty does Austin's definition of law present in a country like Canada?
7. How do modern positivists solve the problem of ascertaining what the law is in a time of revolution?
8. In the case of *Regina v. Dudley and Stephens,* would you acquit or convict the accused men? Why?
9. What is a retroactive law? What difficulties does it create?
10. What essential qualities must a legal system provide to a community?
11. When a law produces an unjust result, what is the first question that we should ask?
12. What view of law do anarchists and Marxists share?
13. Describe Hobbes' view of man's conduct in a state of nature.
14. What was the chief significance of St. Augustine's beliefs for law in the Middle Ages?
15. Describe briefly four important aspects of 19th-century law that lent support to Marx's view of society.
16. What did Marx prophesy would happen to law after the proletarian revolution? What happened to communal societies founded on his thesis?
17. What is your own opinion of his prophecy as it applies to the U.S.S.R. today?
18. Distinguish between retributive and distributive justice.
19. What quality or qualities do you think would prevent men from living in harmony with one another in the absence of enforceable laws?
20. Describe Bentham's principle of utility.
21. Can you perceive an element of natural law in Bentham's theory?
22. Describe what Pound means by "social engineering".
23. Do you believe that law is an entirely passive reflection of society's values? Explain.
24. It has been said that royal commissions and other government "scientific" studies of major problems do nothing but hoodwink the public. Discuss.
25. Do you agree with the description in this chapter of how universal medical care was implemented in Canada? Why or why not?

26. A common complaint of members of Parliament, especially if they are members of the opposition, is that the authority of Parliament is being eroded and displaced by government experts and administrative bureaucracy. Discuss.

CHAPTER 2

The Role of the Courts

AS ARBITER OF THE CONSTITUTION

How effective is a statute in remedying a problem? After years of study, after the careful drafting of legislation, and after exhaustive debate in the legislature followed by final enactment, we might hope that at last the problem has been solved, or at least dealt with as best as the present state of our knowledge will permit. But no — frequently, the problem has just begun. If it is to be of any consequence, a new law must restrict or enlarge someone's activities, or lay down conditions for offering or taking away something of value. Serious difficulties arise when the new law begins to affect people's interests.

When someone becomes unhappy about the application of a statute he may complain to an official charged with administering the law. The matter may well end there: the administrator may change his ruling or give a satisfactory explanation to the complainant or the complainant may be dissatisfied with the answer he receives but decide it is not worth his while to take the matter further. If, however, he decides to press his grievance, he will eventually reach a point where asking informally for a remedy has become futile and he must make a formal complaint, before either a court or an administrative board that regularly hears such matters. A serious dispute, though it begins before an administrative board, will normally arrive before a court and may even be carried on further appeal to the Supreme Court of Canada for final disposition. At this point the statute itself may be attacked as unconstitutional. Before the effect of a statute is ultimately determined, then, the statute may have travelled a long way from its passage through Parliament.

In a federal country such as Canada or the United States, for practical purposes the Supreme Court rather than the legislature has the last word. To understand why this is so we must contrast our federal system with that of a unitary (non-federal) country like Great Britain, where there is a single supreme Parliament with complete jurisdiction over the entire country. In theory the British Parliament can make, amend or repeal any law it wishes, although in practice its scope is restrained by custom, popular opinion, and the possibility of the government's defeat. The supremacy of the British Parliament is so pervasive that city and county councils are its creatures; it retains total power over them. In Canada, by contrast, we have two distinct levels of government, federal and provincial: under the British North America Act, each level has an independent existence and its own sphere of activity. Thus, unlike Britain's, our national Parliament cannot alter the structure of the provincial governments. The division of legislative power made principally under sections 91 and 92 of the B.N.A. Act allocates certain fields of jurisdiction to the federal Parliament and other designated fields (including power over municipalities) to each of the provincial Legislatures. The Act gives residual powers to the federal government, so that all fields not expressly allocated to the provinces are within federal jurisdiction.

A constitution may not only allocate jurisdiction between levels of government, but may also prohibit certain things entirely, thereby removing them from the legislative power of both levels of government. (A prohibition of this type may exist in the constitution of a unitary country, but we are here concerned only with federations.) The United States Constitution contains a lengthy list of prohibitions in the form of a Bill of Rights, and the question has frequently arisen whether either Congress or a state legislature has the power to enact a particular law. In Canada, the British North America Act contains no bill of rights. There may be at most a few prohibitions implied by various sections of the Act, but they are of relatively minor significance and will not affect our discussion. Hence, for most intents and purposes, there are no express prohibitions in the Canadian constitution.

In theory then, each legislature, whether federal or provincial, has absolute power within its fields of jurisdiction, just as the British Parliament has. The difficulty is that problems faced by governments refuse to divide themselves into neat clear-cut subjects for the convenience of federal and provincial jurisdictions. Many problems overlap both jurisdictions, and often both levels of government seem to have concurrent powers to regulate an activity. For example, the federal government has jurisdiction over radio and television broadcasting, and the provincial governments have responsibility for education. Who, then, has responsibility for educational television? Does it matter whether an educational television program is delivered in a taped cassette to be played over an internal closed circuit system within a school, received through a telephone line, transmitted from a provincial government building to a cable-television system, or simply comes over the normal television network? The students in each instance watch the same program but, depending upon the method by which it reaches

them, opinion differs about which government has power to regulate the content
of the program.[1]

Problems of jurisdiction arose in the United States before Canada was
founded. In the early 19th century the Supreme Court of the United States held
that neither the federal nor the state governments could have the last word on interpreting the U.S. Constitution; to give one level the power to interpret the document (doubtless in its own favour) would be to confer supremacy upon it.
Instead, the court declared that it must itself be the final arbiter of the Constitution, the umpire between the two levels of government.[2] This position was accepted by the states and by Congress. In Canada, the Supreme Court came to
play the same role soon after Confederation. As a result, our courts play a key
part in legislative reform.

Illustration:

> The Canadian Parliament has received a report of a special study of abuses
> in the stock market that cause investors to lose their savings. It passes a stat-
> ute prohibiting certain kinds of advertising of securities as being mislead-
> ing, consequently making them criminal in nature. A broker who special-
> izes in these transactions, claiming that his activity is lawful, carries on in
> defiance of the statute. He is charged with an offence under the statute and
> raises the following arguments in defence: (a) that the law is unconstitu-
> tional because it purports to make changes in an area that is exclusively
> within the jurisdiction of the provinces under the B.N.A. Act; and (b) that
> even if his first argument is wrong, the government as prosecuting authority
> has placed an unreasonable interpretation upon the statute and has applied it
> too broadly in charging him with an offence. He argues, in other words, that
> under any reasonable interpretation of the statute his activity would remain
> lawful.

We can see from this illustration that the federal government faces a double
problem whenever it attempts any type of reform. First, it must recognize that if
its entire statute is ruled unconstitutional, it will be void and make no change at
all in the law. (The broker in the illustration would then be subject to no new regulation whatever.) Indeed, even were the Supreme Court to interpret the statute
in such a way as to avoid conflict with the constitution, it might nonetheless restrict its application to certain areas under federal jurisdiction and thus so
emasculate the statute that it would fail to accomplish the desired reform. In effect, the court is then saying: "If these words were given a broad meaning, they

---

[1] Federal and provincial governments are profoundly concerned about who controls the means of
mass communication and education. There have been continual consultation and controversy in
recent years. Both levels of government would like to resolve the conflict by mutual agreement
rather than engage in a constitutional battle, with the attendant difficulties described below.

[2] Marbury v. Madison (1803) 5. U.S. Reports, 1 Cranch, 137.

would attempt to regulate activity beyond the jurisdiction of the federal government. Clearly, Parliament could not have meant to do such a thing. If, however, we restrict their meaning to 'such and such', the regulation will be within federal jurisdiction and valid. We will assume that Parliament meant to do only what is possible under the British North America Act, and accordingly find that these words have a restricted meaning." (Once again the broker would escape regulation, if his activity were outside federal jurisdiction as cut down by the court.)

Secondly, the government must recognize that even if its statute survives the constitutional hurdle, a court may still decide that a reasonable interpretation would limit its application to far fewer instances than Parliament intended, and that as a result its desired reform may be in large measure frustrated. (Again in this event, the broker might be saved by the narrow interpretation of the statute.)

A constitutional defeat in the courts is more serious than a narrow interpretation. There is no way that Parliament can overcome a decision by the Supreme Court that a statute is unconstitutional unless the constitution itself is amended — in Canada at present, an almost impossible process.[3] However, if the problem is simply one of interpretation, the government can subsequently introduce an amendment to preclude future arguments of this kind. The trouble with relying on the ability to amend legislation is that except for emergencies or extraordinary pressure on government, the wheels of Parliament "grind exceeding slow," and a year or several years may pass in the normal course before an amendment is enacted.

When the Supreme Court nullifies legislation on constitutional grounds it can arouse strong feelings and sometimes vehement attacks, both on the judges as individuals and on the concept of a court that can have so much authority. A variety of cries can be heard: ''The Court is a reactionary bastion standing in the

---

[3] A constitution, whether it is of a small social club or a large nation, almost always contains provisions for its own amendment. A "simple majority", that is, any number more than 50 per cent (for example, 50.01 per cent) may pass an appropriate motion to change any earlier motion — or law — also passed by a simple majority. But the provisions of a constitution are usually entrenched: only a "special majority" may amend them. Typically a special majority is two thirds or three quarters of the ballots cast, but sometimes there are quite complex special majorities, giving a specified group the power of veto. Unless the group, even if it comprises a very small minority, approves of a proposed amendment, the amendment will be lost.

The British North America Act, although it is Canada's constitution, was passed simply as an ordinary act of the British Parliament at Westminster, and it may be amended by any subsequent act of that Parliament — at least in theory. In fact, it has been amended a number of times, but only at the request of the government of Canada with the agreement of the provinces (and once, at the request of the federal government alone, for a change not affecting the provinces).

Westminster finds its role as the technical amending body of the constitution of another sovereign country bothersome and potentially embarrassing: what would it do if it received a request for an amendment from all Canadian governments except, let us say, for the vehement opposition of one or two of the smaller provinces? It is unanimously agreed that Britain can rid itself of the problem only at the unanimous request of all governments in Canada for an amendment creating a procedure for amendment within Canada itself. So far, all attempts at agreement on such an amending procedure have failed, the last effort having been made at a federal-provincial conference at Victoria, B.C., in 1971.

way of badly needed reform'' — ''The Court has prevented the federal government from running roughshod over the jurisdiction of the provinces'' (or *vice versa*) — ''The Court has stopped the government from making an unwarranted intrusion on individual liberties.'' Judges of the Supreme Court cannot escape making decisions that play a critical role in political, social, and economic change. As a result, the role and the personality of Supreme Court judges in particular, and of judges generally, have become subjects of great interest to legal theorists, sociologists and psychologists, as well as to the practising lawyers who appear before them.

AS INTERPRETER OF LEGISLATION

The Literal versus the Liberal Approach

We have seen how for a long time, legislatures have sought information and advice before passing legislation. When a court is called on to interpret that legislation, what information and advice, what evidence, will it permit to be brought before it? What will it consider? The long-standing English position has been that the meaning of a statute should be apparent on its face so that ''he who runs can read.'' After all, so this argument goes, a person reading a statute should be able to rely on its words alone, without looking further. If he does not understand a particular word or words he should be able to refer to a standard dictionary for assistance, and if the word happens to be a specialized technical term he should be able to refer to a standard technical dictionary or textbook. But that should be the limit of his outside inquiry.

In theory, the English position is laudable: if it were necessary for a person to read other documents such as a multi-volume report of a royal commission in order to learn what a statute means, it would work a great hardship on him. He would run the risk of misunderstanding the statute if he took it at its face value. Even if he had a large law library available containing the needed material — something few people do have — he would not likely have either the time or the expertise to read and understand it.

In practice, however, the English approach leads to other difficulties. Most words do not have precise meanings like mathematical symbols. Frequently they are ambiguous, capable of different shades of meaning; sometimes they have several distinctly different meanings. A dictionary does not help solve such dilemmas. Furthermore, a statute rarely breaks entirely new ground; new laws almost always affect existing ones. (There are a few exceptions, such as a law to govern rights in outer space.) Most often a statute is passed with the express aim of changing existing law. In these circumstances it will not be possible to understand the new statute without first knowing what the law was before it was passed. An extreme example occurs when a legislature repeals an existing law.

Illustration:

New legislation begins with the following words: ''The Widgets Act, Chapter 49 of the Statutes of 1954, is hereby repealed.'' What is the effect of these words? To understand them one must know what the law was before 1954 when it was changed by the Widgets Act, what change that Act made in the law and how the present repealing act changes the law. It may be less simple than it appears. Suppose that before the Widgets Act was passed the manufacture and sale of widgets was illegal. That Act set out rules for their legal manufacture and sale. Does the repeal of the Widgets Act make those activities illegal again, or does it make them entirely free from any regulation or prohibition?

It may be argued that it is foolish for a legislature to pass an act in such ambiguous terms, but statutes similar to the repealing act in the above illustration occur with disquieting frequency through inadvertence, perhaps as a result of hurrying through a backlog of legislation towards the end of a legislative session. The courts are then left with the problem and they have had to devise methods of dealing with them. The English courts have conceded that it is often necessary to examine the state of the law before a statute was passed in order to determine what change has been made. The result is that a person cannot rely solely on the words of a statute — but by the time this fact is recognized, is the traditional English position not a myth?

Legislative History

How far should a court look into the circumstances surrounding the passing of a statute? Should it examine the report of a royal commission that led to the introduction of a bill in Parliament, at the statements of the minister whose department was responsible for the bill, and at the debates in Parliament itself, in other words at the *legislative history* of a statute? British courts have replied that no royal commission, government minister, or member of Parliament can speak for Parliament as a whole. (Indeed, two leading members of the Commons may have disagreed in debate on the meaning of a key phrase in a bill and yet both may have voted for the bill subsequently without their disagreement being resolved.) The view of the courts is that when Parliament passes a law it represents the "will" of Parliament as a whole. Thus the courts should resolve any ambiguities entirely from "objective" evidence: dictionaries, principles of interpretation already developed by the courts, and ascertainment of the state of the law at the time the statute was passed.

Both English and Canadian courts refuse to hear subjective evidence — legislative history — that purports to interpret the will of Parliament. There would be dangers in its use: in Canada, there have been substantial changes in federal income-tax law following a monumental royal-commission report[4] and a major government white paper (statement of policy) on the subject,[5] but to seek explanations for most of the tax changes in either of those documents would be more likely to mislead than help explain the words of the Income Tax Act. On

---

[4] Canada, Royal Commission on Taxation, *Report*. Ottawa: Queen's Printer, 1966.
[5] Benson, E. J. (Minister of Finance), *Proposals for Tax Reform*. Ottawa: Queen's Printer, 1969.

the other hand, a strong body of opinion insists that the courts examine all information available that may help them to understand a statute and give it the most
reasonable interpretation possible. According to this view, the courts themselves
should be able to decide how much weight to give various aspects of legislative
history. In the United States, legislative history is heard by courts and can sometimes be very influential.

The Brandeis Brief

In 1907, Louis Brandeis, a noted lawyer who subsequently became one of the
most distinguished judges of the United States Supreme Court, prepared his *brief*
(his argument) for an important constitutional law case in a novel manner.[6] He
amassed a great quantity of statistical information, and expert testimony of factory inspectors and others to persuade the court that the most up to date knowledge in health and social science should permit it to distinguish the present case
from an earlier decision that invalidated a statute regulating hours of work.
Rather than argue that the Supreme Court was wrong in its first decision, a difficult thing to do successfully, Brandeis argued that it would not be inconsistent
for the Court to recognize the new information and distinguish a prior decision
that it had made under different circumstances; new circumstances demanded a
new interpretation of the Constitution. The Court accepted Brandeis's argument
and upheld the legislation.

This type of argument has become known as a "Brandeis Brief", and the
submission of socio-economic evidence has become an important part of American constitutional argument ever since, frequently playing a decisive role.
Perhaps the most famous decision occurred in 1954, when that Court reversed its
earlier decision that "separate but equal" schooling facilities for black children
did not conflict with constitutional guarantees given to all citizens.[7] The Court
received exhaustive evidence about the inferior quality of education black
children were *in fact* receiving under the purported equality of the dual education
system in many states. There is no doubt that this information was crucial to the
decision to order desegregation of public schools.

While Canadian courts reject legislative history, they do admit appropriate
"Brandeis Brief" evidence, subject to precautions about verification of facts and
cross-examination of expert witnesses. After all, it may be argued that the state
of the economy and social conditions at any particular time, as well as the results
of scientific investigation, are as much "objective" evidence as the state of the
law at the time of the statute under consideration was passed. Thus, in the 1949
"oleomargarine case", the Supreme Court of Canada considered expert testimony that earlier beliefs about margarine being a nutritionally inferior product
and a possible health hazard were mistaken.[8] As a result, legislation by Parlia-

---

[6] Muller v. Oregan 208 U.S. 412 (1907).
[7] Brown v. Board of Education 347 U.S. 438 (1954), overruling Plessy v. Ferguson 163 U.S. 537
(1896).
[8] Reference re Validity of Section 5(a) Dairy Industry Act [1949] S.C.R. 1, [1949] 1 D.L.R. 433.

ment under the federal power to enact criminal law, prohibiting the manufacture and sale of margarine, was held to be unconstitutional. The decision permitted the provinces to pass legislation to regulate the production and sale of margarine.

We have seen that specialized studies and expert technical advice have become increasingly important and more widely used in planning legislation; to a lesser extent, they are now used by courts called upon to examine the constitutional validity of legislation.

AS PROTECTOR OF CIVIL LIBERTIES

The Various Meanings of Civil Liberties

The phrase "civil liberties" occurs frequently in the news without any clear idea being given of what it means. The term is difficult to define because it comprises a number of quite separate ideas, related only by a general concern for the well-being of the individual citizen. Two other terms — "civil rights" and "human rights" — are often used as synonyms. "Civil liberties" and "civil rights" are the older terms, and date from at least as far back as the 18th century. They have referred traditionally to freedom of the individual in politics and religion. These terms have embraced freedom of expression (both of speech and of the press), freedom of association and assembly, freedom to practise and preach one's religion, freedom from arbitrary arrest and detention, and the right to a fair trial.[9]

We should note, however, that the term "civil rights" has a peculiar meaning in Canadian constitutional law. Section 92 of the British North America Act designates "property and civil rights" as an area of provincial responsibility, and the provinces have relied on it in claiming jurisdiction over a wide variety of matters. The Supreme Court of Canada has generally taken the term, as used in section 92, to mean something like "private rights" relating to the ownership of property, contract law and family relations. Our concern in this chapter is not, of course, limited to this special usage.

Mainly as a result of the horrors of the Second World War — deportation, starvation and genocide — there arose a greatly heightened awareness of human needs beyond the traditional freedoms we have already mentioned. United States President Franklin D. Roosevelt gave eloquent expression to these needs in his statement of "the Four Freedoms" in 1941.[10] They were developed in greater

---

[9] These rights have received international recognition since the Second World War. See: United Nations documents *Universal Declaration of Human Rights* (1948) and *Covenant on Civil and Political Rights* (1966); *European Convention for the Protection of Human Rights and Fundamental Freedoms*, 213 United Nations Treaty Series 221 (1955); Luini del Russo, A., *International Protection of Human Rights*, Appendices A-E, Washington, D.C.: Lerner Law Book Co. Inc., 1971; Stein, E. and Hay, F., *Law and Institutions in the Atlantic Area*, Ch. VIII. New York: The Bobbs-Merrill Co., 1967.

[10] Roosevelt, F.D., *Message to Congress*, January 16, 1941, as reported, for example, in Hardman, J.B.S., *Rendezvous with Destiny: Addresses and Opinions of Franklin Delano Roosevelt*, pp. 171-2. The four freedoms he identified were: freedom of speech and expression everywhere in the world; freedom of every person to worship God in his own way everywhere in the world; freedom from want everywhere in the world; and freedom from fear anywhere in the world.

detail in the United Nations *Universal Declaration of Human Rights,* and the term "human rights" came into general usage at that time. It is concerned in large part with Roosevelt's phrase "freedom from want" and the related idea of equal opportunity for employment and housing, without discrimination. The idea has been further refined to include the assertion that it is society's responsibility to create jobs in order to make adequate employment available to a wage earner in every household. It includes also the opportunity to receive publicly-supported education and the right to reasonable minimum subsistence in food, shelter and clothing, even when unemployed. In addition, Roosevelt's "freedom from fear" has been interpreted in part to mean freedom from discrimination based on sex, race, religion and nationality, not only in housing and employment, but also in access to all public facilities and even to private clubs.

This expanded idea of human rights is not as recent as one might suppose; indeed, it is akin to Aristotle's concept of distributive justice. Certainly, the new awareness of problems of social and economic welfare has helped to raise community standards in many parts of the world. The recognition of these rights depends mainly on the political and social climate within a country, changes in the perception of the role of government, and social legislation. The courts remain primarily concerned with traditional civil liberties related to political and religious freedoms. Since our first concern is a better understanding of the legal system, we shall next examine briefly some legal aspects of political and religious freedom.

Constitutional Protection

The legal base for the protection of civil liberties in Canada is a precarious one and it cannot be adequately explained in the space available here. We can only outline the constitutional problem and refer readers to the short reading list for this topic in the Bibliography at the end of this book.

As we have noted, Canada does not have a bill of rights entrenched in the British North America Act as the United States has in its Constitution. When civil liberties are entrenched in a constitution, they cannot be changed by ordinary statute. They may be varied only by a special amending procedure, usually requiring a majority of two thirds or three quarters of the votes in the legislature or in a popular referendum. Indeed, if any legislature in the country enacts a law that would have the effect of infringing any of the civil liberties provided for in the constitution, that law is invalid and of no effect.

In the absence of an entrenched bill of rights, can civil liberties receive any constitutional protection in Canada? In a rather curious way, a number of civil liberties have been protected by the constitution. Many, though by no means all, attempts to interfere with civil liberties have been made by provincial legislatures asserting jurisdiction under the heading of "property and civil rights in the province" as assigned by section 92 of the B.N.A. Act to the provinces. When these statutes were attacked in court, much of the argument was about the civil liberties infringed, but the decisions have usually turned on the legal issue of which level of government has jurisdiction under the B.N.A. Act. When the Supreme Court of Canada strikes down provincial statutes, it usually declares that jurisdiction over the subject-matter in controversy is federal (frequently because the statutes assert a criminal law power) and hence beyond the powers of the provincial government to regulate or prohibit. On the other hand, when the federal government has been challenged for infringing civil liberties, the question has usually been one of statutory interpretation: did a government agency exceed the powers granted to it under a federal statute? A federal statute has been rarely attacked as unconstitutional; it usually concerns criminal law, immigration, external affairs, or wartime or other national emergencies, where the supremacy of the federal Parliament is unchallenged. In recent years, the existence of another federal statute, the Canadian Bill of Rights, has provided a further base from which federal infringement of civil liberties can be challenged.

The Canadian Bill of Rights

In 1960, the Parliament of Canada enacted a Bill of Rights.[11] It was passed in the same way as other federal statutes and can be amended by normal parliamentary procedure. The value of our Bill of Rights is a subject of controversy. Does it significantly improve the protection of civil liberties in Canada?

Some politicians and jurists believe that it is advantageous to have an explicit parliamentary declaration of civil liberties, and there is now a series of cases showing that the Bill of Rights has influenced our courts. In the 1969 case of *Regina v. Drybones*[12] the Supreme Court of Canada declared that any provision of a federal statute that infringed the rights and freedoms set out in the Bill of Rights would be inoperative unless Parliament had expressly declared that the provision should operate notwithstanding the Bill of Rights. As a result, an Indian accused under a section of the Indian Act of being intoxicated while off a reserve was acquitted, because the section of that Act was held to offend the Bill of Rights: since the section would not apply equally to a non-Indian it was held to be discriminatory.

Thus the Bill of Rights proved to be something more than an ordinary statute; as the *Drybones* case shows, the Bill of Rights could be reasonably effective in establishing standards of respect for civil liberties with which other statutes of Parliament must now comply. However, more recent decisions of the Supreme Court have cast some doubt on how far it may be willing to go in making the Bill of Rights effective against invasions of civil liberties in other sections of the Indian Act and, by implication, in any other federal statute.[13] These cases illustrate the complexity of determining questions of equality.

In any event, critics of the Bill of Rights believe it would be dangerous to rely upon it as a basic protection of civil liberties. The critical time when civil

---

[11] R.S.C. 1970, Appendix III, s. 1.

[12] Regina v. Drybones (1969) 9 D.L.R. (3d) 473.

[13] See Attorney-General of Canada v. Lavell [1974] S.C.R. 1349. See also, Canard v. Attorney-General of Canada and Rees [1972] 5 W.W.R. 678 (C.A.) The latter case was reversed by the Supreme Court of Canada, Attorney-General of Canada et al. v. Canard (1975) 50 D.L.R. (3d) 548, thereby further obscuring the effectiveness of the Bill of Rights.

rights need protecting is when they are called in aid of those who espouse un-
popular causes; in a time of crisis it may prove all too easy for Parliament to pass
new laws that override it. Critics argue that our Canadian Bill of Rights may lull
us into a false sense of security. Moreover, as a federal statute, it does not govern
those large areas of our law reserved to the provincial legislatures under the
B.N.A. Act.[14]

Freedom of Expression

The interest of the individual. The right to speak one's mind is a precious personal liberty, a means of self-realization. In countries that restrict this right for
political or other reasons, the effect is demoralizing and intellectually stifling. A
citizen with a lively interest in the community around him can, perhaps more
readily than he realizes, find himself a member of a minority, dissenting
vigorously from a popular sentiment or equally vigorously advocating an un-
popular cause. Other citizens may take strong exception to his views and, indeed, try to suppress them. Only by his own willingness to tolerate offensive
comment by others can he justify the right to free expression for himself.

As always, the exercise of a freedom cannot be totally unrestrained; it carries with it responsibilities — and limits that may be imposed when those responsibilities are ignored. From the individual's point of view there are three main
restrictions on freedom of expression, the laws of *defamation, sedition* and *obscenity.*

A person may suffer injury not only by the actions of another (as when he is
run down by a carelessly-driven car), but also by the words of another (as when
he is falsely accused of having stolen money). As we shall discuss in Chapter 4, a
person who defames another by unjustifiably injuring his reputation becomes liable to pay compensation for the harm done. If the wrongdoer persists in communicating the defamatory statement, he may be ordered by a court to cease on
pain of imprisonment for failing to comply.

In the eyes of the law, it is one thing to give a critical opinion about another
person but quite another to assert facts that are untrue. In practice, the line between opinion and fact is often difficult to discern, especially in the heat of emotional debate. "I don't think John Doe would be a courageous mayor," is a
statement of opinion. "John Doe stole his partner's profits," is alleging a fact
that if untrue would certainly be defamatory. But what is "John Doe is a thief?"
or "John Doe would steal his grandmother's false teeth if he had the chance?"

---

[14] To date, Saskatchewan has been the only province to enact a provincial bill of rights governing its
own legislative enactments. See Saskatchewan Bill of Rights Act, R.S.S. 1965, c. 378 as
amended by 1970, c. 56 and 1972, c. 104. The other provinces have legislation prohibiting discrimination in housing and employment. See, for example: Human Rights Act, R.S.N.S. 1967,
c. 130; Human Rights Code of British Columbia, St. of B.C. 1973 (2nd session), c. 119; Ontario
Human Rights Code, R.S.O. 1970, c. 318. In Saskatchewan these forms of discrimination are
prohibited separately by The Fair Accommodation Practices Act, R.S.S. 1965, c. 379 and The
Fair Employment Practices Act, R.S.S. 1965, c. 293.

An outspoken critic has sometimes rued his words on finding himself the defendant in a lawsuit for defamation.

Although the law of defamation restricts a person's freedom of expression, it is justified because it helps protect another person's right to freedom from unwarranted and harmful statements. In the area of public debate on government policy and actions, as opposed to statements about specific individuals or groups, the law of defamation hinders freedom of expression very little.

The second restriction comes closer to being an interference with free criticism of the government. The uttering or publishing of a *seditious libel*[15] is an attack upon the government or the institutions of the country (for instance, on the judiciary or Parliament itself) that goes too far and becomes a crime. How far is too far? A placard proclaiming, ''The McGrew Government — a bunch of thugs. Down with McGrew!'' may be vehement but it is not sedition. Nor would an election poster saying, ''Let's kick out the McGrew Gang!'' be seditious. But the same poster carried to the doors of Parliament in front of a crowd armed with clubs and bricks might well amount to sedition. In other words, criticism becomes sedition when it grows so violent as to exhort others to act violently against the lawful government, and when that exhortation calls for immediate action.

It is only slightly less difficult to talk about the purpose of obscenity laws than about the meaning of obscenity itself. In a very general way, the purpose of laws against obscenity is to protect the general public, and more especially the very young, from all forms of communication — verbal, pictorial, or dramatic — that tend to ''corrupt morals'' or ''outrage the moral sense of the ordinary citizen''.[16]

This double standard leads to a paradox: there is no doubt that many people are outraged by certain books, magazines, paintings and dramatic works; on the other hand, there is no objective evidence that a particular piece of allegedly obscene material has had any ascertainable corrupting effect on a specific person or persons. Obscenity is usually associated with pornography and related to sexual conduct, but it has a wider meaning that includes extreme forms of violence and cruelty. One school of thought asserts that sexual obscenity is far less harmful, if indeed it is harmful at all, than obscenity relating to violence and cruelty. Many thoughtful and moderate people have concluded that no such thing as an identifiable, harmful piece of obscene work exists, but that the cumulative effect of obscenity over a period of years does exert a harmful influence on general community standards of moral conduct. Further, they believe that this is a serious problem: individual moral views are subtly changed for the worse by continued exposure to obscenity, especially during the formative younger years.

The issue of obscenity does not often involve material of a direct political nature. Usually it has to do either with profitable commercial pornography marketed by deliberately appealing to some people's taste for sensational or for-

---

[15] Criminal Code, R.S.C. 1970, c. C-34, s. 60.
[16] See Criminal Code, s. 159.

bidden material, or with works defended as having literary or artistic merit in which the allegedly obscene material forms an integral part. The distinction between the two has frequently been debated before the courts. In the years since the Second World War, there has been a steady narrowing of the area prohibited by our obscenity laws, and a growing toleration of material that until recently would have been considered clearly obscene. The role of the courts has on the whole been to support this trend, so that our obscenity laws are now relatively insignificant restrictions on freedom of expression.

The main methods used to suppress obscenity are *censorship* and *seizure and prosecution.* Censorship is carried out by an administrative board before the works reach the public. The board members exercise their discretion about what to prohibit, to release subject to changing or deleting portions, or to pass freely.[17] The process is almost entirely outside the courts. Exhibitors of films and publishers of books usually abide by censorship decisions; to appeal to a higher authority of government, or to the courts, would endanger a continuing cordial relationship with the censors—people they must deal with regularly in earning their living. Prosecution, on the other hand, follows police seizure of offending material that has already reached the public. There may follow a lengthy trial at which the presiding judge must decide whether the material complained of is or is not obscene. In view of the mixed and ever-changing views on this subject, his task is an extraordinarily difficult one.

The public interest. Freedom of expression is the primary civil liberty, not only because it is essential to personal liberty to be able to speak one's mind, but also because it is a fundamental precondition of a democratic system of government. The right to criticize freely — to dissent publicly from the views and actions of the government — provides the only effective means of informing the populace about what government is doing (not just what it says it is doing), and assessing the extent to which its actions are good or bad. Former Chief Justice Lyman Duff of the Supreme Court of Canada said:

> . . . it is axiomatic that the practice of this free right of discussion of public affairs, notwithstanding its individual mischiefs, is the breath of life for parliamentary institutions.[18]

Vociferous public reaction to government proposals has often led to important alterations or even to the abandonment of plans. A government that wins power with a large majority in one election has often suffered defeat in the following contest, when vigilant and critical press, radio and television have illuminated its errors in judgment and insensitivity to social and economic needs.

In any form of totalitarian state, the first concern of the rulers is to suppress free expression as the most dangerous kind of heresy, a poison in the body politic likely to lead to rebellion. Repression invariably takes the same form: the gov-

---

[17] See, for example, Motion Pictures Act, St. of B.C. 1970, c. 27, s. 5; Theatres and Amusements Act, R.S.N.S. 1967, c. 304, s. 3.

[18] Reference re: Alberta Statutes [1938] S.C.R. 100, at 133; [1938] 2 D.L.R. 81 at 107.

ernment accuses its critics of deliberate misrepresentation of government policies and activities, and of reporting events in a distorted and inflammatory manner that is calculated to encourage breaches of the law and violence. Censorship, confiscation of newspapers and journals, and padlocking the premises of opposition media are usually accompanied by repression of opposition political parties and a ban on all forms of public assembly other than those sponsored by the government. The ruling clique makes self-righteous statements characterizing its critics as "criminal elements, enemies of the state". It promises that as soon as the "temporary" unrest and risk of insurrection passes, full civil rights will be restored.

Unhappily, examples of these practices abound throughout the world. It would be unwise to single out one or two examples: no doubt a number of readers would be upset that we had selected some while ignoring others they considered to be worse. In any event, it is well to appreciate that even nations which confidently regard themselves free from these forms of repression remain in danger of succumbing to them in times of crisis. Let us consider, then, some examples from recent Canadian history.

Freedom of the press. The leading judicial opinion on freedom of the press in Canada arose out of the election of a Social Credit government in Alberta in the 1930s under the leadership of Premier William Aberhart. The federal government asked the Supreme Court of Canada for an opinion on the constitutionality of three statutes enacted by the Alberta Legislature in 1937. One of these statutes, entitled the Accurate News and Information Act (generally referred to as the Press Bill), purported to require newspapers published in the province to carry government statements explaining the policies of the government and refuting other published comment on those policies. It required newspapers to report to a government official, when requested, the source of any statements contained in them and the name and address of the writer of any editorial, article or news item. It also authorized the prohibition of further publication by an offending newspaper or of anything written by a specified person.

The explanation for this attempt to interfere with the press was an economic one. The people in the Prairie provinces of Canada had suffered great hardship during the 1930s, and the Social Credit platform offered them a panacea in its system of proposed monetary reform. The advantages of "social credit" would be available, however, only so long as the average citizen had faith in the system and believed it would work, or — so the argument ran — until the system became established and proved itself. Any newspaper comment that induced skepticism would undermine the plan and destroy the currency of the Treasury Credit certificates which were to be substituted for money and become the medium by which Albertans might obtain a free distribution of goods and services derived from the unemployed capacity of the industries and people of the province.

The Supreme Court of Canada was unanimous in its 1938 decision[19] that

---

[19] *Ibid.*, at 100. A review of this and the other cases discussed in this section is to be found in Russell, *Leading Constitutional Decisions*, Part Five, pp. 166-215.

this statute was *ultra vires* (beyond the power of the provincial legislature) and therefore ineffective. It held that criticism of government policy comes within the ambit of criminal law, and noted that the Criminal Code provides that no one shall be deemed to have a seditious intention only because he intends in good faith to point out errors or defects in the government.[20] As one of the judges speaking for the Supreme Court, Mr. Justice Cannon, said in part:

> I agree with the submission of the Attorney-General for Canada that this bill deals with the regulation of the press of Alberta, not from the viewpoint of private wrongs or civil injuries resulting from any alleged infringement or privation of civil rights which belong to individuals, considered as individuals, but from the viewpoint of public wrongs or crimes, i.e. involving a violation of the public rights and duties to the whole community, considered as a community, in its social aggregate capacity. . . .[21]

> Under the British system which is ours, no political party can erect a prohibitory barrier to prevent the electors from getting information concerning the policy of the government. Freedom of discussion is essential to enlighten public opinion in a democratic State; it cannot be curtailed without affecting the right of the people to be informed through sources independent of the government concerning matters of public interest. There must be an untrammelled publication of the news and political opinions of the political parties contending for ascendancy. As stated in the preamble of the British North America Act, our constitution is and will remain, unless radically changed, "similar in principle to that of the United Kingdom". At the time of Confederation, the United Kingdom was a democracy. Democracy cannot be maintained without its foundation: free public opinion and free discussion throughout the nation of all matters affecting the State within the limits set by the criminal code and the common law. Every inhabitant in Alberta is also a citizen of the Dominion. The province may deal with his property and civil rights of a local and private nature within the province; but the province cannot interfere with his status as a Canadian citizen and his fundamental right to express freely his untrammelled opinion about government policies and discuss matters of public concern. The mandatory and prohibitory provisions of the Press Bill are, in my opinion, *ultra vires* of the provincial legislature. They interfere with the free working of the political organization of the Dominion. They have a tendency to nullify the political rights of the inhabitants of Alberta, as citizens of Canada, and cannot be considered as dealing with matters purely private and local in that province.[22]

Freedom of speech. The Supreme Court of Canada decision in *Switzman v. Elbling and Attorney-General for Quebec*[23] is another very important step in the

---

[20] See The Criminal Code, R.S.C. 1970, c. C-34, s. 61.
[21] Reference re: Alberta Statutes, [1938] S.C.R. 100 at 144; [1938] 2 D.L.R. 81 at 118.
[22] [1938] S.C.R. 100 at 145; [1938] 2 D.L.R. 81 at 119.
[23] [1957] S.C.R. 285; (1957) 7 D.L.R. (2d) 337.

delineation of freedom of expression. In that case the constitutional validity of a 1937 act of the Quebec Legislature entitled "An Act Respecting Communistic Propaganda" was in question. The Act purported in part to make it illegal for any person occupying a house within the province to use it or allow any person to make use of it to propagate communism or bolshevism by any means whatsoever, and contained a further provision authorizing the closing of such a house. (For the latter reason, the act became known as the "Padlock Act".) The Act also purported to make it unlawful to print, publish or distribute within the province any newspaper or other document propagating or tending to propagate communism or bolshevism, and provided for the imprisonment of anyone violating this section.

In this case the appellant, Switzman, had been the tenant of premises in Montreal and was sued by his landlady, Elbling, who sought to have Switzman's lease forfeited before its term expired and recover damages from him on the grounds that he had used the premises for the illegal purpose of propagating communism. Switzman pleaded in defence that the "Padlock Act" was unconstitutional. The landlady's action was successful in the trial court and upheld on appeal to the Quebec Court of Queen's Bench; Switzman then appealed to the Supreme Court of Canada.

With only one judge dissenting, the Supreme Court of Canada held that the Act was *ultra vires*. Several of the judges agreed that the Act amounted to legislation in respect of criminal law and was, therefore, a provincial invasion of the power assigned to the federal authority in Canada. Among the judges, Mr. Justice Abbott was the most explicit in relating the issue to an encroachment on fundamental civil liberties. He said, in part:

> The *Canada Elections Act*, the provisions of the British North America Act which provide for Parliament meeting at least once a year and for the election of a new parliament at least every five years, and the *Senate and House of Commons Act*, are examples of enactments which make specific statutory provision for ensuring the exercise of this right of public debate and public discussion. Implicit in all such legislation is the right of candidates for Parliament or for a Legislature, and of citizens generally, to explain, criticize, debate and discuss in the freest possible manner such matters as the qualifications, the policies, and the political, economic and social principles advocated by such candidates or by the political parties or groups of which they may be members.[24]

Freedom of Religion

Does religious freedom come within the jurisdiction of "property and civil rights in the province"? The important question of whether a province can regulate the conditions for the practising and preaching of a religion, or even prohibit a religious sect, arose in *Saumur v. Quebec and Attorney-General for Quebec*.[25]

---

[24] [1957] S.C.R. 285 at 327; (1957) 7 D.L.R. (2d) 337 at 371.
[25] [1953] 2 S.C.R. 299; [1953] 4 D.L.R. 641.

Saumur, a member of the Jehovah's Witnesses, challenged the validity of a Quebec City by-law prohibiting the distribution in the streets of any book, pamphlet or tract without the permission of the Chief of Police. Saumur sought to distribute a pamphlet without obtaining permission. In a subsequent prosecution, the trial court and on appeal the Quebec Court of Queen's Bench both upheld the validity of the by-law. The Supreme Court of Canada, however, by a five-to-four majority, declared the by-law invalid. Two of the dissenting judges held that religious freedom was a "civil right in the province" and, by inference, that the city by-law did not contravene any existing legislation of the province in question. A majority of the judges did not agree, though for different reasons: some thought that the power to restrict religious freedom lay exclusively with the federal government because the British North America Act assigned criminal law to federal jurisdiction; others found in another section of the B.N.A. Act that protected against provincial interference in the educational rights of religious denominations an implication that the provinces had no jurisdiction in laws affecting religious freedom; another attached considerable importance to the existence of statutes antedating the B.N.A. Act which guaranteed the right of citizens of Quebec to profess the religion of the Church of Rome, and inferred from these statutes that the right to religious freedom transcended any assignment of civil rights to the provinces:

> . . . The statutory history of the expression 'Property and Civil Rights' . . . [and] its parallel enactment with special provisions relating to religion shows indubitably that such matters as religious belief, duty and observances were never intended to be included within that collocation of powers [matters of a merely local or private nature in the province]. If it had not been so, the exceptional safeguards to Roman Catholics would have been redundant.[26]

A discussion of this complex case, even in only the barest outline, helps us to see how complicated and uncertain a matter the right to religious freedom in Canada is. It helps underline the fact that although constitutional law is a technical, difficult and often abstruse area of the law, the problems that arise under it can be of great personal importance to us.

Other Civil Liberties

We have limited our discussion of civil liberties to freedom of expression and religion as important examples of the issues confronting the legal system, and especially the courts, in adjusting the competing interests demanding protection. Other examples are freedom from arbitrary arrest and the right to a fair trial, including the rights to remain silent and to object to use by the prosecution of illegally obtained evidence (for instance, by wiretapping).[27] In these areas, the

---

[26] *Ibid.*, per Rand, J. at 329.
[27] Protection of Privacy Act, St. of Can. 1973-74, c. C-50 (Bill C-176).

courts attempt to resolve the conflict between the need of society to protect itself from criminal activity by effective means, and the right of the individual to protect himself from the arbitrary use of governmental power that would deprive him of his freedom.

AS ARBITER OF DISPUTES BETWEEN PRIVATE PARTIES

In this chapter we have considered the role of our courts in arbitrating constitutional issues, in interpreting and applying statutes and protecting civil liberties. Under a legal system such as ours, derived from the English common law, legislation has historically played only a small part in resolving legal disputes between private parties — individuals, corporations or other organized groups not connected with the government. Despite the rapid increase in statutory law in recent years, there remain extensive areas of the law unaffected by legislation. In these areas, the courts apply principles that they themselves have developed in the process of rendering decisions in the past and in novel situations, they develop new principles. These activities of the courts are important and complex. We shall discuss the evolution and continuing importance of court decisions based on principles developed by the courts themselves, in the next chapter.

LEGAL REALISM

While courts are mainly occupied with private lawsuits (motor-vehicle accidents, family conflicts, and commercial disputes) and with criminal prosecutions, it is the constitutional cases that often decide the fate of important social reforms, and in the last few years of the 19th century they focussed the attention of American legal writers on the methods of the courts generally. Led by Oliver Wendell Holmes, the most influential legal thinker of the age and subsequently a great judge of the Supreme Court of the United States, a new, skeptical school of thought known as ''legal realism'' emerged.

Holmes stated that the chief concern of a lawyer when advising a client is to be able to predict which way a court is likely to decide a possible lawsuit. The thing that counts in making a prediction, Holmes asserted, is not to study what judges *say* but what they *do*. To understand this observation, one must first know something about the nature of a court decision.

A court renders its decision by giving *judgment* (making a formal order): let us say for example that the defendant has been found responsible for injuring the plaintiff (the complaining party) through his careless operation of an automobile, and must pay *x* dollars in damages (compensation) to the plaintiff. This formal judgment is what the courts *do* and, as far as the parties to the lawsuit are concerned, it is what counts. In many cases, especially if the case is of considerable importance, the court also gives *reasons for judgment,* aptly described as the judge's justification to the losing side for deciding against it. The reasons for judgment are published in an unending series of books called law reports, found in all law libraries and studied unremittingly by law students, lawyers and other judges. Frequently the *reasons* for judgment are referred to inaccurately as the *judgment*. The reasons then are what the courts *say*. Traditional theory asserts that these reasons form a consistent set of principles from which it is possible to learn what the law is and, in turn, predict how the courts will act in future disputes.

The legal realists claimed that studying only the reasons for judgment as reported in law books creates a mythical view of the law and is harmful both to the practising lawyer (plus his client, of course) and to the cause of law reform. While not denying that general principles and specific rules enunciated by the courts do influence later decisions and *help* predict what may happen, the realists viewed these reasons for judgment as only a small portion of "the law in action". They claimed that at least two other elements are frequently more significant than the principles developed in preceding cases: (a) "facts" are more important than "law", — thus, the lawyer who establishes facts favourable to his client and so creates a sympathy for him is more likely to obtain a favourable decision than one who merely quotes favourable legal principles; and (b) the judge's personal bias is more important than "law" — his opinions, his political affiliation, and a host of other psychological influences. If a judge's moral views tend to be puritanical, therefore, he is more likely than his fellow judges to look with disfavour on a party whose conduct has offended conventional moral standards and, where the conduct was of a criminal nature, to give the accused a more severe sentence. The more extreme legal realists suggested that a judge's conscious or subconscious awareness of popular feeling, and perhaps even the state of his digestion, are likely to influence his decisions more than the rules on which he ostensibly relies.

The realists correctly emphasized that the great majority of lawsuits are decided conclusively at trial, that is, at the first hearing of the case before a single judge. A trial judge hears all the evidence and summarizes it in his *findings of fact* (part of the reasons for judgment); he also listens to the legal arguments of counsel for both sides before he decides what laws apply to the facts as he has found them, and then delivers judgment. It is at the trial stage where the court (the judge and possibly jury) encounters in person the principal parties to the dispute and their witnesses, where a sympathy or antagonism derived from a coincidence or conflict of cultural values is most likely to arise, and where lawyers have the greatest scope for playing on the emotions and prejudices of the court. Of course, if the loser is sufficiently unhappy with the trial judge's decision (sometimes both sides are dissatisfied), he may appeal to a court of appeal. To launch an appeal, however, is a costly and time-consuming process, and the appeal court must be persuaded — no easy task — to overrule the trial judge. Thus most litigants choose not to pursue their cases further than the trial court.

Generally speaking, appeal courts accept the findings of fact of the trial judge and reconsider only his application of the law. Sometimes, especially in criminal cases, a court of appeal may accept an argument that the trial judge excluded important evidence supporting one side of the case, or that he admitted highly prejudicial and improper evidence against one side, or, more rarely, that the evidence does not support the judge's finding of fact. But since the judges sitting on the court of appeal have not had the opportunity to observe the demeanour of witnesses, assess the inflection in their voices and draw conclusions about their credibility, they are hesitant to interfere with a trial judge's findings of fact; they are concerned mainly with what principles of law apply to them. It is precisely because of this generally limited role of appeal courts that the realists focussed their attention upon the trial judge and the fact-finding process. The personal prejudices of a judge are more likely to influence a court's decision when the decision is rendered by a single judge than when it is rendered jointly by two or more judges. It is therefore paradoxical that the trial judge, whose decision is only occasionally appealed from, presides alone, while appeal courts usually have three judges, at least two of whom must agree to render a new decision.

Furthermore, because of the vast number of trial court decisions in the United States, few trial judgments are reported (published), whereas virtually all court of appeal decisions are reported. And it is the judgments of appeal courts that are studied by the legal profession while trial judgments are largely ignored. This criticism is not quite so apt in Canada, where many more decisions at trial are reported in the law reports. We are able to do this not only because we have one tenth the population of the United States, but also because Canadians are less litigious and so have proportionately fewer lawsuits.

The tendency of the realists was to denigrate what judges say — the law in reported cases and in legal treatises — and emphasize the uncertainty, even the irrationality, in the trial process. If the law depends on the state of a judge's digestion it would seem that rules count for very little. But this is not true; the law in books covers a far greater portion of "the law in action" than the realists would admit. It influences and is frequently decisive in a host of legal transactions and relationships that never come before a court. For this reason most legal scholars, supported by the opinions of practising lawyers, reject the excesses of the legal realists.

There are two important areas where people use the law in books continuously without encountering the uncertainties of the trial process. First, they use many legal rules as general guidelines only, simply as a background for a continuing relationship. Neither party stands on his strict rights because it is not in his interest to do so. Instead of fighting his case in a courtroom he prefers to settle any disagreement by informal compromise, as the best means of preserving an amicable and mutually advantageous relationship. Examples can be found in relations among partners and in the field of labour, where some enterprises have had decades of good relations between management and labour without resort to strikes, arbitration or the courts. Secondly, very large areas of the law have highly-developed, predictable and generally fair rules, and people use them as a basis for resolving problems without going to court. Thus a defaulting supplier in a contract to deliver goods realizes full well that he has broken his agreement and may offer to supply different goods of higher quality to make up for his failure; his purchaser may accept willingly rather than resort to a lawsuit.

Even when disputes do go to court, many are decided in a predictable manner, the side with the better case suing in order to enforce its rights against a stubborn defendant. This situation arises frequently in family disputes about the division of assets, or when a spouse sues for an allowance for support. (These decisions are rarely reported because they add nothing new to the evolution of the law.) These predictable cases apart, we are left with an area of genuine uncertainty where the reason for going to court is that either the facts or the law, or both, are acknowledged to be uncertain: the result here is indeed unpredictable. In these circumstances the very fact of uncertainty does increase the potential role of such other factors as a judge's bias. But this part of the law in action is much smaller than the legal realists would have had us believe, and they were unwarranted in using it to demonstrate that the law generally is uncertain.

Nevertheless, the legal realists have made a very important contribution. First and foremost, they made it a legitimate activity to study openly and in a scholarly and objective fashion, those factors that are traditionally considered as non-legal — indeed, improper — but which in reality influence many legal decisions. Certainly, self-knowledge in a judge should help him overcome his own biases and make him a better judge. As well, those responsible for selecting judges (in Canada, the federal and provincial departments of justice) may consider more openly the general character of a prospective judge, in addition to his legal abilities, both to ensure a better choice of individual judges and to achieve a balance of opinion on appeal courts.

In addition, the realists emphasized the importance of facts and the fact-finding process. They gave great impetus to more scientific consideration of the rules of evidence and court procedures to improve the processes, and hence the fairness of the courts. In this respect the realists have been strongly influenced by the social sciences as a whole. Together with the writers in sociological jurisprudence, they have helped break down the barriers isolating law as an independent discipline with its own logic and language, and to place it centrally in society as a major instrument for good or ill. This practical accomplishment has far outweighed any contribution of a theoretical nature. Legal realism has taught us that a hard-headed assessment of such institutions as the courts is a beginning towards their reform.

It has been our goal in Chapters 1 and 2 to introduce the reader to legal theory and persuade him that law shares a common subject matter with the other social sciences in its concern for the effective operation of an immensely complex modern society. The reader may even perhaps have been surprised to learn that the answers to the fundamental questions of law are not any easier to find than they are in economics or in sociology.

QUESTIONS FOR REVIEW

1. How do the courts become involved in the process of legislative reform?
2. Why do British courts refuse to examine legislative history?
3. What is a "Brandeis Brief"?

4. Contrast a judgment with the reasons for judgment.
5. How does the role of an appeal court differ from that of a trial court?
6. Describe briefly the main contentions of the legal realists. Is there a conflict between the perception of legal realists and that of legal positivists?
7. Do statutes ever give rise to judge-made law?
8. What is the argument that justifies a power in the Supreme Court to override the will of Parliament?
9. Give an example of a legal problem that may arise from an attempt in a constitution to divide powers between levels of government.
10. Is it possible for a statute to be held to be constitutional and yet substantially fail in its purpose on constitutional grounds?
11. Is one more likely to be liable for defamation if he says to another person, "Bill Brown stole a car last August," than if he says, "Bill Brown is a thief"?
12. Why is the constitutionality of a statute a more serious issue than its interpretation?
13. What main criticisms can be made of a system of providing protection for civil liberties by means of a Bill of Rights as Canada has done?
14. What was the significance of the *Drybones* case?
15. What arguments can be made, consistent with the protection of civil liberties, for some restraint on freedom of expression?
16. What is the usual form of political argument by which a suppression of free speech is justified?
17. Would you agree that a rule against any form of discrimination has universal validity, or do you think it should sometimes be waived with a view to helping disadvantaged minority groups (as, for example, in admission to universities)?
18. Should corporations have civil rights like individuals?
19. "There is another reason for democracy's commitment to the freedom of the individual — the belief that social progress is more likely to occur in an atmosphere where differences are permitted than in an atmosphere where differences are restricted. Many of the greatest human achievements were conceived in the womb of disagreement." (A. A. Borovoy, *The Fundamentals of our Fundamental Freedoms,* p. 4. Toronto: The Canadian Civil Liberties Education Trust, 1974.) Elaborate with one or two examples.
20. "We have a parliament to pass laws, a government to administer laws, and a police department to enforce laws. Ironically, these potent instruments for the restriction of liberty are necessary for the enjoyment of liberty." (*Ibid.,* p. 5.) Comment on the meaning of this quotation.

CHAPTER 3

The Machinery of Justice

WHO MAKES LAW?

How can we know when rules are also laws? As we have noted, Hume defined positive law as a body of rules for the breach of which sanctions are imposed.[1] His definition has been useful but not complete: the enforcement of rules must be the responsibility of government and not of private persons. Thus, a restaurant owner who makes a rule that male patrons at dinner will not be admitted unless they wear neck ties and jackets, has not made a law. Nor are the rules of a private organization, let us say a tennis club, considered law; a tennis club may impose effective sanctions such as fining or expelling a member who breaks an important club rule, but its rules amount to no more than a private arrangement among club members.

On the other hand, enforcement by government must not be interpreted too narrowly as a requirement. Austin's explanation of law as the command of a sovereign — even of an impersonal sovereign in the form of a written constitution — if taken too literally can mislead us. Many apparent forms of lawmaking seem unconnected with the sovereign. A legal positivist will argue, however, that Austin's definition is broad enough to include even the lowest levels of government and that regulations passed by the licence committee of a town council, for instance, can be shown to emanate indirectly from a sovereign. While it is true that the committee's authority can be traced back through municipal by-laws

---

[1] See Chapter 1 under "Natural Law under Attack — Legal Positivism".

and the town's charter to arrive ultimately at the provincial Legislature, as a practical matter the licence committee itself, acting on its own initiative, creates new law. Many lesser public bodies like licence committees are constantly changing existing law and making new law — and the volume of law generated in this way is growing ever more rapidly.

SUBSTANTIVE AND PROCEDURAL LAW

It is a great help towards understanding a legal system to divide law into broad categories. The two most basic categories are *substantive* and *procedural* law.

Substantive law consists of the rights and duties which each person has in society. Some examples are: the right to own property, to vote, to travel about the country unmolested, to enter into contracts, to sell or give away property; the duty to refrain from injuring others, to perform contractual obligations, to obey traffic laws, customs regulations, and other laws duly passed by the government. These substantive rules are further divided into the fields of *public law* and *private law,* referred to below.

Procedural law is concerned with the protection and enforcement of these rights and duties. For example, the substantive rule decides which of two parties is at fault in an automobile accident, but it is through the rules of procedure that the injured party obtains his remedy against the wrongdoer. Procedural law prescribes the machinery by which the rights and duties recognized in substantive law are actually realized and enforced.

PUBLIC AND PRIVATE LAW

Public law is concerned with the conduct of government and with the relations between government on one side and private persons (including organizations such as companies, clubs, or unions) on the other side. Public law divides into several categories, such as constitutional law, criminal law, and administrative law.

Private law comprises the rules governing the relations between private persons or groups of persons. When a dispute arises, the persons involved may resort to the courts to have their rights against each other decided by the rules of private law. These rules provide the fabric and substance of business law. Private law divides into a number of categories, the largest of which are contracts, torts, property, and trusts. In this book we are mostly concerned with contracts since they are the focus and the essence of business transactions. We cannot consider contracts in isolation, however, and from time to time in contract problems we shall encounter the law of torts, property, and, to a lesser extent, trusts. Frequently the term "civil law" is used to mean "private law". This usage creates unfortunate ambiguity, especially in a country like Canada, because as we explain below, the primary meaning of civil law refers to a different legal system.

THE CIVIL LAW AND THE COMMON LAW

Two great systems of law have grown in western Europe from the Middle Ages, and they have been inherited by most of the lands which the nations of western Europe colonized.

The older of the two systems is called the civil law. It covers the whole of continental Europe and to a large extent Scotland, much of Africa, and the whole of South and Central America. In North America it applies in Mexico and to some degree in several of the southern United States, but particularly in Louisiana, which was French territory until early in the last century. When the English conquered French Canada, they guaranteed the people of Quebec the continued use of French civil law in most areas of private law. To this day most of the private law of the Province of Quebec is civil law.

The other great legal system is called the common law and had its origin in feudal England at the time of the Norman Conquest. It covers the whole of the English-speaking world except Scotland and is a significant part of the law of many non-English-speaking countries that were part of the British Empire, notably India, Pakistan, Bangladesh and the former colonies in Africa.

The civil law has its roots in Roman Law. In the 6th century A.D. the famous emperor of the Eastern Roman Empire, Justinian, decided to codify the law of his vast domains. He brought together the leading jurists of the time and had them draft a comprehensive code based on the laws of Rome in the classical period and incorporating subsequent developments. This tome was a monumental contribution to law and became known as Justinian's Code. It was inherited by the whole of continental Europe and formed the foundation for most of its legal systems. A similiar codification was ordered by Napoleon in 1804. This modern version, the French Civil Code, is best known as the *Code Napoléon,* and was adopted in or greatly influenced the development of codes in such countries as Italy, Spain, Germany, Switzerland and Belgium.

In these countries the theory is that a court always refers to the code to settle a dispute. If the code does not seem to cover a new problem then the court is free to reason by analogy to settle the problem from general principles laid down in the code. In theory a later court need not follow the earlier reasoning in a similar case; the second court may decide that in its view a just result of the law ought to be the reverse of the earlier decision.

Civil law theory presents practical difficulties. If in any system of law judges were to follow their own biases, values and personal prejudices continually, and so contradict earlier decisions, the law would become a jungle. No one could learn what the law on a particular point is. It is a requirement of justice, therefore, that like cases be treated alike.

Illustration:

> *A* contracts to build a house for *B*. *A* fails to carry out his part of the bargain. *B* sues *A* and collects money damages for the breach. *X* makes a similar contract with *Y,* and fails to carry out the contract. *Y* sues *X* for damages but his

suit is dismissed by the court. Either decision, examined entirely separately, might seem reasonable enough: some people might well believe that the builder was justified in backing out; others might favour the owner. But place the two decisions side by side, decided, for example, in adjoining courtrooms on the same day. In these circumstances there would be two very unhappy litigants. *A* would complain because *X* in a similar situation escaped without paying any damages; *Y* would be angry because he obtained nothing while *B* got substantial damages for breach of a similar contract. *A* and *Y* would both feel unjustly treated, and most people would agree with them — either the law should be one way or the other, but not consist of two contradictory rules at the same time.

Equal and consistent treatment in like situations is one of the most important aspects of justice and hence of law as well. Judges must be interested in, and to some extent influenced by, what other judges have decided in similar cases, whether in civil law or in common law countries.

A second major attribute of law is predictability. Suppose, after the contrary decisions we have just discussed, *P* wishes to make a similar contract with *Q*. *Q* asks his lawyer whether the contract is a binding one — if *P* backs out will *P* be liable to pay damages to *Q* for any loss caused by *P's* failing to carry out the bargain? *Q*'s lawyer would have to say, "Maybe yes, maybe no; it depends on whether the court prefers the result in the case of *A* against *B*, or that in *X* against *Y*." One can well imagine the state of confusion if this were the normal advice a client were to receive! If people are to be able to find out where they stand and to act with reasonable certainty, the law itself must be fairly predictable — a strong reason why like cases ought to be decided alike.

An important benefit of the concern that like cases be decided alike is the development by judges of principles that link like cases. These principles accumulate into a body of doctrine — a framework of predictable rules that serves as background for the vast majority of legal relations.

As a result, in civil law countries, judges do decide similar cases in the same way most of the time, although they are under no binding rule to do so. Today, in such countries as France and West Germany, reports of decisions are regularly published so that lawyers and judges can learn what the courts are deciding, and how they are interpreting the Civil Code in modern disputes.

THE THEORY OF PRECEDENT

The common law judges of England discerned these twin needs of consistency and predictability as early as the 13th century. In fact, at certain stages the courts followed previous decisions slavishly, even when the results in new circumstances were nonsensical or manifestly unjust. This custom of following already-decided cases is called the theory of precedent — the doctrine of following precedents already established by the courts. The Latin phrase for the rule is *stare decisis* — to stand by previous decisions. Followed slavishly, such a system, while it has the merits of certainty and uniformity, becomes inflexible, reactionary and stultifying.

Stare decisis has never been an ironclad rule. In the first place, words are at best relatively inaccurate vehicles for thought. This very vagueness of language permits judges to draw distinctions between similar problems and so refuse to follow obsolete precedents. Secondly, no two sets of facts are identical in every respect; even when the same parties are involved, the time must be different. Judges, when they feel it to be truly necessary, can distinguish the case before them from an earlier precedent by dwelling upon minor differences. In this way they are able to adjust the law rather slowly to changing circumstances and values. Nevertheless, the whole spirit of the common law system is bound to the theory of precedent. We look to past decisions to glean principles and to make new laws. Accordingly, a large part of the study of law is the study of decided cases.

Despite its internal flexibility, the theory of precedent hinders the law in accommodating the rapidly increasing rate of change in society. A decision that seemed quite acceptable in, say, 1938, may be entirely out of step with current social standards. The only way for a court to cope with a marked change may be to ignore *stare decisis* and directly overrule a prior decision. A prime example occurred in the school-segregation question in the United States, as noted in Chapter 2, where the Supreme Court took account of social change and reversed its earlier interpretation of the American Constitution.

There is a danger in overruling decided cases too freely, for to do so would undermine the needed consistency and predictability in law. The approach to this problem has been different in the United States, Britain and Canada. The Supreme Court of the United States has never considered itself bound to follow its own previous decisions when the result would be manifestly unjust. In a reversal of its traditional position, the House of Lords (the English equivalent of the Supreme Court) has announced that it will no longer consider itself bound to follow its own decisions.[2] Its announcement is a clear recognition of the need for courts to depart from older decisions when contemporary standards call for change. The Canadian Supreme Court has not committed itself on this subject, but it seems highly likely that following the example of the much respected courts of these senior common-law jurisdictions, it too will accept this needed flexibility.[3] Accordingly, we may look forward to an increasing willingness on the part of our courts to disagree openly with past decisions.

An understanding of these significant limitations on *stare decisis* is important for those who will be proposing answers to the legal cases offered for discussion at the end of Chapters 4 to 31. It is a mistake to assume, when one finds an actual recorded case with facts seemingly identical to those in the case under dis-

---

[2] See announcement, [1966] W.L.R. 1234.

[3] See statement by Cartwright, J. in The Queen v. Binus [1968] 1 C.C.C. 227 at 229: "I do not doubt the power of the court to depart from a previous judgment of its own . . . ." It should be noted, however, that the court did not overrule itself in this case.

cussion, that the conclusion in the recorded case is the most satisfactory one. It is far more useful to consider the case offered for discussion on its legal and social merits and *then* look at the reported case to see what light it may shed on the problem. Some of the reported cases have been severely criticized both by learned writers and by other courts in subsequent cases. They are cited because they offer an opportunity to discuss important problems.

Although both civil and common law reach the same conclusions in most areas of the law, there are some important differences. This book deals only with principles of the common law. Much of what is written here does not necessarily apply to the civil law of Quebec.

THE SOURCES OF LAW

The Variety of Sources

The earliest source of our law is the body of decisions handed down by the judiciary and permanently recorded from Norman times in England to the present day. A second source consists of the statutes passed by Parliament and by provincial Legislatures. The Cabinet, in its formal role of adviser to the monarch, can also "legislate" within certain limited areas by issuing orders-in-council.[4] Every province has also passed statutes providing for the creation of municipal governments and their supervision. These statutes give municipalities the power to make law and to raise revenue for the benefit of their citizens. Municipal by-laws and regulations are thus a form of statute law. In addition to judge-made law and statute law, there is a vast area of *subordinate legislation* usually known as *administrative law*. It derives from authority granted by statute to various administrative agencies of government to make rules and regulations in order to carry out the purposes for which the legislation was passed.

Law Made by Judges

The common law.[5] As we have seen, the common law is based on the theory of precedent, which in turn depends on a constant flow of reported cases. An organized national system of courts was therefore necessary for the development of the common law: before a decision would influence judges in subsequent cases, it was necessary to have a judge with a recognized position in society and a court with a wide jurisdiction. Before the Norman Conquest the courts were mainly local, and varied greatly from county to county. William I gave England its first strong centralized government, and thus laid the foundation for a national system of courts.

---

[4] An order-in-council is issued by the Privy Council (in effect, the Cabinet) in the name of the monarch, either in exercise of the royal prerogative or under authority of a statute.

[5] Unfortunately, the term "common law" has three possible meanings: (1) common law as opposed to equity; (2) judge-made law (including equity) as opposed to statute law; and (3) all the law of a common law country as opposed to a civil law country.

The earliest decisions were, of course, without the benefit of precedent. Courts were often left entirely to their own resources in reaching a decision for the contending parties. For this reason it is not always easy to understand their reasoning, but there is no doubt that local customs, already established, played an important role at the outset. Evidence concerning a local custom would be admitted, influence the judge's decision, and thenceforth be incorporated in the common law. As the body of precedents increased, and as the courts developed into a settled order of importance, prior decisions exerted an ever-increasing influence.

Canon law and Roman law also influenced early judicial decisions in England. The Church created canon law when it had a separate legal jurisdiction and held its own courts in matters of family law and wills. Roman law left its mark particularly in its distinction between possession and ownership of personal property. The influence of these systems of law was inevitable in a day when practically the only literate people were the clergy and scholars trained on the Continent. Still another force, feudal law, affected the common law concerning the ownership of land.

In the early state of commerce, trade was carried on almost exclusively by merchants who were members of guilds. The requirements of trade presented problems which the merchants learned in the first instance to solve for themselves. To facilitate their business activities, they developed a set of rules and acceptable trade practices, and in this way built up a body of business customs known as the *Law Merchant,* which they administered with commendable dispatch through their own courts. Only guild members came within the jurisdiction of these courts. The Law Merchant was developed and shared by all the trading nations of the medieval world.

In the course of time, the monopoly over trade held by merchant guilds broke down, and persons who were not members of guilds began to engage in commerce. The ordinary courts of the land were therefore called upon to adjudicate in disputes between non-guild members. In rendering their decisions, they borrowed from the established rules of the Law Merchant. Our present law of negotiable instruments, for example, originated as a part of the Law Merchant.

Equity. Equity rivals the common law in its contribution to the principles of law developed by our judges. The common law, by its very nature, has always looked to the past for its authority. In its very early stages of development, the common-law judges often sought new remedies when aggrieved parties appeared before them. But as the body of previous decisions grew, the common law became increasingly strict. By the late 13th century, the law had become very formal and was burdened with cumbersome procedure, much of it rooted in ancient customs and superstitions. When an aggrieved person came before the court, he had to find one of the ancient forms, called a "writ", to suit his particular grievance. If he could not, the court would not grant him a remedy. As England developed commercially, these old writs did not provide relief for many wrongs suffered by innocent parties, and great hardship often resulted.

Aggrieved parties without a remedy in the common law courts began the custom of petitioning the king who, in the age of the divine right of the monarchy, looked upon himself as the fountainhead of all law and justice. The king considered the hearing of petitions as an important duty to his subjects and often granted relief. As the number of petitions increased, the king's chancellor (his chief personal adviser, usually a churchman) took over the task of administering them. The flow continued to increase and the chancellor delegated the work to vice-chancellors. Soon it was apparent that another whole system of courts was growing — the courts of the chancellor, or the *courts of chancery* as they became known. These courts were also known as courts of equity, and the rules of law which they administered are called the *principles of equity* or, simply, *equity*.

The whole approach of the chancery courts was at first different from the common law courts, since the medieval chancellor was an ecclesiastic as well as the general secretary of state. ''Equity was a gloss on common law; it was a set of rules which could be invoked to supplement the deficiencies of common law or to ease the clumsy working of common-law actions and remedies.''[6]

An example of what the courts of equity were prepared to do for an injured party, if they thought fit, was to decree *specific performance*. The courts of common law, for their part, would invariably award money damages to a party injured by a breach of contract. Yet there might be circumstances in which money damages would not provide adequate compensation — as where a man had agreed to buy a piece of land which was especially suitable to him for reasons of convenience or health. If the party who had agreed to sell it to him later refused to convey the property, money damages might be an inadequate consolation for him. The courts of equity were prepared to grant specific performance, to order the defendant actually to convey the land.

Remedies available in the courts of equity were discretionary. The relative innocence of the petitioner and the hardship suffered by him determined whether he could hope for equity's special type of intervention on his behalf. As equity developed, however, the principles upon which relief was given became almost as fixed as the rules of common law.

Merger of the courts. For a long time, England had two rival sets of courts, the courts of common law and the courts of equity. In practice, however, a division of labour developed between them, since the advantages of equity came to be associated with those claims for which the common law remedies were inadequate — claims arising out of the administration of estates and execution of trusts, the foreclosure of mortgages, and claims for specific performance, injunction, and the rectification and rescission of contracts. At last, in the late 19th century, Parliament passed an act merging the two systems of courts into the single system we know today. The Canadian provinces passed similar acts shortly afterwards. For convenience the division of labour has been preserved in

---

[6] Jackson, *The Machinery of Justice in England,* 4th ed., p. 7. Cambridge: The University Press, 1964.

England by having two divisions within the High Court of Justice: a Chancery Division and a Queen's Bench Division.

The amalgamation of the courts of common law and equity did not mean the abandonment of the philosophy of equity. Every judge now is supposed to have two minds, one for equity and one for legal precedent. A judge may exercise his prerogative to apply an "equitable maxim" if he feels the circumstances warrant it. Equity has provided a conscience for our modern common law; it prevents the law when applied to particular instances from straying too far from reason and fairness.

Statutes

The second main source of our law, statute law, consists of acts of Parliament and of the provincial Legislatures and of by-laws passed by municipal governments. A statute overrides all the common law dealing with the same point. Although the volume of statute law is increasing rapidly, the common law still constitutes the bulk of our private law and, in particular, of the law of contracts.

Sometimes legislatures enact statutes to *codify* existing common law rather than to change it. This procedure explains, for example, the passing of the Bills of Exchange Act, the Sale of Goods Act, and the Partnership Act. Prior to the passage of these acts, the related law was to be found in a staggering number of individual cases. These acts did away with the labour and uncertainty of searching through the cases for the relevant law.

The traditional attitude of the courts towards the common law is quite different from their attitude towards statutes. The common law is the creation of the courts themselves; statute law, as one writer has put it, is "an alien intruder in the house of common law". The courts are prepared to use principles from earlier decisions, even though their facts may be quite different from the case at issue. On the other hand, the courts are less likely to apply the provisions of a statute unless the facts of the case at issue are covered specifically by the statute. This attitude of the courts is called the *strict interpretation* of the statutes. The courts are often called on to decide whether a statute covers the facts of a case specifically; that is, either to decide on the application of a statute or to interpret it. Their decisions then form part of judge-made law and are often referred to in subsequent cases.

Administrative Law

There are two main classes of legislation. The first and simplest consists of those statutes that change the law: they prohibit an activity formerly permitted or else remove a prohibition, thereby enabling people to carry on a formerly illegal activity. This type of legislation is essentially passive, in that it provides a framework within which people may legally go about their business; it does not presume to supervise and regulate their activities, but leaves it to an injured party or a law-enforcement official to complain about any activity that has violated a statute of this kind, and initiate court proceedings.

The second class of legislation authorizes the government itself to carry on a program: to levy taxes and provide revenue for the purpose stated in the statute, such as building a hospital, paying pensions to the elderly and offering subsidies to encourage a particular kind of economic activity; and to supervise and regulate the related trade or activity. But Parliament itself has never carried on these activities, and is an inappropriate body to undertake any program requiring continuous supervision. It comprises a group of people from ridings across the country whose talents and interests vary greatly, and whose primary responsibility is to enact legislation. From early times in England, Parliament authorized the monarch to levy taxes, pay and equip the armed forces, and construct public works. Thus, projects *authorized* by Parliament were *executed* by the monarch and his officials: hence the term "executive" to describe that arm of government that carries out Parliament's will. Translated into the terms of modern government, this process means that every government department, agency and tribunal is established by the authority of a statute. For example, the Canadian Radio-Television Commission was established under the Broadcasting Act which sets out the purposes of that body and grants it regulatory powers to carry those purposes out.[7]

In exercising its regulatory powers, an administrative agency creates new law, which we have defined earlier as "subordinate legislation". Some subordinate legislation sets down broad criteria regulating the type of guarantee that a licence applicant must supply to engage in a specified form of activity, and the amount and type of investment required to engage in that activity. Other subordinate legislation may be detailed and technical (fees for applications, location of transmitters) and may indeed be a single ruling on a particular application.

Important regulations, normally those setting out broad standards, require the approval of the Cabinet in the form of an order-in-council. The agency itself drafts these regulations and the minister responsible for the agency brings them before the cabinet. Lesser regulations may be authorized by the minister himself, the agency chairman, or even a designated officer of the agency.

As we noted in Chapter 1, the growing complexity of society and government has increased the need for specialized knowledge and control in such areas as environmental protection, energy, transportation, communications, education, and welfare; and the list includes a growing number of business and professional activities which are believed to affect the public interest. As a result, government agencies, each with its own system of regulations and sanctions, continue to proliferate. Although administrative law is not a main area of direct concern in this book, we shall from time to time have to deal with law affecting labour relations, consumer protection, and the financing and operation of cor-

---

[7] Broadcasting Act, R.S.C. 1970, c. B-11, s. 5.

porations, in which government agencies and their regulations play increasingly important roles.

THE SYSTEM OF COURTS IN ENGLAND

We have seen that the substance of the law finds its expression through various institutions — the judiciary, legislature, and administrative agencies. A major part of business law continues to find its expression through the judiciary. It will be necessary, therefore, to have some knowledge of the system of courts and their rules of procedure.

Two reasons make it profitable to begin by studying the English courts: first, much of our own law is derived from English case law, and these cases will thus be easier to understand if we are familiar with the structure of the courts which decided them; secondly, the English system affords a good starting-place because England has a single government, and its system of courts is easier to grasp than the more complicated federal structure existing in Canada.

The Courts of First Instance

Courts of first instance are also sometimes called courts of original jurisdiction because it is in them that actions originate and trials take place. England has many different kinds of courts of original jurisdiction, each having certain types of grievances to decide. Their names differ from those of their Canadian counterparts, and to avoid confusion we shall not list them here, noting only their place in the English system of courts.

The Court of Appeal

The Court of Appeal is the next tier in the English judicial system. It is not a court of first instance: that is, actions never originate in this court. If either of the parties to an action is dissatisfied with the decision of a court of first instance, he may appeal to the Court of Appeal where the decision will be reconsidered. The party who petitions for an appeal is called the *appellant;* the other party, the *respondent*. Trials are not held before the court, nor are witnesses called: the court does not entertain questions of fact because these are for the trial judge to have decided. The Court of Appeal proceeds on the basis of a written record of the trial in the court of first instance. On appeal, lawyers for each side argue only on questions of law, the appellant claiming that the trial judge erred in his interpretation of the law and the respondent arguing to uphold the decision of the trial judge. The court may agree with the trial judge, thereby *dismissing* the appeal; or agree with the appellant and *reverse* the trial judgment; or *vary* the trial judgment in part; or declare that the trial judge erred in failing to consider certain facts, and send the case back for a *new trial* in the lower court. The Court of Appeal usually hears cases in a panel of three judges, but occasionally five judges may hear a very important case.

In England, a Court of Criminal Appeal has a similar task in hearing appeals in criminal law cases.

The House of Lords

It is somewhat surprising to learn that the House of Lords, more widely known as the upper house of the British Parliament, is also the supreme court in Britain. Originally any member of the House of Lords (members of the peerage) could sit with the House when it was convened as a court, but since the mid-19th century, only great lawyers and judges who have been elevated to the peerage actually hear and decide appeals. The court usually consists of the Lord Chancellor and up to nine Lords of Appeal in Ordinary, who are full-time salaried judges. Parties dissatisfied with a decision of the Court of Appeal have one more chance before the House of Lords, which is the ultimate court of appeal and the highest court in the land.

THE SYSTEM OF COURTS IN CANADA

We noted in Chapter 2 that the division of legislative powers between the federal and provincial governments has inevitably led to disputes about which level has jurisdiction over many problems that defy identification with the categories of the B.N.A. Act. Despite the inherent difficulties in federal constitutions, the Canadian constitution has not fared badly. Some aspects show great wisdom and have caused little or no trouble. Others appear rather odd at first sight, but can be explained by circumstances at the time of Confederation.

For example, the B.N.A. Act gives the provinces jurisdiction over the administration of justice — the organization and operation of police forces and the system of courts. At the same time, the Act gives the federal government jurisdiction over trade and commerce, banking, bankruptcy and criminal law — matters frequently litigated before the courts — and also the exclusive right to appoint, and the obligation to pay, all county court and superior court judges.[8]

Why this peculiar division in the administration of the legal system? The explanation lies, at least in part, in the fact that at the time of discussions on Confederation in Canada the United States had just been through a terrible civil war. Many Canadians believed that biased local state legislatures and locally-elected judges (sometimes without any legal training) had fanned internal division in the United States by passing discriminatory laws, and had frequently administered laws unfairly against "outsiders" (citizens of other states). The Canadian constitution sought to avoid the problem of local bias by placing jurisdiction over those matters peculiarly susceptible to local influence in the hands of the national government. Our constitution also requires that only qualified lawyers be appointed to the county and superior court benches. Until retirement, they hold office conditional on good behaviour, and superior court judges can be removed only by

---

[8] The British North America Act, ss. 96 and 100.

"joint address", that is, a vote taken before both House of Commons and Senate. These provisions are designed to keep judges as unbiased and immune from local pressures as possible.

As in England, there are three tiers of courts: the courts of first instance, the intermediate courts of appeal, and the Supreme Court of Canada. The names and jurisdictions of the courts differ somewhat from province to province, but in general they follow the pattern set out below.

The Provincial Courts

The Courts of First Instance

MAGISTRATE'S COURT (OR PROVINCIAL JUDGE'S COURT)

The magistrate or provincial judge decides very little, if any, private law. He hears criminal cases of almost every type except for the most serious offences such as murder, treason, sedition, piracy, rape and manslaughter. No jury trials are held before him. If an accused person elects (as he may) to have a jury trial, the case must be heard in another court.

SURROGATE COURT (OR PROBATE COURT)

This court supervises the estates of deceased persons. It appoints an administrator to wind up the affairs of anyone who dies *intestate* (without leaving a will), settles disputes over the validity of wills and division of assets, and approves the accounts of executors and administrators.

JUVENILE COURT

Children and adolescents who the government feels are too young to be dealt with in the ordinary criminal courts and require special care are brought before the Juvenile Court judge.

FAMILY COURT

Questions of domestic relations (but not divorce) are dealt with by the Family Court.

DIVISION COURT (OR SMALL CLAIMS COURT)

This court handles disputes for small amounts of money. Its procedure is very simple and informal, so that the cost of taking action is slight.

COUNTY OR DISTRICT COURT

The County Court has jurisdiction in actions involving claims of a medium size, whether for debts or for damages for injuries suffered. In Canada, unlike England, each County Court judge also presides at least twice yearly over a court of general session with jurisdiction in most criminal matters, including jury trials. The County Court may also serve as a court of appeal from summary convictions made by magistrates or provincial judges for lesser offences.

HIGH COURT OF JUSTICE OF THE SUPREME COURT	This court is variously known as the Court of Queen's Bench, the Superior Court, the Supreme Court, and the Supreme Court Trial Division. It has unlimited jurisdiction in civil and criminal actions. Judges of the High Court go on *circuit,* that is, one judge tours each of a group of county towns twice a year and tries the cases waiting for him. The High Court sittings are called the *assizes,* and they are held in the county courthouses.
DIVISIONAL COURT	The Divisional Court of the High Court of Justice, created in 1972, is peculiar to Ontario. It consists of the Chief Justice of the High Court and such other judges of his court as he designates from time to time. It sits in panels of three judges, more or less continuously in Toronto, and at various times throughout the year in several other centres. It hears appeals from various lower provincial courts (*not* the County Court, however) and from various provincial administrative tribunals.

Intermediate Appellate Court

THE COURT OF APPEAL	Each province has one intermediate appellate court, called variously the Appellate Division, the Supreme Court *en banc* (the whole bench), and Queen's Bench Appeals, as well as the Court of Appeal. It performs the same function as the Court of Appeal in England, and in addition hears criminal appeals.

The Federal Courts

THE TAX REVIEW BOARD	The Tax Review Board hears appeals of taxpayers against decisions of Revenue Canada. The Board hears only tax appeals, and functions as a court with relatively simple procedures. Either the taxpayer or the department may appeal its decisions to the Trial Division of the Federal Court. There all evidence is resubmitted and the dispute is retried, not as an appeal, but as in a court of first instance.
THE FEDERAL COURT OF CANADA	The federal government maintains the Federal Court of Canada in two divisions, a Trial Division and an Appeal Division. Under a 1970 statute[9] reconstituting

---

[9] The Federal Court Act, St. of Can. 1970-71-72, c. 1.

the former Exchequer Court of Canada, the Federal Court has received expanded jurisdiction, and certain kinds of actions that could formerly be brought in the provincial courts as well are now reserved exclusively for the Federal Court. The Federal Court has exclusive jurisdiction over such matters as patents, copyright and trademarks, disputes concerning ships and navigation, and many sorts of lawsuits against the federal government itself. There remains a large area of concurrent jurisdiction where a plaintiff may still sue in either a provincial or the Federal Court. For example, a person injured by the careless operation of a government motor vehicle may still sue in a provincial court.

THE SUPREME COURT OF CANADA

The Supreme Court is the final court of appeal in Canada, the equivalent of the House of Lords in England. It consists of nine judges and hears appeals both from the provincial courts of appeal and the Federal Court of Canada. In addition it has special jurisdiction under the Supreme Court Act[10] to rule on the constitutionality of federal and provincial statutes when they are referred to the court by the federal cabinet. In private actions the appellant must obtain special leave from the Supreme Court to appeal.[11]

THE SYSTEM OF COURTS IN THE UNITED STATES

Although both Canada and the United States have federal systems of governments, there are considerable differences between the constitutions of the two federations. In the United States, each of the states has more autonomy, and has the residual power which in Canada rests with the federal government. Again, although under the B.N.A. Act the Canadian government has power to create a full system of three-tier federal courts throughout Canada, it has not done so, but has felt content to allow the provincial courts to decide cases of first instance (with the exception of those fields reserved exclusively to the Federal and Tax Courts). On the other hand, the United States has set up a full system of federal courts which handle a large portion of litigation, although much less than the total handled by the state courts. Criminal law, for example, is a state matter, except for cases involving specific fields of federal jurisdiction such as national defence, or unless an offence is committed in more than one state, such as moving stolen goods across state boundaries.

---

[10] R.S.C. 1970, c. S-19, s. 55.
[11] St. of Can. 1974-75, c. 18, s. 5.

The federal courts have jurisdiction in the following cases: bankruptcy, postal matters, federal banking laws; disputes concerning maritime contracts or wrongs; prosecution of crimes punishable under federal laws of the United States or committed at sea; actions requiring an interpretation of the U.S. Constitution, federal statutes and treaties; and disputes between citizens of different states.

The federal courts are organized in the familiar three-tier structure. The court of original jurisdiction is the District Court. There is at least one in each state and several in each of the more populous states. At the next level the county is divided into 11 judicial *circuits* with a Court of Appeals for each circuit. A particular Court of Appeals is often referred to by its number followed by "Circuit Court," e.g., Ninth Circuit Court. Finally, the Supreme Court of the United States hears appeals from the Circuit Courts and acts also as a court of first instance in a few special circumstances provided for in the Constitution. As a general rule, appeals end with the Circuit Courts of Appeals, and may be carried to the United States Supreme Court only at the discretion of the Supreme Court itself: it has usually limited itself to a review of decisions affecting basic human rights or constitutional rights and deciding important legal principles that have received conflicting treatment in different Circuit Courts.

Individual states have authority to create the courts they consider necessary, but in general the system of state courts follows the same pattern as that of the federal courts. Most states have a trial court, an intermediate appellate court, and a final appellate court. A few appeals are brought from the "final" state appellate court to the U.S. Supreme Court, when the appellant can convince the Supreme Court that a "substantial constitutional issue" is involved.

As a result, the great majority of cases commenced in the state courts can go no further than the highest state appellate court, thus permitting wide variations in decisions on the same matter among several states. By contrast, such inconsistencies are often removed in Canada by a decision of the Supreme Court which is then binding on the provincial Courts of Appeal.

We may note that in the United States judges in the federal court system are appointed, just as Canadian and English judges are. Many of the judges in the state courts are elected by popular vote.

USING THE COURTS

Who may sue?

Not everyone has the capacity to start an action. An adult citizen of Canada has the broadest capacity, virtually unlimited access to the courts for any type of action. Generally speaking, non-Canadians may also resort to the courts as freely as citizens. But as we note in Chapter 7 on the Capacity to Contract, during hostilities any person found to be an enemy alien loses the right to sue. A child must be represented in an action by an adult person and is not permitted to bring an action alone. The child may well have a right that should be protected by the courts, and may even have begun an action in ignorance of the fact that an adult representative should be present. If this is discovered, the court will "stay" proceedings until the parent or guardian or the "next friend" is appointed. Similarly, an insane person may use the court only through his court-appointed representative. The reasoning here is that these persons do not have the sound judgment to undertake the risks of court proceedings; they must rely on an adult person to act on their behalf.

Generally speaking, corporations (bodies incorporated by conforming to procedures under a statute) may sue and be sued, although foreign corporations may be subject to strict regulation and required to obtain a provincial licence before bringing an action.

In each of the instances referred to in the above paragraph, action is brought by a "person", either for himself or for the benefit of another person. For this purpose, a corporation is considered to be a legal "person". An incorporated body is referred to as "it" rather than "they"; in other words, it is not thought of as a collectivity but as a single person. Greater difficulties arise when an action is brought by or against an unincorporated collectivity — a group of persons such as a social club, a church, a political party, and perhaps most important, a trade union. In most cases, unincorporated groups are not recognized by the courts and may not sue or be sued. The position of trade unions varies: in some jurisdictions, it is possible to sue and be sued by a trade union, while in others it is not.

Standing to Sue

Suppose a careless landowner pollutes a stream that runs through a municipal park. If the municipality is reluctant to sue the owner, may an individual resident of the city sue on behalf of himself and all other residents for injury to the park? Suppose a board of censors bans a notorious film. May a resident of the province sue on behalf of himself and other residents who are denied the opportunity to view the film? Do individuals in these circumstances acquire "standing" before the court, and can they establish a right to be vindicated? Generally speaking, courts have been reluctant to permit actions by individuals when their rights are no greater than those of the rest of the public. The courts foresee a risk that especially litigious and cantankerous members of the public may choose to litigate many matters in which they have no direct interest. An ordinary citizen may be a member of several organizations including a trade union, hold shares in a company, vote as a taxpayer in a community, own land adjacent to public waterways, be a user of a park and a movie fan. One can imagine numerous other roles in which he might be considered a member of a much larger group. The judiciary has worried that the courts could become clogged by such actions.

On the other hand, with growing awareness of damage to our environment through pollution and failure to practise conservation, with the growing complexity of pharmaceutical products, prepared foods and mechanical devices sold to the public, the risk of serious injury to large groups of persons has grown. Effective means must be available to the public to protect itself from careless and unscrupulous enterprises, especially if no governmental body takes adequate steps to protect the public interest. Some recent decisions of the Supreme Court of Canada have recognized the right of a taxpayer to sue when he believes public revenues are being improperly expended, and the right of a movie viewer to bring an action when he believes his right to see a film has been taken away by a provincial censorship body.[12] This area is in a state of flux, and it is likely to be many years before satisfactory rules have been worked out by the legislatures and the courts to achieve a balance between the public interest and minimizing abuse of the judicial process.

Class Actions[13]

Suppose the owner of a car wishes to sue the manufacturer to recover loss caused by a serious defect in the car, and that the defect is known to exist in several thousand other cars of the same model. May the owner, indeed ought he to, sue not only on his own behalf, but as representative of a class, that is, on behalf of all the other owners — or must each owner bring his own lawsuit? If he fails in his action, will all other owners necessarily fail, or *vice versa?* Courts are reluctant to take away an individual's right to litigate his own claim. On the other hand, it would be unfortunate to clog the courts with hundreds, perhaps thousands, of repetitive claims in which all the salient facts and applicable laws had already been clearly established.

Again, there are no clear rules in this area. A court may first hear argument about whether an individual should represent a group in a class action and thus dispose of the matter for all members of the class at once. If the court so decides, then on handing down a judgment it makes the matter *res judicata* and the case cannot be brought before the court again to contest legal liability. In our example of the defective car, liability having already been established, other owners might then come forward to have the court assess the amount of damage if the parties could not themselves settle on an amount.

Procedural Law

It is not the purpose of this book to instruct its readers in procedural law. Most businessmen will gratefully concede that the intricacies of procedure are properly the province of lawyers. Nevertheless, an overall understanding of what the various steps in legal procedure aim to accomplish should help the business administrator to work more effectively with his legal advisors. Moreover, the business-law student may be needlessly distracted in his study of cases by the occasional reference to procedure if he does not have a general idea of its function.

Just as most primitive religions were concerned more with ritual (tribal dances, sacrifices, witchcraft) than with theology, so primitive law was concerned more with procedure (use of the right words, form of writ and oaths) than

---

[12] Thorson v. Attorney-General of Canada (No. 2) (1974) 43 D.L.R. (3d) 1; Nova Scotia Board of Censors v. MacNeil (1975) 55 D.L.R. (3d) 632.

[13] Kazanjian, "Class Actions in Canada", 1973 *Osgoode Hall Law Journal,* Vol. 11, p. 397.

with substance. Archaic procedure dominated the common law until the early 19th century, when England was swept by a great reform movement. The culmination was reached when Parliament passed the Judicature Act in 1873, unifying the courts and wiping out the last of the old common law procedure. The 1873 Act has been adopted by the common law provinces of Canada and modified to varying degrees. Even so, the rules of procedure remain an important part of the law; a well-defined procedure is necessary to permit the courts to work efficiently. Procedure has now been simplified, and the number of steps in legal proceedings greatly reduced.

Special procedures are still used to bring wills, contracts, and other documents before the court to have them interpreted, and to bring certain proceedings under statutes. Generally speaking, however, the great bulk of litigation proceeds through the courts in one form, called an *action,* and in those provinces that follow the English procedure most closely an action is begun by *issuing* and *serving a writ.*

Settlement out of Court

Disagreements, injuries to persons and property, and breaches of a host of laws, all giving rise to legal "rights", take place daily in vast numbers. Only a small part of these *causes of action* is ever litigated by the aggrieved parties. Even when court proceedings are started, disputes rarely go to trial. (In the City of London, England, less than 1 per cent of legal proceedings continue to trial.) Do all the remaining aggrieved persons simply abandon their rights? On the contrary: the great majority of serious grievances are remedied by *settlement.*

Settlement is an out-of-court procedure whereby one of the parties to an impending court action agrees to pay certain sums of money or do certain things in return for a waiver by the other party of all rights arising from the grievance. This process is especially favoured in commerce as it it is speedy and definite, and avoids the expense of litigation. A party to a settlement also avoids the risk that the court will find against him. Since there are two sides to a story, and since also a dispute is rarely a matter of black and white, there is always a degree of uncertainty in predicting which side the court will favour. Of course, the stronger one party's claim appears to be, the more advantageous a settlement that party will demand, and usually obtain. Often a person will start legal proceedings to convince his adversary that he will not put up with delays or an inadequate settlement. As a result, many actions which are started are settled soon afterwards.

Why then are the courts, and the relatively small body of decisions resulting from an enormous number of disputes, so important? There are two main reasons: first, the decided cases supply the principles by which aggrieved parties may gauge the relative merit of their claims, predict the outcome of a possible court action, and strike a value for their claims; second, the court is the last resort, the decisive tribunal when all compromise fails. It settles the issue when the parties themselves cannot.

Procedure Before Trial

The mere decision to start an action does not end matters; the trial does not follow automatically. After the decision to sue has been made and a writ has been issued by the court, it must then be served on the defendant. The writ informs the defendant by whom and for what he is being sued, so that he can prepare to defend himself; the plaintiff cannot proceed with his claim until the notice has been served. For a businessman, it is axiomatic that as soon as he is served with a writ he should immediately consult a lawyer. It is a long-standing legal maxim that ''he who acts on his own behalf has a fool for a client.'' Lawyers have learned that people are so mesmerized by their own cause that they cannot properly evaluate their claims; in personal matters, one lawyer almost always has another lawyer represent him.

The writ has now been issued by the plaintiff and served on the defendant. Why should they not proceed to trial at once? For one thing, court trials are expensive: the time of the plaintiff and defendant, their *counsel* (lawyer), the judge, and other officers of the court is valuable. It would be wasteful, therefore, to use time in court to do things that can be done just as well out of court. It is worth some preliminary effort to discover exactly what the disagreement is about: otherwise we should have the spectacle of parties arguing about some things on which they agree. The procedure followed after the serving of the writ attempts to narrow the trial precisely to those matters on which the parties are at odds. The necessary steps are as follows:

(a) The defendant gives notice to the clerk of the court that he intends to contest the action, a move called *entering an appearance*. The plaintiff then delivers to the defendant a *statement of claim*, a document in which he sets out in detail the facts which he alleges have given rise to his cause of action, and the damages suffered by him. The defendant replies with a *defence*, admitting those facts not in dispute in the statement of claim and denying all others, and in addition setting out any other facts which the defendant intends to prove in court in support of his defence. The plaintiff then delivers a *reply* countering the added facts alleged by the defendant and adding any further facts believed necessary to cope with the defence. Often the defendant will have a claim of his own arising from the same facts. He will then *counterclaim* as well as defend. In turn the plaintiff will defend the counterclaim. Both claims will then be tried together.

(b) The documents are assembled to form the main body of *pleadings*. Their purpose is to make clear exactly what each party intends to prove in court so that an adequate counter-attack can be prepared if available. The Hollywood element of surprise is contrary to the principle of law that each side should have sufficient notice to put its view of the facts before the court. If a party attempts to introduce surprise evidence, the court may refuse to hear it; or if it admits the evidence, it will usually delay proceedings to give the other side an opportunity to reply, and will also penalize the party with loss of costs. The pleadings often reveal an aspect of the claim which the other side did not know. For example, the plaintiff may claim to have an important receipt book in his possession. The rules of procedure compel the plaintiff upon demand to surrender it to the defendant for inspection. In some circumstances a party may demand further particulars of a claim so that he can evaluate it more clearly.

(c) Some provinces provide for "examination for discovery," a process whereby either party can examine the other to determine whether the trial should be proceeded with and to narrow the issues further.

Once both sides have satisfied themselves that the action should go to trial the case is recorded on the *docket* for the next sitting of the court.

The Trial

The trial is the culmination of the action. Evidence of all facts in dispute is brought before the court. In non-criminal actions the *burden* is on the plaintiff to prove his case. This he must do by bringing all the evidence of favourable facts before the court. Then he must be prepared to argue that these facts, once established, prove his claim in law. (Of course, counsel for the plaintiff must decide beforehand what facts he must prove in support of the claim.) The defendant, on the other hand, must attempt to establish his own version of the facts or at least to minimize the value of the evidence submitted by the plaintiff. The gap between the versions of the two parties is often astonishing. Sometimes the defendant will argue that even if the facts are as the plaintiff claims, they do not support his claim in law. For example, suppose the defendant had swerved his car off the road at night because of oncoming lights; the defendant might then state that although his conduct was as the plaintiff claimed, such acts did not constitute negligence but on the contrary had been quite reasonable under the circumstances.

Evidence is brought before the court by the examination of witnesses. Counsel for the plaintiff will call as witnesses those persons whose testimony is favourable to his client. Counsel for the defendant may next cross-examine those witnesses to bring out any aspects of their testimony which he believes to have been neglected and which may serve his client's position. Counsel for the plaintiff may then re-examine the witnesses to clarify any points dealt with in the cross-examination. Counsel for the defendant may also call witnesses of his own. Certain types of evidence are not *admissible* because they are prejudicial without adding anything to the facts in dispute or because they are *hearsay,* that is, they are words attributed by the witness to a person not before the court. The hearsay rule stems from a belief that the credibility of oral evidence cannot be properly assessed when it is second-hand; and that one who is alleged to have made an assertion should testify in person and be subject to cross-examination and the scrutiny of the court. The rules of admissibility of evidence are intended to winnow bad evidence from good. Unfortunately, in the process they have become technical, more so in the United States than in Canada.

When all the evidence has been heard, counsel for each side will present the argument in law favouring his client. In simple cases the judge may give his decision at once or after a short recess, but in complicated and important cases he will usually *reserve* judgment so that he may have time to study his notes of the facts and the legal arguments, and to compare the opinions in decided cases and textbooks. When judgment is finally handed down, it is often delivered orally in the court; important cases are invariably given in written form as well, and are reprinted in the law reports of that particular court or jurisdiction.

Appeals

If either or both parties wish to appeal, they must make up their minds and serve notice within a time limit, usually thirty days or less.

As we have seen, most appeals take the form of a review, by an appeal court, of evidence forwarded to it from the trial courts. An appeal court will also review proceedings of the trial court when it is contended that the trial judge erred in instructing the jury or in admitting or excluding certain evidence; in these instances the appeal court may order the case sent back to a new trial, directing the judge to correct the shortcomings of the first hearing.

THE LEGAL PROFESSION

In England the profession is divided into two groups, *solicitors* and *barristers*. Solicitors are "office" lawyers. They spend almost all their time interviewing clients and carrying on the legal aspects of business and family affairs. They look after the drafting of wills, deeds, and contracts, the incorporation of companies, arrangements for adoption of children, and other domestic documents. They also prepare cases for trial, draft pleadings, interview witnesses, and make copious notes for trial. In addition, they argue cases in some of the lower courts. Barristers only take *briefs,* that is, cases handed to them by solicitors, to be presented in court. They are a much smaller group and have their offices mainly in London around the central law courts.

In Canada from very early times, lawyers became both barristers and solicitors. In the common-law provinces, lawyers are qualified to carry on the duties of both professions and often do, especially in smaller cities and towns. In larger cities, lawyers tend to specialize and to be either "office" lawyers or "litigation" lawyers. Under the civil law of Quebec the profession is divided in approximately the same way as in England. Quebec has *notaries* (solicitors) and *advocates* (barristers). In the United States the distinction has broken down completely. A lawyer is not called "barrister and solicitor" as he is in Canada, but is simply an *attorney*.

The legal profession is organized on a provincial basis in Canada. Each province has its own "bar" (barristers' society), and by provincial statute one must be a member if he or she is to practise law. Membership in one provincial bar does not permit a lawyer to practise in another province. He or she must meet the standards and pay the fees of any other provincial bar before practising in that province. A member of any provincial bar may appear, however, before the Supreme Court of Canada.

QUESTIONS FOR REVIEW

1. What factors may discourage a litigant from appealing to a higher court?
2. What are the restrictions on appeals to the Supreme Court of Canada?
3. In what respects does the operation of an appeal court differ from that of a trial court?
4. Why has subordinate legislation come to prominence?
5. What are the chief differences between the systems of courts in the United States and in Canada?
6. What are the advantages of a settlement over a court trial?
7. Motion pictures and television programs are responsible for a misconception about the way in which trials proceed. Elaborate.
8. What court procedures are designed to make the evidence received as reliable as possible?
9. Define: appellant; respondent; counterclaim; counsel; bench; writ; settlement; pleadings; assizes.
10. Is a legal rule in one province necessarily the same in another province? Explain.
11. How does a judge decide a case when there is no precedent available in earlier decisions?
12. A student is assigned a hypothetical case with a requirement that he offer an opinion about what the court's decision would be. He discovers that many of the facts are similar to those in an actual case reported in the law reports of thirty years ago. Is it sufficient for him to rely on the judge's opinion in the reported case?
13. One of the major purposes of private law is to settle disputes between businesses. How can the settlement of a particular private dispute make a contribution to the business community as a whole?
14. "Under a system of *stare decisis,* in which a court has frequently to say, 'Whatever the anachronism or inconvenience, we must abide by the established rule,' it is extremely difficult for changing social needs to be met promptly and systematically." (Allen, *Law in the Making,* p. 352.)
    (a) Develop briefly the meaning of this quotation in your own words and explain the rationale or logic underlying the doctrine of *stare decisis.*
    (b) Explain how the courts have managed to apply this doctrine to permit some adaptation to changing social conditions.
    (c) Do the courts ever abandon the doctrine?

CHAPTER 4

The Law of Torts

SCOPE OF TORT LAW

The law of torts is a wide-ranging subject, almost impossible to define. Interestingly enough, however, while the leading writers in the field cannot agree upon an entirely satisfactory definition, they have no difficulty in agreeing upon a lengthy list of torts. An examination of the more important ones gives a better clue to the nature of torts than does any attempt at a dictionary definition.

The law of torts is concerned with the ever-expanding variety of harm suffered by individuals incident to all the activities necessarily carried on in our increasingly complex society.[1] Automobile accidents, industrial accidents and pollution are among the more important causes of harm. The basic issue is who should bear the loss: the unfortunate victim, the particular person whose act caused the harm, the group that benefits most directly by a common activity such as all motor vehicle owners (through insurance premiums), or a larger group such as taxpayers generally (through government compensation). We should note that the primary purpose of tort law is to compensate victims of tortious activities, not to punish the wrongdoers. Punishment is left to the criminal law when particular tortious conduct happens also to amount to a crime. For ex-

---

[1] For a fuller discussion of the purposes of tort law, see especially Fleming, *The Law of Torts* (4th ed), Sydney: Law Book Company of Australasia, 1971. See also Linden (ed.), *Studies in Canadian Case Law,* Toronto: Butterworths, 1968; Prosser, *Handbook of the Law of Torts* (4th ed.), St. Paul: West Publishing Company, 1971; Salmond, *Law of Torts* (15th ed.), Heuston, ed., London: Sweet and Maxwell Ltd., 1969. For an excellent shorter account see Fleming, *An Introduction to the Law of Torts,* Oxford: Oxford University Press, 1967.

ample, when a drunken driver collides with a parked vehicle, its owner may sue
him in tort and the state may charge him with drunken driving.[2]

DEVELOPMENT OF THE TORT CONCEPT

In the early stages of development, societies have rules of liability for injurious
conduct that are usually very simple: anyone who causes direct violent injury to
another has to pay compensation. No inquiry is made into the reasons for his injury or whether the injurer is justified in his conduct. Such liability for injury is
usually called *strict liability*. There are accurate medieval records of the amount
of compensation considered adequate, according to the kind of injury and the importance of the injured party.

Gradually, the idea grew that a person ought not to be responsible for harm
caused to another if he or she acted without *fault*. For example, suppose *A* were
driving a wagon down a road and a snake frightened his horses, causing them to
bolt and run down *B*, a passerby. At this stage, the law began to excuse *A* from
liability in these circumstances. Both parties were equally innocent, so the loss
was left to lie where it had fallen — upon the unfortunate victim, *B*.

In addition, the courts began to consider the way in which the harm had
arisen. At first, as we have noted, only direct, violent injuries were recognized
by the courts — running down another person or striking a blow. Gradually the
courts began to recognize indirect or *consequential* injuries.

Illustration:

> *A* carelessly drops a log on the travelled portion of road near sunset, and
> does not bother to remove it. After dark, *B*'s horse trips over the log and is
> seriously injured. In early law, *B* would have been without a remedy. Even-
> tually, however, the courts recognized *A*'s act was as much responsible for
> the injury to *B*'s horse as if he had struck the horse by throwing the log at it.
> They allowed *B* to recover damages.[3]

We can see then that early tort law changed in two ways: the law took into
account the *fault* (or blameworthiness) of the defendant; it also took into account
causation — whether the defendant could be considered the operative cause of
the harm in a much more sophisticated sense than direct violence would indicate.
Both these developments present difficult, continuing problems for society and
they are being energetically debated at the present time. We shall examine them
more closely.

---

[2] In relatively rare circumstances, a court may do more than simply compensate a victim of a tort; it
may also award *exemplary* (or *punitive*) damages against the wrongdoer when his conduct has been
intentional and malicious.

[3] This example was discussed by Fortesque, J. in Reynolds v. Clarke (1726), 93 E.R. 747, and has
been cited many times since by both the courts and leading writers as a classic statement of the
law.

BASIS FOR LIABILITY

Fault

Fault, in the setting of tort law, refers to blameworthy or culpable conduct — conduct which in the eyes of the law is unjustifiable because of intentional or careless disregard for the interests of others. There is by no means universal agreement that fault is a sound basis for liability in many areas of tort law. As we noted at the beginning of this chapter, there is a broad, general problem concerning the distribution of loss caused as an inevitable consequence of such activities as the operation of automobiles. Statistically, we know that each year there will be thousands of victims of car accidents. Is it fair that the victim or his family should bear the financial loss, or that the unlucky driver or owner of the vehicle physically responsible should bear the financial burden? In fact, the almost universal prevalence of insurance has done much to shift and distribute the burden already; in a majority of cases neither party suffers the main financial loss.

One justification for basing liability upon fault is the deterrent effect this approach should have on careless people. However, there is no statistical evidence to support this theory. It may be argued that only careful drivers are deterred by such penalties; the irresponsible driver is no more deterred by them than is a habitual criminal. Schemes have been put forward proposing that all injured parties in motor-vehicle accidents, regardless of fault, should receive compensation at least to certain minimum standards — for example, up to $10,000 in damages — and that only claims for larger sums should be litigated on the basis of fault.[4] These schemes contemplate that a more rigorous system of penalties, including banning certain drivers completely from the roads, would do more to reduce the accident rate than the present system of liability based on complex rules governing the determination of fault.

Strict Liability

A system of strict liability already exists under our workmen's compensation legislation.[5] Under this system, industrial accidents are assumed to be the inevitable price of doing business. Employers are compelled to make contributions to a fund which in turn compensates victims of industrial accidents, even when the employer has been blameless and the injury has resulted from the carelessness of the employee himself.

Strict liability regardless of fault exists in other areas as well. A person who collects potentially dangerous things on his land, from which they subsequently escape, is liable for any resulting damage even if he was blameless in his care of

---

[4] Keaton and O'Connell, *Basic Protection for the Traffic Victim,* Boston: Little, Brown and Company, 1965; Keeton and O'Connell, *After Cars Crash: The Need for Legal and Insurance Reforms,* Homewood: Dow Jones-Irwin, 1967.

[5] See, for example: Workmen's Compensation Act, 1968, St. of B.C. 1968, c. 59; R.S.O. 1970, c. 505; R.S.N.S. 1967, c. 343 as amended.

them.[6] Thus, if a landowner stores water in a large cistern, and the cistern is punctured by a visitor's truck accidentally colliding with it, thereby flooding and damaging a neighbour's building, the owner of the cistern will be liable to compensate his neighbour. The risk of such damage is a burden the landowner must bear as the price for storing water on his land.

Social Policy

It by no means follows, however, that strict liability is a satisfactory approach to all areas of tort law. Many homeowners would boggle at the prospect of being liable for every harm done to a visitor on their property, especially if the injury was caused solely by their guest's negligence. A friend's or neighbour's child might climb a tree or a fence without permission and suffer a serious injury. There are many such circumstances, not involving major social and economic problems, where liability based on fault is the fairest principle. Accordingly, in most areas of tort law, liability remains firmly based on a finding of fault. Whether liability should be based on fault or on other principles is an important question of policy, constantly changing as our social standards change. These social standards force the law to adapt in many ways, ranging from direct legislative intervention, as in workmen's compensation statutes, to more subtle influences on judge and jury in determining liability and the amounts of damages awarded.

Vicarious Liability

The law has responded pragmatically to the pressure of social needs with respect to torts committed by employees in the course of their employment. An employer may be personally at fault for a tort committed by his employee. For example, he may knowingly assign an employee to perform a dangerous task for which he is not trained, and thus be liable for injury to others. It does not follow logically, however, that an employer should be liable when he is not himself at fault, especially if he has done his best to train the employee to avoid anything that might constitute a tort. Nevertheless, the common law has evolved a basis for making the employer liable for harm caused by the tortious acts of an employee when these acts arise in the course of employment. These developments have two main justifications. First, it is true that an employee is personally liable for the torts he commits while acting for himself or his employer. Yet employees generally have very limited assets available for the redress of the potential harm they can cause — an engineer of a locomotive can operate it so negligently that it injures hundreds of passengers. Secondly, there is the strong argument based on fairness: he who makes the profit should also be liable for the loss. Accordingly, the courts have developed the principle of *vicarious liability*, whereby an em-

---

[6] Rylands v. Fletcher (1868) L.R. 3 H.L. 330; Heintzman & Co. Ltd. v. Hashman Construction Ltd. (1973) 32 D.L.R. (3d) 622; O'Neill v. Esquire Hotels Ltd. (1973) 30 D.L.R. (3d) 589; Gersten et al. v. Municipality of Metropolitan Toronto et al. (1974) 41 D.L.R. (3d) 646.

ployer is liable to compensate persons for harm caused by his employee in the course of his employment. The employee remains personally liable for his torts, but the best chance for recovery usually lies against the employer.

A consequence of the development of vicarious liability has been that employers ordinarily insure themselves against such losses and take into account the cost of the insurance in pricing their products, thus distributing the loss as discussed at the beginning of this chapter. We shall discuss an employer's liability further in Chapter 21.

ELEMENTS OF A TORT ACTION

As a practical matter in establishing his right to recover compensation, a plaintiff must prove three things to the court's satisfaction: (a) that the defendant owed him a duty to refrain from the injurious conduct in question, (b) that the defendant broke that duty by acting as he did, and (c) that the defendant's conduct *caused* the injury. All three requirements may create major difficulties for the plaintiff; lawyers debate all of them with great energy. The first element requires a policy decision or *value judgment* by the court — is the conduct complained of such that it *ought* to create liability? As our social values change, so does public policy as expounded by the courts. The second question is a mixed question of policy and fact — did the defendant's conduct actually go so far as to amount to a breach of duty recognized by the court? The third question is one not only of fact but also of philosophy, as we shall see in the next section. Legal cause is a subtle subject about which whole volumes have been written.[7] We must be careful not to jump to the conclusion that a defendant caused the plaintiff's injury in law.

CAUSATION

The most extreme view of the theory of causation can link one act to every other act in the world. An example will illustrate this contention: *A* breaks a china plate from a dinner set. The following day, his wife makes a special trip by car to a shopping centre to replace the plate. On the way she has a collision. It could be argued that *A*'s carelessness in dropping the dinner plate the previous evening "caused" the accident. Had he not dropped the plate, there might not have been a collision. Yet in the eyes of the law *A* clearly did not "cause" the accident. In the first place, many intervening voluntary acts occurred to bring Mrs. *A* and the driver of the other car to the same place at the same time. Mrs. *A* might have chosen to go at another time, as might the other driver. The interposition of these voluntary acts removes any legal blame from *A*. Secondly, the accident might have occurred because Mrs. *A* or the other driver or both of them made mistakes in judgment. Had they driven carefully, no accident would have taken place. Thus we can see that the interposition of careless conduct — neglect — may well absolve the earlier conduct of *A* from legal responsibility.

---

[7] Hart and Honoré, *Causation in the Law*, Oxford: Oxford University Press, 1959.

Generally speaking, the closer in time a person's conduct occurs to the inflicting of an injury, the less chance there is of significant intervening acts happening that would absolve the defendant and the more likely he is to be found the "cause" of the injury. For example, suppose X swerves across the road to make a left turn in front of Y at the last moment. Y may react unwisely and collide with X, yet the suddenness of X's action may make him wholly the "cause". If X had made the same maneuver five seconds earlier, so that Y had time to examine the situation and decide what to do, then Y's act might be the "cause" of the collision. At this point we can see that "cause" in the physical sense becomes confused with "cause" in the moral sense of responsibility and confused too, in turn, with "fault" in its legal sense. In discussing the physical closeness or *proximity* of a particular act to a subsequent injury we must eventually decide, as a matter of policy, at what point we cut off the process and pronounce that the actor is or is not responsible. The practical necessity of drawing reasonable limits for liability means that a court must decide to break the chain of causation at some point. In choosing that point, the court makes a social judgment.

BURDEN OF PROOF

In common with plaintiffs in other actions, a plaintiff in a tort action must prove his case; in certain kinds of cases, however, he is in a peculiarly difficult position. A pedestrian knocked down by a car or a consumer poisoned by a dangerous substance in a can of food, for example, may be unable to ascertain exactly how the defendant driver's or manufacturer's conduct contributed to his injury. The law has taken these difficulties of proof into account. The injured party need only establish that the defendant's car or product physically caused the injury. The burden is then cast upon the defendant to exculpate himself. He is presumed to have been in breach of a duty owed to the plaintiff and also to be in possession of any information that might establish him to be innocent of any breach. Once the burden has been *shifted* to him he will be found liable, unless he adduces the necessary evidence to satisfy the court that on balance he was not in breach of a duty to the plaintiff.

NEGLIGENCE

Foreseeability

We noted at the beginning of this chapter that in early tort law, it was enough simply to establish that a person had physically caused harm to another — he would be found liable. The question of his moral responsibility did not arise. As soon as we introduce the idea of fault, however, we must establish criteria for proving fault. The principal criterion is whether an alleged wrongdoer, whom we shall here call A, should have realized his actions would do harm. Another way of putting it is to ask, "Should A have foreseen that his actions would cause harm?'' Of course it would be unfair to expect *A* to have the vision of a prophet or a genius; his ability to foresee the consequences of his act need not be exceptional. Thus the question becomes, ''Would a normally intelligent and alert person — a reasonable person — have foreseen that *A*'s conduct would likely harm someone?'' or, more succinctly, ''Were the harmful consequences reasonably foreseeable?''

Illustration:

A carelessly throws a lit cigarette into a trash can. An explosion follows, causing serious injury to *B,* a bystander. A bottle of gasoline had been put into the receptacle earlier by an unknown person.

Only if the harmful consequences were reasonably foreseeable would *A* be under a duty to refrain from the activity.

In examining the problem of duty, we find two levels of foreseeability. First, *A* may claim that he was under no duty because his conduct would not be considered likely to produce harm. That is, it would not generally speaking be considered as dangerous conduct. Secondly, even if his conduct is considered dangerous and he is under a general duty to refrain, in *A*'s particular case he could not reasonably be expected to have foreseen the specific type of harm that actually resulted. In other words, the harm was unusual and not foreseeable. Thus, in our illustration, *A* would have been liable for a fire caused by his act if normal rubbish such as cellophane and dry paper were present, but it does not follow that he should be liable for damage caused by an explosion, an extraordinary event that is not reasonably foreseeable.

It has been argued that when the law lays down a standard of conduct and a person acts in breach of that standard, he should be liable for whatever injuries flow physically from his acts, regardless of whether the injuries could reasonably have been anticipated.[8] The contrary view is that a person should be responsible only for the reasonably foreseeable consequences of his acts, and that when the harmful results are unforeseeable, even though he is the physical cause, he should not be considered to be at fault; therefore he is not legally responsible.[9] The second view has become the one primarily favoured by our courts.[10]

Standard of Care

The problem we have been discussing above is central to the tort of negligence. The law places a general duty on every person to conduct his activities taking

---

[8] Re Polemis [1921] 3 K.B. 560.

[9] Overseas Tankship (U.K.) Ltd. v. Morts Dock & Engineering Co. (The Wagon Mound) [1961] A.C. 388; Overseas Tankship (U.K.) Ltd. v. Miller Steamship Co. Pty. Ltd. (The Wagon Mound No. 2) [1966] 2 All E.R. 709; MacMillan Bloedel (Alberni) Ltd. et al. v. British Columbia Hydro and Power Authority et al. (1973) 33 D.L.R. (3d) 538.

[10] *Ibid.* See also the excellent discussion in Fleming, *The Law of Torts,* (4th ed.) pp. 169 ff.

reasonable care not to injure other persons or their property. Whether or not a person has acted with reasonable care is a question of foreseeability of harm: if a reasonable man would foresee that by failing to be careful in his activity he is likely to injure another, then he is under a duty to take due care. If he fails to do so and injures another, he is guilty of negligence and liable for the injury he has inflicted. The question of reasonable foreseeability — or, put in its classic legal form, whether a reasonable man would foresee the danger — may seem a vague standard, very difficult to apply. Indeed it is; but it is the most useful test yet devised, and it has the redeeming feature of being capable of gradual adjustment by the courts as the standards of what is reasonable in the community change. Critics often say that the courts have not responded well to social change, but few have suggested that the test of the reasonable man be narrowed to hem the courts in further.

Contributory Negligence

Although the principles of liability for negligence are much younger than many other areas of tort law, they are old enough to have acquired certain rigid and undesirable strictures that have required statutory reform. Early in the development of the principles of negligence, the courts recognized a defence that the plaintiff was the author of his own misfortune as sufficient to excuse the defendant. This defence seems reasonable enough: if the defendant shows, for example, that the plaintiff carelessly stepped out from behind a parked car and the defendant could not have avoided the accident even if he had been driving very slowly, then it is not unjust to excuse the defendant. However, the courts took a rather narrow and mechanical approach to the subject. If the defendant could establish even a small measure of blame on the part of the plaintiff, indicating that the plaintiff contributed in some measure to his own loss, the plaintiff would fail even if the defendant was mainly at fault. Thus, a defence showing *contributory negligence* on the part of the plaintiff became a severe and unjust stricture in negligence law.

In the 19th century, the courts attempted to ease the harshness of the contributory negligence rule by permitting the plaintiff to recover if, despite the plaintiff's negligence, the defendant nevertheless had the *last opportunity* or *last clear chance* to avoid the injury. Again, theoretically, the idea seems sound enough; it gave the court another chance to help a plaintiff who would otherwise fail (because he was to some degree negligent), especially when it felt that the defendant was mainly responsible for the loss. But the rule was still an all-or-nothing solution: the plaintiff either recovered all the damages assessed by the court or none of them. Worse still, application of the rule became mired in complicated and unjustified nuances that were a nightmare to judges and lawyers. Since *last clear chance* is based on a chain-of-events theory, it is not realistic to apply it to "instantaneous" accidents such as most highway mishaps. As a result, reasoning about who theoretically had the last clear chance became so illogical at one stage as to appear to have reversed the rule completely.

The way out of these difficulties was first established in marine law by international convention,[11] and was finally applied to negligence actions in general by statutory reform pioneered in Canada.[12] These statutes, known as *comparative negligence* or *apportionment of loss* legislation, required courts to apportion damages according to the respective degree of responsibility of the parties. The acts do not set out in detail the basis for making the apportionment, but leave it to be decided by judges and juries according to their opinion of what is fair in the circumstances. Within the framework of ''fault'' or ''responsibility'' as the basis for liability, the legislation has been a great improvement towards awarding compensation more equitably. But the entire system is subject to reservations discussed earlier, concerning the appropriateness of fault as a basis for liability in such areas as automobile accidents.

Hazardous Activities

An underlying assumption made in every case of negligence is that the particular activity is not in itself considered dangerous if carried on with reasonable care. However, some activities are inherently dangerous regardless of the care taken — for example, transporting high explosives. A strong argument may be made that in these circumstances, a person carrying on an inherently dangerous activity should be strictly liable for damage, regardless of fault. In other words, a person so engaged should charge for his services according to the degree of hazard, and should carry insurance to compensate for harm done to others. There is no reason why an innocent victim should suffer a loss caused by a dangerous activity carried on by another person for his own benefit. Although some United States courts have reached this conclusion, Canadian courts, in common with most other jurisdictions, still apply the principles of negligence. However they have raised the *standard of care* proportionally as the danger increases. As a result, in many cases of hazardous activities the defendant finds the standard of care so high that it is virtually impossible for him to show that he has satisfied it. The effect is much the same as if he were strictly liable.

Carrying high explosives is a clearcut case for such strict liability. Few would question a policy that makes carriers of these materials liable regardless of fault. Many activities, however, are much more difficult to assess. Hence the controversy concerning road traffic. Is driving — or even walking — on public roads and sidewalks an inherently dangerous activity (as it seems to be statistically)? Should liability, therefore, be strict and not based on negligence? Although it is too early to be certain, opinion seems to be moving toward such a policy in this area.

---

[11] Maritime Conventions Act, 1911, 1 and 2 Geo. 5, c. 57.

[12] Ontario passed the first statute in the field: The Negligence Act, St. of Ont. 1924, c. 32.

Product Liability

Who should bear the loss in the following situations?

(a) *X* runs a small refreshment booth at a beach and buys his supplies from
Y Bottling Co. Ltd. He sells a dark-green bottle of ginger ale to *A* who
gives it to his friend *B*. *B* drinks half the contents and becomes violently
ill. The balance is found to contain a decomposed snail. *B* is hospital-
ized and is unable to return to work for several weeks.

(b) *P* buys a *Q* Company sports car from *R* Dealer. On being driven away
from the showroom, the car loses a defective front wheel and collides
with a parked vehicle, injuring the occupant, *S*.

(c) *M* buys from the *N* Ski Shop a set of thermal underwear manufactured
by *O* Company. The underwear proves to contain a toxic acid which
when it comes in contact with perspiration causes *M* to have a severe
and debilitating skin burn.

As we point out in Chapters 12, 13 and 16, the retailer in each of our examples is liable to the buyer for breach of a warranty of fitness. But in example
(a), *X* may well have insufficient assets to compensate for the loss. In any event,
he sold the soft drink to *A* rather than *B*, the injured party. Accordingly, *B* is not a
buyer entitled to the protection of a warranty of fitness. Similarly, in example
(b), the injured person, *S*, has no contractual relationship with *R* Dealer. In these
circumstances, contractual remedies are not available. If the injured parties are
going to be compensated, it must be by imposing liability in tort law. Since the
manufacturer allowed the defective product to reach the market, public policy
would seem to require that he should be liable.

Not until 1932 did the British courts recognize the duty of manufacturers to
ultimate consumers of their products as an obligation in tort law; the House of
Lords did so in the famous case of *Donoghue v. Stevenson*,[13] in which the facts
were analogous to those in example (a). Example (b) is drawn in part from the
United States case *MacPherson v. Buick Motor Co.*,[14] decided by the New York
Court of Appeals in 1916, a decision that must have influenced the later House of
Lords decision. In the years since *Donoghue v. Stevenson*, its principle has been
applied by the courts in an ever-widening ambit of circumstances to protect the
consumer and other members of the public who may be harmed. The increasing
complexity and sophistication of manufactured products, and the resultant increasing inability of the consumer and even of the intermediate distributor to detect dangers in these products, places the manufacturer in a position of growing
responsibility for the safety of the consumer. On the whole, the courts have
recognized this development and widened the application of the duty accordingly.

An interesting aspect of this problem concerns the question of proof. The
basic principle in Anglo-Canadian law is that the manufacturer is liable only for

---

[13] [1932] A.C. 562.
[14] (1916) 111 N.E. 1050.

defects caused by his proven negligence. By contrast, the prevailing view in parts of the United States is that the manufacturer warrants his products to be free of defects regardless of negligence. We can see, then, that our courts have based liability on fault, while some American courts have favoured the principle of strict liability for defects. Thus, a manufacturer in the United States may find himself liable to compensate the victim of a defect even when it was undetectable with the best technology available to him at the time.[15] Except for these extreme cases, our law has approached a similar position as a result of the burden of proof cast upon a manufacturer: if certain defects are foreseeable, then he must take every reasonable precaution in production and inspection to prevent defective goods from slipping into his distribution system. In example (c), based on the leading case of *Grant v. Australian Knitting Mills,*[16] the manufacturer was caught on the horns of the following dilemma: if his inspection process permitted such underwear to pass through undetected, the system was inadequate and he was therefore negligent; if his inspection process was virtually foolproof, as indeed the manufacturer claimed, then surely one of his employees must have been personally at fault, making the manufacturer vicariously liable in any event. Accordingly, the present state of our law appears to make manufacturers liable for all product defects of which the present state of technology can reasonably be expected to make them aware. If they take economic advantage of sampling inspection and risk allowing defective products to reach the consumer, they thereby assume responsibility for harm caused. In turn, the increased probability of injury will eventually be reflected in increased insurance premiums paid by the manufacturer, thus raising the price of his product.

Negligent Misrepresentation

An interesting aspect of negligence, which our courts did not recognize until 1963, concerns negligent misstatements causing purely economic loss (as distinguished from injury to persons or property).[17] As we note in our discussion of misrepresentation in Chapter 10, wilful or fraudulent misrepresentation constitutes the tort of deceit, and damages are clearly recoverable by the victim who relies on such statements. But the courts drew back from holding persons liable for negligent misstatements except where they had contracted to provide a service to the injured party or, apart from contract, owed him a special duty such as an accountant owes a client to whom he does not charge a fee. Their reluctance to find persons guilty of this type of negligence extended especially to those who

---

[15] The rationale for the position taken by the U.S. courts has been summed up as follows: "It is needlessly circuitous to make negligence the basis of recovery and impose what is in reality liability without negligence. If public policy demands that a manufacturer of goods be responsible for their quality regardless of negligence there is no reason not to fix that responsibility openly." Escola v. Coca Cola Bottling Co. of Fresno, 150 P. 2d 436 (1944) per Traynor, J. at 441.

[16] [1936] A.C. 85.

[17] Negligent misstatements causing *physical* injury have long been actionable. For example, it would be a tort to assure an inquiring motorist that the road ahead of him is safe, while carelessly forgetting to say that there is a deep uncovered ditch across the road just over the brow of the next hill.

made a profession of giving financial advice and information, such as accountants, bankers, trust company officers and stockbrokers — persons whose statements may reach large numbers of the public.

A person owes a general duty of honesty to all persons with whom he has dealings; a deliberate misstatement brings with it liability for injury so caused. But the duty was limited to being honest and did not extend to being diligent and careful. Thus, in a leading case in England in 1951,[18] the English Court of Appeal held that an accountant who carelessly prepared a misleading balance sheet of a company, knowing that it would be shown to a person interested in investing in the company, was not liable to compensate the investor for the loss caused by his reliance on the statement. The court expressed a fear that a general liability for careless words would create such an overwhelming risk as to drive certain activities out of existence. Suppose, for example, that a stockbroker were advising a friend, while they were at lunch, about the value of a certain company's shares, and a stranger at the next table overheard the advice, unintentionally and without trying to eavesdrop. Would the stockbroker be liable to compensate the stranger for a loss suffered because he invested in the company? This kind of unexpected liability to third persons for advice casually given to and intended for a friend might make the risk so wide as to severely limit the reasonable freedom of people in such occupations. Lord Justice Denning, who dissented from the majority opinion in the case, minimized such risks; the duty should be owed not to every conceivable person, but confined to a particular person or group of persons whom the author of the statement would reasonably expect to rely on the information provided.[19] The majority of the court had an understandable fear of virtually unlimited liability and did not accept the argument that reasonable limits could be set.

Denning's position was vindicated by the House of Lords 12 years later in the case of *Hedley Byrne v. Heller*.[20] In that case, the plaintiff requested that his bank obtain a credit report from the defendant bank on one of the defendant bank's clients before advancing a line of credit for an expensive advertising campaign. The bank made a superficial check and reported — with a disclaimer of responsibility — that the customer was financially sound. At no time did the bank deal directly with, or even know the identity of, the plaintiff. It dealt only with the plaintiff's bank. Nevertheless, the House of Lords held that the defendant should have foreseen that its information would be relied upon by a client of the other bank and accordingly owed that client a duty to take reasonable care in giving information about the creditworthiness of the prospective debtor. The House concluded that the defendant would have been liable to compensate the plaintiff for his large loss, except for the fact that the bank had quite clearly disclaimed any liability.

The result of the case seems to be that anyone who makes a negligent misstatement may be liable for losses suffered by a considerably wider group; he

---

[18] Candler v. Crane, Christmas & Co. [1951] 2 K.B. 164.

[19] *Ibid.*, at p. 184.

[20] [1964] A.C. 465.

may be held to owe a duty to those whom he should reasonably expect to rely and who do rely upon his misstatement. But further, a party making a statement may make it clear that he gives the information upon the condition that he accepts no liability for it, and such a disclaimer will be effective. This decision has been widely acclaimed by jurists.[21] It remains to be seen whether the principle will be expanded to widen the ambit of persons to whom the maker of a careless statement will become liable. Meanwhile there is little doubt that the standard of conduct required of people who give financial advice has been raised considerably by the decision.[22]

Occupier's Liability

Common sense might lead us to assume that an occupier of land and buildings (owner or tenant) would be liable for injuries inflicted upon visitors to his premises according to the ordinary rules of negligence; a visitor should have a claim against the owner or tenant of a piece of real property for any harm caused by unreasonable conduct, such as creating or leaving unexpected hazards in places where they might injure an innocent visitor. Unfortunately, this area of the law became bound up with concepts of land law and, as we see in Chapter 24, land law developed from ancient common law concepts, often rigid and irrational. Distinctions grew up dividing visitors on land and in buildings into several categories; the obligations of the occupier to take care vary according to the category to which the visitor belongs. The categories in descending order are: invitee, licensee and trespasser. The distinctions between invitee and licensee were abolished by statute in England in 1957,[23] but remain in Canada.

The highest obligation is owed to an invitee. An invitee is a person permitted by the occupier to enter as a matter of business, and the occupier obtains some material benefit or at least probability of a benefit from the invitee's presence.[24] For example, a customer entering a retail store is an invitee. Since the definition is highly artificial, the distinction between invitees and licensees is irrational, at least in some circumstances. Courts have disagreed on whether an invitee of a tenant is also an invitee when he passes over the landlord's premises in order to reach the tenant's premises — for instance when walking along a corridor in the landlord's building. We shall not attempt to discuss all the vagaries of this area of the law, but simply note that the duty owed by an occupier to his invitee is to take care to prevent injuries from hazards of which he is aware and also those of which as a reasonable person he *ought* to be aware. Thus, an occupier will be liable for an injury caused to an invitee by a hazard of which he had no knowledge, but would have known about had he taken reasonable care.

---

[21] For a discussion of its application in Canada, see Haig v. Bamford [1974] 6 W.W.R. 236.

[22] For a discussion of the liability of public accountants to third parties in respect of financial statements on which they have expressed an opinion, see: Dickerson, *Accountants and the Law of Negligence,* Toronto: The Canadian Institute of Chartered Accountants, 1966.

[23] Occupiers' Liability Act, 1957, 5 and 6 Eliz. 2, c. 31 (U.K.).

[24] Fleming, *The Law of Torts* (4th ed.) pp. 389-95.

The licensee category includes all other visitors who enter with the tacit or express permission of the occupier. Ordinarily a licensee enters premises for his own benefit, rather than for the benefit of the occupier. How apt is this distinction? For example, is a guest invited to dinner for his benefit or the benefit of the host? The question is inappropriate. A social guest is considered to be merely a licensee, even if his host expects ultimately to receive a pecuniary benefit as a result of the hospitality he has shown. The duty of an occupier to a licensee upon his premises is to remove concealed dangers of which he has knowledge; he has no liability for hazards unknown to him, even though a reasonable person in his place ought to have realized that a hazard existed. Thus the duty owed to licensees is less in this significant respect.

A trespasser is one who enters upon premises unlawfully; he enters without any invitation or permission of the occupier and is either unknown to the occupier or, if known to him, would be refused permission. The duty owed in these circumstances is minimal: the occupier must not set out deliberately to harm the trespasser or recklessly disregard the possibility that his acts might injure a trespasser. Thus, he must not set out traps in an open field, or fire a gun in the general area where he knows a trespasser to be present.

OTHER TORTS

One Tort or Many?

The general opinion of lawyers is that tort law is ever changing and expanding; as new forms of conduct arise and increase to the point where they cause unreasonable harm to members of the public fairly frequently, the law eventually brands the conduct as unlawful and grants a remedy to the aggrieved parties. Today an aggrieved party need not find a ''pigeon-hole'' into which his complaint will fit in order to hold his wrongdoer liable for a loss. As a result, it is not possible to enumerate a definitive list of torts or a comprehensive description of all conduct for which the law imposes liability. Some writers attempt to rationalize a general principle of tort law: that all conduct that causes unreasonable harm to others is tortious and creates liability. But such a general principle is not very helpful without examining particular torts. For our purposes a discussion of specific areas of tort law is useful. The torts discussed below by no means constitute an exhaustive list.

Some torts, for example, are examined in the context of other subjects; we shall discuss them as they arise and need mention them only briefly here. An outsider who incites a party to break an existing contractual obligation commits a tort known as *inducing breach of contract*. As we see in Chapter 8, any contract pursuing such a result is illegal as being against public policy. The tort of *deceit* takes the form of knowingly making a false statement with a view to inducing another to act upon it to his detriment. We discuss it in Chapter 10 under its alternative name of fraudulent misrepresentation as it affects contract law. The tort of *conversion* consists in the wrongful exercise of control over goods, inconsistent with the ownership, or against the wish, of the party entitled to them. We encounter the tort of conversion twice in Chapter 17, when examining the liability of a seller who wrongfully disposes of goods which no longer belong to him and of a carrier who disobeys instructions and wrongfully delivers goods. We meet it again in Chapter 30 in describing the liability of a buyer of goods under the instalment plan when he wrongfully disposes of them before completing his payments.

The most ancient and familiar tort is that of *trespass,* the act of entering on the lands of another without consent or lawful right or, after a lawful entry, refusing to leave when ordered to do so by the owner. In less civilized and less well-policed times trespass was often an incitement to violence. Hence it was originally considered a crime, a breach of the peace. Now, however, an owner is restricted to fencing his lands and to using no more than reasonable force in ejecting a trespasser. He may also bring an action against the trespasser, but he will often get little more than nominal damages unless he can prove that actual harm was done to his property. A brief discussion of this tort arises in Chapter 25 in relation to the rights of landlord and tenant against one another, and again in Chapter 30 as a restraint on an unpaid seller in asserting his right to repossess goods while they are on the land of a defaulting buyer.

Nuisance

A major problem confronting our society, indeed the whole world, is pollution of the atmosphere and water resources. In common law, the mere discharge of noxious substances into the atmosphere or into water is not itself a breach of duty, either to the community at large or to individuals who may subsequently be harmed by these materials. It may in fact be very difficult to establish that the conduct of any one person or industry has caused a harm. We can see this difficulty in the build-up of carbon monoxide and other noxious substances in the atmosphere from the operation of internal combustion engines in automobiles. We may read, for example, that the level of carbon monoxide in the city of Montreal has reached dangerous and alarming proportions. Those who breathe these fumes over an extended period of time may suffer serious injury to health, but it is impossible to conclude that any one automobile is responsible for the harm. In the first place, hundreds of thousands of vehicles contribute to the danger and, secondly, the effect is cumulative. For these reasons, effective control over pollution can only be obtained through legislation that carefully defines standards limiting the escape of noxious substances and that prescribes heavy penalties for failure to comply with these standards. Growing awareness of the problem is now bringing about increased government regulation.

A small group of public offences known as *public nuisances* includes such misconduct as blocking public roads, interfering with other public amenities such as the use of marketplaces or parks and, in a few instances, emitting dangerous substances in public places. Actions against the wrongdoer may ordinarily be brought only by an organ of government on behalf of the public as a whole. Occasionally, when an individual has shown a special injury considerably greater than that sustained by other members of the public in general, he may successfully maintain an action for compensation against the wrongdoer. These common law public nuisances are of limited significance today.

On the other hand, the common law has long recognized an *occupier's right* to the normal use and enjoyment of his land, free from such interference as noxious fumes, soot, contaminating liquids poured into rivers and streams or percolating through the soil, and also such things as noise and vibration. The term "occupier" includes not only the owner of land but tenants as well. Since most members of the public qualify as owners or tenants of their homes, they may legally complain of *private nuisances*.

Does the law give an occupier a right to absolute freedom from these various annoyances? A leading writer has said, "One can no more claim an absolute right to noiselessness than a right to absolute noiselessness."[25] The answer must be a relative one, weighing competing interests in society. It turns on two main issues: the degree of interference with the occupier's use and enjoyment of his land, and the economic importance of the offending activity.

The level of interference that a community as a whole already tolerates, and hence that individual members of it must tolerate as *reasonable use* (justified use not considered tortious), varies according to local conditions. The standard of reasonable use of adjoining lands in an industrial area such as Hamilton, Ontario, might be quite unreasonable and amount to tortious use in a holiday resort area such as Ingonish, Cape Breton. No matter what the local standard, however, an interference may be so severe as to rise above that level and be declared a nuisance.

Even when an activity clearly amounts to a nuisance and seriously affects a plaintiff's use of his land, the question arises whether it would be too high a price for the community to pay to grant him an injunction forcing the offending user to cease business. In theory, the court has two options open to it: it may grant the injunction, or it may only award the plaintiff damages without restraining the defendant's continued activity. Where the nuisance is so severe as to make his land unusable, the second decision amounts virtually to an expropriation of it in return for his damage award. Both Canadian and United States courts have been uncertain about the extent of their discretion in granting injunctions as a device for balancing social and economic interests in the community. Sometimes they have concluded that the offending industry is too important to restrain by injunction and have left the plaintiff to his remedy in damages.[26] At other times they have been less flexible and felt bound to grant an injunction, thus leaving it to the legislature to decide whether to legalize the defendant's impor-

---

25 Fleming, *An Introduction to the Law of Torts,* p. 187.
26 Bottom v. Ontario Leaf Tobacco Co. [1935] 2 D.L.R. 699; Mountain Copper Co. v. United States (1906) 142 Fed. 625.

tant industrial activity by dissolving the injunction and awarding the plaintiff compensation.[27]

The discussion above illustrates the difficulty in adjusting such questions by private litigation. In almost every action by an individual against a great industrial enterprise there loom the larger public issues of the economic viability of the industry should it be excessively restricted, and the dangers presented by unabated pollution.

Assault and Battery

One of the oldest torts recognized by English medieval law is the tort of *trespass to the person*. Initially this tort consisted of direct and violent attack against the victim, a tort easily understood by both the citizen and the courts. Acts of violence against the person are not uncommon today. The present-day legal term is *assault* (the threat of violence) and *battery* (the actual attack), although the word assault is frequently used by itself in non-legal discussions to include the battery. Except for rare cases, assaults are usually committed in the course of a crime; the attacker, if he is caught, is usually imprisoned and, although he may be clearly liable, he usually has no assets for the victim to seize in order to satisfy a judgment. Accordingly, assault cases are rarely litigated as private actions and the details of this area of the law are of little practical importance. Suffice it to say that no one is justified in assaulting another person in response to a verbal insult and that in repelling an attacker one is legally justified in using all *reasonable force,* but *no more force* than is reasonably necessary in the circumstances.

False Imprisonment

A more interesting aspect of trespass to the person is the tort of *false imprisonment. (False arrest,* a phrase often used in the same context, ordinarily includes a false imprisonment, but contains the additional feature of holding the victim with the intention that he be turned over to the police authorities for prosecution.) False imprisonment consists of "intentionally and without lawful justification subjecting another to total restraint of movement by either actively causing his confinement or preventing him from exercising his privilege of leaving the place in which he is".[28] Typical examples of false imprisonment occur when a store detective mistakenly detains a customer in the belief that he is a shoplifter (actively causing confinement), or when a motorist refuses to stop a moving vehicle to allow a passenger to get out in response to a reasonable request to stop (thus preventing him from exercising his privilege of leaving).

Physical restraint, or even the threat that it will be applied, is not neces-

---

[27] K.V.P. Co. Ltd. v. McKie [1949] 4 D.L.R. 497 and subsequent legislation, K.V.P. Company Limited Act, St. of Ont. 1950, c. 33.

[28] Fleming, *The Law of Torts,* p. 28.

sary: it is enough that the victim is given the idea that disobedience of a command not to leave will lead to humiliation in a public place. A reasonable fear that a store detective or other employee might shout, "Stop, thief!" would be enough restraint to amount to an imprisonment. Accordingly, there is a considerable risk in confronting a member of the public with the charge of a crime without very strong evidence. The policy of the law is not to encourage self-help remedies, such as a citizen's arrest, except in fairly clear cases. Does a person who falsely imprisons another have any means of absolving himself of liability? A private citizen may successfully defend a charge of false imprisonment only if a crime had been committed and he had reasonable cause to believe the plaintiff had committed that crime; in other words, the only good defence is that he apprehended the wrong person, and did so with reasonable cause. He will be liable if no crime was committed, despite an honest and reasonable belief on his part that a crime had been committed. Thus, the store detective who arrests a suspected shoplifter when no shoplifting has in fact occurred at that time has no defence against an action for false imprisonment.

On the other hand, the very limited defence available to private citizens when they have mistakenly arrested an innocent person would unduly restrict police officers in the performance of their duties; policemen will be excused so long as they have reasonable and probable cause to believe a crime has been committed, even when in fact none has been.[29] A policeman might be justified in arresting a "prowler" attempting to enter a building at night, even though the "prowler" turns out to be the owner of the premises.

Malicious Prosecution

By contrast, a private citizen who makes a complaint to the police about a suspected crime is not liable for false imprisonment (nor is the policeman) when the person is arrested by the police as a result of his complaint and the complaint turns out to be unfounded. Thus, if a store detective reports his suspected shoplifter to a policeman and the policeman arrests the alleged shoplifter the policeman is not liable, since he relied reasonably upon the complaint of the detective. The detective is not liable either, since he did not attempt to arrest the shoplifter but merely reported his suspicions to a law officer. The only circumstances in which the detective would be liable for malicious prosecution would be when he did not have an honest belief that a crime had been committed, but had some improper motive such as a wish to harass the victim. A charge of malicious prosecution is very difficult to prove, because in order to succeed the plaintiff must satisfy the court of the defendant's malicious intention, a subjective and nebulous matter that courts do not lightly accept as established. In the absence of an overt criminal act, it is much less hazardous to report suspicious activity to the police

---

[29] Criminal Code, R.S.C. 1970, c. C-34, s. 435(a). We should note that the protection discussed above, for anyone who mistakenly imprisons an innocent person, applies to the more serious offences known as *indictable offences*. Defences are much more limited when the crime is a petty one, such as being drunk in a public place. See Criminal Code, ss. 436 and 437.

and let them decide whether an arrest is reasonably justified, rather than attempt a citizen's arrest and learn too late that no crime has been committed.

Defamation

Defamation, better known as *libel* (written defamation) or *slander* (spoken defamation), is perhaps the most notorious form of tort. Generally speaking, defamation consists of unjustified injury to the reputation — private, professional or business — of another person.

> The law of defamation seeks to protect individual reputation. Its concern is not so much with insult or hurt to personal feelings as with injury to the respect and esteem in which one is held by one's fellows. The offensive imputation must have been conveyed to someone other than the person defamed.[30]

In cases of slander, the law is not concerned merely with soothing injured feelings; the aggrieved party must show that the defamer has made serious allegations about his character, ability or business reputation, before it will award damages. A complete defence against a charge of defamation is that the alleged defamatory statements are true. The problem for a defendant in this instance is the difficulty in establishing to the satisfaction of a court of law that the statements are true. The burden of proof makes it hazardous to make defamatory statements in the vague hope of later being able to establish their truth.

The public interest requires that in some circumstances there shall be *absolute privilege,* a complete immunity from defamation suits. Thus, words spoken in parliamentary debate, in proceedings in law courts and inquests, and before royal commissions, are absolutely privileged in the hope of promoting vigorous and candid discussion without the inhibiting effect of defamation laws. While there is the possibility of abuse resulting in innocent persons being defamed, the public good requires unfettered discussion in these functions of government. As a result, even intentional and malicious falsehoods uttered in Parliament are completely immune from action in the courts.

On numerous family, social and business occasions, a person may have an obligation to disclose information or give an opinion about another. The obligation is rarely a legal duty, yet the effect of the disclosure may be important both to the person receiving the information and the one about whom it is given. A letter of reference from a former employer, a teacher or a bank manager may be solicited by an applicant with full knowledge that the letter will be frank and may contain some uncomplimentary things. Yet the person supplying the letter would be hard pressed to prove everything he has stated. If he were in constant danger of having to defend his statements in a court of law, he would rarely be willing to give a letter of reference unless it could be couched in the most flattering terms. Obviously, such a situation would not be in the interests of applicants who often

---

[30] Fleming, *The Law of Torts*, (4th ed.) p. 455.

willingly accept less than a saintly and implausible reference, or those who must rely on such letters to choose among applicants. The law extends a *qualified privilege* to anyone giving such information. Provided they give it in good faith with an honest belief in its accuracy, they can successfully defend an action of defamation even if their statements prove to be untrue.

Qualified privilege arises in many other situations. Fair and accurate reports of proceedings in Parliament, courts, administrative tribunals, public inquiries and meetings enjoy qualified privilege. The common law also tolerates, as a necessary function in a democratic society, statements made as fair comment and criticism in matters of public interest. The basic requisite for a critic is to establish that he had an honest belief in his opinions, but the cases often turn on subtle questions concerning the accuracy of the facts used by the critic to form his opinions.

QUESTIONS FOR REVIEW

1. What are the purposes of tort law?
2. What must a plaintiff in an action for damages be able to prove if he is to succeed?
3. What is the significance of shifting the burden of proof in certain kinds of negligence cases?
4. Is automobile insurance that provides protection against liability to third parties consistent with a doctrine of fault? Explain.
5. Is it correct to say that a person is liable in damages to an injured party for the consequences of his conduct, regardless of whether he could have foreseen those consequences at the time he acted?
6. Why is it necessary to resort to tort law in product liability cases?
7. Do the ideas of ``fault'' and ``causation'' lead to the same conclusions in determining liability for a tort?
8. By what logic can an employer be held liable for the negligent conduct of an employee whom he has instructed *not* to act in the manner that causes the loss?
9. In determining liability for negligence a court will ask itself whether a reasonable man, given an opportunity to contemplate the probable consequences of the conduct in question, would have foreseen any danger in his conduct. It does not ask whether the defendant *in fact* foresaw any danger. Why would a court reject the latter question as a test for liability?
10. Why was the contributory negligence rule a harsh one? In what way has our law now alleviated its severity and unfairness?
11. Discuss the consequences of the recently extended liability of professional accountants.
12. What public policy may be related to the attitude of the law with respect to the tort of false imprisonment?
13. Why would a legislature grant damages when it dissolves a court injunction

obtained in an action to restrain a nuisance? Why would it dissolve an injunction in the first place?

14. What are the implications of sampling inspection for the liability of a manufacturer?
15. In what ways are courts incapable of coping with some of the more serious problems raised by nuisances? How can the law tackle such problems?
16. Distinguish between absolute and qualified privilege.
17. *A* insults *B* in a telephone conversation. Has *A* committed slander? What additional facts might affect the answer?
18. *X,* a customer in a department store, sees *Y* running to the store exit with an unwrapped toaster, and shouts, ''Stop thief!'' *Y* continues running but *Z,* a policeman who heard the shout, apprehends him. As it turns out, *Y* had purchased the toaster and was merely rushing home to afternoon tea. What causes of action might *Y* have and against whom?
19. The owner of a wax museum places the wax figure of a prominent living politician in a display of figures of notorious convicted criminals. What legal risk, if any, does he take?
20. ''Be the exceptions more or less numerous, the general purpose of the law of torts is to secure a man indemnity against certain forms of harm to person, reputation, or estate, at the hands of his neighbours, not because they are wrong, but because they are harms . . .'' (Oliver Wendell Holmes, *The Common Law* (1881), pp. 144-5). Explain the meaning of this quotation in your own words.
21. ''. . . the existence of a duty to take reasonable care no longer depends on whether it is physical injury or financial loss which can reasonably be foreseen as a result of a failure to take such care.'' (*Ministry of Housing and Local Government v. Sharp* [1970] 2 Q.B. 223 per Salmon, J.J. at 278.) Explain with illustrations the meaning of this quotation.

CASES FOR DISCUSSION

Note: The cases presented below and those at the end of all subsequent chapters sometimes contain references to actual reported decisions. It may be helpful to consult the decisions for a discussion of the principles involved, but it is wrong to assume that the specific results necessarily apply to the cases for discussion. As pointed out in the Preface and in Chapter 3, there are often significant variations in the facts, and in any event the reported decisions may be opposed by conflicting judgments. In other words, the references *do not* supply the answers.

CASE 1

While en route to work on his motorcycle, Yardley collided with an automobile and later died from injuries. The evidence showed that Yardley was at fault.

At the time of the accident Ms. Hill, who was eight months pregnant, was standing on the far side of a bus, and while not a witness to the accident, heard the impact and later saw blood on the road and the injured parties in pain.

Ms. Hill brought an action for damages against the executor of Yardley's estate. She claimed she had sustained nervous shock and wrenched her back and testified that her child had been stillborn.

Discuss the merits of Ms. Hill's argument, indicating whether you think her action should succeed. (See *Bourhill v. Young* [1943] A.C. 92; [1942] All E.R. 396.)

CASE 2

Chandler and Alfredo, buyers for another store, entered the shop of Park Avenue & Yorkville Fashions Ltd. and were recognized. The manager of the shop, Silverberg, became angry and in the presence of a number of interested customers accused Chandler and Alfredo of spying. There followed an exchange of insults. Silverberg called the shop detective, telling him to keep an eye on Chandler and Alfredo, and then telephoned the police, referring to Chandler and Alfredo as "suspicious characters". No one touched the two buyers, but they came to the conclusion that they would be detained if they were to try to leave. In due course three policemen arrived and escorted Chandler and Alfredo from the shop while Silverberg declared that he intended to press charges, although he did not specify what the nature of these charges would be. The two men were led away amid a further exchange of invective, and business at the shop returned to normal.

Chandler and Alfredo brought an action against Silverberg for false imprisonment and Silverberg counter-claimed for damages for trespass. Discuss the relative merits of the claim and counter-claim. (See *Chaytor et al. v. London, New York and Paris Association of Fashion Ltd. and Price* (1961) 30 D.L.R (2d) 527.)

CASE 3

A passenger plane operated by Saltwater Air Lines Ltd. on a flight from Sydney to Dartmouth deviated somewhat to the south of its normal path to avoid some clouds and give a smoother ride. In doing so the aircraft passed over a hill, on the other side of which was a mink ranch operated by Scotia Mink Ltd. The noise of the plane caused panic among the mink and, because it was the whelping season, the female adults killed their young in large numbers. Between 175 and 200 animals valued at $10,000 were lost as a result of the incident. Scotia Mink Ltd. brought an action for $10,000 damages for negligence against Saltwater Air Lines Ltd.

The main building of the ranch had the words MINK RANCH painted in large white letters on a red roof. From the evidence it was unlikely, however, that the pilots could have avoided flying over it because of its location on the opposite side of the hill. The evidence also showed that the aircraft's altitude at the time was between 400 and 2,000 feet and not in violation of the Air Traffic rules in the Regulations under the Aeronautics Act. The pilot and co-pilot were preoccupied with making an approach to the Dartmouth airport and had no opportunity to survey the ground beneath the plane.

It was also brought out in evidence that the Department of Transport in Ottawa had published and issued to all pilots and aircraft owners an information circular advising of the way in which mink ranches were to be marked so that they would be visible from the air, though the circular did not disclose the location of any mink ranches. The evidence showed too that the pilots in this case had ignored the information circular.

Should the action succeed? Discuss the principles of tort liability that would seem to apply. (For reference, see *Nova Mink Ltd. v. Trans-Canada Airlines* [1951] 2 D.L.R. 241.)

CASE 4

In the late spring of 1972, C. P. Oliver, a letter carrier employed by the Canada Post Office, set up a group of mail boxes with 20 compartments to serve a trailer court. He located the boxes at the side of a busy highway just adjacent to the entrance to the trailer court. Because of the condition of the ground at the time he placed them in position, Oliver did not secure them permanently, intending to return at a later time to complete the installation. What he did was place a large stone under one of the legs; soon after he left, however, the stone sank in the soft ground so that the mail boxes tilted at a considerable angle. Oliver had delivered mail in the district for some time and was acquainted with many of the residents of the trailer court.

The next day, Bobby Smith, a six-year-old boy who lived in the trailer court, climbed on top of the mail boxes along with a four-year-old playmate, Jimmie Lee. The boxes fell on the younger child. They proved to be too heavy for Bobby Smith to lift and it was not until some thirty minutes later that a passerby who saw what had happened removed them from the injured child. As a result of the accident Jimmie Lee sustained a broken leg and a fractured skull. For some days he remained in serious condition, but after two months in hospital recovered completely except for a small scar on his scalp.

Jimmie Lee's father brought an action for damages jointly against the Crown (specifically the Canada Post Office) and Oliver. He claimed $3,000 on behalf of his child as compensation for his suffering, and an additional $350 compensation for baby-sitting costs and travel expenses required by his frequent visits to Jimmie in a hospital ten miles distant.

Discuss with reference to these facts the questions of duty of care and vicarious liability in determining the defendants' liability for negligence.

CASE 5

The Popular Furniture Company Ltd. was a small concern turning out wooden furniture and doing contract work on interiors of offices and private residences. It required some new equipment and its manager and owner, Mr. Craftsman, approached his bank for a term loan. The bank manager agreed to approve a loan of $30,000 on the condition that an additional $20,000 be invested in the company as well. The bank manager then introduced a local venture capitalist, Mr. Richman, to Mr. Craftsman.

Mr. Richman toured the plant of the Popular Furniture Company Ltd. and was impressed with its efficiency. He told Mr. Craftsman he would favourably consider buying newly issued company shares that would provide it with an additional $20,000 in cash, if he were made a director and if he were also satisfied with the company's audited financial statement for the business year just ended.

In previous years McAdam & McCollum, a firm of practising public accountants whose partners were members of a leading professional accounting body, had done the audit of the Popular Furniture Company Ltd. Mr. Craftsman got in touch with Mr. McAdam, explained the situation to him, and pleaded for an early audit of the company's accounting records. The accounting firm was very busy preparing income tax returns for clients at the time, but eventually sent Henry Postwell, a junior audit clerk who had done the audit for the past two years, to do the work. In due course a set of financial statements was prepared in collaboration with the company's bookkeeper, and McAdam & McCollum prepared on their firm letterhead an auditor's report addressed to the owners of the Popular Furniture Company Limited. In their report the auditors expressed the opinion that the attached financial statements fairly presented the financial condition and results of operations of the company. The financial statements showed a profit for the year of $10,000 and a barely adequate working capital position as at the year end. Mr. Craftsman gave a copy of them and the auditor's report to Mr. Richman and the latter then invested $20,000 in a new issue of the company's shares.

The company ran into severe financial difficulties in the following period and became insolvent. It then came to light that just before the end of the preceding year, an advance deposit of $25,000 had been received from a department store towards a future shipment of furniture; the amount had been recorded as a sale for the year without any shipment of the goods having been made, so that the goods had also been included in closing inventory. As a result, the reported profit of $10,000 should have been reported instead as a substantial loss, and the working capital was in fact inadequate. The transaction with the department store was the first of its kind in the history of the company and Henry Postwell had simply missed its significance in the course of his audit.

Richman lost his investment in the company and brought an action against McAdam & McCollum for damages of $20,000. Offer an opinion about whether his action might succeed. (See *Candler v. Crane, Christmas & Co.* [1951] 2 K.B. 164; *Hedley Byrne & Co. v. Heller & Partners* [1964] A.C. 465, [1963] 2 All E.R. 575; *Haig v. Bamford et al.* [1972] 6 W.W.R. 557; reversed on appeal, [1974] 6 W.W.R. 236.)

PART TWO
Contracts

CHAPTER 5

Formation of a Contract: Offer and Acceptance

THE ROLE OF CONTRACT LAW

We tend to think of law as a body of rules that constrain and control individual activity for the best interests of society as a whole. This tendency is natural enough, since it reflects the purposes of such important and familiar areas of law as criminal law and torts, where obligations are placed *involuntarily* on each member of society. Yet the law has another important role: it enables individuals to enter voluntarily into obligations by following legal rules established for the purpose.

Why do people voluntarily enter into obligations? Why not remain free of all obligations not imposed by law? The answer is simple enough: the ability to enter into obligations voluntarily *expands* a person's freedom of choice. If a person wishes to acquire certain advantages, he can bargain for them by entering into an obligation for the benefit of others in exchange for the advantage he desires. In Chapter 2, we noted that many legal rules work as guidelines to form a background for voluntary legal relationships such as business partnerships. In this context, law is a facilitative process, a passive framework within which parties can decide upon and bargain for their own legal obligations. In a sense, it is an area where people make law for themselves and where they can express their individual preferences. Contract law is the prime example of law in its facilitative role.

We must not make this picture appear too idealized. As we shall see, there is often great inequality between parties to contracts in terms of bargaining power, expertise and intelligence, and in some circumstances there is no opportunity whatever to bargain. Thus, many unfair bargains are made. Secondly, the rules of contract law are human rules subject to human frailties — sometimes they lead to unintended or unjust results. In a few instances, it seems beyond the ken of the legal mind to devise a fair solution for a manifestly difficult problem. On the whole, however, contract law responds well — perhaps better than most areas of the law — to the individual's needs and wishes, and it accommodates most relationships with a minimum of conflict.

THE NATURE OF A CONTRACT

All contracts begin with a promise, but not all promises become contracts. Although there may be a moral obligation to keep all promises seriously made, it does not follow that there will be any legal obligation. Contract law is concerned with legally binding promises. "The most popular description of a contract that can be given is also the most exact one, namely that it is a promise or set of promises which the law will enforce."[1] These are the words of a great English lawyer in the opening paragraph of his treatise on the law of contract.

It is one thing to learn a simple definition, however, and quite another to apply it to a set of facts. The definition does not tell us what types of promises the law will enforce; before we can discuss how the law "enforces" a contract, we must be able to decide whether there is a contract. Accordingly we shall concern ourselves with two aspects of the definition through this and the following ten chapters of this book: first, a description of the promise or promises that may form a contract, and second, an investigation of the resources available in the law to enforce them.

A contract cannot come into existence until an offer has been made by one party and accepted by the other party. The first essentials of a contract are therefore offer and acceptance.

THE NATURE OF AN OFFER

An offer is a tentative promise made by one party, the offeror, subject to a condition or containing a request to the other party, the offeree. When the offeree accepts the offer by agreeing to the condition or request, a contract is formed: the promise is no longer tentative. The offeror is then bound to carry out his promise while the offeree is bound to carry out the condition or request.

The form of an offer is of no importance as long as the offeror conveys his proposal to the offeree. He could say, "I offer to sell you my car for $500," or, "I will sell you my car for $500," or even, "I'll take $500 for my car." All are equally good offers. In each instance the tentative promise is to sell the car if the condition of agreeing to pay the stipulated price is met.

---

[1] Pollock, *Principles of the Law of Contract* (13th ed.), p. 1. Winfield, ed., London: Stevens & Sons Limited, 1950.

We are accustomed to thinking of an offer as being communicated orally or in writing, but an offeror can also express his offer by conduct without words. Holding up one's hand for a taxi, raising a finger at an auction, and the gestures of floor traders at a stock exchange are examples that come to mind. As we shall see, it may even be possible for an offeror to communicate an offer by proceeding with performance to the knowledge of the party benefiting, though without any formal request having been made for his services.

A mere invitation to do business is not an offer to make a contract. The display of a shirt in the window of a men's shop does not amount to an offer to sell; a mail-order catalogue does not guarantee that the goods pictured or described will be delivered to all who try to order them. These are merely merchandising or advertising devices for introducing possible customers to an arena in which negotiations towards the formation of a contract may conveniently be started. Perhaps it will fall to the prospective customer, acting in response to the invitation, to make an offer — an offer which the businessman may in his turn accept or refuse. On the other hand, it may be the businessman who confronts the prospective customer with an offer as soon as he shows interest.

Newspaper advertisements generally are presumed to be mere invitations to do business. An advertisement to sell goods at a certain price is an invitation to the public to visit the advertiser's place of business with a view to buying. Obviously, the advertiser does not intend to sell to everyone who reads the advertisement — his supply of goods is limited, and he cannot accurately predict the number of readers who will be seriously interested. If the advertisement were taken to be an offer and many people accepted it, the advertiser would be liable for breach of contract with all those who accepted his offer and whom he could not supply with goods as offered. On the other hand, there is no rule that advertisements can never be offers; the courts have on occasion held them to be offers, when their wording reasonably favoured this intention. An advertisement to sell a fixed number of items at a fixed price to those who accept first, an offer of a reward for information or for the return of a lost object, or a reward to any person using a preventive medicine who still catches an illness, all may be valid offers. Obviously this group of advertisements forms only a very small proportion of newspaper advertisements; they are the exceptions rather than the rule.

In an English case[2] the court had to decide whether, in a self-service drug store, the display of merchandise constituted an offer and the act of the customer in taking the merchandise from the shelf amounted to an acceptance, or whether the display was merely an invitation to the customer to make an offer by taking the merchandise to the cashier. The matter was of importance, because by an English statute it is unlawful to sell any poison unless the sale is effected under the supervision of a registered pharmacist. The court held that the statute was not violated because in this instance a registered pharmacist was at hand near the

---

[2] Pharmaceutical Society of Great Britain v. Boots Cash Chemists (Southern) Ltd. [1952] 2 All E.R. 456.

cashier with authority to refuse a customer's offer to purchase any drug. The judge said:

> The mere fact that a customer picks up a bottle of medicine from the shelves in this case does not amount to an acceptance of an offer to sell. It is an offer by the customer to buy, and there is no sale effected until the buyer's offer to buy is accepted by the acceptance of the price.[3]

An offer cannot be accepted by the offeree until he has first learned of it. This is not the trite proposition it appears to be at first glance. A man may find and return a lost article to its owner and afterwards learn that a reward has been offered for the return of the article. The finder is not entitled to the reward because he did not act in response to the offer of it. The offer must have been communicated before it can be accepted.

Crossed offers provide a further illustration of this rule. If *A* writes to *B* offering to *sell* his car for $1,500 and *B* meanwhile has written a letter crossing *A*'s letter in the mail offering to *buy* *A*'s car for $1,500, there is no contract. *B* was unaware of *A*'s offer when he wrote, and accordingly *B*'s letter could not be an acceptance; *A* was unaware of *B*'s offer — *A*'s letter, too, could not be an acceptance. Unless either *A* or *B* sends a subsequent acceptance, no contract will be formed.

Similarly, we cannot be obligated by people who do work for us without our knowledge. We are entitled first to receive an offer to do the work, which we may then accept or reject. A person for whom work has been done without his request, and without his knowledge, may well benefit from it; but as he has not accepted any offer to do the work, he has no contractual obligation to pay for it. In *Taylor v. Laird*[4] the facts were that Taylor had been engaged to command Laird's ship and that during the course of a voyage he gave up his command of the ship but helped to work the vessel home in another capacity. Laird refused to pay Taylor for these services. The court held that Laird was within his rights because he was not given the option of accepting or refusing Taylor's services.

AN OFFER MADE BY TENDERING A WRITTEN DOCUMENT TO THE OFFEREE

Very often, offerors who deal with the general public present the terms of their offers in written documents handed to their offerees, or they post notices containing them on their business premises. Sometimes both methods are used together, the delivered document referring to the terms posted in the notice. Common examples of such documents are tickets for theatres, railways, and airlines, receipts for dry cleaning, fur storage, watch repairs, and checked luggage, as well as insurance policies and bills of lading. Almost without exception, a person receiving any one of these documents is not asked to read or approve of its terms. If he

---

[3] *Ibid.*, per Lord Goddard at 458.
[4] (1856) 25 L.J. Ex. 329.

were to take time to read it and suggest changes, the offeror would probably become very annoyed. He would say, "Take it or leave it." Thus, in fact, the offeree cannot change any terms of such a *standard form contract:* no real element of bargaining is involved. He must accept the offer as is or not at all. Often — as in a contract with a railway when there is only one practical means of transportation between two points — the offeree does not even have the choice of refusing. He *must* accept if he is to make his journey. In these circumstances the offeror has the tempting opportunity to disregard the interests of his offerees, the general public, and give himself every advantage; he rarely resists. On the other hand, the standard form contract is an indispensable tool. Imagine waiting in a queue at a railway ticket office while each would-be passenger bargains separately for each term in his contract!

> . . . Too often, the standard form is presented as an evil. The form is a facet of the efficiency and standardization of modern business; in some situations a form may provide an accumulation of experience and a thorough job of drafting that could not be gathered for one deal alone. But the concentration of economic power, and in particular the rise of the large business corporation, has led to many situations in which bargaining power is grossly unequal. Power corrupts. Forms are often used in situations where contract in fact is distorted or denied. They are dictated, not negotiated.[5]

The public has two means of protection. First, if the business carried on by the offeror falls within one of the classes of business regulated by government boards or commissions, the terms of these documents will be subject to their approval. When these boards operate effectively, the public is usually well protected, and unreasonable and onerous terms are excluded. Secondly, in the vast range of unregulated activity the public receives whatever protection the courts can muster from the general law of contract. On the whole the latter form of protection is unsatisfactory, but unless we are to sanction government regulation of every niche of business activity, no other means is readily available. What protection does the court offer?

As a starting point, the law presumes that an unqualified acceptance of an offer is an acceptance of every term of that offer. Suppose, however, that the offeree in fact does not know that the offer contains a certain term. He purchases a ticket to attend a baseball game. The ticket contains a clause stating that the management reserves the right to remove the ticket-holder at any time without giving reasons. The ticket-holder does not know or suspect that the ticket contains such a term. Is he bound by the term? If he establishes in court that he did not know of the term, then the court will inquire what steps the management took to bring the term to the attention of its customers generally. If it decides that the steps were insufficient, the ticket-holder will not be bound by the term; and if he has been wrongfully ejected from the baseball park, he will have the same remedy as if the

---

[5] Risk, "Recent Developments in Contracts", *Special Lectures, Law Society of Upper Canada, 1966*, p. 256.

term had not been on the ticket. On the other hand, if the court holds that the management had done what was reasonably necessary in the circumstances to bring the term to the notice of its customers, then the ticket-holder will be bound by the term whether he knew of it or not. The "ticket" cases always turn on their individual facts, and it is difficult to set down any firm guides of what is or is not sufficient notice. It should help us to understand the way the courts have reasoned on this matter if we look at some of the leading cases.

In *Parker v. South Eastern Railway Co.*[6] the contract was for the storage of a suitcase in a cloakroom of a railway station for a fee. Parker deposited his bag and received from the attendant a ticket on the face of which were the words, "See back." On the reverse side of the ticket was a printed condition that the railway should not be liable for loss in excess of £10. The bag was lost, and Parker sued the railway for the value of its contents, £24. On appeal, the court decided that the issue was whether the railway had done what was reasonably necessary to notify customers of the term. The court ordered a new trial because the trial judge had not asked the jury to decide this question.

The fact that the ticket given in *Parker v. South Eastern Railway Co.* contained on its face the words, "See back" is important. If a ticket or other document given to the customer at the time of his purchase contains a short and clear reference to other terms appearing either on the reverse side, or posted on a nearby wall in the form of a notice or sign, there is much greater likelihood that "reasonably sufficient notice" of those additional terms has been given. Thus, a sign in a parking lot in which the operator disclaims liability for loss or damage to car or contents may not in itself be reasonably sufficient notice to be binding on the owners of cars who park their vehicles there. We have to ask whether the ticket or voucher which a patron receives when he parks his car contains a clear reference to the sign and whether, in the circumstances, each customer ought to recognize the term stated on the sign as part of the contract he is making with the operator of the lot. A printed ticket or receipt which contains the words "subject to the conditions as exhibited on the premises" may serve to tie the sign in with each contract. The sign must, of course, be displayed prominently, but this in itself may not be sufficient; it must be brought home to the customer *at the time of the contract*. The operator of the parking lot, garage, or other place of storage cannot assume that he may exempt himself from liability merely by putting up a sign.[7] Lord Justice Denning has summed up the law on this subject as follows.

People who rely on a contract to exempt themselves from their common law liability must prove that contract strictly. Not only must the terms of the contract be clearly proved, but also the intention to create legal relations —

---

[6] (1877) 2 C.P.D. 416.

[7] Watkins v. Rymill (1883) 10 Q.B.D. 178. It may be more difficult for the operator of a parking lot to exempt himself from liability when the customer leaves his keys in the car at the request of the parking lot operator. See also Brown v. Toronto Auto Parks Ltd. [1954] O.W.N. 869 and Dewart v. 400 Parking Systems Ltd. [1954] O.W.N. 154; Samuel Smith & Sons Ltd. v. Silverman (1961) 29 D.L.R. (2d) 98.

the intention to be legally bound — must be clearly proved. The best way of proving it is by a written document signed by the party to be bound. Another way is by handing him, before or at the time of the contract, a written notice specifying certain terms and making it clear to him that the contract is in those terms. A prominent public notice which is plain for him to see when he makes the contract would, no doubt, have the same effect, but nothing short of one of these three ways will suffice.[8]

An insurance policy is another example of a standard form contract. Usually a purchaser of insurance will be presumed to have notice of all the terms contained in the policy. Too often, a person who has purchased protection under health, accident, automobile, or other types of insurance contract assumes blandly that he is completely covered. When a loss occurs, he may be disillusioned to discover that the insurance policy contains a term exempting the insurer from liability for loss under the very circumstances of his claim. Nevertheless, the insurance contract as written will be binding, and the insurance company will not be liable.

The problem of reasonably sufficient notice arises only when the customer has not signed the document which contains the terms exempting the seller from liability. If the purchaser signs the document, he cannot claim insufficient notice. He can only hope to avoid the whole contract, and it is exceedingly difficult to do this. Chapter 8 deals with this problem under the heading *non est factum*.

THE LAPSE AND REVOCATION OF AN OFFER

Lapse

An offer may lapse in any of the following ways:
(a) when the offeree fails to accept within a time specified in the offer;
(b) when the offeree fails to accept within a reasonable time, if the offer has not specified any time limit;
(c) when either of the parties dies or becomes insane prior to acceptance.[9]

When an offer has lapsed, the offeree can no longer accept the offer. This result follows whether or not he realizes the offer has lapsed, for it has become a nullity.

Students of business law frequently have difficulty understanding how the courts determine what constitutes a "reasonable time", and the answer, "It depends upon the circumstances of each case" may not seem helpful. Mr. Justice Estey of the Supreme Court of Canada has pointed out how the subject-matter of

---

[8] Olley v. Marlborough Court Ltd. [1949] 1 All E.R. 127, per Denning, L.J., at 134. Also quoted by Roach, J., in Pickin v. Hesk and Lawrence [1954] 4 D.L.R. 90.

[9] There appears to be some doubt about lapse in one circumstance: when an offeree accepts without knowledge that the offeror has died. See Cheshire, Fifoot and Furmston, *The Law of Contract* (8th ed.), pp. 51-3. London: Butterworth & Co. Ltd., 1972; Anson, *Principles of the English Law of Contract* (23rd ed.), pp. 55-6. Guest, ed. Oxford: Clarendon Press, 1969.

the contract may provide a clue for deciding whether a reasonable length of time has elapsed in an offer to buy or sell:

> Farm lands, apart from evidence to the contrary . . . are not subject to frequent or sudden changes or fluctuations in price and, therefore, in the ordinary course of business a reasonable time for the acceptance of an offer would be longer than that with respect to such commodities as shares of stock upon an established trading market. It would also be longer than in respect to goods of a perishable character. With this in mind the fact, therefore, that it was land would tend to lengthen what would be concluded as a reasonable time which, however, must be determined in relation to the other circumstances.[10]

The "other circumstances" which help to determine the length of a reasonable time include the manner in which an offer is made, and whether its wording indicates urgency. Often when a prospective purchaser makes an offer to buy property, he specifies that the offer must be accepted within twenty-four hours. The restriction is in his interest because it prevents the vendor from using this "firm offer" as a means of approaching other possible purchasers and bidding up the price.

Revocation

An offeror may be able to revoke (that is, withdraw) his offer at any time before acceptance, even when he has promised to hold the offer open for a specified time.

Illustration:

> *A* sends a letter dated January 15 to *B* offering to sell his house to *B* for $30,000. He states that the offer is open only until January 19, and that he must have heard from *B* by then. *B* receives the letter on January 16, and immediately prepares a letter of acceptance. Before he mails his reply on the morning of January 17, *A* changes his mind and telephones *B* saying that he wishes to withdraw his offer.
>
> The revocation is valid because it has reached *B* before he has accepted. Accordingly, *B* can no longer accept *A*'s offer.

In the above illustration, the offeror clearly revoked his offer before its acceptance: his personal communication of the revocation left no doubt about the offeree's knowledge of it. The legal position of the parties is less certain if the offeree merely hears rumours that the offeror has revoked, or hears that the offeror has made it impossible to carry out his offer because he has sold the property to someone else. The court will consider the offer revoked if it would be unreasonable for the offeree to suppose that the offeror still intended to stand by his offer.[11]

---

[10] Barrick v. Clark [1950] 4 D.L.R. 529 at 537.

[11] See Dickinson v. Dodds (1876) 2 Ch. D. 463.

An offeree may bind an offeror to keep his offer open for a specified time in one of two ways: (1) he may obtain a written offer under seal; (2) he may make a special contract called an *option* to keep the offer open. We shall consider the use of a seal in the next chapter. In an option, the offeree makes a contract with the offeror in the following general terms: the offeree agrees to pay a sum of money; in return the offeror agrees (1) to keep his offer open for a specified time (that is, not to revoke his offer) and (2) not to make contracts with other parties which would prevent him from fulfilling his offer (that is, to give the offeree the exclusive right to accept the offer). The exclusive right to such an offer may be very valuable to an offeree, even though he realizes he may eventually decide not to accept.

As an example, a manufacturer may purchase a number of options from property owners whose lots would, in the aggregate, provide a suitable location for a plant. The manufacturer might offer $300 to Farmer *A* for the right to buy his farm within three months for $50,000 and obtain similar option agreements from other farmers in the vicinity. In this way he can determine at modest cost whether all the necessary property will be available and what his total cost will be. The manufacturer need not "take up" or exercise the options, that is, accept the offers to sell the farms. On the other hand, he would be within his rights to require each of the farmers who had sold him these options to sell at the agreed price, provided he accepts the offers contained in the options within the specified time. In this illustration, the farmers are in the position of offerors who for an agreed period of time are not free to withdraw their offers without being in breach of contract. There are really two contracts in contemplation: first, the option agreement itself and second, the actual sale which will materialize if the option is exercised.

REJECTION AND COUNTER-OFFER BY THE OFFEREE

We have noted that a contract is not formed until an offer has been duly accepted. In many business negotiations the parties make a number of offers and counter-offers, but until a specific offer by one side is accepted without qualification by the other there will be no contract, and the parties will have no legal obligation to one another.

When an offer is put forward and the offeree, though interested, chooses to vary some of its features, he has not accepted; rather he has rejected the offer and made a counter-offer of his own. In this manner, the initiative in bargaining may shift back and forth until one of the parties finds the last proposal of the other quite satisfactory and accepts it without qualification. A contract is formed only when one party makes such an unqualified acceptance.

The making of a counter-offer amounts to a rejection of the original offer and brings it to an end. Further, the original offer does not revive if the counter-offer is in turn also rejected. The offeree can only accept the former offer if the offeror agrees to renew it; and this he may be unwilling to do because of changed circumstances. The courts have held, however, that the offeree's merely inquiring whether the terms offered are the best he can expect does not amount to a rejection.

Illustration:

> *A* wrote to *B* offering to sell his car for $1,000. *B* replied by mail, "I will give you $900 for the car." Two days later *B* wrote again to *A* saying, "I have been reconsidering. I will accept your offer of $1,000 after all."
>
> There is no contract. *B*'s counter-offer of $900 brought the original offer to sell for $1,000 to an end. While *B* has phrased his final statement in the form of an acceptance, he is doing no more than making a fresh offer of his own which *A* may or may not wish to accept. Perhaps someone else has offered *A* $1,050 for the car in the meantime. If when *A* made the offer to sell for $1,000 *B* had simply inquired whether this was the lowest *A* would go, the offer would have continued to stand. *B* would continue free to accept it within a reasonable period of time provided *A* did not withdraw his offer first.

THE ELEMENTS OF ACCEPTANCE

Its Positive Nature

Acceptance must be made in some positive form, whether in words or in conduct, with one exception which we note below. If acceptance is by conduct, the conduct must refer unequivocally to the offer made. One's conduct may happen to comply with the mode of acceptance set out in an offer and yet not constitute an acceptance. The offeree may habitually perform the act requested in the offer: he need not abandon his normal conduct to avoid accepting the offer. Suppose Smith always walks his dog around the park each evening, and Jones stipulates that Smith will have accepted Jones's offer to sell his car for $2,000 if Smith walks his dog in the park the next evening. Smith need not abandon his normal habit the next evening to avoid having the contract foisted on him.

For the same reason, an offeror cannot by himself stipulate silence as a mode of acceptance, thus forcing the offeree to act in order to reject the offer.

Illustration:

> A salesman for Ion Electric Supply Co. demonstrated a new high-speed Auto-analyzer for Glover, the owner of Speedy Car Repair Service. The price was $2,500. Glover thought the device was useful but overpriced: "At $1,500 I might consider buying it." The salesman said that he could not reduce his price and removed the machine.
>
> Two weeks later, an Auto-analyzer arrived with a letter from the salesman as follows: "When I reported how impressed you were with our analyzer to the manager, he said it would be worth selling one even at a loss just to break into the market in your city. We know what an excellent repu-

tation you have and it would be a good move to have our product in use in your shop. Our price is reduced, only to you, to $1,750. That is below cost. If we don't hear from you in ten days we shall assume you have accepted this exceptional buy and will expect payment of our invoice.''

There will be no contract even if the offeree, Glover, does not reply and simply allows the machine to sit idle; but he may well be bound if he takes the risk of using the machine, even to experiment with it.

Silence can be a sufficient mode of acceptance only if the parties have habitually used this method to communicate assent in previous transactions, or have agreed between themselves that silence shall be sufficient.

Its Communication to the Offeror

Generally speaking, an offeree must communicate his acceptance to the offeror. Some types of offers, however, can be validly accepted without such communication because the offeror asks only that the offeree perform an act, and implies that the act shall constitute acceptance. The offeror is bound to the terms of his proposition as soon as the offeree has performed whatever was required of him in the offer. The offeror may, in other words, dispense with notice to himself of the fact of acceptance.

This idea is illustrated by the decision in *Carlill v. Carbolic Smoke Ball Company*.[12] The Smoke Ball Company had placed an advertisement in a newspaper promising to pay £100 to anyone who used one of its smoke balls three times daily for two weeks and still contracted influenza. Mrs. Carlill used the smoke ball following the instructions supplied and contracted influenza. She sued the Smoke Ball Company on its promise to pay £100 — and succeeded. As a part of its defence the company pleaded that Mrs. Carlill had never communicated her intention to accept its offer. The court held that the offer had implied that notice was not necessary. All the company had asked was that readers should buy and use the smoke balls. Performance of the conditions set out was a sufficient acceptance without notification to the company.

The *Carlill* case also established that an offer may be made to an indefinite number of people who remain unknown to the offeror even after they have accepted. This result simply follows from the nature of the offer, a newspaper advertisement read by thousands of people. If the offer had been addressed to one particular person, then only that person could have accepted.

The Moment of Acceptance

The moment that a contract is formed by offer and acceptance, each party is bound to its terms. A person may withdraw from a business arrangement only if he can show that the arrangement is still tentative, that is, has not yet ''ripened into a contract''. We must, therefore, be able to analyze business negotiations so that out of all that is said between the parties, we can identify a specific offer when it is made and the acceptance of that offer if and when it is given.

---

[12] [1892] 2 Q.B. 484.

The common business practice of *inviting tenders* affords a useful illustration of the need for analyzing the various stages in a business deal to determine the point at which acceptance takes place. The purpose of inviting tenders may be to obtain firm offers from the tenderers for a fixed quantity of goods and services over a stated period, or it may be to explore the market of available suppliers and ascertain the best terms on which a given project may proceed. When the object is to obtain firm offers, the inviter of the tenders will accept the most satisfactory tender and a contract will be formed forthwith. This is normal practice when a company or government calls for tenders for the construction of a building. Often, however, no formal contract is contemplated as soon as the tenders are received; the procedure aims at accomplishing nothing more than a recognition of one supplier as the appropriate source of future work to be done or goods to be supplied, as required. Thus, a municipal corporation may advertise for the submission of tenders by contractors for the paving of a number of streets. In these circumstances the selection of the successful bid does not constitute acceptance of an offer made by the supplier. The supplier is in the position of having made a *standing offer,* and the party inviting the tender may avail himself of the offer by later placing specific orders. Each order so placed will be an acceptance of the standing offer of the supplier; and to that extent the supplier will have a contractual obligation to perform. The supplier remains free, however, to withdraw from the standing agreement if he finds it unsatisfactory, and he will have no liability to fill any further orders after his revocation.[13]

TRANSACTIONS BETWEEN PARTIES AT A DISTANCE FROM EACH OTHER

When the parties are at a distance, an acceptance should be made in the way suggested by the offer. An offer made by mail may reasonably be taken as inviting an acceptance by mail if no other mode of acceptance has been suggested. Understandably, a more efficient mode may be used — a telegram or telephone call in response to a letter can be valid acceptance.

Contracts made through the post are such a common incident of business life that it is important to have a rule which clearly sets out how the time of acceptance is determined. The rule which the courts have adopted is that acceptance is complete when a properly-addressed and stamped letter of acceptance is dropped in the mail. This rule is probably as practical and convenient as any alternative, when we consider that during the time required for a letter to reach its destination there must of necessity be a period of uncertainty in which the parties will not know whether a contract exists. The rule may be justified logically, because an offeror who is prepared to use the mails to communicate his offer ought to be willing to have the same medium used for acceptance, and to take his chance that the post office will be efficient in bringing him word of acceptance. If the offeror invites acceptance by mail, he must also be prepared to take the risk that the letter of acceptance may go astray; harsh though this may seem, it follows that he would be bound by a contract without notice of its existence.

---

[13] See Great Northern Railway Co. v. Witham (1873) L.R. 9 C.P. 16.

An offer may, of course, invite acceptance by post although it was not sent through the mails itself. Whenever acceptance by mail constitutes a reasonable response to an offer, the acceptance is complete at the time of mailing. Circumstances may, for example, make it reasonable that an offer made orally in the presence of the offeree be accepted by letter. The English courts have held:

> Where the circumstances are such that it must have been within the contemplation of the parties that, according to the ordinary usages of mankind, the post might be used as a means of communicating the acceptance of an offer, the acceptance is complete as soon as it is posted.[14]

When an offer indicates that acceptance should be made by some means other than post as, for example, by telephone or in person, the offeree may still accept by post but the offeror will not be bound unless and until the acceptance reaches him. Further, it must reach him before the offer has lapsed. When the mode of acceptance specified is speedier than mail, the danger that the offer will lapse before a letter arrives is increased. In other words, the acceptance is not valid when dropped in the mailbox (as it would be if acceptance by mail were reasonably contemplated), but only when received. Of course, an offeror may stipulate that an acceptance by letter will be effective only if received, or he may go further and state that acceptance will not be valid by letter at all. Such stipulations are effective, and unless the offeree accepts by complying with them he cannot bind the offeror.

The rule that applies to acceptance by mail applies also to acceptance by telegram — a telegram of acceptance is valid at the time it is delivered to the telegraph company. Except for these two modes of offer, however, an offeror will not be bound unless and until he received the acceptance. When businessmen use instantaneous means of communication such as telephone, radio, or teletype, the offeror must receive the acceptance before he is bound. In an English decision, the judge considered what would be the result if the telephone line were to go dead so that the offeror did not hear the offeree's words of acceptance. The judge concluded that the acceptance would be ineffective and that the offeror would have no contractual liability.[15] The common sense for this rule is that the offeree would know that the line went dead and that his acceptance might not have been heard. He must then verify that his acceptance was received.

The usual rule concerning the time of acceptance by mail differs from the rule concerning withdrawal of an offer. Revocation by mail is effective only when notice is actually received by the offeree, not when it is dropped in the

---

[14] Henthorn v. Fraser [1892] 2 Ch. 27 per Lord Herschell, at 33. The law in Canada is probably accurately represented by this case. There is some confusion caused in a Supreme Court of Canada decision on appeal from the Quebec courts where the post office is referred to as an "agent". See Charlebois v. Baril [1928] S.C.R. 88. See also Loft v. Physicians' Services Inc. (1966) 56 D.L.R. (2d) 481, where a letter posted in a mailbox but never received was held to be adequate notice to the defendant.

[15] Entores, Ltd. v. Miles Far East Corporation [1955] 2 Q.B. 327, per Denning, L.J., at 332.

mailbox. As a result, the offeree may accept and a binding contract be formed after revocation of the offer has been mailed but not yet received.

Illustration:

Able, in a letter posted January 15, offered to sell his business to Baker for $7,000. The letter was received by Baker on January 17. On January 19, Baker posted his letter of acceptance, which did not reach Able until the 21st. On January 18, however, Able had decided to withdraw his offer and posted a letter to Baker revoking it. This letter did not reach Baker until January 20.

Able's revocation arrived too late. There was a valid contract on January 19 when the acceptance was posted. Able was bound from the moment the letter was dropped into the mailbox.

Occasionally it may be important to know what is meant by the requirement that a revocation be ''actually received''. Is the revocation of an offer ''received'' if delivered to the place of business or residence of the offeree, or must it reach him in person? The general rule is that unless the offeror has knowledge that the revocation will not reach the offeree at his usual address, then delivery at that address establishes the fact and time of revocation, and the offeree is deemed to have notice from that time.

In contracts made by post, telegram, or other long-distance communication, the offeror and the acceptor are often in different provinces or countries at the time. In case of a dispute it may be important to know where the contract was formed. If the law in the two places is different, as sometimes it is, the place where the contract was formed is one of the criteria for deciding which law applies. The general rule is that a contract is formed at the place where the acceptance becomes effective. This is determined by the moment in time when the contract is effective. Thus, when an offeror invites an acceptance by mail or telegram, the contract is formed at the moment the acceptance is dropped into the mailbox or delivered to the telegraph company. Accordingly, it is formed at the place where the mailbox or the telegraph office is located. When an instantaneous means of communication such as telephone, telex, or teletype is used, the contract is not formed until the offeror receives the acceptance, and these contracts are formed at the place where the offeror receives the acceptance.

UNILATERAL AND BILATERAL CONTRACTS

The Offer of a Promise for an Act

As we have seen in the *Carlill* case, an offer may invite acceptance simply by the performance of its conditions and without a separate communication of that acceptance. When we leave a note on the doorstep requesting a quart of milk, we expect the milkman simply to leave the milk, thereby making a contract of sale. We should be annoyed if he were to ring the doorbell at 6:00 a.m. to tell us that he wished to accept our offer to purchase. In circumstances of this kind no reply is expected: the leaving of the quart of milk is all that is contemplated or needed in the way of acceptance.

An offer of a reward is accepted by anyone to whom the offer is made if he performs the conditions stipulated, such as providing information or returning a lost article. If the reward is for providing information, the courts have decided that only the person who first gives the information will be deemed to have accepted and be entitled to the reward.[16]

The offers in the above examples are part of a class of offers which require acceptance by performance of an act. Once the offeree has performed the act, he is not obligated to do anything more. All obligation now rests with the offeror to perform his half of the bargain: he is the only party under a contractual duty. These contracts are often called *unilateral contracts*.

Some unilateral offers require the offeree to perform a series of acts over a long period, as for example an offer to pay $2,000 to the offeree if he will build and deliver a trailer to the offeror by a certain date. The offeree may only accept by actually delivering by that date, and until then there is no contract. What would happen if the day before delivery the offeror revoked his offer? Strictly speaking, the offeror may always revoke before acceptance, and early judges seemed to accept this view. It was apparent that the offeree might suffer considerable hardship, but the answer was, "He knew the risk of revocation was present and accepted the risk." Since, however, parties often do not address themselves to such possibilities, the hardship still occurs. Today, courts try to avoid this unfairness where possible by treating offers "as calling for bilateral rather than unilateral action when the language can be fairly so construed."[17] The advantage of treating an agreement as bilateral is that both parties are bound from the moment the offeree indicates his intention to perform.

Where the courts find it impossible to construe an offer as bilateral, they may still try to help the offeree by implying a *subsidiary promise* that the offeror will not revoke once the offeree begins performance in good faith and continues to perform. Thus, as soon as the offeree starts performance, a subsidiary contract is formed in which the offeror undertakes not to revoke while the offeree proceeds reasonably with his performance. Accordingly, revocation will be a breach of the subsidiary contract. By this reasoning the court would probably hold that the offeror could not revoke in the preceding example of the trailer.[18] Of course, this subsidiary promise is merely implied, and its existence is rebutted by an express term to the contrary. Thus if *A* offers to pay *B* $100 for the delivery of a typewriter to his son provided it is delivered at exactly 10:00 p.m. at a birthday party and provided *A* does not change his mind, *A* can revoke the offer before delivery.

---

[16] Lancaster v. Walsh (1838) 150 E.R. 1324.

[17] Dawson v. Helicopter Exploration Co. Ltd. [1955] 5 D.L.R. 404, per Rand, J., at p. 410.

[18] See Brackenbury v. Hodgkin (1917) 102 Atlantic 106, 116 Maine 399 and Errington v. Errington [1952] 1 All E.R. 149.

The Offer of a Promise for a Promise

While unilateral contracts are important, they form only a small proportion of all contracts. Most offers require the giving of a promise rather than the performance of an act as the means of acceptance. For example, if *A* Motors offers to sell a truck to *B* Co. Ltd. for $8,500 and *B* Co. Ltd. replies accepting the offer, a contract has been made though neither *A* Motors nor *B* Co. Ltd. has as yet performed anything. In effect *A* Motors has promised to sell the truck for $8,500, and *B* Co. in return has promised to buy it for $8,500; the two parties have traded promises. If *A* Motors should refuse to perform its promise, then *B* Co. Ltd. would have a right to sue. Similarly if *B* Co. Ltd. should refuse to perform its promise, *A* Motors would have a right to sue. The contract consists of the two promises and both parties are bound to perform. This type of contract is called a *bilateral contract*.

The most commonplace of all business transactions, the credit sale, affords an illustration of the bilateral contract: at the time of the contract, and often for some time thereafter, the goods may be neither delivered by the seller nor paid for by the buyer. Again, a contract of employment comprises a promise by the employer to pay a wage or salary and a promise by the employee to work for a future period of time.

A characteristic of bilateral contracts is that each party will be both a *promisor* and a *promisee,* since each has an obligation to perform for the other and each has a right to performance by the other. For the purpose of describing proceedings in a court action, however, we find it convenient to think of the party who alleges that he has not received the performance to which he is entitled as the promisee. The promisor, in his turn, may have one or more defences which he offers to the court as a reason why his conduct should be excused and why he should not be ordered to pay the promisee damages for breach of contract.

PRECISION IN THE WORDING OF AN OFFER

A vague offer may prove to be no offer at all, and the intended acceptance of it cannot then form a contract. If the parties enter into a loosely-worded arrangement, not having been specific in the terms of the offer, it is possible that a court will find the agreement too ambiguous to be enforced. In *Taylor v. Portington,*[19] Portington wrote to Taylor offering to take a lease of Taylor's house for three years at a rent of £85 "if put into thorough repair" and the drawing-rooms "handsomely decorated according to the present style; paint is required both inside and outside although perhaps for some parts, one coat might be sufficient." Taylor replied accepting the offer. Later a dispute arose over the adequacy of the repairs, and Portington refused to proceed with his promise to rent the house. In the final hearing of the case, an appeal judge ruled that the expressions Portington had used in his letter "imported uncertainty into what might otherwise have amounted to an agreement sufficiently definite for the court to enforce".

---

[19] (1855) 44 E.R. 128.

Other examples of lack of certainty in the terms of a contract are: a promise to give a "fair" share in the profits of a business; a promise to "favourably consider" the renewal of the present contract "if satisfied with you";[20] a promise made by the buyer of a race horse to pay an additional amount on the price "if the horse is lucky".[21]

Uncertainty in the wording of the terms of a contract may be more apparent than real. It may be possible to adduce evidence of local customs or trade usage which gives a new precision to the terms. With the object of giving effect to contracts wherever possible, the courts have held (1) that anything is certain which is capable of being calculated or ascertained, and (2) that where a contract may be construed as either enforceable or unenforceable, they will favour the interpretation which will see the contract enforced. We shall examine these problems in greater detail in Chapter 11, which discusses the interpretation of contracts.

THE EFFECT OF AN INCOMPLETE AGREEMENT

In *Friesen v. Braun*,[22] there was a lease of land for a term of one year from July 1, 1947. The lease included an option clause entitling the tenants to purchase the property for the sum of $1,200 less the amount of rent received by the landlady up to the time the option was exercised. The option clause read in part, "The purchase money shall be paid as follows: On terms to be discussed and decided upon by the parties at date of acceptance." The tenants served a notice of acceptance of the option within the time specified and tendered the full sum in cash. The landlady refused the tender of payment, and the tenants brought an action against her for breach of the option clause. The court held that the option clause was invalid, and the tenants' case failed. One of the judges observed that ". . . an agreement which leaves one of the essential terms to be determined by the parties mutually at a future time is unenforceable." The same principle is expressed in the words, "The law does not recognize a contract to enter into a contract."[23]

We should, however, distinguish between a contract for the sale of goods and a contract for the sale of land in this respect. The Sale of Goods Act provides that the price in a contract of sale of goods "may be left to be fixed in manner thereby agreed, or may be determined by the course of dealing between the parties" and that, "Where the price is not determined in accordance with the foregoing provisions the buyer must pay a reasonable price."[24]

---

[20] Montreal Gas Co. v. Vasey [1900] A.C. 595.

[21] Cuthing v. Lynn (1831) 109 E.R. 1130.

[22] [1950] 2 D.L.R. 250.

[23] Von Hatzfeldt-Wildenburg v. Alexander [1912] 1 Ch. 284, per Parker, J., at 289. See also National Bowling and Billiards Ltd. v. Double Diamond Bowling Supply Ltd. and Automatic Pinsetters Ltd. (1961) 27 D.L.R. (2d) 342: Re Pigeon et al. and Titley, Pigeon, Lavoie Ltd. (1973) 30 D.L.R. (3d) 132. For a fuller discussion see Cheshire, Fifoot and Furmston, *The Law of Contract* (8th ed.), pp. 32-36.

[24] See, for example: R.S.B.C. 1960, c. 344, s. 14; R.S.O. 1970, c. 421, s. 9; R.S.N.S. 1967, c. 274, s. 10.

QUESTIONS FOR REVIEW

1. What is the relationship between a promise and a contract?

2. What must happen to an offer before a contract is formed?

3. How may an offer be made by conduct other than spoken or written word?

4. "We cannot be obligated by people who do work for us without our knowledge." Why?

5. What is the legal effect of a counter-offer?

6. What does it mean to "purchase an option"?

7. When does the selection of a successful bidder following an invitation for tenders create a contract?

8. Can the time of acceptance date from the time a letter of acceptance is mailed when the offer was not itself made though the mails?

9. When exactly is a letter withdrawing a previous offer effective?

10. What principles of law does the *Carlill* case illustrate?

11. Did the *Carlill* case concern a unilateral or a bilateral contract? Why? Under which type does a purchase on credit usually fall?

12. What is the effect of an agreement in which the parties state that certain terms will be discussed and agreed upon at a later date?

13. To what extent does the law protect the interest of the public in standard form contracts?

14. What is the difference between the revocation and the rejection of an offer? Between the revocation and the lapse of an offer?

15. What does it mean to say that the conduct of an offeree will constitute his acceptance only if the conduct refers unequivocally to the offer? When might his conduct be "equivocal"?

16. Give an example of circumstances in which the rule, "An offer must be communicated before it can be accepted," would operate.

17. Is it also true that an acceptance must be communicated before a contract can be formed?

18. May a person withdraw a bid he makes at an auction sale before the fall of the hammer?

19. X offers to subscribe for 100 shares in Y Co. Ltd., which is issuing further stock. He makes his offer in June. He does not receive a letter of allotment (acceptance) from Y Co. Ltd. until the following November. Must he pay for the shares? (*Ramsgate Victoria Hotel Co. v. Montefiore* (1866) L.R. 1 Ex. 109.)

20. An amendment to existing criminal legislation makes it an offence "to manufacture, sell, or offer for sale" flick knives. The Sundries Shop exhibits a flick knife in its shop window. Its proprietor is prosecuted for violation of the statute. Should he be held guilty?

CASES FOR DISCUSSION

CASE 1

A by-law of the City of Winnipeg prohibits the sale of horsemeat within the city limits for human consumption. The penalty for violation is a fine of $50 and costs or ten days in jail.

Lalonde operated a butcher shop, La Boucherie Franco-Canadienne, in St. Boniface, outside the Winnipeg city limits. Onasis, who owned a restaurant in Winnipeg, telephoned Lalonde and asked whether he could deliver some horse-meat ("la viande chevaline") to his restaurant. Lalonde agreed to supply the meat. After the meat was delivered to the restaurant Lalonde sent Onasis an invoice for $17.65. Subsequently a patron of the restaurant who had ordered filet mignon complained that he had instead been served *filly* mignon.

The City of Winnipeg charged Lalonde with a violation of the by-law. What rule affecting the formation of contracts is relevant? What would be the result?

CASE 2

Daly, a United States citizen, entered into negotiations with Stevens of Vancouver with a view to arranging an investigation and staking of mineral claims at the head of the Leduc River in British Columbia. Daly had discovered evidence of deposits there some twenty years earlier.

On January 13, Daly wrote, "A large mining company in Boise is showing an interest. To protect my interest it will be necessary for me to arrive at some definite arrangement soon." Stevens replied on January 17, "Perhaps we can make some arrangement this summer to finance you in staking claims for which I would give you an interest. I would suggest that I should pay for your time and expenses and carry you for a 10 per cent interest in the claims." Daly replied on January 22, "Your proposition appeals to me as being a fair one."

Thereafter, Daly was called to active duty in the United States Naval Reserve Engineering Corps and was sent to the Marshall Islands. Correspondence continued with some difficulty, but on February 28 Daly wrote, "As I informed you in a previous letter, your offer of a 10 per cent interest for relocating and finding these properties is acceptable to me, provided there is a definite agreement to this effect in the near future."

On March 5, Stevens wrote, "I hereby agree that if you will take me in to the showings, and I think they warrant staking, I will stake the claims and give you a 10 per cent interest. The claims would be recorded in my name and I will have full discretion in dealing with them — you are to get 10 per cent of the vendor interest. I can arrange to get a pilot here." Daly replied on April 12, "If you will inform me when you can obtain a pilot, I will immediately take steps for a temporary release in order to be on hand."

On June 6, Stevens wrote, "I was talking to a prospector who said he had been over your showings at the head of the Leduc River, and in his opinion it would be practically impossible to operate there, as the showings were behind ice fields which, along with the extreme snowfalls, make it very doubtful if an economic operation could be carried on. I now have so much work lined up that I doubt if I would have time to visit your showings and do not think I would be warranted in making the effort to get in there due to the unfavourable conditions. I must advise you, therefore, not to depend on making this trip, and suggest if you are still determined to go in, to make some other arrangements.''

Daly did not reply. On his return from the Marshall Islands the following year, he did, however, follow up his interest in the property. He then discovered that in July, Stevens had sent prospectors into the area and, as a result of their investigations, had staked claims in his own name which he had later sold to a mining development company. Daly brought an action against Stevens claiming damages for breach of contract. Should Daly succeed in his action? Explain.

CASE 3

Lambert purchased a car last year and placed his insurance with the Reliable Insurance Company, for whom Drake is the local agent. On July 29 last, Drake wrote as follows to Lambert, who was at his summer cottage: "As you know, your automobile insurance policy with us expires on August 15. We will renew this policy on the same terms unless notified to the contrary by you. You may sign the application form and pay after you return to the city."

On his way back from his holidays on August 16 Lambert struck and injured a pedestrian with his car. The pedestrian has claimed $50,000 damages from Lambert, and on referring the matter to the Reliable Insurance Company, Lambert was informed that his policy of insurance had expired without renewal on August 15.

Describe Lambert's legal position.

CASE 4

Superior Used Cars Ltd. has as the most prominent display on its lot an immaculate, highly-polished model which rotates slowly on a raised circular platform under powerful floodlights. The price is on the windshield, $2,700. Walking home one evening, Williams noticed the display and stopped and asked a salesman for a demonstration. The salesman then proceeded to try to interest him in several other models which, he urged, were "really better" than the one displayed. When Williams persisted in wanting to see the one displayed, the salesman replied that it was not actually for sale, but was being used as an advertising gambit. Has Williams any claim in law?

CASE 5

Smith saw an automobile which he liked in a dealer's premises. At Smith's request the dealer promised to put the car aside and not to sell it until the next day when Smith was to return and tell the dealer whether he would buy the car. While on his way to the dealer's premises on the following day, Smith met his friend

Williams. Williams told Smith that he had bought the automobile in question late the previous evening. Smith went to the dealer's premises and told him that he had come to take the car away. The dealer told Smith that the car had been sold to Williams. Is the dealer liable to Smith for breach of contract? (See *Dickinson v. Dodds* (1876) 2 Ch. D. 463.)

CASE 6

Henwood was desirous of purchasing from Foley certain property in the village of Cataraqui some three miles west of Kingston. Henwood is a resident of Kingston and Foley a resident of Cataraqui.

In May, Henwood went to Cataraqui to see Foley and make him an offer of $14,750 for the property. This offer was refused by Foley. On July 7 Henwood went again to see Foley, and this time Foley offered to sell the property for $15,500 and said he would hold the offer open for fourteen days at that price.

Early on the morning of July 8, another person called to see Foley and offered him $16,000 for the same piece of property. Foley accepted, subject to a condition for avoiding the contract if he found he could not withdraw from his contract with Henwood.

Between 12 and 1 o'clock on July 8, Foley posted a letter to Henwood, stating, "Please take notice that my offer to you of July 7 is withdrawn."

This letter was delivered at Henwood's Kingston address the following morning about 10:30, but as he was at work, it did not reach his hands until noon. On the same morning Henwood's solicitor, by his direction, wrote to Foley as follows: "I am instructed by Mr. Henwood to write to you and accept your offer of July 7, to sell at the price of $15,500. Kindly have the contract prepared and forwarded to me." This letter was posted at 10:00 a.m. that morning (July 9). When Foley received it on July 10, he replied stating that the offer had been withdrawn.

Henwood brought an action for breach of contract against Foley. State with reasons what you think the court's decision would be.

CASE 7

The Tomkins Well Co. Ltd. was engaged by Norman Food Products Ltd. to drill a well for it on some property adjoining the sea; Norman Food Products Ltd. required a freshwater well for a factory which it expected to have in operation there. In the negotiations Tomkins Well Co. Ltd. quoted a price of $8 per foot plus the cost of casing, but refused to guarantee that the well drilled would produce fresh water. A representative of the well-drilling company did, however, express the view that they would probably be able to exclude any sea water by proper casing. The well was subsequently drilled at a cost of $1,500 but produced salty water which could not be shut out. The project was abandoned; but some time afterwards the Tomkins Well Co. Ltd. returned its equipment to the property without the knowledge of Norman Food Products Ltd. and drilled two more holes in an attempt to obtain a freshwater well; neither drilling was successful. Then the Tomkins Well Co. Ltd. rendered a bill for $4,200 to Norman Food Products Ltd., its total price for all the work done to date. Norman Food Products Ltd. refused to pay the $4,200 but offered to settle for $1,800; when this offer was refused by Tomkins Well Co. Ltd., the food company paid the sum into court, awaiting a judgment on the action brought by Tomkins Well Co. Ltd. for the full $4,200.

In your opinion, what should be the result of this action? Would your opinion have been different if Tomkins Well Co. Ltd. had obtained a good fresh-water well on drilling the third hole? (See *Trask Well Co. Ltd. v. Northern Food Products, Inc.* (1953) 31 M.P.R. 325.)

CASE 8

Clark in Saskatchewan opened correspondence on September 9, 1947, with Barrick in Ontario for the purchase from Barrick of Saskatchewan farm land. There followed an exchange of letters on the subject. The land was under lease so that a purchaser could not get possession until March 1, 1948, and in any case farming operations could not be carried on until spring.

Finally, by letter of October 30, 1947, Clark offered $14,500 cash for the property. Barrick replied as follows:

Toronto, Ont.,
Nov. 15, 1947.

Mr. F. J. Clark,
Luseland, Sask.

Dear Sir:

In reply to your recent letter, in which you offer $14,500 cash for the [land] . . . I have delayed answering in order to consult with those interested in the Estate and thereby be in a position to give something concrete.

We are prepared to sell this land for $15,000 cash. If this price is satisfactory to you, the deal could be closed immediately by preparing an agreement for sale to be given you on receipt of the initial payment of $2,000 — transfer of clear title to be given you on January 1st, 1948 on receipt of balance of purchase price of $13,000. The present tenant Kostrosky's lease expires March 1st, 1948.

Trusting to hear from you as soon as possible.

Yours truly,
R. N. Barrick

Clark was away when Barrick's letter arrived, but Clark's wife wrote on November 20 telling of his absence on a hunting trip and asking that the deal be kept open as she expected him home in ten days.

A new party, Hohman, became interested in the property, and on December 3 Barrick and Hohman contracted for its sale at $15,000. Clark returned home on December 10 and that evening mailed a letter to Barrick in which he accepted Barrick's offer. The following day Clark heard of Hohman's purchase and on that date wired Barrick as follows:

RETURNED HERE YESTERDAY MORNING FROM BIG GAME HUNTING TRIP AIR-
MAILED LETTER TO YOU LAST NIGHT ENCLOSING TWO THOUSAND DOLLARS
THIS MORNING TOWN GOSSIP CLAIMS WILLIAM HOHMAN HAS BOUGHT THE
THREE QUARTERS PRESUME YOU RECEIVED MRS CLARK'S LETTER NOVEMBER
TWENTIETH TRUST THAT REPORT IS NOT CORRECT WOULD APPRECIATE REPLY
BY WIRE

Barrick replied that he had received an offer of $15,000 from Hohman
which he had accepted on December 3, having had no reply from Clark, and
noted that if Hohman failed to pay the $15,000 he would then be at liberty to sell
to someone else. He concluded, "I am very sorry this hitch has occurred, and I
shall return your $2,000 immediately upon receipt of same."

Clark then sued Barrick for breach of contract.

Should Clark succeed? (See *Barrick v. Clark* [1950] 4 D.L.R. 529.)

CASE 9

Evans wrote to Livingstone offering to sell him a farm for $68,000 on certain
terms of credit. Upon receipt of this offer Livingstone immediately wired back:
"SEND LOWEST CASH PRICE. WILL GIVE $45,000 CASH." Evans replied by telegram,
"CANNOT REDUCE PRICE." Immediately on receipt of this telegram Livingstone
wired his acceptance of $68,000. Evans refused to sell the land to Livingstone,
claiming that Livingstone had rejected his offer and so terminated it. Has Livingstone any claim against Evans? (See *Livingstone v. Evans et al.* [1925] 4 D.L.R.
769.)

CASE 10

Moore, a resident of Oshawa, Ontario, read the following notice in the *Oshawa
Herald:* "Those wishing to drive new automobiles to west coast contact P. T.
Jones, 54 Totem Blvd., Vancouver. Expenses en route will be paid for." Moore
wrote for information and received the following reply: "If you will deliver a
super-six Pontiac Glidemaster four-door sedan to me by September 1, I will pay
you $6,000 for it." When Moore read the letter he bought the car specified and
set out for Vancouver. On arriving in New Westminster on August 15, he
decided to telephone Jones to get the directions to 54 Totem Blvd. When Jones
answered, he said: "Oh, it's you, Moore. I waited and waited to hear from you,
and eventually bought a Cadillac I found on sale. I'm sure you can find someone
else here to take the Pontiac off your hands."

If Moore were to sue Jones for breach of contract, would he succeed?

CASE 11

Early in August, 1974, the Great Prairie Railway had constructed its line to the
southerly boundary of K. C. Jones' land, near the town of Carmen, Manitoba.

The railway company had not intended to enter upon Jones' land at all, but to terminate the railway just south of it. It decided ultimately, however, to build across Jones' land up to the right of way of the C.P.R.

On August 9 the company opened negotiations with Jones through its right-of-way agent for the purpose of obtaining possession of the necessary land for the construction of its railway across his farm. Jones refused to give possession until the terms of sale of the right of way were settled and determined. At length Jones handed to the agent a written statement of the terms upon which he would sell. These terms were that, first, the company was to be responsible for damage for trespassing or straying cattle in consequence of its interfering with the fences; second, the company was to put up proper railway fences in due course; third, the price for the land taken was to be $1,000 an acre; fourth, the company was to put in a level crossing when required to do so by Jones at the point he should indicate; fifth, the company was to pay damages for the crop then growing on the land, and to pay Jones' solicitors' costs in connection with the business; and finally, the whole matter was to be completed within two months of the time when possession was given and interest at ten per cent was to be paid after two months from the completion day.

When Jones handed these terms to the right-of-way agent for Great Prairie Railway, he notified the agent that if the railway took possession of the land, he would understand from that act that the company accepted and agreed to his terms. A few days after this and without further communication with Jones, the company took possession and proceeded to and did complete the construction of the railway across Jones' land. About two weeks afterwards Jones was advised by letter from the right-of-way agent that the company did not propose to abide by the terms stated but proposed to proceed by expropriation. Jones, claiming that the railway company had accepted his offer, sued the railway for damages for breach of a contract containing the terms of his offer.

During the course of the trial the court was referred to s. 156 of the Railway Act, R.S.C. 1970, c. R-2, which reads as follows:

EXPROPRIATION PROCEEDINGS
Notice

Notice of expropriation to be served

156. Preliminary to proceeding to arbitration to fix compensation or damages, the company shall serve upon the opposite party a notice containing

(a) a description of the lands to be taken, or of the power intended to be exercised with regard to any lands therein described;

(b) a declaration of readiness to pay a certain sum or rent, as the case may be, as compensation for such lands or for such damages; and

(c) a notification that if within ten days after the service of this notice, or, where the notice is served by publication, within one month after

> the first publication thereof, the party to whom
> the notice is addressed does not give notice to the
> company that he accepts the sum offered by the
> company, either he or the company may apply to
> have the compensation fixed by arbitration as
> provided in this Act.

What would be the railway company's defence? Should Jones succeed? Do the facts of a case like this raise any public policy issue? (For reference, see *Carr v. Canadian Northern Railway Co.* (1907) 6 W.L.R. 720.)

CHAPTER 6

Formation of a Contract: Consideration; Intention to Create Legal Relations

THE MEANING OF CONSIDERATION

At the root of our idea of a contract is the concept of a bargain, that one party must pay a price, that is make some contribution, for the promise he obtains from the other party. In a unilateral contract the price paid for the promise of the offeror is the act done by the acceptor. In a bilateral contract, the price paid by each of the parties for the promise of the other is his own promise. This price is called *consideration*. In short, consideration is "the price for which the promise [or the act] of the other is bought".[1]

When a party bargains for consideration, it usually brings him a benefit, such as a promise to pay him money or to deliver goods or render services to him; but it need not always confer a benefit directly upon him. So long as he bargains for an altered course of action or a promise of an altered course of action by the other party, he will have received consideration.

Illustration:

Adams, a creditor of Brown, threatened to sue Brown for the amount of an overdue account. Cox, a friend of Brown, then promised to pay Adams the amount due if Adams would refrain from suing, and Adams agreed.

If Cox failed to pay Adams as agreed and Adams sued him for breach of contract, Adams would succeed. To establish consideration Adams need only show that he adopted a different course of action, that is, that he for-

---

[1] Pollock, *Principles of Contract* (13th ed.), p. 133.

bore suing Brown, in return for Cox's promise. In this sense the "price" which Adams agrees to pay may confer no direct benefit on the other contracting party, Cox.

GRATUITOUS PROMISES

Consideration is essential to make a contract binding in law. A person may, however, make a promise to another when the element of a bargain is completely absent. A promise made in the absence of a bargain is called a *gratuitous promise* and, although accepted by the person to whom it is made, does not constitute a contract and is not enforceable in law. A promise to make a gift and a promise to perform services without remuneration are common examples of gratuitous promises. Such "contracts" are void for lack of consideration, which is another way of saying that they never amounted to a contract.

The law does not hinder the performance of a gratuitous promise. It simply asserts that if the promise is not performed, the promisee has no remedy at law to compensate him for his disappointed expectations. As a matter of honour most people do, of course, perform their gratuitous promises.

Then what of a charitable donation? Charities seldom find it in their interest to sue those who have made subscription pledges. Their experience shows that they may rely upon their subscribers' sense of honour to a large extent; in their budgeting they are wise to discount the balance. They believe that people would become reluctant to give pledges if there were a probability of legal action to enforce them. Occasionally, however, subscribers have died before honouring large pledges, and charities have sued their estates.[2]

In looking for consideration in this type of subscription pledge, we have to ask, "What price did the charity pay for the subscriber's promise?" Our answer must be, "None," if the charitable organization did not change its future course of action and incur additional expense in return for the promise. A sense of disillusionment and loss of faith in human nature on the part of its officers is not enough to constitute consideration, pitiful though it may be. In some circumstances we might find consideration if the charity undertook a specific project, such as the construction of a building, in response to the subscriber's promise. The court must, however, be able to find an implied request from the subscriber that the charity undertake the project as the "price" of his subscription. When donations are for general funds, the charitable organization can only make the pledges it receives legally binding if it adopts the use of a seal on its pledge cards. We shall discuss the use of a seal in a later section of this chapter.

As long as the promise of a gift remains unperformed, the promisee is without recourse. But suppose the promise is performed — a gift is actually made: may the donor later change his mind and demand it back on grounds of lack of consideration? Generally speaking, no. Once he has voluntarily made the

---

[2] See, for example: Governors of Dalhousie College v. Boutilier [1934] 3 D.L.R. 593.

gift, it is no longer his property and he has no control over it. In exceptional circumstances the donor may show that he made the gift as a result of threats or undue influence, and the court may then restore it to him or award damages to the value of the gift. We shall consider the consequences of undue influence in Chapter 10.

Though a promisor is not bound by his gratuitous promise, once he undertakes the performance of it he is under a duty to carry it out without negligence. If, through his negligence, he injures the promisee or the promisee's property, he will be liable to compensate the promisee for the loss. A defence that the donor received no consideration for his promise will be of no avail. The standard of care is imposed upon him not by the promise but by the rules of the law of torts; indeed, he may be liable for any damages caused by his negligence whether the damage is done to the promisee or a stranger. Thus, if a doctor offers to give free aid to an injured person and negligently aggravates the man's injuries, he will be liable for damages. Similarly, a public accountant who gratuitously undertakes an audit for a charitable organization is liable for damages caused to the organization through his negligence. He is under no obligation to do the audit, but once he commences the work he must proceed with care.

ADEQUACY OF CONSIDERATION

In developing the concept of consideration, the courts have insisted that the consideration must always have some value in the eyes of the law; but they have refused to concern themselves with whether the promisor has made a good bargain. They have taken the view that it is not for them to make a bargain for the parties, and if a party requests a totally inadequate consideration for his promise, that is up to him. To assess the adequacy of consideration requires a personal value judgment; and the courts would have to relinquish their role of impartial arbiter if they were to concern themselves with adequacy. They might otherwise find themselves penalizing the business acumen of one of the parties and comforting the stupidity of the other. Much has been made of the judge's observation that a creditor can agree to accept a "canary or a tomtit" in settlement of his account if he chooses.[3] The adequacy of the consideration is not for the courts to determine.

This is not to say that a court will never be interested in the nature of the consideration. If, for example, the consideration is grossly inadequate for the promise and if other evidence points to fraud, duress, or undue influence exerted on the promisor, the court may hold that the promise is voidable at his option.[4]

An important question of adequacy of consideration arises whenever parties to a dispute agree upon a settlement out of court. Suppose that subsequent to making a settlement one party should discover that he was mistaken about either

---

[3] Jessel, M.R., in Couldery v. Bartrum (1881) 19 Ch. D., at 399.
[4] See Chapter 10.

the law or the facts: he promised to pay a sum of money to the other party when he really was not bound to pay anything. The threat of the other party to sue was without merit since he would have lost in court. Is his promise not to sue, therefore, worthless and hence not really consideration for the promise to pay something in settlement?

Illustration:

> In an automobile collision between Jones and Brown, Brown's car suffers $800 damage. The parties engage in an extended argument by mail about which of them is responsible for the accident. Finally after many months Brown threatens to sue Jones unless Jones will agree to pay 75% of Brown's damages, that is, $600. Jones promises to pay this sum in full settlement of all Brown's claims. Subsequently Jones realizes that at the time he made his promise to pay Brown, more than twelve months had passed since the accident had occurred. The provincial Highway Traffic Act states: "No action shall be brought against a person for the recovery of damages occasioned by a motor vehicle after the expiration of twelve months from the time when the damages were sustained."
>
> Jones now refuses to perform his promise to pay Brown $600. He states that since Brown could not have successfully sued him for damages, Brown's promise under the settlement not to sue him is no consideration for Jones's promise to pay $600. It is well settled, however, that Brown's promise not to sue Jones is good consideration, and he will succeed in an action against Jones.

Provided the promisee has an honest belief in his right to sue, giving it up is good consideration for the promisor's promise.[5] If this were not the rule, no one could ever be sure that a settlement was binding; subsequent information might upset a settlement made in good faith. Indeed, it could even be argued that until a dispute was actually decided by the courts, neither side could be sure that he had given anything of value as consideration for the promise of the other. Aside from being an intolerable situation for the parties, such a state of affairs would conflict with basic principles of the law: to discourage unnecessary lawsuits and to promote certainty in the law.

MOTIVE CONTRASTED WITH CONSIDERATION: PAST CONSIDERATION

Consideration is the *price* for the promisor's promise, however inadequate it may be in a financial sense. His reason for making such a promise, his *motive,* is irrelevant. Indeed, motive does not affect the question of consideration either way: it cannot change a gratuitous promise into a contractual obligation, nor can it trans-

---

[5] Haigh v. Brooks (1839) 113 E.R. 119; Famous Foods Ltd. v. Liddle [1941] 3 D.L.R. 525; Fairgrief v. Ellis [1935] 2 D.L.R. 806.

form a binding promise into a merely voluntary, moral obligation. A promisor's motive, whether it be gratitude, a sense of honour, duty, affection or charity, or even part of an unworthy scheme, does not affect the question of whether his promise is binding in law.

From an ethical point of view, we may say that it is wrong to break *any* promise seriously made and that every promisor has a moral duty to perform his promise. However, the doctrine of consideration would virtually cease to exist if every promise were legally enforceable simply because the promisor had a moral duty to do as he said he would. Although the doctrine of consideration has been attacked as causing unfair decisions in some instances (and undoubtedly it does, as we shall see), it has the virtue of being an external and objective test of whether a promise should be binding. In other legal systems, where moral obligation — called *moral cause* — may be substituted for the idea of a bargain, other difficulties arise in trying to probe into a promisor's motive in order to establish moral cause.

This point is illustrated in *Eastwood v. Kenyon.*[6] Eastwood had been guardian of Mrs. Kenyon while she was a child and had borrowed money, giving his promissory note, in order to finance her education and to maintain the estate of which she was sole heiress. On coming of age she promised that she would reimburse him, and after her marriage, her husband Kenyon promised Eastwood that he would pay his promissory note for him. This Kenyon failed to do. In bringing his action, Eastwood insisted upon Kenyon's moral duty to honour his promise, but his action failed because of lack of consideration. What price had Eastwood paid for Kenyon's promise? The court could find none. The explanation for Kenyon's promise was not found in a bargain made with Eastwood but in motive, a sense of gratitude, a feeling of moral duty that was strong enough to lead to a declaration of noble intent though not strong enough to be binding at law when the intention failed to materialize in performance.

If a promise is made to reward a person who has previously done an act gratuitously or given something of value to the promisor, the promise is not binding. The promise is, in its turn, gratuitous, just as the benefit which the promisee had earlier conferred upon the promisor; and as we have seen, gratuitous promises are not binding. Another approach is to say that the motive of the promisor was to return the kindness of the promisee, and, of course, motive and consideration are not the same thing. The benefit previously conferred upon the promisor is often called *past consideration*. But since there is no element of bargain, that is, of the benefit being performed *in return for* the promise, the expression is really a contradiction of terms, for "past consideration" is no consideration.

Illustration:

Adams saved Brown from drowning. Afterwards Brown promised to pay Adams $100 out of gratitude.

Brown may change his mind at any time before he actually pays

---

[6] (1840) 113 E.R. 482.

Adams the money, and Adams will be helpless to enforce the promise. In saving Brown's life, Adams did not act in response to an offer to pay him for doing so. Brown's promise was made after the event and was therefore made for "past consideration". In the circumstances Adams did not pay any price for Brown's promise.

RELATION BETWEEN EXISTING LEGAL DUTY AND CONSIDERATION

Where *A* is bound by an existing contractual duty to *B,* a later promise by *B* to pay *A* something extra to perform the same obligation is not binding. The performance by *A* of his obligation is not good consideration for the later promise because he was already bound to perform — his failure to do so would have been a breach of contract. For example, a promise to members of a crew to increase their pay if they do not desert their ship is unenforceable.[7] There is an existing contract of employment between the crew and the employer which binds the crew to perform their duties faithfully. On the other hand, a term of such contracts is that the ship is seaworthy. If it proves unseaworthy, the crew are released from their obligation, and then, of course, there will be consideration for the promise to pay an extra sum if the crew stay with the ship.[8]

The problem often arises in the following circumstance: *A* may threaten to default on his obligation and leave *B* to his remedy for the breach, in the courts. If *B* is anxious to have *A* carry out his part of the bargain, he may agree to pay *A* more money. A typical example occurs when a building contractor discovers he has agreed to erect a building for too low a price, or runs into unexpected difficulties. The owner may be depending upon completion at a certain date, and if the contractor abandons the job, the owner may lose valuable time, perhaps even putting himself in breach of other contracts, as where he has leased out large parts of the building. Some U.S. courts have taken the view that the contractor is at liberty to abandon the job if he chooses, and pay damages. In this view there is good consideration for a fresh promise from him to proceed, and the owner is bound to pay the additional sum promised. Most courts, including all the English and Canadian courts, take the view that this conduct smacks of extortion by the party threatening to abandon the contract. Accordingly, they hold that there is no consideration for the promise to pay an extra sum.

A different problem arises when an agreement to perform an existing contractual duty is made with a stranger to that contract, as where *A* is already bound to perform under a contract with *B,* and *C* promises to pay *A* a sum of money if he will perform his existing obligation to *B.* Suppose *A* has promised to construct an office building for *B.* Is there consideration for a promise made by *C,* a prospective tenant, to pay *A* a sum of money if he completes the building on

---

[7] Stilk v. Myrick (1809) 170 E.R. 1168.
[8] Turner v. Owen (1862) 176 E.R. 79.

time?[9] *A* is already bound to *B* to perform his contract to construct the building on time: what further price does he give for *C*'s promise to pay him if he does carry it out? This problem has seldom arisen, but the courts seem to agree that *A* can enforce *C*'s promise, and also that if *A* failed to perform, he would be liable to actions by both *B* and *C*.[10] We must therefore distinguish between the situation where the later promise is made by one of the parties to the original contract, and where it is made by a stranger to the original contract.

The problem is slightly different when *A*'s duty to perform is a public duty cast upon him by law, as for example where *A* is a policeman. If *B* promises to pay *A* for his services as a policeman, the court is confronted with two problems — the questions of public policy and of consideration. If the policeman has been asked to do something which he is already bound to do or something which will interfere with his regular duties, the court will probably be concerned that the promise to pay him tends to corrupt public servants and will find the promise unenforceable. On the other hand, if the court finds that he has been requested to do something beyond his duties and not in conflict with them, it will probably find consideration and hold the promise to pay for the services binding. Thus, in *Glasbrook Brothers v. Glamorgan County Council*[11] a company agreed to pay for a special police guard during a strike and was held to be bound by its promise.

GRATUITOUS REDUCTION OF A DEBT

The necessity for consideration to make a promise binding at law can lead to unexpected results, especially in business transactions. In the leading English case of *Foakes v. Beer*[12] a debtor owed a large sum of money already overdue. His creditor agreed to take payment by a series of instalments of principal and to forgo her right to interest if the debtor paid these instalments promptly and regularly. The debtor paid the full principal sum by instalments as agreed, but the creditor then sued for the interest. She succeeded, on the grounds that her promise to accept less than the total sum to which she was entitled amounted to a promise to give away her right to interest, and as the promise was gratuitous, it did not bind her.

The practical application of this rule is unsatisfactory. There are a number of reasons why a creditor (whom we shall call *C*) may find it more to his benefit to settle for some reduction in the debt owing to him than to press his claim for payment in full. For one thing, such a compromise may avoid placing the debtor in bankruptcy; it is quite possible that by the time all creditors' claims have been recognized, *C* might realize less out of bankruptcy than if he had agreed directly to a reduction of his claim. Secondly, the proposed reduction may make it possible for the debtor to prevail upon his friends to lend him enough to take advan-

---

[9] Shadwell v. Shadwell (1860) 142 E.R. 62.
[10] Scotson v. Pegg (1861) 158 E.R. 121.
[11] [1925] A.C. 270.
[12] (1884) 9 App. Cas. 605.

tage of it, and make a fresh start. Thirdly, the debtor may simply not have the assets to enable him to pay in full, so that a court judgment against him could not in any event realize more than the reduced amount. Finally, C may well need at least part of the sum owed him urgently for other commitments: he may be happier to take the lesser amount at once, even though he might collect the full account with all the delays inherent in a legal action.

The rule in *Foakes v. Beer* may be avoided in several ways. In the first place, payment before the due date is sufficient consideration to make a reduction in the debt binding on the creditor if he so agrees. Thus if the debtor pays $600 one day in advance in settlement of a $1,000 debt due the next day, the agreement to accept $600 will be binding. As we have seen, the court will not inquire into the adequacy of the consideration; if the creditor chooses to reduce the debt by $400 in order to receive it one day in advance, he may bind himself to do so.

Secondly, the rule in *Foakes v. Beer* applies only to payments of money. It does not apply to the transfer of goods or to the rendering of services. Since a man may make a contract for a totally inadequate consideration if he so desires, he may agree to pay $1,000 for a trinket, a cheap watch, or a package of cigarettes. Similarly, he may agree to cancel a $1,000 debt upon receipt of any one of these objects. In effect, he is trading the debt for the object, and such an agreement is perfectly valid, provided he enters upon it voluntarily. The result of this reasoning creates a paradox: if a man agrees to accept $900 in full settlement of a $1,000 debt, he may later sue for the balance successfully; if a man accepts $500 and a string of beads worth ten cents in full settlement of a $1,000 debt, he will fail if he sues for the balance.

Thirdly, the rule in *Foakes v. Beer* applies only to agreements between the creditor and the debtor. A third party, who is not bound to pay anything to the creditor, may offer to pay the creditor a lesser sum if he will cancel the debt. A creditor who accepts such an offer is bound by his promise and cannot sue the debtor afterwards.[13] The result is the same as if the third person had purchased the debt from the creditor.

Illustration:

A Co. Ltd. has an account receivable from B for $1,000, and sells it to X for $800. A Co. Ltd. no longer has any rights against B.

The result would have been different, however, if X had lent $800 to B and B had then paid the $800 to A Co. Ltd. in full settlement of its account of $1,000. A Co. Ltd. would not be bound by this settlement and could later sue B for $200 (apart from the statutory exceptions discussed below).

It would not matter whether X was purchasing the account receivable as a business proposition or whether he wished merely to help the debtor; X's motive is irrelevant. If he deals directly with the creditor, the debt for

---

[13] Hirachand Punamchand v. Temple [1911] 2 K.B. 330.

$1,000 can be settled for $800. If he were instead to hand the $800 over to *B*, the creditor might still sue for the balance, unless the statute discussed below applies.

Finally, as we shall see shortly, the rule in *Foakes v. Beer* is avoided if the creditor agrees in writing and under seal to reduce the debt.

The rule in *Foakes v. Beer* has been modified in British Columbia, Alberta, Saskatchewan, Manitoba, and Ontario by statute.[14] Under any of these acts, if a creditor agrees to accept part performance (that is, a lesser sum of money) in settlement of his debt, once he has accepted this part performance, he is bound. On the other hand, he may be able to go back on his promise to accept a lesser sum of money before the sum is actually paid; the cases interpreting this situation are unclear on the point.

INJURIOUS RELIANCE (EQUITABLE ESTOPPEL)

Not infrequently, one person makes a promise to another fully intending to keep it. The promise is clearly gratuitous; yet the promisee, believing the promisor to be a trustworthy person, relies on that promise and incurs expenses he would otherwise not have made. What happens if the promisor subsequently defaults? According to the strict rules of common law, the answer is "nothing at all". The gratuitous promise remains gratuitous, the promise cannot be enforced, and the promisee suffers the burden of his expenses.

Illustration:

A, who has just ordered a new 90-hp. outboard motor, tells his friend *B* that he will give him his old 35-hp. motor as soon as the new one arrives. Before *B* can make use of *A*'s old engine, he will have to make expensive modifications to his small boat. Instead, at *A*'s suggestion he buys a new boat for $800. Subsequently, *A*'s brother reminds him that he had promised the old motor to him, and rather than promote a family quarrel, *A* tells *B* he cannot carry out his promise. *B* has no right in contract law to enforce *A*'s promise.

Some parts of the United States have adopted a principle whereby *A* would be bound to carry out his promise.[15] Courts in these jurisdictions argue that since *A* by his conduct *induced B* to rely on his promise and *B* did rely upon it, to his injury, *A* must now honour his promise to prevent an injustice. This principle, known as *injurious reliance,* is based on rules similar to the tort rules concerning

---

[14] The Laws Declaratory Act, R.S.B.C. 1960, c. 213, s. 2(33); The Judicature Act, R.S.A. 1970, c. 193, s. 34(8); The Queen's Bench Act, R.S.S. 1965, c. 73, s. 45(7); The Mercantile Law Amendment Act, R.S.M. 1970, c. M-120, s. 6; and The Mercantile Law Amendment Act, R.S.O. 1970, c. 272, s. 16. For cases interpreting this section see Rommerill v. Gardener (1962) 35 D.L.R. (2d) 717 and others referred to therein.

[15] Ricketts v. Scothorn (1898) 77 N.W. 365.

foreseeability of harm in negligence actions. The classic expression of the doctrine is as follows:

> A promise which the promisor should reasonably expect to induce action or forbearance of a definite and substantial character on the part of the promisee and which does induce such action or forbearance is binding if injustice can be avoided only by enforcement of the promise.[16]

Thus, although a promisor has not *requested* the acts of reliance of the promisee in return for his promise, inducement alone, as in the circumstances described in the above statement, becomes a substitute for the request. (If he had requested the act of reliance in return for his promise, there would be an offer, an acceptance and consideration in all common law jurisdictions.) This position, as we are about to discuss, has been recognized in a limited way in England and Canada.

When one person asserts as true a certain *statement of fact* and another relies on that statement to his detriment, the maker of the statement will be *estopped* (prevented) from denying the truth of his original statement in a court of law, even if it turns out to have been untrue.

Illustration:

(a) *A* has purchased a retail shoe business from *X* in rented premises owned by *B*. After a few months, *A* mentions to *B* that the business does not have an adequate sales area. He remarks that he would like to turn a back room into a display and fitting salon, but that the room contains a number of pieces of old furniture belonging to *B* that he would like to get rid of. *B* then says to *A*, "That furniture belonged to *X* and you acquired it when you purchased the business. You can do as you like with it." *A* replies, "I thought that the furniture was yours. That's what *X* told me." "No, it's yours," *B* answers. *C*, the next-door tenant to *A*, is present and hears the conversation.

That evening, when *B* reports the incident to his wife, she becomes furious and reminds *B* that several antique pieces given to them by her grandmother are stored in the back room of the store. When *B* arrives at the shoe store the next morning he discovers that the furniture has been taken away to the city dump and compressed by a bulldozer. He then sues *A* for the value of the antique furniture.

B would fail because *A* can prove in his defence that *B* had asserted that the furniture was *A*'s, and the court would estop *B* from asserting the true state of facts.

(b) Estoppel applies to an assertion of existing fact; but does it also apply to a promise of future conduct? Suppose, that instead of stating the furniture was *A*'s, *B* had replied, "I wouldn't mind seeing that ugly furni-

---

[16] American Law Institute, *Restatement of Contracts*, Section 90, Washington, 1932.

ture of ours in the city dump, as long as you don't tell my wife. I promise not to interfere.'' The following morning, *B*'s wife was shopping in the vicinity and saw the furniture being removed from *A*'s premises. Before she could stop the workmen, several of the best pieces were damaged beyond repair. *B* reluctantly sued *A* for the value of the destroyed pieces and the return of the remainder. *B* would recover the remaining furniture, but would he succeed in getting damages?

To answer this question, we must examine the original meaning of estoppel and its subsequent enlargement. For practical reasons, the common law restricted the use of estoppel to assertions of fact. When an assertion of fact has been made, its truth or falsity at the time of its assertion is an objective matter that can be determined by evidence. The essence of estoppel is reliance on facts as they were at the time of the statement. Only if they were untrue at that time would the maker be estopped. If instead of an assertion of existing facts a promisor should make a promise of future conduct, the essential element of common law estoppel would be missing.

A promisee may claim that a promise made to him was not a ''true'' promise because at the time he made it the promisor had no intention of keeping it. As we have noted, the common law courts strongly resisted examining a person's motives; motives are not subject to proof by external evidence, except in those rare instances where a dishonest promisor gives himself away by his own admission. In any event, the harm suffered by the promisee is the same whether the promisor originally intended to keep his promise and later changed his mind, or originally intended to mislead because he never meant to keep his promise. While the question of intention is germane to the punishment of a wrongdoer in criminal law, it has little to do with the concern of contract law to seek external standards in order to determine when a promise is binding as a contractual bargain.

Despite these arguments, the courts found themselves unable to ignore the plea of an innocent party who had relied in good faith on a gratuitous promise only to find later that the promisor had changed his mind. In part (b) of our illustration above, *A* relied on *B*'s implied promise that he would not demand the return of his furniture, and it can certainly be argued that *A*'s reliance differs in its effect little, if at all, from his reliance on *B*'s assertion in part (a) that the furniture belonged to *A*. Solely on the grounds of fairness, the court would exercise its equitable jurisdiction to estop *B* from claiming that he was not bound by his gratuitous promise as it applied to the furniture already destroyed. Such reasoning appears to extend the idea of estoppel to promises. (The argument has been called *promissory estoppel* but the more common phrase is *equitable estoppel,* because the court is acting as a court of equity to override a common law rule.) The American term ''injurious reliance'' and the English term ''equitable estoppel'' are essentially two sides of the same coin: injurious reliance looks at the situation from the point of view of the promisee, while equitable estoppel views it from the position of the promisor.

The English doctrine of equitable estoppel has not been carried as far as the

American doctrine of injurious reliance, at least in its present state of development. It appears to be limited to a defence against a claim by the promisor where a legal relationship already exists between the parties. The English courts have not permitted a gratuitous promisee to rely on equitable estoppel in order to make the promise to him a binding one. (Hence, in our earlier illustration of the gratuitous promise of an outboard motor, the promisee would not succeed in an English court.)

Although the doctrine of equitable estoppel originated a century ago in the leading case of *Hughes v. Metropolitan Railway Co.*[17] very little change took place in it until recent years. In the *Hughes* case, a tenant under a 99-year lease of a large block of buildings was under an obligation to keep the building in good repair. The penalty for failure to honour a notice to repair given by the landlord (Hughes) would be forfeiture of possession. Hughes served the tenant with notice that repairs were needed and the tenant had six months in which to make them. The tenant then suggested that perhaps Hughes might be interested in buying back the remaining years of the tenant's 99-year lease. Evidently the lease was a valuable one, as rents to subtenants had risen greatly over the long years of the master lease. Serious negotiation began when Hughes expressed interest in the proposal. All repairs were delayed with Hughes' acquiescence, as repairs would simply have increased the tenant's investment in the property and thus the sale price of the lease. After several months negotiations broke down, and the tenant then proceeded with the repairs. They were not finished within six months of the original notice, but were complete within six months of the termination of negotiations. Hughes sued for forfeiture of the lease, the effect of which would be to give him the remaining years free. In refusing Hughes' claim, the House of Lords stated that by entering into negotiation Hughes had impliedly agreed to a suspension of the notice, and he could not subsequently go back on his word and revert to his strict legal rights in the lease; the notice became effective again only on negotiations being broken off, when the tenant could no longer rely on Hughes' implied promise not to pursue his strict rights.

The immediate post-Second-World-War period saw a flurry of cases in England in which Lord Denning sought gradually to expand the use of this doctrine.[18] More recently, Canadian courts have taken notice of it, and in particular the decision of the Supreme Court of Canada in *Conwest Exploration Co. v. Letain*[19] has pushed the doctrine quite far indeed; it can even be argued that the decision conceded that equitable estoppel might be used as a cause of action. The facts were complicated, but the essential ones for our purposes can be summarized as follows:

> *A* held an option to purchase certain mining claims. Before the date of expiry of the option, *B,* the grantor of the option, impliedly agreed to its exten-

---

[17] (1877) 2 App. Cas. 439.

[18] See, for example, Central London Property Trust, Ltd. v. High Trees House, Ltd. [1947] K.B. 130.

[19] (1964) 41 D.L.R. (2d) 198.

sion. (As in the *Hughes* case, it appeared to be in his interest to do so.) As a result, *A* did not hurry to complete the required task under the option before the original expiry date, but he did try to exercise the option shortly afterwards, and before *B* had given any notice that he wished to return to his strict legal rights. In an action brought by *A* asking the court to permit him to exercise his option, the court did not allow *B* to assert the original expiry date, and *A*'s action succeeded.

The promise to extend the period was impliedly made during the original option period and thus while legal relations existed between the parties. On the one hand, therefore, it can be concluded that this decision amounts to no more than an application of the *Hughes* case. On the other hand, there is an opposing view that once the original option had expired, without an extension having been granted for additional consideration, there was then no subsisting legal relationship between *A* and *B;* they were as strangers. Thus, to permit *A* to succeed is to permit him to use equitable estoppel as a cause of action, as in American cases of injurious reliance. It remains to be seen whether in future cases the Canadian courts will favour this second view.

THE EFFECT OF A REQUEST FOR GOODS OR SERVICES

When one person requests the services of another, and the other performs those services, the law implies a promise to pay. Although there is no mention of price, the implied promise is for payment of what the services are reasonably worth, that is, for payment *quantum meruit*.[20] Difficult though it may be when the services are not usual professional services with a recognized scale of fees, the court will nonetheless endeavour to find what is reasonable. A promise to pay will be implied in a request between strangers or even between friends, if the services are rendered in a customary business transaction. But such a promise is not usually implied when the services are performed between members of a family or close friends; the surrounding circumstances may show that although the services were requested, the parties expected them to be given gratuitously because of friendship, kindness, or family duty.

After services requested in a business relationship have been performed, the parties may agree on what they consider to be a reasonable price. If so, neither of them can later change his mind and ask the court to fix a reasonable price. In effect, each party has given up his right to refer the matter to the court by agreeing to a price.

Illustration:

A asks lawyer *B* for legal advice. Afterwards, *A* asks *B* what his fee is and *B* suggests a certain sum. *A* refuses to pay it. In an action for payment for ser-

---

[20] *Quantum meruit* means, "the amount he merits for his services".

vices performed, the court may give judgment in favour of *B* in the amount he requested or for some other amount which it deems reasonable.

If instead, *A* had agreed to the figure suggested by *B* but later changed his mind about paying, the court would not concern itself with what *it* considered reasonable; it would give judgment in favour of *B* for the amount earlier agreed upon. Only if the figure were obviously exorbitant would the court reopen the matter of what is reasonable.

The performance of services at the request of a party creates from that time an *existing obligation* to pay a reasonable price for them. When the parties later agree upon a fixed price, they have done away with the need for an implied price; and the subsequent payment of the fixed price satisfies all obligations owed by the party who requested the services. We must be careful to distinguish this position from that arising when a promise is made for a past consideration.[21] If, for example, *A* promises to pay *B* $100 because *B* has given him and his family an excellent dinner, *A* is not bound — he is under no existing legal obligation at the time he makes his promise. If, however, *A* promises to pay *B* $100 because *B* has catered a dinner for him at his request, *A* would be bound — in fact, *A* was already bound to pay *B* a reasonable price, and he and *B* have merely agreed later upon what this price should be.

The principle of *quantum meruit* applies to goods supplied on request as well as to services rendered; generally, a court has less difficulty ascertaining the reasonable worth of goods than of services.

THE USE OF A SEAL

In medieval times, when few men could read or write, a serious promise or *covenant* was often recorded by a clergyman. He would read the covenant over to the convenantor, who would then show his consent by impressing his coat of arms into a pool of hot sealing wax poured at the foot of the document. Usually the coat of arms was worn on a signet ring. By impressing his seal in this way, the covenantor adopted the document as *his act and deed*. To this day a document under seal is still called a deed. After a time, other methods of sealing a document came to be used, including embossing the coat of arms directly on the paper. Today the usual method is to affix a small red gummed wafer to a document, but almost any mark identifiable as a "seal" will do, even the word "seal" simply written in.

A seal, however, must be affixed (or the word "seal" written) on the document at the time the party signs it. The word "seal" printed on the document in advance presents difficulties: it may simply indicate the place where the parties are to place a red paper wafer. In *Royal Bank of Canada v. Kiska*[22] the bank used a printed form of guarantee which included the word "seal" and also the words,

---

[21] Lampleigh v. Braithwait (1615) 80 E.R. 255.
[22] (1967) 63 D.L.R. (2d) 582.

"Given under seal at . . ." and, "Signed, sealed and delivered in the presence of . . ." The bank manager did not affix a red paper wafer, however, until some time after the guarantor had signed, and without the guarantor's instructions to do so. Mr. Justice Laskin (as he then was) commented:

> The respective words are merely anticipatory of a formality which must be observed and are not a substitute for it. I am not tempted by any suggestion that it would be a modern and liberal view to hold that a person who signs a document that states it is under seal should be bound accordingly although there is no seal on it. I have no regret in declining to follow this path in a case where a bank thrusts a printed form under the nose of a young man for his signature. Formality serves a purpose here and some semblance of it should be preserved . . .[23]

A promise made properly under the seal of the promisor does not require consideration to make it binding. Historically, signing under seal was taken as an act of great deliberation. It is still considered so today. The seal says in effect, "I fully intend to be bound by this promise." Its presence means that the court will not, as it otherwise would, insist upon consideration to hold the promisor bound.

Although a seal is an alternative to consideration in binding the promisor, it does not do away with any other requirements needed to make a promise enforceable. Other essentials for a binding contract (its legality, for example) remain the same.

Certain documents, such as a deed of land and a mortgage, may require a seal even if there is consideration. These documents will be explained as they arise in later chapters.

AN INTENTION TO CREATE LEGAL RELATIONS

Even when an apparently valid offer has been accepted and consideration is present, there may be no contract in law. An intention on the part of both sides to create a legally enforceable agreement must also be present. Of course, parties do not often direct their minds to the legal effects of their bargains, but the law presumes that the necessary intention is present in almost all instances where an agreement is seriously made. This presumption is especially strong in dealings between strangers, and in commerce generally. On the other hand, it is easier to rebut this presumption in arrangements between friends or members of a family, where it is often obvious that there was no intention to create legal relations. For example, claiming that a failure to show up for a dinner invitation would give the host a right to sue for breach of contract — even though the host went to considerable trouble and expense — would be highly unreasonable. Many domestic arrangements between husband and wife are on the same footing.[24] In a United

---

[23] *Ibid.*, at 594.
[24] Balfour v. Balfour [1919] 2 K.B. 571.

States case,[25] a farmer from whom a $15 harness had been stolen announced in the indignation and frustration of the moment, "I will give $100 to any man who will find out who the thief is." Thereupon someone present named the thief. When the informer sued to recover the $100, the court ruled that the farmer's statement was "the extravagant exclamation of an excited man" and could not be construed as a serious offer which, when accepted, would create a legal relationship.

We may note that the law *presumes* that the parties to a contract intend to be legally bound. The law takes this position because it is impractical, if not impossible, for a court to inquire into the state of mind of both parties at the time they made the agreement and to decide whether they truly had such an intention. Instead, the court uses the external or objective test of the reasonable bystander: if to such a person the *outward* conduct of the parties showed a serious intention to make an agreement, then in the eyes of the law a legally binding contract results.

The requirement that a promise must be seriously meant before it has legal consequences is important in interpreting the legal effect of advertisements. A seller is allowed considerable latitude under the law in the nature of the claims he may make for the goods he offers for sale; and a buyer must learn to treat the enthusiastic and extravagant assertions of sellers with urbanity. An action brought by a disappointed buyer whose cotton shirt did not, after all, "wear like iron," is unlikely to succeed. The point was relevant also in *Carlill v. The Carbolic Smoke Ball Company* considered in the preceding chapter. Indeed, the company pleaded in defence that its undertaking to pay a £ 100 reward was no more than a "mere puff" and was not to be taken seriously. This defence might well have succeeded, but for the fact that the company had included in its advertisement the statement, " £1,000 is deposited with the Alliance Bank, Regent Street, showing our sincerity in the matter."

Apart from promises which do not imply legal relations, the parties may always include in their agreement an express term that in the event of its breach neither party may sue the other. Such an understanding, though rare in business contracts, is recognized by the courts and is an effective defence to any action brought under the contract.[26]

QUESTIONS FOR REVIEW

1. What is the consideration for the promise of the offeror in a unilateral contract? In a bilateral contract?
2. How may a gratuitous promise be made enforceable?
3. Is there consideration for a promise to reward the promisee for performing what is already his contractual duty to the promisor? Does it make any difference if the promisee owes the contractual duty to someone other than the promisor?

---

[25] Higgins v. Lessig, 49 Ill. App. 459 (1893).
[26] Rose and Frank v. Crompton [1925] A.C. 445.

4. Does the use of a seal answer for a failure to satisfy all essentials of a binding contract?
5. In what way may the common law rules about the need for consideration be unsatisfactory for business purposes? How can the defect be remedied?
6. Under what circumstances might a promised donation to a charitable organization be enforceable?
7. If past consideration were to be acknowledged as good consideration, what basic notion about consideration would be violated?
8. What is the nature of the obligation of a person who requests services?
9. Does a court ever concern itself with the adequacy of the consideration? If so, when?
10. What three essentials of a binding contract have we considered thus far?
11. A firm of public accountants has for years been auditing the accounts of a charitable organization without charge. It now appears that the treasurer of the organization has absconded with a sizeable amount of money and that an application of generally accepted auditing standards would have disclosed the defalcation in time to avoid the loss. Has the charitable organization any recourse against its auditors in these circumstances?
12. A supplier's invoice for goods has the following common term printed on it: "Terms — Net price thirty days; two per cent discount if paid within ten days." If the buyer pays the price less two per cent within ten days, can the supplier later sue successfully for the sum deducted?
13. Can there be consideration in a contract without the parties having expressly agreed upon what it is to be? Explain.
14. What question remains unresolved in the application of the concept of equitable estoppel by the Canadian courts?

CASES FOR DISCUSSION

CASE 1

MacGregor, who was in private dispute with his neighbour, O'Toole, called upon an acquaintance of his, Smith, who happened to be a lawyer. In the course of a conversation about world affairs and the weather MacGregor casually mentioned his dispute, and wondered audibly whether a legal action against O'Toole for trespass and slander might not be feasible. Smith advised against it. Subsequently MacGregor received a bill for $35 from Smith "for professional services rendered".

Has Smith contractual grounds for making this claim?

CASE 2

Prior to his death Mr. C. S. Cameron owned substantial property but did not make a will, because all his property was held jointly with his wife and would pass to her as survivor. He did, however, express to his wife a wish that she should make some provision for his brother, Mr. D. J. Cameron, and his children, because of their poverty. Shortly after Mr. C. S. Cameron's death, his wife, Mrs. Grace Cameron, went to a lawyer and told him that she had promised her late husband that she would give certain things to his brother and that in case anything happened she wanted to get it in writing "so it could not be upset". Accordingly, she signed a written undertaking prepared for her by the lawyer, promising that as soon as the business affairs of her late husband were settled she would give $10,000 to Mr. D. J. Cameron in pursuance of a promise made by her to her late husband. The document contained a seal adjacent to her signature, and was delivered to Mr. D. J. Cameron.

A misunderstanding subsequently developed between Mrs. Grace Cameron and her brother-in-law, and Mrs. Grace Cameron refused to pay him the $10,000. Mr. D. J. Cameron sued for the money.

State whether Mr. D. J. Cameron would succeed in his action.

CASE 3

Atlas Limited advertised its body-building course in *The Man's Magazine* in the following words which appeared beside a picture of Mr. Universe: "Are you underweight? Ten more pounds in three weeks with our Magic Body Building Kit or double your money back."

Whimple paid $150 cash for the course and used the related exercising equipment and pills as directed for three weeks with no other result than that he felt very tired. He then sued Atlas Limited for $300.

Discuss the respective arguments for the plaintiff and the defendant and render a decision.

CASE 4

Miss Sarah Binks, a prominent local citizen in the town of Crocus, undertook to contribute $50,000 towards the expansion programme of the local university. On the occasion on which Miss Binks signed the subscription card, the president of the university stated that the university would now be able to undertake the construction of an additional building, which it would name after Miss Binks in recognition of her contribution. A picture of Miss Binks and the university president appeared in the *Crocus Daily Bugle* with a news item about Miss Binks's generous contribution to the university campaign.

Unfortunately Miss Binks died shortly afterwards, before she had paid the amount. The executor of her estate, on instructions from her next of kin, advised the university that he did not propose to pay the amount. The university sued Miss Binks's estate for $50,000.

Examine the possible arguments for the plaintiff and the defendant, and state what you think the decision would be.

CASE 5

(a) Roberts was a business consultant and was recommended by a bank manager to Matthews. Matthews wished to buy the control of a business and was prepared to pay a sum in the neighbourhood of $30,000 if he could find a business which he regarded as satisfactory.

Matthews identified three companies in which he was interested, and at Matthews's request Roberts devoted most of his time from May to February of the following year investigating the three businesses. Roberts's rate of remuneration for performing these services was not discussed. Finally, after consultation with Matthews, Roberts attempted to obtain, and did obtain, an option for Matthews to purchase the shares of the A. C. Electrical Co. Ltd., one of the three companies in which Matthews was interested. When Matthews learned of Roberts's success in obtaining the option, he promised to pay Roberts $6,000 for his services. Roberts expressed his approval of this amount.

Matthews subsequently decided not to exercise the option, and refused to pay Roberts the $6,000. Roberts brought an action against Matthews for this sum. In defence Matthews asserted that it was expressly agreed that if, as a result of Roberts's services or efforts, Matthews actually made a purchase, he would pay a suitable commission to Roberts but unless he made such a purchase, Roberts would be entitled to nothing. Roberts denied that Matthews's undertaking had been qualified in this manner. Faced with this conflict of evidence, the trial judge stated that he accepted the evidence of the plaintiff in preference to that of the defendant.

What is the main issue? Should Roberts succeed? (See *Roche v. Marston* [1951] 3 D.L.R. 433.)

(b) Suppose instead that the parties had discussed $6,000 as the appropriate fee *before* the services were rendered and then when Matthews learned of Roberts's success in obtaining the option, he was so elated as to promise him $2,000 more. What issue would arise if Roberts found it necessary to sue Matthews for the $8,000?

CASE 6

Mrs. Pays owned a house in which she lived with Miss Esme Pays, her granddaughter, and Miss May Simpkins, a paying boarder. The three took part together each week in a fashion competition organized by a Sunday newspaper, the *Sunday Empire News,* in which readers were invited to place in order of merit eight fashions or articles of attire. They sometimes discussed the possibility of winning in a way which assumed they would all share equally. The entries were made in Mrs. Pays' name, but there was no regular rule for the payment of postage and other expenses. One week the entry was successful, and Mrs. Pays obtained a prize of £750. Miss Simpkins claimed a third of this sum, but Mrs. Pays refused to pay it. Miss Simpkins brought legal action to recover.

What is the main issue in this case? Should the action succeed? (See *Simpkins v. Pays* [1955] 3 All E.R. 10.)

CASE 7

Mr. and Mrs. Balfour were married in August, 1900. Balfour, a civil engineer, had a position as Director of Irrigation under the Government of Ceylon, and after their marriage he and his wife went to Ceylon and lived there together until 1915. In November, 1915, Mrs. Balfour returned to England with her husband, who was on leave. They remained in England until August, 1916, when Balfour's leave was up. His wife, however, was suffering from rheumatoid arthritis, and her doctor advised her to remain in England for some months. Before sailing for Ceylon on August 8, 1916, Balfour consulted with his wife about her needs and said that he would send her £30 a month for her maintenance until she returned to Ceylon. Some time afterwards differences arose between the husband and wife, and Balfour wrote to his wife suggesting that they had better remain apart. Balfour became in arrears on his monthly payments.

In March, 1918, Mrs. Balfour commenced proceedings against her husband for alimony. On December 16, 1918, she obtained an order for alimony, and then proceeded to sue her husband for money past due in respect of the agreed allowance of £30 a month.

Mrs. Balfour failed. (See *Balfour v. Balfour* [1919] 2 K.B. 571.) Would a court today be likely to decide the case in the same way?

CASE 8

Harris N. Dealer was sole proprietor of a profitable computer data centre which he sold as a going concern to Irwin B. Wheeler for the price of $80,000. The purchase consideration was paid with $20,000 in cash and the balance in the form of a contract under Wheeler's seal which read in part as follows:

> For value received Irwin B. Wheeler promises to pay Harris N. Dealer the sum of sixty thousand dollars ($60,000) in ten years from April 1, 1975 together with interest at 9% per annum from April 1st 1975 payable monthly on the first day of May, 1975 and on the first day of each and every month thereafter until payment of the principal sum on April 1, 1985.
>
> After ten (10) days' default in any interest payment due under this agreement the whole amount payable shall become immediately due.
>
> Irwin B. Wheeler [SEAL]

Dealer and Wheeler remained on friendly terms throughout the balance of 1975. Wheeler was somewhat dilatory in making his monthly payments of $450 interest, so that by the end of the year he had made six of the eight monthly payments required by then on dates more than ten days after they were due; Dealer had acquiesced in the arrangement without complaint, though the parties had never expressly agreed on any change in the due dates and Dealer seemed merely to have been indulgent with his debtor. Unfortunately, however, the parties had a serious personal disagreement early in 1976. On February 5, 1976, the January 1st interest payment then being 35 days overdue, Dealer wrote to Wheeler as follows:

> This letter will serve to inform you that, an interest payment due under the terms of the contract dated March 29, 1975 being in default for more than 10 days, the whole amount under the contract is now due.

I hereby demand immediate payment of the principal amount of $60,000 and outstanding interest.

H. N. Dealer

When Wheeler failed to pay the full amount Dealer brought an action against him for that sum.

What is the legal issue raised by these facts? State with reasons whether the action should succeed. (For reference, see *John Burrows Ltd. v. Subsurface Surveys et al.* (1968) 68 D.L.R. (2d) 354; *Hughes v. Metropolitan Railway Co.* (1877) 2 App. Cas. 439; *Conwest Exploration Co. Ltd. et al. v. Letain* (1964) 41 D.L.R. (2d) 198.)

CASE 9

Krohm and Sterling incorporated Old Colony Silver Mines Ltd. for the purpose of acquiring mining properties and claims owned by them. They received 40% of the voting shares of the company as consideration for the transfer to the company of their interests. The remaining 60% of the shares were held by others who had acquired them from the company for cash.

In the first year of the company's operations Krohm and Sterling personally advanced sums totalling $39,500 to the company to help it defray development costs. They received promissory notes from the company and the amounts were included in the company's general ledger in an account entitled "Notes Payable". By the end of the year it appeared that the company's prospects were good, but that to realize its potential the company would require additional outside financing.

At the first annual meeting of shareholders, Krohm stated that he and his fellow shareholder Sterling, for whom he was also speaking, had considered the company's financial position and concluded that it was imperative that the debt-equity ratio appearing on the company's balance sheet be improved if the company were to succeed in obtaining the additional financing it needed. He therefore wished the meeting to take note of the intention of both Mr. Sterling and himself to forgive the two promissory notes of Old Colony Silver Mines Ltd. in the amounts of $19,750 each. Sterling then spoke briefly to confirm Krohm's statement; the notes, he said, "would never be enforced". At this juncture, another shareholder rose to propose a motion of appreciation to Krohm and Sterling for "this most selfless, altruistic and loyal gesture". The motion was duly seconded and unanimously approved by the meeting, and recorded by the secretary in the minutes.

The next quarterly financial statements of Old Colony Silver Mines Ltd. omitted the notes payable to Krohm and Sterling from the company's liabilities as presented on its balance sheet, and showed the amount forgiven as an extraordinary item of income in the income statement, after operating profit for the quarter. The company submitted these financial statements with an application to its bank for a term loan. Krohm and Sterling did not, however, surrender the company's promissory notes to it for cancellation, nor did they sign any statement acknowledging their expressed intention not to enforce the notes. The application for the term loan was not successful.

A few weeks later Old Colony Silver Mines received from another mining company an offer of $300,000 for its individual assets. At a special general meeting of shareholders, Krohm and Sterling opposed the acceptance of this offer on the grounds that the company had not exhausted the possibilities for outside financing, but they were voted down. A resolution was then approved instructing Old Colony to accept the offer and proceed to distribute the proceeds of the sale to its creditors and shareholders in the course of winding up the company. At this stage Krohm and Sterling insisted that the sum of $39,500 they had previously lent to the company be first paid to them as creditors before any amount should be distributed to shareholders. The majority shareholders then passed a resolution directing the company treasurer not to pay these notes, in view of the statement made by Krohm and Sterling at the preceding meeting.

Krohm and Sterling thereupon commenced legal proceedings against Old Colony Silver Mines Ltd., submitting the promissory notes in their possession as evidence of the company's indebtedness to them. Outline fully the defence which the company could offer, and then comment upon its validity.

CHAPTER 7

Formation of a Contract: Capacity to Contract

THE MEANING OF CAPACITY TO CONTRACT

Under the common law some types of people lack the ability, competence, or *capacity* in certain respects to enter into contracts which will be binding upon them. We are now to consider the persons affected and the circumstances under which they may or may not succeed in making themselves parties to a contract which can be enforced against them.

MINORS (OR INFANTS)

Contracts Creating Liability for a Minor

For the purposes of the law of contract a minor or infant is a person who has not attained the age of majority in his province. At common law this age was deemed to be 21, but it has now been varied by legislation in the provinces, an example of their jurisdiction over property and civil rights.[1] The general rule is that the contract of a minor is unenforceable against him but enforceable by him against the other side. In consequence, a minor may often disregard his promises with impunity. In addition, when a minor owns considerable assets, his father or

---

[1] For example: Age of Majority Act, St. of B.C. 1970, c. 2 (19 years of age); St. of N.S. 1970-71, c. 10 (19); St. of Man. 1970, c. 91 (18); Age of Majority and Accountability Act, St. of Ont. 1971, c. 98 (18).

mother is ordinarily empowered to look after his affairs or, with supervision of the court, may make contracts concerning his property; if his parents are deceased or are unable to manage his affairs the court will appoint a guardian to do so.

The object of these rules is to protect minors, but if the rules had no exceptions they would defeat their purpose: businessmen might refuse to rely upon *any* promise of a minor, causing him great hardship. A minor might require food or clothing in an emergency but be unable to find a merchant willing to sell him these things on credit. Accordingly, the courts have come to regard *necessaries* and *beneficial contracts of service* as exceptions.

Necessaries. A minor will be bound to pay a reasonable price for all necessaries he buys. Two criteria determine whether a particular purchase by a minor has been for necessary goods:

(1) the goods must be necessary in relation to the minor's station in life;
(2) the minor must not already have an adequate supply of them.

The first of these criteria was the issue in *Ryder v. Wombwell*.[2] The minor, Wombwell, had purchased on credit from Ryder a silver-gilt goblet and a pair of ornamental studs "made of crystals set in gold and ornamented with diamonds representing a horseshoe in which the nails were rubies". Wombwell was the younger son of a deceased baronet of means and moved in the highest society. He purchased the items as a gift for a friend, but declined to pay for them. Ryder's attempt to collect the price by legal action failed. The court ruled that although "necessaries" may vary according to one's position, the articles in question could not be necessary for a minor in any station of life, even one as exalted as that of Wombwell. "The burden lay on the plaintiff to give evidence of something peculiar making them necessaries in this special case and . . . he has given no evidence at all to this effect."

The decision in *Johnstone v. Marks*[3] illustrates the second of the criteria. A tailor sued for the price of clothes supplied on credit to a minor who, in defence, pleaded infancy. The court held that the minor was entitled to produce evidence which showed that at the time of the purchase he was already well supplied with clothes. In dismissing the tailor's claim, Lord Esher said, "It lies upon the plaintiff to prove, not that the goods supplied belong to the class of necessaries as distinguished from luxuries, but that the goods supplied *when supplied* were necessaries to the infant."

The courts have in particular identified the following types of subject-matter as necessaries: food, clothing, lodging, medical attention,[4] legal advice,[5] and transportation.[6] But "transportation" includes only the means of getting him to

[2] (1869) L.R. 4 Ex. 32.
[3] (1887) 19 Q.B.D. 509.
[4] Huggins v. Wiseman (1690) 90 E.R. 669.
[5] Helps v. Clayton (1864) 144 E.R. 222.
[6] Clyde Cycle Co. v. Hargreaves (1898) 78 L.T. 296.

work, and does not include liability for the purchase price of vehicles required by the minor in the exercise of his trade or business.[7]

The minor's liability for necessary goods is not for the contract price, as such, but rather for a reasonable price. In the absence of evidence that the minor has been exploited, the court usually regards the contract price as evidence of what a reasonable price should be.

Beneficial contracts of service. An infant is bound to the terms of contracts of employment deemed to be for his benefit. But not every contract which associates a minor with a trading or business venture will be deemed for his benefit and so bind him. Particularly is this so when the minor is in business for himself[8] or in a partnership with others. As yet, only service or apprenticeship contracts have been enforced against minors; other business arrangements, even though for their benefit, have not been binding upon them.

It is remarkable how little litigation arises in practice as a result of attempts by minors to repudiate their contracts. An important non-legal sanction operates to persuade them, in spite of their opportunity to avoid liability, to perform their promises: if they should repudiate on grounds of incapacity, they would all but eliminate their chances of finding people willing to transact business with them.

Contracts Creating No Liability for a Minor

A minor may always repudiate a contract for *non-necessaries* even in circumstances where the non-necessaries are clearly beneficial to him. The purchase of a truck for use in his business may well be of great benefit to a minor; nevertheless, the truck is not a necessary.[9] We can only determine the nature of non-necessaries negatively, that is, from a review of the circumstances of cases which have decided whether a particular subject-matter *was* a necessary. A fairly large number of things have been held to be necessaries; beyond these things each case must be decided on its own facts, and the judges are reluctant to enlarge the group of necessaries. When a minor is living at home and supported by his parents, his purchases are less likely to be considered as necessaries than when he is on his own. The courts assume that a minor living at home is provided for.

Although there are no decisions on the point, it would appear that a minor will not be liable for necessaries which he has ordered but not yet received. Accordingly, he can repudiate a contract of sale before delivery of the goods.[10] The point is underlined in the Sale of Goods Act which defines necessaries for an infant in terms of goods sold *and delivered*.[11]

The minor who repudiates his liability for non-necessary goods may, if the goods are still in his possession, be required to restore the goods to the seller in

---

[7] Mercantile Union Guarantee Corp. v. Ball [1937] 2 K.B. 498.

[8] *Ibid.*

[9] *Ibid.*

[10] See Cheshire, Fifoot and Furmston, *The Law of Contract* (8th ed.), p. 393.

[11] See, for example: R.S.B.C. 1960, c. 344, s. 9; R.S.O. 1970, c. 421, s. 3; R.S.N.S. 1967, c. 274, s. 4.

whatever condition they may be at that time. In *Louden Manufacturing Co. v. Milmine,* Chief Justice Meredith said:

> Upon principle and the authorities cited . . . it must be that if an infant avails himself of the right he has to avoid a contract which he has entered into and upon the faith of which he has obtained goods, he is bound to restore the goods which he has in possession at the time he so repudiates. If that were not so, a man might buy a farm for a large sum of money, give a mortgage upon it shortly before coming of age, then repudiate the contract, and insist upon holding the property. The authorities are all the other way, and establish that the effect of repudiating the contract is to revest the property in the vendor.[12]

Similarly, when the minor is a seller rather than a buyer in a contract for the sale of goods, he cannot repudiate the contract to recover the goods delivered unless he returns the money paid.[13]

There is nothing to prevent a minor from purchasing non-necessaries if he can find a merchant who is prepared to rely entirely upon the minor's honour for payment or, where he purchases goods for cash, not to return them for refund.

Ordinarily a minor does not have implied authority to pledge his parents' credit in purchases he makes.[14] Authority may sometimes be implied from the fact that a parent has paid the account for a previous purchase by his child without complaint. Apart from this possibility, a merchant needs express authority from the parent before he can bind him.

Contracts Indirectly Affecting a Minor

If a minor has received benefit as a result of a contract for non-necessaries, he will not be able to recover money which he has already paid, though he will be able to repudiate his remaining liability. In *Valentini v. Canali*[15] a minor became tenant of a house under an agreement by which he was to pay a certain amount for the furniture in it. He paid part of the sum and gave a promissory note for the balance. He occupied the premises and had the use of the furniture for several months. Then he brought an action to have the contract rescinded and to recover the money he had paid. The Court held that he might avoid his liability on the note, but that he was not entitled to a return of what he had paid.

An adult can recover money lent to a minor only if the minor in fact devoted the proceeds of the loan to the purchase of necessary goods.[16] If he spends the

---

[12] (1908) 15 O.L.R. 53, at 54; McGaw v. Fisk (1908) 38 N.B.R. 354; Williston, *A Treatise on the Law of Contracts* (3rd ed.), Vol. 2, p. 35. Jaeger, ed. Mount Kisco: Baker, Voorhis & Co. Inc., 1959.

[13] Williston, *A Treatise on the Law of Contracts* (3rd ed.), Vol. 2, s. 238, pp. 35-43. The right to repudiate may be lost when the infant comes of age.

[14] Halsbury, *The Laws of England* (3rd ed.), Vol. 21, p. 201. Simonds, ed. London: Butterworth & Co. Ltd., 1960.

[15] (1889) 24 Q.B.D. 166.

[16] Halsbury, *op. cit.,* p. 144.

borrowed money at the races, the lender cannot recover the debt. At the same time, we should note that the voidability of minors' contracts is a part of the common law and can always be altered by statute for certain types of contracts. For example, the Canada Students Loans Act[16a] provides that a guaranteed bank loan to a student "is recoverable by a bank from the borrower as though the borrower had been of full age at the time the loan was made".

A minor's freedom from liability in private law is limited to contract; he remains liable for torts such as negligence, assault, slander, libel, or deceit. If, however, the minor causes a loss while performing the very acts contemplated by the contract, the court will decide the case under the law of contract and not of torts, and the minor will escape liability for the consequences. The other contracting party will not, in other words, be permitted to circumvent the rules protecting minors in contract by suing for damages for a tort, where he would fail if he sued for breach of contract.

Illustration:

A minor hires a horse for a period of time for the purpose of riding, undertaking as a term of the contract that he will handle the animal with care. The infant in his youthful exuberance injures the horse by riding it too hard.

The owner of the horse may realize that if he sues the infant for breach of contract he will fail, since the subject-matter of the contract is a non-necessary. It may, therefore, seem preferable to sue the infant for the tort of negligence. The owner will not be allowed this evasion.[17] He will fail whichever approach he takes.

Suppose, however, that the infant had injured the horse by entering it in a ploughing match, something not at all contemplated in the contract of hiring. If the minor's act which results in loss was outside the scope of the contract, as would be true in these circumstances, the owner may then sue the minor for damages for negligence.

The Contractual Liability of Minors upon Attaining Majority

Naturally, a minor's liability to pay for necessaries and beneficial contracts of service continues after he attains majority. In addition, he may *become* liable for obligations which could not be enforced against him while he was a minor. When he attains majority, this latter group of obligations become part of a class called *voidable* contracts, of which there are two types.

In the first type the minor acquires "an interest of a permanent or continuous nature." He must repudiate such a contract promptly upon coming of age, or it will be enforceable against him thereafter and he will be liable on it just as if he had entered into it after coming of age. The courts have decided that interests of a permanent or continuous nature are found in contracts for rights in land, for the

---

[16a] R.S.C. 1970, c. S-17, s. 15.
[17] Jennings v. Rundall (1799) 101 E.R. 1419.

subscription to shares in a company, and in partnership agreements; this class of contracts is quite narrow. An infant partner will not be held liable for partnership debts contracted while he was a member of the firm and under age, but he will become liable for debts incurred by the firm after he attains full age if he does not repudiate the partnership agreement. In contracts of this nature, the minor loses his right to repudiate if he does not do so promptly after becoming of age, or if he accepts the benefits of the contract after that time.

The second and more common type of voidable contract does not create an interest of a continuous nature. It will not be binding upon the minor unless he expressly ratifies the contract after attaining his majority. In addition, some provinces require that to be enforceable the ratification must be in writing and signed by him.[18] Contracts of this class include a minor's promise to pay for non-necessary goods and his promise to pay for services previously performed at his request. An earlier promise to pay for necessary goods not delivered to him by the time he becomes of age will also require his ratification.

There is a small group of contracts which the courts have held by their very nature to be prejudicial and unfair to minors. Accordingly, they have declared that these contracts are absolutely *void* rather than merely voidable. The effect of this distinction is that ratification by a minor after he attains majority will be ineffective and his promise to pay, merely gratuitous and unenforceable. In other words, in these circumstances there is never any contract which would be capable of ratification. Examples of this type are contracts which include forfeiture clauses and penalty clauses.[19]

LUNATICS AND DRUNKARDS

The law protects a lunatic or drunk person (or person similarly incapacitated through the use of drugs) in the same way as a minor by making his contracts, except for necessaries, voidable at his option but enforceable by him against the other contracting party. An insane or drunk person is liable for a reasonable price for the necessary goods.

In practice a drunk or insane person, upon becoming sober or sane, has a problem of evidence which a minor does not have in proving his incapacity at the time of the contract. Proof of age is more readily established than the fact that one was so intoxicated or insane that he did not know what he was doing — though the terms of the contract may well encourage that presumption.

The burden of evidence is the greater yet for the reason that the party seeking to avoid the contract must show, not only that he was incapable of a rational decision at the time of the agreement, but also that the other party was aware of his condition. Unfortunately, if one is so insane or drunk that he does not know what he is doing, his own observations about the other contracting party are un-

---

[18] The Statute of Frauds: for example, R.S.O. 1970, c. 444, s. 7, R.S.N.S. 1967, c. 290, s. 8.
[19] Beam v. Beatty (1902) 4 O.L.R. 554; Phillips v. Greater Ottawa Development Co. (1916) 38 O.L.R. 315.

likely to be reliable, and the necessary evidence must then be adduced from all the surrounding circumstances.

As with voidable contracts generally, the party entitled to avoid must act promptly upon emerging from his state of incapacity. Unless repudiation comes within a reasonable time, the privilege is lost. It will also be too late to repudiate if, after regaining sanity or sobriety, the afflicted party accepts the benefits of the contract.

CORPORATIONS — *Limitations of Capability of responsibles*

Since a corporation is a legal fiction, a mere creature of the law, it has no physical existence — it cannot think or act or sign its name in the same way that a natural person can. But this kind of impotence is a mere technical handicap. The law could give corporations the capacity to make any contract or enter into any obligation that a natural person possesses. In fact, however, the law has not extended to all corporations the widest possible contractual capacity. Public corporations, such as municipalities and crown corporations, are restricted in the range of their contractual activity because of the limited power conferred by the statutes creating them. Obligations which they purport to undertake but which are outside the ambit of the statute will, if challenged, be declared by the court to be *ultra vires* (beyond their powers) and, therefore, void. The promisee cannot enforce such obligations against the corporation. The legal consequences of *ultra vires* contracts are often complex and difficult.

In Canada, the determination of the contractual capacity of business corporations (limited companies) is further complicated because several methods of incorporation are in use, and each is subject to different rules about *ultra vires* transactions. We must defer a discussion of this problem until we deal with limited companies in Chapter 28.

We must wait also until we deal with the law relating to principal and agent in Chapter 20 to determine whether the person or persons purporting to act on behalf of a corporation have the power to bind it in contracts. The matter is of special importance for a corporation because it is not a natural person and must make all its contracts through agents. Assuming that the officers do have the necessary authority, the corporation's signature is easily enough accomplished. Its name is signed to particularly important contracts and to formal documents, such as share certificates, bonds, debentures, deeds, and mortgages (and certified copies of any of these), by its officers' impressing the company seal with an embossing device. For ordinary day-to-day business the signature of an authorized officer of the company will suffice.

LABOUR UNIONS

To have a contractual capacity, a labour union must be regarded in law as a separate legal person. For the most part the status of trade unions in this respect remains equivocal, though the law varies significantly from province to province and is changing quite rapidly.[20] On the other hand, the legal status of limited companies as employers is clearly settled. The discrepancy makes uncertain the enforceability of collective agreements between limited companies and labour unions. However, most provinces do have statutes[21] that provide for an arbitrator in the event of a dispute arising out of the collective agreement. If the employer does not implement the decision of the arbitrator, the union may apply to a labour relations board for permission to prosecute, and for this purpose is vested with a separate legal status. If a union rejects the arbitrator's decision and causes an illegal strike, damages have occasionally been awarded against it; the enforceability of such decisions is currently a matter of debate. In those provinces where an employer may seek permission to prosecute a union for such a strike, this ability derives from a statutory provision and not from the contractual capacity of the union in general.

Despite their indefinite status, trade unions may bring actions or defend against them when they so wish. By a legal technique known as a *representative action,* a union may expressly or impliedly authorize one or more persons to represent it in court simply as a group of individuals having a common interest in a particular case. As a result, the officials of a trade union may bring or defend a representative action on behalf of its members.

MARRIED WOMEN

At one time a married woman had no contractual capacity, all her contracts were void, and she could not own property independently of her husband. All her contractual capacity and property were vested in her husband, and he assumed complete control of business affairs for the family.

Within the last hundred years a series of statutes has gradually conferred upon a married woman all the contractual capacity of an adult man. Subject to certain exceptions in the province of Quebec, she may now hold or dispose of her property, earnings, and money as she pleases, free from her husband's control. What is equally important, none of her property, unless it was conveyed to her by her husband with the object of defrauding his creditors, is subject to seizure for payment of her husband's debts.

In Quebec a married woman's contractual capacity and right to dispose of her property may be determined by the particular terms of a separate formal contract made in contemplation of marriage and executed before a notary public. If no special advance arrangement of this kind is made before marriage, the provisions of the Quebec Civil Code as to community of property will apply.[22]

---

[20] See Chapter 21, under "Legal Status of Trade Unions."

[21] See, for example: Labour Code, St. of B.C., c. 122, s. 93; The Labour Relations Act, R.S.O. 1970, c. 232, s. 37; The Trade Union Act, St. of N.S. 1972, c. 19, s. 40.

[22] See the Quebec Civil Code, articles 1272 ff. for a statement of things which constitute the assets and liabilities of the "community" which exists between husband and wife.

The creditors of a married woman may look only to her separate property as security for the debts she incurs from contracts made in her own name and from pledging her own credit. Over and above debts of this kind, a wife may have implied authority to make contracts for the purchase of domestic requirements in her husband's name, pledging his credit for the purchases. These contracts belong to a discussion of the law relating to principal and agent, and we shall consider them again in Chapter 20.

ENEMY ALIENS

Ordinarily, an alien has the same rights as a citizen in making contracts and in all other matters of private law. The enemy alien, however, loses all his contractual capacity during hostilities, apart from any special licence granted by the Crown. For the purposes of contracts the enemy alien is identified not by his citizenship, but by the fact that either his residence or business interests are located in enemy territory.

Whenever there is the slightest suggestion that a contract made between an enemy alien and someone else is detrimental to the public interest, the contract is void as being against public policy, and the rights and liabilities created by it are wholly dissolved. In a few exceptional instances where the public interest is thought not to be affected, the contract may be regarded as being merely suspended for the duration of hostilities.

In the past the federal government has passed a number of statutes and orders-in-council after the outbreak of war describing the status of aliens in detail. It is necessary to refer to these when a party to the contract may be an enemy alien.

INDIANS

In Canada, Indians living on reserves are wards of the Crown. The property comprising the reserve is held by the Crown in trust for the benefit of the Indian band. It is not available as security for the claims of creditors, and any disposition of such property to an outside party is void unless the transaction has been approved by the Minister of Indian Affairs and Northern Development. Indians on reserves may manufacture and sell chattels to outsiders, although in the Prairie provinces, sales of produce must have the approval of a superintendent under the Minister. The legal position of Indians on reservations is set out in detail in the Indian Act.[23] An Indian may be enfranchised after leaving the reservation, and his contractual capacity then becomes the same as that of any other citizen.

---

[23] R.S.C. 1970, c. I-6.

BANKRUPT DEBTORS

A bankrupt debtor, until he receives a discharge from the court, is under certain contractual disabilities. We will discuss these disabilities more fully in Chapter 31.

QUESTIONS FOR REVIEW

1. Does the fact that one of the parties to a contract is under age prevent him from enforcing the contract against the other (adult) party?
2. What is the purpose of the general rule concerning the enforceability of infants' contracts? What is the purpose of the exceptions which are made to this rule?
3. What two criteria must we apply to determine whether goods which a minor has bought and received are of a type for which he must pay?
4. Are foods and clothing the only things which may be necessaries for an infant?
5. If a minor is operating a business of his own and enters into contracts pertaining to the business which are of general benefit to him, are these contracts enforceable against him?
6. What two types of minors' contracts must be distinguished for the purpose of determining the liability of the minors after they become of age?
7. Are minors' contracts for non-necessaries always voidable when the minors attain majority?
8. What two points must be established before a person intoxicated at the time of a contract may avoid his liability under it?
9. Under what circumstances may a contract voidable at the option of one of the parties cease to be voidable?
10. What does *ultra vires* mean in relation to a contract to which a corporation is a party?
11. What is the nature of the legal problem that adds to the uncertainty of an action against a trade union?
12. When may the property of a married woman be seized for payment of her husband's debts?
13. How is the status of an enemy alien determined for purposes of contract?
14. Under what circumstances do Indians have restricted contractual capacity?
15. (a) When Jones was 17 years old, he took his hi-fi set into the Mariposa Service Centre for an extensive repair job, to cost $75. If he does not pay, can the Mariposa Service Centre sue him successfully?
    (b) After Jones becomes of age he picks up the repaired radio and does nothing to repudiate his liability to the Mariposa Service Centre. Can the Mariposa Service Centre recover the money now?
    (c) Upon becoming of age, Jones tells the manager of the Mariposa Service Centre in a telephone conversation that he will pay the $75. Can the Mariposa Service Centre recover now?
16. Brown, while 17 years of age, orders a new suit of clothes which are neces-

sary for him, in view of both his station in life and his present supply of clothing. The suit is to cost $175. Before the suit is quite finished, Brown changes his mind about the style and advises the tailor that he does not propose to accept or pay for the suit. Is he liable?

17. Smith, a student 17 years of age, bought a suit of clothes for $250 and took it home. He then refused to pay the price, alleging it to be too high. The tailor sued for $250. It was established that the suit was a necessary article for Smith, but his lawyer produced witnesses who testified that an identical suit might have been purchased elsewhere for $125. What will be the result of the action?

18. An adult lends a minor money which the minor spends on a necessary suit of clothes. If the minor fails to repay his debt, can the adult recover in a court action?

19. At 17 years of age Watson entered into a contract of employment with an oil company which has a one-year training and familiarization program for its promising young employees. Shortly after Watson went to work for the company, it proposed to send him, with an adequate living allowance, to its oil fields in the Northwest Territories for a few months as part of the training program. Is Watson liable for breach of contract if he refuses to go?

20. An adult lends a minor money which the minor spends on the midway at the local fair. Can the adult recover?

21. In what respects does our present law affecting the contractual capacity of minors seem illogical?

CASES FOR DISCUSSION

CASE 1

For most of a year, Harrison acted as agent for the purpose of obtaining options on property on an island in British Columbia on behalf of the Western Development Company, which planned to develop the island industrially. These plans became known to the property owners on the island, and some of them, believing their holdings to be indispensable to the plan, sought to obtain prices a good deal higher than the market value established there for farm or residential purposes.

Harrison obtained, for a consideration of $1, an option to purchase within one year the property of Mrs. Foy for $50,000. Harrison had negotiated the price with a Miss Foy and a widow, Mrs. Sheridan; he had offered $500 an acre, which was the maximum he had been authorized to offer, and the two women had insisted upon $1,000 an acre; he had then reluctantly agreed to take an option at the price demanded, explaining that his principals would not likely take up the option at such an exorbitant price; Miss Foy had next insisted that a further $4,000 be added to the price for the barn; Harrison had agreed to that, too. It was only when the option agreement was prepared for signing that Harrison learned that he had not been dealing with the registered owner of the property, but with her daughters, both of whom resided there. He was informed that the owner, Mrs. Foy, was a very old lady and was in bed. Harrison was taken to the bedroom where he explained, carefully and accurately, the terms and effect of the option. Mrs. Foy appeared to understand what he was saying, nodding and smiling and from time to time saying, ''Yes.'' She did not sign her name but made a cross under one of her daughters' direction, it having been explained to Harrison that she used to be able to sign her name but her hand was now too unsteady.

Harrison's principals did, in fact, elect to take up the option and sought within the year to obtain this property at the agreed price of $50,000; they had taken up the options on the adjoining properties and needed Mrs. Foy's property to complete the section of land they required. They were immediately met with the defence, on the part of the two daughters, that the option agreement was ''not worth the paper it was written on'' because Mrs. Foy was insane at the time of her signing. The principals brought an action to have the option agreement enforced. It was brought out in evidence that Mrs. Foy was, indeed, insane, a fact of which Harrison denied any knowledge at the time; it was also shown that the fair market value of the property, as a farm, at the date of the option agreement was about $32,000.

Render a decision. (See *Hardman v. Falk* [1955] 3 D.L.R. 129.)

CASE 2

Sam West, having obtained his licence to drive, went to Drive-Yourself Ltd., showed his licence, and signed a contract for the hiring of a car in which there was a clause to the effect that the hirer should return the car in good condition. West was a kitchen helper in a restaurant and 16 years of age.

Sam West then gathered up seven friends and took them for a drive. In attempting to pass another car, the car which he was driving went out of control and was wrecked against a stump.

(a) Drive-Yourself Ltd. brought action against West for the value of the wrecked car. What would be the arguments for the plaintiff in this case? Would they succeed? (See *Dickson Brothers Garage & U-Drive Ltd. v. Sam Woo* (1957) 10 D.L.R. (2d) 652; affirmed on appeal (1958) 11 D.L.R. (2d) 477.)

(b) Suppose instead that West had managed to enter the rented car in a car rally, and that as a result of his handling of it the car was demolished in the course of competition. Would the result of the action be different?

CASE 3

Hunter, while boarding with his parents, was employed during the summer by a lawyer whose offices were located five miles away. Hunter was 17 years old. Primarily as a means of getting back and forth to work, Hunter bought a deluxe ten-speed bicycle from the Rover Cycle Co. The price of the bicycle was $375, payable on the following terms: a down payment of $75 on delivery and the balance in 12 monthly instalments of $25 each.

Hunter used the bicycle for the summer and then returned it to the Rover Cycle Co. At that time he still owed $200 under his contract. The sales manager for the company agreed to allow him $50 off the balance owing. Hunter failed to pay the reduced amount of $150.

Rover Cycle Co. brought an action against Hunter for the full $200 owing. Evidence given at the trial established that Hunter had not only used the bicycle for going to work but had entered four races with it, and won two prizes.

What factors must the court take into consideration? What would be the likely result of the action? Would it have made any difference if Hunter had attained majority one month after he bought the bicycle?

CHAPTER 8

Formation of a Contract: Legality of Object

THE ROLE OF LEGALITY IN THE FORMATION OF A CONTRACT

We have seen that offer and acceptance, an intention to create legal relations, consideration, and capacity to contract are necessary, each and every one, to the formation of a contract. In addition, the object of the contract must be "legal". In the absence of evidence to the contrary, the courts presume that business transactions neither offend the public good nor violate any law. Evidence may, of course, show that this presumption is wrong. If it does, the contract will at least be *void*, which means that in law it was never formed at all. In some circumstances the courts will stigmatize the contract by finding that it is also *illegal*.

THE DIFFERENCE BETWEEN A VOID AND AN ILLEGAL CONTRACT

No stigma attaches to the parties if their contract is void; they have just not succeeded in creating a binding agreement. If they have partly performed their undertakings, the court will do its best, taking all the circumstances into account, to restore them to their respective positions before the contract was attempted. It may order the return of money paid or of property transferred if the party complaining can show cause why he should have it back. Further, each party is released from the performance of any further obligations under the agreement.

When a contract is not only void but also illegal, the court will refuse to aid a party who knowingly agreed to the illegal purpose. Not only may he not sue for money promised, but if he has transferred property to the other party, he will also be unable to recover it. If both parties are tainted with the illegal object, the fact that a court will assist neither of them has the effect of rendering the plaintiff impotent and thereby of assisting the defendant. The effect is summed up in the legal maxim that where both parties are equally in the wrong, the position of the defendant is the stronger.

The law is not as helpful as it might be in providing an objective criterion for deciding when a given contract is illegal as well as void. Generally, the more reprehensible the object of a contract, the more likely it is that the contract will be regarded as illegal and a plaintiff's claim dismissed.

CONTRACTS AFFECTED BY STATUTE

Significance of the Wording of a Statute

The legislature may wish merely to deprive a particular type of contract of legal effect, or it may wish to go further and express positive disapproval. It can achieve the former object by providing in a statute that such agreements shall be void. To accomplish the second purpose it may describe the type of agreement as "unlawful" or "illegal" in the wording of the statute. It may even stipulate that performance of the agreement shall be a criminal offence, subject to prescribed penalties of a fine or imprisonment.

Agreements Void by Statute

The Workmen's Compensation Act, for example, specifies that any provision in an agreement between employer and employee purporting to deprive the employee of the protection of the Act is void.[1] Other statutes declare particular types of transfers of property to be void. In these instances the law says that despite the intention of the parties, the ownership does not pass from the transferor and that the property may be recovered from the transferee and applied according to the terms of the statute. Thus, the Bankruptcy Act contains a provision that if a person transfers property either by gift or for an obviously inadequate compensation and becomes bankrupt within one year, the transfer is void against the trustee in bankruptcy.[2] The trustee may recover the property and apply it to the claims of the bankrupt person's creditors. The same statute provides that a transfer of property by an insolvent person to one of his creditors with a view to

---

[1] See for example: St. of B.C. 1968, c. 59, s. 13; R.S.O. 1970, c. 505, s. 16; R.S.N.S. 1967, c. 343, s. 50.

[2] R.S.C. 1970, c. B-3, s. 69(1). S. 3 of the Bankruptcy Act also provides, "For the purposes of this Act, a person who has entered into a transaction with another person otherwise than at arm's length shall be deemed to have entered into a reviewable transaction." Under s. 78 a court may give judgment in favour of the trustee against the other party to such a transaction for the difference between the actual consideration given or received by the bankrupt and the fair market value of the property or services concerned. The provisions of the Bankruptcy Act are dealt with in more detail in Chapter 31.

giving that creditor a preference over other creditors is "fraudulent and void" if it occurs within three months preceding bankruptcy.[3]

Some provinces have statutes which specifically provide that all types of bets are void.[4] Betting is not thereby made a criminal offence; these statutes do not prescribe fines or imprisonment for those who make bets.[5] They simply make it impossible for a winner to collect his bet through court action. Betting agreements have long been regarded by the courts as a nuisance, and not the kind of agreement deserving their attention when more urgent disputes await solution. Thus, the winner of a bet cannot enforce a promise (even in the form of a promissory note or a cheque) given by the loser to pay a wager, nor can a loser who has paid his wager recover it through the courts.[6] An innocent third person who purchases a note or cheque for valuable consideration may, however, be able to enforce payment.

A wager is an agreement between two parties in which each has at the time some probability of winning or losing. Organizations that manage lotteries and race tracks accept and redistribute money as a type of stakeholder, and it has been held that they are not a party to a wagering agreement. They do, however, remain legally accountable for performing their task as stakeholder.[7] For many years, provincial legislation has permitted the placing of bets at authorized race courses,[8] and there has recently been further legislation to permit the holding of lotteries.[9] With these important exceptions, wagers are generally simple agreements between individuals and seldom if ever made between businesses. The subject would hold little interest for our purposes, were it not for the fact that a number of contracts commonly regarded as being of a legitimate business nature have an element of speculation in them — insurance contracts, stock exchange transactions, and "futures" transactions in commodities. To be enforceable, these contracts must not be interpreted as wagering contracts.

Contracts of insurance form a large and important class of commercial transactions. In an insurance contract one does not, of course, *hope* that he will win his "bet" with the insurance company. Herein lies the purpose of insurance: that the party contracting with the insurance company will receive some measure of compensation should the feared loss occur. The insurance acts of the various

---

[3] S. 73(1)

[4] See, for example, The Gaming Act, R.S.O. 1970, c. 187, s. 4; Insurance Act, R.S.B.C. 1960, c. 197, s. 10. The early Gaming Acts of England which declare wagering contracts to be void are in force in the other provinces. See also: Halsbury, *The Laws of England* (3rd ed.) Vol. 20A (Canadian Converter), p. 221.

[5] The Criminal Code, R.S.C. 1970, c. C-34, does, however, make certain betting activities illegal. It is a criminal offence to keep a gaming house (s. 185) or to operate a pool (s. 186) or a lottery (s. 189) unless within specified exceptions within the Act.

[6] By way of an exception, s. 3 of the Ontario Gaming Act permits a loser at "cards, dice, tables or other game" to sue for recovery when he has lost $40 or more at one sitting and brings his action within three months.

[7] Ellesmere v. Wallace [1929] 2 Ch. 1; Tote Investors Ltd. v. Smoker [1968] 1 Q.B. 509.

[8] See, for example, Racing Commission Act, R.S.O. 1970, c. 398.

[9] The Criminal Code, R.S.C. 1970, c. C-34, s. 190.

provinces state that an insurance contract is invalid unless the party making the contract has an *insurable interest* in the property or life insured. For a person to have such an insurable interest, he must have a pecuniary benefit from the continued existence of the property or life insured or suffer some pecuniary detriment from its loss or destruction.

Statutes may simply declare where an insurable interest exists: for example, with respect to life insurance, provincial statutes provide that every person has an insurable interest in his own life, in the life of his child or grandchild, in the life of a husband or wife, in the life of another on whom he is wholly or in part dependent for support or education, in the life of his employee, or in the life of another person in which he has a pecuniary interest. It would indeed add nothing to the peace of mind of a person if he were to learn that a stranger who stood to suffer nothing in the way of personal bereavement or pecuniary loss from his death was insuring his life with a life insurance company. There is, however, an exception to the requirement of an insurable interest under the Uniform Life Insurance Act which has been passed by all the common law provinces. The Act waives the requirement if the person whose life is insured consents in writing to the placing of the insurance.[10] The statute makes all other policies void even assuming an insurance company was willing to provide them, but it preserves the validity of insurance contracts in which there is a legitimate insurable interest. Thus, a creditor may insure the life of his debtor for the amount of the debt, as a means of ensuring repayment should the debtor die; a landlord may insure the life of his tenant for an amount sufficient to reimburse him should the tenant die and the premises be unsuited to other occupants; partnership funds may be used to insure the lives of partners and thus make available the money needed to buy the share of a deceased partner from his estate. Often the person receiving the proceeds of an insurance contract (that is, the *beneficiary*) is someone other than the party making the contract. It is necessary only that the maker of the contract, not the beneficiary, have an insurable interest in the life or property insured. *stock*

Stock exchange transactions are among the more speculative of business *Exchange* contracts. But while they are no doubt often explained by a difference of opinion between the buyer and the seller about the future price of the shares traded, the essence of the contract is an actual sale of personal property. Bona-fide contracts for the purchase and sale of shares are therefore valid and enforceable. If, however, the subject of an agreement is a wager about what the price of a particular stock will be at a specified future time, without an actual purchase or sale of the shares, the agreement is void.[11]

Whenever goods are purchased or sold for future delivery at a price agreed upon in advance, one contracting party may gain at the expense of the other because of price changes between the time of the contract and the time of delivery. Again the speculative element in these contracts is incidental to a larger

---

[10] See, for example: Insurance Act, St. of B.C. 1962, c. 29, s. 121 (2) (b); R.S.O. 1970, c. 224, s. 152 (2); R.S.N.S. 1967, c. 148, s. 137(2)(b).

[11] The Criminal Code, R.S.C. 1970, c. C-34, s. 341.

purpose, and the contracts cannot be impeached on the ground that they amount to wagers.

Agreements Illegal by Statute

Some statutes, as we have noted, have the effect of making agreements of a specified type illegal. Examples are the Lord's Day Act and the Combines Investigation Act. We shall discuss the Combines Investigation Act briefly in a separate section below. The Lord's Day Act (Canada) states that it shall not be lawful for any person to sell or offer for sale or purchase any goods, or to perform his ordinary business, or employ anyone to do so on Sunday.[12] However, the Act excludes any work of necessity or mercy, and the tendency has been to broaden the meaning of "necessary works". Furthermore, it is subject to qualifications imposed by related statutes of individual provinces.

A number of statutes do not deal directly with contracts but simply describe certain kinds of conduct for which they provide penalties. The most important of these statutes is the Criminal Code. Further examples are the Income Tax Act, which imposes penalties for false returns and evasion,[13] and the Customs Act, which exacts penalties for smuggling.[14] Any contract which contemplates the performance of such acts is itself illegal, not because the statute directly prescribes this result (it may say nothing about contracts) but because the common law holds that when the *object* of a contract is illegal by statute, then the *contract* is illegal.

Provincial statutes require licensing or registration of various classes of business and professional people, such as moneylenders, partnerships, real estate agents, investment advisors and stock brokers, optometrists, and public accountants.[15] It is a good defence to an action brought by any of them in the attempt to collect his accounts or fees that he has not been properly registered. In *Kocotis v. D'Angelo*[16] an electrician sued for work done and materials supplied. The customer pleaded in defence that the electrician was not licensed as an electrical contractor as required by local by-law. The court held that the object of the by-law was to protect the public against mistakes and loss that might arise from work done by unqualified electricians and accordingly that the contract was

---

[12] R.S.C. 1970, c. L-13, ss. 4, 11. See also, Neider v. Carda of Peace River District Ltd. (1962) 25 D.L.R. (3d) 363.

[13] St. of Can. 1970-71-72, c. 63, s. 239.

[14] R.S.C. 1970, c. C-40, ss. 174-182.

[15] See, for example, the following Ontario statutes: Partnership Registration Act, R.S.O. 1970, c. 340, s. 9; Real Estate and Business Brokers Act, R.S.O. 1970, c. 401, s. 3; Securities Act, R.S.O. 1970, c. 426, s. 6; Optometry Act, R.S.O. 1970, c. 335, s. 9; Public Accountancy Act, R.S.O. 1970, c. 373, s. 14; and others.

[16] (1958) 13 D.L.R. (2d) 69. But see Sidmay Ltd. et al. v. Wehttam Investments Ltd. (1967) 61 D.L.R. (2d) 358 for a case in which a mortgagor was required to honour his mortgage obligations even though the mortgagee was a corporation not authorized to lend on mortgages under the Loan and Trust Corporations Act (Ontario).

unlawful. The court would not assist the electrician in his attempt to collect the account.

On the other hand, an action brought *against* a person who has not been licensed will not fail on that ground: the defendant cannot claim that his own misconduct in not complying with a statute is a defence to an action by an innocent person. This result is but an application of a general principle that a person (whether as plaintiff or defendant) will not be permitted to use evidence of his own wrongdoing for his advantage before the courts.

CONTRACTS ILLEGAL BY THE COMMON LAW AND PUBLIC POLICY

The Common Law

Over the years, the common law has condemned certain types of conduct and has granted remedies, usually in the form of damages, to parties aggrieved or harmed by that conduct. Generally this conduct is considered a private wrong or tort, and whenever a contract contemplates the commission of a tort, the contract is illegal.

Among the private wrongs or torts which may conceivably form the subject-matter of an agreement are slander and libel, trespass, deceit (fraud), and incitement to break an existing contract with someone else. In *Wanderers Hockey Club v. Johnson*[17] the plaintiff hockey club learned that Johnson had signed a contract to play for the 1912-13 season with another club managed by Patrick. It persuaded Johnson to enter into a second contract with it for the same season by offering him a higher salary. Johnson tore up his contract with Patrick, but as things turned out he failed to perform his new contract with the plaintiff. It then sued him for breach of contract. The action failed on the grounds that no cause of action can arise out of a wrongdoing; it had been obvious to both parties that the second contract could not be performed without breaking another existing contract.

It may be that the agreement does not have as its primary object the commission of a wrongful act but contains an undertaking by one party to indemnify the other against any damages arising from a private wrong should it be committed in the course of performance. In *Smith v. Clinton,*[18] the English firm of W. H. Smith & Son had agreed to print a weekly newspaper, *Vanity Fair,* for Clinton on the terms that they should have a letter of indemnity from Clinton against claims arising out of publication of libellous matter in the paper. In June, 1907, an article was published containing statements libellous to Parr's Bank. W. H. Smith & Son settled the claim against them by paying Parr's Bank a sum of

---

[17] (1913) 14 D.L.R. 42. See also Fabbi et al. v. Jones (1972) 28 D.L.R. (3d) 224.
[18] (1908) 99 L.T. 840.

money. They in turn sought to recover the money from Clinton, but the action failed because the court refused to assist in the recovery of money to indemnify a wrongdoer.

There is, however, a familiar arrangement in which the law makes an exception. A contract of insurance is neither void nor illegal because it proposes to indemnify a motorist for the damages he may have to pay to third parties as a result of his negligence in the operation of the vehicle; automobile insurance for public liability and property damage is valid. Other policies of insurance have been designed to protect professional people against the consequences of their negligence in the course of practice and such policies are also valid.

In addition, a person may exempt himself from liability for negligence by the terms of a contract. Thus a railway or other carrier may state in its standard form contract for the shipment of goods (bill of lading) that it shall not be liable for damage to goods in excess of a stated amount, whether caused by the negligence of its employees or not. The temptation to stipulate for such exemptions is great, and as a result these contracts are often subject to government regulation.[19]

Public Policy

A contract may be regarded as illegal even though it does not contemplate the commission of a crime or of any of the recognized private wrongs. Public policy alone dictates the result. If the court decides that a particular contract is prejudicial to the interests of Canada, its relations with foreign countries, its national defence, its public service, or the administration of justice within the country, the contract will be declared illegal although the performance of such a contract is neither a tort nor a crime in itself.

An agreement which has the perversion of justice as its object will be illegal on grounds of public policy. A promise to pay a witness either for appearing or for not appearing to give evidence in criminal proceedings is illegal.[20] In *Symington v. Vancouver Breweries and Riefel*,[21] the plaintiff made an agreement with the defendants (who were anxious to see one Ball convicted of illegal manufacture of alcohol) to give evidence which would assure Ball's conviction. A term of the agreement was that the plaintiff should receive from the defendants $1,000 for each and every month of imprisonment called for in the sentence of Ball. As a result of the plaintiff's testimony at the trial, Ball received a sentence of 12 months' imprisonment. The plaintiff received part payment but found it necessary to sue for the balance. The action failed on grounds of public policy and in particular because of the tendency of the agreement to pervert justice. One of the appeal judges noted that Ball might have received a much longer term and

---

[19] See, for example: Railway Act, R.S.C. 1970, c. R-2, ss. 294, 310.
[20] Collins v. Blantern (1767) 95 E.R. 847.
[21] [1931] 1 D.L.R. 935.

that "no doubt the leniency of the court was disappointing." In summarizing, Mr. Justice Martin said in part:

> There is a peculiar and sinister element in this case which distinguishes it from all the others that have been cited to us, *viz.*, that it provides for remuneration upon a sliding scale corresponding in amount to the amount of the sentence secured by the informer's evidence. This is so direct and inevitable an incentive to perjury and other concomitant nefarious conduct that it cannot be in the public interest to countenance a transaction which is dangerous to such an exceptional degree to the administration of criminal justice.[22]

The arrangements by which a person accused of a crime may be released under bail are intended to be fair and humane.[23] Their rationale requires, however, that the party putting up the bail shall stand to suffer the personal loss of forfeiture of the bail money should the prisoner abscond. Accordingly, a promise either by the accused or by a third party to indemnify the party putting up bail is illegal.[24]

The most common crime committed within the business world is embezzlement, the so-called "white-collar crime". It is often committed by persons without previous criminal record who succumb to temptation or personal misfortune and "borrow" funds without permission. On discovery, these wretched individuals usually repent and promise to repay every cent if they are not turned over to the police. In many cases, either through sympathy or in the hope of recovering the loss, the victim of the embezzler agrees to such an arrangement. As charitable as the motives of the injured party may be, it must be emphasized that the embezzler has committed a major crime for which the law demands conviction and punishment, though in fact it may turn out to be lenient in many cases. In failing to inform the police of the commission of the crime, the victim is himself in breach of the criminal law. Accordingly, an agreement to repay the embezzled funds in return for a promise not to carry out a duty to inform the police is an illegal agreement; the promise not to inform is void.[25]

In the above circumstances, the victim is not in fact contemplating the commission of a crime. He may be ignorant of the fact that his failure to inform the police is a wrong. Nevertheless, since the agreement tends to pervert justice, it is illegal. Indeed, the most a businessman can do is to assure the embezzler that if restitution is made, he will testify to that effect as a mitigating factor in the

---

[22] *Ibid.,* at 937.

[23] See Friedland, *Detention Without Trial.* Toronto: University of Toronto Press, 1965; Bail Reform Act, R.S.C. 1970 (2nd Supp.), c. 2.

[24] Herman v. Jeuchner (1885) 15 Q.B.D. 561; Consolidated Exploration and Finance Co. v. Musgrave [1900] 1 Ch. 37.

[25] See: Russell, *Russell on Crime* (12th ed.), pp. 339-41. Turner, ed. London: Stevens & Sons Ltd., 1964; also, U.S. Fidelity and Guarantee Co. v. Cruikshank and Simmons (1919) 49 D.L.R. 674; Keir v. Leeman (1846) 115 E.R. 1315.

court's assessment of the crime. The court considers restitution in these cases to be of great weight in arriving at a just punishment.

Agreements which promote unnecessary litigation amount also to an obstruction of the course of justice. They take up the time of the law courts when more serious matters are awaiting decision.

An incentive sometimes exists to stir up litigation because of its advertising value, on the theory that any kind of publicity is good publicity. In *Dann v. Curzon,*[26] money was promised a party for intentionally creating a disturbance in a theatre and then suing the theatre manager for assault. The scheme was carried out and the summons for assault dismissed. When the theatre management failed to make the promised payment, the parties who had carried out the scheme brought action against him. The action failed on grounds of public policy.

In addition, agreements are illegal if their performance is sexually immoral. Those who have made a business of sponsoring such activities[27] or of publishing pornographic literature[28] have found the courts uncooperative in enforcing their supposed contractual rights.

AGREEMENTS IN RESTRAINT OF TRADE

Types of Restraint

Perhaps the most common reason for business agreements being challenged on grounds of public policy is that they may be in restraint of trade. The courts have long considered competition a necessary element of our economic life, and regard agreements that diminish competition as undesirable. Of the agreements that may be in restraint of trade, some are at worst simply void. Others are illegal, because they are prohibited by the Combines Investigation Act.

Though a contract contains a *restrictive covenant* (a term in restraint of trade) that is found to be against public policy, the term may not invalidate the entire contract. The courts may refuse to enforce the offending term while treating the remainder of the contract as valid.

The following classification of terms is helpful in sorting out the various effects of contracts in restraint of trade:[29]

(a) An agreement between employer and employee in which the employee undertakes that after leaving his present employment he will not compete against his present employer, either by setting up his own business or by taking a position with a competing business.

---

[26] (1911) 104 L.T. 66.

[27] Pearce v. Brooks (1866) L.R. 1 Ex. 213.

[28] Poplett v. Stockdale (1825) 172 E.R. 90.

[29] This basic classification has been adopted by leading English authorities on contract, *viz.,* Cheshire, Fifoot and Furmston, *The Law of Contract* (8th ed.), p. 367, and Anson, *Principles of the English Law of Contract* (23rd ed.), pp. 339-48.

(b) An agreement between the vendor and the purchaser of a business whereby the vendor undertakes not to carry on a similar business which will compete with the purchaser.

(c) An agreement among manufacturers or merchants to restrict output or fix the selling price of a commodity.

The courts make an initial presumption that any term in restraint of trade is against public policy and void. But this presumption is not absolute. It may be *rebutted* (overcome) by the party seeking to enforce the covenant if he can demonstrate that it is a reasonable arrangement between the parties and does not adversely affect the public interest. We may note that public policy is virtually the sole consideration of the courts in judging type-(c) covenants. In types (a) and (b), the interests of the parties themselves are dominant.

Agreements Between Employee and Employer

Of the three types of covenants, it is most difficult to convince courts that covenants between employee and employer restricting the future economic freedom of the employee are reasonable and not in restraint of trade.[30] Frequently there is no equality of bargaining power, and an employer is able to impose terms on an employee which the latter must accept if he wants the position. Later he may find that the covenant, if valid, makes it virtually impossible for him to leave his employer in order to accept another position in the vicinity: he would have to sell his house and move his family to establish himself in another city. In protecting employees by striking down unreasonable restraints, the courts at the same time serve a second public interest — they protect the mobility of labour and thereby encourage the more efficient allocation of human resources.

We must distinguish agreements which try to govern an employee's means of livelihood *after* he leaves his present employment from those in which the employee undertakes not to compete directly or indirectly *while* he remains in the service of his employer. The law recognizes an employee's primary duty of loyalty to his employer, and an absolute promise not to engage in any other business during the term of the employment is valid, whether that business competes with the employer or not. Similar agreements between partners which are operative during the life of the partnership are also binding.

A plaintiff seeking to enforce a restrictive covenant will usually ask the court for the equitable remedy of an injunction to restrain the defendant. A restrictive covenant may be enforced if it can be shown to be reasonable as between the parties and not injurious to the public.

The courts will more readily accept as reasonable certain restraints placed upon an employee who has access to valuable trade secrets or a knowledge of secret processes in his employment[31] or who has acted as the personal represent-

---

[30] Mason v. Provident Clothing & Supply Co. Ltd. [1913] A.C. 724.

[31] Reliable Toy Co. and Reliable Plastics Co. Ltd. v. Collins [1950] 4 D.L.R. 499. For an interesting case that compares covenants both during employment and after termination, see Robinson (William) & Co. Ltd. v. Heuer [1898] 2 Ch. 451.

ative of his employer in dealings with the customers of the business.[32] In such circumstances, a promise by the employee not to work for a competing business or to set up a business of his own after leaving his present employment is more likely to be binding upon him.

Agreements between Vendor and Purchaser of a Business

Often an important asset of a business is its goodwill, that is, the trade and commercial connections that it has established through years of carrying on business under a particular name and in a particular location. The vendor of a business can only realize this value in a sale if he is permitted to covenant with the purchaser that he will do nothing in the future to diminish or destroy the value of what he is selling. He can command a higher price for the business if he is free to covenant with the purchaser that he will not in future enter into any business which is likely to compete with the business he is selling: there will then be no danger that he can attract old customers and thus diminish the value of the business being sold. After the sale, it is important that the law enforce reasonable undertakings of this kind made by the vendor, or else the purchaser will be deprived of a part of the property right which he has purchased.

The law recognizes that the purchaser and vendor of a business may find a mutual advantage in a restrictive covenant, and that such a restraint need not be against the public interest. The vendor's covenant not to compete with the purchaser, as a term in an agreement for the sale of a business, may be enforced if it can be shown that the restrictions placed on the vendor are reasonable in view of the nature of the trade or practice sold.

Whether a particular restriction is so broad that if offends the public interest is for the court to decide. On the one hand, a clause forbidding the vendor ever to enter business again anywhere would, for most types of business, be more than is needed to protect the purchaser and would be considered to deprive the public of the benefits of the vendor's abilities: accordingly, it would be void. On the other hand, a term by which the vendor undertakes for a specified period of time (or perhaps even within his lifetime) not to set up business again within specific geographic limits which reasonably describe the area of competition may well be reasonable in the opinion of a court, and consequently valid. The size of the area and the period of time denied to the vendor vary with the nature of the business.

Illustration:

> A dentist in Saskatoon sells his practice to a young graduate, promising that he will not practise again anywhere in Canada. The retiring dentist has a change of heart, however, and two years later sets up practice in the same city. The other dentist brings an action to obtain a court injunction restraining him from doing so.

---

[32] Fitch v. Dewes [1921] 2 A.C. 158.

In these circumstances a restrictive clause which denies the seller a right to practise anywhere in Canada is in excess of what is necessary to protect the interests of the purchaser. To argue that a covenant in restraint of trade is not against public policy, it is necessary to show at least that it is reasonable between the parties. The scope of this covenant, in view of the nature of a dental practice, is unreasonable, and it is therefore void. The purchaser would fail to obtain his injunction, although if his covenant had been confined to the city of Saskatoon for, say, a period of three years, it would probably have been valid.

With rare exceptions, the courts have refused to take on themselves the task of narrowing to a "reasonable scope" the area within which the seller is not to set up business.[33] The basic objection to narrowing a covenant is that it discriminates in favour of one of the parties: it gives a purchaser who has demanded an unreasonable restriction the benefit of the court's opinion about the maximum area which is not detrimental to the public interest. Accordingly, this possibility ought not to be relied upon in framing the terms of an agreement. If a restrictive clause is held to be too wide, it is highly unlikely that courts will narrow it to a reasonable scope; the clause will be void and a seller who might otherwise have been bound by a reasonable restriction is free of the restraint. The lesson for the purchaser is that he should demand no more than a reasonable restriction, erring on the conservative side rather than demanding too much.

The case of *Nordenfelt v. Maxim Nordenfelt Guns and Ammunition Co. Ltd.*[34] illustrates how the nature of the business may be important in determining what is a reasonable restriction on the vendor of a business. Nordenfelt had been a manufacturer of guns and ammunition. He transferred his patents and business to Maxim Nordenfelt Guns and Ammunition Co. Ltd. for £287,500 and covenanted that for 25 years he would not engage, except on behalf of this company, either directly or indirectly in the business of a manufacturer of guns or ammunition *or* in any other business competing or liable to compete in any way with the business for the time being carried on by the company. Thereafter, Nordenfelt entered into an agreement with other manufacturers of guns and ammunition, and the plaintiff company brought an action to enforce the covenant. The House of Lords, considering the clause, decided that it could be broken into two parts: first, the promise not to engage in the manufacture of guns or ammunition, and second, the promise not to engage in *any other business* competing or liable to compete with the plaintiff company. The court held that the second promise was an unreasonable restriction and declared it void. But they also held that they could *sever* the second promise from the first and that the first promise was a reasonable restriction. Accordingly, they granted an injunction to restrain Nordenfelt from working for any other business which manufactured guns and ammunition.

---

[33] See Goldsoll v. Goldman [1920] 3 K.B. 571.
[34] [1894] A.C. 535.

We should note that although the courts will not redraft or in any way narrow a restriction that is unreasonable to save it, they will sever an unreasonable restriction from one that is reasonable even if the restrictions occur in the same sentence, provided they are two distinct ideas and can be severed without changing the meaning of the reasonable restraint. In enforcing the restraint concerning guns and ammunition, the court pointed out that improved communications and transportation facilities had enabled orders to be directed to, and filled from, distant sources of supply, and had greatly broadened the market in which competition might be effective in certain lines of business. The decision, though handed down in 1894, recognized that the whole world had become a market in the ammunitions business. In expressing the opinion of the court, Lord Macnaghten set the law in its present mould:

> All interferences with individual liberty of action in trading, and all restraints of trade of themselves, if there is nothing more, are contrary to public policy and therefore void. That is the general rule. But there are exceptions: restraints of trade . . . may be justified by the special circumstances of a particular case. It is sufficient justification, and indeed it is the only justification, if the restriction is reasonable — reasonable, that is, in reference to the interests of the parties concerned and reasonable in reference to the interests of the public, so framed and so guarded as to afford adequate protection to the party in whose favour it is imposed, while at the same time it is in no way injurious to the public.[35]

Agreements among Existing Businesses

Agreements involving two or more businesses to restrict competition among themselves are governed by statute as well as by the common law in Canada.[36] The most effective part of the Combines Investigation Act has been the "conspiracy section,"[37] which has been primarily concerned with price-fixing agreements, including tendering schemes. It provides that contracts among businesses in the same line of activity, or between producing or supplying concerns and their retail outlets, are illegal if they lessen competition *unduly*. The lessening is "undue" if the object of the parties is to eliminate competition.[38] Agreements among businesses to fix prices, restrict output, standardize quality, allocate markets or customers, or prevent the admission of new businesses into the industry, for example, may have the effect of lessening competition unduly. It is not necessarily an offence, however, for businesses to exchange production and sales statistics and credit information, define product standards, agree to co-operate in

---

[35] *Ibid.* at 565.

[36] See Gosse, *The Law of Competition in Canada,* Chapter 1. Toronto: Carswell & Co., 1962; Rosenbluth and Thorburn, *Canadian Anti-Combines Administration 1952-1960,* Chapters 4, 5, 7, 8, 9. Toronto: University of Toronto Press, 1963.

[37] R.S.C. 1970, c. C-23, s. 32. (Sections quoted below refer to this Act.)

[38] Howard Smith Paper Mills Ltd. v. Rex (1957) 8 D.L.R. (2d) 449, at 472-4.

research, or agree to restrict advertising. It may often be difficult to distinguish between those agreements which are in violation of the Act and those which are permitted practice.

A merger of businesses or a monopoly may be illegal under the Act if it takes the form of a business expansion or consolidation whereby competition is lessened ''to the detriment or against the interest of the public, whether consumers, producers or others''.[39] It has been very difficult to obtain convictions in Canada under either the merger or monopoly provisions.[40] We cannot assume that this singular lack of success in obtaining convictions implies a high degree of competition among businesses in this country. In the authors' view, the law will only become effective when major changes are made to our competitions legislation.

The Combines Investigation Act also makes it an offence for a producer or supplier to stipulate in selling to its retail outlets a minimum price at which the article may be sold to the public.[41] This prohibition against *resale price maintenance* is, however, qualified by a provision that the producer does not violate the Act if he refuses to sell to a retail outlet because it uses his article as a *loss leader* or fails to provide a level of servicing which purchasers of such articles might reasonably expect. An article is used as a loss leader when it is sold at a very low price for the purpose of advertising and attracting customers and selling them other articles.

UNFAIR TRADE PRACTICES

In addition to its concern with agreements between or among existing businesses, the Combines Investigation Act prescribes penalties for a limited number of unfair trade practices which might be employed by a single business with a view to enhancing its position in the market. These offences include predatory pricing, discriminatory allowances, and misleading advertising about price.[42] *Predatory pricing* consists in the practice of selling an article at an unreasonably low price with a view to eliminating competitors. *Discriminatory allowances* take the form of rebates, discounts, or price concessions which are not also offered on proportionate terms to competing purchasers. No decisions have been reported on predatory pricing and discriminatory allowances, which may indicate that the

---

[39] Ss. 2, 33.

[40] For two interesting cases in which the government failed to obtain a conviction under the merger provision, see Reg. v. Canadian Breweries Ltd. (1960) 126 C.C.C. 133, and Reg. v. British Columbia Sugar Refining Co. (1960) 32 W.W.R. 577. The case in which a conviction was obtained against a monopoly is Rex. v. Eddy Match Co. (1951) 104 C.C.C. 39 (trial); (1953) 109 C.C.C. 1 (Court of Appeal). Convictions on both merger and monopoly charges were obtained at trial in Reg. v. K.C. Irving Ltd. (1974) 13 C.P.R. (2d) 115. This decision has been reversed on appeal at date of publication.

[41] S. 38 See Reg. v. Moffats Ltd. (1957) 7 D.L.R. (2d) 405; Reg. v. Sunbeam Corporation (Canada) Ltd. (1967) 59 D.L.R. (2d) 321; 62 D.L.R. (2d) 75.

[42] Ss. 34, 35, 36.

sections are difficult to apply. *Misleading advertising about price* consists in a materially misleading misrepresentation to the public concerning the "regular" price of an article; other forms of misleading advertising are dealt with in a separate section of the Act[43] and we shall refer to them again in a later chapter dealing with the contract of sale.[44]

The Act makes the directors and officers of companies personally liable for failure or refusal to co-operate with the Restrictive Trade Practices Commission in its investigation of the affairs of the company.[45] The usual practice has been to prosecute only the corporations for violations of the main provisions of the Act, but there appears to be no reason why the officers of the corporations who were responsible for the agreements could not also be charged; it could be contended that they are party to the conspiracy under the conspiracy section.[46]

QUESTIONS FOR REVIEW

1. Why may it be important to a party to a dispute to show that the contract is merely void and not also illegal?

2. How can we tell whether the intention of the legislature is to make a certain type of agreement illegal as well as void?

3. In what way does the Gaming Act inhibit wagering contracts?

4. What quality must an insurance contract possess to prevent it from being a wager and therefore void?

5. What kinds of business contract may have an element of wagering incidental to the main purpose of the transaction?

6. What exception is there to the rule that an agreement is illegal if it purports to indemnify a person against the consequences of his own wrongdoing?

7. What is the most help an employer can legally offer an employee who has been guilty of a theft?

8. How is the public interest affected in an agreement which stirs up litigation? In an agreement in restraint of trade?

9. State the nature of the restrictive covenant that may occur in each of the following types of contract:
   (a) an employment contract;
   (b) a contract for the sale of a business;
   (c) an agreement between existing businesses.

10. In what ways may businesses "unduly lessen competition" by an agreement among themselves?

---

[43] S. 37
[44] Chapter 17, under "Scope of the Seller's Liability".
[45] S. 42.
[46] In Regina v. Electrical Contractors Association of Ontario and Dent (1961) 27 D.L.R. (2d) 193, the president of a trade association was prosecuted along with the trade association and made subject to a court order prohibiting the continuation or repetition of the offence.

11. A newspaper advertisement reads:

    SPECIAL! SPECIAL!
    For limited time only: $2.98
    Regular price: $12.00

    What facts would determine whether this advertisement is legal?

12. *A* leases an apartment to *B*, a prostitute, for one year. After several months, *B* decides that she does not like the apartment and tells *A* that she intends to break the lease by moving out and paying no more rent. Are *A*'s rights against *B* under the lease different from his rights against other tenants?

13. What is the policy of the law that justifies a stricter view of restraints in employment contracts than in contracts for the sale of a business?

14. In a decision given in 1875, an English judge said, "If there is one thing which more than another public policy requires it is that men of full age and competent understanding shall have the utmost liberty of contracting and that their contracts when entered into freely and voluntarily shall be held sacred and shall be enforced by courts of justice." (Jessel, M.R., in *Printing & Numerical Registering Co. v. Sampson* (1875) 19 Eq. 462.) Explain how a conflict may arise between the attitude represented in this quotation and a willingness on the part of the courts to expand the types of contract that may be void or illegal for reasons of public policy.

15. In a pari-mutuel system, all the bets made on each horse in a race are registered on a machine which calculates the odds in such a way that the total amount of money paid in, less a percentage for expenses, is divided among those who bet on the winning horses. Is it possible for the organization that manages the pari-mutuel system to refuse to account for the money deposited with it, on the grounds that it is a party to a void contract? *N₂*

CASES FOR DISCUSSION

CASE 1

B. Flatt and F. Major made a wager about the spelling of *Cavalleria Rusticana* with the result that Flatt lost. Flatt then gave Major his cheque for $50 in payment. When Major attempted to deposit the cheque in his bank account, he learned that Flatt had instructed his bank to stop payment on it. What are Major's rights? *O*

Would it make any difference if Major had cashed Flatt's cheque with his corner druggist and the druggist was then confronted with Flatt's stop-payment order? *yes*

CASE 2

Rhodes, a civil engineer, entered into an employment contract with Newton Brothers, a firm of engineering consultants located in the borough of Park Forest. In his work, Rhodes acquired an expert knowledge of costs for the purpose of submitting tenders on various types of construction projects and the sources of supply of the necessary materials. He worked almost entirely in the offices of the firm: the partners handled most negotiations with the firm's clients.

Rhodes' contract of employment stated that for a period of five years after the termination of his employment he would not "engage in the professional practice of engineering either alone or in association with or as an employee of any persons within Park Forest or two miles thereof". Park Forest is a residential suburban borough in the largest metropolitan area in the province: there are two other firms of engineering consultants in Park Forest and some two hundred firms in the whole metropolitan area.

Within a few days of terminating his employment with Newton Brothers, Rhodes advised the firm's partners that he considered the restrictive covenant unenforceable and that he intended to open his own office as a professional engineer within Park Forest. Newton Brothers then sued Rhodes to obtain an injunction to restrain him from breaking the contract.

(a) Identify the legal issues present and state the principles that would affect the decision (without coming to a conclusion at this point). *Restraint of trade – legal*

(b) What is the role of public policy in this problem?   *Employer – Employee*

(c) To what extent does the law recognize the respective interests of the employee and employer?

(d) Should the action succeed?

CASE 3

Hall insured the life of his mother, who was residing with him as his housekeeper, for $5,000. He also supported her and paid amounts for her maintenance that equalled or exceeded the costs of a housekeeper's services. He was the proprietor of a successful business.

Hall had purchased this insurance after having been approached in confidence by an agent for the Perpetual Life Insurance Co. The agent had reminded him of his moral obligation to arrange a respectable funeral for his mother when she died. The insurance policy was intended to reimburse Hall for these costs. The annual premium was $225.

Hall paid the premiums for seven years until Mrs. Hall died. The Perpetual Life Insurance Co. then refused to pay Hall the $5,000. Hall sued the insurance company. Discuss the legal arguments available to Hall and to the Perpetual Life Insurance Co. Having in mind the possibility of a failure to recover the face value of the policy, what claim might Hall have made in the alternative when bringing his action? (For reference, see *Harse v. Pearl Life Insurance Co.* [1904] 1 K.B. 558; *Martin v. Sitwell* (1691) 89 E.R. 509.)

CASE 4

While driving his motor car in September, Turner was involved in an accident with another car and suit for damages was threatened against him both by the owner of the other car and by a passenger who happened to be riding with Turner in his car at the time. Turner did not have any automobile insurance.

Before action was started against Turner, Turner transferred to his acquaintance, Brown, the sum of $2,500, representing the balance in his savings account at the Crown Bank. Turner also delivered to Brown a promissory note dated August 15, preceding the accident, for $1,750 made by Turner in favour of Brown and stating on its face that the title to a specified 1975 Ford car (the car which Turner was driving at the time of the accident and which in fact belonged to him) should remain in Brown's name until the note was paid: this "lien note" did not represent any real transaction. The car and the bank balance comprised the sum total of Turner's assets.

In due course a writ was issued against Turner by the owner of the other motor car involved in the accident and a judgment of only $200 was obtained against Turner. The passenger did not sue. Turner then sought to recover the $2,500 he had transferred to Brown, but Brown refused to return the money, alleging that Turner had boarded and roomed with him for four years without ever paying anything. Turner sued Brown for recovery of the money, claiming that he had given Brown the money to hold in trust for him while convalescing from the effects of the accident, and that he had repeatedly demanded its return and been refused. In the course of the trial the court was referred to the following provision in The Criminal Code, R.S.C. 1970, c. C-34:

350. Every one who,
(a) with intent to defraud his creditors,
   (i) makes or causes to be made a gift, conveyance, assignment, sale, transfer or delivery of his property, or
   (ii) removes, conceals or disposes of any of his property, or
(b) with intent that any one should defraud his creditors, receives any property by means of or in relation to which an offence has been committed under paragraph (a),
is guilty of an indictable offence and is liable to imprisonment for two years.

Should Taylor succeed? (For reference, see *Toohey v. Toohey* [1941] 2 D.L.R. 520.)

CASE 5

Mandrake Electric Ltd., manufacturers of small electric appliances such as toasters and electric frying pans, started a "co-operative advertising plan" with their retail dealers across Canada. The essentials of the plan were as follows: Mandrake Electric agreed to pay 50 per cent of the cost of advertisements published by its authorized dealers advertising its products, provided that in such advertisements these products were suitably described to the satisfaction of the manufacturer and that the price designated in the advertisement was not less than the price specified by the manufacturer for use in such advertisements.

At the same time, Mandrake Electric sent out letters to all its retail outlets specifying suggested prices for each of its products, and advising them that in its opinion, the sale of such articles could not be made at a price less than that specified and still permit the retailer a profit. The letters then stated that any retail store selling at a lower price could be considered by Mandrake Electric as using its products as loss leaders and that it would have to reserve the right to decide whether it could continue to supply such articles to the offending store. As a follow-up, company salesmen devoted considerable time to bring recalcitrant retailers into line with others who had adopted the suggested prices.

The Attorney-General for Canada started a prosecution against Mandrake Electric for a violation of sub-sections (2)(b) and (3)(b)(i) of s. 38 of the Combines Investigation Act, R.S.C. 1970, c. C-23. The court was referred to the following parts of s. 38:

(2) No dealer [including manufacturer] shall directly or indirectly by agreement, threat, promise or any other means whatsoever, require or induce or attempt to require or induce any other person to resell an article or commodity . . .

(b) at a price not less than a minimum price specified by the dealer or established by agreement . . .

(3) No dealer shall refuse to sell or supply an article or commodity to any other person for the reason that such other person . . .

(b) has resold or offered to resell the article or commodity
    (i) at a price less than a price or minimum price specified by the dealer or established by agreement . . .

(4) Every person who violates subsection (2) or (3) is guilty of an indictable offence and is liable on conviction to a fine in the discretion of the court or to imprisonment for a term not exceeding two years or to both.

(5) Where, in a prosecution under this section, it is proved that the person charged refused or counselled the refusal to sell or supply an article to any other person, no inference unfavourable to the person charged shall be drawn from such evidence if he satisfies the court that he and any one upon whose report he depended had reasonable cause to believe and did believe

(a) that the other person was making a practice of using articles supplied by the person charged as loss-leaders, that is to say, not for the purpose of making a profit thereon but for purposes of advertising;

(b) that the other person was making a practice of using articles supplied by the person charged not for the purpose of selling such articles at a profit but for the purpose of attracting customers to his store in the hope of selling them other articles;

(c) that the other person was making a practice of engaging in misleading advertising in respect of articles supplied by the person charged; or

(d) that the other person made a practice of not providing the level of servicing that a purchaser of such articles might reasonably expect from such other person.

In defence, Mandrake Electric established: that retailers could advertise Mandrake's products in any other manner and at any other price they wished, without taking advantage of the co-operative plan; that retailers were at liberty to sell Mandrake's products at any price they wished despite the price in a co-operative advertisement; and that it was quite usual for retailers to sell Mandrake's products at less than the price in the co-operative advertising.

Discuss the merits of this defence and offer an opinion about whether it should succeed.

CASE 6

Dadson arrived at Toronto International Airport on a trip from Paris, and on leaving the building at the "Arrivals" level was approached by Carman, the owner and operator of a taxi licensed by the Municipality of Metropolitan Toronto. The airport is in Mississauga, where a by-law forbids taxis not licensed by that municipality to pick up fares in Mississauga. (Mississauga is outside the boundaries of Metropolitan Toronto.)

Dadson, unaware that Carman was not licensed in Mississauga, got in the taxi. On his way to his home in Mississauga, Dadson learned from notices posted inside the cab that Carman did not have a Mississauga licence.

When he arrived home safely, Dadson refused to pay for his ride. Carman sued Dadson in the First Small Claims Court of Peel County (Mississauga). Should he succeed? Give brief reasons for your opinion.

CASE 7

Flanders & Co., a Montreal firm of wine importers, chartered the ship *Bacchus* from its owners, Swan Ltd., to transport a cargo of wine from Madeira to Montreal. The contract of charter party included a term to the effect that the charterer, Flanders & Co., should be liable for an additional $1,000 for each additional day at the port of destination if the unloading of the ship were delayed for any reason. Unknown to either party, the wine was a prohibited product under the federal Food and Drugs Act because of a preservative used its production.

When the ship reached Montreal, customs officers refused permission to unload pending determination of the cargo's compliance with the federal Act. The investigation and report from the government laboratory in Ottawa took ten days; it was determined by customs officials that it would be illegal to import the wine, and the cargo was finally transferred at dockside to another ship for shipment to New York.

When Flanders & Co. refused to pay the additional $10,000 caused by the delay, Swan Ltd., sued for the amount. What defence might Flanders & Co. offer? Would Swan Ltd. succeed? (See *Waugh v. Morris* (1873) L.R. 8 Q.B. 202.)

CHAPTER 9

Grounds Upon Which
a Contract May be
Impeached: Mistake

THE DIFFERENCE BETWEEN VOID AND VOIDABLE AGREEMENTS

Vitiating Elements

In the preceding chapters we have been concerned with the essential elements of
a contract, the *absence* of any one of which will prevent the formation of a contract. In this and the following chapter we shall discuss a number of elements
which are vitiating elements, the *presence* of any one of which may make the
contract voidable or even completely void.

 The difference between voidable and void contracts first arose in our discussion of infants' contracts. The distinction is important throughout the law of contract, and especially in this chapter, for the results that flow from a void contract
may be entirely different from those flowing from a voidable one.

Void Contracts

As we have noted, to decide that a contract is void is to say that in law it was
never formed at all: in this sense calling an agreement a void contract is a contradiction in terms — if it is void, it is no contract. Nevertheless, through custom
and convenience the term has long been used to describe agreements which have
been declared void from the beginning.

 The results flowing from a declaration that a contract is void, although logical, are often surprising and sometimes unjust. If *A* sells goods to *B* and the sale
is declared void, it follows that the ownership never went from *A* to *B*. If *B* still

has the goods, *A* simply recovers them. But if *B* has resold the goods (which in law he did not own) to an innocent third party, the second sale is equally void. Under common law *B* has no greater right to the goods than a thief would have. *B* cannot sell *A*'s goods. Consequently, the third party has not acquired ownership: although he paid fair value for the goods and was unaware of the void sale between *A* and *B,* he must nevertheless restore them to *A.* If he cannot restore them, he must pay damages to *A* equal to their value. The common law recognized no half measures: either *B* acquired title (ownership) and thus could pass title on to a third party, or he did not acquire title and could not destroy *A*'s right to recover his goods from a third party.

Voidable Contracts

It is important at this time to understand that the courts of common law provided little or no contractual remedy for an aggrieved party when a contract was formed as a result of misrepresentation, duress, undue influence, or certain types of mistake. None of these grievances was sufficient reason for saying that the contract was void. The contribution of the courts of equity was in providing a remedy for such grievances. They did so by recognizing an intermediate type of contract which, while not void, might yet be repudiated by the aggrieved party: they created the concept of the *voidable* contract and the related remedy of *rescission.*

In a contract of sale the title to goods passes from *A* to *B* in spite of the existence of misrepresentation, duress, undue influence and a few instances of mistake. In the days when the courts of common law and those of equity existed separately, there was no way by which the victim, *A,* might recover his goods from *B* by appealing to the courts of common law. The courts of equity, on the other hand, were not inhibited by the fact that the common law courts had recognized the contract and that title had passed; if they saw fit they would *set aside*[1] the contract and order the property restored to *A.* In cases where a common law court would say, "There has been a sale and a transfer of title in the goods from *A* to *B;* we will not interfere," a court of equity might say, "We agree that title has been transferred to *B,* but because there is a vitiating element (misrepresentation, for example), we will order that the goods be restored to *A.*" Equity might permit *A* to repudiate the contract if he wished.

On the other hand, equity will only intervene when the dispute concerns the original parties to the contract. As soon as the rights of a third party are affected, it will draw back and leave the parties in their common law position. If, in our example, *B* has resold the goods to an innocent third party, equity will permit the third party to keep them. *A* will have to pursue other remedies, such as damages, that may be available against *B.* Unfortunately, *B* is often impecunious or the

---

[1] The terms *to set aside, to rescind* (obtain rescission), *to avoid, to lawfully repudiate* are used interchangeably to mean the right which the injured party seeks in a voidable contract.

perpetrator of a fraud who has absconded and cannot be found. Since both *A* and the third party are innocent, equity will not decide between them: it will let the loss lie where it has fallen. The third party has received title to the goods at common law, and equity will allow him to retain it. It is important to note, however, that the third party must be *innocent* and have *paid value* for the goods. *B* cannot simply sell the goods to a friend or relative who knows about the fraud worked on *A* and by this means frustrate *A*'s attempt to recover them. Equity will consider such persons as standing in the shoes of the original party, *B*, and may order recovery. Similarly, equity will not permit a party who has received the goods *as a gift* to retain them against the victim of fraud, undue influence, or duress. Thus if *B* has made a gift of the goods to *C*, *A* may recover them from *C* whether *C* is innocent of the fraud or not.

As we shall see, a contract may sometimes be voidable because of mistake, but we must be careful: sometimes mistake has the effect of making a contract voidable and other times of making it void.

Summary

Illustrations:

> (a) *A* sells goods to *B* under a contract which is subsequently held to have been *void* from the outset for one of the reasons described later in this chapter: *A* may recover the goods from *B*. In the event that *B* has already resold the goods to *C*, an innocent third party, *A* may recover them from *C*.

> (b) *A* sells goods to *B* under a contract which is *voidable* for one of the reasons described later: *A* may recover the goods from *B*. If *B* has already resold the goods to *C*, an innocent third party, *A* cannot recover them from *C*.

We can see that where a contract concerns only the two original parties, it may not matter whether the court declares it void or merely voidable. In either event, the court may order the return of property which has passed between the parties. But if the property has passed to an innocent third party, the original owner will seek to have the contract declared void so that he may obtain the return of the property.

THE RESTRICTED MEANING OF MISTAKE

A party sometimes discovers unhappily that a contract he has made is quite different from what he intended — and he wishes to free himself from it. If there is a practical lesson to be gained from a review of the cases on mistake, it is that the possibility of avoiding a contract for this reason is both precarious and unlikely.

Mistake as a reason for avoiding a contractual obligation has had a narrow construction placed upon it in law, and we must guard against using the word in its more general meaning. The sanctity of contracts is an important principle in our society. If our courts permitted their decisions to be influenced by the layman's idea of mistake, there would be a danger that anyone who was for any reason disappointed with the results of a contract might claim mistake and thus avoid the contract. Contractual obligations would then mean little or nothing. In a United States case the judge said in part:

> Contracts are the deliberate and voluntary obligations of parties capable of contracting and they must be accorded binding force and effect. Those who enter into them must understand that they have a meaning and that they cannot lightly be tampered with. . . . The owner of property is supposed to know what it is worth and at least know what he is willing to take for his property. The purchaser may likewise exercise his free will and choice as to whether he will purchase property at a given price. After he has received the property, understanding that he is to pay a fixed price for it, he cannot be compelled to pay a different and greater price simply because the vendor was careless and negligent in the transaction of his own business [and had sold it for too little].[2]

Illustrations:

(a) The owner of a car writes, "I will sell you my car for $890." The offeree then pays the cash price. A few days later the seller realizes that he had intended to quote a figure of $980.

The seller would not succeed if he were to sue for the $90. A reasonable third person without access to the actual state of mind of the two parties at the time of the contract would conclude that they had intended to contract in respect of a specific car at the price mentioned, $890. The only circumstance in which a court might intervene on behalf of an offeror in a situation of this kind would be where the error is an obvious one and it is apparent that the offeree was aware of the error and snapped up the offer.

(b) A novice in stamp collecting sells an ugly-looking one-cent black-on-magenta stamp of British Guiana dated 1856 to another collector for $25. The stamp proves to be a second copy of "the world's rarest stamp".

The contract is binding whether the purchaser is aware of the great worth of his acquisition or not. (At least a part of the fascination of philately derives from this rule.)

A purchaser may prove to be wrong in his estimate of the value of the property. He may have paid a high price because he wrongly supposed that the property would have, or continue to have, a certain use or value; yet the contract will stand. A mistaken motive is not mistake in the eyes of the law. Similarly, if a vendor later discovers that he has sold his property for too little, his self-castigation is not equivalent to mistake.

Mistake as to the law itself is not mistake of the kind that entitles a party to seek rescission of the contract, though in practice the distinction between a mis-

---

[2] Tatum v. Coast Lumber Co. (1909) 101 P. 957 at 960. See also Scott v. Littledale (1858) 120 E.R. 304.

take of fact and a mistake of law can be difficult to draw.[3] In a clear case of mistake as to the law, the maxim, ''Ignorance of the law is no excuse'' would apply; one is bound to know the law or take the consequences.[4]

TYPES OF MISTAKE

Perhaps the most difficult task in the law of contract is to state clearly the circumstances in which the courts will afford a remedy for mistake. The problem has exercised the authors of the leading works on contract.[5] In the opinion of the authors of this book, the most helpful approach recognizes three types of mistakes — common mistake, mutual mistake, and unilateral mistake.[6]

Common mistake arises when both parties understand each other but both are commonly mistaken about certain facts. They are thinking of the same thing and fully intend to make the contract they have made. But unknown to both, the subject-matter of their contract is in fact very different from what they believed it to be. A common mistake is a mistake shared by both parties.

Mutual mistake arises when one party is thinking about one type of subject-matter and the other about another type of subject-matter, and neither party is aware that he is misunderstanding the other. In contrast to common mistake, here the parties do not understand each other. Hence the adjectives ''common'' and ''mutual'' have different meanings in this context.

Unilateral mistake arises when one party is mistaken about an important fact concerning the contract: the other party knows the true fact and is also aware that the first party is mistaken.

COMMON MISTAKE

If the basis of the common mistake is not merely that the subject-matter was in fact different from that contemplated by the parties, but rather that it did not exist at all at the time of the agreement, the resulting contract is void. In *Couturier v. Hastie,*[7] the parties arranged for the sale of a cargo of corn which they supposed at the time to be en route from Salonica to England. Unknown to both parties, the cargo had become overheated and was in danger of spoiling. The ship had had to put into the port of Tunis, and the corn had been sold. An action by the seller to

---

[3] The problem comes to a head in the interpretation of the rights set out in a written document. ''The whole relationship of law and fact remains incoherent and continues to embarrass many branches of English law,'' (Cheshire, Fifoot and Furmston, *The Law of Contract* (8th ed.), p. 638.)

[4] It is, for example, no defence to an action for recovery of money paid under a gaming bet (as permitted under the Gaming Act of Ontario) to claim that the statutory provision is an obscure and little-used one. See McGillis v. Sullivan [1947] O.R. 650 and [1949] 2 D.L.R. 305.

[5] Compare, for example, Anson, *Principles of the English Law of Contract* (23rd ed.), Chapter VIII, and Cheshire, Fifoot and Furmston, *The Law of Contract* (8th ed.), Part IV, Chapter 1.

[6] This classification of mistake follows Cheshire, Fifoot and Furmston.

[7] (1852) 155 E.R. 1250; affirmed by the House of Lords (1856) 10 E.R. 1065.

recover the agreed price for the cargo failed because the contract was held to be void.

This rule, in so far as it applies to contracts for the sale of goods, is incorporated in the Sale of Goods Act which provides that "where there is a contract for sale of specific goods and the goods without the knowledge of the seller have perished at the time the contract is made, the contract is void."[8]

If a common mistake arises because the parties have made a false assumption about a fundamental aspect of the subject-matter but the subject-matter is in existence, their mistake does not render the contract void.[9] The contract may, however, be voidable in equity. The court may set it aside in whole or only in part; rescission is a discretionary remedy to be used as a means of reaching a fair and equitable result. For example, the court may give one of the parties a choice of two specified courses of action. In the English case *Solle v. Butcher,*[10] the contract was for the lease of a flat at a yearly rental of £250. The landlord had renovated the flat substantially, and both parties mistakenly assumed that the renovation had removed the lease from the provisions of the rent-control laws then prevailing in England. In fact, the maximum permissible rent under the law was £140, though the landlord might have obtained permission for a higher rent had he reported the reconstruction of the flat to the rent-control authorities, and applied for and obtained authority to increase the rent, before entering into the lease. After occupying the premises for two years, the tenant sued to recover the amount of rent he had overpaid. Both parties had made a common mistake through their false assumption about a fundamental aspect of the subject-matter; they had believed that they were leasing a flat exempt from rent control, but in fact they were leasing a flat subject to rent control. The court held that the contract was not void but put the tenant "on terms". He was given the choice of either vacating the premises or remaining under a new lease for the remainder of the term of the old lease at the full rent that would be permitted on a new application to the rent-control authorities, but not to exceed £250. In other words the tenant, as plaintiff, failed in his action to recover overpayment of the rent. The fairness of the decision becomes more apparent on looking further into the facts. The tenant had been engaged in the real estate business with the landlord, and before he decided to enter into the lease, which was for one of five flats in the renovated building, he had investigated the rental status of the property as a part of his work and had advised the landlord that in his opinion he could charge £250.

Sometimes the equitable remedy of *rectification* provides an appropriate means of resolving a common mistake. Rectification is a remedy requiring a written document to be altered to express the real intention of the parties. It is only available when the following conditions are satisfied:

---

[8] R.S.N.S. 1967, c. 274, s. 8; R.S.O. 1970, c. 421, s. 7; R.S.B.C. 1960, c. 344, s. 12.

[9] See: Bell v. Lever Bros. Ltd. [1932] A.C. 161; Harrison and Jones Ltd. v. Bunten and Lancaster Ltd. [1953] 1 Q.B. 646; Rose v. Pim [1953] 2 All E.R. 739.

[10] [1950] 1 K.B. 671.

(1) There must be a completed original agreement which was itself free from any ambiguity when made and which clearly expressed the intention of the parties.

(2) There must have been no change in the agreement of the parties in the interval between their completed agreement and its reduction into written form.

(3) The party seeking rectification must be able to convince the court that because of an obvious mistake the written instrument does not embody the terms of the original agreement.

The case of *Rose v. Pim*[11] shows how a court insists upon the satisfaction of these conditions before it rectifies a written instrument. The buyer acted on the strength of a request from his branch in the Middle East to buy five hundred tons of "Moroccan horsebeans described here as feveroles" to be delivered for resale in Alexandria. Both the buyer and his supplier entered into an agreement under the illusion that horsebeans were the same thing as feveroles. The parties first made an oral contract of sale of horsebeans and later incorporated the same terms in a written agreement. They subsequently discovered that horsebeans (the goods ordered) were not the same thing as feveroles and not suitable for the purposes of the buyer. In fact, feveroles are a special medium size of horsebean, more valuable than other types. The buyer sought to have the written contract rectified by changing "horsebeans" to read "feveroles" and then to enforce it on the latter terms. He failed because the subsequent written document *did* accurately express the terms of the prior oral agreement. The mistake was made before the parties had even arrived at their oral agreement. Their oral agreement was for sale of horsebeans, as was the subsequent written agreement. In the course of this judgment, Lord Justice Denning said, "In order to get rectification it is necessary to show that the parties were in complete agreement upon the terms of their contract, but by an error wrote them down wrongly."[12] Rectification having been refused, it was held that the supplier had satisfied the contract by delivering horsebeans.

MUTUAL MISTAKE

The court does not hold that a contract is void because of mutual mistake: rather, it decides between the two meanings claimed by the parties by asking which is the more reasonable. If an offeror makes an offer in certain terms and these are understood by the offeree in a way different from that intended by the offeror, the court will strive to discover the more reasonable interpretation. In some cases it will decide that the meaning given by the offeror to his own words was the more reasonable one. If so, the offeree will be bound on the terms as understood by the offeror. In other cases the court will decide that the offeror was imprudent to use the words as he did and that the offeree interpreted them more reasonably. In that event the offeror will be bound by the contract as the offeree understood it.

---

[11] [1953] 2 All E.R. 739.
[12] *Ibid.* at 747.

In *Lindsey v. Heron*[13] the seller asked the buyer, "What will you give me for 75 shares of Eastern Cafeterias of Canada?" The buyer said he would make inquiries and then make an offer. Later in the day he replied, "I will give you $10.50 a share for your Eastern Cafeterias." The seller replied, "I accept your offer." The seller delivered the shares for his Eastern Cafeterias of Canada Ltd. and received a cheque in full payment. Subsequently, the buyer realized that Eastern Cafeterias Ltd. and Eastern Cafeterias of Canada Ltd. were two different companies, and further, that he had the former company in mind when he made his offer to buy the shares. He stopped payment on his cheque. In defending an action by the seller, the buyer claimed that his offer to buy Eastern Cafeterias was ambiguous. He could have meant either company. Since the buyer and seller were talking about different companies, ignorant of the misunderstanding between them, there was never any agreement and no contract was formed.

This defence was rejected by the court. It held that in the light of the unambiguous statement of the seller when he referred to Eastern Cafeterias of Canada, the offer must be construed to refer to those shares. In giving the decision of the court, Mr. Justice Middleton said:

> I think that, judged by any reasonable standard, the words used by the defendants manifested an intention to offer the named price for the thing which the plaintiff proposed to sell, i.e., stock in the Eastern Cafeterias of Canada Limited. Had the plaintiff spoken of "Eastern Cafeterias," the words used would have been ambiguous, and I should find no contract, for each might have used the ambiguous term in a different sense; but the defendants, by use of these ambiguous terms in response to the plaintiff's request couched in unambiguous language, must be taken to have used it in the same sense.[14]

In rare cases the court is faced by an insoluble set of facts: both parties have been equally reasonable (or unreasonable) in the meaning they attributed to the words, and it would be unjust to hold one party to the other's interpretation. The classic example occurred in the case of *Raffles v. Wichelhaus*.[15] The contract was for the sale of cotton to arrive in England from Bombay on board the ship *Peerless*. By a remarkable coincidence two ships called *Peerless* were sailing from Bombay, one in October, the other in December. The seller believed he contracted to sell cotton on the later ship; the buyer believed he contracted to buy cotton on the earlier ship. It was important to the buyer to have early delivery, and when the cotton was delivered from the later ship he refused to accept it or pay for it. The seller sued for breach of contract, and the buyer pleaded mistake in defence. The defence succeeded because the court could not decide which ship *Peerless* was meant. A reasonable man would have been helpless to decide that the contract was for cotton on one ship rather than the other.

---

[13] (1921) 50 O.L.R. 1.

[14] *Ibid.* at 9.

[15] (1864) 159 E.R. 375. See also Angevaare v. McKay (1960) 25 D.L.R. (2d) 521.

As suggested by Mr. Justice Middleton in *Lindsey v. Heron,* two parties may use an ambiguous phrase, both being equally careless, and the court will refuse to decide between them. The practical result, then, is that the position of the defendant is the stronger: the party who tries to enforce the contract will fail. In *Falck v. Williams*[16] a Norwegian shipowner communicated by cable with an Australian ship-broker arranging contracts of carriage for the Norwegian's ships from various ports in the Pacific. To save money, they used a code system in which single words stood for phrases or even whole sentences. The shipowner sent an ambiguous message in code. The court held it could equally have been interpreted that cargo was to be picked up in the Fiji Islands or at Sydney, Australia. The sender of the cable intended the ship to load in the Fiji Islands; the receiver intended the port to be Sydney. In rejecting the shipowner's action for breach of contract, Lord MacNaghten said:

> In their Lordships' opinion there is no conclusive reason pointing one way
> or the other. The fault lay with the . . . [appellant]: if he had spent a few
> more shillings on his message, if he had even arranged the words he used
> more carefully, if he had only put the word "estcorte" before the word
> "begloom" instead of after it, there would have been no difficulty. It is not
> for their Lordships to determine what is the true construction of . . . [the]
> telegram. It was the duty of the appellant as plaintiff to make out that the
> construction which he put upon it was the true one. In that he must fail if the
> message was ambiguous, as their Lordships hold it to be. *If the respondent
> had been maintaining his construction as plaintiff he would equally have
> failed.*[17]

UNILATERAL MISTAKE

About an Essential Term of a Contract

Unilateral mistake is best explained by an example. Suppose *A* offers to sell certain goods to *B*. *A*'s offer is clear and unequivocal; he refers to specific goods, say a quantity of cloth, at a definite price. Unfortunately *B* believes that the cloth has a certain characteristic, namely that it is imported and not domestic; in fact, the cloth does not have this quality and *A* has not represented that it has. Nevertheless, *A* realizes that *B* is mistaken in this respect. In these circumstances he is under no duty to disillusion *B,* and if *B* accepts the offer, he is bound by the contract whether he later discovers his mistake or not. He is subject to the risks of commerce expressed by the Latin maxim *caveat emptor,* "Let the buyer beware." If a seller makes no representation about the quality of his goods, the buyer must take them as he finds them.

On the other hand, the buyer might mistakenly believe that the seller has

---

[16] [1900] A.C. 176.
[17] *Ibid.* at 181 (authors' italics).

made the quality of the cloth (that it is imported) a term of his offer: the buyer believes that the seller is contracting to sell *this imported cloth,* not just *this cloth.* The buyer has misunderstood the scope of the offer rather than the nature of the goods. If the seller realizes this misunderstanding and fails to clear it up, the buyer may subsequently have the contract declared void.

The distinction is subtle in theory: in the first instance, the buyer under-stands the offer correctly but has a mistaken belief about the quality of the *subject-matter* — and he has no remedy; in the second instance, the buyer misunderstands an essential term of the *offer* and believes that the seller is con-tracting that the subject-matter has the quality he desires — and he has a remedy.

In practice we should expect to find the distinction even more difficult, since the court must decide not only the state of mind of the mistaken buyer but also the knowledge of the seller about the buyer's mistake. Fortunately, in most cases it is actually a much easier task, for if the buyer is mistaken about the term of the offer, the seller has usually encouraged the mistake by actively misleading the buyer or by acquiescing in such a way that the court will find him guilty of misrepresentation. In these cases of sharp practice or bad faith, the courts are more easily persuaded to give the buyer a remedy. But when the seller has made no misleading statements and the buyer has simply jumped to his own conclusions about the goods, the buyer is without a remedy. If the court concludes that the parties have agreed in the same terms on the same subject-mat-ter, they are bound. The traditional attitude of the courts has been that if a buyer wishes to be certain that the goods have the quality he wants, he can stipulate that the quality be made a term of the contract.

About the Identity of the Other Party to a Contract

The English case of *Cundy v. Lindsay*[18] decided that unilateral mistake about the identity of the other party may render a contract void. Lindsay, a manufacturer in Ireland, was induced to ship goods on credit to a thief, Alfred Blenkarn. Blenkarn signed an order for goods with an indistinct signature that appeared to be ''Blenkiron & Co.,'' a reputable firm with offices on the same street but at a different number from that of Blenkarn. Lindsay did not check the street number but simply shipped the goods to Blenkarn, who then sold the goods to Cundy for cash and absconded. Cundy was unaware of the fraud. The facts came to light when Lindsay attempted to collect payment: he subsequently sued Cundy for the goods. Lindsay claimed that the sale to Blenkarn was void. The court accepted this argument. It held that as Lindsay intended to sell to ''Blenkiron & Co.'' and only to them, Blenkarn obtained the goods entirely without Lindsay's consent. Thus, there was no contract between Lindsay and Blenkarn, and the ownership of the goods remained with Lindsay: Cundy was required to return them or pay damages.

---

[18] (1878) 3 App. Cas. 459. Note that the order of the names in the case citation does not necessarily indicate who was plaintiff and who defendant, or appellant and respondent. The practice varies in different jurisdictions.

Unfortunately, the decision in *Cundy v. Lindsay* offends the general principle that as between two innocent persons, both victims of a fraud, the loss should be borne by the more careless of the two. Lindsay had shipped goods on credit without a careful check of the street address of Blenkiron & Co., and it was as a result of this carelessness, however slight, that Blenkarn came into possession of the goods. On the other hand, Cundy was completely blameless. As between Cundy and Lindsay we should have expected that it would be Lindsay who would bear the loss, yet such was not the result. The decision that the contract was void led to a hardship upon Cundy. It is not surprising, therefore, that the courts have attempted to limit the application of this case.

In *King's Norton Metal Co. v. Edridge,*[19] once again goods were obtained on credit as a result of a fraud perpetrated on their manufacturer. This time the fraud was effected more shrewdly: a letterhead bearing the picture of a large factory and purporting to be that of a nonexistent firm, Hallam & Co., with international offices, was used by the author of the fraud, one Wallis, to order and obtain goods from the plaintiffs, a firm of metal manufacturers. Wallis resold the goods and absconded. The metal manufacturers, claiming that their contract with Hallam & Co. was void, sought to recover the goods from the innocent purchaser; but the action failed. It was held that they had intended to contract with someone, and since there was no "Hallam & Co.," it could only be with the writer of the letter, even though he was a very different person from the party they had in mind. Accordingly, the court held that the contract was only voidable for fraud and that title to the goods had passed to Wallis. The plaintiff could recover the goods from Wallis while he had them, but Wallis could pass title to an innocent purchaser in the meantime. In other words, the plaintiffs could not recover the goods from the innocent purchaser. The decision is technically distinguishable from *Cundy v. Lindsay* because in the *King's Norton* case there was only one party with whom the vendor might have contracted (Wallis alias Hallam & Co.) and not two separate entities as in *Cundy v. Lindsay* (Blenkarn, and Blenkiron & Co.). Though an innocent party may perhaps be excused for failing to appreciate the significance of this distinction, the *King's Norton* case has the virtue of limiting the application of *Cundy v. Lindsay* to fewer situations.

In *Cundy v. Lindsay* and the *King's Norton* case, the parties dealt by mail at a distance. The same difficulty about identity can occur when the innocent party and the rogue confront each other in person. And unfortunately the same judicial confusion can arise. In 1918 in *Phillips v. Brooks,*[20] the English Court of Appeal held that the plaintiff jeweller intended to deal with the man who appeared in his shop, even though the man falsely identified himself as a reputable and wealthy member of the community whom the jeweller knew by name, but not in person. The contract was voidable and not void. As a result, a subsequent innocent purchaser from the rogue was able to maintain his right to keep the fraudulently obtained pearls, despite the jeweller's claim that he intended to deal only with the reputable named person and not the rogue who had appeared in his shop.

[19] (1897) 14 T.L.R. 98.
[20] [1918-19]All E.R. Rep. 246.

More than a half-century later and after some contradictory decisions, the English Court of Appeal in *Lewis v. Averay*[21] confirmed the reasoning in *Phillips v. Brooks*. In the later case, a rogue had obtained a car, paying for it with a bogus cheque, while impersonating a well-known English movie actor. The Court held the contract was merely voidable and protected an innocent purchaser who acquired the car from the rogue.

Canadian courts have followed the reasoning in *Phillips v. Brooks*. In one case,[22] the facts were very much like those in *Lewis v. Averay*. In another case, the Supreme Court of Canada held that a car-rental company had "consented" to the rental of a car to a rogue who gave a false identity.[23] On this basis, it would appear that innocent subsequent purchasers are better protected when the first transaction takes place face to face than when the transaction takes place through the mails.

About the Nature of a Signed Document

Unilateral mistake arises when a person is induced to sign a document which has been misrepresented to him either innocently or fraudulently. The victim may raise the plea known as *non est factum* ("it is not my doing"). If the court accepts the plea, it is good even against third parties who believe they have acquired rights under the document. In this respect the effect of a successful plea of *non est factum* is similar to the result in *Cundy v. Lindsay:* an innocent third party may suffer. The plea originated in medieval times when most men could not read or write. A man would bind himself to a written document by making a mark or impressing his family seal, but he had to rely on the honesty of the literate party who presented the document to him. If he were later sued for breach of the terms of the document, he could only deny that it was his deed because of the misrepresentation. In medieval times the result was reasonable. The result would still be reasonable today if it were limited in application to illiterate or blind persons.

Unfortunately, the plea of *non est factum* was later extended to literate men who were simply duped into signing documents without reading them. As harsh as the result is from the point of view of innocent third parties who rely on the document without knowledge of the misrepresentation, the signer can none the less escape liability. The doctrine of *non est factum* seems to apply, however, only to unilateral mistake about the *nature* of the document.

Illustration:

B induces *A* to sign a document which he tells *A* is an application to join a society for the advancement of business ethics. *A* does not read the document. *A* in fact signs an undertaking in favour of a third party, *C,* that he

---

[21] [1971] 3 All E.R. 907.

[22] Ellyatt v. Little [1947] 1 D.L.R. 700.

[23] Terry v. Vancouver Motors U-Drive Ltd. and Walter [1942] 1 W.W.R. 503.

will guarantee debts incurred by *B* up to $1,000. On the strength of this guarantee *B* borrows $1,000 from *C*. *B* fails to repay the loan and absconds. *C* sues *A* on his guarantee. *A* may successfully use the defence of *non est factum* to avoid liability. He was misled about the nature of the document.

If, on the other hand, *B* had told *A* that the document he was signing was a guarantee for $500 when in fact it was a guarantee for $1,000, *A*'s mistake is about the *content* but not about the *nature* of the document. Accordingly, the defence of *non est factum* is not available to *A*, and he will be bound by his guarantee for $1,000.

The distinction is as irrational as that drawn between the cases of *Cundy v. Lindsay* and *King's Norton Metal v. Edridge,* discussed above. The innocent third party does not know of the misrepresentation, yet depending on the kind of misrepresentation of which he is unaware, he may or may not be able to enforce the terms of the document. The best that can be said for a distinction between nature and content is that it cuts down the number of cases of injustice to innocent third parties: they will be safe when the court holds that the mistake is only about the content of the document. The distinction is often very difficult to draw, however, and in hard cases will necessarily be somewhat arbitrary.[24]

In *Foster v. Mackinnon,*[25] a person who had placed his signature on a negotiable instrument attempted to avoid liability to a third party, an innocent holder of the instrument. The document had been misrepresented to the signer as a guarantee instead of a negotiable instrument, and the court regarded the difference between these types of document as one of nature rather than of content. The signer pleaded *non est factum* and succeeded in the trial court. On appeal the court held that it was also important to determine whether the signer had been careless in not reading over the document. Since he was "a gentleman far advanced in years," the court of appeal acknowledged that his age might excuse conduct that would be careless in a younger man. The trial court had not considered whether the signer had been careless; the court of appeal, therefore, sent the case back for a new trial to determine whether he had in fact been careless. It said that if the signer had been careless he could not rely on *non est factum,* and would be bound by his careless act.[26] This rule seemed satisfactory: innocent signers, such as illiterate, blind, or infirm persons, who must rely on someone's honesty, would be protected. Other persons would have great difficulty in avoiding liability, for ordinarily it would be careless to sign a document without reading it.

---

[24] See Howatson v. Webb [1908] 1 Ch. 1, where the signer executed a mortgage believing it to be a deed. The documents are very similar: in each instance the signer conveys the title to the piece of land, but in a mortgage he also promises to pay money. The court held that the signer was mistaken only about the content, and not about the nature, of the document, and accordingly he was held liable to an innocent third party to whom the mortgage was assigned.

[25] (1869) L.R. 4 C.P. 704.

[26] The result of the new trial is unreported. In any event it would not affect the statement of the law by the court of appeal: if the signer was found not negligent by the trial court, he would escape liability; if he was found negligent, he would be liable.

Unfortunately, this sensible rule was modified in an important respect in a later case, *Carlisle and Cumberland Banking Co. v. Bragg.*[27] That case held that the signer owes a duty of care to a third party when the document is a negotiable instrument, but *in no other circumstance.* The unhappy result has been that though the signer be utterly careless, he is not bound, provided: (1) he was mistaken about the nature of the document, and (2) the document is not a negotiable instrument. This unsatisfactory development was followed rather blindly by the Supreme Court of Canada[28] and appears to be a statement of our present law on the subject, although the English courts have recently overruled the *Bragg* case.

In *Gallie v. Lee,*[29] a widow 78 years of age signed a deed which she was unable to read because she had just broken her glasses. The deed was supposed to be a gift of her house to her nephew. The dishonest defendant had made the deed out to himself as a sale and subsequently mortgaged the property. The House of Lords rejected the plea of *non est factum* by the widow in her attempt to recover the property. In so doing, it effectively overruled both of the much criticized branches of the decision in *Carlisle and Cumberland Banking Co. v. Bragg.*

In the first place, the House of Lords disapproved of the distinction between nature and content. The judges were more concerned with the effect of the document signed by the widow. Was its effect radically different? Did it entirely change the substance of her obligation? If so, but only then, would the plea of *non est factum* be available.

Secondly, in circumstances where the plea is available, the law lords expressly overruled the *Bragg* case with respect to the effect of careless conduct. They stated that in raising the plea of *non est factum,* the reasonableness of a person in caring for his own welfare may determine the issue: a person who is careless in looking after his or her own affairs will lose the benefit of a *non est factum* plea.

It remains to be seen whether the Canadian courts will follow the improvement in this area of the law brought by the case of *Gallie v. Lee.* Eventually, the Supreme Court of Canada may face the choice of overruling its own decisions in *Prudential Trust v. Cugnet.*

It may be helpful at this point to recall that the arguments available to a person who has signed a document are different from those available to one who has not signed. When the document is signed, the only grounds on which the signer can avoid liability are *non est factum* or the pleas of fraud, undue influence, or duress, discussed in the chapter to follow. As we have seen in Chapter 5, when the document is *not* signed, a party may also be able to avoid liability by showing that he did not have reasonable notice of the terms — a separate legal problem.

---

[27] [1911] 1 K.B. 489. The court reasoned that a necessary ingredient of negligence (as in the law of tort) is that there must be a duty of care owed to someone and that duty must be breached before there can be liability for carelessness. It then went on to argue that the only document which implies a duty of care to prospective third parties is a negotiable instrument.

[28] Prudential Trust Co. v. Cugnet (1956) 5 D.L.R. (2d) 1.

[29] [1971] A.C. 1004.

About the Wording of an Offer

An offeror may write his offer down mistakenly; the offeree realizes that the offeror has made an error and accepts hoping to take advantage of the mistaken terms. This is another instance of unilateral mistake—the offeror is unaware of his mistake, but the offeree is quite aware of it. In these circumstances the court will resist any attempt by the offeree to enforce the contract. In *Webster v. Cecil*[30] the parties had at one time negotiated about the possible sale to Webster of land belonging to Cecil. Cecil had refused Webster's offer of £2,000. Later Cecil wrote to Webster mistakenly offering the land for £1,250, and Webster posted an acceptance by return mail. Immediately after he had mailed the letter, Cecil realized his error and wrote that the price should have been £2,250, but his letter arrived after Webster's acceptance was posted. The court refused Webster's request for specific performance. If Webster had sued for damages for breach of contract, he would have failed as well, for the contract was void, and he could acquire no rights under it.

QUESTIONS FOR REVIEW

1. What are the three types of mistake distinguished in this chapter?
2. In what circumstances will neither party have a remedy for mutual mistake?
3. What is the difference between a void and a voidable contract in so far as a third party is concerned?
4. In what circumstances is a contract void for common mistake? In what circumstances is it voidable for common mistake?
5. What is meant by "snapping up an offer"?
6. Under what circumstances is the remedy of rectification appropriate? What conditions must be satisfied before the court will order rectification?
7. What are the tests to decide whether a plea of *non est factum* will succeed against a third party?
8. In what way is the result in *Cundy v. Lindsay* unsatisfactory? Does the *King's Norton Metal* case cure the problem?
9. May the carelessness of a person who has mistakenly signed a document be relevant in determining whether he can avoid his promises in the document?

CASES FOR DISCUSSION

CASE 1

Brown was the owner of a service station located on a two-lane highway. He learned that a new, four-lane freeway would bypass his service station, and then put it up for sale. Smith purchased the property from Brown for $25,000 and two months later learned that the highway on which it was located would be superseded for the purpose of long-distance traffic by the new highway, to be con-

---

[30] (1861) 54 E.R. 812.

structed within the next four years. Smith then commenced action to have the contract set aside. Should he succeed? (See *Bell v. Lever Brothers, Ltd.* [1932] A.C. 161 per Lord Atkin at 224.)

CASE 2

Brown, acting as an agent for an undisclosed principal, secured an option on a farm belonging to Wright. By the terms of the option agreement Wright undertook for a money consideration of $200 to hold open for six months an offer to sell the farm for $25,000 and not to dispose of it otherwise in the meantime.

After Brown had obtained this and similar options on adjoining property, he disclosed that he was acting for Canada Steel Car Co. Ltd., which would build a large plant in the district. As the company was an important one, the value of the property in the area was generally enhanced. When Canada Steel Car Co. Ltd. sought to exercise its options, Wright refused to convey his property according to the option he had given. Canada Steel Car Co. Ltd. then brought an action against him for specific performance. In defending the action, Wright claimed that Brown's failure to disclose the name of the purchaser induced him to sell at too low a price. Discuss the merits of this defence.

CASE 3

Through the negligence of employees, an airliner engaged for a charter flight caught fire and its passengers were severely injured. Each passenger had signed a contract in the form of a ticket containing a condition that he agreed to exempt the company entirely from any liability for injury to his person or property, whether caused by negligence or misconduct of employees. At common law, a carrier is normally responsible for any loss or injury caused by such negligence. A passenger injured in the fire sued the airline for negligence, claiming that he was not bound by the terms of the contract because he had not read the document, and that the term was written in very fine print which the court would not expect an ordinary, prudent person to read. The court agreed that as a fact there was insufficient notice of the term and that even a prudent person would not have read it. Nevertheless, they held that the passenger was bound by the term and could not recover. Explain. (See, for example, *Luddit v. Ginger Coote Airways Ltd.* [1947] A.C. 233.)

CASE 4

In negotiations preliminary to the sale of Argentine hare skins by Messrs. Colin & Shields to Hartog, the parties had discussed price on the basis of price per skin, the way in which Argentine hare skins are generally bought and sold. Afterwards Colin & Shields wrote to Hartog offering to sell to him 10,000 Argentine hare skins, winters, at 10¼d. per pound. There are approximately three pieces to a pound of Argentine hare skins. When Colin & Shields realized they had mistakenly quoted a price in terms of pounds instead of pieces, they attempted to withdraw their offer, but by this time Hartog had already mailed his letter of acceptance. Colin & Shields refused to deliver the skins on the basis of "per pound" price. Hartog sued for damages for breach of contract of a sale of goods. Should he succeed? (See *Hartog v. Colin & Shields* [1939] 3 All E.R. 566.)

CASE 5

Powell was a middle-aged farmer with a Grade 4 education: he could read only with difficulty. Arthurs, an employee of the Fiduciary Trust Company, visited Powell with a printed form of agreement concerning oil rights in Powell's farm, and urged Powell to sign it. Such agreements do not affect ownership of the surface of the land but give the purchaser the right to remove oil and make minimum necessary use of the surface to bring in drilling rigs, pipes, and other equipment. They usually provide that the owner of the land will receive a royalty, that is, a series of payments during the currency of the agreement varying with the value of the oil removed.

From the conversation, Powell was led to believe that the agreement made the trust company his agent to negotiate royalty contracts with interested oil companies. He believed that the agreement reserved to him a royalty equal to 50% of the value of all oil removed from his land by an oil company, and that the trust company, acting as his agent for the purpose of collecting these royalties, would deduct a maximum annual $1,000 fee from the royalties as reimbursement for its services. These arrangements sounded like a "good deal" to Powell—he had not been offered terms nearly as favourable by anyone else. Arthurs persuaded him to sign the printed form and then took the form away. A year passed before Powell received a copy of it, and he then put it away without examining it.

Several months after receiving his copy, Powell discovered the true significance of the document: instead of merely appointing an agent he had made an outright sale of 50% of the oil rights to Fiduciary Trust Company for the sum of $1,000. In addition, the agreement contained a clause appointing the trust company Powell's agent for the sale of the remaining half of the oil rights. The agreement did not provide for any royalty payments to Powell at all. In fact, because the trust company had bought half the oil rights for so little, it was prepared to part with them for a quick profit. Acting as agent for Powell and selling its own interest as well, the trust company transferred the whole of the oil rights in Powell's farm to Interior Oils Limited for $25,000. Having made a tidy profit on the transaction, Fiduciary Trust Company sent a cheque for $13,500 to Powell in full settlement.

Powell refused to accept the money. He brought an action against both the trust company and the oil company to have the court declare that the transfer was void and that he was still the owner of the oil rights in his farm. At the trial, a conflict of testimony occurred over what Arthurs had said to Powell in their original conversation before Powell signed the agreement. The court accepted the evidence of Powell as being the correct version. Should Powell succeed? What, if anything would have been the significance of additional evidence suggesting that as at the time Interior Oils Limited purchased the oil rights, one of its senior officers had been aware of the circumstances under which Fiduciary Trust Company had obtained its contract with Powell? (For references, see: *Perry and Perry v. Prudential Trust Co. Ltd.* (1958) 11 D.L.R. (2d) 689; *Saunders v. Anglia Building Society* [1970] 3 All E.R. 961; [1971] A.C. 1004.)

CASE 6

Powelson was interested in purchasing a commercial building owned by Samuelson and early in January told Samuelson that he would like to take an option on the building for a period of six months. In pursuit of this objective, Powelson prepared a form of written option agreement in which he set out for himself the opportunity to acquire the building at a price of $60,000: both parties signed the agreement and Powelson paid Samuelson the agreed option price of $500. It was dated January 24 and stated in part, "The term of the option is to be for 171 days from the date hereof, expiring at the hour of 11:50 p.m. on the 24th day of July, next."

On July 23 Powelson advised Samuelson in writing of his decision to exercise the option and to purchase the building for $60,000. In the meantime, property values had increased and Samuelson refused to convey the property, claiming that the option period of 171 days from the date of the document had expired on July 14. Powelson brought an action asking for rectification of the option contract and for specific performance.

Outline the arguments for each of the parties in this dispute and indicate whether the action should succeed.

CHAPTER 10

Grounds Upon Which a Contract May be Impeached: Misrepresentation, Undue Influence, and Duress

INNOCENT MISREPRESENTATION

Distinguished from Fraudulent Misrepresentation

Misrepresentation is a false assertion of fact which induces another party to enter into a contract. If the assertion was made with knowledge of its falsity, or at any rate without an honest belief in its truth, the misrepresentation is fraudulent; if the assertion was made in the belief that it was true, the misrepresentation is innocent. It is the duty of one who has innocently made a misstatement, and who later learns of its falsity, to inform the other party of the true situation if it is not already too late to avoid injury. Innocent misrepresentation becomes fraudulent if the party responsible fails to correct his statement when he is in a position to do so.

Relation to a Subsequent Contract

Misrepresentation takes place in the preliminary bargaining which precedes the actual formation of the agreement, and it need not be made a term of the contract which follows; the court may nevertheless declare the contract voidable and grant the remedy of rescission. In addition, the false assertion may sometimes be regarded as being a term of the contract: the injured party may then claim damages for breach of the term. The two remedies, rescission for misrepresentation and damages for breach of a term, are quite separate. The circumstances of the misrepresentation will determine which remedy is available (or in some cases whether both are available). Often it is difficult to convince the court that the false assertion was embodied in the contract as one of its terms, and in these circumstances the victim should seek his redress by claiming rescission of the contract. In many cases it is advisable to seek each remedy in the alternative; the court may deny damages and still grant rescission.

Remedies

Upon learning the true facts, the party who relied on the misrepresentation may repudiate the contract and free himself from his obligations under it. He must, however, renounce the agreement promptly: if he allows an unreasonable length of time to elapse without repudiating, or else takes further benefits under the contract, he will lose his right to repudiate. In addition, he may bring an action himself to have the contract set aside and to recover money or property in the hands of the other party. If he has sustained out-of-pocket expenses in his performance of the contract before he becomes aware of his right to repudiate, he may be entitled to a money award known as an *indemnity* or *compensation*.[1] The loss thus compensated must arise directly out of his performance of the contract, and the indemnity will not cover nearly as wide a variety of loss as an award of damages.

In *Corbeil v. Appell*,[2] a salesman was engaged by Appell to arrange a sale of Appell's business. The salesman represented to Corbeil, a prospective purchaser, that the gross receipts were from $35 to $40 daily. Corbeil asked if there were any records showing this daily turnover, and the salesman replied that Appell had no records but that the former owners of the business did have such records. Corbeil was introduced to the former owners, who did not produce any records but who confirmed in a general way the information given by the salesman about daily gross receipts. Corbeil then purchased the business, delivering his motor car to Appell at the agreed value of $1,000 as a down payment, and began to operate the business as of February 2, 1949. When he discovered that its revenue did not approach the amount indicated, he repudiated the purchase by letter dated February 8, 1949. He then sued for recovery of his car and damages for loss of its use, alleging fraud. The court held that fraud was not proved by these circumstances but that the contract might still be rescinded for innocent misrepresentation. The purpose of rescission is to restore the parties as nearly as possible to their position before they entered into the contract. Hence Corbeil was entitled to the return of his car and also to *compensation* for its loss of value by depreciation through use or accident. In these circumstances Corbeil was not entitled, however, to *damages,* either on grounds of fraud (a tort) or on grounds of breach of contract; he could prove neither.

The remedy of rescission has one implication that may at first seem surprising: the party who seeks the remedy must himself be both willing and able to make restitution even though he may have been the victim of fraud, duress or

---

[1] Whittington v. Seale-Hayne (1900) 82 L.T. 49.
[2] [1950] 1 D.L.R. 159.

undue influence. Thus, if one has been induced to buy goods on the strength of the seller's false assertion of fact, he might by the time he seeks to repudiate the contract have consumed the goods or else used them in a larger project so that they are unrecoverable, as in the case of building materials. Provided the change has occurred as a consequence of the buyer's treatment of the goods or with his consent, he will have lost his opportunity to rescind the contract. If, however, the goods have merely deteriorated somewhat in value, though they remain of substantially the same character as when purchased, a court may grant rescission on terms that the party seeking it pay compensation for the deterioration.[3]

As we have seen, a party will lose his right to rescind when title to property has passed to an innocent purchaser. The right to rescind will also be lost when a third party has relied on the contract in good faith and when rescission would cause a loss to the third party. Once a company is adjudged bankrupt, shareholders who have subscribed and promised to pay for shares in the company cannot rescind their contracts and avoid paying for the shares by alleging misrepresentation in the prospectus which induced them to buy the shares.[4] Although the contract could have been set aside if the shareholder had acted promptly on learning of the misstatement and before bankruptcy, once bankruptcy or winding-up proceedings have started, it is too late. Creditors of the company may well have extended credit to it on the faith of the shareholders' subscriptions for the price of their shares. In these circumstances the rights of the creditors are given precedence, and the shareholders must pay in the full amount of their subscriptions to the company for the benefit of the creditors.

In contracts for the sale of land, the right to rescission for innocent misrepresentation is lost once the transaction is completed and the title to the property has been transferred. The reasons for this rule are not clear: perhaps it is because of the danger that an outstanding right to rescission would not be apparent to the third party who investigated the ownership of the land and relied on it, say, to extend credit on the security of a mortgage. At any rate it seems firmly established that a court will not grant rescission in such contracts unless the misrepresentation is fraudulent.

Opinion versus Fact

A false assertion is a misrepresentation only if it is made as a statement of fact. Mere statements of opinion do not constitute misrepresentation and afford no remedy for those whom they may persuade. Thus, the attitude of the law is indulgent towards sellers who rhapsodize about their wares. A booksellers' claim that "this is the best textbook in its field" would leave a disillusioned purchaser without any remedy.

We can see most clearly the distinction between an expression of opinion

---

[3] For a fuller discussion, see "Limits to the Rights of Rescission", Cheshire, Fifoot and Furmston, *The Law of Contract* (8th ed.), pp. 263-67.

[4] Oakes v. Turquand (1867) L.R. 2 H.L. 325. In a number of jurisdictions now, however, shares must be issued as fully paid from the outset.

and one of fact by contrasting two statements. If *A* says to *B*, "That property is worth at least $5,000 today," his remarks are no more than an expression of opinion. But if he says instead, "That property cost me $5,000," he has made a representation of fact.

Unfortunately, it is not always so easy to distinguish between statements of fact and opinion, Suppose a merchant wishing to sell some foreign goods says, "In my opinion these goods can be imported under the lower tariff rate in section — of the statute." It later appears that they cannot be imported under that section. In these circumstances the court might hold that the seller merely gave his opinion. But if in the view of the court the merchant is an expert in marketing such goods, or has purported to be one, the court may conclude that he made a misrepresentation; in this context an expert opinion is equivalent to a statement of fact.

The phrase *assertion of fact* normally implies a representation in words, whether oral or written. It is conceivable, however, that conduct not expressed in words may constitute an assertion of fact. If a prospective buyer asks to see goods of a certain specification and in response a seller shows him some goods, the seller may by this conduct have asserted the fact that the goods meet the buyer's specifications.

FRAUDULENT MISREPRESENTATION

Remedies of the Injured Party

We have noted that in most circumstances innocent and fraudulent misrepresentation give a common remedy, because the resulting contract is voidable at the option of the victim. If the misrepresentation is fraudulent, however, the injured party has an additional remedy. He may sue for money damages based upon the tort known as *deceit*.

Money damages for deceit may often be a valuable supplement to rescission. Nevertheless, a contracting party is unwise to assume that the law will always provide adequate compensation for the loss he may sustain as the victim of a fraud; not only must the guilty party be apprehended and a judgment secured against him, but he must also have assets that can be seized to satisfy the judgment.

Prerequisites for an Award of Money Damages

To obtain a judgment for money damages, the onus is on the party alleging misrepresentation to show that it was fraudulent. If he does not prove fraud, the misrepresentation will be presumed innocent. The court will not lightly find a defendant guilty of fraud, with the injury to reputation that follows such a decision. The decision in *Derry v. Peek*[5] has provided a helpful test for fraudu-

---

[5] (1889) 14 App. Cas. 337.

lent misrepresentation. The directors of a proposed tramway company issued a prospectus soliciting subscriptions for shares in the company from the public. The prospectus stated that by its special act of Parliament, the company had the right to use steam power instead of horses. In fact, this "right" was really contingent upon the approval of the Board of Trade, but the directors assumed that approval would be given without question. Unfortunately the Board of Trade refused to give its consent, and the company failed. A shareholder brought this action against the directors for damages on grounds of fraudulent misrepresentation. The action failed because the court was satisfied that the directors had an honest belief in the truth of their statement. Lord Herschell stated his now famous test: "Fraud is proved when it is shown that a false representation has been made (a) knowingly, or (b) without belief in its truth, or (c) recklessly, careless whether it be true or false." The court was not convinced that the facts in this case corresponded with any of these criteria for fraud.

As we have seen in Chapter 4, the courts are now prepared to recognize the possibility of negligent misrepresentation as grounds for damages in tort distinct from fraudulent misrepresentation. The decision in *Hedley Byrne v. Heller*[6] extended the duty of a person making a representation from a duty of being honest to a duty of also being diligent and careful.

A general rule is that a plaintiff will not be granted a remedy he does not claim. If he sues for damages for fraudulent or negligent misrepresentation but does not also ask for rescission of the contract, he can secure only damages; if he fails to prove the fraud or negligence, he receives nothing. On the other hand, if he asks for rescission of the contract because of fraudulent or negligent misrepresentation and fails to prove his case, he may still be granted rescission on grounds of innocent misrepresentation.

Contracts Requiring Utmost Good Faith

In a few classes of contract, the concept of misrepresentation has been enlarged to include a failure to disclose pertinent information. In these contracts, the circumstances are such that one of the parties has access to vital information not available to the other. If this information were known to the other party, he might well change his decision to enter into the contract. It then becomes a duty of the party "in a superior position of knowledge" to declare the facts to the other, so that he may have an adequate idea of the risks which would attach to his obligations under the proposed contract.

The most important contract requiring *utmost good faith* is the contract of insurance: the party seeking insurance must disclose to the insurance company all pertinent aspects of the risk he is asking it to assume so that it may make an informed judgment about whether to provide the insurance coverage requested and fix a rate commensurate with the risk. A person who is applying for life insurance. for example, must disclose everything about his state of health that will be

---

[6] [1964] A.C. 465.

of value to the insurer in deciding whether to accept or reject his application. An insurance company can avoid its obligation to pay the insurance money to his estate or beneficiaries if the insured withheld such information when applying for the insurance. Similarly, an applicant's failure to disclose that he has been refused life insurance by other companies constitutes a breach of good faith and hence a misrepresentation.

The necessity for the utmost good faith in applying for fire insurance is governed by statute in each of the provinces.[7] In *Sherman v. American Insurance Co.*[8] the policy-holder, when applying for fire insurance, failed to disclose that he had had a previous fire and that the insurance company affected had then refused to continue the insurance protection. The insured property was damaged by fire again, and the insurance company refused to pay the insured, alleging these facts. It was held that the insured's conduct constituted a fraudulent omission within the terms of the Insurance Act: the insurance company was not obligated to pay the insurance money.

Another type of contract in which one of the parties typically has special access to information is a subscription for the purchase of shares or bonds in a company. The promoters or directors naturally know more about the company's affairs and prospects than do the investing public from whom they are soliciting subscriptions. Information to investors about a new issue of shares or bonds is usually given to the public in a statement issued by the company called a *prospectus*, or sometimes in other documents such as circulars, letters, or notices published in newspapers. All these documents present tempting opportunities for misrepresentation of a company's financial position by non-disclosure.[9] The various statutes comprising our companies and securities legislation now require a disclosure of information in such documents in sufficient detail that directors, by simply omitting pertinent information, are more likely to be liable for violating the statute than for violating the common law.[10] Indeed, as we shall see in Chapter 29, the securities acts of most of the provinces require that in many instances prospectuses be approved by the provincial securities commission or another government body before the shares can be offered to the public.

We have noted that the buyer of goods must take them with their defects unless their quality has been misrepresented. There are certain qualifications of this doctrine of *caveat emptor* which are discussed in Chapter 16 on the sale of goods. *Caveat emptor*, however, applies only to quality or condition of the

---

[7] See, for example: The Insurance Act, R.S.B.C. 1960, c. 197, s. 208 as amended by St. of B.C. 1969, c. 11; R.S.O. 1970, c. 224, Part IV, s. 122; R.S.N.S. 1967, c. 148, Sched. to Part VII, s. 1.

[8] [1937] 4 D.L.R. 723.

[9] See Gower, *The Principles of Modern Company Law* (3rd ed.), p. 325. London: Stevens & Sons Ltd., 1969. "Contracts to acquire securities, whether from the company itself or from an existing holder, are not within the traditional category of contracts under which there is a positive duty to disclose all material facts. Nevertheless the difference between them and fully-fledged contracts *uberrimae fidei* [utmost good faith] is perhaps more apparent than real. Especially is this so when the content of the prospectus is prescribed by law."

[10] See, for example, The Securities Act, R.S.O. 1970, c. 426, ss. 41, 42, 43, 47, 137.

goods, not to ownership. A seller implies that he has the right to sell goods and to pass clear title free from any claims, simply by offering the goods for sale. His failure to disclose an outstanding claim will entitle the buyer to rescission. Although the buyer's right to rescind arises from a breach of an implied term rather than from a duty to disclose, the result is the same as if utmost good faith about ownership had been required of the seller.

The purchaser of an interest in land has, if anything, less protection against undisclosed faults of the property. If the vendor has made no representations, the purchaser must take it with all its faults. Even if the vendor's ownership is subject to the claims of other persons, he need not disclose these claims. In the absence of representations by the vendor, the law presumes that the vendor offers to sell only the interest he has in the land. The purchaser has no remedy and to protect himself should make a thorough investigaton of title. In some cases, however, the court may willingly imply a representation if the fraud practised is blatant. For example, *A* purports to sell a piece of land to *B* when in fact *A* is only a tenant, not the owner. The court would imply that *A* represented himself as owner, and grant rescission to *B*.

UNDUE INFLUENCE

Undue influence is the domination of one party over the mind of the other party to such a degree as to rob him of his free will. A contract formed as the result of undue influence is voidable at the option of the victim. The victim may only avoid the contract if he acts promptly after he is freed from the domination. If he acquiesces or delays, hoping to gain some advantage, the court will refuse to assist him.

Generally, undue influence arises where the parties stand in a special relationship to each other; one party has a special skill or knowledge causing the other to place his confidence and trust in him. Typical examples of this relationship are doctor and patient, lawyer and client, clergyman and parishioner, parent and child. Sometimes undue influence arises when one party is temporarily in dire straits and will agree to exorbitant and unfair terms because he is desperate for aid.

Illustration:

A whaling ship three years at sea sailed into a thick fog near Bering Strait and ran upon rocks. The coast was barren and the ocean navigable only two months in the year: winter was expected within two or three weeks. Then another ship came along, rescued the crew, and bought the cargo of whale oil at a bargain price, to which the captain of the wrecked ship readily agreed. The owners of the wrecked ship later successfully repudiated the contract for the sale of the whale oil.[11]

---

[11] Post v. Jones (1856) 60 U.S. 618.

The party alleging undue influence must satisfy the court that the circumstances were such that domination was probable. He may do so relatively easily if a special relationship existed: the law presumes that undue influence was exerted in contracts advantageous to the party in the dominant position, as for example in a contract between a doctor and his patient in which the patient promises to pay the doctor more than a usual sum for treatments. The absence of a special relationship makes it rather more difficult for the party alleging undue influence to make his case, but he still may be able to show, for example, that he was in a desperate state of misfortune at the time of the contract.

Once the alleged victim shows that circumstances likely to lead to undue influence existed, the burden shifts to the dominant party. If he is to save the contract, the dominant party must then prove that undue influence was *not* exerted by him. He will often find this task very difficult. The courts are concerned that these circumstances should not be used as a device to exploit the weaker party. Sometimes the advantage taken of weakness on the other side is referred to as "fraud", but as Lord Selborne has put it:

> Fraud does not here mean deceit or circumvention; it means an unconscientious use of the power arising out of these circumstances and conditions; and when the relative position of the parties is such as *prima facie* to raise this presumption, the transaction cannot stand unless the person claiming the benefit of it is able to repel the presumption by contrary evidence, proving it to have been in point of fact fair, just and reasonable.[12]

The most important factors in determining whether there is undue influence are: (a) the degree of domination of the stronger party, and (b) the extent of the advantage he has received (that is, the unfairness of the bargain). The degree of domination is often difficult to ascertain. Domination involves questions of personality; by contrast, unfairness can generally be measured against the market value of the goods or services traded in a contract and is more easily ascertained.

Undue influence is somewhat more difficult to prove in the relationship of husband and wife than in the other relationships referred to, because the law presumes that at various times each party may well desire to confer a benefit on the other without exacting a good "price" in return. In some circumstances, however, undue influence may arise, especially if the husband has persuaded his wife to pledge her separate wealth as security for his business transactions. Two Canadian cases illustrate how undue influence may be found in the husband-wife relationship. In the first, a broker to whom a sum of money was owing either suggested or acquiesced in misrepresentation and cajolery by a husband to secure his wife's promissory notes, payable to the broker. The wife later avoided her liability on the notes.[13] In the second case a wife surrendered to a bank all her extensive separate estate in settlement of her husband's debts, in a series of transactions extending over a period of eight years. She was a confirmed invalid

---

[12] Aylesford v. Morris (1873) L.R. 8 Ch. 484, at 490.

[13] Cox v. Adams (1905) 35 S.C.R. 393.

who had never had any advice that could be called independent, and she had acted in passive obedience to her husband. The only lawyer with whom she had any dealings was the solicitor of the bank and of her husband. The transfers of her property were set aside and recovered for the benefit of her estate.[14]

Sometimes a person chooses of his own free will to confer a benefit on another by contract, but subsequent events bring a change of heart and a claim of undue influence; or the promisor may die, and his executor or heirs may then try to avoid the contract on grounds of undue influence. After the benefit has been promised but before it is actually conferred, the alleged dominant person, relying on the contract, may enter into further obligations. He may, for example, make a contract with a builder to erect a house on a piece of land, relying on an earlier contract with another person to sell him the land at a very low price. A subsequent judgment setting aside the contract for the sale of the land because of undue influence would necessarily cause the dominant party to break the second contract for the construction of the house, and render him liable for payment of damages to the builder.

To avoid such a result whenever undue influence is a possibility, the dominant party should take the precaution of asking the other party to obtain independent legal advice about his rights and duties before making the agreement. Not only will the suggestion to get such advice tend to refute undue influence, but testimony of the independent lawyer, not associated with the transaction, that he explained the nature of the transaction and that the other party freely and with full knowledge made the commitment, will usually be conclusive evidence against the claim. A lawyer, confronted with a situation where undue influence may exist, will almost always send the weaker party to some other completely independent lawyer. The circumstance often arises when a husband brings his wife to sign documents in which she is to guarantee proposed loans for her husband's business. The lawyer will usually suggest several lawyers' names and ask the wife to choose one at random. She will then visit the other lawyer with all relevant documents, have them explained carefully, pay the lawyer for his time, and return with a certificate signed by the lawyer stating exactly what took place in his office. Although this procedure seems overly cautious, it is inexpensive and may save the husband or the creditor untold difficulties later if the possibility of undue influence is raised.

A situation that invites undue influence often arises in contracts of loan. The borrower may be in a financial crisis and desperate for money: he agrees to any exorbitant rate of interest at the time. Later he finds that he cannot repay the debt because the interest is so high: he has all he can do to pay the interest regularly. The result of these loans is almost a form of bondage. In some countries with a poor peasant population, the practice has led to the enslavement of large numbers of people. In India especially, it has become a chronic problem. The common law remedies discussed above are available, of course, but many jurisdictions have recognized that loans present a special problem and have passed statutes to

---

[14] Bank of Montreal v. Stuart [1911] A.C. 120.

provide additional remedies. Among the most important acts are the federal Small Loans Act,[15] which regulates the maximum rate of interest chargeable on loans up to $1,500, and the federal Interest Act,[16] which sets out the method by which interest must be calculated in various types of loans. Several of the provinces have passed acts providing for the relief of debtors generally from highly oppressive transactions.[17]

Undue influence may also arise through fear of prosecution of a near relation.[18] A parent may be prepared to go to great lengths to save his or her child from prosecution for a misdemeanour, and sometimes a person in possession of the necessary evidence has elected not to press for prosecution following a promise of money from the parent. The matter is very close to the criminal offence of blackmail even though no express threat may have been made; presumably such activities would not come to light until the parent dies and the executor refuses to pay, or until the child dies and the possibility of prosecution ceases.

Undue influence is often an issue in disputes not involving contracts: it is frequently raised in cases where a gift has been made and the donor wishes to recover the gift, and perhaps most often where a bequest has been made under a will. Generally speaking, the principles governing undue influence in these circumstances are the same as in contract.

DURESS — *Threat of violence, imprisonment - Coercion*

Duress consists in actual or threatened violence or imprisonment as a means of coercing a party to enter into a contract. The effect of duress is similar to that of undue influence: the contract is voidable at the option of the victim. The threat of violence need not be directed against the party being coerced — it may be a threat to harm his wife, parent, or child.

A situation closely resembling duress arises when one party has possession of the goods of another and wrongfully refuses to return them unless the owner promises to give the wrongful possessor some benefit. Suppose *A* lends his car to *B* for a weekend. When he requests *B* to return it, *B* demands $100. After paying the $100, *A* receives his car. If he wishes to sue *B* for the return of the money, he need not rely on duress; he can more easily prove that there was no consideration for the payment. There was in fact no contract at all. Since the payment was certainly not a gift, *A* would recover his money. In addition, he could recover damages for *B*'s wrongful conduct in refusing to give up the car. Accordingly the remedies available are adequate to protect *A* without using duress as a cause of action.

---

[15] R.S.C. 1970, c. S-11, ss. 2-6.
[16] R.S.C. 1970, c. I-18, ss. 4-10.
[17] See Unconscionable Transactions Relief Act, R.S.M. 1970, c. U20, s. 3; R.S.O. 1970, c. 472, s. 2; Money-Lenders Act, R.S.N.S. 1967, c. 188, ss. 2, 3.
[18] Kaufman v. Gerson [1904] 1 K.B. 591.

Historically, duress was a concept recognized by the common law courts and was narrowly construed in the usual manner of those courts. Today duress is still strictly confined by the courts to the circumstances described above. In contrast, the concept of undue influence was developed by the courts of equity to fill a gap and give remedies in circumstances not encompassed by the concepts of fraudulent misrepresentation and of duress. Consequently, the concept of undue influence is wider ranging and more flexible than the other two concepts and, as Lord Selborne noted, includes circumstances which would not otherwise be called fraud.

QUESTIONS FOR REVIEW

1. What is the difference between innocent and fraudulent misrepresentation?
2. Under what circumstances may it be important for a victim of misrepresentation to show that it was fraudulent?
3. In what circumstance will a court consider the adequacy of consideration as relevant?
4. In what respect is the application of the rule "let the purchaser beware" *(caveat emptor)* modified in our law?
5. Which remedy provides the greater recourse to a victim of misrepresentation — damages or "compensation"?
6. Under what circumstances does the victim of misrepresentation lose his right to rescind?
7. What is a prospectus?
8. Why does the law distinguish a separate category of contracts requiring "the utmost good faith"?
9. If a man sues for damages for fraudulent misrepresentation and the court decides that the misrepresentation was innocent, will it set the contract aside for him? Why should the court adopt this position?
10. What is the difference between undue influence and duress?

CASES FOR DISCUSSION

CASE 1

Watts purchased a car from Botswell Motors Ltd. on a representation of a salesman that the car was new except for some minor use as a demonstrator. Botswell Motors Ltd., however, gave no warranty as to satisfactory performance of the car for any period of time. Two days after his purchase Watts took the car to a garage man, Morris, because of trouble with the gearshift, and learned that the car was not new but had been repainted. In fact, the car had been previously sold to a third party and Botswell Motors Ltd. had taken it back because of alleged defects.

Three weeks after he bought the car Watts wrote a letter to Botswell Motors Ltd. claiming rescission of the contract and offering to return the car on repayment to him of the payments he had made to date on the price. Botswell

Motors Ltd. refused. Watts continued to use the car for a further four months incurring more expense at Morris's garage because of the gearshift. He then commenced action against Botswell Motors. What remedies, if any, are available to Watts?

CASE 2

Smart was Hull's lawyer for many years. The nature of their relationship was such that Smart not only handled legal matters for Hull, but gave him important advice on business matters as well. At one stage, Hull owed Smart about $3,500 for professional services and Smart suggested to Hull that the account could be conveniently settled in full if Hull would transfer his new 33-foot sailboat to Smart. Hull demurred at first, but realizing how indispensable his relationship with Smart had been and how important it was that Smart should continue to respect the confidential nature of his private business affairs, he transferred the sailboat to Smart.

A few months later Hull's son, who greatly enjoyed sailing, returned from a year's post-graduate studies in Europe and persuaded his father to institute proceedings for recovery of the sailboat. Explain how the onus of proof will operate in the resulting legal action, and indicate the probable outcome.

CASE 3

Matheson told Eastman, the owner of a large number of rented houses, that he wished to buy a house containing an extra suite suitable for renting. Eastman showed Matheson one of his houses with a separate basement suite. Matheson liked it and signed a contract to purchase the property from Eastman. Unknown to Matheson the suite was unlawfully rented, because no permit had been obtained to build the suite; nor could a permit be obtained, because the ceiling was lower than the local by-laws allowed. Eastman was aware of these facts when he showed Matheson the house and also that Matheson was ignorant of them. He further realized that Matheson believed the house was being offered as a house with a rentable basement suite, although Eastman had done nothing more than show the house to him after Matheson had made his initial inquiry. Upon learning the true facts, Matheson sued for rescission of the contract and for damages.

Give the argument for both sides and state what the decision should be. (See *Graham v. Legault* [1951] 3 D.L.R. 423.)

CASE 4

In response to an advertisement offering a free trial lesson in modern dancing, Miss Galt, a graduate nurse 22 years of age, entered into a contract with the Modern Dancing Studios for 15 two-hour lessons for $350. Before she had taken all these lessons, the dancing instructor, Valentino, told her that she would become a wonderful dancer if she would go on and that if she agreed to more lessons she would "probably get the bronze medal for dancing". On St. Valentine's Day he gave her a rose, and in the course of a lesson whispered in her ear how wonderfully she danced. She eventually signed a second contract to take another 35 hours of dancing lessons for $650. A new instructor was thereupon assigned to her, and all compliments and personal attentions ceased. Miss Galt brought action for rescission of the contract and return of the $650.

On what ground might such a contract possibly be avoided? Should the action succeed? (For references, see: *Greisshammer v. Ungerer and Miami Studios of Dancing* (1958) 14 D.L.R. (2d) 599; *Gaertner v. Fiesta Dance Studios Ltd.* (1973) 32 D.L.R. (3d) 639.)

CASE 5

Lambert advertised his Mercedes car for sale for $6,200. A rogue introducing himself as Glover called on Lambert in the evening, tried the car and said he liked it. They then went to the apartment of Lambert's fiancée, where in the course of general social conversation the prospective purchaser represented himself as being connected with professional football, where R. A. Glover was a well-known coach. He said he would like to buy the car and take it away that night and wrote a cheque for $6,200 which he signed "R. A. Glover". In response to Lambert's request for some identification be brought out a pass to the local stadium bearing the name of R. A. Glover, a photograph of himself, and an official-looking stamp. Thereupon Lambert transferred his passenger motor-vehicle permit to him and allowed him to take the car. Two days after Lambert deposited the cheque, his bank advised him that it had been forged and that the credit in his account was being cancelled.

A few days later, Adams, who had advertised for a car of this type, received a visit from a man who said he was Lambert and produced a motor-vehicle permit bearing Lambert's name and address. Adams bought the car for $5,400. Within the next three or four days, Adams discovered that the usual driver's manual was missing from the glove compartment and telephoned Lambert to ask for further information about the car. The whole story was then revealed in an excited conversation.

His telephone call proved a fateful one for Adams, because Lambert then brought an action against him for return of the car. Discuss with reasons the probability of this action's succeeding.

CASE 6

X. Turpi Company Ltd. was in financial difficulty and was being pressed by its bank to reduce its loan. As a "solution" to this problem the company's general manager had duplicate invoices prepared for some sales and reported this sales revenue twice in the accounts: the bank continued to extend credit for a further month on the strength of the falsified financial position.

At this juncture Miss Good, the company's accountant, realized what was going on, refused to prepare further financial statements for the bank, and resigned. She then went to the bank manager and reported these matters to him.

The financial position of the X. Turpi Company Ltd. continued to deteriorate. In a desperate move, its officers (including the general manager) approached a local businessman, Rich, to urge him to invest some capital in the company. They showed him a list of the inflated accounts receivable. Rich then went to the company's bank to inquire about its present standing with the bank. The bank manager told him that there was no risk because the company's receivables were comfortably in excess of the bank loan, and intimated that the company's problems were merely those of temporary lack of financing. Rich then guaranteed the company's bank loan and deposited $20,000 in marketable shares as security for his guarantee.

In the course of his regular examination, the auditor for X. Turpi Company Ltd. discovered the falsification in the accounts and insisted on their correction as a condition for expressing an unqualified opinion on the fairness of the company's financial statements. On learning the facts, Rich spent several days at the company's office in the hope of straightening out its tangled affairs. He interviewed several present and former employees, including Miss Good. He then sought to recover the $20,000 in marketable securities he had pledged to the bank. The bank manager advised him that the bank had already sold the shares and applied the proceeds to the liquidation of the company's bank loan.

Rich brought an action against the bank for damages equal to his loss. In defence, the bank pleaded that it owed no duty to him because he was not a customer of the bank. Should his action succeed?

CASE 7

Mrs. McGraw, a young widow of 35, inherited a fruit farm in the Okanagan Valley when her husband died some five years ago. Two years ago, she befriended Mr. Val Lawton, a used-car salesman, and allowed him to operate the fruit farm on the understanding they would live there together when they were married.

Lawton operated the farm at a loss but concealed the mounting debts from Mrs. McGraw by intercepting her mail. He did his business at the Tower Bank, where from time to time he filed statements of largely fictitious assets as a basis for increasing loans. His main security seems to have been an affable and suave appearance, Mrs. McGraw's indulgence, and his long friendship with the bank manager.

The bank took possession of Mrs. McGraw's car when Lawton defaulted in his bank loan: he had offered her car as collateral security, asserting that it was his. Mrs. McGraw was sympathetic when the matter was explained to her at the bank, and she then applied to her credit union to borrow enough money to repay the bank and recover her car. Some three weeks later she returned to the bank with her fiancé Lawton and the money required to get her car back. The bank manager then asked her if she wouldn't mind signing "these bunch of papers," which she obligingly did.

Six months afterwards, the bank claimed from Mrs. McGraw a half year's interest on a mortgage on her fruit farm, and it emerged that the mortgage in question had been among the papers she had signed at the bank. The bank proposed to use the mortgage in substitution for amounts still owing by Val Lawton.

At this juncture Mrs. McGraw terminated arrangements with Lawton, and on the advice of her lawyer brought an action against the Tower Bank. In her action she sought to have the mortgage set aside, and in addition claimed $1,000 damages in tort, as compensation for costs incurred as a result of the wrongful seizure of her car and loss of its use.

Explain with reasons whether, in your opinion, this action would succeed.

CASE 8

Mrs. Sarah Burke was the owner of a 1,000-acre farm in Manitoba. She was 85 years old, inclined to be forgetful, and easily led by her family and persons in whom she had confidence. Her daughter and son-in-law lived with her on the farm.

Kerr, a neighbour of long standing, had for several years been trying to persuade Mrs. Burke to sell him her farm. One afternoon he called on her again for this purpose while she was alone in the house and asked her how much an acre she would want: she replied that she was not anxious to sell and would insist upon as much as $35 an acre. Kerr thereupon drove her to the nearest town in his car and they visited a real-estate agent. He signed an offer to purchase the farm at $35,000 and Mrs. Burke accepted it with her signature.

When Mrs. Burke revealed the afternoon's business to her daughter and son-in-law the same evening, they were greatly disturbed. They prevailed upon her to repudiate the contract, pointing out that she had agreed to a price that would have been appropriate twenty-five years earlier, and that prevailing prices were at least twice as great. The next morning they took her to the family lawyer who prepared a statement of renunciation and delivered it to Kerr.

Explain the nature of the legal remedies that Kerr might seek in these circumstances and discuss the validity of the defences, if any, available to Mrs. Burke. (For reference, see *Knupp v. Bell* (1966) 58 D.L.R. (2d) 466.)

CHAPTER 11

The Requirement of Writing

THE DISTINCTION BETWEEN SUBSTANCE AND FORM

Contractual duties, like all other obligations in law, are abstract concepts. Although we speak of the formation of a contract, we mean it in a legal, not in a physical, sense. The parties must, of course, be aware of the terms of their contract. The contract may exist only in their recollection of the spoken words, or it may be recorded in a written document, on a magnetic tape, or stored in a computer. Thus the *substance*, the terms of the contract, may have a variety of physical *forms* or even no form at all, other than in the minds of the parties. The distinction between the substance of the contract and the form in which it is known to the parties is crucial: we must not confuse the two. For the purpose of this chapter the following categories of form are important:

(a) contracts whose terms are entirely oral;
(b) contracts some of whose terms are oral and some in writing;
(c) contracts whose terms are entirely in writing, whether all in one document or spread through several documents, such as a series of letters.

The terms of a contract remain the same whatever form they may take, but from a practical point of view it is almost always advantageous to have them in written form. In good business practice some record is kept of even the simplest transaction at the time it is made. Of course, the more complicated a contract becomes, the greater will be the convenience of a written record. Human memories are fallible, especially when burdened with many details, and common sense tells us that it is better to trust to written records than to mere memory whenever a contract is complicated or will take effect over a very long time. Many disputes may be avoided by keeping accurate records. At this point, however, we must distinguish between records kept as good business practice and the legal significance of these records. Records that are a valuable aid in business may not satisfy the legal requirement of writing, which we are about to discuss. Furthermore, as we shall see, a business record may even assist the other party in enforcing his claim if he should obtain possession of it.

In disputes before the courts, written evidence of a contract will aid the judge in determining what the terms are and in resolving a conflict of testimony by the parties, each with his own remembered version of the contract. But written evidence does not resolve all problems. Even when the court has ascertained the exact words of the contract, these words themselves may be open to several interpretations, and the court must decide their meaning in the particular contract before it. The interpretation of contracts will be the subject of the next chapter.

At common law, once the terms are ascertained, a contract is equally effective whether it is in writing or merely oral. However, in 1677 the English Parliament passed a peculiar act known as the Statute of Frauds. It was passed apparently for special reasons arising out of the turmoil of the times and was concerned mainly with ownership and the transfer of ownership in land. After the civil war and the restoration of the monarchy, Parliament wished to settle title to real property by eliminating perjured testimony in suits concerning lands — hence the use of the word "frauds" in the title of the Statute.[1] Two sections in the Statute particularly affected contracts, and almost immediately after they came into force judges were unhappy about their effect on this area of the law. The Statute was poorly drafted and did not accomplish its vague purposes. Unfortunately, it became so much a part of the law that it was re-enacted or adopted virtually unchanged in most common law jurisdictions, including those of Canada and the United States. A notable change in the law occurred when England amended the act in 1954: British Columbia has since passed a similar amendment.[2] In the remaining common law provinces the Statute is in force in its original form.

The effect of the Statute of Frauds is to render certain types of contracts unenforceable unless they are in writing. Unfortunately, neither the logic nor the policy used in selecting the types of contracts is observable today. As a result, parties to oral contracts have often been able to avoid their obligations solely because these contracts have been held to come within the scope of the Statute: the contracts might be perfectly valid in every other respect. It has often been said that by defeating the reasonable expectations of parties, the Statute of Frauds promotes more frauds than it prevents. For this reason the courts have striven to limit the application of the Statute wherever possible. The results have not always been logical, but the Statute has certainly been hemmed in by exceptions.

---

[1] See Cheshire, Fifoot and Furmston, *The Law of Contract* (8th ed.) pp. 172 ff.

[2] Statute of Frauds, R.S.B.C. 1960, c. 369, s. 5.

The problem of deciding whether a contract is affected by the Statute of Frauds arises only when an otherwise valid contract has been made. The mere fact that a promise is in writing as required by the Statute does not make the promise binding. There is no contract even to be considered unless all the requirements for the formation of a contract, which we have discussed in earlier chapters, are fulfilled.

THE TYPES OF CONTRACT AFFECTED BY
THE STATUTE OF FRAUDS

A Promise by an Executor or Administrator to Answer Damages out of His Own Estate

The executor or administrator of an estate may discover that a debt owing by the deceased is due at a time when it is not convenient to pay it out of the estate assets, possibly because these assets have not been realized in cash. In these circumstances the executor may promise the creditor that he will pay the debt out of his own money if the creditor does not press his claim, intending to claim a reimbursement from the estate later. The creditor will not be able to enforce the executor's promise unless the executor has expressed it in writing and has signed it.

This class of contract is relatively unimportant because it applies to a narrow group of circumstances. We deal with it first only because we are considering the types of contract affected by the Statute of Frauds in the order in which the Statute lists them.

A Promise to Answer for the Debt or Default or Miscarriage of Another

In attempting to limit the application of the Statute, the courts have distinguished between two types of promise that are similar, a promise of *guarantee* and a promise of *indemnity*. A guarantee is a promise to pay only if the debtor defaults: "If he does not pay you, I will." The creditor must look to the debtor for payment, and only after the debtor has defaulted may the creditor claim payment from the guarantor. In contrast, a person who makes a promise to indemnify a creditor makes himself primarily liable to pay the debt. Accordingly, if it suits his purpose, the creditor may claim from the person who has given the promise to indemnify even when he has given up any rights he had against the party whom the indemnity has accommodated. "Give him the goods and I will see that you are paid," would usually be a promise to indemnify.[3] A promise by a purchaser of a business to its employees to pay back wages owed by the former owner would also be a promise to indemnify.

---

[3] As Cheshire, Fifoot and Furmston point out in *The Law of Contract* (8th ed.) at p. 178, it is the intention of the parties and not their language which determines whether the promise is a guarantee or an indemnity.

The courts have applied this part of the Statute of Frauds only to guarantees. A guarantee must be made in writing to be enforceable, but a promise to indemnify is outside the Statute and is enforceable without being in writing.

Even the class of guarantees which falls within the Statute has been narrowed: the courts have excluded those guarantees incidental to a larger contract where the element of guarantee is only one among a number of more important rights and duties created by the contract. In *Sutton & Co. v. Grey,* [4] Sutton & Co. were stockbrokers and members of the London Stock Exchange with access to its facilities. Grey was not a member, but he had contacts with prospective investors. The parties made an oral agreement by which Grey was to receive half the commission from transactions for his clients completed through Sutton & Co. and was to pay half of any bad debts which might develop out of such transactions. A loss resulted from one of these transactions. Sutton & Co. sued Grey for half the loss according to the agreement. Grey pleaded that his promise to pay half the loss was a guarantee and was not enforceable against him because it was not in writing. The court ruled that the whole arrangement between Sutton & Co. and Grey had been a much broader one than merely guaranteeing the payment of a debt owing by a particular client, and that the Statute of Frauds should not apply. The agreement was thus enforceable, and Sutton & Co. obtained judgment against Grey for half the loss.

A further illustration of this approach concerns the liability of a *del credere agent*. Not only does he arrange the sale of his principal's goods, but he also guarantees payment by the buyer. Upon default of payment he himself must pay for the goods. For this additional service the *del credere* agent receives a higher commission than an ordinary salesman. The courts have held that the main aspect of the contract by which he is employed is an agency relationship and that his promise of guarantee is merely subsidiary. Accordingly, an oral contract for the services of a *del credere* agent (including his guarantee of customers' debts) does not come under the Statute and is enforceable.

In amending the Statute of Frauds in recent years, England and British Columbia have retained the requirement of writing for contracts of guarantee. In addition, British Columbia has done away with the judge-made distinction between indemnity and guarantee by requiring that both types of promises be in writing. [5]

In contrast to the restricted meaning given to the words "debt" and "default", the courts have given the word "miscarriage" a wider meaning. They have interpreted a promise to "answer for the miscarriage of another" to mean "to pay damages for injury caused by the tort of another person," for example by his negligence or fraud. Thus to be enforceable, the promise, "I will pay you for the injury *B* caused you if he doesn't settle with you," must be in writing. On the other hand, the promise, "I will pay you for the injury *B* caused

---

[4] [1894] 1 Q.B. 285.
[5] Law Reform (Enforcement of Contracts) Act, 1954, 2 & 3 Eliz. 2, c. 34, s. 1 (United Kingdom), and Statute of Frauds, R.S.B.C. 1960, c. 369, s. 5.

you if you will give up absolutely any rights you have against *B*,'' is a promise of indemnity and need not be in writing to be enforceable.[6]

An Agreement Made in Consideration of Marriage

A promise to marry need not be in writing to be enforceable: each party to an oral agreement to marry has a right to sue for breach of the promise by the other. But a promise made for which the marriage is consideration must be in writing to be enforceable. "I will give you $10,000 if you will marry my daughter," or, "I will pay the cost of looking after your invalid father if you will marry me," must be in writing to be enforceable.

A Contract Concerning an Interest in Land

Unlike most provisions of the Statute, this provision has received general approval as a necessary protection of property interests. The special qualities of land, in particular its virtual indestructibility, are discussed later, in Chapter 24. These qualities make it important that we be able to ascertain readily the various outstanding interests and claims against land. It is important, therefore to have written records of transactions affecting interests in land verified by the signatures of the parties and available over long periods for inspection by interested persons. To this end we have systems of public records where interested parties may "search" and discover who owns or claims to own the interests that may arise in land.

We must distinguish between contracts concerning land to which the Statute applies and those too remote in their connection with land to be under the Statute. The courts have held that agreements to repair or build a house and to obtain room and board are outside the Statute, while agreements to permit taking water from a well, to lease any land, house, or other building or an apartment are within the Statute. Thus, an agreement to rent an apartment will be unenforceable if not in writing, while an oral agreement to repair the apartment will be enforceable. We discuss the enforceability of leases again in Chapter 25.

England and British Columbia have retained the requirement of writing for contracts concerning interests in land.[7]

An Agreement not to be Performed by Either Party within One Year

The purpose of this part of the Statute is clear enough: Parliament did not wish to trust to memory the terms of a contract which would be performed over a long period of time. Unfortunately, the choice of a definite cut-off date, one year, does not accomplish this purpose — if indeed any provision, no matter how

---

[6] Kirkham v. Marter (1819) 106 E.R. 490. Read v. Nash (1751) 95 E.R. 632.

[7] Law of Property Act, 1925, 15 & 16 Geo. 5, c. 20, s. 40 (United Kingdom), and Statute of Frauds, R.S.B.C. 1960, c. 369, s. 2.

carefully drawn, could accomplish it. The injustice of enforcing a wholly oral contract extending exactly one year while not enforcing a similar contract lasting a year plus a day became evident to the judges immediately after the Statute was passed. Again they strove to cut down the effect of the Statute. They held that the Statute did not apply to a contract, though it might well extend beyond a year, unless the terms of the contract specified a time for performance clearly longer than a year. The effect of this ruling is to exclude from the Statute contracts for an *indefinite* period.

Illustration:

> Ajax Co. Ltd. hires Smith as supervisor for setting up an electronic data-processing system. Although the project may well take longer than a year, it is not certain to do so. Accordingly the contract is outside the Statute and need not be in writing.

On the other hand, if the contract is by its terms to extend beyond one year, it is governed by the Statute even though it may be brought to an end in less than one year.

Illustration:

> The Trojan Co. Ltd. has hired Brown as general manager in an oral contract for two years, provided that either party may bring the contract to an end by serving three months' notice on the other. Brown has been working for the company for some months when he receives one month's notice of dismissal. He will be unable to enforce the term entitling him to three months' notice.

The courts have further interpreted the Statute not to apply to a contract that shows an intention that *one* of the parties should wholly perform his obligations within a year, even though the *other* party will necessarily require more than a year to perform.

Illustration:

> Green agrees to repair promptly a leaking roof on Brown's warehouse for $3,000, the money to be paid in four annual instalments of $750 each. Green completes the repairs within five weeks. At the end of the year Brown refuses to pay, claiming that their oral agreement is unenforceable because performance by him of the act of payment could not be wholly performed within one year. Green can enforce the contract. The court has again excluded the Statute where it can find the slimmest reason for doing so — in this case because the parties intended that one of them, Green, should complete performance within a year, and did so.

Where the obligations of the other party clearly extend beyond the year, the intention that one of the parties should wholly perform within one year must be clear from the terms of the contract or from the surrounding circumstances: it is not enough that he *might* perform within one year. Hence, an oral promise by *A* to pay *B* a sum of money in three years' time if *B* will tutor *A*'s son in accounting until he obtains a professional qualification will not be enforceable, unless it can clearly be shown from the surrounding circumstances that the tutoring was to be done within the succeeding few weeks or months and *not* to continue beyond one year.

The provision of the Statute of Frauds concerning agreements not to be performed within one year illustrates better than any other the absurd lengths to which the courts must go to prevent the Statute from working an injustice. They cannot invariably circumvent the Statute, however, and injustice often results when the plaintiff fails only because the Statute of Frauds bars him. It may be hoped that the remaining provinces will follow the lead of British Columbia in amending the Statute.

Ratification of an Infant's Contract

Contracts requiring ratification by an infant upon coming of age (that is, contracts which are not for a permanent interest in property) must in some jurisdictions be ratified in writing to be enforceable.[8] The requirement of writing does not, however, apply to the other class of minor's contracts which are valid unless disaffirmed: for these contracts, mere acquiescence is sufficient to bind the infant after coming of age.

ESSENTIALS OF A WRITTEN MEMORANDUM

We have discussed the classes of contract affected by the Statute of Frauds. Now let us assume that a contract falls clearly within its scope. What must the memorandum contain in order to satisfy the Statute and permit a party to maintain an action upon the contract? The Statute requires a "note or memorandum" of the contract "signed by the party to be charged" or his authorized agent.

The memorandum must contain all the essential terms of the contract, including the identity of the parties. If the contract is for the sale of land, for example, the memorandum must name the parties, adequately describe the subject-matter (the land), and set out the consideration to be given for it.

Illustration:

A gives *B* a signed offer to purchase Summerhill. *B* accepts by signing. The offer to purchase states the price to be simply $50,000 and does not say how the money is to be paid. In previous conversations the parties had agreed

---

[8] See, for example: Statute of Frauds, R.S.O. 1970, c. 444, s. 7; R.S.N.S. 1967, c. 290, s. 8; also Chapter 7 of this book.

orally that payment should be made $20,000 in cash and $30,000 by way of a ten-year mortgage. The memorandum is insufficient: the method of payment is an essential term and it has been omitted.

If *A* and *B* had previously agreed that the whole price should be paid in cash, then the memorandum would be sufficient, for by naming the price to be paid, without more, they imply that it should be paid in cash at the time the property is transferred.

The Statute of Frauds makes an exception for contracts of guarantee by providing that the consideration for that type of promise need not appear in the writing.[9]

The memorandum need not be wholly contained in one document; several written notes may be taken together to satisfy the requirements of the Statute. No problem arises when one or more of the documents refer directly to the others. The plaintiff will have considerably more trouble if there is no cross-reference within the documents themselves. The courts have gone as far as to hear evidence that a signed letter beginning with "Dear Sir" was contained in a particular envelope which bore the name and address of the plaintiff, and in this way to link the two pieces of paper as a sufficient memorandum.[10] The court justified its decision on the grounds that even without oral evidence, it could reasonably assume that the letter was contained in an envelope: it admitted oral evidence merely to identify the envelope. Thus, the court did not rely solely on the testimony of the parties, a step it will not take. In the words of Baron Blackburn:

> If the contents of the signed paper themselves make reference to the others so as to show by internal evidence that the papers refer to each other, they may be all taken together as one memorandum in writing . . . but if it is necessary, in order to connect them, to give evidence of the intention of the parties that they should be connected, shown by circumstances not apparent on the face of the writings, the memorandum is not all in writing, for it consists partly of the contents of the writings and partly of the expression of an intention to unite them and that expression is not in writing.[11]

Illustration:

> *A* wrote to *B* on May 4 saying that he would give $1,000 for *B*'s estate and at the same time stating the terms in detail. *B* wrote back in a signed letter addressed to *A*, "I will accept your offer of May 4." The agreement is enforceable by either party. The two letters may be taken together as providing the necessary written evidence because they relate to each other and contain all the terms.

---

[9] See, for example: R.S.B.C. 1960, c. 369, s. 6; R.S.O. 1970, c. 444, s. 6; R.S.N.S. 1967, c. 290, s. 7.

[10] Pearce v. Gardner [1897] 1 Q.B. 688.

[11] Blackburn, *A Treatise on the Effect of the Contract of Sale*, p. 47. London: W. Benning & Co., 1845, as quoted in North Sea Trawl... Pearl ... 1962, 120 E.R. 777, per Williams, J., at 782.

The Statute requires that the note or memorandum be signed *by the party to be charged*. Only the person who is to be sued need have signed the document; the plaintiff need not have signed it. On the other hand, if only the plaintiff has signed, he cannot enforce the contract against the other party. It is the defendant's signature that the Statute requires.

The courts have been lenient in prescribing what amounts to a sufficient signature — it need not be in the handwriting of the defendant. A printed name will suffice as long as it is intended to validate the whole of the document. A letterhead on an invoice is designed to authenticate the goods described below it, and suffices; but a letterhead on stationery would probably not be a sufficient signature if the written contents indicated that the letter was to be signed and it was not signed, as when the letter ends with a complimentary closing "Yours truly" and no signature.

THE EFFECT OF THE STATUTE ON CONTRACTS WITHIN ITS SCOPE

What do we mean when we say that an oral contract which falls within the Statute of Frauds is *unenforceable*? First, the contract is not thereby made void. It still exists as a valid contract though a court action to enforce it specifically or to obtain money damages for breach of its terms will fail. Is this not the same thing as to say it is void? The answer is a definite "No," for although no action may be brought on the contract, it may yet affect legal relations between the parties.

Illustration:

P agrees orally to buy Blackacre from V for $5,000 and gives a deposit of $800, the balance to be paid in 30 days.

(a) Suppose P changes his mind and refuses to pay the balance. The Statute of Frauds applies and V cannot enforce the contract. On the other hand, P cannot by court action require V to return the deposit; for although the contract is unenforceable, it is still valid and existing. V may retain the deposit by claiming that it was properly owing and was paid under the contract.

(b) Suppose instead that V refuses to either complete the sale or return the deposit. P can sue successfully for the return of the deposit. The court in these circumstances will not permit V both to repudiate the contract and yet keep the deposit he has received under its terms.

In the above illustration, we can see that although the contract is unenforceable it nevertheless exists, and the court is concerned with the conduct of the parties under it. The court will not permit the party who repudiates the contract to gain a further advantage, in case (a) by allowing him to recover his deposit after his own breach, and in case (b) by permitting him to retain the other party's deposit after his breach. If the contract were found instead to be void, the problem of breach would not arise: there cannot be a "breach" of a void contract. Thus, if the contract had been void, say, for uncertainty (so that the requirement of offer and acceptance were not met), P could recover his deposit whether it was he or V who refused to complete the transaction.

Secondly, as we shall see in Chapter 15, when there is an express term in a contract to pay a specified price for goods or services, an implied term to pay a reasonable price, as in *quantum meruit,* is excluded. Accordingly, even when an oral contract is clearly within the Statute of Frauds, it still exists and governs the price to be paid by its terms. Thus, if *A* performs work for *B* under an oral contract calling for the work to be done over a two-year period for $20,000 payable on completion, since *B* has acquiesced in *A*'s full performance, the court will treat the contract as a unilateral one, accepted by performance: on *A*'s completing his part of the bargain, the price immediately becomes payable by *B* and the Statute does not apply — yet another example of the lengths to which the courts go to prevent the Statute from working an injustice. At the same time, *A* cannot refuse *B*'s tender of $20,000 and sue *quantum meruit* because he believes the work is worth more than the agreed price. The oral contract, although neither party may sue upon it directly for breach, still limits the price *A* may recover.

On the other hand, if after *A* performed three quarters of the work, *B* repudiated the contract and refused to let *A* enter his business premises to complete the work, *B* would be in breach of the oral contract. As we shall also see in Chapter 15, such repudiation by one party permits the aggrieved party, *A*, to treat the contract as being at an end. *A* may now sue *quantum meruit* for the work he has done.

Thirdly, the written memorandum may come into existence *after* the contract has been formed and the memorandum will still satisfy the Statute. As long as the memorandum comes into existence before the action is brought on the contract, it will provide the necessary evidence.

Illustration:

> *P* agrees orally to buy Blackacre from *V*. *P* then refuses to complete the contract, and *V* sends him a letter outlining the contract and demanding that he carry out his obligations. *P* replies by letter saying that he has decided not to go through with the contract referred to in *V*'s letter and that he is not bound since the contract is not in writing. Even though the statements in *P*'s letter were intended as a denial of liability, the two letters taken together would amount to a sufficient memorandum to satisfy the Statute and make the contract enforceable.

Fourthly, a defendant who is sued upon an oral contract must plead the Statute as a defence to the action. If he fails to plead it, the court will decide the case without reference to the Statute. The plaintiff will then succeed if he establishes that the contract, though oral, was validly formed.

Fifthly, an oral contract may effectively vary or even dissolve a prior written contract although the oral contract could not itself be enforced. An oral contract within the Statute is effective as long as a party does not have to bring an action to have it enforced. This result may seem surprising, but it is logical upon careful examination. When an oral contract purports to rescind a previous written contract, an action on the oral agreement to enforce the rescission would fail because its subject-matter (the same as in the previous written contract) is within the Statute. On the other hand, although the oral contract does not comply with the Statute, it still *exists;* for this reason, it successfully rescinds the prior written contract.

Illustration:

> *P* agrees to buy Roselawn from *V* under a written contract containing a promise by *V* to give vacant possession on a certain day. Subsequently, *V* has unexpected difficulty in removing his tenants; he informs *P* that he will not be able to give vacant possession. *P* then finds another property equally suitable to him and available with vacant possession. Rather than get into a dispute the parties make a mutual oral agreement to call off the contract: *P* releases *V* from his promise to transfer Roselawn with vacant possession in return for a release by *V* of *P*'s promise to pay the purchase price. Afterwards *V* succeeds in removing his tenants and sues *P* to enforce the original written contract. *P* may successfully plead that the subsequent oral contract validly terminated the written contract.
>
> On the other hand, the oral contract cannot be sued upon directly. Suppose that in addition to terminating the prior contract *V* had orally agreed to give *P* an option on another property in settlement of *V*'s default in not giving vacant possession. Although the oral contract effectively dissolved the prior written contract, *P* could not sue upon the promise to give an option because otherwise the court would be enforcing an oral promise for an interest in land.[12]

Finally, as we have seen, a party to a contract who has signed a memorandum can himself be sued, whereas he cannot sue the other party who has not signed a memorandum: if the contract were void, neither party would have any rights under it.

THE DOCTRINE OF PART PERFORMANCE

We have examined how the courts struggled to cut down the scope of the Statute of Frauds, severely limiting the circumstances in which it would apply. Nevertheless, even a strict interpretation of the Statute did not prevent it from thwarting a large number of contracts in the common law courts. The courts of equity (often known as courts of conscience) were prepared to go further within their own jurisdiction. These courts were often used in disputes concerning the sale of land because of their special power to grant the remedy of specific performance in such contracts if they felt the circumstances warranted it.[13] Within a few years after the Statute of Frauds was passed, the courts of equity developed and

---

[12] See Morris v. Baron [1918] A.C. 1 for a similar result.
[13] See Chapter 3 and Chapter 15.

applied the doctrine of part performance to contracts concerning an interest in land: if the plaintiff could show that he had begun performance of the contract in reliance on it, the court would accept such performance as evidence of the contract in lieu of a written memorandum. Although the courts of equity and the courts of common law are now fused, our modern courts still employ this doctrine in cases concerning an interest in land.

Not every act of performance under a contract is considered a substitute for a written memorandum. The following conditions must be satisfied before the court will enforce the contract:

(a) As we have seen, the contract must be one concerning land.

(b) The acts of performance must suggest quite clearly the existence of the alleged contract; they must not be ambiguous and just as readily explained as part of a quite different transaction. Thus, a payment of a deposit on the price of land, by itself, while certainly an act of part performance, is not a sufficient substitute for writing: the payment could refer to almost any kind of contract between the parties — a contract for the sale of goods or for services to be rendered.[14] (A preceding illustration has shown that the purchaser may at least obtain the return of his deposit.) However, if the plaintiff has taken possession of the land with the acquiescence of the defendant and has begun to make improvements on it, the court will consider this a sufficient act of part performance to satisfy the Statute. It would be most extraordinary for a stranger to enter on another's land and make improvements unless there were a contract in relation to the land to explain this behaviour.

(c) The plaintiff must perform the acts, not the defendant, and he must suffer a loss by his performance if the contract is not enforced. The plaintiff's performance in reliance on the oral contract and the defendant's refusal to carry out the contract combine to create the hardship which equity recognizes and seeks to remedy.

Once the act of part performance is accepted by the court as sufficient evidence, the contract will be enforced. Even though the act of part performance does not disclose all the terms of the contract, the court will enforce the contract according to the terms orally agreed.

Rawlinson v. Ames[15] illustrates the operation of the doctrine of part performance. Mrs. Ames entered into an oral contract for the lease of a flat to which Rawlinson, the landlord, was to make certain alterations. During the course of the alterations (performed by Rawlinson), Mrs. Ames inspected them and offered suggestions. On completion of the alterations she refused to proceed with the lease, claiming that the agreement was for an interest in land and should have been in writing and signed by her to be enforceable against her. As plaintiff,

---

[14] See Ross v. Ross, Jr. et al. (1973) 33 D.L.R. (3d) 351.
[15] [1925] 1 Ch. 96.

however, Rawlinson was permitted to offer evidence of his part performance in lieu of a written memorandum, and succeeded in his action for breach of contract.

EVIDENCE REQUIRED BY THE SALE OF GOODS ACT

For over two hundred years, from the time of its enactment until 1893, the English Statute of Frauds contained a provision requiring contracts for the sale of goods priced at £10 or more to be evidenced by a written memorandum or by one of three types of conduct. This provision of the Statute of Frauds was repealed and replaced by a similar one in the Sale of Goods Act passed in 1893. When the Canadian provinces adopted the Sale of Goods Act, they followed the English example.

What is a sale of goods for the purposes of the Act? The question is not always easy. Is, for example, a contract in which a carpenter agrees for a stated price to provide materials and erect a garage a contract for *the sale of goods* or a contract for *work and materials?* If it is one for work and materials, it is enforceable without reference to the Sale of Goods Act. If it is one for the sale of goods, to be enforceable it must comply with the requirements which we have just examined. The problem of defining a sale of goods is also of importance for other provisions of the Act, and we shall consider it again in Chapter 16.

The various provinces have translated the £10 minimum into different amounts varying from $30 to $50.[16] Otherwise the wording remained the same as the English wording. When a number of items are purchased at one time, the *aggregate* price of the order is the deciding amount for the purposes of the Act. In *Baldey v. Parker*,[17] Parker visited Baldey's linen shop and bargained for various articles. A separate price was agreed upon for each, and no single article was sold for £10 or more, though the aggregate was considerably more than £10. Later a dispute arose about discounts, and when the goods were delivered, Parker refused them. Baldey brought an action against Parker for breach of contract. He maintained that the price of the articles should be considered item by item so that the amount of each sale was not large enough to come within the Act; and that accordingly the contract, though oral, was enforceable. The court rejected the seller's contention and held that the contract was unenforceable.

The Sale of Goods Act provides: "The price in a contract of sale may be fixed by the contract or may be left to be fixed in a manner thereby agreed, or may be determined by the course of dealing between the parties."[18] In other words, the Act permits consideration to be determined in other ways than by stat-

---

[16] The amount is $40 in Nova Scotia, New Brunswick, and Ontario; $50 in Newfoundland, Manitoba, Saskatchewan, and Alberta; $30 in Prince Edward Island.

[17] (1823) 107 E.R. 297.

[18] See, for example: Sale of Goods Act, R.S.B.C. 1960, c. 344, s. 14; R.S.O. 1970, c. 421, s. 9; R.S.N.S. 1967, c. 274, s. 10.

ing a fixed price. With this exception, the Sale of Goods Act requires the same content in writing as the Statute of Frauds.

Unlike the Statute of Frauds, however, the Sale of Goods Act provides specifically that a party to a contract for the sale of goods who cannot produce the required memorandum may still enforce the contract if he can show one of the following kinds of conduct:[19]

(a) "acceptance" and actual receipt of the goods by the buyer;
(b) part payment tendered by the buyer and accepted by the seller;
(c) something "by way of earnest" given by the buyer to the seller.

(a) We have placed the word "acceptance" in quotation marks because the term has a special meaning in this context. It means any act on the part of the buyer in relation to the goods which recognizes a pre-existing contract of sale. The buyer will have accepted the goods, thus making the contract enforceable against him, when he does anything tantamount to admitting that he has a contract with respect to them. He may be neither satisfied nor willing to keep the goods, and yet if he does anything which recognizes them as goods ordered, he will not be able to claim that the contract is unenforceable for lack of evidence. For example, proof that the buyer has inspected the goods or sampled them to see if they are what he ordered will establish his "acceptance". Of course, he may still protest against the quality of the seller's performance; if the goods are not according to the terms of the contract, he may obtain remedies for breach of the contract. A buyer's remedies are examined later, in Chapter 17.

(b) There may even be some doubt about whether a buyer has made a part payment, and the courts have to decide each case on its own merits. One point is clear: a part payment which will have the effect of making the contract enforceable must be a separate act subsequent to the formation of the contract. Thus, if the buyer agrees to set off a present debt owed to him by the seller as the equivalent of a deposit on the goods, the court will not regard this arrangement as a part payment. In the words of Baron Alderson, ". . . [the buyer] must have done two things; first, made a contract, and next, he must have given something . . . in part payment or discharge of his liability. But where one of the terms of an oral bargain is for the seller to take something in part payment, that term alone cannot be equivalent to actual part payment."[20]

Illustration:

A offers orally to sell his typewriter to *B* for $150. *B* accepts orally and then hands *A* a deposit of $10 which *A* accepts. The act of handing *A* the deposit immediately after the contract was formed is a sufficient act of part payment subsequent to the contract and satisfies the provisions of the Act.

---

[19] R.S.O. 1970, c. 421, s. 5; R.S.N.S. 1967, c. 274, s. 6.
[20] Walker v. Nussey (1847) 153 E.R. 1203 at 1205.

If, instead, *B* had replied, "I'll buy the typewriter at that price if you will deduct the $10 you owe me from the price and consider it as a deposit," and if *A* had agreed to these terms, there would not be sufficient part payment.

We must contrast a sale of goods (moveable, tangible property) with a sale of an interest in land (including the buildings thereon). Part payment is acceptable evidence as a substitute for a written memorandum in contracts for the sale of goods, but is insufficient in contracts for an interest in land.

(c) "Earnest" differs from part payment in that it is not deducted from the price to be paid. Rather it is a token sum (or article) given to seal the bargain. Although the giving of something by way of earnest was common at one time, it is now rarely if ever done, and the reference to the practice remains as a relic in the Act.

Both the Sale of Goods Act and the Statute of Frauds may apply to the same contract. They will both apply, for example, where there is an oral agreement to sell goods which are to be delivered and paid for by instalments over a period of time exceeding one year. Such an agreement may satisfy the requirements of the Sale of Goods Act by virtue of acceptance and receipt by the buyer, or part payment, but it will not comply with the Statute of Frauds because it is an oral contract which neither party can wholly perform within one year. It is therefore unenforceable because of the Statute of Frauds, though not because of the Sale of Goods Act.

The requirement of a written memorandum in the Sale of Goods Act is open to the same criticism as the comparable provision in the Statute of Frauds. In 1937 the English Law Revision Committee complained:

> A man who by an oral contract buys or sells £10 worth of goods cannot . . . [subject to the special conduct accepted in lieu of a memorandum] enforce the bargain, yet a man who orally contracts to do work or to sell shares or to insure property . . . can enforce his bargain, and have it enforced against him *however great the amount involved.*[21]

In 1954, when the English Parliament amended the Statute of Frauds, it also repealed the section in the Sale of Goods Act requiring special types of evidence to enforce contracts for the sale of goods, and British Columbia followed suit in 1958.[22] At the time of writing, the requirements are still in effect for the other common law provinces in Canada.

Many other legal aspects of a contract for the sale of goods exist besides questions of evidence. We shall turn to these later, in Chapters 16 and 17.

---

[21] The Law Revision Committee, *Sixth Interim Report,* 1937 (Reprinted 1955), Cmd. 5449, p. 9 (authors' italics).

[22] Law Reform (Enforcement of Contracts) Act, 1954, 2 & 3 Eliz. 2, c. 34, s. 1 (United Kingdom), and Statute Law Amendment Act, 1958, St. of B.C. 1958, c. 52, s. 17.

CONSUMER PROTECTION LEGISLATION

A growing concern for the protection of consumers in our increasingly complex market for goods and services has resulted in a recent flurry of legislative activity. All the common law provinces have now passed statutes varying both in name and application.[23] These statutes are novel in that they are concerned with the protection of only one party to a consumer contract—the buyer. An example is the Ontario Consumer Protection Act, which covers not only goods but services. The significant sections of this Act with regard to the requirement of writing are section 1 paragraphs (c) and (f) which state, respectively:

> "buyer" means a person who purchases goods for consumption or services under an executory contract and includes his agent, but does not include a person who buys in the course of carrying on business or an association of individuals, a partnership or corporation.

> "executory contract" means a contract between a buyer and seller for the purchase and sale of goods or services in respect of which delivery of the goods or performance of the services or payment in full of the consideration is not made at the time the contract is entered into;

and section 16, which states:

> (1) Every executory contract . . . shall be in writing and shall contain . . . [detailed information about the subject matter of the contract, details of credit arrangements and costs and any warranty or guarantee given].
> (2) An executory contract is not binding on the buyer unless the contract is made in accordance with . . . [subsection (1) among other requirements] and is signed by the parties and a duplicate original copy thereof is in the possession of each of the parties thereto.

These sections are intended to give consumers wide protection in the form of complete disclosure by sellers. Although there are few reported decisions interpreting them,[24] the provinces have passed detailed regulations and set up agencies to hear consumer complaints as well as investigate or even negotiate on the consumer's behalf.

QUESTIONS FOR REVIEW

1. What does it mean to say that a contract "comes within" the Statute of Frauds? What are the types of contracts so affected?

---

[23] See, for example: St. of B.C. 1967, c. 14, as amended; R.S.O. 1970, c. 82; R.S.N.S. 1967, c. 53 as amended by St. of N.S. 1970-71, c. 32.

[24] See, for example: Household Finance Corp. Ltd. v. McEllim et ux. [1970] 5 W.W.R. 187, where a husband and wife were joint signers of a promissory note. Only one copy of the detailed information on credit was given to the husband; plaintiff lender thought this was sufficient. The action was dismissed against both parties because the wife had not received her own copy of the credit information.

2. Explain the criticism that "on the whole they [the provisions of the Statute of Frauds and Sale of Goods Act requiring written evidence] promote rather than restrain dishonesty." (The Law Revision Committee, *Sixth Interim Report,* 1937)
3. For what reasons might a defendant who is sued on an oral contract within the Statute of Frauds not plead the Statute in defence?
4. Give examples of oral promises that are enforceable.
5. In what ways may an unenforceable contract differ from a void one?
6. When a contract must be evidenced by a written memorandum to be enforceable, what facts about the agreement must the memorandum contain?
7. Granted that certain types of conduct may sometimes provide sufficient evidence of a contract, in what respects does a written memorandum still have a practical advantage?
8. State which of the following contracts are affected by the Statute of Frauds or the Sale of Goods Act:

   (a) *A* and *B,* the purchaser and vendor of a piece of land, agree to call off the sale.

   (b) *C* enters into a contract with *D,* a contractor, to build a house for *C.*

   (c) *E* is the proprietor of a business which requires a bank loan. *E*'s father, *F,* advises the bank that if it will lend the money to *E* and *E* does not repay the loan, he (*F*) will.

   (d) *G,* on bended knee, says to Miss *H,* "My dear, will you marry me?" Miss *H* replies, "Oh *G,* yes."

   (e) *J,* having just graduated from a university, goes to work for a large Canadian manufacturing concern. Nothing is said about the duration of his employment.

   (f) *K* agrees to buy a talking parrot from *L,* who has taught the bird to talk. Its price is $100.

9. Are there any circumstances in which an oral contract for the sale of goods may still be enforceable?
10. In *Baldey v. Parker,* if the plaintiff had succeeded, would the application of the Sale of Goods Act have been narrowed or broadened?
11. What does the doctrine of part performance achieve? What points must a plaintiff establish to become entitled to its benefit?
12. Review the facts in Case 11 in Chapter 5. Would the Statute of Frauds affect your decision?

CASES FOR DISCUSSION

CASE 1

On January 15, Trotter made a lease with Logan, signed by both parties, in which Logan undertook to rent his apartment to Trotter at $200 a month for three years, commencing February 1. In March of the same year Trotter and Logan agreed orally that Trotter would pay an additional $15 a month rent upon the completion of certain alterations and repairs to the premises within three months.

Logan completed the alterations and repairs in April, but Trotter refused to pay anything but the $200 a month specified in the lease. In August, Logan sued Trotter for the additional rent.

What points must the court settle in reaching its decision, and what should the decision be? (See *Donellan v. Read* (1832) 110 E.R. 330.)

CASE 2

After being interviewed for a position with Passmore, a lawyer with an established practice, Bidgood, who was just recently called to the bar, received a letter stating: "I offer you a starting salary of $1,000 per month. As we discussed in our conversation, in accepting this offer you agree that for a period of two years after termination of employment you will not engage in law practice within a one-mile radius of my office. If you find this offer satisfactory, please come to the office next Monday morning."

Bidgood reported for work and remained in Passmore's employ for several years. The parties mutually terminated the employment, and Bidgood immediately started a law practice across the street. Can Passmore enforce the promise not to compete? (See *Reeve v. Jennings* [1910] 2 K.B. 522.)

CASE 3

In February, Baldwin Co. Ltd., a woollen manufacturer, contracted to sell 500 pieces of blue serge to Martin Bros., tailors, at a price of $40,000 stated in a written memorandum signed by both parties. After 220 pieces of the cloth had been delivered under the contract, a dispute arose between the parties: Martin Bros. complained of delay in delivery, and Baldwin Co. Ltd. complained of failure to pay for the goods delivered to date. Baldwin Co. Ltd. started legal proceedings against Martin Bros. for the price of the goods delivered, and Martin Bros. counterclaimed for damages for non-delivery.

In August, before the case came to trial, the parties agreed to a settlement and agreed orally to substitute a new contract for the original one, in which Martin Bros. would have an additional three months to pay for the goods and have an option of buying the remaining 280 pieces at the prices specified in the earlier contract. The following November, Martin Bros. paid the amount due on the original 220 pieces of cloth and placed an order for the remaining 280 pieces under the option agreed to in the substituted contract. Baldwin Co. Ltd. refused to deliver these pieces, the agreed price being no longer profitable to them. Martin Bros. then brought an action against Baldwin Co. Ltd. for damages for breach of contract (failure to deliver). Should this action succeed? (See *Morris v. Baron* [1918] A.C. 1.)

CASE 4

Carter left a position where he was earning $30,000 a year to accept a position as general manager of Buildwell Limited at the same annual salary. All negotiations leading up to his appointment were carried on orally between Carter and Webster, the president of Buildwell Limited. Both parties assured each other in various conversations that the employment would last "for life"; they agreed further that each year Carter would receive a bonus, and that if he was not satisfied with it he could terminate his employment, but that the company could not terminate his employment unless he "did something wrong".

Over the succeeding few years Carter's salary was increased from $2,500 to $3,500 per month, and he received in addition annual bonuses of up to $4,000. A letter to Carter announcing his last bonus was signed by both the president and vice-president of the company and included the words, "And we want you to know that with all the experiences we are going through in connection with the business, your efforts are appreciated."

Subsequently Webster died, and immediately thereafter the company dismissed Carter from his position as general manager without explanation, paying him one month's salary. Carter then attempted to go into business for himself but without success. He brought action against Buildwell Limited for wrongful dismissal, claiming breach of his employment contract. Should he succeed? (See *Campbell v. Business Fleets Limited* [1954] 2 D.L.R. 263; *Shaver et al. v. Hamilton Cooperative Creameries Ltd.* [1937] 1 D.L.R. 489.)

CASE 5

The late John Brown, in a conversation with Mrs. Barber, proposed to her that if a house could be found which would be suitable and if she would move into the house, occupy it as a housekeeper and operate it as a rooming house, and take care of him, he would then give her the house on his death. In the following month Mr. Brown purchased a house which he operated as a rooming house until his death five years later. Throughout this period Mrs. Barber served as housekeeper, making the necessary food and other household purchases and turning over to Mr. Brown the balance of the board money received from the tenants. She received no remuneration for these services other than her own board and an occasional allowance for clothing.

Mr. Brown made no provision in his will for Mrs. Barber, and following his death Mrs. Barber brought an action against the executors of his estate for specific performance of his promise. In evidence, Mrs. Barber offered the testimony of her two daughters, her son, and her son-in-law who were present at the time of the original conversation between her and Mr. Brown. The executor contested the action.

(a) What legal considerations are relevant to a decision in this case? State whether Mrs. Barber's action would succeed. (See *Baker v. Guaranty Trust Co.* (1956) 1 D.L.R. (2d) 448; *Maddison v. Alderson* (1883) 8 App. Cas. 467.)

(b) Suppose that instead of remaining in the house until Brown's death, Mrs. Barber and Mr. Brown had decided to part company after Mrs. Barber had served as his housekeeper for three years. At that time Brown wrote and signed a memorandum to Mrs. Barber which stated, "I hereby promise to pay you $5,000 in consideration for the surrender by you of any rights to my house according to our earlier agreement.'' When Brown failed to pay the $5,000 to Mrs. Barber, she sued him for this amount. What defence might Brown offer? Should Mrs. Barber succeed? (For reference, see *Fairgrief v. Ellis* [1935] 2 D.L.R. 806.)

CASE 6

The manager of Jiffy Discount Stores ordered a carload of refrigerators from Colonel Electric Company by telephone. When the refrigerators arrived at the warehouse, the transport employees and Jiffy's employees began unloading them. When about half of them were unloaded, the manager arrived and asked to examine one. An employee uncrated one refrigerator, and after looking it over, the manager stated it was not the right model. He ordered the transport employees to take them back. The refrigerators were returned to Colonel Electric Company, and the company sued Jiffy Discount Stores for breach of contract. It was proved that the manager was mistaken, and the refrigerators did conform to the telephone order. What should the result be? (See *Page v. Morgan* (1885) 15 Q.B.D. 228.)

CASE 7

Pearce offered to buy Greenacre from Vincent for $15,000 and gave Vincent a deposit of $2,000. Vincent accepted orally and promised to arrange a formal transfer of ownership in two weeks. Several days later he discovered that an exit to a new super-highway was to be built along the front of Greenacre, substantially increasing its value. It appeared probable that the purchaser, Pearce, had known about the exit but had not told Vincent. Vincent refused to transfer the land unless Pearce would pay an additional $10,000, and further refused to return the deposit.

Pearce brought an action for specific performance or in the alternative for the recovery of his deposit. What should be the result?

CASE 8

In October, 1970, Nicholson approached Knowles and discussed the purchase from Knowles of a lot of woodland outside the city of Fredericton. Knowles agreed to a price of $12,000, the transaction to be completed on December 1, 1970. Upon payment of a $500 deposit by Nicholson, Knowles gave him the following receipt:

October 12, 1970.

Thomas Nicholson.
Received five hundred and .... xx/100 dollars for purchase of woodland approx. 25 to 30 acres. Balance $11,500. Completion date, December 1, 1970.
$500.

(*signed*) James A. Knowles.

Shortly thereafter, Knowles showed Nicholson the property and walked with him over the lines of the property on three occasions. On one of these occasions they were accompanied by Mrs. Nicholson. Since, however, Knowles was not sure about the actual area he had agreed to sell, he suggested having a survey made. Nicholson then secured a surveyor who, with Knowles' consent, was engaged in blazing and clearing the property lines for about two days. Knowles refused to pay the survey costs of $200 and Nicholson absorbed them.

On December 1, Nicholson went to Knowles' house and advised him that he had come prepared to pay the balance of the price. Knowles told him that he had changed his mind and would not sell the woodland lot.

Nicholson brought an action for specific performance or for damages in the alternative. Indicate with reasons whether the action should succeed.

CASE 9

Brian Kelly, a student in his third year of Commerce & Business Administration, looked after banking arrangements for his older brother Paul, who was in the hair-dressing business, and Paul helped Brian to a significant degree with his tuition and living expenses. Paul Kelly owed the bank $6,000 payable on demand in connection with his business, and as collateral security the bank held some mining shares registered in Paul's name. The bank brought pressure to bear on Paul to repay the loan, and intimated that the shares would have to be sold if repayment were not forthcoming.

At this time Paul prevailed on Brian to go to the bank and sign a form of guarantee to the extent of $4,000 of his (Paul's) indebtedness. Brian signed a printed form presented to him by the bank at the foot of which there appeared the word "(SEAL)" in a place reserved for the affixing of a red gummed wafer, though none was in fact affixed until afterwards by the bank manager. A customer in the bank at the time, known to Brian, also signed as a witness. The printed form included the proviso, "The Bank may deal with the principal debtor, Paul Kelly, and with all his securities as it sees fit."

One year later, Paul failed to respond to a demand by the bank that he repay the loan, and the bank asked Brian to make good his guarantee. Brian protested that he had been led to believe that the shares in the bank's possession were sufficient to repay the loan. The bank manager advised that the shares had since declined in price and were worth only $1,800. When these facts were brought to his attention Brian became upset, and in the belief that without his signature the guarantee would not be enforceable, tore a strip from the bottom of the guarantee and swallowed the portion bearing his signature. When the bank officers present told him that his conduct had been foolish and futile because the witness could still prove that his signature had been on the document, Brian tore off a further portion of paper on which the witness's signature appeared and swallowed that too. At this stage, the police were called in. Brian was told that he would go to jail if he did not immediately sign another guarantee to replace the mutilated one. He eventually did so, and this time a red paper wafer was affixed when he signed.

Brian paid ten monthly instalments of $50 each in reduction of his alleged liability under the guarantee, but failed to pay further amounts. The bank brought an action against him for the balance owing. It produced both the remnant of the first document and the second document as evidence of the guarantee.

(a) Discuss the validity of the defences available to Brian Kelly in these circumstances;

(b) Identify the major issue in the case;

(c) Indicate, with reasons, the probable result of the legal action.

CHAPTER 12

The Interpretation of Contracts

THE RELATIONSHIP BETWEEN FORMATION AND INTERPRETATION OF CONTRACTS

We have seen that the formation of a valid contract requires an offer and its acceptance, consideration, an intention to be legally bound, the capacity to contract, and legality of object. An understanding of these elements is essential to an understanding of contract. But the large majority of disputes, both in and out of court, are over the meaning of the contract, not about its formation. Indeed, very often the reason a party disputes the formation of a contract is that he disagrees about its interpretation.

Illustration:

Smith offers to build a set of kitchen cabinets for Doe for $100, and Doe accepts. The next day Smith appears and asks where the lumber is. Doe says, "You are supposed to supply it." Smith replies, "My price was for the work only, not for the materials."

At this point the dispute may take one of two different courses. The first possibility is that either party may claim that the offer was too vague because it omitted an essential term indicating who should supply the lumber: such an offer is not capable of acceptance, and accordingly no contract is formed. The second possibility is that each side will concede that the agreement "to build a set of kitchen cabinets for $100" is valid, but Smith will claim that the proper meaning is that Doe should supply the lumber, and Doe will claim the contrary. The problem of *construing* or *interpreting* the contract is the subject of this chapter.

We are not dealing here with fraud or deceit, though each party believes passionately that his is the only sensible interpretation of the contract and that the other party must be dishonest to suggest that there is any other. Often a lawyer's most difficult task is to show his client that the view held by the other side has some merit. Only then may the lawyer broach the possibility of a compromise or, if the dispute goes to court, be in a position to counter all the arguments of the other side.

A cynic may observe how strange it is that the interpretation by each party invariably favours himself. We may answer him in two ways. First, either party might well have rejected the terms at the outset had he realized they would be construed less favourably towards him. Words are at best inefficient vehicles for communicating thoughts: they can be ambiguous without the parties realizing it, and people tend to give themselves the benefit of the doubt even when they sense a possible ambiguity. Secondly, contracting parties do not "invariably" find themselves in conflict on questions of interpretation: in the vast majority of contracts no dispute arises because the parties have understood each other.

When parties appear before a court to have a question of interpretation settled, the court must choose the most reasonable meaning that can be attributed to the words in the circumstances. This is no easy task. The difficulties the courts experience with problems of interpretation are responsible for much criticism of the law. Learning that his "sensible and just" interpretation has been ignored, the losing party blames the law, the judge, the dishonesty of his opponent, and his lawyer. The winning party regards the legal proceedings as superfluous, and a waste of his time and money in confirming a meaning for the contract which he accepted from the outset. To the outsider the dispute appears as a mere quibbling over words — an unlikely approach to justice. Yet the litigation is caused because the parties could not agree on the meaning of the words *they* used, and the dispute has to be solved by the court. These difficulties may arise even in relatively simple contracts. In complicated and important contracts, prevention in the form of legal advice in drafting the terms is likely to be far cheaper than the cure. Of course, lawyers themselves are not immune to the inherent problems of language, but their training and experience make them especially aware of the areas of danger.

To return to our illustration of the kitchen cabinets, the misunderstanding might have been avoided had Doe asked Smith, "Does your offer include supplying the lumber?" or better still, "What does your offer include besides the labour needed?" He might also have asked, "When shall I pay you: in advance, in instalments, or after the work is completed?" It is understandable but unfortunate that people do not always direct their minds to all the terms, even all the important terms, which may affect their contracts. The list of possible questions is a long one, and while the parties can reduce the chances of a later dispute over interpretation by carefully discussing the implications of their contract at the time of its formation, they cannot always eliminate such a dispute.

THE INTERPRETATION OF EXPRESS TERMS

What precisely did Smith promise when he agreed "to build a set of kitchen cabinets for $100"? In attempting to answer such a question, lawyers have often argued that there are two approaches to the interpretation of words: the *strict* or *plain-meaning* approach and the *liberal* approach.

The plain-meaning approach restricts the interpretation to the ordinary meaning, the dictionary meaning of the word. In fact, however, few words have a "plain" or "ordinary" meaning. A glance at the dictionary will show how many words have two or more completely different definitions. In addition, the meaning of words changes from time to time and place to place, or the context of the words in a contract may make it obvious that they have been used in a special sense.[1]

The liberal approach, by contrast, looks to the purposes of the parties in drafting their agreement — what did they intend to say? It stresses the circumstances surrounding the contract, the negotiations leading up to it, the knowledge of the parties, and any other relevant facts. It minimizes the importance of the words actually used. The liberal approach also has its limitations. In its extreme form, it too may lead to unsatisfactory results by inviting endless speculation about what the parties may have intended but never expressed. The particular words one chooses to use are a part of his conduct in relation to the contract, and in law one's conduct (including his words) must continue to serve as the primary guide to his intentions.

In the result there are not really two distinct approaches to interpretation, one of which is used to the total exclusion of the other: rather than choosing directly between them, a court will simply emphasize one approach more than the other. In other words, the court must decide in relation to the circumstances of each case how far it should look beyond the words used to explain their meaning.

In our illustration of the kitchen cabinets Smith promised "to build" the cabinets. Does "to build" include "to supply materials"? Literally, "to build" means only "to construct", but in practice it usually includes "to supply materials". When a contractor undertakes to build a house, the price usually includes the price of materials as well. In the illustration, the words themselves are not conclusive either way; there is an ambiguity. The court will then more willingly look outside the contract to the surrounding circumstances as a means of clearing up this ambiguity. For example, it will hear evidence of any past transactions between the parties to learn whether materials have been included in previous building contracts between them. It will hear evidence of the negotiations leading up to the contract: perhaps Smith had quoted different prices varying with the kind of lumber to be used; perhaps Doe had made it clear earlier that he wanted an inclusive price. Any of these facts, if established in court, would support the claim that "to build" in this contract meant "to supply materials" as well as labour.

There is an inaccurate but widespread belief that when the two principals in

---

[1] See Chafee, "The Disorderly Conduct of Words", 20 *Can. B. Rev.*, p. 752 (1942).

a dispute give conflicting evidence in court and there are no other witnesses, the court will not accept either account but will apply the popular maxim, "One man's word is as good as another's." Normally reputable men have sometimes been tempted into making extravagant or distorted statements on the false assumption that the court has no recourse but to accept their story on an equal footing with their opponents' testimony. True, the court is reluctant to accept direct testimony of one party rather than the other, and will seek corroboration if possible from a third party or from the actions of the parties in relation to the contract other than those disclosed in their own testimony. As a last resort, however, the court will choose between them. It will then base its decision on the credibility of the parties themselves, taking all the circumstances into account — in other words, it simply decides which story seems more reasonable. With their experience in this type of problem, judges, though certainly not infallible, develop an intuitive ability for assessing the credibility of witnesses.

The dictionary definition of the words used, their meaning in the context of the contract, the surrounding circumstances of the contract, and the judge's ability to weigh the evidence, are all means by which the court endeavours to interpret the express terms of a contract. Another important aid in deciding the meaning of words is evidence of special usage of words in particular trades and in particular areas of the country. In our illustration, Smith might produce expert witnesses who testify from their experience that in the carpentry trade standard usage of the word "build" means labour only. Or he might show that in that part of the country the word always had that meaning. In *Brown v. Byrne* Mr. Justice Coleridge said:

> What words more plain than "a thousand", "a week", "a day"? Yet the cases are familiar in which "a thousand" has been held to mean twelve hundred, "a week" a week only during the theatrical season, "a day" a working day. In such cases the evidence neither adds to, nor qualifies, nor contradicts the written contract; it only ascertains it, by expounding the language.[2]

Evidence of special usage is not, however, conclusive: a court may well decide that the word was used in a general rather than a special way, perhaps because the tradesman was aware that the other party was not familiar with trade usage. In general, the courts construe words most strongly against the party who has suggested them, in order to prevent him from having a choice of whichever of two possible meanings ultimately proves to his advantage.

One should realize that there are no hard and fast rules of interpretation. At one time the courts were quite mechanical in applying ancient canons of interpretation, but today they try to look for the most reasonable interpretation in the circumstances — an approach that requires flexibility and common sense. For a businessman to be able to predict the decision a court is likely to reach if the meaning of a contract is challenged, he must know what a "reasonable interpretation" of it would be. His personal interest deprives him of the ability to reach

---

[2] (1854) 118 E.R. 1304 at 1309.

an objective conclusion about the reasonable meaning of the contract. He needs unbiased advice. The court, in searching for the objective meaning of words, seeks the advice of the mythical reasonable man — the personification of an informed, objective bystander. The businessman's imperfect approximation of this legendary figure[3] must be his lawyer. If he finds his interpretation of a contract challenged, he should immediately obtain legal advice. By doing so he will have the benefit of an unbiased external opinion, at a time when it will be of most help to him. His protection is then twofold: if his interpretation of the contract is correct, he will learn how best to enforce it; if it is incorrect, he may avoid a costly breach of contract.

A court must render a decision, difficult though it may be, and the best available solution often is not entirely satisfactory. Frequently, the easier course would be to declare an agreement unenforceable because of an ambiguity in its wording; but if the courts took this attitude they would not be performing the role assigned to them in the community. Instead they lean towards keeping an agreement alive rather than brushing it aside as being without force at law. Equivocal words are assigned that meaning which makes the contract enforceable, if at all possible. Lord Wright, one of the most respected of English judges in commercial law, has given a classic statement of the rule in a House of Lords decision:

> The object of the court is to do justice between the parties, and the court will do its best, if satisfied that there was an ascertainable and determinate intention to contract, to give effect to that intention, looking at substance and not mere form. It will not be deterred by mere difficulties of interpretation. Difficulty is not synonymous with ambiguity, so long as any definite meaning can be extracted.[4]

THE PAROL EVIDENCE RULE

The Meaning of the Rule

Before a contract is made, there is very often a process of bargaining and negotiation, offer and counter-offer, with each party making concessions until finally they reach a suitable compromise. The bargaining may be carried on orally or in writing. In important contracts, the parties usually put their final agreement into a more formal document signed by both sides. One party may later discover that the document does not contain one or more terms he believed were part of the agreement. It is possible, of course, that the omission is due to a mistake in reducing into writing the terms actually agreed upon — a typing error, for example. The equitable remedy of rectification, as explained in Chapter 9, may then be available. Where, however, there is no clear evidence that the term was

---

[3] For an amusing account of all the attributes of the "reasonable man" see Herbert, *Uncommon Law*, London: Methuen & Co., 1948, in the fictitious case of Fardell v. Potts.

[4] Scammel v. Ouston [1941]1 All E.R. 14 at 25.

omitted by error—as when the complaining party admits that he read the document over and approved it — he will be held to the contract as it is written.

The parol evidence rule states that a term, previously agreed upon between the parties but not included in the final form of the contract, will not later be permitted to add to or contradict the contract. In this context the word "parol" means *extrinsic to* or *outside of* the written agreement.[5] The rule applies both to an oral agreement which has been reduced to writing and to a written agreement which has been reduced to a formal document under seal.

The parol evidence rule operates to exclude *terms* which one party claims should be added to the contract. It does not exclude evidence pertaining to the formation of the contract such as its legality, the capacity of the parties, mistake, duress, undue influence, or fraud. In other words, it does not affect evidence of any of the circumstances surrounding the contract — it operates only to exclude the introduction of terms not found in the written document.

Sometimes parties agree to omit a term from the final form of the contract, still intending it to be part of their whole agreement. They are most likely to do so when they are using a standard form contract, such as a conditional sale agreement, a short-term lease, a mortgage, or a grant of land. One party may persuade the other to leave a term out because it will be confusing or because a third party may object to it.

Illustration:

> Smith sells Mrs. Gulliver a vacuum cleaner on the instalment plan for $160. They agree orally that Mrs. Gulliver will give the names of several friends to Smith and that Smith will give her a $20 rebate for each sale made to one of her friends. Mrs. Gulliver signs a standard form instalment contract containing her promise to pay $160 for the vacuum cleaner. Smith explains that the contract contains no reference to the rebate term because the finance company will not accept the contract if alterations have been made to its standard form. Smith sells the contract to the finance company.
>
> Mrs. Gulliver is liable to the finance company for the full $160 even though Smith sells vacuum cleaners to some of her friends. Her only remedy is to sue Smith for deceit; because of the parol evidence rule, she cannot sue either the finance company or Smith for breach of the oral term.

Though a party may suffer hardship, the courts are reluctant to relax the parol evidence rule because they fear that any relaxation would tempt parties who are unhappy with their contracts to claim that favourable terms, discussed during negotiations but not agreed upon, are part of their contracts. The courts would create serious difficulties for the business community if they showed any disposition to upset written agreements deliberately made. For this reason, it is the height of folly to allow any term of importance to be omitted from the final written form of an agreement. If the term is important and the other side insists on

---

[5] For a more complete discussion of the meaning of the parol evidence rule, see Cross, *Evidence* (4th ed.), pp. 532 ff. London: Butterworth & Co., 1974.

excluding it from the final document, it is better to break off negotiations than to enter into the contract with the term excluded.

The Scope of the Rule

We have seen that once the parties have reduced their agreement to a document intended to be its final form, the parol evidence rule precludes either of them from offering evidence of other terms not in that final agreement. There are some circumstances where at first sight it would appear that the rule applies, but where the courts have decided that a written document was not intended to embody the *whole* contract, and have therefore admitted evidence of its oral terms. In the preceding chapter we learned that the terms of a contract may be partly in writing and partly oral. If a party can show that the writing was not intended to be a reduction of the whole oral contract into writing but was merely a part of it, then he may introduce evidence of those terms of the contract which are oral.[6]

Illustration:

A, the owner of a fleet of dump trucks, agrees orally with *B,* a paving contractor, to move 75,000 cubic feet of gravel within three months from Harrowsmith to Yarker for $15,000, and to provide any related documents that *B* may require for financing the project. To finance his paving operations *B* applies for a bank loan, and the bank requests evidence that the paving work can be started immediately. *B* therefore asks *A* to sign a statement to the effect that he will deliver 25,000 cubic feet from Harrowsmith to Yarker within the next month for $5,000. Soon after *A* starts to make the deliveries, he discovers that he has quoted too low a price per cubic foot. He claims that his agreement with *B* has been reduced to writing and that he need only move the 25,000 cubic feet referred to in the writing.

The parol evidence rule does not apply. The written document for the bank was not intended to be a complete statement of the contract. Rather it was drawn up as part of *A*'s performance of his obligation under it. Accordingly, *B* may sue *A* for damages if *A* refuses to perform the balance of the contract, and for this purpose *B* may offer evidence of the terms of the original oral agreement.

There are two further circumstances where the rule by definition does not apply. First, it does not hinder the interpretation of express terms already in the contract. As we have seen in the preceding section, the court does accept evidence to explain the meaning of the words used in a written contract — to determine the meaning of the word "build" in the contract to build kitchen cabinets, for example. As one English judge has put it:

There cannot be the slightest objection to the admission of evidence . . . which neither alters nor adds to the written contract, but merely enables us to ascertain what was the subject matter referred to therein.[7]

---

[6] DeLasalle v. Guilford [1901] 2 K.B. 215, is an extreme example of the lengths to which the courts will go in avoiding the parol evidence rule on these grounds.

[7] Macdonald v. Longbottom (1863) 120 E.R. 1177 at 1179.

Secondly, the rule does not exclude evidence of an oral agreement that the parties may reach *after* they have entered into the written agreement. The subsequent oral agreement may change the terms of the written agreement[8] or, as we have seen in the preceding chapter, even rescind the prior contract altogether.[9] In either event, the court will hear evidence of the subsequent oral contract.

Collateral Agreement

An argument often made by a party is that there was a collateral agreement (sometimes called a collateral term) — an entirely separate undertaking upon which the parties were agreed and which they did not incorporate in their written contract, probably because the written contract seemed an inappropriate place for it. Such a collateral undertaking, the argument runs, may be enforced as a separate contract quite independently of the written document. Allowed much scope, this argument would provide an easy evasion of the parol evidence rule. The acceptance of this argument by a Canadian court seems to depend upon whether a separate consideration is given for the collateral promise.

Illustration:

A offers to sell his residence, Rainbow End, to *B* for $10,000. *B* replies that he will buy Rainbow End for that price only if *A* will include an old dining-room set. *A* agrees to this request, and the parties draw a written contract for the sale of Rainbow End but do not mention the dining-room set in it because they believe they should not do so in a contract for the sale of land.

The consideration for the dining-room set is the payment of the $10,000 purchase price for Rainbow End, and thus the promise to include the set is an integral part of the contract: it must be in the written agreement, or it is excluded by the parol evidence rule.

If, instead, *B* had agreed to pay *A* an extra $35 for the dining-room set, there would be a separate consideration for it. In effect there would be two separate contracts — a written contract for the sale of Rainbow End for $10,000 and a collateral oral contract for the sale of the dining-room set for $35. Because there is a separate consideration, the court will very likely consider the oral agreement outside the scope of the parol evidence rule and enforce it.

Condition Precedent

We come next to a surprising historical exception to the parol evidence rule — the effect of a separate understanding about a *condition precedent*. A condition precedent is any set of circumstances or events which the parties stipulate must be satisfied or must happen before their contract takes effect. It may be an event

---

[8] See Johnson Investments v. Pagritide [1923] 2 D.L.R. 985.

[9] Morris v. Baron [1918] A.C. 1.

beyond the control of either of them. An agreement to have a contract subject to a condition precedent need not be in writing. If the party alleging that a condition precedent was stipulated and not met can adduce evidence to support his claim, the court will recognize this understanding in the face of a complete written form of contract, and declare the contract void. The courts are prepared to recognize and enforce a condition precedent agreed to orally even when the subject-matter of the contract falls within the scope of the Statute of Frauds or the Sale of Goods Act.

Illustration:

> *B* offers to sell a car to *A* for $2,000. *A* agrees to buy it provided he can per-suade his bank to lend him $1,500. The parties agree that the contract will only operate if the bank makes the loan, and that otherwise the contract will be void. They then make a written contract in which *A* agrees to pay *B* $2,000 in ten days and *B* agrees to deliver the car to *A* at that time. The writ-ing does not mention that the contract is subject to the ability of *A* to obtain the bank loan. The bank refuses to lend *A* $1,500, and *A* informs *B* that the sale is off. *B* sues *A* for breach of contract and contends that their oral under-standing about the bank loan is excluded by the parol evidence rule.
>
> The parol evidence rule does not apply, and *B* will fail in his action. In his defence, *A* may show that there was an oral understanding suspending the contract of sale unless and until he could obtain the necessary bank loan.

Summary

In practice it is difficult to convince a court that the parol evidence rule does not apply: often, the parties have misunderstood the effect of their agreement, and their later evidence about the alleged oral terms is in sharp conflict. It is hazard-ous for a businessman to count on the possibility of an exception to the rule, either at the time the contract is being formed and put in writing or at a later time when he must decide whether to go to court over a difference of opinion about the interpretation of the contract.

IMPLIED TERMS AS A METHOD OF INTERPRETATION

We have noted that the parties to a contract cannot direct their minds to all those possibilities which may turn out to be a source of contention between them after their contract is formed. When we discussed the interpretation of express terms above, we were considering one of the approaches the courts use in trying to resolve a dispute which arises for this reason. A second approach to the problem is for the court to consider whether the intention of the parties can only be given effect by acknowledging the existence of a term that is implied. An *implied term* is a term the parties have not expressly included in their agreement but which, in the opinion of the court, they would *as reasonable men* have included when they made their contract had they thought of the possibility of the subsequent difficulty arising. Thus, in our illustration of the contract to build kitchen cabinets the court might choose to concentrate upon the meaning of the express words "to build", or it might instead consider whether the contract taken as a whole implies a term that the carpenter is to supply the lumber necessary to build the cabinets. Sometimes, as here, the distinction between these two approaches is more apparent than real: the meaning of the word "build" is likely to be an important factor in deciding whether a term can reasonably be implied. In other instances the *type* of the contract will determine whether a term should be implied. Contracts for the sale of goods contain an implied term that the goods will be suitable for the purpose for which they have been purchased if that purpose has been made known to the seller and it is in the course of the seller's business to supply such goods;[10] but a contract for the sale of land carries with it no such implied term.

Implied terms are usually the result of long-established custom in a particular trade or type of transaction. They exist in almost every field of commerce. They came to be recognized among businessmen because they made good sense or because they led to certainty in transactions without the necessity of spelling out every detail of the transactions. In time, the courts fell into line with this business practice. When a party failed to perform in compliance with such an implied term, the courts would recognize the existence of the implied term and enforce the contract as though it had been an express term.

Illustration:

A asks *B,* a tire dealer, to supply truck tires for his five-ton dump truck. *B* then shows *A* a set of tires and quotes a price. *A* purchases the tires. The sales slip merely sets out the name and the price of the tires. Later *A* discovers that these tires are not safe on trucks of over three tons' capacity, and claims that he is the victim of a breach of contract.

On these facts there was no express undertaking by *B* that the tires would be safe for a five-ton truck or any other type of truck. Nevertheless, the court would hold that in the circumstances there was an implied term that the tires should be suitable for a five-ton truck. It would say that in showing *A* the tires after he had made his intended use of them clear, *B,* as a regular seller of such tires, implied that they would be suitable for *A*'s truck.

We still, of course, have a problem of knowing in what circumstances the courts are likely to regard an implied term as an appropriate interpretation of a contract. As a general rule, they will imply terms reasonably necessary to give effect to a contract when otherwise the just expectations of a party would be defeated. This approach applies to all kinds of contracts, but in some fields, especially the sale of goods, insurance, partnership, and landlord and tenant relations, a large and complex body of customary terms has grown up. In many jurisdictions these customary terms have been codified in a statute which sets out in one place all the rules previously established by the courts. Thus the court's

---

[10] The various implied terms in a contract of sale are discussed in Chapter 16.

decision in the illustration above follows a specific provision in the Sale of Goods Act.

A case which is often cited on the subject of implied terms is known as *The Moorcock*.[11] The defendants were owners of a wharf and jetty on the river Thames, and the plaintiff was owner of the steamship *Moorcock*. It was agreed between them that the ship should be loaded at the defendants' jetty, the plaintiff paying for the service. While the ship was docked there, the tide ebbed; she came to rest on a hard ridge beneath the river mud and was damaged. The owner sued and recovered damages on the ground that the defendants must be taken to have implied that the facilities were reasonably safe for the ship at low tide, a necessary provision for carrying out the contract. In giving his opinion Lord Justice Bowen said:

> I believe if one were to take all the cases, and there are many, of implied warranties or covenants in law, it will be found that in all of them the law is raising an implication from the presumed intention of the parties, with the object of giving the transaction such efficacy as both parties must have intended that at all events it should have. In business transactions such as this, what the law desires to effect by the implication is to give such business efficacy to the transaction as must have been intended at all events by both parties who are business men . . . .[12]

These famous words have been quoted and misquoted innumerable times both by judges and lawyers. The doctrine is an assurance that the court will not permit the legitimate and reasonable expectations of the parties to a contract to be defeated simply because the contract does not deal expressly with a serious contingency that affects the basis of the transaction. On the other hand, the court will not go further than is necessary, and will not make a new contract for the parties. Nor will it imply a term which is contrary to the expressed intent of the agreement. Lawyers are sometimes inclined to resort to the *Moorcock* doctrine when all else has failed for their client. Consequently, the courts insist that the case for implying a term be made clearly. The parties do well, therefore, to consider carefully what assumptions underlie their performance of the contract and to bring as many of the important possibilities as they can think of into the open so that they may be made the subject of an express understanding. The courts have become more cautious than formerly about finding an implied term on the authority of the *Moorcock* decision. In the words of Lord Justice Jenkins:

> I do not think that the court will read a term into a contract unless, considering the matter from the point of view of business efficacy, it is clear beyond a peradventure that both parties intended a given term to operate, although they did not include it in so many words.[13]

A Canadian decision illustrates the resolution of the courts to restrict the

---

[11] (1889) 14 P.D. 64.

[12] *Ibid.*, at 68.

[13] Sethia (1944) Ltd. v. Partabmull Rameshwar [1950] 1 All E.R. 51 at 59.

circumstances in which they will find an implied term on grounds of business efficacy. In *Douglas Bros. and Jones Ltd. v. MacQueen*, [14] the owner of certain property in Nova Scotia engaged the plaintiffs to dig and drill a well at $3 per foot plus the cost of pipe. A well was drilled to the depth of 385 feet, at which level the operation closed when the owner refused to pay for the work done and materials supplied because no water had yet been found. In defence of an action for the value of the work done and materials supplied, the owner claimed that the contract contained an implied term that he should have to pay only if clear water was obtained. The court rejected this argument. It held that the contract contained no implied term to this effect either from trade custom or for reasons of business efficacy. Accordingly, the owner was liable for the work done and the materials supplied.

QUESTIONS FOR REVIEW

1. What is the difference between the *plain-meaning* and the *liberal* approach to the interpretation of contracts?
2. What kinds of evidence may help a court to decide upon the meaning of an ambiguous term in a contract?
3. What is a common explanation for parties' omitting an agreed term from the final written expression of their contract?
4. What does the word "parol" mean in the "parol evidence rule"?
5. What is the difference between an express term and an implied term?
6. What is a condition precedent?
7. Suppose that at the time a contract is formed, some of the terms are stated in a letter and other terms are agreed upon orally. Will the parol evidence rule operate to exclude any later testimony about these oral terms?
8. In a written contract *A* promises to pay *B* $1,000 if *B* will bring a truckload of certain cases from Vancouver to *A*'s residence in Thunder Bay. *B* does so. *A* fails to pay *B* the $1,000, and *B* sues. In defence *A* offers evidence that *B* knew that the cases contained liquor and that their importation into Ontario was in violation of the Liquor Control Act (Ontario). Will such evidence be admitted so as to affect the court's decision?
9. In what types of contract are implied terms of special importance?
10. What was the principle declared in the *Moorcock* case?
11. How do the courts justify the parol evidence rule? Do you agree with them?
12. ". . . it is now generally recognized that a party to a contract is held to assume an obligation not because he voluntarily consents to be bound, but because the law attaches that consequence on the basis of his manifested conduct, with or without his consent." (Fleming, *The Law of Torts*, [2nd ed.], p. 3.) Cite a case mentioned in the text which might be used as an illustration of this idea, and explain why.
13. "The normal contract is not an isolated act, but an incident in the conduct of business or in the framework of some more general relation such as that of

---

[14] (1959) 42 M.P.R. 256.

landlord and tenant.'' (Cheshire, Fifoot and Furmston, *Law of Contract*, [8th ed.], p. 122.) Show how the idea expressed in this quotation is applied in the interpretation of contracts.

14. By what logic can one reconcile the doctrine of the implied term with the parol evidence rule, when oral testimony is required to establish the circumstances necessary for the operation of an implied term?

15. What did Lord Wright mean in his judgment in *Scammel v. Ouston* when he said, ''Difficulty is not synonymous with ambiguity''?

CASES FOR DISCUSSION

CASE 1

In response to an advertisement by Mrs. Atkinson to sell her house, Kirby made a written offer to purchase it for $24,000. The parties discussed the offer several days later, and Mrs. Atkinson stated that she would also like to sell her furniture. After discussion about the amount of furniture for sale and its price, Mrs. Atkinson accepted in writing Kirby's offer to purchase the house. The offer in writing made no reference to the furniture and required Kirby's certified cheque for $2,000 as an immediate payment on account of the agreed price for the house. In fact, Kirby gave Mrs. Atkinson a cheque for $4,950, the excess being the price they had agreed upon orally for Mrs. Atkinson's furniture.

When Kirby occupied the house, he found that Mrs. Atkinson had removed the grand piano from the living room and had taken it with her. He thereupon commenced legal proceedings for breach of contract, alleging that in their oral negotiations about the furniture he and Mrs. Atkinson had specifically included the grand piano, and that he had even tried it out in the presence of Mrs. Atkinson. In defence, Mrs. Atkinson pleaded that she had never intended to sell the piano, and that in any event evidence of the oral agreement about the furniture would be inadmissible.

With what issues must the court deal before reaching a decision? Should Kirby's action succeed? Give reasons for your opinion. (For reference, see *Kaplan v. Andrews* [1955] 4 D.L.R. 553.)

CASE 2

In July, Messrs. Saunders and Dimmock entered into a partnership for carrying on a grocery and provision business on Dundee Street East in Toronto. They dissolved the partnership two years later with a view to the continued operation of the business by Saunders. Dimmock then wrote out an agreement dissolving the partnership, including his covenant as retiring partner that he would not ''during a term of five years from the date hereof commence and carry on a butcher and grocery business, neither directly nor indirectly, nor shall he work as an employee in such business within a radius of one half-mile from the said premises at 346 Dundee Street East, in the City of Toronto.''

Shortly thereafter, Dimmock opened a grocery and provision business at

258 Dundee Street East, less than a half-mile away, and operated it as sole proprietor. Saunders brought an action to restrain Dimmock from continuing to break the covenant. In defence Dimmock admitted that the half-mile restriction on employment was a reasonable restraint. He further conceded that if the restriction on carrying on business (owning a business) were also limited to one half-mile, it would be a reasonable restraint, but he argued that the words "half-mile" applied only to *employment* and that there was no geographic limit to his covenant not to *carry on business*. Therefore, the first half of the covenant was void because it was an unreasonable restraint, and accordingly he was free to carry on business as owner. Did Dimmock break the contract? (See *Sotiroff v. Dimitroff* [1933] O.W.N. 249.)

CASE 3

Schnabel purchased a piano from Keyes for $575 on an instalment plan and signed a printed contract. The parties had agreed orally that if Schnabel should find that the piano was priced higher than its market value, Keyes would take the piano back and refund Schnabel his $10 deposit. Schnabel asked to have this understanding put in the agreement, but Keyes said that because their contract was a printed one he could not change it; he said that Schnabel could accept his word that the contract would be cancelled and that he would take the piano back if it was overpriced. Schnabel hesitated: he was a recent immigrant and unfamiliar with Canadian prices. He said he wished to come back with a man competent to judge the piano's value, but Keyes persuaded him to sign by saying that if he did not sign immediately the price would go up to $650. (It was subsequently proved in court that the market value of the piano was about $400, a price that would give the dealer a good profit.) The piano was delivered to Schnabel. Afterwards Schnabel sent it back and relied on the oral agreement with Keyes to claim that the contract was void.

Keyes sued Schnabel for breach of contract and contended that it was improper to receive oral testimony of terms outside the writing, especially so because printed at the bottom of the contract were the words, "This contract contains the whole agreement between myself [Schnabel] and J. Keyes." Should Keyes succeed? (See *Long v. Smith* (1911) 23 O.L.R. 121.)

CASE 4

Brooks gave the following guarantee to Haigh in respect of purchases on credit from Haigh by John Lees & Sons:

> Messrs. Haigh:
>   In consideration of your being in advance to Messrs. John Lees & Sons in the sum of £10,000 for the purchase of cotton, I do hereby give you my guarantee for that amount on their behalf.
>
>   (signed) "John Brooks"

When the question of the validity of Brooks' guarantee arose at a later time, the court had to interpret the meaning of the words "in consideration of your being in advance". If the words "being in advance" meant "already being in advance" or "already having a sum owing to you from past credit purchases by John Lees & Sons," the guarantee would have been given for a past consideration (assuming, at any rate, that its purpose was not to obtain Haigh's forbearance from suing). If, on the other hand, the words "being in advance" meant "becoming further in advance," the debt to be guaranteed was a future debt, and there was consideration for the guarantee because Haigh, without the guarantee, might not have supplied goods to John Lees & Sons.

If no further evidence is offered to clarify the meaning of these words, what rule will the court follow in choosing between the two possible meanings? (*Haigh v. Brooks* (1839) 113 E.R. 119.)

CASE 5

Henry Doubt operated a business as a merchant tailor in Port Perry. He sold all the interest and goodwill of his business, stock-in-trade, and fixtures to Stone for $2,000 and covenanted with Stone that he would:

> . . . neither for himself nor for any other person or company engage in the cutting or manufacture or repair of gentlemen's clothing, either tailor-made or ready-made, or in the merchant tailoring business in the village of Port Perry, or within eight miles of the said village, as long as the purchaser [Stone] shall carry on the business of tailor in the said village. But it is expressly understood that [the vendor is] not barred from the sale of ready-made goods or conducting a general store; also [the vendor] may act as a journeyman tailor, but not as either cutter or salesman in a merchant tailor business.

About a year later, Doubt bought out another business in Port Perry which sold ready-made clothing, gents' furnishings, shoes, rubbers, furs, hats, and caps. He had on hand a stock of fifty or more ready-made suits purchased by him from the manufacturer in Hamilton. To fit a particular customer it was sometimes necessary to lengthen, shorten, let out, or take in part of the suit. Occasionally, none of the clothing on hand would fit a customer, who would then be shown samples of cloth from which to select the material and a chart of different styles of suits made by the manufacturers from which he might make his choice. Doubt would then take the customer's measurements and forward them on a standard form to the manufacturers, who maintained a much larger assortment of goods and styles, sizes and patterns than a small retailer such as he could afford. In special instances, when the customer was quite "out of proportion," the manufacturer would have to make a suit up especially for him. Doubt sold about three hundred suits a year, of which about ten on the average had to be ordered from the manufacturer.

After Doubt had been engaged in the new business for three years, Stone brought an action against him for damages for breach of contract. The court heard evidence from Mr. Walters, another retailer in the same business as Doubt, which established that the practice followed by Doubt was customary. It was also established that the term "repairing" in the tailoring trade applies to damaged or worn goods. List the strongest points in Doubt's defence with reasons. (*Stone v. Doubt* (1909) 14 O.W.R. 459.)

CASE 6

Campbell proposed to buy from Pym a three-eighths share in a machine invented by Pym provided that two engineers, Ferguson and Abernethie, were prepared to recommend the invention. They arranged a meeting to be attended by all four men, at which the engineers might examine the machine and have Pym explain it to them. Confusion arose about the time of the meeting, and after several of the men had departed and returned, a meeting was held with one of the engineers, Abernethie, absent. The other engineer, Ferguson, approved of the machine, and the meeting agreed that as they were together and might find it troublesome to meet again, an agreement should be drawn up and signed which, if Abernethie later gave his approval, should be the final agreement. The agreement for the purchase of the three-eighths share was set out in the writing and signed by Campbell: it made no reference to the necessity for Abernethie's approval of Pym's invention.

Abernethie refused to recommend the purchase of an interest in the machine when he saw it at a later time. Campbell then refused to proceed with the purchase. Pym brought an action against Campbell to enforce the contract as written. Should he succeed? (*Pym v. Campbell* (1856) 119 E.R. 903.)

CASE 7

Chiswell sold the surface and minerals in his land in Alberta for $11,300 to Werner under an agreement for sale (an instalment sale which reserved the ownership in the property of Chiswell until a specified amount of the price was paid). Werner became in arrears, thus giving Chiswell the right to recover possession by court action. Chiswell commenced proceedings, but they were not yet complete when it became apparent that the land was very valuable. Werner entered into a petroleum and natural gas lease with Imperial Oil Ltd. and received a cash bonus of $12,000, which he proposed to use in settlement of his debt to Chiswell. About the same time Chiswell, anticipating the recovery of his property by court order, entered into a similar lease of the same property with California Standard Oil Co. At the time Chiswell gave his lease to California Standard Oil Co., he told the company's agent that his ability to lease the property depended upon a favourable outcome of his pending court action against Werner and that he could give the lease only on one consideration — that the company's agent give him a signed statement acknowledging that he (Chiswell) did not have any right to lease the mineral rights until the court action against Werner went through. The agent gave him a statement to that effect, and Chiswell and California Standard Oil Co. entered into a lease of the mineral rights which made no reference to the proviso signed by the company's agent and which, furthermore, contained a paragraph stating that the lease contained the whole of the agreement.

Werner tendered the balance of the purchase price to Chiswell, but Chiswell refused it and proceeded with his court action. The court dismissed Chiswell's petition for recovery of the property. He was, therefore, unable to lease the property to California Standard Oil Co. and that company sued him for breach of contract. Should the action succeed? (*California Standard Oil Co. v. Chiswell* [1955] 5 D.L.R. 119.)

CASE 8

Burgoyne and Murphy made a contract for sawing lumber, containing the following terms: "Burgoyne agrees to saw for Murphy approximately one million feet of birch and maple logs during the fall of 1948 and winter and spring of 1949. . . . The price to be $18.00 per thousand feet. . . . On the 20th of each month Murphy will pay for lumber that is sawn up to the 15th of each month . . . final payment when all lumber is sawn and piled." Both parties signed the contract. Murphy delivered only 560,000 feet of lumber for sawing, although Burgoyne requested the balance. Burgoyne then sued for the profit lost through Murphy's failure to deliver the remainder of the lumber for sawing. Murphy contended that there was no promise in the contract that he should deliver one million feet. In reply Burgoyne claimed that he could not saw any logs unless they were supplied. Should Burgoyne succeed? (*Burgoyne v. Murphy* [1951] 2 D.L.R. 556.)

CASE 9

Fitzgerald had sold a large quantity of oil to the federal government to be shipped from Ontario and delivered at Halifax. He then made an oral agreement with the Grand Trunk Railway to carry the oil to Halifax in covered cars. (At the time it was apparently common to carry oil both in open and in covered cars.) A term of the oral agreement was that the oil would be carried in two shipments. The first shipment of oil was delivered to the railway, and the agent gave Fitzgerald a bill of lading for the oil shipped. The bill of lading did not state that the oil would be carried in covered cars. The railway shipped the oil in open cars, and as a result it was destroyed by weather.

Fitzgerald sued the railway for loss resulting from the breach of the oral agreement. The railway defended by claiming that the contract had been reduced to writing and the writing did not include a term that the oil should be carried in covered cars. Should Fitzgerald succeed? (*Fitzgerald v. Grand Trunk Railway* (1880) 4 O.A.R. 601. This decision discussed other issues, in particular the negligence of the railway, but they are not relevant to the above problem.)

CASE 10

In September, Knowles, the owner of a professional hockey club, entered into negotiations with Martin, a professional hockey player, for Martin's services for the following two years. A salary of $2,000 a week during the training and playing seasons was agreed upon orally. Martin inquired at the time whether players would be covered by workmen's-compensation insurance if injured. Knowles replied that he thought not, but that in any event he was having written contracts drawn up by his lawyer in which a clause would provide that every player would be insured against injury and that if a player were disabled he would be looked after.

Written contracts were subsequently prepared and presented to all the players (including Martin) for signing. The contracts in their written form specified the agreed salary for each player, respectively, and outlined the usual conditions regarding the player's obligations, but made no reference to insurance protection against injury or the employer's obligation in the event a player were disabled.

Martin played for the team for six weeks and then received a serious injury to his eye during a hockey game. He was immediately taken to the hospital. At the end of the game, Knowles announced to Martin's teammates in the dressing room that he would pay Martin's salary to the end of the season.

Knowles paid Martin's salary to the date of his injury and refused to pay anything additional. Martin brought an action for damages claiming (a) $30,000 representing his salary for the remaining 15 weeks of the playing season; (b) $500 for the cost of an artificial eye; and (c) $10,000 general damages as compensation for the loss of his eye.

Discuss the issues raised by these facts and explain whether the action should succeed.

CHAPTER 13

Privity of Contract and The Assignment of Contractual Rights

PRIVITY OF CONTRACT

When parties make a contract, they create a little body of law for themselves by its terms. Looked at in this way, it seems fair that the jurisdiction of the contract or its power to affect relations should be confined to the parties who created it: persons outside the contract, who had no say in the formulation of its terms, should have no rights or duties under it.

In theory this reasoning seems sound, and in fact it represents the general attitude of the common law as well as of other systems of law. But in practice a number of situations arise where the purposes of justice generally, and of business convenience in particular, require that a contract be allowed to affect persons outside it. In the law of contract, a person who is not a party to a contract is called a *third person* or *third party,* or sometimes a *stranger* to the contract. In this chapter we are going to explore the effect of contracts on third persons. In other words, we are to examine the "sphere of influence" of contracts.

The general rule of the common law is that a contract should not confer any benefits or impose any obligations on a stranger to the contract. To succeed in an action on contract, the plaintiff must therefore be able to prove *privity of contract* with the defendant: he must be able to show that they are both parties to the same contract.

Illustration:

> *A,* a carpenter, owes $1,000 to *B.* Subsequently, *A* offers to renovate *C's* kitchen if *C* will promise to pay off *A's* debt to *B. C* accepts the offer, and *A*

then completes the renovation. As a third party to the contract for renovation *B* cannot enforce *C*'s promise; there is no privity of contract between them.[1] Consequently, if a dispute arises, two court actions will be necessary to enforce the objects of the contract: *B* cannot sue *C*, but he may still sue *A* for the debt *A* owes him; *A* may then sue *C* for his failure to carry out his promise to pay *B,* and will recover damages equal to $1,000 plus the costs he suffered when *B* sued him.

An additional argument sometimes made against permitting a third person to sue on a contract is that he has not given consideration for the promise. Whatever the validity of this argument, it does not make the result any more satisfactory for the third person. Suppose in our illustration that in addition to *A* and *C, B* was also a party to the contract to renovate the kitchen. There would now be privity of contract between *B* and *C* because *C* would have made his promise of payment to *B* as well as to *A*. However, *B* still could not sue because he would not have given consideration for *C*'s promise. Not only must consideration for the promise be given by some party to the contract, it must be given by that party who is trying to enforce the promise.

We have seen in the preceding chapter that when a consumer purchases goods from a merchant, he receives the benefit of an implied term that the goods are reasonably suited for the purpose for which they are sold. Thus, if a person buys a can of salmon which turns out to be poisonous and seriously injures him, he may recover damages for breach of the implied term that the fish was suitable to eat. But members of his family who were also injured cannot recover damages against the merchant. The merchant's contract was with the buyer, and only the buyer can sue successfully for breach of contract. Other members of the family have no privity of contract with the merchant and no rights under the contract. Indeed, the buyer himself may not be compensated for his loss if the merchant has few assets and is unable to meet the claim.

What about an action against the manufacturer instead of the merchant? This course would seem reasonable since the merchant has no way of knowing that sealed goods are not up to standard — it is the manufacturer who has caused the product to be poisonous. But the consumer bought the salmon from the merchant, not the manufacturer. There is no privity of contract between the consumer and the manufacturer: therefore, the consumer has no remedy for breach of contract against the manufacturer. Fortunately, as we have noted in Chapter 4, the consumer does have a remedy in another field of law: he may sue the manufacturer for negligence under the law of tort. In perhaps the most famous case of the century, *Donoghue v. Stevenson,*[2] the House of Lords decided that manufacturers are liable in tort for damages caused by their products when the products are most likely to be used without intermediate examination. While in a shop, the plaintiff drank ginger beer poured from an opaque bottle into her glass. She drank one glassful, and when more ginger beer was poured from

---

[1] Price v. Easton (1883) 110 E.R. 518.

[2] [1932] A.C. 562.

the bottle a decomposed snail also came out. The plaintiff became violently ill. A friend had bought the beverage for her so that there was no privity of contract between her and the shopkeeper. Nor could she sue the shopkeeper in tort, for he had not been negligent: he had received the sealed bottle from the manufacturer and had passed it on to the consumer, merely opening the bottle as is customary. The plaintiff sued the manufacturer for negligence. The court held that manufacturers of goods used without intermediate inspection are under a high duty of care to make their products safe. It held that if the defendant company had not lived up to this standard, that is if it were negligent in permitting the snail to get into the bottle, it must pay damages for the loss suffered.

A comparable question is whether a landlord owes a similar duty to persons who use premises occupied by a tenant. This time the answer is less satisfactory. A landlord has no liability to repair unfurnished premises unless he expressly promises to do so in the lease.[3] Even if he does promise to repair the property, he makes his promise only to the tenant as the other contracting party. Accordingly, if the tenant's wife is injured because of the landlord's failure to repair as promised, she cannot maintain an action against the landlord for damages; there is no privity of contract between her and the landlord.[4] The courts have also held that there is no duty upon the landlord in tort, either to the tenant or to others, to repair unfurnished premises. In contrast to the liability of a manufacturer, a landlord may leave premises occupied by the tenant in disrepair without fear that he may be held liable in tort for injuries suffered by the tenant himself or by his family or guests.

The privity of contract rule appears in its harshest complexion when it prevents a third person from enforcing a contract the whole object of which was to benefit him. Yet this was the decision in *Tweddle v. Atkinson*.[5] There the contract was between the respective fathers of a young married couple: the father of the husband promised the father of the bride that he would pay £100 to the married couple, and in return the father of the bride promised that he would pay them a further £200. The father of the bride died before he had paid the £200, and his executor, Atkinson, refused to pay it. The husband, Tweddle, brought an action to enforce the promise but failed because he was a stranger to the contract between the two fathers. The court rejected the argument that the plaintiff's kinship to one of the contracting parties made him something more than a ''stranger'' to the contract.

---

[3] This common-law rule may however be altered by statute. For example, the Landlord and Tenant Act, R.S.O. 1970, c. 236, s. 95, provides that in respect of *residential* tenancies only, a landlord is responsible for providing and maintaining the rented premises in a good state of repair and fit for habitation. See also St. of B.C. 1970, c. 18, s. 49; St. of Man. 1970, c. 106, s. 98; St. of N.S. 1970, c. 13, s. 6, para. 1.

[4] Cavalier v. Pope [1906] A.C. 428.

[5] (1861) 121 E.R. 762. The court based its decision on the rule that consideration must move from the promisee and that since the husband, Tweddle, could not show that he had given any consideration, his action must fail. But our definition of consideration also implies that the plaintiff to an action (in this case, Tweddle) must be a party to the contract; since he was not a party, he could not have given consideration in any event.

NOVATION

The common law has long recognized a procedure by which an outside party may achieve a contractual status as a replacement for an existing party who wishes to be relieved of his rights and duties. The process is known as *novation,* and it takes the form of a termination of the original contract and the substitution of a new contract for it. Novation must be voluntary: one party cannot insist upon it over the objections of the other. The new contract formed by novation may differ from the original either by a change in the parties to it or by a change in its terms. In business usage novation is usually confined to a change of parties, and we shall use the term in this sense. A new party introduced by novation may sue or be sued on the new contract, and the former party no longer has any rights or obligations; this result is consistent with the rule requiring privity of contract.

VICARIOUS PERFORMANCE

A promisor cannot escape his liability to the promisee by imposing a substitute for himself without the consent of the promisee. In other words, he cannot transfer or "assign" his liability, even assuming he can find someone willing to assume the liability for him. The promisee may, of course, consent to a new contract with a change of parties, but then the arrangement is not within the terms of the original contract — it is novation.

There are nevertheless, many circumstances in which it is open to a party to obtain someone to carry out his actual duties for him, though he remains accountable to the promisee for proper performance. Performance of this type is known as *vicarious performance;* an employee of the promisor performs vicariously (that is, on his behalf). Vicarious performance must be distinguished from personal performance. In vicarious performance the promisor assumes the role of employer and engages someone to undertake the work for him. If the work is not done satisfactorily, the promisee will seek a remedy against the promisor, and not the promisor's employee. In turn, the employee can look only to his employer (and not to the promisee) for payment for the work he has done. The performance of the original contract is accomplished by means of a second contract, a contract of employment. The results are consistent with the rule of privity of contract.

The promisor may employ a third party to vicariously perform the work if it is of such a nature that the personal performance of the promisor was not the reason why the promisee entered into the contract. The party entitled to performance generally cannot complain if someone other than the promisor turns up and does the work equally well. In fact, many contracts are created with the understanding that they must by their very nature be performed by a large number of persons who are not parties to the contract: contracts for the construction of buildings, the manufacture of goods, and the transport of people, for example.

Illustrations:

(a) *A* Co. Ltd. contracts with a public accountant, *B,* to have its accounts audited. *B* sends *C,* a senior accountant, to carry out the audit program. May *A* Co. Ltd. object? This is a type of work which can be carried out competently by a qualified accountant and ordinarily would not require *B*'s personal performance unless *A* Co. Ltd. had expressly bargained for it. Consequently, the vicarious performance by *C* is permissible, and *A* Co. Ltd. is not entitled to reject the tender of such performance. (We may, of course, assume that a final review of the audit would always be made by *B*.)

(b) Suppose that *C* does such an inadequate job that he fails to detect a material error in the accounts and as a result *A* Co. Ltd. suffers a loss. What is the recourse of *A* Co. Ltd.? It must look to *B* for redress. Vicarious performance by *C* does not relieve *B* from liability if the performance is unsatisfactory.

(c) Suppose instead that *C* performs satisfactorily and *B* dies insolvent without paying *C* his salary. *C* then brings an action for his wages against *A* Co. Ltd. as the beneficiary of the services he has rendered. Will he succeed? There is no privity of contract between *C* and *A* Co. Ltd. on which he may base his action. The arrangement has involved two contracts, one between *A* Co. Ltd. and *B,* and one between *B* and *C,* but none between *A* Co. Ltd. and *C*.

An instance of vicarious performance arises when goods are shipped to a destination which requires the services of a number of carriers. Thus, a shipment by rail from Toronto to New York City may be made by Canadian National Railways and the New York Central. The shipper contracts with a carrier whose franchise area includes the point of shipment and that carrier arranges for completion of the shipment with connecting carriers who operate outside its area of franchise.

Performance may in fact be undertaken vicariously when it should have been undertaken personally, and the promisee may have no opportunity to protest until the work is finished. What has happened then is that the promisor is guilty of a breach of a term in the contract (his implied or express promise to perform personally), and he may be sued for money damages of such an amount as will compensate the promisee for whatever loss he can show resulted from vicarious, rather than personal, performance.

TRUSTS

We may best introduce the idea of a trust by an example. Suppose a father wishes to provide for his daughter in the event of his dying while she is still an infant. In his will, he leaves a fund to be invested in securities, and directs that the income is to be used to care for his daughter. Since he requires someone to administer the fund and to pay the money out for her care, he appoints a *trustee*. To give effect to this plan he provides in the will that the fund be paid over to the trustee and placed under his control.

Suppose the father in our example then dies and the fund is handed over to the trustee. If the trustee refuses to pay the income out for the benefit of the daughter, what rights has she as *beneficiary* of the trust? The old common law courts took the position that the trustee was the sole owner of the property, and refused to recognize the interest of the beneficiary in the fund. To redress this injustice, the courts of equity recognized that the trust fund was set up by the father for the benefit of the daughter and not the trustee. In effect, equity decided that the daughter was the true owner of the fund. Equity developed procedures by which a beneficiary could compel a trustee to carry out his duties faithfully. As we have noted in Chapter 3, the conflict between the courts of equity and the courts of common law was resolved when the courts were amalgamated: the equitable principles recognizing beneficial interests in trusts prevailed in the new courts.

The trust concept has important applications in business. A trust is created when the creditors of a business convince the court that their debtor is no longer capable of paying his debts as they fall due. The court will order that the property of the bankrupt debtor be transferred to a trustee in bankruptcy for realization and distribution to the creditors. Again, a company may transfer the title to its fixed assets to a trustee for the bondholders as security for the repayment of money borrowed by an issue of mortgage bonds; and a company may pay annual instalments to a sinking fund trustee who will use the money to redeem and cancel a part of the bonds payable by the company.

A trust has been defined as "any arrangement whereby property is transferred with the intention that it be administered by a trustee for another's benefit."[6] In this definition and in all of the examples given above, the trust is created by the transfer of some kind of *property* to the trustee. How, then, is the concept of a trust related to contracts and the rights of third parties? The beneficiary of a trust is in a position analogous to that of a third party to a contract, being neither the person who created the trust nor the person who is appointed to administer it; yet the beneficiary has been given a means of enforcing the trust in his favour. In time the courts of equity developed an ingenious extension of the idea of the trust: they noted that the legal right to demand performance of a promise in a contract is a thing of value — a type of property, in other words. The next step was to say that a promisee who has extracted a promise for the benefit of a third person can be regarded as a trustee for the third person of the benefit of that promise. The way was then open for permitting a third party to enforce the contract in his or her favour. A trust of this kind is called a *constructive trust*. When a court accepts this argument the strictures of the privity of contract rule are avoided.

Illustration:

A, B, and *C* enter into a partnership agreement. A term of the agreement is that if one of the partners should die his widow would receive a share of the

[6] Black, *Law Dictionary* (rev. 4th ed.), St. Paul, Minn.: West Publishing Co., 1968.

future profits of the firm. On the death of *A,* the surviving partners *B* and *C* refuse to pay a share of the profits to *A*'s widow. Will she be successful in enforcing the term? The facts here are based on the case of *Re Flavell,* [7] where the court held that while the widow was not a party to the partnership agreement, the agreement had created a trust in her favour. It held that her husband as promisee of the term in the partnership agreement had become a trustee of her interest. On his death his executor became the trustee in his place, and the executor was successful in obtaining the share for the widow.

Unfortunately, parties to a contract are not likely to be aware of the subtleties of a constructive trust, nor are they likely to create a trust expressly to ensure that a third party beneficiary will have rights enforceable in court. In an action by a third party to obtain a declaration that a trust was created, the court often must proceed only by inference from the contract: in many cases the party who intended to confer the benefit has died or is unavailable to give testimony of his intentions. As a result the courts have experienced considerable difficulty in deciding when a constructive trust has been created — even when the facts have been ascertained, it is hazardous to predict the decision.

One of the main obstacles to finding a constructive trust is the rule that once created, a trust cannot be revoked by those who created it without the consent of the beneficiary. Before a court will find a constructive trust, it must be satisfied that the contracting parties intended that the benefit for the third party should be binding on them *without the possibility of later revision or revocation by them.* The courts have naturally been reluctant to imply such an intention. [8] In the result, the constructive trust has not become a reliable vehicle for circumventing the privity of contract rule.

The difficulties inherent in this branch of the common law would seem to require revision by statute. In England, the Law Revision Committee has proposed as a solution that a separate statute be enacted which provides:

> . . . where a contract by its express terms purports to confer a benefit directly on a third party, the third party shall be entitled to enforce the provision in his own name, provided that the promisor shall be entitled to raise as against the third party any defence that would have been valid against the promisee. The rights of the third party shall be subject to cancellation of the contract by the mutual consent of the contracting parties at any time before the third party has adopted it either expressly or by conduct. [9]

The proposal has not yet been enacted in England or in any of the Canadian provinces. In several of the United States the courts have for many years followed a rule like that recommended by the Law Revision Committee.

---

[7] (1883) 25 Ch. D. 89.

[8] See Re Schebsman [1944] Ch. 83.

[9] Law Revision Committee, *Sixth Interim Report,* 1937, p. 30.

EXCEPTIONS TO THE PRIVITY OF CONTRACT RULE

Insurance

When one insures his life, he enters into a contract of insurance with an insurance company. This contract or *policy* may indicate that the insurance money is to be paid to a specified person, say a spouse, who is not a party to the insurance contract. Each of the provinces has a statute which gives the beneficiary a right against the insurance company to enforce the insurance contract according to its terms.[10] Similarly, in a contract of automobile insurance, the company may promise to indemnify not only the owner but also anyone driving with his consent. If a person driving with the owner's consent injures a pedestrian and is required to pay damages, he may in turn sue the insurance company for indemnity against his loss, even though he was not a party to the insurance contract.[11]

The Undisclosed Principal

A further modification of the rule requiring privity of contract occurs when one of the contracting parties, unknown to the other, proves to be only an agent of someone else: this latter person, known as an *undisclosed principal,* may sue or be sued on the contract. The subject is of sufficient complexity that we must defer a discussion of it for separate consideration in Chapter 20.

Contracts Concerning Land

The idea of privity of contract does not apply generally in land law. If the owner of land leases it to a tenant who promises to pay rent and keep the property in good repair, and the owner subsequently sells it, the tenant must perform his promises for the new owner. The value of the land on the market would be substantially lowered if the tenant could ignore his promises to the former owner. Similarly, the new owner must respect the tenant's rights to remain on the property until the lease expires. Otherwise tenants would always be in jeopardy of being evicted when land is sold. Accordingly, we find that persons who acquire interests in land are often subject to earlier contracts relating to the property and can often take benefits under them as well.

There has been some debate about whether liabilities arising out of the chartering of ships may also affect subsequent purchasers of the ships.[12]

---

[10] See, for example: The Insurance Act, R.S.O. 1970, c. 224, s. 169; R.S.B.C. 1960, c. 197, s. 144(2); R.S.N.S. 1967, c. 148, s. 154.

[11] See, for example: The Insurance Act, R.S.O. 1970, c. 224, s. 207; R.S.B.C. 1960, c. 197, s. 232, as amended by St. of B.C. 1969, c. 11, s. 225; R.S.N.S. 1967, c. 148, s. 90.

[12] See: Lord Strathcona Steamship Co. v. Dominion Coal Co. [1926] A.C. 108, and Port Line Ltd. v. Ben Line Steamers Ltd. [1958] 2 Q.B. 146.

Special Concessions to Commercial Practice

A few recent English decisions point to a tendency in the courts to enlarge the sphere of a contract so that persons who are closely associated with a whole business transaction, though not strictly a party to a specific contract, may nevertheless be subject to the terms of the contract.

In *Shanklin Pier, Ltd. v. Detel Products, Ltd.*[13] the owners of a pier consulted Detel Products, Ltd., paint manufacturers, about the best type of paint to use in repainting the pier. Detel Products recommended one of their paints as suitable. The owners of the pier then made a contract with a firm of contractors to do the work on the understanding that the contractors would use the paint recommended by Detel Products, Ltd.; the contractors purchased the paint from Detel Products. The paint proved unsuitable for the purpose. The owners of the pier sued Detel Products and succeeded in recovering damages though they had no specific contract with that company. Detel Products had, of course, made a contract for the sale of the paint to the firm of contractors. Nevertheless, the owners of the pier were held to be entitled to the benefit of an implied term in this contract that the goods were suitable for their purpose. Although the precise grounds for reaching the decision are at present debated by legal writers, the justice of the decision is generally commended.

In *Pyrene Co. Ltd. v. Scindia Navigation Co. Ltd.*[14] the Pyrene Co. sold certain aircraft tenders to a department of the Indian government on the terms that the Indian government should arrange for their shipment from London to India and that the goods should be at the risk of the Pyrene Co. until they were loaded on board ship. The Indian government then contracted with Scindia Navigation Co. as carrier to ship the goods, and it was a term of that contract that the carrier should not be liable for damages in excess of £200. As a result of the negligence of the carrier in attempting to load one of the tenders, before it crossed the ship's rail it was severely damaged to the extent of £900. The Pyrene Co. Ltd., since the goods were at its risk, was obliged to make good this loss to the Indian government. The Pyrene Co. then sued the carrier for negligence to recoup its loss of £900. In defence the carrier claimed that the Pyrene Co. was bound by the term of the contract of shipment with the Indian government restricting the carrier's liability to £200. Since the Pyrene Co. was a stranger to the contract of shipment, it claimed that the rule requiring privity of contract meant that it was not bound by the term restricting liability, and that it should recover the full £900. The court ruled, however, that the effect of the whole transaction, and in particular of the agreement that the Indian government should arrange for shipping, was to make the Pyrene Co. a participant in the contract of shipment. Accordingly, it could not recover more than £200 damages.

These two cases illustrate a growing sensitivity of the courts to the substance of commercial transactions and an inclination to grant appropriate remedies.

---

[13] [1951] 2 K.B. 854.
[14] [1954] 2 Q.B. 402.

THE NATURE OF AN ASSIGNMENT OF RIGHTS

We have seen that apart from land law an assignment of liabilities to a third person is not possible. An assignment of contractual rights is, however, a common form of business transaction.

Illustration:

> *A,* a building contractor, has erected a building for *B.* Under the terms of their contract, *B* still owes *A* $10,000 to be paid one month after the completion of the building. *A* has purchased $12,000 worth of materials from *X.* In payment of his debt to his supplier *X, A* gives $2,000 in cash and assigns in writing his rights to the $10,000 still owing by *B. X* then notifies *B* that he should pay the money to him rather than to *A* when the debt falls due.

In the above illustration, the contractor *A* is the *assignor* of his right to the payment of $10,000. He has assigned the right to *X,* his *assignee,* for a valuable consideration. The consideration is *X*'s promise to accept the assignment in satisfaction of *A*'s debt. Given proper notice, the promisor *B* must perform for the assignee *X* instead of for the original promisee *A.*

As we noted in our discussion of constructive trusts, contractual rights are often valuable and may be considered a type of personal property along with the ownership of goods. The main difference is that tangible property, such as goods, may be possessed physically — it has a concrete existence, whereas a right to demand performance of a contract has no concrete existence — it is valuable only in so far as it is enforceable in the courts. The rights to tangible property which may be possessed physically are known as *choses in possession;* the rights to intangible property, to those things which have value only because they may if necessary be enforced by action in the courts, are called *choses in action.* There are many types of choses in action, including such things as patents, copyrights, stocks, bonds, rights to collect the proceeds of an insurance policy in the event the risk should occur, rights of action against persons who have caused injury, and rights under contracts generally.

A willingness to accept the ownership of choses in action as a form of personal wealth is the mark of a modern industrial society. By utilizing this concept, people may own a valuable type of personal property and at the same time place their savings at the disposal of companies through the ownership of shares and bonds; in other words, this device relates personal savings within a community to business investment. It has been a major problem in some of the under-developed countries to persuade wealthy residents to abandon their preference for investment in gold, jewels and real estate and accept a portfolio of mortgages, shares and bonds as an alternative form of property. The problem is closely related to the development of active capital markets. In this chapter we are concerned with the assignment of rights arising under contracts generally: a discussion of the specific features of such choses in action as mortgages, shares, bonds and negotiable instruments is reserved for later chapters.

A similarity exists between an assignment of rights (choses in action) and a sale of goods (choses in possession). In an assignment the subject-matter is the transfer of contractual rights: in a sale the subject-matter is the transfer of ownership in goods. Although we would expect the law to give equal recognition to each of these transfers, this was not so in the old courts of common law. The common law courts ruled that choses in action were personal rights and could not be transferred as could choses in possession. This rule grew steadily more inconvenient and obsolete as commerce increased. The courts of equity, on the other hand, were much more flexible; they recognized the efficacy and fairness of enforcing assignments of contractual rights. Equity required only that a clear intention to assign a benefit be shown either orally or in writing by the assignor, and then it would permit the assignee to recover from the promisor. Because of this conflict between the rules of the common law courts and those of the courts of equity, the courts of equity required in every action brought by an assignee that he make the assignor a party as well. The action then had three parties — the assignee, the assignor, and the promisor.

EQUITABLE ASSIGNMENTS

A basic principle of law is that a court will not decide a dispute unless all the persons directly affected by its decision have been made parties and have had an opportunity to argue on their own behalf. Thus, if the assignor assigns *part* of his rights only, he is vitally interested in the result of an action by the assignee against the promisor: if the court should decide that the promisor is not bound to perform any part of his obligations, its decision would adversely affect the assignor as well as the assignee.

Illustration:

> *A* owes $1,000 to *B* under a contract. *B* owes $600 to *X*. *B* assigns $600 of his account receivable from *A* to satisfy *X*. Subsequently, *X* sues *A* for the $600. If the court were to decide that *A* was not bound to pay anything on the debt because, say, the contract between *A* and *B* was within the Statute of Frauds and there was an insufficient memorandum of it, *B* would be affected, for he could not claim his remaining $400 of the debt either. The court requires that *B* be made a party to the action by *X* so that he may take part in it. In an assignment of part of a debt, both the assignee and the assignor are equally anxious that the court find the debtor (that is, the promisor) liable. Accordingly, the assignor *B* must have his own chance to argue and to adduce evidence. For example, it might well be that he would have in his possession a memorandum sufficient to comply with the Statute of Frauds, and his evidence might be decisive in holding the debtor liable.
>
> Similarly, in an action brought by *B* against *A*, the court would require that *X* also be made a party.

Let us assume that the assignor assigns only part of his rights and the promisor is willing to perform his obligation, but he does not know what part he should perform for the benefit of the assignee and what part for the benefit of the assignor.

Illustration:

> *A* owes $10,000 to *B* due in twelve months. *B* needs some money now and borrows $8,000 from X Bank, repayable in one year, giving the X bank a *conditional assignment* of his account receivable from *A* as security for repayment of the loan. *B* and the bank have agreed that as long as *B* pays the interest on his loan every three months, the bank will not be entitled to notify *A* of the assignment; but if *B* fails to pay the interest or fails to pay the $8,000 on the due date, the bank may advise *A* to pay it that sum plus unpaid interest, in reduction of his debt to *B*. In other words, the assignment is conditional upon the default of the borrower, *B*. If at the end of the year, the bank notifies *A* that *B* has assigned his account and it demands that *A* pay the bank, *A* cannot afford to do so until he has verified the default and the amount owing. He must check with *B*. Suppose *B* claims that he has paid the bank $6,000 of the debt. *A* is in a quandary: he is aware of the competing claims and fears that if he pays one party and guesses wrong, the other may sue him successfully and collect the money a second time. In such a case *A* should hand the money over to the court as custodian and let *B* and the bank settle their dispute before a judge.

In each of the above illustrations all three parties have a vital concern in the assignment, and it is necessary that all should be bound by a decision of the court. Thus, the requirement of equity that all three should be made parties to the action is a just one in cases where the assignor retains an interest in the contract.

STATUTORY ASSIGNMENTS

In many business transactions an assignor does not wish to retain any rights under the contract assigned. He assigns it wholly and absolutely to the assignee and has no further interest in it. If later the assignee wishes to sue the promisor, the requirement of making the assignor a party may be inconvenient and may even cause considerable hardship; the assignor may be out of the country for a time, or he may have died (in which case it would be necessary to make his personal representative a party). In any event it increases the expense of the action by bringing in a party who has no real interest. In 1873, when the British Parliament amalgamated the courts of common law and equity by passing the Judicature Act, they included a section remedying this defect. The section permits an assignee to sue the promisor to a contract without the assistance of the assignor provided (a) the assignment was absolute (unconditional and complete), (b) the assignment was in writing, and (c) the promisor received notice in writing of the assignment. Most of the provinces of Canada have since passed similar statutes.[15] Assignments that comply with these requirements have become known as *statutory assignments*. All other assignments are today called *equitable assignments*. We should note, however, that the statute did not create any new type of assignment. It merely provided a streamlined procedure for hearing actions on assignments which meet the requirements laid down by statute.

The requirements of the statute about the need for writing are reasonable: if the assignment were oral, the assignee would ordinarily have to call the assignor as a witness anyway, to prove that the assignment was actually made. As we noted in Chapter 3, evidence given by other persons of what the assignor said is *hearsay*, and for this reason the court will not allow such evidence when the assignor himself is able to testify. A written assignment signed by the assignor is as good in most cases as his personal appearance in court. It may be tendered to the court, and only if there is a rare allegation of a serious fraud, such as forgery, will further evidence be required to prove the assignment. The requirement of notice of assignment in writing similarly is helpful and simplifies proving that the promisor knew of the assignment. It is good business practice and common sense to send written notice by registered letter when important rights are in question in any transaction.

NOTICE TO THE PROMISOR

The Effect of Notice on the Promisor

All assignments, whether equitable or statutory, require notice to the promisor. But we must observe that notice to the promisor is not the same thing as requiring his consent. Indeed, a debtor ignores a notice of an assignment at his peril. Confronted with a demand for payment from one who claims to be an assignee, the debtor should, of course, require proof of the fact of assignment to protect himself against a possible fraud, but once he has had an opportunity to satisfy himself that there has been an assignment, he must make further payments to the assignee. If he persists in making payment to his original creditor in the face of such information, he can be sued by the assignee and required to pay the amount a second time.

Illustration:

Akron Manufacturing Co. has sold and delivered a large quantity of its product to Brian Wholesalers Ltd. on credit. Brian Wholesalers Ltd.

---

[15] See, for example: The Conveyancing and Law of Property Act, R.S.O. 1970, c. 85, s. 54; The Judicature Act, R.S.A. 1970, c. 193, s. 34(15); The Laws Declaratory Act, R.S.B.C. 1960, c. 213, s. 2(25); The Judicature Act, St. of N.S. 1950, c. 65 s. 19(5). The statutory provisions are somewhat different in certain provinces. See, for example: The Choses in Action Act, R.S.S. 1965, c. 395, s. 2 and the Law of Property Act, R.S.M. 1970, c. L90, s. 32(1) and (5).

defaults payment and offers to pay Akron Manufacturing Co. by assigning to it certain accounts receivable for goods Brian Wholesalers Ltd. has delivered to retail merchants with excellent credit ratings. Akron Manufacturing Co. agrees to this settlement and takes an absolute assignment of these debts, the largest of which is owed by Woolridge's Department Store. Akron Manufacturing Co. sends a notice to Woolridge's stating that the account has been assigned to it, and encloses a request to pay Akron Manufacturing Co. signed by an officer of Brian Wholesalers. Woolridge's inadvertently ignores the request and notice, and pays Brian Wholesalers Ltd., which shortly afterwards is adjudged bankrupt. Akron Manufacturing Co. sues Woolridge's for payment of the debt again.

In these circumstances Akron Manufacturing Co. would succeed in its action; Woolridge's paid Brian Wholesalers Ltd. at its peril after receiving valid notice of the assignment.[16]

The Effect of Notice from Contending Assignees

The recognition of the assignability of contractual rights is an important modification of the doctrine of privity of contract: someone other than the original party to a contract may emerge to claim the benefit of rights the contract has created. Indeed, more than one person may claim to be the assignee of the same right. Mercifully, the promisor need perform his obligation but once. In order to determine who is entitled to his performance, the court must ascertain the validity and extent of every right claimed against him by various contending assignees.

An unscrupulous creditor can gain a temporary prosperity by assigning to two different persons for valuable consideration the right to collect the same debt. The debtor is then faced with demands for payment from two sources. Which of the two innocent assignees is entitled to payment by the debtor? And which has only an action against the assignor for fraud? The cases are unanimous in deciding that the assignee who first gave notice to the debtor is the one entitled to payment. This rule, like the rule that the debtor must at least receive some notice of assignment before it affects him, offers the only fair treatment to the debtor. Otherwise a debtor would be in a most insecure position, never being sure when he makes payment that someone else may not turn up later to whom he should have paid the money.

When there are two assignees of the same debt, the one who receives his assignment from the assignor first may delay in notifying the debtor, so that the second assignee succeeds in notifying the debtor first. The second assignee is entitled to payment by the debtor unless he knows of the prior assignment at the time of the assignment to him. If he knows of the prior assignment, he is a party to the fraud, and cannot take payment ahead of the first assignee without becoming liable to him.

---

[16] See Brandt's Sons & Co. v. Dunlop Rubber Co. Ltd. [1905] A.C. 454.

THE ASSIGNEE'S TITLE

One of the most important rules affecting assignments is that the assignee can never acquire a better right to sue the promisor than the assignor himself had. In legal terms, the assignee "takes subject to the equities". The result is that a person who acquires a right under an assignment takes it subject to any right arising between the original parties before the promisor receives notice of the assignment. In suing the promisor, the assignee may be met by any defence which the promisor could have put up against the assignor, the party with whom he originally contracted. Consequently, if a person takes an assignment of rights under a contract originally induced by the fraudulent misrepresentation of the assignor, the assignee will have no better chance to enforce his claim than if he had been the perpetrator of the fraud himself. In other words, if a debtor is the victim of fraudulent misrepresentation, the contract remains voidable at his option despite any assignment of the contractual rights. The debtor cannot, however, sue the assignee for *damages* for the tort of deceit: he must sue the assignor, the person actually guilty of the fraud.

We should contrast the position of a person who obtains title to *goods* by fraud with that of a person who obtains *contractual rights* by fraud. We have seen that in spite of fraud a person may obtain title to goods so that, in turn, he may pass on valid title to a subsequent innocent purchaser. The innocent purchaser may retain the goods against the claim of the original defrauded vendor.[17] In contrast, a person who obtains contractual rights by fraud does not, by assigning these rights, give an innocent assignee the right to enforce them against the defrauded promisor. An innocent assignee of a chose in action is in a much more vulnerable position than an innocent purchaser of goods.

Fraudulent misrepresentation is not, of course, the only defence a promisor may apply against an assignee — mistake, undue influence, duress, and a right to set off a debt owed by the assignor to the promisor are equally effective. The promisor may also defend by showing that he received no consideration for his promise. The right to set off a debt requires further explanation:

Illustration:

> *A* is employed by *B* at a salary of $275 per week, payable at noon Saturday when the business closes. On Thursday, *A* borrows $80 from *B*. On Saturday, *A* fails to appear at work on time. When he telephones an hour late an argument ensues, and *B* informs *A* that he is fired and not to bother to come back. On Monday, *A* sues *B* for $275 in the small claims court. *B* may set off both the $80 loan and the $25 *A* would have earned had he appeared at work on Saturday morning. *A* obtains a court judgment for $170.
>
> Suppose, instead of suing *B*, *A* had assigned his claim for salary to his neighbour *X* for $250. *X* would take it subject to the equities between *A* and *B*, and even though *X* did not know of *B*'s loan to *A* and of *A*'s failure to

---

[17] This result follows because fraud makes the contract voidable, not void. See Chapter 9 and King's Norton Metal Co. v. Edridge (1897) 14 T.L.R. 98.

work on Saturday, *B* would be able to set off these amounts in an action by *X*. Thus *X* would recover $170 from *B,* the same amount as *A* could recover.

Until the assignee gives the promisor notice of the assignment, acts of either the assignor or the promisor or their agents may prejudice the assignee's rights. Thus, it is important that the assignee give notice as soon as possible. If he delays, his rights may well deteriorate.

Illustration:

> Williams owes Turner $300. Turner assigns the debt to Young on May 1. Young neglects to notify Williams, and on May 11 Williams pays Turner $125 on account, unaware of the assignment. Because of his failure to notify Williams, the assignee, Young, may now recover from Williams only $175 and must look to Turner for the $125 already paid.

When a creditor assigns rights under a contract before he has completed performance, an assignee may be subject to an additional risk. Even when he has given notice to the debtor, the debtor may be able to use defences based upon developments after the time of notice. Thus, the assignor's failure to complete performance may cause the debtor damages which he can set off against the assignee's claim. In other words, an assignee's rights under a yet incomplete contract are imperfect, and subject to proper completion of the contract.[18]

A general assignment of book debts is an important business device for securing credit. The common law provinces each have statutes rendering such assignments void as against the assignor's creditors unless the assignment is registered in a public office where its terms are available for inspection. The purpose of these statutes is to protect prospective creditors: they may inspect the registry to discover whether some assignee has a prior claim against the assets of a person who has applied to them for credit. We shall consider the reasons for providing public notice more fully in Chapters 24 and 30.

ASSIGNMENTS BY OPERATION OF LAW

Upon the Death of a Party

When one dies, the law automatically assigns his or her rights and obligations under outstanding contracts to a personal representative. If the deceased person leaves a will naming a representative, the representative is called an *executor*. If he or she fails to name an executor in the will (or the executor refuses to assume the position) or else leaves no will (that is, dies *intestate*), the court will appoint a personal representative called an *administrator*. There is no obligation for a representative to perform a contract requiring personal services — the skill of the deceased cannot be demanded of his representative. We need only contemplate the executor of a deceased violinist to understand the need for this rule.

---

[18] Young v. Kitchin (1878), 3 Ex. D. 127.

The task of the executor or administrator is to pay all just claims against the deceased's estate, to complete performance of any outstanding contractual obligations of the deceased not requiring his personal skill, to prosecute all claims the deceased had against others, and to distribute the assets according to the will — or in the case of an intestate person, distribute the assets to his heirs according to statutory provisions.[19]

Bankruptcy

An insolvent businessman, on realizing that his position is hopeless, may voluntarily apply for bankruptcy proceedings to avoid further loss to his creditors and injury to his name. In many instances, however, bankruptcy proceedings are instituted against a debtor by creditors who petition the court for an order known as a *receiving order*. If the creditors present convincing proof of the insolvency of their debtor, the court adjudges him bankrupt and appoints a licensed trustee to take charge of his property. It is then the duty of the licensed trustee to liquidate the assets and to settle the creditors' claims.

We are to deal with bankruptcy again in Chapter 31. We raise the topic at this point simply to emphasize the relationship between a bankrupt person and a trustee in bankruptcy. The proceedings require an assignment to the trustee of the bankrupt person's assets, including his contractual rights and his liabilities as well.[20]

Since presumably one wishes neither to die nor to become bankrupt, the assignments caused by death and most bankruptcy proceedings differ from other assignments in that they are involuntary; they take place "by operation of law". One's affairs are seldom completely in order on either of these occasions, and the assignment achieves an artificial extension of the assignor's legal existence until his affairs can be wound up.

NEGOTIABLE INSTRUMENTS

Their Nature and Uses

A negotiable instrument — for example, a draft, promissory note, or cheque — is a written contract containing a promise, express or implied,[21] to pay a specific sum of money to the order of a designated person or to "bearer".

---

[19] The way in which the estate of an intestate person will be distributed to his heirs is set down in provincial statutes. See, for example: The Devolution of Estates Act, R.S.O. 1970, c. 129; Intestate Succession Act, R.S.N.S. 1967, c. 153; The Administration Act, R.S.B.C. 1960, c. 3, Part VII.

[20] The licensed trustee may, however, with the permission of inspectors appointed by the creditors, disclaim any lease of property of the bankrupt debtor. The Bankruptcy Act, R.S.C. 1970, c. B-3, s. 14(1)(k).

[21] According to the wording of a cheque, the drawer does not directly promise to pay its amount, but he does promise by implication that sufficient funds will be available in his account to pay it when it is presented.

Generally speaking, a negotiable instrument arises from a contract that precedes it: a buyer delivers a negotiable instrument in payment for goods or services received. But delivery of the instrument does not complete the promisor's obligation. If he does not honour the instrument when it falls due and is presented to be paid, the promisee's rights, under the original contract of sale or for services, revive. Often the promisee chooses to sue for failure to honour the negotiable instrument rather than breach of the original contract, because the procedure for suing on a negotiable instrument is somewhat simpler.

The unique aspects of the law of negotiable instruments arise when a promisee assigns an instrument to a third party.

Negotiability Compared with Assignability

The process of assigning a negotiable instrument is known as *negotiation*. A promisee or payee of an instrument may negotiate it in one of two ways: if the instrument is payable to bearer, he need only deliver it to a third party; if the instrument is payable to his order, he must endorse his name upon it and then deliver it. Negotiation is really a special type of assignment in which the new holder of the instrument acquires from the transferor the rights which the instrument has to convey.

Chapters 21 and 22 of this book examine the law affecting negotiable instruments in more detail. Since, however, negotiation is a special application of assignments, we can better understand both concepts by reviewing their differences here. In a sense, negotiation is a privileged type of assignment which is released, for reasons of business convenience, from certain of the strictures that apply to an ordinary assignment of contractual rights. It therefore differs from an assignment of rights generally in the following important respects:

(i) Notice to the Promisor. We have seen that notice plays two important roles in assignment generally: first, written notice is necessary before an assignee may take advantage of a statutory assignment; second, notice protects an assignee against the consequences of payment by the promisor to the assignor or other assignees. Notice, however, is of no consequence in the transfer of a negotiable instrument — indeed, it is irrelevant. This result stems from the fact that the promisor in a negotiable instrument is liable to pay only one person, the holder of the instrument for the time being. Thus, even if he receives notice of the assignment, neither he nor his bank will pay the assignee unless the assignee presents the instrument. The promisor pays his debt only once — to the holder of the instrument for the time being *and* in exchange for the instrument. In effect he pays for the return of his negotiable instrument. "The idea of 'embedding' legal rights in a document, such that the abstract rights move in unison with the physical certificate, has been very potent in commercial law, especially in regard to debt obligations."[22]

---

[22] Baxter and Johnston, "New Mechanics for Securities Transactions", (1971) 21 *University of Toronto Law Journal*, 358.

Illustration:

Steele receives his monthly pay cheque of $1,000 from Union Foundry Co. Ltd. He negotiates it to Comfy Furniture Mart for $700 worth of furniture and $300 cash. Steele then tells his employer that he has inadvertently destroyed the cheque by throwing the envelope containing it into a fire, and he persuades the company to pay him a second time. When Comfy Furniture Mart presents the original cheque for payment, the foundry company must honour it even though the furniture dealer gave no notice of the assignment.

If instead Steele had assigned to the furniture dealer a claim against the foundry for arrears of wages (a contractual right not represented by any negotiable instrument) and if the furniture dealer did not immediately notify the foundry of the assignment, the foundry could defeat the claim of the furniture dealer, as assignee, by establishing that it had already paid Steele before receiving notice.

(ii) Defences of the Promisor. An assignee for value of a negotiable instrument may succeed in an action against the promisor where the assignor himself would not have succeeded. For example, even when a party is induced to undertake liability on a negotiable instrument as a result of fraud or undue influence, he may be sued successfully by a subsequent innocent holder who has given consideration for the instrument; yet the party guilty of the fraud could not himself enforce the promise in the instrument.[23] Similarly, a person who has given a negotiable instrument in payment for an illegal consideration loses his defence of illegality against an innocent holder of the instrument for value. By contrast, in an ordinary assignment of rights, the assignee never acquires a better right than the assignor had; the debtor retains his defences against the assignee.

Illustration:

Bacchus contracted with Hermes for the illegal transportation of liquor into Ontario and gave Hermes his cheque for $2,000 for services rendered. The police discovered and confiscated the liquor, and Bacchus then advised his bank to stop payment on the cheque to Hermes. In the meantime, Hermes had used the cheque in payment of a debt to an innocent trade creditor, Argus, who knew nothing of the circumstances under which it had been obtained. Argus learned that payment of the cheque had been stopped when he attempted to cash it at the bank. Argus sued Bacchus on the dishonoured instrument.

Bacchus might have used the defence of illegality in an action brought against him by the party with whom he contracted — Hermes. But he must pay the holder of the cheque, Argus, assuming (as appears probable) that Argus can prove he took the instrument unaware of its illegal origin and gave value for it.

---

[23] But see The Bills of Exchange Act, R.S.C. 1970, c. B-5, as amended by St. of Can. 1969-70, c. 48, s. 190, restricting the rights of finance companies to assert the status of a holder in due course.

By contrast, if Hermes' claim for $2,000 against Bacchus had remained simply in the form of an account receivable, no one to whom Hermes might have assigned the debt would have obtained a better right to collect it than Hermes himself had.

(iii) Form of Action. A holder of a negotiable instrument can sue in his own name without joining any of the other parties to the instrument.

Commercial Importance of Negotiability

For hundreds of years, merchants have found it to their mutual advantage to recognize negotiable instruments as a special class of readily assignable promise, free from the formalities and many of the risks which attend an ordinary assignment of contractual rights. Business experience has shown that the concept of negotiability has a convenience that far outweighs the probable cost of its abuse. As we have noted, one of the ways the law restricts the possibility of abuse is by the rule that before a holder of a negotiable instrument can succeed in the face of such defences as fraud, undue influence, duress, and illegality, he must have been innocent of the origin of the instrument, and he or some previous holder of the instrument must have given value for it.[24]

Modern banking practice is based upon the relatively secure position of an innocent holder for value of a negotiable instrument. Banks, as innocent holders for value, are able to cash cheques or accept them for deposit without exhaustive inquiry into the background of the transactions out of which they arose: for example they are entitled to collect the amount from a drawer even if his cheque originated as a result of fraud, undue influence, or duress practised upon him, or as a result of an illegal transaction. Without such a rule, banking facilities would be much less accessible to business and the public generally.

Currency

The familiar Bank of Canada note is a special type of instrument authorized by statute and designed to circulate with maximum ease of transferability. We shall refer to it again briefly in Chapter 22.

QUESTIONS FOR REVIEW

1. Define: assignee; vicarious performance; novation; constructive trust; beneficiary; chose in action.
2. Under what circumstances may a promisor obtain the services of another to perform his obligation?
3. What are the chief respects in which the privity of contract rule has been modified?

---

[24] In fact, the requirements are somewhat more technical than we can conveniently describe here: the holder must be a *holder in due course*. See *infra*, Chapter 28.

4. Apart from law, what objection might an employer have to his employee's assigning a part of his salary in payment for a debt?
5. By what legal rule could the old courts of common law refuse to enforce the rights of an assignee of a chose in action?
6. *A* fraudulently sold to *B* shares in a company which proved to be non-existent.
   (a) *B* signed an agreement for the purchase of the shares in which he promised to pay *A* $300. *A* assigned this debt to *C*.
   (b) *B* gave his promissory note for $300 payable to the order of *A*. *A* endorsed the note over to *C*.
   (c) Instead of promising to pay money, *B* delivered to *A* his stereophonic radio in payment for the shares. *A* sold the radio to *C*.

   In each of the above unrelated instances *C* was an innocent third party who gave consideration to *A*. What are *C*'s rights?
7. A debtor owed his creditor $200. The creditor assigned his right to collect this debt to another person, *X*. The assignee (*X*) delayed in sending notice to the debtor that he was now the party entitled to payment. The debtor, before receiving any notice of assignment, paid his original creditor $125 on account. What is the nature of *X*'s recourse?
8. Anderson, a skilled mechanic, agreed to do some car repair work for Bartlett. Anderson was busy when the car was delivered for repair and gave his friend Gauche the work to do, without consulting Bartlett. Gauche sent Bartlett a bill for his services. Bartlett refused to pay. Is he justified?
9. "If it were asked what discovery has most deeply affected the fortunes of the human race it might probably be said with truth — The discovery that a debt is a saleable commodity." (McLeod, *Theory and Practice of Banking,* (5th ed.), I:200.) Explain and elaborate this quotation.
10. (a) Give a brief example illustrating the operation of the rule: "The successive assignees of an obligation rank as to their title, not according to the dates at which the creditor assigned his rights to them respectively, but according to the dates at which notice was given to the party to be charged." (*Anson's Law of Contract* (23rd ed.), p. 416.)
    (b) Explain the reason for this rule.
    (c) Why is this rule irrelevant for negotiable instruments?

CASES FOR DISCUSSION

CASE 1

Rigoletto, an operatic singer of great renown, was engaged to give a concert in Montreal. A hall was rented, a stage crew hired, and much advertising undertaken. The day before he was to perform, notice was received in Montreal to the effect that he proposed to send his understudy, Tremolo, to sing in his place. The reason advanced for this change in plans was that one of Rigoletto's friends was leaving on an extended trip and Rigoletto wished to attend a farewell party in his honour. Tremolo was not, of course, nearly as well known as Rigoletto, but a noted music critic had recently observed that he was quite as good.

Can Rigoletto's sponsors in Montreal sue him for breach of contract? Give reasons.

CASE 2

Gamble purchased from Brown a building for business purposes. In their agreement Gamble convenanted that he would insure the property and assign the insurance to Brown, the vendor, as security for the amount which remained owing on the purchase price.

Gamble insured the property with the Standard Insurance Company but neglected to advise it that the proceeds in the event of a claim should be paid to Brown. The building was later destroyed in a fire.

Immediately following the fire, three of Gamble's trade creditors sought payment of their claims and agreed to accept from him an assignment to them of the proceeds of the fire insurance. The trade creditors gave notice to Standard Insurance Company at once, before the amount of the loss had been established and before that company had admitted any liability under the policy. Thereafter Brown, learning of these circumstances, advised the insurance company that he wished to claim the insurance money due, and supported his claim by reference to the terms of the agreement for sale. The insurance company paid the money into court for settlement of the dispute. Who is entitled to the money? (See *Gordon v. Gordon* [1924] 1 W.W.R. 903.)

CASE 3

Kerr was a schoolteacher employed at a private school operated by Humphries. Kerr became indebted to a money-lender, Jones, for about $450. In consideration for the loan, he assigned to Jones as much of his salary as should be necessary to repay the sum borrowed with interest and any further sums for which he might thereafter become indebted to Jones. Is Jones, as assignee, entitled to sue Humphries without the assistance of Kerr's testimony? (See *Jones v. Humphries* [1902] 1 K.B. 10.)

CASE 4

On January 15 Benson, a contractor, undertook the installation of frozen-food cabinets in Ross's grocery store, for which his bill was $95. Through the period January 1 to 31 of the same year, Benson purchased groceries on credit from Ross to the value of $135. On January 31, Benson assigned to Kilby his claim of $95 against Ross, as a means of repayment of a sum of money lent by Kilby to Benson. Kilby notified Ross of the assignment on February 2. Ross refused to pay Kilby. Is he entitled to do so? (See *Burman v. Rosin* (1916) 26 D.L.R. 790.)

CASE 5

Leeder sold his taxi business to Fisher, covenanting not to directly or indirectly carry on or be engaged in as principal, partner, or servant of another taxi business within five miles of the place of business for five years from the date of sale. The agreement contained the usual clause extending the benefit of the contract to the "assigns" (assignees) of the parties. Before the five years had elapsed, Fisher resold the taxi business to Pivnick, and Leeder entered into another taxi business within the five-mile area. Pivnick brought an action against Leeder for an injunction to restrain him from operating a competing business within the five-mile area. Should Pivnick succeed? (*Pivnick v. Leeder* (1932) 41 O.W.N. 143.)

CASE 6

York Bridge Co. Ltd. undertook construction work for the City of Toronto in July. A month later, when the construction work was partly completed, York Bridge Co. Ltd. assigned to Southern Ontario Foundries & Steel Co. Ltd. the amount of $6,800 then due to it in respect of work completed by that time. Southern Ontario Foundries & Steel Co. Ltd. immediately notified the City of Toronto of the assignment but did not immediately pursue its rights when the City was slow in paying.

York Bridge Co. Ltd. abandoned the contract in September following, and its non-performance occasioned a loss to the City of Toronto in the order of $25,000. When Southern Ontario Foundries & Steel Co. Ltd. then attempted, as assignee, to collect $6,800 from the City, it was met with the defence that the City now owed no money in respect of the construction work because the damages it had sustained from breach of the contract exceeded the sum owing for the part of the work that had already been done. In reply, Southern Ontario Foundries & Steel Co. Ltd. contended that the sum of $6,800 was due and payable at the time the City of Toronto had been notified of the assignment.

Explain the issues raised by these facts and the applicable rules of law, and express an opinion whether Southern Ontario Foundries & Steel Co. Ltd. should be able to recover $6,800 from the City of Toronto. (For references, see *Young v. Kitchin* (1878) 3 Ex.D. 127; *American Bridge Co. v. City of Boston* 202 Mass. 374, 88 N.E. 1089.)

CHAPTER 14

The Discharge of Contracts

THE WAYS IN WHICH A CONTRACT MAY BE DISCHARGED

To discharge a contract means "to cancel or unloose the obligation of a contract; to make an agreement or contract null and inoperative".[1] In this chapter we shall consider four ways in which the discharge of a contract may occur. These are by performance, agreement, frustration, and operation of law. In addition, a contract is sometimes said to be "discharged" by its breach, but this topic is reserved for separate treatment in the following chapter.

DISCHARGE BY PERFORMANCE

The Nature of Discharge by Performance

Performance is the type of discharge anticipated when the parties make their agreement. A contract is at an end when the parties have performed their respective obligations satisfactorily. For a discharge to be effected, performance must have been completed by both parties and not merely by one of them. A bilateral contract, formed by the offer of a promise for a promise, goes through three stages: first, when neither party has performed his promise; second, when one but not the other party has performed; and third, when both parties have performed. Only at the final stage is the contract discharged by performance. In a unilateral contract, formed by the offer of a promise for an act, the first of these

---

[1] Black, *Law Dictionary* (4th ed.).

stages never exists and the second takes place in the very formation of the contract: the last stage is still necessary for discharge by performance.

Performance may take several forms, depending on the contract. It may be services rendered, goods delivered, a cash payment made, or any combination of these.

Tender of Performance

Occasionally a party attempts to perform, but the other party refuses to accept his performance. An attempt to perform is called a *tender* of performance, whether accepted or rejected by the other party.

If a seller properly tenders delivery of the goods and the buyer refuses to accept them, the seller is under no obligation to attempt delivery again and may immediately bring an action for breach of contract.

In a tender of payment, if the debtor makes an unsuccessful but reasonable attempt to pay, he will be free from further liability for interest on the amount owing and generally will not have to pay court costs if he is later sued for the debt. To be sure of this result, he should offer the money in the form of *legal tender*. Legal tender consists of Bank of Canada notes (or "bills" as we call them) and coins to the following limits: silver coin to $10, nickel coin to $5, and coppers to 25¢.[2] A creditor is legally within his rights in refusing to accept payment in silver of a debt of, say, $100: he may also refuse any negotiable instrument, including even a cheque certified by a bank. In practice, however, payment is often made in a form which is not legal tender, and the majority of business debts are now settled by cheque. Only when there is a possibility of dispute does a legally correct tender of payment become important. The debtor will then make a formal legal tender of cash to his creditor to avoid any later claim that he was unwilling or unable to meet his obligations.

Illustration:

> *S* agrees in writing to sell $10,000 worth of flour to *B*, cash on delivery. Before the date of delivery the price of flour rises substantially. *S* becomes anxious to discover a means of avoiding the contract; and hearing a rumour that *B* is in financial difficulties, he uses the argument that *B* may be unable to pay as a pretext for notifying *B* that he is terminating the contract. *B*, on the other hand, wishes to go through with the sale at the agreed price. He takes the contract to his bank and borrows sufficient cash (in legal tender) to pay the purchase price. He then appears at *S'*s place of business and tenders the money in the presence of a witness. If *S* does not deliver the flour and *B* sues him for breach of contract, *S* cannot claim in defence that *B* was unable to pay.

If a creditor is foolish enough to refuse a legal tender of payment, any subsequent action to recover the money will be at his own expense. On the other

---

[2] The Currency and Exchange Act, R.S.C. 1970, c. C-39, s. 7.

hand, the debtor is not discharged of his debt by having had his tender of payment refused. He will still have to pay it, but no interest will accrue after the date of tender. It is possible that if the debtor tenders payment in a reasonable fashion (though not strictly speaking in the form of legal tender), a court may, in its discretion, still award the costs of any subsequent litigation against the creditor.

There is a legal maxim that the debtor must seek out his creditor. He is not excused from tendering payment because his creditor is shy or diffident about asking for it: the onus is on the debtor to find his creditor and pay him.

DISCHARGE BY AGREEMENT

Waiver

A contract may not run its course through performance but may be discharged prematurely because the parties agree between themselves not to perform it. A waiver is an agreement not to proceed with performance of a contract already in existence, when one or both of the parties has yet to perform his part of it. If neither party has performed fully at the time both agree to call off the bargain, there will automatically be consideration for waiver of each party. Each still has rights and obligations outstanding, and his promise to waive his rights is sufficient consideration for his release from his obligations.

On the other hand, if one party has already performed his part, he receives no consideration for his waiver of the other party's duty to perform. To be enforceable, his promise to release the other party should be under seal.

Illustration:

> Atwater agrees to build a high-fidelity radio for Kent for $450. Kent's right under the contract is to receive the benefits of the work, and his obligation is to pay for it. Atwater's right is to receive his money, and his obligation is to do the work required. Consequently, if they should mutually agree to call their contract off before Atwater completes the work, there is consideration for the waiver. From Kent's point of view, the consideration for Atwater's abandonment of a claim for payment is giving up Kent's right to Atwater's services. From Atwater's point of view, the consideration for Kent's abandoning a claim for Atwater's services is giving up his claim for payment by Kent.
>
> But suppose that Kent has paid Atwater the $450 and that to date Atwater has only partly built the radio. At this stage any undertaking by Kent that he will ''require neither completion of the work nor a return of any money'' will be without consideration and not binding unless under seal.

Of course, neither party can impose a waiver on the other. If one party fails to perform without securing a waiver of the other, he commits a breach of the contract. As we shall see in the following chapter, the consequences of breach are quite different from discharge by agreement.

Substituted Agreement

Material alteration of the terms. If the parties agree to a material alteration of the terms that goes to the root of the contract, they have in effect agreed to a discharge of their original contract and its replacement with a new one. Minor changes in the terms do not have this sweeping effect. To bring a substituted agreement into existence, a major alteration of the original agreement must be made with the consent of all parties.

In *Thornhill v. Neats*[3] a building contract provided a penalty against the contractor if he did not have the work done by a certain date. Before its completion the contractor and the owner agreed that additional work should be undertaken by the contractor on the same project. The change made it impossible to complete the building by the date originally set. In settling a dispute about the total price of the project, the court held that the new agreement had discharged the old and that the penalty clause had disappeared with it.

Accord and satisfaction. Sometimes a promisor finds he cannot perform his obligation according to the terms of his contract. He may offer the promisee a money payment or some other substitute if the promisee will discharge him from his original obligation. For example, a seller may find that he cannot obtain certain imported goods to fill an order and may offer other goods of equal quality, perhaps at a lower price, if the buyer will release him from his original promise. Accord and satisfaction often takes the form of a compromise out of court. One of the parties may have been preparing to sue the other when a money settlement is reached.

The distinction between a material alteration of the terms and accord and satisfaction is as follows: in a *material alteration* the parties are basically preoccupied with the new arrangement, and the discharge of the old contract is incidental — they may not even direct their minds to this problem; in *accord and satisfaction* the parties are directly concerned with the discharge of an existing contract — the new arrangement is for that very purpose.

A party may concede liability for damages though he and the other party still differ about the *amount* of the damages he should pay. The party admitting liability may tender payment of an amount in settlement and have it refused on the grounds that it is insufficient. He may then pay into court the amount he has offered. If the other party proceeds with an action for damages and the court awards him no more than what has already been tendered in settlement, he will have to pay the court costs as the penalty for his insistence upon litigation; and the defendant will not be liable for interest on the sum due from the time he tendered it. On the other hand, if the damages awarded are greater than the sum paid

---

[3] (1860) 141 E.R. 1392.

into court by the defendant, the judge may apportion the court costs between the parties, or if the amount of the defendant's tender was unreasonable, he may order the defendant to pay all the costs.

Novation. Novation is another method of discharge: a replacement of one of the parties discharges the original contract and substitutes a new one. A common example of novation arises when a businessman purchases a going business and assumes its outstanding liabilities as a part of the purchase price for the assets acquired. If the creditors accept the new owner as their debtor, either by an express agreement with him or by applying to the new owner for payment of their claims against the former owner, the liability of the former owner will be discharged and replaced by that of the purchaser. In the words of Mr. Justice Fisher:

> Where the business of a partnership is taken over by a new company [new owner] and the creditor of the partnership applies to the new company for payment, his claim is admitted and they promise to pay the debt, that is sufficient in my opinion to make the new company liable, as slight circumstances are sufficient to show an adoption by the creditors of the new company as their debtor.[4]

It is fair to add, however, that there must be evidence of consent to the novation on the part of both the creditors and the new owner.[5]

In good business practice, neither the vendor nor the purchaser of a business relies upon implied novation with creditors. The two parties to the sale agree upon what debts the new owner should assume and then call in the creditors to obtain their express consent to the substitution of a new debtor. In addition, to protect himself, the purchaser of a business makes a careful examination of public records, requires the vendor to provide a declaration setting out the names of all his creditors and the amounts owing to them, and advertises the sale. We shall examine the statutory reasons for these procedures more fully in Chapters 30 and 31, which discuss creditors' rights.

The Contract Provides for its Own Dissolution

At the time the parties draw up their contract, one of them may foresee the possibility of some event affecting his ability or willingness to perform. If the other party is agreeable, they may include an express term to allow for this eventuality. Alternatively, there may be a similar term implied by trade usage or by the surrounding circumstances of the agreement. The subject-matter of the term may be a condition precedent, a condition subsequent, or an option to terminate.

Condition precedent. In Chapter 12 we noted that a condition precedent is a future or uncertain event which must either happen or not happen before the promisor's liability is established. In that chapter we were concerned with the in-

---

[4] Re Star Flooring Co. Ltd. [1924] 3 D.L.R. 269 at 272.
[5] Toronto Star v. Aiken [1955] O.W.N. 613.

terpretation of contracts and the operation of the parol evidence rule, so that in our references a condition precedent was the subject of an oral understanding. It may also be the subject of a term within a written contract.

Illustration:

> *A* Co. Ltd., located in Moncton, writes to *B* in Winnipeg offering him a good position. *B* replies by letter that he will take the position if *A* Co. Ltd. will first find satisfactory living accommodation in Moncton for his wife and seven children. *A* Co. Ltd. accepts *B*'s counter-offer by mail. The employer's act of finding the specified living accommodation is the condition precedent.

Some have argued that a contract never even comes into existence when there is a condition precedent, and that to be capable of discharge a contract must first have existed. Yet there is a real sense in which the contract is formed from the time of the offer and the acceptance, even though the condition precedent is not resolved until later. A contract subject to a condition precedent does have a binding force from the outset, and the parties are not free to withdraw from their promises unless and until the condition precedent becomes impossible to fulfil. The arrangement is therefore much more than an outstanding offer which can be revoked prior to acceptance.

A series of conditions precedent may arise in one contract when a party for whom work is to be done stipulates that as work progresses it must be approved at specified stages by a designated architect or engineer. If after the work at any stage is completed, the architect or engineer states that he is not satisfied with the quality of performance, the obligation to pay for that stage and for further work under the contract ceases. His approval is a condition precedent to payment for the preceding stage and for continuing with all remaining stages. When a person agrees to do work on these terms, he exposes himself to the judgment and reasonableness of the architect or engineer. Unless he can show that there has been fraud or collusion between the architect or engineer and the other contracting party, he is subject to the verdict reached; and he cannot claim a breach of contract if the work is brought to an end prematurely because the architect or engineer, acting in good faith, refuses to approve what has been done.[6]

A promisor would be in an even more difficult position if he gave the right to approve or disapprove of performance to the promisee himself rather than to a third party such as an engineer or architect. The promisee's opinion of what is satisfactory is far more likely to be highly prejudiced in his own favour. The courts have held that the promisee can withhold approval and avoid liability under the contract. It does not matter that the promisee's judgment is unreasonable, or that the judge or jury believe that in the circumstances they themselves would have approved of the performance: so long as they find that the promisee is honestly dissatisfied, the promisor has no rights against him.[7]

---

[6] Halsbury, *Laws of England* (3rd ed.), Vol. 3, 456, para. 871.
[7] Truman v. Ford Motor Co. [1926] 1 D.L.R. 960.

Condition subsequent. A condition subsequent is an uncertain event the happening of which brings the promisor's liability to an end. Liability is established when the contract is formed but one of the parties has reserved for himself an "out" in certain circumstances. A patron of professional baseball has the benefit of a term in his contract for the purchase of admission that if the game is rained out before a stated inning he will have his money refunded (or, possibly, be given a ticket for another game).

Illustration:

> Norton is the holder of a baseball season's ticket which, because of his habits known to the management, was sold to him on terms that he must watch his conduct at the games.
>
> Norton attends a game and conducts himself in such a way as to be a source of annoyance and nuisance not only to the operators of the ball park but also to other patrons and to the persons selling tickets. He has a loud, resonant voice and insists on telling other fans things they do not want to know, and by moving about, obstructs the views of others. The management advises Norton of the cancellation of his season's ticket and tenders him the *pro-rata* portion of the purchase price pertaining to the remaining games. Norton brings an action against the management for breach of contract.
>
> The contract has contained a term relating to a condition subsequent — Norton's objectionable conduct. It is therefore discharged by agreement rather than by breach, and Norton's action will fail. [8]

In contracts for the shipment of goods the so-called "act of God" (the raging of the natural elements) may be a condition subsequent if it results in the total destruction of the shipment. When a railway, trucking line, airline, or steamship company accepts goods for shipment, it undertakes to be liable for any damage to the extent that the goods arrive at their destination in a poorer condition than they were received by the carrier; but there is a term that the carrier will be discharged from this liability if an act of God occurs which destroys the goods. If the goods are only partly destroyed, the contract is not discharged completely; instead the carrier is absolved from liability to the extent that the damage was caused to the goods by an act of God and must deliver them as they are. Such a term is in fact implied by trade custom, but most carriers take the added precaution of making the term express in the writing of their bills of lading. Accordingly, it is wise for a party who has goods shipped at his own risk to contract for insurance against such loss.

Option to terminate. A contract may include a term which provides that one party or perhaps both will have the option of bringing the contract to an end before performance has been completed, usually by giving notice. The operation of the term results in discharge by agreement because the means of discharge

---

[8] See: North v. Victoria Baseball & Athletic Co. [1949] 1 W.W.R. 1033.

have in fact been agreed upon in drawing up the contract. For example, a contract of employment of indefinite duration usually contains an option clause, either express or implied, entitling the employer to dispense with the services of his employee on giving the required notice, as explained in Chapter 21. Again, many mortgages have an option clause entitling the mortgagor to pay off the principal sum before maturity by tendering an additional payment of interest.

DISCHARGE BY FRUSTRATION

Effect of Absolute Promises

The English common law originally held a party responsible in every instance for a failure to perform his promise — even when the failure had not been his fault. Of course, a party could avoid such consequences, if he foresaw them, by insisting at the time of agreement upon an express term absolving him from liability under given circumstances. In fact, the argument for holding a party responsible was that he could have provided for the event in the contract but did not do so. Unfortunately, many people would not think to take this precaution, nor is it possible to foresee all the eventualities that may occur.

As we point out later, the law now excuses a party for his failure to perform in a wide variety of circumstances where he is not at fault. Nevertheless, a few types of promise remain which the law regards as being of such a positive or inviolable nature as to preclude the defence of frustration, regardless of the reason for failing to perform. The tenant's covenants in a lease to keep the property in repair and to pay rent are promises of this kind, with the result that tenants have found themselves liable for damages caused by fire, storms, and enemy action, and liable for rent for the duration of the lease when the property was no longer of use to them.[9] In addition, it is open to a party in any type of contract to express his promise in such an absolute and unconditional way as to rule out any possible reservation for his benefit and thus forfeit the defence of frustration.[10]

Several of the provinces have enacted legislation to overrule the common law and provide that the doctrine of frustration applies to tenancy agreements for residential premises.[11] The legislation does not, however, extend the doctrine to leases of commercial, as opposed to residential, premises.

Doctrine of Frustration

As we have seen, an overriding consideration in our law is that contracts in general should have binding force and effect: for the courts to condone a failure to

---

[9] Paradine v. Jane (1647) 82 E.R. 897; Redmond v. Dainton [1920] 2 K.B. 256; Foster v. Caldwell [1948] 4 D.L.R. 70.

[10] Budgett & Co. v. Binnington & Co. [1891] 1 Q.B. 35; Hills v. Sughrue (1846) 153 E.R. 844.

[11] See, for example: The Landlord and Tenant Act, St. of B.C. 1970, c. 18, s. 41; St. of Man. 1970, c. 106, s. 90; R.S.O. 1970, c. 236, s. 88.

perform on slight pretext would be to import uncertainty into business affairs. The doctrine of frustration qualifies this general proposition. Accordingly, judges have given much thought to the problem of defining the scope of the doctrine and the instances in which it can be applied.

The courts have offered a variety of explanations for the doctrine of frustration. In *Davis Contractors Ltd. v. Fareham*, Lord Radcliffe said:

> Frustration occurs whenever the law recognizes that without default of either party a contractual obligation has become incapable of being performed because the circumstances in which performance is called for would render it a radically different thing from that which was undertaken by contract. . . . It is not hardship or inconvenience or material loss itself which calls the principle of frustration into play. There must be as well such a change in the significance of the obligation that the thing undertaken would, if performed, be a different thing from that contracted for.[12]

In another case, Mr. Justice Goddard said:

> If the foundation of the contract goes, either by the destruction of the subject-matter or by reason of such long interruption or delay that the performance is really in effect that of a different contract, and the parties have not provided what in that event is to happen, the performance of the contract is to be regarded as frustrated.[13]

Again, Lord Sumner has put it this way:

> It is really a device by which the rules as to absolute contracts are reconciled with a special exception which justice demands.[14]

A decision that a contract has been discharged by frustration may be viewed, then, as a practical and reasonable solution to be imposed authoritatively by a court under circumstances that were not contemplated by the parties.[15]

The simplest cases are those in which performance becomes literally impossible, and it is understandable that it was through them the courts first began to develop the doctrine of frustration. In *Taylor v. Caldwell*[16] the producer of a concert contracted for the use of a music hall, but it was destroyed by fire prior to the date on which the concert was to be given. The producer sued the owner for damages to compensate for losses sustained in having to cancel the concert and festivities planned. The court held that the contract had been discharged by frustration, with the result that the action for damages failed. Had the court found

---

[12] [1956] A.C. 696 at 729.

[13] Tatem Ltd. v. Gamboa [1939] 1 K.B. 132 at 139.

[14] Hirji Mulji v. Chong Yue Steamship Co. [1926] A.C. 497 at 510.

[15] The theories underlying the doctrine of frustration are discussed in Cheshire, Fifoot and Furmston, *The Law of Contract* (8th ed.), Part VII, Chapter 3; and in Anson, *Principles of the English Law of Contract* (23rd ed.), Chapter XIV.

[16] (1863) 122 E.R. 309.

instead that the contract had been broken by the owner of the music hall, it would have ordered him to pay damages.

Again, in *Robinson v. Davison*[17] Robinson had engaged Mrs. Davison, a pianist, to give a concert on the evening of January 14, 1870. He incurred expenses in preparing for the concert. About 9:00 a.m. on the morning of the 14th he received a letter from Mrs. Davison advising that a sudden illness would prevent her from performing. Robinson incurred further expenses in cancelling the concert. When he sued for damages for his loss, the court held that the contract had been discharged by frustration, and the action failed.

The doctrine has required its most careful statement in a number of later cases in which performance *could* be physically undertaken, though performance had come to have a very different meaning for the parties from that which they conceived at the time of their agreement. *Metropolitan Water Board v. Dick, Kerr & Co.*[18] was such a case. In July 1914 the English contractors Dick, Kerr & Co. agreed to construct certain reservoirs for a local water board within six years at an agreed price; they commenced work immediately. In February, 1916, the Minister of Munitions, acting under wartime statutes, ordered the contractors to cease work. The greater part of their plant and materials was then sold under his directions. After the war ended, the water board insisted that the contractors should resume their work under the original terms, and the contractors refused to comply. Prices and conditions of supply were then very different from what they had been in 1916. The court held that the contract had been discharged by frustration, with the result that the water board failed in its action.

On the other hand, hardship is not a sufficient excuse for failing to perform. The mere fact that the contractual obligations prove to be more onerous than anticipated will not, by itself, discharge the contract by frustration. It follows that a promisor who finds himself deprived of the most convenient or inexpensive method of performance is not excused if other means remain by which he may reasonably perform. To excuse a promisor in these circumstances would, in the words of Lord Wright, be "to impair the authority of written contracts . . . by lax or too wide application of the doctrine of frustration. Modern English law has recognized how beneficial that doctrine is when the whole circumstances justify it, but to apply it calls for circumspection."[19]

Lastly, we may note that for a contract to be discharged by frustration performance must become impossible or purposeless *after the agreement was made*, for reasons beyond the control of the parties. We must distinguish this situation from one in which performance was impossible or purposeless at the very time the agreement was made. If the subject-matter has ceased to exist at the time of the agreement, the agreement is void for common mistake, as Chapter 9 has shown: it is not discharged by frustration.

---

[17] (1871) L.R. 6 Ex. 269.

[18] [1918] A.C. 119.

[19] Twentsche Overseas Trading Co. v. Uganda Sugar Factory Ltd. (1945) 114 L.J.P.C. 25 at 28.

Self-induced Frustration

A party to a contract cannot wilfully disable himself from performing and then claim successfully that the contract has been frustrated. Such *self-induced frustration* is a breach of the contract. In many circumstances the distinction between true frustration and self-induced frustration is readily apparent.

Illustrations:

> (a) *A* contracts to transport earth for *B*. Upon discovering that he has made a bad bargain, he sells his dump truck and claims that he cannot fulfil the contract because of frustration. We have no difficulty in deciding that *A* has broken the contract.

> (b) *A* contracts to transport earth for *B* in an isolated northern community. Shortly after the contract is made, his one truck (the only available one in the area) is stolen and wrecked. The contract is discharged by frustration, and *A* is freed from his obligation to perform.

> (c) *A* contracts to transport earth for *B*. His dump truck breaks down because of his negligence, and there will be a long delay in its repair as the parties are in a small northern community. Because the situation is attributable to *A*'s negligence, he will be liable for breach of contract.

Not every degree of fault or irresponsibility, however, will bar a party from claiming that the contract has been frustrated. As Lord Russell said in his judgment in a leading House of Lords case:

> The possible varieties are infinite, and can range from the criminality of the scuttler who opens the sea-cocks and sinks his ship, to the thoughtlessness of the prima donna who sits in a draught and loses her voice.[20]

Perhaps the most subtle variation of the problem arises when the frustrating event is only partly in the hands of the promisor.

Illustration:

> *A*, a building contractor, makes a contract to erect a house for *B* on a lot in a neighbouring town. Before he begins actual construction, *A* follows the usual procedure of applying for a building permit from the municipality where the house is to be built. He is informed that the town has just passed a by-law requiring any contractor who intends to build within the town limits to deposit $20,000 in cash to ensure compliance with all local regulations. *A* refuses to make the deposit on the ground that it was not part of the contract and that the hardship involved would make it uneconomical for him to go through with the contract. Has the contract been frustrated? There appears to be no clear answer; the courts must decide each case on its own facts.

---

[20] Joseph Constantine Steamship Line Ltd. v. Imperial Smelting Corp. Ltd. [1942] A.C. 154 at 179.

The Effect of Frustration

Until now, we have assumed that frustration discharges the contract and frees both parties from the duty of further performance. In the very simple situation where neither party has performed at all, a complete discharge of both is a fair settlement. But often the circumstances are not so simple, and discharging both parties may lead to injustice. When, for example, performance is spread over a period of time and is to be paid for on completion, a frustration of the contract before its completion may cause serious hardship for the performer or his estate. The harsh results in the old case of *Cutter v. Powell*[21] serve as an illustration. A seaman was to be paid on *completion* of a voyage from Jamaica to Liverpool. He died en route when the voyage was nearly three-quarters complete. An action by his widow to recover a proportionate part of his wages failed on the grounds that he had not performed as promised.[22]

The early decisions concerning frustration were harsh in another respect: the frustrating event was considered to terminate the contract and future obligations under it from the time of the frustrating event, but any performance already due was still enforceable. In the unhappy case of *Chandler v. Webster*[23] the plaintiff rented a room to view the coronation procession of Edward VII. The price was £141 payable at once, though the plaintiff paid only £100 and owed the remaining £41. Subsequently the contract was frustrated by the cancellation of the procession. The plaintiff not only failed to recover his £100, but the court held that since the remaining £41 was due and owing before the frustrating event occurred, he was still liable for that sum too! The solution proposed in this decision was to let the loss lie where it had fallen at the time of the frustrating event.

The 1943 decision of the House of Lords in the *Fibrosa* case[24] altered the rule in *Chandler v. Webster;* it permitted a purchaser of goods or services who had prepaid money to recover the money provided he had received no benefit from the other party before the frustrating event took place. This solution seems eminently reasonable from the purchaser's point of view — but is it always so from the point of view of the other party? While a seller may not have delivered any of the fruits of his labour, he may well have done considerable work towards the completion of the contract at his own expense; according to the *Fibrosa* decision the buyer can still demand the return of his deposit in full. In fact, in the *Fibrosa* case the defendant had partially built expensive, custom-built machinery, and not only was he unable to require the buyer to share in his loss, but he had to return the entire deposit he had received.

It follows from the *Fibrosa* decision that if the seller cannot succeed in retaining a deposit merely because he has incurred expenses, he certainly cannot

---

[21] (1795) 101 E.R. 573.

[22] The harshness of this rule has since been mitigated to some extent by the doctrine of substantial performance, discussed in the next chapter.

[23] [1904] 1 K.B. 493.

[24] Fibrosa Spolka Akcyjna v. Fairbairn Lawson Combe Barbour, Ltd. [1943] A.C. 32.

recover these expenses from a buyer who has made no deposit. On the other hand, the judgment asserted that if the seller had conferred even the slightest benefit on the buyer (for example, if the seller had delivered a small advance shipment of spare parts), the seller could retain the whole deposit. The common law did nothing to apportion the loss between the parties: it was a matter either of retaining the whole of the deposit or of returning it entirely.

At this point it became apparent that only legislation could correct the law. In 1943 the English Parliament passed the Frustrated Contracts Act in an attempt to remedy the inequities. Subsequently, the provinces of Prince Edward Island, New Brunswick, Ontario, Manitoba, Alberta and Newfoundland have passed similar acts with some improvement on the original English Act.[25]

In the first place, these acts provide that a party who has undertaken performance may retain money already paid by the other party to the extent that he has incurred expenses to the time of frustration. Secondly, the performing party may recover for such expenses even when the money has not been paid but should have been paid (and is in arrears) at the time of the frustrating event. In neither of these situations may the performing party retain or recover any money in excess of the payment made or already due to him, even when his loss has been greater; and the other party may recover any amount by which his payment exceeds the performing party's actual loss. Thirdly, the acts authorize a court to award to the performer a just amount in remuneration for any valuable benefit *received* by the other party regardless of whether a deposit has been paid.

The Frustrated Contracts Acts do not, however, provide for one important situation. A party who has expended time and money in performance of the contract prior to its frustration must bear the loss wholly himself where the other party who is intended eventually to receive the benefit of the work done has (a) made no deposit and (b) has not yet received any benefit. In these circumstances the party who has made the expenditures is still without remedy, and cannot require the other party to share in the loss.[26]

The Sale of Goods

Where the Sale of Goods Act applies. Circumstances may arise in a contract for the sale of goods where we might expect the doctrine of frustration to apply. We must, however, consult the Sale of Goods Act to determine whether it deals directly with the particular circumstances of the sale:

> Where there is an agreement to sell specific goods and subsequently the goods without any fault of the seller or buyer perish before the risk has passed to the buyer, the agreement is thereby avoided.[27]

---

[25] The Frustrated Contracts Act, R.S.P.E.I. 1951, c. 66; R.S.N.B. 1973, c. F-24; R.S.O. 1970, c. 185; R.S.M. 1970, c. F-190; R.S.A. 1970, c. 151; St. of Nfld., 1970, c. 144.

[26] The point may be illustrated by the facts in Appleby v. Myers (1867) L.R. 2 C.P. 651. Even if the Frustrated Contracts Act had been passed at that time it would not presumably have altered the decision.

[27] R.S.B.C. 1960, c. 344, s. 13; R.S.O. 1970, c. 421, s. 8; R.S.N.S. 1967, c. 274, s. 9.

Three conditions must be present for this section to apply. Firstly, the goods must be *specific,* that is "they must be identified and agreed upon at the time the sale is made." Secondly, the risk must still be with the seller, that is, he must still be responsible for their safety. Thirdly, the cause of the frustration must be the perishing of the goods.

Illustration:

> *A* sends a letter to *B* offering to sell "the carload of number one flour sitting at my rail siding for $10,000, risk to pass to you on delivery of the shipping documents in seven days' time". *B* accepts by return mail. Three days later a shunting locomotive on adjacent tracks is derailed and knocks over the freight car containing the flour. The contents are spilled out and ruined by rain, thereby frustrating the contract.
>
> Both parties are immediately discharged from liability under the contract: *A* cannot sue for the price, nor can *B* sue for failure to deliver. *B* can recover any deposit he has made. *A*'s only recourse is against those responsible for the accident.

In the above illustration, all three elements mentioned in the Sale of Goods Act are present: the Sale of Goods Act applies and the Frustrated Contracts Act does not. If any one of these elements is missing, the Sale of Goods Act will not apply.[28] In those provinces having the Frustrated Contracts Act that Act will apply to all other contracts for the sale of goods where the contract has been frustrated. In the remaining provinces the parties will be left with the common law position up to and including the *Fibrosa* case. We may now discuss the position of the parties in each of these circumstances.

In provinces where the Frustrated Contracts Act applies. The application of the Act is more easily understood if we begin with some illustrations.

Illustrations:

> (a) *A* sends a letter to *B* offering to sell "one thousand sacks of number one flour from my warehouse stock for $5,000, risk to pass to you on delivery of the shipping documents in seven days' time". *B* accepts by return mail. Three days later, the warehouse and contents are destroyed by fire without any negligence on *A*'s part. In this instance the goods are not specific because they have not been segregated from the larger stock and earmarked for the buyer.
>
> (b) *A* sends a letter to *B* offering to sell "the carload of number one flour sitting at my rail siding for $10,000, risk to pass to you on delivery of the shipping documents in seven days' time". *B* accepts by return mail. Three days later, the government requisitions all of *A*'s flour, including the carload sold to *B,* in order to help feed the victims of a flood disaster. Here the contract is frustrated by an event other than the perishing of the goods.

In neither of the above cases does the Sale of Goods Act apply. Under the

---

[28] See, for example: R.S.O. 1970, c. 185, s. 2(2)(c).

Frustrated Contracts Act, if *B* had made a deposit and sued for its return, the court would consider whether *A* had incurred any expenses towards the completion of the contract and take these into account in determining how much of the deposit *B* would recover. If *B* had made no deposit, *A* could only recover for the value of any benefit already conferred upon *B*. Thus, if *A* had delivered one sack of flour to *B* as a sample, he could recover the price of that sack, but no more.

Secondly, the Frustrated Contracts Act states that the courts shall give effect to any special provisions made by the parties in contemplation of a frustrating event.

Illustration:

(c) *A* sends a letter to *B* offering to sell "the carload of number one flour sitting at my rail siding for $10,000, risk to pass to you upon acceptance of this offer. Delivery in seven days' time." *B* accepts by return mail. Three days later the flour is destroyed in a derailment accident. The risk has passed to the buyer when the frustrating event takes place.

In the above example, the parties have provided expressly that the risk should pass to the buyer. This seems to indicate that the buyer would be liable for any loss caused by a frustrating event after the risk has passed and must then pay the price to the seller; there are no reported cases directly on this point.

Where the common law applies. We may consider again the above three illustrations as if they had occurred in a province not having the Frustrated Contracts Act. In Illustrations (a) and (b) the *Fibrosa* decision applies. If *B* had made a deposit, he could recover it in full regardless of whether or not *A* had incurred any expenses towards the completion of the contract. If, however, *B* had received the slightest benefit, such as one sack of flour as a sample, he could recover none of his deposit.

The *Fibrosa* case did not consider situations where the seller had conferred a benefit upon the buyer (for instance, by an advance delivery of part of the goods) and where no deposit had been made. In these circumstances the older cases would govern: both parties would be immediately discharged by the frustrating event, and the seller would have no right of recovery against the buyer for the goods already delivered when, by the contract, none are to be paid for until all are delivered. This result conforms to the law as stated in *Cutter v. Powell* and shows the value of the Frustrated Contracts Act in avoiding a harsh result.

The result in Illustration (c) would be the same under the common law; the common law as well as the statute respects the intention of the parties as contained in their contract of sale.

Where the source of the goods is destroyed. Another way in which frustration may affect the sale of goods arises when the source of the goods, rather than the goods themselves, is destroyed. In a contract of sale containing no terms about how the goods shall be produced, the destruction of the *source* of the subject-matter will not frustrate the contract. If, for example, the parties make no stipulation about where the goods shall be made but the factory contemplated by them is destroyed by fire, the supplier will probably not be excused from liability for failing to deliver goods according to the contract.[29] He must then either purchase them elsewhere for delivery to the buyer or pay damages for non-delivery. On the other hand, if the parties stipulate a *particular source* and the source is destroyed, the contract will be frustrated, and the buyer cannot demand delivery. In *Howell v. Coupland*[30] the contract was for the sale of 200 tons of potatoes to be grown in a particular field. The crop failed. When the buyer sued for damages for non-delivery, the court held that the contract had been frustrated, and the action failed.

The general rule is that the frustrating event must defeat the common intention of both parties. A contract of sale is not frustrated when the seller only (and not the buyer) has a particular source of supply in mind and that source proves ineffectual. In *Blackburn Bobbin v. Allen*,[31] the buyer had ordered a quantity of Finnish birch timber to be delivered to him at Hull, England. He had no thought except that the seller would supply him from existing stocks and was unaware that the seller had to obtain it directly from Finland. The outbreak of World War I made it impossible to fill the order. In an action for damages for non-delivery, the English Court of Appeal held that there had not been frustration and that the action should succeed.

An interesting 1968 Ontario decision falls between the *Howell* and the *Blackburn Bobbin* cases.[32] In that decision, a trucker in Parkhill contracted with a Toronto corn merchant to deliver a quantity of corn to shipping points specified by the corn merchant in the Parkhill area. The parties appear to have understood that the trucker was to purchase the corn from certain Parkhill farmers when the crop matured. Unfortunately, however, the trucker was unable to obtain the required quantity of corn because of a local drought. The corn merchant sued for damages for failure to deliver according to the contract. The Court of Appeal agreed with the defendant trucker that if the source of the goods formed a term of the contract the failure of the crop would have amounted to a frustrating event excusing the trucker from performance. The majority of the court found that the contract had not expressly provided that the corn should be from a particular source and was unwilling to find an implied term to that effect. It held that the trucker should have obtained the corn from other suppliers and that he was accordingly in breach of contract. In dissent, Mr. Justice Laskin (as he then was) took a more liberal view of the defendant's obligations. He said, in part:

---

[29] See Twentsche Overseas Trading Co. case, above. But see also Dow Votaw, *Legal Aspects of Business Administration* (2nd ed.), p. 162, Englewood Cliffs: Prentice-Hall, Inc., 1961. The author notes that in the United States, "there is an increasing trend in the courts towards *implying* an agreement that goods are to be manufactured in a particular factory which the parties reasonably understand is to be the source of the subject-matter of the contract."

[30] (1876) 1 Q.B.D. 258.

[31] [1918] 2 K.B. 467.

[32] Parrish & Heimbecker Ltd. v. Gooding Lumber Ltd. [1968] 1 O.R. 716.

I cannot agree that these contracts should be viewed in the absolute terms
in which the majority [of the court] has treated them. I think it is clear that
the original attitude of the common law that a contract duty is absolute has
been considerably modified over the past one hundred years as we have
come to recognize that mutual assumptions by parties that underlie their
commercial relations cannot be ignored, and that, in the enforcement of a
contract, allowance must be made if a failure of those assumptions super-
venes, without fault of the contracting parties, after the contract has been
made. . . .

It is . . . material to the basis on which these contracts were
concluded that the price to be paid by the defendant for the corn obtainable
from the farmers was a price fixed by the plaintiff and the plaintiff also fixed
the trucking charge that would be paid to the defendant for the transportation of the corn to the specified destinations set out in the written confirmations. It seems to me, therefore, that in the circumstances it would be
changing the fundamental character of the contract to require the defendant
. . . to obtain the grain from some other area and at the same time insist that
it accept payment on the basis of a price and trucking arrangement which
contemplated that the grain would come from the area about which the representatives of the parties had reached an understanding.[33]

DISCHARGE BY OPERATION OF LAW

The Bankruptcy Act operates to discharge a bankrupt debtor from his contractual
liabilities after the processes of bankruptcy have been completed. The debtor is
discharged, however, only if he qualifies for a certificate stating that the bankruptcy was caused by misfortune and without any misconduct on his part.[34]

A debt or other contractual obligation that has been neglected by a creditor
for a long time becomes *statute barred,* that is, the creditor loses his right to
bring an action on it. Each province has a *Limitations Act* setting out the time at
which a creditor loses his remedy.[35] The Limitations Act "bars" (rather than
completely discharges) a right of action if the promisee fails to assert it within the
time specified. In so doing, it gives effect to the legal principle that the public interest requires a definite end to the opportunity for litigation. The effect of the
statute is really to banish the right of action from the courts rather than to pass a
death sentence upon it. The distinction is important because the claim may be re-
habilitated and rendered enforceable by certain conduct of the promisor, as we
shall see in Chapter 31.

---

[33] *Ibid.,* at pp. 719-20.
[34] R.S.C. 1970, c. B-3, s. 145.
[35] See, for example: The Statute of Limitations, R.S.B.C. 1960, c. 370; The Limitations Act,
R.S.O. 1970, c. 246; Limitation of Actions Act, R.S.N.S. 1967, c. 168.

QUESTIONS FOR REVIEW

1. Define: accord and satisfaction; condition precedent; condition subsequent; waiver; tender of performance.
2. Is a debtor freed from his liability if the creditor refuses payment? For what reasons might a creditor refuse payment?
3. How may a creditor prejudice himself by being unreasonable about the form in which payment must be made to him?
4. Suppose a party, guilty of breach of contract, offers to settle for a given amount of money, and the other party refuses it. What steps should he take?
5. What element of a binding contract is lacking in a waiver of a contract already performed on one side?
6. In what respect does the arrangement known as accord and satisfaction involve a discharge of a contract?
7. How can you explain the fact that there have been legal disputes over contracts which have been discharged by *agreement?*
8. Both common mistake and discharge by frustration may relate to a nonexistent subject-matter. What is the difference? In what respects, if any, do the remedies differ?
9. Give an example of a promise to which the doctrine of frustration will not apply.
10. May a contract be frustrated though the promisor might still be able to perform it?
11. Does an unforeseen difficulty or expense constitute frustration?
12. What might be the undesirable consequences of extending the applicability of the doctrine of frustration to a wider variety of circumstances?
13. Describe several ways in which a contract for the sale of goods may be frustrated.
14. What contribution does the Frustrated Contracts Act make to the law governing discharge by frustration?
15. In what respect does bankruptcy bring about a discharge of contracts?
16. (a) Gilbert owed Sullivan $100. Sullivan pressed Gilbert for payment and in a moment of irritation Gilbert tendered the entire sum in 25¢ pieces. Need Sullivan accept payment in this fashion? Would it make any difference if Gilbert had instead tendered payment in the form of a certified cheque?

    (b) Suppose Sullivan claimed that the amount was $125 instead of $100 as offered by Gilbert. Gilbert deposited $100 with the proper court official, and Sullivan sued him for $125. The court only awarded Sullivan $100. Who should have to pay the court costs, Gilbert or Sullivan? What would be the result if the court had instead given judgment for $115?

CASES FOR DISCUSSION

CASE 1

Smith, the owner of a steamship, received from Nugent a valuable horse to be carried from London to Aberdeen. In the course of the voyage the ship met with rough weather, and the horse, being much frightened and struggling violently, suffered injuries of which it died. It was shown that the accident could not have been prevented by any amount of foresight and care reasonably to have been expected of Smith.

Should Nugent succeed in an action against Smith for damages to compensate him for this loss? (*Nugent v. Smith* (1875) 1 C.P.D. 423.)

CASE 2

Maritime National Fish Ltd. operated five trawlers each of which was fitted with an otter trawl for catching fish and could only operate with this equipment. Maritime National Fish Ltd. owned four of the trawlers and chartered the fifth, the *St. Cuthbert,* from Ocean Trawlers Ltd. for one year from October 25, 1932, at the rate of $591 per month.

At the time the parties entered into the charter agreement they were aware of an amendment to the Fisheries Act (Canada) which required the licensing of all fishing vessels using an otter trawl; the legislation was intended as a method of controlling the extent of this type of operation and of conserving the fisheries resources of Canada. Operators of boats using an otter trawl were required to apply for a separate licence in respect of each such boat.

In 1933 it became government policy to reduce the number of licences granted, and Maritime National Fish Ltd. was advised that it would be granted licences for only three of the five trawlers it was operating. In April 1933, the fish company applied for licences for three vessels without naming the *St. Cuthbert* as one of them. It then advised the *St. Cuthbert's* owner, Ocean Trawlers Ltd., that the agreement for charter had become impossible of performance on and after April 30, 1933, and that it did not propose to pay further monthly hire from that time. Ocean Trawlers Ltd. sued Maritime National Fish Ltd. for the value of hire for the period May 1 to October 25, 1933. Should the action succeed?

CASE 3

Kennedy undertook to rent from Howard a room in Halifax along the route scheduled for the procession of the Royal Family for the day on which they would appear. The agreement was in writing and the rent for the room was for a substantial sum, payable at the time of the procession. In the meantime Howard redecorated the room for the occasion. Later it was announced that the route of the Royal Family through the city was changed and would not pass Howard's building. Kennedy thereupon refused to pay the rent for the room, and Howard sued for the amount. Should Howard succeed? How would it affect the outcome if at the time Kennedy undertook to rent the room he had paid a $100 deposit? (See *Krell v. Henry* [1903] 2 K.B. 740.)

Suppose that the place in which these events occurred had been Saint John, New Brunswick instead of Halifax, Nova Scotia: would the result be different?

CASE 4

Summers, a building contractor, agreed with Davis to build him a house for $40,000 to be paid in full on completion. The contract contained an unqualified promise by the contractor to complete the house at that price. When the house was three-quarters finished, a fire took place in it, causing considerable damage.

Davis had some expensive furniture stored in the house at the time and had taken out $10,000 in insurance against the possibility of its destruction by fire. Summers had not insured the house during its construction although he could have done so to the value of the contract.

After the fire Summers learned that Davis had received $8,000 in insurance money, and when Davis asked him to go ahead and complete the house, Summers objected to going on without some kind of assurance that he would get this insurance money. Davis demurred as he had lost considerably by the destruction of his furniture, but finally said, "All right, go ahead and do the work."

When the house was completed Davis paid Summers $40,000 but refused to pay the additional insurance moneys. Summers sued Davis for $8,000 claiming that the original contract had been frustrated by the fire and that in effect there was a new contract for $48,000. Decide whether he would succeed.

CASE 5

Adams leased to Coastal Airlines Ltd. an aircraft known as *Nanaimo Comet* for a period of four months at a rental of $25 an hour. There was a clause in the agreement that there should be a minimum payment for 200 hours whether the aircraft was used that much during the four months or not. The aircraft was to be used by Coastal Airlines Ltd. in fishery patrol service on the B.C. coast.

A month later when the aircraft had flown about 50 hours under the lease, it was wrecked in an accident in which both the pilot, an employee of the airline, and a patrol officer of the Department of Fisheries were killed.

Adams sued for the full $5,000 due under the contract as a minimum rental. Coastal Airlines Ltd. denied liability for the 150 hours still short of the minimum.

Indicate the grounds upon which Coastal Airlines Ltd. might base its defence, and state whether the defence should succeed. (See *McDonald Aviation Co. v. Queen Charlotte Airlines Ltd.* [1952] 1 D.L.R. 291.)

CASE 6

McArthur contracted in writing with Reeve, the owner of a business called Demographic Services Ltd., for the purchase of that business. The terms were that McArthur should pay Reeve $24,000 in monthly instalments of $400 over the next five years. The only business done by the company was the preparation of an annual voters' list for the City of Saskatoon for which it was paid $12,000 a year by that municipality. At the time of the contract the parties discussed orally the possibility that the law requiring this voters' list might be changed, concluding only that "in that event the whole agreement would have to be reconsidered and altered."

After McArthur had paid 14 monthly instalments, the Legislature of the Province of Saskatchewan amended the Urban Municipality Act so that the annual preparation of voters' lists would no longer be required for cities within the province. McArthur then repudiated the contract. When sued by Reeve for damages for breach of contract he counterclaimed for a return of the two monthly instalments he had already paid in respect of the current year in which the business would be earning no revenue and during which the company had already incurred some expense in the preparation of the next voters' list.

Offer, with reasons, your opinion as to the probable outcome of this action.

CASE 7

The *Kingston Daily Times* sold its daily newspapers for many years to Paul Jones, proprietor of the Jones Drug store. The drug store resold the papers to its customers. Jones retired and sold the business to Frontenac Pharmacy Ltd. The parties to the sale made no agreement concerning the payment of newspaper accounts, although Jones had run up an account payable of $250 to the *Kingston Daily Times*. Frontenac Pharmacy Ltd. purchased further newspapers, which it paid for promptly. Jones died shortly after the sale of the drug store. After several months the *Kingston Daily Times* applied to Jones's executor for payment of its account, but he refused to pay, maintaining that the account had become a debt of Frontenac Pharmacy Ltd. The latter company insisted that it had purchased only the assets of the drug store and had never undertaken to pay outstanding liabilities. The *Kingston Daily Times,* relying on this assertion of Frontenac Pharmacy Ltd., sued Jones's executor for $250. Should the action succeed?

CASE 8

Manson contracted in writing with Urban Construction Co. for the erection of a small two-storey office building for $135,000. The contract contained a clause that the agreed price would be reduced by $300 for every business day the building was not completed after April 1. The price was to be paid on completion of the building.

During the course of construction, Manson asked Urban Construction Co. to alter certain specifications so that a complete air-conditioning system might be installed at a later time with a minimum of inconvenience and so that there would be an additional washroom on the second floor.

The building was completed April 17. Urban Construction Co. refused Manson's tender of a cheque for $136,100 (comprising $135,000 less $3,900 for 13 business days, plus $5,000, the agreed price for the extra work). Urban Construction Co. brought action for $140,000, the full price without deduction.

Examine the validity of the arguments Manson might use in defending the action.

CASE 9

In 1954 the Dryden Construction Co. contracted with the Ontario Hydro Electric Power Commission to build an access road seven miles long from its Manitou Falls generating station to provincial Highway No. 105. The contract contained the following clause:

> The contractor agrees that he is fully informed regarding all of the conditions affecting work to be done and labour and materials to be furnished for the completion of the contract and that his information was secured by personal investigation and research and not from the Commission or its estimates and that he will make no claim against the Commission. . . .

In fact, the area over which the road was to be built was under heavy snow at the time and the temperature was very low. The description of the property proved to be inaccurate, there being much more muskeg than indicated. After these facts came to light, the contractor sought to be excused from the contract, alleging that it had been frustrated and that what was required amounted to an entirely different contract.

Is there a binding contract to build the road? (*Dryden Construction Co. Ltd. v. Hydro Electric Power Commission of Ontario* (1957) 10 D.L.R. (2d) 124. This decision was reversed on other grounds not concerning frustration: (1960) 24 D.L.R. (2d) 529.)

CASE 10

Mr. Watson was employed as a clerk by Kilby, Farmer & Co., wool merchants, for forty years. During this period he was not a party to any pension scheme and neither he nor his employers made any contribution to such a plan. Just prior to his retirement he received the following letter from his employers:

> Dear Mr. Watson,
>
> Upon your retirement on June 30, next, we have decided to grant you a pension of $1,200 a year, payable by monthly instalments.
>
> You are at liberty to undertake any other employment or enter into any business anywhere in the world on your own account except in the wool trade, and the only other stipulation we attach to the continuance of this pension is that you do nothing at any time to our detriment.
>
> Wishing you every happiness and success in the future, we remain,
>
> Yours sincerely,
> S. Holmes [signed]
> for Kilby, Farmer & Co.

Mr. Watson received his full salary to June 30 and thereafter a payment of $100 a month. Nine years later new owners acquired the business, and two years thereafter Mr. Watson received the following letter:

> Dear Mr. Watson,
>
> In going through our accounts we were greatly surprised to find that an

allowance of $1,200 was being paid to you, whereas drastic steps have had to be taken of late to reduce business expenses, which have become excessive in relation to present-day values of wool and pressures of foreign competition in the textile business generally.

After due consideration we have come reluctantly to the conclusion that this allowance must be discontinued as from June 30, next. Will you please therefore take note of our decision. We remain,

Yours sincerely,
P. Moriarty [signed]
for Kilby, Farmer & Co.

In August, following the termination of payment, Mr. Watson, then 78 years of age, commenced legal action against Kilby, Farmer & Co. for damages for breach of contract.

Outline the possible defences of Kilby, Farmer & Co. and state with reasons whether Mr. Watson's action should succeed.

CHAPTER 15

Breach of Contract

IMPLICATIONS OF BREACH

In our discussion of the ways in which a contract may be discharged, we noted that breach is sometimes described as a method of discharge. This statement must be qualified in two ways: first, not every breach may discharge a contract; secondly, in any event breach does not discharge a contract automatically (as does frustration or completed performance, for example). Even when the breach is sufficient to discharge the contract, it will only be discharged if the party who suffered the breach elects to treat it as doing so.

An injured party cannot elect to treat every breach as discharging the contract and freeing him from his own obligation to perform. The breach must be of either the whole contract or an essential term of the contract, so that the purpose of the agreement is defeated and performance by the aggrieved party has become pointless. Breach of a minor term may entitle an aggrieved party to damages, but it does not entitle him to abandon his obligations. If he does so, it is at his peril, and the other party may in turn sue him successfully for his failure to carry out his promises.

Illustrations:

(a) *A* agrees to sell 10,000 bags of potatoes to *B* and to deliver them in yellow paper bags with green labels. Through a mistake, the labels are printed in blue rather than green. *B* may feel annoyed and believe that his merchandise display will not be as effective. He may sue *A* and collect damages for such

291

loss as he can show the breach has caused him. But he cannot reject the potatoes without himself committing a breach that might make him liable for heavy damages.

(b) *A* agrees to sell 10,000 bags of potatoes to *B* and to deliver them to *B*'s warehouse on Wednesday in time for *B* to distribute them to his supermarket chain for a weekend special. *A* does not attempt to deliver until late Friday afternoon. By his delay he has committed a breach of an essential term of the contract — delivery on Wednesday. *B* may reject the potatoes and discharge the contract, thereby freeing himself from any obligation to pay for them. In addition, he may sue *A* for damages caused by his failure to deliver on time. In the alternative, *B* may accept the potatoes if he decides he still wants them. In this event the contract is *not* discharged: *B* is liable to pay the price for the potatoes, but he may still sue *A* for damages for the failure to deliver on time. If *B* should accept the potatoes and then refuse to pay for them, *A* could sue *B* for the price, and *B* could counterclaim for his damages.

Thus we see that breach does not discharge the contract: if the breach is of a minor term, the contract is still binding on both parties; if the breach is of a fundamental term, the party committing the breach is still bound, but the injured party may then elect to discharge the contract and free himself, or else affirm the contract so that it continues to bind both parties.

It is not always easy to determine whether a term of a contract is essential to it or of lesser importance. Nevertheless in any dispute concerning a breach, the first task is to ascertain to which class the term in question belongs.

We must here note an unfortunate development in terminology concerning essential and non-essential terms: for a variety of reasons stemming from 19th-century developments in contract law, essential terms became known as *conditions* and non-essential terms as *warranties*. These names are unfortunate because ''condition'' may easily become confused with ''condition precedent'' (where the word ''condition'' means a happening or event rather than a term of an agreement) and ''warranty'' may be confused with its special meaning in a sale of goods (where it means a guarantee of quality of the goods or of their ownership — usually an essential term). Despite the confusion, the use of ''condition'' and ''warranty'' to distinguish essential from non-essential terms has now acquired a wide usage that we cannot ignore. We must therefore take care to ascertain the meaning of these words each time we meet them.

HOW BREACH MAY OCCUR

A party may break a contract by (a) repudiating his liabilities expressly, (b) by acting in a way that makes his promise impossible to perform, or (c) by either failing to perform at all or tendering an actual performance that is not equivalent to his promise. We may now discuss these ways in turn.

EXPRESS REPUDIATION

An express repudiation is a declaration by one of the parties that he does not propose to perform as he had promised. It has this to be said for it: it is the most forthright way in which breach may take place. The promisee is entitled to treat the contract as being immediately at an end, find another party to perform, and sue for whatever damages he sustains in delay and higher costs because the original contract will not be performed. Before making other arrangements for the work to be done, however, the promisee should advise the repudiating party that he treats the contract as terminated and reserves his rights to sue for damages.

A promisee may continue to insist on performance after the promisor has repudiated until the date agreed originally for performance passes. If he elects to insist on performance and waits until the time scheduled without receiving it, he is still entitled to damages for breach of contract. However, by continuing to insist on performance he takes the chance of intervening events providing the other party with an excuse for not performing.

Avery v. Bowden[1] shows what can happen when a promisee insists upon performance. A ship was chartered to sail from England to Odessa and to pick up a cargo at Odessa. On reaching Odessa, the ship's master requested his cargo, and the charterer's agent refused to give him one. The charterer was entitled by custom to a period of grace to provide a cargo. As soon as he repudiated his intention to provide one, however, the ship's master could have treated himself as freed from further liability and sailed immediately for England. Instead, he elected to wait out the period and make further demands for a cargo. Before the period of grace elapsed, war broke out between England and Russia, and it then became impossible to complete the contract. The ship's owner was unsuccessful when he sued the charterer for damages caused by the futile trip. The contract had been discharged by frustration and not by breach. The court noted that the decision would have been different had the ship's master elected to treat the express repudiation as an immediate breach of contract.

Repudiation may also occur after performance has begun. In *General Billposting Co. v. Atkinson*[2] Atkinson had been employed under a contract which contained a clause that he should not work in competition with the company within a given period after the termination of his employment with it. Atkinson was dismissed without cause in breach of this employment contract. He sued and recovered damages for wrongful dismissal, and then began to trade as a billposter on his own account within the district. The General Billposting Co. brought an action for a court injunction restraining him from competition, but the action failed. The court held that the company had, by its repudiation of the employment contract, entitled Atkinson to consider his own contractual obligations at an end.

---

[1] (1855) 119 E.R. 647.
[2] [1909] A.C. 118.

In our examples repudiation has been a declaration affecting the performance of the *whole* of the contract. There are many business situations, however, in which one party repudiates only a minor term of the contract. As we have seen, such a breach does not entitle the other party to abandon the contract and declare it discharged. A wise businessman will notify the other party that he is unable to perform exactly as promised as soon as he is aware of the situation, so that the other party may take immediate steps to reduce any loss which the breach may cause him.

Illustration:

> *A* Co., a wholesale hi-fi and electronic distributor, has agreed to supply *B* Co., a chain of hi-fi stores, with a large quantity of new, cartridge-type tape recorders and also to supply sample demonstration cartridges with spectacular sound effects and advertising for the new product. Several days before delivery the manager of *A* Co. ascertains that he has the tape recorders on hand but that the demonstration cartridges have been lost in shipment. Knowing that *B* Co. plans to feature the new product, he would be wise to notify *B* Co. at once of the expected breach of this minor term. *B* Co. may then arrange in advance for an alternative supply of good demonstration tapes. If *A* Co. were to deliver without prior indication of its inability to supply the tapes, *B* Co. might suffer a greater loss for which *A* Co. would be liable.

ONE PARTY RENDERS PERFORMANCE IMPOSSIBLE

An act constituting a breach of contract must be a wilful act of the promisor and not an involuntary response to forces beyond his control. Performance may be rendered impossible in either of these ways, but only the former amounts to breach of contract. A deliberate act which makes performance impossible is a form of repudiation: although not declared by the promisor in so many words, it is none the less implied. It is the self-induced frustration we referred to in the preceding chapter.

An interesting example of this type of breach occurred in *Shirlaw v. Southern Foundries*.[3] Shirlaw was employed by the company as its managing director (the English equivalent of a general manager) for ten years beginning in 1933. A general requirement of the company was that the managing director must always be elected as a director of the company, and Southern Foundries, having its shares closely held, undertook to keep Shirlaw elected. The company got into financial difficulty during the depression and accepted an offer to join a new group called Federated Foundries. In so doing it transferred the controlling interest in its shares to Federated Foundries, which subsequently refused to keep Shirlaw as a director. Then, on the excuse that Shirlaw was no longer a company

---

[3] [1939] 2 K.B. 206.

director, Southern Foundries dismissed him as managing director as well. Shirlaw sued for damages for breach of his contract of employment. The House of Lords held that Southern Foundries had indeed broken its contract: the court stated that when the company put control out of its hands and permitted Federated Foundries to oust Shirlaw from its board of directors, it had repudiated its contract with Shirlaw by necessary implication.

As with express repudiation, conduct that makes performance impossible may take place either before or during performance. Whenever breach occurs in advance of the time for performance, it is known as an *anticipatory breach*. Thus, if *A* contracts to deliver a particular car to *B* for an agreed price, but a week before the agreed delivery date *A* sells and delivers the car to a third person, he has committed an anticipatory breach of his contract with *B*. *B* need not wait until the delivery date to sue, nor can *A* defend by claiming that he might still buy the car back in time to deliver it as promised. The courts have recognized that a promisee is entitled not only to performance of the contract at a future date but to a continuous expectation of performance in the interim between formation of the contract and its performance.

FAILURE OF PERFORMANCE

Types of Failure

Unlike the other two types of breach, failure of performance can never become apparent until the time arrives for performance, or during the course of it. The failure may be of various degrees: it may be a total failure to perform, it may be a grossly inadequate performance, or it may be failure in a minor particular. It may take the form of a satisfactory performance of all but one of the terms of the contract. It may take the form of performing only part of a main term. The extent of the failure always has an important bearing on the nature of the remedies available to the injured party.

The problems created by failure of performance arise typically when the party guilty of the breach is required by the terms of the contract, or by usual trade practice, to perform his part first. We have then to decide whether the injured party is excused from performance of his own part of the bargain. This question arises often in contracts calling for the delivery of goods by instalments when the quantity delivered in a particular instalment is not up to schedule. The issue is whether the balance left undone amounts to a sufficient breach to free the injured party from his part of the bargain, or the breach is so minor as to entitle the injured party only to damages, with the agreement itself continuing. Partial delivery may be merely inconvenient, or it may be completely unsatisfactory.

Illustrations:

(a) A contract of sale calls for the delivery of 6,000 tons of coal in 12 monthly instalments of about 500 tons each. One of the terms is that the buyer will provide the trucks to take the coal away. In the first month the buyer sends only sufficient trucks to take away 400 tons. The buyer's default would not be sufficient to discharge the seller from his obligation to stand ready to provide the remaining 5,600 tons over the following 11 months.[4]

(b) A seller is required by a contract of sale to deliver 150 tons of iron per month. He delivers only 21 in the first month. His default is sufficient to discharge the buyer, who may then turn to another source of supply and sue for such damages as he has sustained from the breach.[5]

In a contract where one party is to perform by instalments, the other may regard himself as freed from liability only if he can offer convincing affirmative answers to each of these questions:

(a) Is there good reason to think that future performance will be equally defective?

(b) Is either the expected deficiency or the actual deficiency to date important relative to the whole performance promised?

The Doctrine of Substantial Performance

The courts have grown more willing to recognize a substantial performance by the promisor, though defective or incomplete in some minor respects, as sufficient to bind the other party to his part of the bargain. The doctrine of *substantial performance* asserts that the promisor is entitled to enforce the contract when he has substantially performed, even though his performance does not comply in some minor particular with the requirements of the contract. The promisor's claim is, however, subject to a reduction for damages caused by his defective performance. The effect of this doctrine is that a promisee cannot seize upon a trivial failure of performance to avoid his own obligations.[6]

When the Right to Rescind is Lost

Two situations may occur where a breach of an important term would ordinarily give the aggrieved party a right to discharge (rescind) the contract but where he is entitled to damages only. First, he may have elected to proceed with the contract and accept benefits under it in spite of the breach of the condition. Second, performance may be such that he cannot learn of the breach until the performance is complete and he has received the benefit of the contract.

Illustrations:

(a) *A* chartered a ship from *B* for a voyage from Liverpool to Sydney, the price being £1,550 for the use of the vessel. The contract contained a term

---

[4] See Simpson v. Crippin (1872) L.R. 8 Q.B. 14, where in similar facts the buyer took delivery of only 158 tons in the first month, and yet the seller was held to the contract.

[5] Hoare v. Rennie (1859) 157 E.R. 1083.

[6] Dakin & Co. Ltd. v. Lee [1916] 1 K.B. 566.

that the ship should be capable of carrying a minimum cargo of 1,000 tons. The vessel proved incapable of carrying such a cargo, but *A* permitted it to load what it could and made an advance payment on the freight. Subsequently, he refused to pay any of the balance, claiming that the contract was discharged for breach of a condition. In an action by *B* for the balance of the price agreed upon, the court noted that while there may have been a breach of condition, in these circumstances the acceptance of performance meant that the charterer, *A*, could not treat the contract as at an end and refuse to pay anything. Instead, he must pay the agreed price subject to a counterclaim for such damages as he could establish.[7]

(b) *A* purchased seed from *B* described by *B* as "common English sainfoin". After it was sown, it proved to be "giant sainfoin," an inferior type. This was a defect which by its nature could only be discovered by *A*, or by anyone to whom he resold the seed, after the seed came up. Though there had been a breach of condition, *A* was obviously not in a position to return the seed and demand the price back. His remedy instead was to sue for damages for the breach.[8]

These illustrations show that the right to consider a contract at an end may depend upon the contract's being capable of rescission.[9] When this requirement cannot be met, the aggrieved party remains bound to perform, subject to his right to claim damages.

Exemption clauses

Their purpose. In many types of transaction one party ordinarily runs a substantial risk that failure to perform on his part, sometimes even in a relatively minor respect, may lead to substantial harm to the interests of the other party. We shall discuss the extent of liability in the section on damages below. A party running these risks has several alternatives when he strikes a bargain: (a) he may obtain insurance against the risk and raise his price accordingly; (b) he may be a "self-insurer", that is, charge a higher fee and build up a reserve to pay any claim that arises later from harm to a customer; (c) he may insist on an *exemption clause* in the contract, in effect excluding himself from any liability for the risk and putting the risk of harm upon his customer. As we noted in our discussion of the ticket cases in the opening chapter on the law of contract, the last alternative is usually the most attractive.

---

[7] Pust v. Dowie (1863) 122 E.R. 740 and 745.

[8] Wallis v. Pratt [1911] A.C. 394. In a contract of sale the buyer's remedy is confined to money damages "where a contract of sale is not severable and the buyer has accepted the goods or part thereof," by virtue of the Sale of Goods Act. See, for example: The Sale of Goods Act, R.S.O. 1970, c. 421, s. 12(3); R.S.B.C. 1960, c. 344, s. 17(3); R.S.N.S. 1967, c. 274, s. 13(3).

[9] For a discussion of the limits of the remedy of rescission for breach of contract, as distinguished from rescission for misrepresentation, see Cheshire, Fifoot and Furmston, *The Law of Contract* (8th ed.), pp. 577-82.

There are several reasons why exemption clauses are widely used. In the first place, they permit a supplier of goods and services to keep his price low — he need not increase his price to protect himself against the risk of liability to his customer. Secondly, even if he is sued for damages despite the exemption clause, he will utterly disclaim liability and thereby seek to avoid the difficult question of the extent of his liability for the harm done. Finally, if he is in the position of using a standard form contract (especially if it is a detailed printed form with many other terms) he will in most circumstances have a distinct advantage over his customer; the customer may be quite knowledgeable about competitive pricing and drive a hard bargain, but will usually have little or no expertise in legal issues. A customer will gladly accept a lower price without realizing the implications of an exemption clause.

In some circumstances, exemption clauses make good sense and work reasonably well. If bargaining power and knowledge of the law is relatively equal between the parties, one party may wish to assume the risk in return for a lower price. For example, he may already have adequate blanket insurance coverage. Or the activity may be extremely hazardous: a charter airline may be unwilling to fly a client into northern mountain regions in winter except at the client's own risk. Generally speaking, however, exemption clauses are drafted to the clear advantage of the party preparing the standard form contract, and the courts have developed techniques to cut this advantage down wherever reasonably necessary.

Attitude of the courts. When an exemption clause is placed in a document which a customer does not sign — such as a ticket or receipt, or a sign displayed on a wall — the first defence against it is to deny adequate notice of the term. If this defence succeeds, then the term is not considered to be part of the bargain between the parties. Even if a person signs a document containing an exemption clause, in those very limited circumstances described in Chapter 9 on mistake he may plead *non est factum* and escape the consequences of the term. In most cases where a person signs a contract, however, he is bound by all the terms contained in it; so too, if he actually knew or should reasonably have known the terms of a document he is not expected to sign. Assuming adequate notice, what effect does an exemption clause have if the party who has drafted it fails in some significant way to perform the contract as agreed, apart from the exemption clause?

Exemption clauses are typically drawn in very wide terms, exempting, let us say, a supplier of machinery from all liability for defects in the product supplied and any negligence of its employees or any guarantees implied by custom or trade usage, except only those guarantees expressly set out in the contract, such as replacing any defective parts for three months. Courts have taken the view that exemption clauses should be very strictly construed against the party who draws them because they permit parties to evade legal responsibility ordinarily placed on suppliers of goods and services. Even so, the courts respect the theory of freedom of contract, and in the absence of special rules (such as exist for common carriers) or special statutory protection (as in consumer protection legislation), will not make a new contract for the parties to protect the one in a weaker position. If an exemption clause squarely excludes liability for the breach that has occurred, the injured party — subject to the discussion that follows — will have no remedy. Thus, if one day after an express guarantee expires a piece of machinery breaks down for the first time, the supplier will not be liable, even if at common law he would have been liable under an implied warranty of fitness.

Exemption clauses are strictly construed by the courts, in ways not apparent on first impression. Thus, a clause exempting a supplier from liability under the contract has been held not to exempt him from liability in tort.[10] Similarly, if a clause exempts a carrier from liability for negligence by its employees, the carrier will escape vicarious liability but the customer who has suffered injury or loss may still sue employees personally for their negligence, since they were not parties to the contract.[11] Again, if a warehouseman agrees to store goods in building *A*, but for his own convenience stores them in adjoining building *B*, and they are lost under circumstances that would have been covered by an exemption clause had they been in building *A*, the warehouseman will be liable because he has performed a different contract from that agreed between the parties.[12]

Fundamental breach. The most difficult cases arise where even on careful examination the exempting clause appears to protect the supplier of goods or services, but where, apart from this clause, his breach has been so serious as to defeat the purpose of the contract. In the absence of the clause, the aggrieved party could immediately have treated the contract as discharged, and sued for rescission and damages. In recent years, a large number of English and Canadian cases have dealt with this problem under the rubric of *fundamental breach*. For some time, the courts treated the doctrine of fundamental breach as a rule of law: if the breach amounted to non-performance of the contract, it went to the *core* of the contract — of the bargain between the parties — and to treat an exemption clause as exonerating one party from performance was repugnant to the idea of a contract; the clause must therefore be struck down by the court and the aggrieved party will have his remedy. This approach was seriously questioned in a 1964 judgment of the English Court of Appeal, when Pearson, L.J. said:

> As to the question of "fundamental breach", I think there is a rule of construction that normally an exemption or exclusion clause or similar provision in a contract should be construed as not applying to a situation created by a fundamental breach of contract. This is not an independent rule of law imposed by the court on the parties willy-nilly in disregard of their contractual intention. On the contrary, it is a rule of construction based on the presumed intention of the contracting parties. It involves the implication

---

[10] White v. John Warrick & Co. Ltd. [1953] 2 All E.R. 1021.
[11] Adler v. Dickson [1955] 1 Q.B. 158.
[12] Lilley v. Doubleday (1881), 7 Q.B.D. 510.

of a term to give to the contract that business efficacy which the parties as reasonable men must have intended it to have. This rule of construction is not new in principle but it has become prominent in recent years in consequence of the tendency to have standard forms of contract containing exceptions clauses drawn in extravagantly wide terms, which would produce absurd results if applied literally.[13]

This statement was generally approved of by the House of Lords in a 1967 case.[14] The facts of that case were found not to raise the issue of fundamental breach, but the law lords took the opportunity to discuss the subject exhaustively. The result of the English cases appears to be this: that as a matter of law, exemption clauses that might excuse a fundamental breach could still be valid if it were absolutely clear that the parties had so agreed. As a practical matter, however, this can rarely be the result. An examination of recent Canadian cases bears out this conclusion. Although the courts pay lip service to the reasoning of the House of Lords, when the breach is truly fundamental to the contract they consider the contract as if it were repudiated by the defaulting party — this repudiation including repudiation of his own exemption clause — and the aggrieved party has all the usual remedies. English courts have applied the law in the same way, even when rescission is not possible. Thus in *Harbutt's "Plasticine" Ltd. v. Wayne Tank and Pump Co. Ltd.*:[15]

A supplier contracted to install equipment for storing and dispensing heavy wax liquefied under heat for a manufacturing process. A clause in the contract limited the supplier's "total liability for loss damage or injury . . . [to] the total value of the contract," which was £ 2,330. The supplier designed a system wholly inadequate for the purpose and was careless in testing it. A fire resulted that totally destroyed the plaintiff's factory with damage assessed at almost £ 150,000. Despite the exemption clause, the court held that the breach went to "the very root" of the contract and was "so fundamental as to bring the contract to an end and thus disentitle the defendants from relying on the limitation clause".[16] The plaintiff recovered a substantial sum for loss of the factory, many times in excess of the £ 2,330 limit based on the value of the contract.

It would appear that even where an aggrieved buyer exhorts the seller to continue his efforts to remedy the defects and tries his best to continue the contract, if the fundamental breach discharges the original contract any subsequent acceptance by the buyer does not destroy his right to damages. He may elect to

---

[13] U.G.S. Finance Ltd. v. National Mortgage Bank of Greece, S.A. [1964] 1 Lloyd's Rep. 446 at 453.
[14] Suisse Atlantique Société D'Armement Maritime S.A. v. N.V. Rotterdamsche Kolen Centrale [1967] 1 A.C. 361.
[15] [1970] 1 Q.B. 447.
[16] *Ibid.*, per Lord Denning, M.R. at 466.

give up his right to rescind the contract, and accept damages only.[17] The breach must, however, be found to be fundamental by the court. If the breach was of a minor nature, covered by the exemption or limiting clause, his rights will be restricted by it.

Three possible arguments may be made to defeat an exemption clause when the clause appears to excuse a fundamental breach of contract. The first two we have already mentioned:

(i) that it is repugnant to the idea of contract that one party should pay valuable consideration for the other party's promise to perform or not perform at his option — accordingly, the court will almost invariably construe the clause as *not* excusing non-performance or clearly inadequate performance;

(ii) that fundamental breach is tantamount to express repudiation of the contract and that repudiation is of the whole contract including the exemption clause, so that the other party is left with all usual remedies for breach.

A third argument is as follows:

(iii) that if the exemption clause is held to be effective, one party is really bound to do nothing. Thus there is a total failure of consideration and the other party's promise is merely gratuitous; he is therefore not bound by his promise to pay.

This third argument is subject to two criticisms. First, it may be argued that a mere promise by one party even to *consider seriously* performing his part may be legally sufficient consideration, although it makes no sense from the other party's point of view and could hardly have been what he intended to bargain for. Secondly, and more serious, however, if the total failure of consideration argument is accepted, it leads only to recovery by the aggrieved party of benefits conferred. Since there is no contract, there can be no recovery for breach of contract. Thus in our example above from the *Harbutt* case, the plaintiff could have recovered his payment to the supplier, but would not have been allowed the much larger sum in damages for business loss based on failure to deliver equipment that was safe and adequate for the job.

REMEDIES FOR BREACH

When a contract is broken, the injured party may have several remedies open to him, depending on the type of breach committed and the subject-matter of the contract. They are as follows:

(a) damages,

(b) *quantum meruit,*

(c) the equitable remedies of specific performance and injunction.

---

[17] R.G. McLean Ltd. v. Canadian Vickers Ltd. [1971] 1 O.R. 207; Canso Chemicals Ltd. v. Canadian Westinghouse Co. Ltd. (1975) 10 N.S.R. (2d) 306.

In addition, as we have seen, the injured party may be freed of his own contractual obligations, depending on the circumstances.

DAMAGES

Prerequisites for an Award of Damages

The purpose of an award of damages is to place the injured party in the same position as if the contract had been completed. Damages must, however, "flow naturally from the breach". The loss which results from the breach must be within the compass of what the parties would have expected as a likely consequence of a failure to perform, assuming they had thought about the possibility of breach when they drew up their contract. Damages will not generally be awarded to compensate an injured party for some unusual or unexpected consequence of breach.

One of the leading cases on this point is *B.C. Saw Mill Co. v. Nettleship.*[18] A carrier failed to deliver a vital piece of machinery promptly to the sawmill as instructed by an employee of the mill; the result was that the sawmill had to suspend operations until the part arrived. The owners of the sawmill failed to recover damages as compensation for this loss of time. The carrier had not been advised of the special nature of the machinery when it undertook to transport it. If the carrier had been told of the importance of the item it would presumably have been liable for the loss. In all probability it would also have placed the item in a much higher category of freight to ensure greater care in delivery, and charged a higher rate for its services.

On the other hand, there are circumstances in which a party does enter into a contract with a knowledge of special liability if he fails to perform. In *Hydraulic Engineering Co. v. McHaffie Goslett*[19] the plaintiff had to make a machine to be delivered by a given date. Under a subcontract, the engineering company arranged with the defendant firm for the manufacture of part of the machine. In doing so, the engineering company made it clear that the entire machine had to be completed for its customer within a specified time. The defendant subcontractor did not manufacture its part until after the agreed date, however, claiming it had no foreman competent to prepare patterns for it. Because of the delay the customer of the engineering company refused to accept the machine. The engineering company successfully sued its subcontractor for damages which included the loss of profit on the contract and the expenditure it had incurred uselessly in making the machine.

In general, a seller or manufacturer of goods will have a better idea of the consequences of late supply to the buyer than will a carrier who transports the goods. A supplier is more likely to know the needs of his customer in order to

---

[18] (1868) L.R. 3 C.P. 499.
[19] (1878) 4 Q.B.D. 670.

sell to him: a carrier usually knows only that the goods are to be picked up at one point and delivered to another, according to the terms of the contract of carriage.[20]

The breach of a contract may spark a chain of events which eventually materializes in a significant loss for the promisee. To an outsider, the logical relationship between the breach and the loss may be a tenuous one. The critical test, however, is to ask whether, from the past business dealings between the parties and the actual and supposed knowledge of the promisor at the time of the contract, he should reasonably have expected such a loss to be a result of breach on his part. If so, damages may be awarded against him to compensate for the loss.

We find an example of damages that "flow naturally from the breach" in a contract for the sale of goods which are not accepted by the buyer on delivery. Assuming that the goods correspond with those ordered, the buyer has broken the contract and may be sued for damages. The damages will be set either at the excess of the contract price over the price the seller may now obtain on the open market, or at some more appropriate amount which measures the pecuniary loss sustained by the seller. There may, of course, be no significant difference between market price and contract price, and yet if the seller is a regular dealer in the article, he will have lost a sale. His lost profit will then be the damage which flows naturally from the buyer's breach.[21]

Damages may also flow naturally from a breach on the part of a seller who fails to deliver the goods as he promised. These damages may often be measured as the excess of the price the buyer must pay elsewhere over the price specified in the broken contract. But again, a formula of this type is only a first approach to the measure of the appropriate damages. If, to the seller's knowledge, the buyer has purchased the goods for the purpose of resale, the damages flowing naturally from the breach may be the profits lost in the interval between the failure to deliver and the replacement of the goods by other suppliers.

Illustration:

A makes a written contract with *B* to supply *B*'s restaurant with ice cream twice weekly, on Tuesdays and Fridays. *A* fails to deliver on a Friday at the beginning of a hot summer weekend. Other suppliers are busy servicing their own customers and refuse to supply ice cream to *B*. He runs out of ice cream Saturday morning and cannot obtain a fresh supply until Monday. *B*'s loss is not the extra cost of obtaining ice cream elsewhere; it is the loss of profits on ice cream sales over the weekend.

The seller's breach of contract may consist instead in a delivery of defective goods. In these circumstances, still other tests must be applied to assess the damages that flow naturally from the breach.

---

[20] See Victoria Laundry (Windsor) Ltd. v. Newman Industries Ltd. [1949] 2 K.B. 528, per Asquith, L.J., at 537.

[21] Thompson (W. L.) Ltd. v. Robinson (Gunmakers), Ltd. [1955] Ch. 177; Mason & Risch Ltd. v. Christner (1920) 54 D.L.R. 653.

Illustration:

A supplier delivered sugar for the manufacture of beer. It turned out that the sugar contained arsenic, a circumstance which rendered the beer unsaleable. In an action against the supplier of sugar the brewer was awarded damages based on the selling price, rather than the cost, of the beer which he had to destroy.[22]

The Duty To Mitigate Damages

A person who has sustained a loss as a result of breach of contract must do what he can to mitigate the extent of the loss: the damages he can recover at law will not include what he might reasonably have avoided. Thus, a seller who has had perishable goods refused upon tender of delivery will only prejudice himself by continuing to insist on their acceptance. He must try to dispose of them at the best obtainable price as quickly as he can, and may then recoup the resulting loss in an action for damages. Similarly, when a buyer is satisfied that the seller will not deliver, he should move to replace the goods from other suppliers as soon as he can. The same rule applies when a contract of employment is broken. An employee in suing for damages for wrongful dismissal must show that he has taken the best available alternative employment as a means of mitigating his loss. All the more, an aggrieved party who acts in a manner that aggravates the damages and increases his loss cannot recover these additional damages by court action.

The Assessment of Damages

Damages for breach of contract are intended merely to compensate an injured party for his loss, not to punish the party who has committed the breach. Of course, knowledge of the fact that he will have to compensate another party for breach of contract usually deters a person from committing a breach he can avoid. The rule is similar in the law of torts. When a party commits a tort such as negligence, trespass, or fraud, damages are intended chiefly to compensate injured persons for the loss suffered. An important difference exists between tort and breach of contract in assessing damages: in tort, the relevant time for judging foreseeability is when the offence occurs, while in contract it is the time of making the contract and *not* the time of the subsequent breach. When a party commits a tort flagrantly or with malice, the court will sometimes assess *punitive* or *exemplary damages* against him to make an example of his conduct to the community and to discourage any similar behaviour.[23] The law of contract knows no such principle: damages are strictly limited to an assessment of the loss suffered.

In assessing the loss suffered, the courts adopt a purely impersonal and dispassionate approach. Their test is simply actual sustained pecuniary loss. In only one instance — a promise to marry — does a consideration for the feelings

---

[22] Holden Co. Ltd. v. Bostock & Co. Ltd. (1902) 18 T.L.R. 317.
[23] See Fridman, "Punitive Damages in Tort", 48 *Can Bar Rev.*, 373 (1970).

of a victim of a breach of contract affect the amount of damages, although today breach-of-promise actions are rare. Even where employees have been dismissed without cause and in breach of an employment contract, the courts have declined to include an amount to compensate the employee for his humiliation or hurt feelings, or for the fact that dismissal makes it more difficult to find a position elsewhere.

Damages may be *speculative,* as when they attempt to allow for a profit which would have been realized had the contract not been broken. Before a court can award speculative damages, it must have a reasonable basis for determining, in dollars, what the difference in result would have been if the contract had been completed. Where the loss suffered takes the form of profits forgone, it may be possible to establish its amount in dollars by reference to the profits of a comparable former period, or of a former transaction entered into under similar circumstances.

Occasionally an award of *nominal damages* serves to acknowledge a breach of contract where no appreciable loss measurable in money has been sustained by the promisee. A court award of one dollar will at least establish the validity of the plaintiff's claim. More importantly, it may serve as a means of vindicating his character, as in an action brought by an employee for wrongful dismissal. In general, the possibility that the plaintiff may still have to pay or share the court costs discourages litigation when the amount in dispute is small.

Liquidated damages for breach constitute an attempt by the parties themselves to measure their remedy in advance, should either of them fail to perform. They are to be found in a term of the contract specifying an amount payable in the event of breach. The actual loss from the breach may bear no relation to the agreed liquidated damages — it may prove to be far greater or far less. Nevertheless, if the term was a genuine attempt by the parties to estimate the loss, it will conclusively govern the damages that can be recovered. In the same way, the parties may by a term in their contract state an upper limit to the amount of damages payable in the event of breach, and if the actual loss sustained exceeds the amount specified, the court will abide by the limit.

On the other hand, we must distinguish between a genuine attempt to anticipate or "liquidate" the consequences of a breach of contract and a *penalty clause.* If a term in the contract specifies an amount payable for breach which is exorbitant, out of all relation to the probable consequences of breach, and intended merely to inhibit a party and frighten him into performance, it is a penalty clause. The court is not bound to award the amount specified in a penalty clause: it will award damages based upon the actual loss suffered.

Methods of Enforcing Judgment

What happens when a party obtains a judgment for damages? How may he enforce his claim? When a plaintiff obtains judgment for a sum of money, he becomes a *judgment creditor,* and the defendant a *judgment debtor.* If the judgment debtor is sound financially, the mere force of the court judgment is usually sufficient: he will raise the money and pay it voluntarily. If, however, he is recalcitrant or in financial difficulty and unable to raise the money readily, the judgment creditor must then move to enforce payment. We must be clear that a judgment debtor is not considered a criminal. He cannot be imprisoned for debt as he once could, provided he does not attempt to commit a fraud, as by absconding and taking his assets with him. (Some jurisdictions provide for detaining a fleeing debtor temporarily to extract the assets he is escaping with.) The law provides procedures whereby the judgment creditor may seize as much of the debtor's property as is necessary to satisfy the judgment. If the assets are insufficient, the creditor is without further recourse for the time being. He may wait in the hope that the debtor will obtain more assets in the future so that he may seize them as well. Generally speaking, however, the creditor gets whatever he can soon after the judgment is obtained and writes off any expectation of further satisfaction at a future date.

The most usual procedure when the judgment debtor does not pay promptly is to register the judgment with the office of the sheriff of the county where the debtor resides, and request the sheriff to *levy execution* against the assets of the debtor to satisfy the judgment. An *execution order* gives the sheriff authority to seize and sell various chattels and arrange for a sale of the debtor's lands after an appropriate period of grace.[24] More complicated procedures are necessary to seize a bank account, the contents of a safety-deposit box, or an income from a trust fund. A creditor may also obtain a *garnishee order* against a debtor's wages. The order requires the employer to retain a portion of the debtor's wages each pay-day and surrender the sum to the creditor to be applied against the judgment.

Besides money damages, a court may make two other types of money awards for breach of contract. As we shall see in Chapter 17, a seller may be awarded the price of goods sold instead of damages for non-acceptance. Again, a lender of money may recover the amount of the debt by court action. Each of these awards is analogous to a decree of specific performance in which the performance is to take the form of a payment of money owed.

QUANTUM MERUIT

We will recall from Chapter 6 that when one person requests the services of another and obtains performance, the law implies a promise to pay a reasonable price for the services. It provides the party who has performed with the remedy of *quantum meruit*. The law permits a *quantum meruit* remedy only in the absence of an agreed price stated in an existing contract. If, however, one of the parties breaks a contract which has fixed a price and thus discharges it, the law permits the aggrieved party to treat the contract as if it had never existed; the contract no longer stands in the way of a *quantum meruit* remedy.

---

[24] For a description of property exempt from seizure, see, for example: The Execution Act, R.S.O. 1970, c. 152, s. 2; R.S.B.C. 1960, c. 135, ss. 24-32.

Illustration:

> *A*, a contractor, agrees to erect a building for *B* for a price to be paid upon completion (a lump-sum payment). After the work is well under way, the owner *B* gets into financial difficulty and repudiates the contract. *A* may sue for his loss sustained through *B*'s breach of contract or, alternatively, he may elect to consider the contract nonexistent and sue on a *quantum meruit* claim for the value of the work he has done.

A *quantum meruit* remedy will be of less value when the contractor or workman is paid regularly as the work progresses. In these circumstances he would be substantially, if not completely, paid up to date at any time the work ceases.

For a *quantum meruit* claim to arise when the contract states a price for the services, the following two situations must normally obtain:

(a) the work is only partly finished; and

(b) the contract has been broken by the defendant in such a way as to entitle the plaintiff to cease work, and he must have elected to do so.

While a contractor may sue for *quantum meruit* if *any* part of the work remains unfinished, he would not bother with the remedy if he had substantially performed the contract. He could sue on the contract for the price of his services less an amount which measures the minor respect in which the work is not completed. This result follows from the doctrine of substantial performance which we discussed above.

Discharge of the contract by breach on the part of the employer is generally required for a *quantum meruit* remedy. In *Appleby v. Myers*[25] the plaintiff was hired to erect machinery on the defendant's premises. Before the work of installation was completed, the premises and contents were entirely destroyed by fire. The agreement provided that the work was to be paid for on completion. The court held that the plaintiff could not recover the value of the work he had already done because the contract had been discharged by frustration instead of by the other party's breach. The case also illustrates the importance of obtaining insurance protection against risks undertaken in the performance of a contract.

In the absence of expressly agreed progress payments, the normal presumption is that nothing is due until completion, and that a contractor who abandons after part performance, for whatever reason, cannot recover anything. There appears to be one important exception to this rule that applies to workmen. Cheshire, Fifoot and Furmston note that ". . . [in] a contract to work materials into the property of another the *prima facie* rule, failing an express agreement to the contrary [that is, for a lump sum payment], is that payment can be demanded for what has already been done."[26] They quote Blackburn, J. as follows:

> Bricks built into a wall become part of the house; thread stitched into a coat which is under repair, or planks and nails and pitch worked into a ship under

---

[25] (1867) L.R. 2 C.P. 651.

[26] Cheshire, Fifoot and Furmston, *The Law of Contract* (8th ed.), p. 522.

repair, become part of the coat or the ship; and therefore, generally and in the absence of something to show a contrary intention, the bricklayer, or tailor or shipwright is to be paid for the work and materials he has done and provided, although the whole work is not complete. It is not material whether in such a case the non-completion is because the shipwright did not choose to go on with the work.[27]

EQUITABLE REMEDIES: SPECIFIC PERFORMANCE AND INJUNCTION

Circumstances in Which the Remedies Are Granted

Historically the Courts of Chancery (or equity) developed their ''equitable'' remedies for breach of contract when attempting to deal with cases where money damages seemed incapable of adequately compensating the injured party. An award of money damages was the only remedy available in the courts of common law before the two systems of courts were merged. The courts of equity granted their special remedies when justice demanded them, instead of leaving aggrieved parties to their remedy of damages in the common law courts. These equitable remedies were discretionary, but the principles governing the exercise of this discretion have become well settled and follow as a matter of course to a plaintiff who establishes his claim for an equitable remedy.

The sanction for an order of specific performance or injunction is different from that for a judgment awarding money damages. To disobey an order in equity is to be in contempt of court. The penalty may be a fine or imprisonment or both, until the defendant agrees to comply.

Because equitable remedies are within the discretion of the court, a plaintiff who requests them must present a claim that is above reproach. If there is an element of sharp practice on his part, the court will refuse him an equitable remedy, and his remedy will be at most a question of money damages. Again, the plaintiff must be a type of person against whom the remedy could be awarded were he the defendant instead. For this reason, a court will not grant specific performance or an injunction *in favour of* an infant since neither remedy could be decreed *against* him, his contracts being generally voidable. Nor will a court grant either of these remedies where there has been no consideration for the defendant's promise, even though his promise is under seal: money damages only will be awarded. The plaintiff must have given a consideration of real worth for the promise he is seeking to enforce if he is to have an equitable remedy.

Specific Performance

Specific performance will not be granted where the court might be obliged to

---

[27] Appleby v. Myers (1867) L.R. 2 C.P. 651 at pp. 660-1. Note that in this case the court did find an express agreement that no payment would be due until the whole work had been completed.

supervise the performance. It follows that contracts in which performance depends upon the personal skill or judgment of one of the parties do not lend themselves to a decree of specific performance. The plaintiff will have to content himself with an award of money damages. Thus, an artist engaged to give a concert would not be ordered to give the concert: to decree specific performance would only be to invite a disgruntled performance.

The remedy of specific performance is most often applied to contracts for sale of land. As we saw in Chapter 3, the courts granted specific performance originally on the argument that each piece of land is unique, and that consequently money damages are an inadequate remedy. Though we may doubt the validity of this reasoning when applied to a lot in a modern subdivision in a suburb, the principle is firmly established that when requested, specific performance will be granted as a matter of course in contracts for the sale of land. The reader may be surprised to learn that the vendor of land may obtain judgment for specific performance just as the purchaser may. The reasons are first, that the general principle giving parties mutual remedies wherever possible should be followed; and second, that damages may well be an inadequate remedy to the vendor. If damages were awarded, he would still be left with the land; he would have the problem of looking after the land, paying taxes, and maintaining buildings, and would have to find another purchaser in order to rid himself of these burdens. Therefore, the court may order the purchaser to specifically perform the contract, that is, to pay the vendor the full sale price and accept the land.

By contrast, the courts will not ordinarily grant specific performance of a contract for the sale of goods — damages are an adequate compensation. On a rare occasion the court will grant specific performance of a contract for the sale of a chattel having a unique value. Antiques, heirlooms, and rare coins are possible examples. If the buyer succeeds in his plea, the court will order the seller to deliver the property as he promised.

Injunction

An injunction is a court order restraining a party from acting in a specific manner: when granted in relation to a contract, it restrains a party from committing a breach of the contract. It is sometimes possible for a court to grant an injunction when it could not decree specific performance. A court does not have the problem of supervising actual performance when it grants an injunction; instead, it simply orders that there shall be no further breach of the contract. Thus, when a hotelkeeper promised to buy all the beer he required exclusively from one source of supply and then purchased some elsewhere, the court granted an injunction restraining him from making further purchases from other suppliers.[28] The court did not say, ''You must buy all your supply from this source, and we will see that you do.'' Instead, it said in effect, ''In future you must not buy from any other source, and if we hear of your doing so, you will be in serious trouble.''

Injunctions are sometimes granted when a tenant has used the premises for

---

[28] Clegg v. Hands (1890) 44 Ch. D. 503.

some purpose not authorized in the lease and objectionable to the landlord. A tenant might, for example, rent a building on the express understanding that it be used as a motion-picture theatre. If after occupying it he uses it as a night club, the landlord may obtain an injunction prohibiting him from doing so.

In some situations an injunction may have the effect of specific performance. It may leave the defendant with the alternatives of performing specifically or suffering serious consequences, possibly loss of livelihood. Accordingly, a court is loath to grant an injunction against an employee who has promised his exclusive services to one employer but has broken the contract by working elsewhere. Injunctions have been granted, however, when an employee in possession of trade secrets of great value left his employer in breach of his contract of employment and went to work for another in the same line of business,[29] and when a singer had promised her exclusive services to an employer for a limited period only and expressly undertook not to sing anywhere else.[30] But the effect of the injunction must not be to confront the employee with a choice between performing specifically and becoming a pauper. The granting of such injunctions is best regarded as an exception to the general rule that the court will not grant this remedy where the subject-matter of the contract comprises personal services and where the effect would be to leave the employee no alternative but to work for his original employer or remain unemployed.

For the remedy of an injunction to be available the contract must contain a *negative covenant* of some kind, that is, a promise not to do something. Such a promise need not be expressed as a prohibition: it may be implied as an inescapable consequence of an express promise made in the contract. Thus, as we have seen, an express promise to purchase all the supplies of a particular article required for a given time *exclusively* from the other party to the contract necessarily implies a negative covenant — a promise not to purchase from any other source of supply.

POSSIBLE CRIMINAL CONSEQUENCES OF BREACH

A breach of contract may be criminal when a party breaks the contract with a knowledge that his action will endanger human life, cause bodily injury, expose valuable property to damage, deprive the inhabitants of a place of its supply of light, power, gas, or water, or delay or prevent the operation of a train by a common carrier.[31]

QUESTIONS FOR REVIEW

1. Define: anticipatory breach; liquidated damages; judgment creditor; condi-

---

[29] Robinson (William) & Co. Ltd. v. Heuer [1898] 2 Ch. 451.
[30] Lumley v. Wagner (1852) 42 E.R. 687; also, Warner Bros. Pictures v. Nelson [1937] 1 K.B. 209.
[31] The Criminal Code, R.S.C. 1970, c. C-34, s. 380.

tion; *quantum meruit;* injunction; nominal damages; lump sum payment; garnishee order.

2. There are various ways in which the law of contract reflects economic or social policy. Describe two of these ways briefly.

3. Why may the difference between a condition and a warranty be important?

4. In what circumstances is the victim of a breach of a condition limited in his remedy to money damages?

5. Contrast the doctrine of substantial performance with the doctrine of part performance.

6. In a contract for the delivery of goods by instalments, one of the deliveries is short in the quantity specified. What tests should we apply in deciding whether the buyer can regard himself as discharged from the contract?

7. Who enforces a judgment on behalf of a judgment creditor? How does he proceed?

8. What is the purpose of an award of money damages?

9. When might a court award only nominal damages?

10. Under what circumstances is a *quantum meruit* remedy appropriate?

11. When will a court refuse to decree specific performance as a remedy?

12. Under what circumstances is a plaintiff likely to seek an injunction as his remedy?

13. On May 12, *A* contracts to deliver goods to *B* by May 31 with payment due June 30. On May 25, *B* closes up his business and moves to another district. Has any breach of contract occurred before May 31? If so, what would be the measure of damages?

14. Shaw contracts with Universal Travel Services for an advertised conducted three-week tour through western Canada, including five days at Banff. The itinerary includes a stop at Mount Eisenhower. Instead of visiting this mountain Universal Travel Services takes its patrons for a brief visit to Mount Assiniboine. Is the contract discharged? Would the contract have been discharged if, instead of accommodating its patrons for five days at Banff, Universal Travel Services had booked its patrons into a small hotel in Calgary for that period?

15. In a conversation between an engineer and a professor, the professor contends that some understanding of the law of contract is essential for the successful operation and management of a modern business. The engineer replies that he cannot see why; that in his experience it is much more important to know the reputation of the person with whom one is transacting business than to rely upon a detailed drafting of a written document, and that business depends much more upon the goodwill of the parties than upon the right to take court action if a contract is broken. Discuss the extent to which the engineer's argument is valid, and suggest some of the weaknesses in his position.

16. Why can a promise of *future* performance have *present* value in the business world? Give two examples of such promises. How is the answer relevant to the doctrine of anticipatory breach?

CASES FOR DISCUSSION

CASE 1

Brown, a painting contractor, entered into an oral contract with Hilton to paint the interior of Hilton's house for $350, to be paid on completion of the work. Brown encountered difficulty when he painted the walls of the living room because the paint was sucked into the wall by the porous plaster. He applied a second coat to the living-room walls, with the same results. At that stage he realized what was causing the trouble and applied what is known as a "sealer", so that the next coat might adhere properly. Leaving the living room in that condition until the sealer was dry, he proceeded to paint the dining room. When the painting in the dining room had been partly completed, Mrs. Hilton inspected the work and complained to Brown that the colour of the paint was not the colour she had selected. This displeased Brown, and he emphatically announced his intention of quitting the job. Mrs. Hilton urged him not to abandon the work without first seeing her husband, but without further ado he removed his materials and equipment. When he abandoned the work, Brown had still to finish painting the living room and had not begun to paint several other rooms in the house. It also appeared that the woodwork had been painted without having been sanded, and would have to be repainted. Brown brought an action against Hilton for $300, claiming $80 for materials and $220 for 55 hours work by himself and his helper. Should he succeed? (See *Bradley v. Horner* (1957) 10 D.L.R. (2d) 446.)

CASE 2

Jones contracted with the Martin Floor Covering & Tile Co. to have his kitchen floor tiled. Before entering into the contract, Jones asked the manager of the company whether, once the job was started, the workmen would be left on it without interruption until it was completed. The manager replied: "Why, of course. We never pull a man off a job until it's finished." Jones then said: "All right, but I would not go ahead with this work on any other terms."

After the work was begun, the workmen, under the direction of the company, were transferred to another "emergency job" at a new house which had to be completed by the end of the week because the owners were moving into it then from out of town. As a result, the Jones family was unable to use their kitchen for a week and had to eat in restaurants.

In due course, the workmen returned and finished tiling the kitchen floor in the Jones home. Jones then refused to pay for the work done. The Martin Floor Covering & Tile Co. sued Jones for the price agreed on for the job. Jones counterclaimed for damages to compensate him for the cost of meals for all members of his family at Winston's Gourmet Restaurant for ten days, $400, taxi fare each night to and from the restaurant, $60, and $50 medical and hospital cost incurred as a result of one of his children falling on the restaurant stairs.

Examine the possible arguments for the defendant and the plaintiff and state, with reasons, what the probable decision would be.

CASE 3

On June 30, Sampson, a professional football player, signed a three-year contract with the Mariposa Football Club Ltd. The contract contained the following clause:

> The Player promises and agrees that during the term of this contract he will not play football or engage in activities related to football for any other person, firm, corporation or institution, except with the prior written consent of the Club, and that he will not during the term of this contract engage in any game or exhibition of basketball, baseball, wrestling, boxing, hockey, or any other sport which endangers his ability to perform his services hereunder without the prior written consent of the Club.

In July of the following year Sampson accepted an offer from another professional football club, the Orillia Wildcats, and moved to Orillia with the intention of playing with that club for the coming football season. He also arranged to play hockey in Orillia after the football season ended.

Shortly after learning these facts, the officials of the Mariposa Football Club brought an action for damages and for an injunction restraining Sampson from continuing to break his contract. The Mariposa Club alleged that it had sustained irreparable injury in having to locate another player of Sampson's calibre, and that it had in the past spent considerable money in training Sampson as a professional football player. In defence, Sampson testified that he would be unable to earn his livelihood if prevented from playing football and hockey. Discuss the legal issues the court will consider in reaching its decision. (See *Detroit Football Club v. Dublinski* (1957) 7 D.L.R. (2d) 9.)

CASE 4

Suppose that Sampson had insisted on a clause in his contract with Orillia Wildcats that should he have to pay damages for breach of his contract with the Mariposa Club, the Orillia Club would reimburse him. If damages were awarded against Sampson in favour of the Mariposa Club, would he succeed if he sued the Orillia Club on its promise to reimburse him?

CASE 5

The Hickorytown School Board required a new school building and engaged Kane, an architect, to advise them and prepare the necessary plans. The contract between Kane and the school board provided that the school building must not cost in excess of $100,000 and that Kane's total fee should be $6,000, payable when construction of the school building was complete.

Kane made preliminary studies, sketch drawings, working drawings, and specifications. The town council passed the necessary by-law to obtain the funds. Tenders were called for from contractors, and the lowest received was for $160,000. Kane revised the plans for the school so as to eliminate certain classrooms in an endeavour to bring the cost within the by-law estimate. Tenders were again called for on the revised specifications, and the lowest was for $135,000. By this time Kane had performed services which normally constitute seventy per cent of those required of an architect by the time the construction is completed.

The Hickorytown School Board dispensed with Kane's services and engaged other architects who prepared plans for a new type of school. The school was eventually built for a contract price of $95,000 using the new plans.

Kane brought an action against the school board for his fees. On what grounds might he base such an action? Would it succeed? (See *Savage v. Board of School Trustees of School District No. 60* [1951] 3 D.L.R. 39.)

CASE 6

In November, Tanton entered into an oral contract with Marsh to cut and haul to Marsh's mill approximately 500,000 board feet of lumber at a price of $20 per thousand delivered to the mill. It was also a term of the contract that on its completion Tanton should be reimbursed for the cost of the construction of camps and roads necessary for the lumbering operations.

In January next, after Tanton had delivered 200,000 board feet to the mill, he found that he was in financial difficulties and was unable to pay his men their wages. At that time Tanton had been paid up to date for the logs delivered, but had not been paid for the camps and roads he had had to construct for the purpose. Tanton thereupon advised Marsh that he was quitting and that he considered the contract as having been frustrated by his inability to pay his men. Tanton next brought an action to recover the value of the work done in the construction of camps, roads, and bridges during the lumbering operations up to January.

Should Tanton succeed? (See *Tingley v. McKeen* [1954] 4 D.L.R. 392.)

CASE 7

The plaintiffs were millers at Gloucester. Their mill was stopped by a breakage of the crankshaft of the steam engine by which the mill was worked. The steam engine was manufactured by Messrs. Joyce & Co., the engineers, at Greenwich, and it became necessary to send the shaft as a pattern for a new one at Greenwich. The plaintiffs sent one of their servants to the office of the defendants, who were well-known common carriers, and requested them to carry the shaft to Greenwich. The plaintiffs' servant told the clerk that the article to be carried was the broken shaft at the mill. He asked when the shaft would be taken and was told that if it was sent up by twelve o'clock any day, it would be delivered at Greenwich on the following day. On the following day the shaft was received by the defendants before noon, for shipment to Greenwich, at a charge of £2 4s. At the time the carrier's clerk was told that if necessary he should make a special note to speed the delivery. The delivery of the shaft at Greenwich was delayed through fault of the carrier and as a result the plaintiffs did not receive the new shaft until several days after they would otherwise have done. The working of their mill was thereby delayed, and the plaintiffs meanwhile lost profits of several hundred pounds.

The defendants acknowledged some liability for having failed to deliver the shaft within a reasonable time and offered to settle for £25; the plaintiffs refused, claiming damages well in excess of this in the way of profits lost. The defendants then paid the £25 into court, and the plaintiffs sued. Should they succeed? (See *Hadley v. Baxendale* (1854) 156 E.R. 145.)

CASE 8

Leander owns extensive greenhouses in which he grows flowers and plants for retail florists. On October 25, Jason, a retail florist, contracted with Leander to supply him with 1,000 poinsettias for the Christmas trade, the plants to cost 50¢ each and to be available between December 10 and December 20. Jason requested delivery on December 11. At that time Leander advised him that he did not propose to perform the contract, since he could obtain 60¢ each for the plants elsewhere. Jason refused to pay more than 50¢ a plant and continued to insist upon delivery. On December 16, an extreme cold spell arrived and Leander's heating system broke down and all the poinsettias he had on hand froze. Jason then purchased the 1,000 poinsettias from another wholesale florist but had to pay 62¢ a plant.

Has Jason any remedy? Discuss the arguments in his favour and the defences which Leander might offer. Would it make any difference if the contract had provided instead that the plants should be available between December 10 and December 15?

CASE 9

The Complicated Machinery Co. Ltd. manufactures and assembles heavy equipment for industry. It received an order for a large machine from the Northern Paper Co. to automate certain processes, and the two companies entered into a contract, one of the terms of which was that the machine was to be completed by October 31 of the same year. The contract further stipulated that if the machine was not completed by October 31, the Complicated Machinery Co. Ltd. must pay the Northern Paper Co. "liquidated damages" at the rate of $500 a week for the duration of the delay. The Northern Paper Co. manager had said in a letter accompanying the offer: "Until the machine is in full operation it is hard to say what our savings will be. Five hundred dollars a week is a rough guess."

Complicated Machinery Co. Ltd. failed to deliver until December 26, eight weeks late. It billed the paper company for the full price less $4,000 (eight weeks at $500). The paper company discovered that the machine actually saved $1,200 weekly in production costs. It therefore tendered as payment the full price less $9,600 (eight weeks at $1,200). By agreement between the parties the machinery company accepted payment of the lesser sum and applied for a decision on which party was entitled to the difference of $5,600. What should the court's decision be?

CASE 10

Hunter was the owner of a resort hotel at Twillingate Harbour, Newfoundland. During the summer he contracted with Burns, a plumbing and heating contractor, to enlarge the heating system of the hotel. The proposed work required moving the existing furnace, adding to the present network of ducts, and providing additional hot-air outlets in various specified rooms. It was a term of the contract that the total price of the work and parts required should be $7,500 and that payment was ''due on the full completion of the work''.

By August 15, Burns' employees had proceeded with performance of the contract to the point that the furnace had been relocated and the main trunk line of ducts had been installed; one or two branch lines to individual rooms had also been constructed. The work remaining to be done comprised about one third of the total performance contracted for, consisting of running most of the branch lines to various rooms and installing heating outlets there. On August 16, a fire broke out and the entire hotel building and contents were destroyed. Burns brought action against Hunter for $5,000, representing the value of services and parts supplied to the time of the fire.

The Frustrated Contracts Act, 1956, St. of Nfld., c. 29, included the following provisions:

> *S. 3(2)(c).* This Act does not apply to a contract for the sale of specific goods where the goods without the knowledge of the seller have perished at the time when the contract is made or where the goods without any fault on the part of the seller or buyer perish before the risk passes to the buyer.
>
> *S. 4(3).* If before the parties were discharged any of them has by reason of anything done by any other party in connection with the performance of the contract obtained a valuable benefit other than a payment of money, the court if it considers it just to do so having regard to all the circumstances may allow the other party to recover from the party benefited the whole or any part of the value of the benefit.
>
> *S. 4(7).* Where it appears to the court that a part of the contract can be severed properly from the remainder of the contract, being a part wholly performed except for the payment in respect of that part of the contract of sums that are or can be ascertained under the contract, the court shall treat that part of the contract as if it was a separate contract that had not been frustrated and shall treat this section as applicable only to the remainder of the contract.

Discuss the relevance, if any, of these statutory provisions. Should Burns succeed? Can your conclusion be justified in the light of good business practice?

CASE 11

The Fowler Engineering Co. agreed to supply Supreme Soap Co. with a machine of specified design for the manufacture of soap-chips from liquid soap. The essential terms of the contract were as follows:

> *Fowler agrees:* To supply the machine and supervise its installation; to supervise the installation of all motors and pipes supplied by Supreme Soap; to test the machine and put it in good working order.

> *Supreme Soap agrees:* To supply all necessary motors and pipes and labour; to pay $3,000 on delivery of the machine by Fowler; to pay the balance of $4,500 on completion of the installation.

When the machine was fully installed but had not yet been tested, Fowler demanded payment of the balance of $4,500. The manager of Supreme Soap Co. refused to pay until the machine had had a trial run and had proved satisfactory. Fowler said he did not want payment held up, because there might be some minor adjustments. Both parties were adamant. Supreme Soap Co. then employed another engineering firm to test the machine. The machine did not operate satisfactorily, although it was ascertained that the defect could be remedied for about $45. The test also indicated that a different type of equipment would be better for the purposes of the soap company.

Supreme Soap Co. brought an action for return of the $3,000 deposit and for damages for breach of contract including the value of the floor space occupied by the machine, the value of the materials and labour it had supplied towards its completion, and the fees of the other engineering firm employed for the trial run. Fowler Engineering Co. counterclaimed for the balance owing on the price. What should be the result? (See *Fairbanks Soap Co. v. Sheppard* [1952] 1 D.L.R. 417.)

CASE 12

The Town of Crestwood Heights entered into a contract with the Ajax Construction Co. for the construction of a storm relief sewer. A term of the contract was that Ajax Construction Co. should conform to the decisions and adopt the methods of an engineer appointed by the town to supervise the project. As designated sections of the project were completed to the satisfaction of the engineer, the town was to pay for the work done.

Immediately after the work was begun, the engineer appointed by the town insisted upon a different grade for the sewers from that proposed by the construction company and demanded a jointing compound of better quality. An unfortunate conflict of personalities developed between the engineer and the manager for the construction company. The construction company refused to comply with the engineer's demands and removed its equipment from the project, specifying as a condition for resumption that the engineer be replaced. The town replied at once that abandonment of the work at this stage constituted a serious threat of property damage to homeowners in the event of a heavy rainfall, and that unless the work was resumed within two days the town would have it completed by other contractors. There followed a number of inconclusive meetings between the mayor and other representatives of Crestwood Heights and the manager of the Ajax Construction Co., which failed to resolve these differences. These meetings took place sporadically over a period of about a week. Without further notice to Ajax Construction Co., the town then engaged another contractor with equipment available in the district, and the project was completed. The town brought an action against Ajax Construction Co. for $10,000, being the excess paid to the second contractors over the contract price agreed upon by Ajax Construction Co. in respect of the work completed by the other contractor. Ajax Construction Co. claimed, as one of its defences, that the town failed to give it notice that a new contractor had been hired.

The following is an extract from the evidence at the time of the trial when the judge questioned Miller, the manager of Ajax Construction Co.:

> His Lordship: But you have already said when you signed the contract that you would agree that the engineer's ruling shall be final and binding?
>
> Mr. Miller: That's quite possible, but to my mind that contract is an unfair contract from beginning to end.
>
> His Lordship: That may be.
>
> Mr. Miller: That's not for me to judge.
>
> His Lordship: No, but it is for me.

Further evidence indicated that while there might be room for a difference of opinion about the adequacy of the work done by Ajax Construction Co., the engineer engaged by the town had nevertheless acted in good faith in insisting on a different type of performance.

What should the court's decision be? (See *Kamlee Construction Ltd. v. Town of Oakville* (1961) 26 D.L.R. (2d) 166; *Rickards (Charles), Ltd. v. Oppenheim* [1950] 1 K.B. 616; [1950] 1 All E.R. 420.)

PART THREE
Special Types of Contract

CHAPTER 16

The Contract of Sale:
Its Nature and Effect

THE SALE OF GOODS ACT

History

The modern business organization has been described as "a bundle of contracts".[1] The production and marketing of goods today proceeds by a succession of contracts, many of which are contracts of sale. We find, for example, a contract of sale in the acquisition of raw materials, and again at each stage in the distribution of manufactured goods to wholesalers, retailers, and consumers.

Only in modern times has the contract of sale enjoyed such a position of pre-eminence, however. The economic activity of medieval England was mainly agrarian, and much of the law was concerned with feudal rules for holding land. Not until the late 18th century, when England had become the world's first industrial power, did the law governing the distribution and sale of goods become the subject of frequent decisions in the courts. In succeeding years, general principles began to emerge from the decisions of the courts, and in the latter part of the 19th century these principles were well established. By this time the body of case law was immense. Lengthy and learned treatises were written in attempts to digest and rationalize the cases into a logical pattern. In 1893, the British Parliament simplified the case law by codifying it into a comprehensive statute called

---

[1] See Hunt, Williams, and Donaldson, *Basic Business Finance* (3rd ed.), p. 33. Homewood, Illinois: Richard D. Irwin, Inc., 1966.

320

the Sale of Goods Act. All the common law provinces in Canada have since adopted this Act almost word for word.

The Sale of Goods Act resembles the Partnership Act (which we shall discuss in Chapter 27) in that it made no attempt to change the law: its purpose was to set out succinctly the law as it then existed, with clarification where necessary to resolve conflicts between competing principles. In particular, the cases decided before the Act was passed had recognized a number of important implied terms which formed a part of every contract for the sale of goods, unless those terms were inconsistent with the purposes of the contract or were expressly excluded by the parties. The terms implied by the courts in these decisions were codified: they are now implied under the Sale of Goods Act just as they were implied by case law before the Act was passed. We shall discuss these implied terms in the next section of this chapter.

Ownership and Possession

The words "ownership" and "possession" signify to the legal historian and jurist some of the most difficult analytical problems in the whole of law. For our purposes, it is sufficient to note that in primitive societies possession was considered the equivalent of ownership, with a great premium placed on physical strength in retaining possession. A sophisticated system of law separates the two concepts. We assume the separation in everyday activity, as when we lend possession of an object to a friend yet retain ownership of it. We automatically assume that if a friend refused to return our car, we would have a remedy in the courts against him to protect our ownership or *title*. We have seen also in our discussion of mistake in Chapter 9 that in English law, the distinction between possession and ownership of goods is carried to its logical conclusion, in that the owner may recover his goods from an innocent purchaser after they have been stolen.

The separation of ownership and possession is a common occurrence in a contract for the sale of goods: when the contract is a sale which passes title to the buyer immediately, possession often remains with the seller or a common carrier for some time afterwards; and, as we shall see, under instalment-sales contracts, a vendor often retains title to goods as security for payment of the price, while possession passes to the buyer. Transactions other than sales, such as pledges, consignments, and rental arrangements, also separate ownership from possession. In this and the succeeding chapter we shall often have occasion to refer to the passing of title independently of possession, and to a change in possession without a transfer of title.

Definition of Goods

In these two chapters we shall discuss only those contracts that are governed by the Sale of Goods Act; we must therefore discover the limits of the Act's application. For the Act to apply, the subject-matter of the contract must be "goods".

As we shall see in Chapter 24, property is divided into two main classes — real property and personal property. Real property is confined to interests in land. All other property is called personal property, which in turn has two categories, choses in action and goods or *chattels*. We have already discussed the nature of choses in action in Chapter 13 in relation to the assignment of contractual rights. In contrast to choses in action, which obtain their value because they represent binding obligations of persons, goods derive their value intrinsically, that is simply because people wish the goods themselves, for the utility or satisfaction they furnish.

When discussing the requirement of writing in Chapter 11, we noted that the courts have interpreted the Sale of Goods Act to exclude the sale of items whose final value is attributable mainly to the skill and labour that have gone into their preparation at the request of the buyer. These contracts have been held to be for work and materials and not for ''goods'' within the meaning of the Act: accordingly, they are outside its scope. All other goods come within the definition of goods in the statute.

Types of Contract of Sale

In the Sale of Goods Act, a contract of sale ''is a contract whereby the seller transfers or agrees to transfer the property in the goods to the buyer for a money consideration, called the price . . .'' Money must form a part of the transaction; it therefore follows that a straight barter of goods where no money changes hands is not a sale within the compass of the statute.

The Sale of Goods Act distinguishes between a *sale* and an *agreement to sell*. In a sale, the ownership or title in goods passes from the seller to the buyer at the moment the contract is made. In an agreement to sell, the transfer of ownership or title to the buyer is deferred until a future time; that time is either a specified or an indefinite date, depending on the fulfilment of a particular requirement. The Sale of Goods Act applies to both sales and agreements to sell. An agreement to sell may be formed even when the goods are nonexistent. A contract to sell goods to be manufactured in three months' time, or to sell a crop at a stated price per bushel when it has grown in a certain field, are examples of this type of agreement to sell. An agreement to sell is a binding contract just as are all other contracts containing promises of future conduct.

At this point we may conveniently distinguish a contract of sale from another type of transaction known as a *consignment*. A consignment is a shipment of goods from one location to another: the shipper is the *consignor* and the recipient the *consignee*. There are two common varieties of consignment. First, the consignor may ship the goods in performance of a contract of sale; here, the consignor is a seller and the consignee a buyer (or possibly, someone financing him). Secondly, the consignor may ship the goods to an agent who will offer them for sale at their new location. In this instance it is not necessary for ownership in the goods ever to pass between the consignor and consignee: if the consignee sells them, the title passes directly from the consignor to the purchaser.

Expensive items displayed in the window of a jeweller's shop, for example, may not be part of the jeweller's stock-in-trade, but simply held by him on consignment from the manufacturer.

Required Evidence

We have discussed in Chapter 11 the circumstances in which a contract of sale may be unenforceable for lack of a memorandum in writing, or alternatively, for lack of evidence of certain conduct by the buyer. It would be helpful to review the relevant sections of that chapter at this time.

TERMS IN A CONTRACT OF SALE

Conditions and Warranties

In Chapter 15, we noted the unfortunate confusion caused by the use of one word "condition" in entirely different senses in the law. The Sale of Goods Act has used "condition" to mean a major or essential term of the contract, the breach of which relieves the injured party from further duty to perform the contract if he so elects. It uses "warranty" to mean a minor or non-essential term, the breach of which does not relieve the injured party from the bargain — he must perform his side but may sue for damages. We shall use the two words in this chapter with the same meanings as those given by the Act. Some terms implied by the Act are conditions and others are warranties; we must be careful to note which terms fall into each class.

In the remainder of this section we shall discuss the more important terms of a contract of sale implied by the Sale of Goods Act, and also those terms that are usually expressly agreed upon by the parties.

Statutory Protection for the Buyer: Limitations on Caveat Emptor

Scope of caveat emptor. We encountered the Latin maxim *caveat emptor* briefly in Chapter 9 in our discussion of unilateral mistake, and Chapter 10 in discussing fraudulent misrepresentation. It would be wise at this point to be sure we understand the phrase. As a learned Irish judge has pointed out, *"Caveat emptor* does not mean in law or Latin that the buyer must 'take chance'; it means that he must 'take care'."[2] In other words he must be reasonably cautious when he buys goods in circumstances where a buyer can, and usually does, exercise his own judgment. *Caveat emptor* is, however, not a rigid rule but a flexible general principle, subject to limits put on it by common sense and customary business practice.

Caveat emptor applies where the goods are in existence, and are specific items which may be inspected by the buyer, and where the seller has made no

---

[2] Wallis v. Russell [1902] 2 I.R. 585 per Fitzgibbon, L.J., at 615.

misrepresentations about them. In these circumstances *caveat emptor* is a sensible rule: the buyer has the opportunity of exercising his judgment in examining the goods; if he distrusts his own judgment or has doubts, he may choose to bargain for an express term that the goods have a particular quality required by him.

Illustration:

> Hard-Sell TV Ltd. advertises: "Used TV sets for sale. 17-inch to 23-inch sets all one price — $50. Take your choice." Adams enters the store and asks a salesman to show him a 17-inch portable he can use in his basement recreation room. The salesman leads him to the sets and says: "Here are all our portables. Some are pretty good buys. See for yourself."
>
> Adams examines several and finds one that appears to be in good condition from the outside. He turns it on and gets quite a good picture from the local station. When he asks whether the set is connected to an outside antenna, he is told that it is not. Adams says: "Well, it looks pretty good to me. I'll take it. Here's the $50. Just place it in the back seat of my car." When Adams gets the set home and attaches it to his outdoor antenna, he finds he can still bring in only the local station, whereas his living room set brings in four other channels.
>
> He has no recourse against Hard-Sell TV. Had he wished an undertaking that the set would bring in other channels he needed to request it. At the price of $50 it is very unlikely that the seller would have agreed to give that undertaking.

Caveat emptor encourages buyers to take care and to determine that the goods are what they want before they contract to buy them. On the other hand, there are special circumstances in which the principle, if not qualified, would invite abuse by unscrupulous sellers. For example, a buyer must sometimes rely to some extent upon the knowledge or expert judgment of the seller, or by mutual consent a buyer may sometimes place special confidence or trust in the seller. Accordingly, a series of implied terms to protect buyers were evolved in the decided cases and are now found in the Sale of Goods Act.[3]

Seller's title. Caveat emptor applies to the qualities of goods, not their ownership. The buyer must rely in almost every instance on the seller to be able to transfer good title to him. In offering to sell goods, the seller impliedly represents that he has the right to do so. The Sale of Goods Act states (s. 13):

> In a contract of sale, unless the circumstances of the contract are such as to show a different intention, there is
>   (a) An implied condition on the part of the seller that in the case of a sale he has a right to sell the goods, and that in the case of an agreement to

---

[3] Although the wording of the various provincial Sale of Goods Acts is virtually the same, the numbering of sections differs considerably. For simplicity of reference in the remainder of this chapter, we shall prefix each section quoted with the number used in the Ontario act, R.S.O. 1970, c. 421.

sell he will have a right to sell the goods at the time when the property is to pass;

(b) An implied warranty that the buyer will have and enjoy quiet possession of the goods; and

(c) An implied warranty that the goods will be free from any charge or encumbrance in favour of any third party, not declared or known to the buyer before or at the time when the contract is made.

Illustration:

Adams purchases a second-hand refrigerator from Blake. It then emerges that Cowan and not Blake was the owner of the refrigerator. Cowan thereupon takes possession of the refrigerator from Adams.

In the contract of sale between Adams and Blake there was an implied undertaking by Blake that he had a right to sell the refrigerator, that Adams should have quiet possession of it (that is, not have his physical possession of it interrupted), and that it would be free from any encumbrance in favour of a third person. None of these requirements was satisfied. Adams is therefore entitled to recover money damages from Blake for *breach of warranty of title*. We should remember, however, that the practical value of Adams's right to sue Blake depends upon whether he can find him and whether Blake has enough assets to satisfy a court judgment: for this reason, a prospective buyer ought to take every reasonable precaution to ascertain that the seller has title before entering into a contract of sale.

Description. The Sale of Goods Act sets out the circumstances for an implied term as to description, as follows (s. 14):

Where there is a contract for the sale of goods by description, there is an implied condition that the goods will correspond with the description, and, if the sale is by sample as well as by description, it is not sufficient that the bulk of the goods corresponds with the sample if the goods do not also correspond with the description.

Illustration:

On entering the nursery business, Wallace purchases from Powell, a seed dealer, some seed described as "Rose of Heaven Petunias". When the seed grows, it proves instead to be "Pride of Barcelona Onions". Wallace may sue Powell for damages based on a breach of an implied term to the effect that the goods shall correspond with the description, whether he has inspected a sample of the seeds or not.

Suitability and quality. The Sale of Goods Act makes two exceptions to the general rule that the buyer must exercise care as to the suitability and quality of the goods (s. 15):

Subject to this Act and any statute in that behalf, there is no implied warranty or condition as to the quality or fitness for any particular purpose of goods supplied under a contract of sale, except as follows:

1. Where the buyer, expressly or by implication, makes known to the seller the particular purpose for which the goods are required so as to show that the buyer relies on the seller's skill or judgment, and the goods are of a description that it is in the course of the seller's business to supply (whether he is the manufacturer or not), there is an implied condition that the goods will be reasonably fit for such purpose, but in the case of a contract for the sale of a specified article under its patent or other trade name, there is no implied condition as to its fitness for any particular purpose.

2. Where the goods are bought by description from a seller who deals in goods of that description (whether he is the manufacturer or not), there is an implied condition that the goods shall be of merchantable quality, but if the buyer has examined the goods, there is no implied condition as regards defects that such examination ought to have revealed.

Part 1 offers protection to a buyer who has a *particular* purpose in mind for the goods. To have the advantage of this provision he should declare this purpose specifically if it is not one of the general uses to which such goods are customarily put. It is not necessary, however, for him to state his purpose in so many words if this is obvious. Thus, if one were to buy a dozen buns in a bakeshop, he need not announce to the clerk, ''I propose to eat these, and so they must be edible.'' The essential requirement for Part 1 is that the buyer shall have relied upon the seller's skill and judgment.[4]

Illustration:

Slack enters a hardware store, asks for and obtains 100 feet of clothesline wire. He then uses it as a cable for a home-made elevator in his barn. Subsequently the wire breaks with him in the elevator, causing him injury and shock. He sues the hardware dealer for damages equal to his medical expenses.

Slack will not succeed because: (a) he did not expressly state the particular purpose for which he intended to use the wire, and so did not rely on the seller's skill and judgment, and (b) his damages were not of a kind likely to have occurred to the seller as a possible consequence of breach.

A Canadian court has held that a contract for work and materials is subject as a matter of common law to an implied condition of fitness which is analogous to the condition of fitness implied in contracts for the sale of goods as described above.[5]

In *Baldry v. Marshall,* the court had to consider the circumstances in which the buyer might lose the protection afforded him by this part of the section because he had referred to the article by its trade name. Lord Justice Bankes said:

---

[4] Chaproniere v. Mason (1905) 21 T.L.R. 633.

[5] A.G. of Canada v. Laminated Structures & Holdings Ltd. et al. (1961) 28 D.L.R. (2d) 92, per Macdonald, J., at 100-1. For a U.S. and an English case on this point, see: Perlmutter v. Beth David Hospital (1955), 123 N.E. 2d. 792, and Dodd v. Wilson [1946] 2 All E.R. 691. See also Atiyah, *The Sale of Goods* (4th ed.), pp. 10-11. London: Pitman, 1971.

The mere fact that an article sold is described in the contract by its trade name does not necessarily make the sale a sale under a trade name. Whether it is so or not depends upon the circumstances. . . . In my opinion the test of an article having been sold under its trade name within the meaning of the proviso is: did the buyer specify it under its trade name in such a way as to indicate that he is satisfied, rightly or wrongly, that it will answer his purpose, and that he is not relying on the skill or judgment of the seller, however great that skill or judgment may be?[6]

Part 2 of this section indicates when a seller is responsible for the quality of goods in their *general* uses. Under Part 2, to establish a breach of condition by the seller, the buyer need not show that he relied on the seller's skill and judgment.[7]

Illustration:

Payne purchases some canned peas at the Pure Food Grocery Store. When he heats and eats the peas, they poison him. He loses wages for one week while recovering from the incident. Payne sues the Pure Food Grocery Store for damages equal to these costs.

The contract of sale has been broken by the store because of the implied condition that the article should be of merchantable quality. The Pure Food Store may in turn recover from the manufacturer or wholesaler who supplied the canned peas because there will also have been a contract of sale between them with a similar implied term.

It will be helpful to explain the use of the word "merchantable". To paraphrase an English judge,[8] goods of merchantable quality should be in such a state that a buyer, fully acquainted with the facts and having found the goods in reasonably sound condition, would buy them without abatement of the current market price and without special guarantees.

Sale by sample. The last of the implied terms recognized in the Sale of Goods Act is explained in these words (s. 16(2)):

In the case of a contract for sale by sample, there is an implied condition

    (a) that the bulk will correspond with the sample in quality;

    (b) that the buyer will have a reasonable opportunity of comparing the bulk with the sample; and

    (c) that the goods will be free from any defect rendering them unmerchantable that would not be apparent on reasonable examination of the sample.

---

[6] [1925] 1 K.B. 260 at 266-7.

[7] Wren v. Holt [1903] 1 K.B. 610.

[8] Bristol Tramways v. Fiat Motors [1910] 2 K.B. 831.

Illustration:

The plant foreman at High Grade Printing Company examines a sample of choice quality paper supplied by Universal Paper Co. Ltd. and approves its purchase. When the paper is used in one of the fine books printed by High Grade Printing Company, it turns yellow a month afterwards so that the entire run must be done over again. High Grade Printing Company brings an action against Universal Paper Co. Ltd. for damages to compensate it for its loss. In defence, Universal Paper Co. Ltd. pleads that the paper supplied was exactly the same as the sample on which the purchase was based, and that a chemical test of the sample would have revealed the defect.

The printing company should succeed in its action if it can show that the defect would not have been apparent in the sample on an ordinary examination, and that an ordinary examination in this business would not include a chemical test.

Exemption clauses

The Sale of Goods Act contains the following provision (s. 53):

Where any right, duty or liability would arise under a contract of sale by implication of law, it may be negatived or varied by express agreement or by the course of dealing between the parties, or by usage, if the usage is such as to bind both parties to the contract.

As a result, a seller may insist that a contract of sale shall contain an express term exonerating him from the liability normally imposed by its implied terms. A prospective buyer may, of course, refuse to enter into a contract containing such an exemption clause; if he agrees to the clause, he loses the protection afforded a buyer by the Sale of Goods Act.

In the belief that the terms implied by the Act are fair and equitable, the English courts have been zealous in restricting the circumstances in which a seller may absolve himself of his liability under the Act: if the words he uses do not precisely describe the type of liability he is disclaiming, the courts will declare that the implied liability is still part of the contract. Thus, if a seller makes it an express term that "all warranties implied by statute are hereby excluded," he will avoid liability under all those implied terms which are *warranties* but not under those which are *conditions*. Moreover, if the seller expressly promises that the goods shall be of a certain quality or type, an exemption clause that refers only to *implied* terms will not free him from his obligations under this *express* term.

Illustration:

Allan agrees to purchase a car from Lambeth Motors Ltd. In the contract the car is described as "a new, 90-h.p., 6-cylinder Vintage sedan". There is also a clause, inserted at the instance of the seller, that "All conditions, warranties, and liabilities implied by statute, common law, or otherwise are hereby excluded.'' After taking delivery, Allan discovers that the car is not new and has only four cylinders, and he sues for damages.

The exempting clause refers only to implied terms. The undertaking that the car is new and has six cylinders is an express term in this contract of sale. The seller has, therefore, failed to exempt himself from liability and must pay damages.[9]

The courts have declared, moreover, that a seller cannot so completely exempt himself from liability that he may default on his bargain with impunity. (We have already discussed the doctrine of fundamental breach with respect to exemption clauses in contracts generally in Chapter 15.) Consequently, the courts would not give effect to an exemption clause that gives a seller immunity from action if he delivers goods entirely different from those contracted for by the buyer or if he delivers goods to which he did not have good title.[10]

With respect to consumer sales, some provinces now prevent sellers exempting themselves from liabilities under implied conditions and warranties as stated in the Sale of Goods Act. In these jurisdictions, the implied conditions and warranties of the Act apply to the transaction, giving the consumer a remedy even when he has signed a contract expressly exempting his seller from liability.[10a]

Payment

In many contracts of sale the time of payment is set out expressly, and in others may be implied from the terms of the contract in the particular circumstances. Where the contract itself gives no guidance about when the buyer is to pay, the law presumes that delivery and payment are concurrent conditions; the transaction must be a cash sale. Of course, a large proportion of goods are bought on credit, an arrangement that sets a time for future payment. The buyer may then require delivery before the time for payment.

The courts interpret the time set for payment as a warranty unless the parties have expressed themselves otherwise. Consequently, a seller is not entitled to rescind the contract of sale and have his goods back, though he is not paid on time. He must content himself with an action for the price of goods. But the parties often agree otherwise. The seller may require the inclusion of a term entitling him to retake possession in the event of non-payment. This provision is characteristic of the instalment sale, which we are to consider separately in Chapter 30.

---

[9] Andrews Bros. Ltd. v. Singer & Co. Ltd. [1934] 1 K.B. 17.

[10] Pinnock Brothers v. Lewis and Peat Ltd. [1923] 1 K.B. 690; Rowland v. Divall [1923] 2 K.B. 500; Kersales (Harrow) Ltd. v. Wallis [1956] 2 All E.R. 866; Canadian-Dominion Leasing Corporation Ltd. v. Suburban Superdrug Ltd. (1966) 56 D.L.R. (2d) 43; Western Tractor Ltd. v. Dyck (1970) 7 D.L.R. (3d) 535.

[10a] See, for example, St. of Ont. 1971, c. 24, s. 2(2).

Delivery

The terms in a contract of sale relating to delivery are mainly of three kinds: terms relating to quantity to be delivered, the time of delivery, and the place of delivery. We shall deal with them in turn.

A term specifying the quantity of goods to be delivered is a condition. If the term is broken, that is, if the seller delivers the wrong quantity, the buyer is free to reject the goods. His right to do so exists whether a greater or lesser quantity is delivered than promised. The buyer may, of course, choose to treat the contract as not having been discharged by breach of condition and take all or part of what is in fact delivered. If he does so, he must pay for what he takes at the contract rate.

The time specified for delivery is also usually a condition, so that if the goods are not delivered on time the buyer may rescind the contract. He is free to look elsewhere for the goods he needs as soon as he learns they will not be available. If the parties agree that the goods are to be delivered as soon as they are available without specifying a time, then the time for delivery is a reasonable time taking into account all the circumstances. Reasonable time of delivery may vary according to the place of delivery: delivery may occur at the seller's place of business, the buyer's place of business, or some intermediate point.

Often a commodity wholesaler or importer keeps his goods stored in the warehouse of a storage company, and a buyer of the goods may wish to leave the goods there until he has arranged to store them himself or until he has resold them. In these circumstances, where the seller and buyer do not arrange a physical delivery of the goods, when does the delivery take place? The Sale of Goods Act states (s. 28(3)):

> Where the goods at the time of sale are in the possession of a third person there is no delivery by the seller to the buyer unless and until such third person acknowledges to the buyer that he holds the goods on his behalf . . .

Thus, delivery takes place when the warehouseman sends a notice to the buyer that he is holding the goods on the buyer's behalf.

The place of delivery is normally either the seller's place of business or wherever the goods happen to be located at the time of the contract. The parties may, however, express a different intention, or their intention can be implied from trade custom. Thus, when we order goods from a department store and give the clerk our address, the agreed place of delivery is our residence.

In offering his goods for sale, a seller commonly states the terms of delivery in short form along with his asking price. He may, for example, quote wheat at so much per bushel *f.o.b. Winnipeg,* or steel at so much for a shipment of a specified number of tons *c.i.f. Hamilton.* There are other forms of quotations, but f.o.b. and c.i.f. are the most important. The place mentioned in an f.o.b. quotation is often the seller's place of business, though it need not be. This method of quoting price means that the seller will place the goods "free on board" the type of transport specified by the buyer. The seller's duty of delivery is complete when he arranges the kind of transportation requested and delivers the goods to the place of business of the carrier.

When a c.i.f. (cost, insurance, freight) price is quoted, the seller undertakes to arrange insurance in the name of the buyer, ship the goods, and send an insurance policy, bill of lading, and invoice for the total price to the buyer. This type of price quotation tells the buyer what the total cost of the goods will be laid down at the place named in the quotation, usually the buyer's place of business. The seller's duty of delivery is not complete until he has arranged insurance and freight, delivered the goods to the carrier, and tendered the necessary documents to the buyer "so that he may know what freight [and insurance] he has to pay and obtain delivery of the goods if they arrive or recover for their loss if they are lost on the voyage".[11]

A c.o.d. (cash on delivery) contract differs from the f.o.b. and c.i.f. contracts in that the seller's duty of delivery is not complete until he tenders the goods at the buyer's place of business or residence.

Risk of Loss

The buyer and seller may expressly agree about when the risk for loss caused by damage to or destruction of the goods shall pass from the seller to the buyer, or it may be possible to imply such a term from the contract as a whole. Thus, in f.o.b. and c.i.f. contracts it is reasonably implied that the goods remain at the risk of the seller until he has delivered them to the carrier, and in c.o.d. contracts, until the seller or his carrier has delivered them to the buyer. But the parties may not think to include an express term concerning the passing of risk, and it may often be impossible to discover an implied term on the subject from the terms of the contract. Such an omission, though unfortunate, is understandable, since the great majority of contracts of sale proceed without any loss occurring between the time of making the agreement and receipt of the goods by the buyer.

When such a loss does occur, however, we have the curious spectacle of both parties disclaiming any interest in or responsibility for the goods. The reason for their disclaimers is that the risk of loss follows the title to the goods (unless the parties have agreed otherwise): he who has title must suffer the loss. Somewhere, Solomon-like, the law must provide rules for resolving the dispute when the parties have not provided their own. The general rules evolved to determine who has title have been embodied in the Sale of Goods Act, and we may now turn to a discussion of them.

TITLE TO GOODS

Specific Goods

The first four of the rules set down in the Sale of Goods Act (s. 19) for the passing of title relate to *specific goods,* that is, to goods in existence and identified and agreed upon as the subject-matter of the sale at the time the contract is formed.

---

[11] Biddell Brothers v. E. Clemens Horst Co. [1911] 1 K.B. 214 per Hamilton, J., at 220.

These four rules apply only when the parties have not expressed a contrary intention about when title shall pass.

Rule 1

Where there is an unconditional contract for the sale of specific goods in a deliverable state, the property in the goods passes to the buyer when the contract is made, and it is immaterial whether the time of payment or the time of delivery or both are postponed.

Illustration:

> Maple Leaf Appliances Ltd. is having its annual January sale. Late on a Saturday afternoon, Hardy contracts to buy a new television set displayed on the floor. He agrees to pay for it in 30 days, and the set is to be delivered on Monday. On the intervening Sunday, however, the premises of Maple Leaf Appliances Ltd. are broken into, and the television set is stolen. The parties have not discussed who should have the risk of loss until the set was either delivered or paid for. Maple Leaf Appliances sue Hardy for the price of the set.
>
> The action will succeed. The title passed to Hardy on Saturday and the loss is his. Hardy might, of course, be able to argue in defence that the loss was attributable to the negligence of Maple Leaf Appliances — for example, that they failed to lock the premises. However, it is not negligence on the part of a seller to fail to insure the goods unless the buyer has instructed him to do so.[12] Nevertheless, a retail merchant may carry insurance that reimburses customers for loss or damage to their goods remaining on his premises, and in any event, for reasons of goodwill, he will usually replace lost goods before insisting upon the price.
>
> If, in this illustration, Maple Leaf Appliances had delayed delivery without Hardy's request or consent and the theft had occurred instead on Monday night, so that the loss might have been avoided if the set had been delivered to Hardy as agreed, Hardy would not be liable.

Rule 2

Where there is a contract for the sale of specific goods and the seller is bound to do something to the goods for the purpose of putting them into a deliverable state, the property does not pass until such thing is done and the buyer has notice that it is done.

Illustration:

> In the course of the same January sale described in the preceding illustration, another customer, Oliver, agrees to buy a second-hand television set

---

[12] Halsbury, *The Laws of England* (3rd ed.), Vol. 2, p. 116.

which Maple Leaf Appliances Ltd. displays, but a term of the agreement is that Maple Leaf Appliances shall replace the picture tube. It has not done so when the set is stolen. The title has not passed to Oliver, and he is not liable for the price.

Even if Maple Leaf Appliances had replaced the picture tube shortly after Oliver left the store, Oliver would not have the title unless he had also been *notified* that this had been done before the set was stolen. Often, when the seller undertakes to deliver the goods, he will not communicate separately with the buyer to advise him that the goods are now in a deliverable state but will simply deliver them. In these circumstances, the required notice to the buyer is satisfied by delivery, and the title passes at the time of delivery.

Rule 3

Where there is a contract for the sale of specific goods in a deliverable state but the seller is bound to weigh, measure, test, or do some other act or thing with reference to the goods for the purpose of ascertaining their price, the property does not pass until such act or thing is done and the buyer has notice.

Illustration:

The firm of McTavish, Frobisher & Co. agrees to buy a pile of beaver skins from Peter Pond, a trapper, at $6.50 per skin. Before Pond counts the skins, most of them disappear mysteriously. The title has not passed to McTavish, Frobisher & Co., and in the absence of any special agreement between the parties, the loss is Pond's.[13]

The result would have been different, however, if the parties had agreed in the first instance to a provisional price of $1,300 for the entire pile, the exact price to be determined later by counting and valuing the skins at $6.50 each. When the parties agree on a provisional price, the court infers that the transfer of title does not depend on the counting.[14]

Rule 4

When goods are delivered to the buyer on approval or on "sale or return" or other similar terms, the property therein passes to the buyer:

    (a) when he signifies his approval or acceptance to the seller or does any other act adopting the transaction;

    (b) if he does not signify his approval or acceptance to the seller but retains the goods without giving notice of rejection, then, if a time has been fixed for the return of the goods, on the expiration of such time, and if

---

[13] See Zasbury v. Furnell (1809) 170 E.R. 1142; Simmons v. Swift (1826) 108 E.R. 319.

[14] See Chalmers, *Sale of Goods Act, 1893* (14th ed.), pp. 109-10, 115. Sieghart, ed. London: Butterworth & Co. (Publishers), Ltd., 1963.

no time has been fixed, on the expiration of a reasonable time, and what is a reasonable time is a question of fact.

We can see from this rule that a buyer may accept goods and acquire ownership of them without having expressly communicated that intention to the seller. As our discussion of bailment in Chapter 19 will show, a prospective buyer who has custody of goods on approval owes a duty of care in looking after them: therefore he does have some liability even though he is not yet liable for the price.

Unascertained Goods

The Sale of Goods Act prescribes a separate rule about when title passes in goods that are unascertained at the time of the contract. The extreme example of unascertained goods occurs when they have not yet been produced, that is, when they are *future goods;* but they may also be unascertained even when they are in existence, provided they have not yet been selected and related categorically to a particular contract. Goods are ascertained once they have been set aside or earmarked and agreed upon as the subject-matter of the sale. When unascertained goods are the subject of a contract, by definition the contract must be an agreement to sell, for title cannot pass to the buyer until the goods are ascertained. Nor can the parties effectively insert a term in their agreement purporting to pass the title before that event. The rule is as follows:

Rule 5

(a) Where there is a contract for the sale of unascertained or future goods by description and goods of that description and in a deliverable state are unconditionally appropriated to the contract, either by the seller with the assent of the buyer, or by the buyer with the assent of the seller, the property in the goods thereupon passes to the buyer, and such assent may be expressed or implied and may be given either before or after the appropriation is made.

(b) Where in pursuance of the contract the seller delivers the goods to the buyer or to a carrier or other bailee (whether named by the buyer or not) for the purpose of transmission to the buyer and does not reserve the right of disposal, he is deemed to have unconditionally appropriated the goods to the contract.

Illustration:

Prentice orders from Hall's automotive supply store four truck tires, size 750 x 20. Hall has a large number of such tires in his stockroom. Later in the day, a clerk removes four such tires from the rack where Hall keeps his stock. He sets them aside in the stockroom, attaching a note, "For Mr. Prentice." The clerk's act of separating these tires from the larger bulk does not amount to an unconditional appropriation of the goods. If the contents of the stockroom were to be destroyed in a fire, the loss of the tires would be the seller's because title has not yet passed to the buyer.

Suppose, however, that Prentice had left his truck at the garage on Hall's premises, and Hall's employees subsequently installed the four tires on the truck. Such installation of the tires would amount to an unconditional appropriation of the tires to the contract. It would in fact be tantamount to a delivery of the tires to Prentice. If, before Prentice called for his truck, a fire destroyed the garage including the truck and tires, Prentice would be liable for the price of the tires, as title in them would have passed to him.

Unconditional appropriation of goods to a contract does not take place until the seller can no longer change his mind and substitute other goods for delivery to the buyer. In other words, some act must be done that conclusively determines the election about what goods are appropriated to the contract. It seems that nothing less than delivery of the goods — or at least an act that virtually amounts to delivery — will constitute unconditional appropriation, as when the tires were installed in the above illustration.

The buyer's assent to appropriation can be presumed from his prior order. Accordingly, title may pass to the buyer even before he receives notice of the unconditional appropriation, as illustrated above. In this respect, then, the rule for unascertained goods differs from some of the rules we discussed earlier for specific goods.

Rule 5 above refers to the possibility of a seller's "reserving the right of disposal". We shall consider this right in the following chapter, when we deal with the bill of lading.

The Effect of Agency

When an owner ships goods to his agent for the purpose of sale by the agent, the effect of the consignment is to give the agent (the consignee) the appearance of ownership in the eyes of the public. Consequently, statutes in the various provinces provide that the agent has authority to deal with the goods as though he were their owner.[15]

He may therefore validly pass title to anyone who purchases the goods from him in good faith, even though he sells them in a manner forbidden by the owner (the consignor). Again, he may pledge the goods as security for a loan, and the owner is bound by the transaction. We shall encounter the law on this point again in Chapter 20 on agency.

A similar though more complex problem arises when a seller gives a buyer possession but retains the title as security for payment, as he does in an instalment sale. We shall discuss the effect of an instalment sale in Chapter 30.

---

[15] See, for example: Factors Act, R.S.O. 1970, c. 156, s. 2; R.S.N.S. 1967, c. 97, s. 2; Sale of Goods Act, R.S.B.C. 1960, c. 344, ss. 31 and 59; R.S.O. 1970, c. 421, s. 25; R.S.N.S. 1967, c. 274, s. 27. See also the Criminal Code, R.S.C. 1970, c. C-34, s. 286 for the circumstances under which a factor or agent does not commit theft by pledging or giving a lien on goods or documents of title to goods that are entrusted to him for the purpose of sale.

QUESTIONS FOR REVIEW

1. Is the sale of every type of chattel necessarily governed by the Sale of Goods Act?
2. Distinguish two types of consignment.
3. Does the term *personal property* embrace a larger range of assets than the term *chattels?*
4. In what respect may the amount of a sale be important?
5. Do the terms relating to delivery comprise the sole obligations of the seller?
6. Have the parties any control over the terms implied by the Sale of Goods Act?
7. Is there any difference between *specific* goods and *ascertained* goods?
8. Is the purchase of a valuable portrait from an art collector a contract of sale of goods or a contract for work and materials?
9. Is a contract for the sale of a prefabricated cottage a contract of sale of goods or a contract of sale of real property?
10. If a buyer and seller agree expressly that title is to pass at a specified time in advance of delivery, and the goods are destroyed in the interval between the passing of title and the delivery date, who sustains the loss?
11. State which of the following terms are conditions and which are warranties: time of payment; time of delivery; an implied term as to description.
12. Assume all the facts in the illustration in this chapter for Rule 1 under "Title to Goods" except that the dealer had agreed to deliver the same model of television set "from my stock". Would the buyer then be liable for the purchase price?
13. Farmer *A* wanted to sell his goat for $10, and farmer *B* agreed to buy it. *B* put $10 on the table, and *A* suggested a glass of beer to celebrate the deal. While they were drinking, the goat ate the ten dollars. (News item, May 13, 1961.) Who owns the goat?

CASES FOR DISCUSSION

CASE 1

Barnsworthy agreed to buy from Ajax Co. Ltd. 1,000 barrels of oil which was stored in a large tank on the company's premises. The tank in question contained in all 25,000 barrels of oil. Before Ajax Co. Ltd. had the opportunity to withdraw the 1,000 barrels for delivery to Barnsworthy, the tank developed a leak, and 5,000 barrels were lost before the leak was discovered and repaired. Ajax Co. Ltd. then refused to make delivery to Barnsworthy, claiming that the oil that had leaked out of the tank included the 1,000 barrels purchased by Barnsworthy and that the loss was accordingly Barnsworthy's. Barnsworthy refused to pay, and Ajax Co. Ltd. sued him for the price. Should the action succeed?

CASE 2

Baldwin was dissatisfied with his present car because it was uncomfortable and unsuitable for taking his wife out in. He wrote to Martin, the proprietor of a business selling a variety of foreign cars, "Can you tell me if the Bugatti eight cylinder is likely to be on the market this year, and if so will you send particulars?" Martin replied, "As you no doubt are already aware, we specialize in the sale of these cars and are in a position to supply you with all the information necessary." In a subsequent interview, Baldwin made plain to Martin the purpose for which he required the car. Baldwin then signed a printed document in the form of a request by him to Martin to supply him with "one eight-cylinder Bugatti car fully equipped and finished as standard specification as per the car inspected." It was a term of this agreement that Baldwin should pay $1,200 in cash and the balance of the price in sixty days. On the back of the contract there was printed under the heading, *Guarantee,* the words: "Guaranteed against breakage of parts due to faulty material. Cars are sold on condition that the foregoing guarantee is accepted instead of, and expressly excludes, any other guarantee or warranty statutory or otherwise."

An eight-cylinder Bugatti was delivered to Baldwin but proved to be uncomfortable and useless for ordinary touring purposes. Baldwin claimed either (1) to reject the car and recover back the purchase money he had paid, or (2) to be entitled to damages for breach of contract substantially equal to the price of the car. What should the court's decision be? (See *Baldry v. Marshall* [1925] 1 K.B. 260.)

CASE 3

Smith purchased a motor car from Goral, a dealer, who had purchased it from a third party. The contract between Smith and Goral contained an express term that the car "is, to the best of the seller's knowledge, free from any charge or encumbrance". It was later seized from Smith by the Crown as having been forfeited under the Customs Act for unlawful importation into Canada without the payment of customs duty. Neither Smith nor Goral was aware of the outstanding claim for duty, and they were innocent of the unlawful importation. Smith brought an action against Goral to recover the purchase price he had paid for the car.

State whether Smith should succeed. (See *Smith v. Goral* [1952] 3 D.L.R. 328.)

CASE 4

In December, Winnipeg Seafoods Ltd. orally agreed to purchase from Lakehead Fish Wholesale Co. a lot of 1,000 ten-pound boxes of frozen Lake Superior herring at 15¢ per pound. The fish was then in the cold storage warehouse of a third party, the Bailey Co. of Thunder Bay. The Bailey Co. operated as a storage company which processed and stored fresh fish. At the time it held some 1,500 boxes of this type of fish in storage.

Because Winnipeg Seafoods Ltd. was short of storage space, it did not want the fish shipped to it, but desired to have it remain in the warehouse at Thunder Bay. Lakehead Fish Wholesale Co. then arranged with the Bailey Co. to transfer the storage account to the name of Winnipeg Seafoods Ltd. in respect of the 1,000 boxes; and Lakehead Fish Wholesale Co. sent an invoice for $1,500 to Winnipeg Seafoods Ltd. which indicated that the merchandise was in storage at the Bailey Co., Thunder Bay. Immediately afterwards, Bailey Co. sent its invoice to Winnipeg Seafoods Ltd. for one month's storage charges, payable in advance. Winnipeg Seafoods Ltd. did not pay either of these accounts. The price of frozen herring started to fall in the middle of January. The fish was held in storage until the end of January and then processed to prevent spoilage. On February 2, Winnipeg Seafoods Ltd. returned the invoice of Lakehead Fish Wholesale Co. with an accompanying letter to the effect that it had decided to "cancel the order". Lakehead Fish Wholesale Co. then sued Winnipeg Seafoods Ltd. for the price of the fish, $1,500, or in the alternative for damages for non-acceptance. Should it succeed?

CASE 5

On March 20, Mrs. Jackson entered into a contract for the purchase from Tip Top Motor Sales Ltd. of a previous year's model Ford car that had been used as a demonstrator. The terms of the contract were that Mrs. Jackson was to turn in two used cars which she then owned (a three-year-old Rambler and a six-year-old Chevrolet) and pay the balance of $500 in cash. It was also a term of the contract that before delivery certain necessary repairs should be made to the Ford car purchased and that a new battery recently acquired for the Rambler should be installed in the Ford. The parties had agreed that Mrs. Jackson should at once deliver the Rambler to Tip Top Motor Sales Ltd. but that she could continue to use the Chevrolet until she took delivery of the Ford car on March 28 or 30. She transferred the ownership papers of the Rambler and Chevrolet to Tip Top Motor Sales Ltd. and paid the cash balance of $500 on March 21.

All repairs except for the changing of the battery were completed on March 27, and the Ford car was put in the showroom of Tip Top Motor Sales Ltd. Early next morning a fire destroyed the showroom, and the Ford car was badly damaged. Mrs. Jackson brought an action against Tip Top Motor Sales Ltd. for the $500 she had already paid and for the trade-in value of the Rambler, which Tip Top Motor Sales Ltd. had resold. Should she succeed? (See *Jerome v. Clements Motors Sales Ltd.* (1958) 14 D.L.R. (2d) 745; (1959) 15 D.L.R. (2d) 689.)

CASE 6

Wilby purchased a second-hand Oldsmobile from True-Blue Auto Dealers under a contract that contained the following clause:

> No condition or warranty that the vehicle is roadworthy or as to its age, condition, or fitness is given by the seller or implied herein.

Wilby had inspected the car, which he found to be in excellent condition, but it took him three weeks to arrange all the financing. The car was then delivered by the seller to Wilby's house late at night and left outside the garage. When Wilby inspected it the next morning, he found that it had the same serial and engine numbers and licence plates but had been badly damaged and stripped. It had evidently been towed to his place. The new tires had been taken off and old ones put on; the AM/FM radio had been removed; the chrome strips around the body were missing; the cylinder head was off the engine; all the valves were burnt; and there were two broken pistons.

Wilby had agreed to pay $2,750 for the car but the mechanic at his neighbourhood service station estimated that it would cost him a further $1,300 to restore the car to its former condition. Wilby immediately returned the car to True-Blue Auto Dealers. The finance company to which the dealer had assigned the contract then brought an action against Wilby for the amount due under it.

Discuss the legal issues raised by these facts and, with reasons, suggest a verdict.

CASE 7

Jonah was accompanying his wife on a food-shopping trip in one of the supermarkets of Pause & Purchase Groceterias, and his wife had taken three 30-ounce bottles of "Swinger Cola" from the shelves and placed them in the shopping cart he was pushing, when there was an explosion. Jonah felt a piece of glass strike him in the left eye. One of the three bottles in the cart was shattered, with the bottom and some ragged sides remaining upright, and a pool of beverage was on the floor below. The other two bottles were intact.

Jonah suffered a scarred cornea and permanently impaired vision in his left eye with its overall efficiency reduced to about 75%. The effect was to make him sensitive to glare, cause headaches, and reduce his perception in reading. He was a relatively young chartered accountant and it appeared that his ability to undertake any more senior responsibilities in his firm was now diminished. He brought an action jointly against Pause & Purchase Groceterias Ltd. and Swinger Cola Ltd.

Explain whether the plaintiff in this case would have any remedy under the Sale of Goods Act. Discuss also the nature of any other type of liability that might form the basis for the action. Indicate the probable outcome without regard to the question of the amount of damages.

CASE 8

In February, 1976, Gantry visited the small workshop of Marley, a cabinet-maker, and orally ordered some furniture for a price of $950. The furniture comprised a coffee table, three end-tables, and a built-in bookshelf and cabinet. Gantry supplied a sketch setting out in some detail the design of the items of furniture he was ordering.

In May, 1976, the coffee table was delivered to Gantry, who kept it overnight and then returned it with the complaint that the finish did not correspond with what had been ordered and a request that a different finish be applied. The other pieces were delivered over the following two weeks, with the same results. Gantry refused to pay anything for the furniture and Marley brought an action against him for the price of $950.

At the trial, a conflict of evidence developed about whether the finish on the furniture as supplied corresponded with what Gantry had specified. The trial judge found that the plaintiff had performed the contract according to the defendant's specifications.

Outline the nature of the defence available to the defendant and the arguments that the plaintiff might use. Indicate the probable decision of the court.

CASE 9

Dawson was in the business of land clearing, which involved knocking down bush, piling it up and burning it. He used a heavy-duty tractor for the purpose and could earn gross revenue of $150 a day.

A salesman for Vincible Tractors Ltd. sold Dawson a tractor for this work for the price of $32,000. The contract of sale contained the following clause:

> The Vendor warrants the tractor described herein to be free from defects in material and workmanship under normal use and service, the Vendor's obligation under this warranty being limited to making good any parts which examination shall disclose to the manufacturer's satisfaction to have been defective, provided that such parts shall be so returned to the factory within six months after delivery of such tractor and that at the time of such return the tractor claimed to be so defective shall not have been operated in excess of 1,500 hours.
>
> The above warranty is in lieu of all other warranties, express or implied.

After its delivery, the tractor was used from 18 to 20 hours a day with three skilled operators for six days a week. It worked well for a few weeks but then, while still under warranty, began to fail under the heavy pressure of work. Dawson had to return it repeatedly to the tractor company's nearest service and repair depot for repairs. He had to take it from his place of work some 40 miles into Nanaimo on 20 occasions in its first year and, after the first six months, he paid about $2,500 in repair bills to keep it in operation. After about 1,700 hours of work, it eventually became clear that the tractor was basically useless for the purpose for which it had been purchased, being unable to develop enough power to do this type of work; and that the company had made every effort to make it work, without success.

At this stage Dawson returned the tractor and brought an action against Vincible Tractors Ltd. for recovery of the price paid and for damages for breach of contract in the amount of $10,000, representing his net earnings lost while the tractor was in the company's hands being repaired and the cost of repairs in excess of normal maintenance. Should this action succeed?

CHAPTER 17

The Contract of Sale: Remedies of the Parties

SCOPE OF THE SELLER'S LIABILITY

Misrepresentation

The Common Law. We have considered the remedies for misrepresentation in Chapter 10, but a review of that chapter is worth while at this point. We noted there that when the misrepresentation is innocent, the only remedy, rescission, is often impossible or at least impractical for the buyer; and to have the more extensive remedies available for fraudulent misrepresentation, the buyer must clearly establish fraud.

The type of false assertion that comes within the definition of misrepresentation has two important characteristics for our present purposes. First, the assertion must be part of the preliminary bargaining, and not be incorporated as a term in the contract of sale — if it were embodied in the contract, the buyer's recourse would be for breach of contract. Secondly, the false assertion made by the seller must be made as a statement of fact — the law provides no remedy for a buyer induced to enter into a contract by a mere expression of opinion, or commendation of the goods.

Advertising can be misleading in a general way and still not amount to misrepresentation as we have defined it. While to many, the common law may seem inadequate in this respect, several factors help both to explain this state of affairs and to minimize potential abuse. In the first place, much of business proceeds with reasonable responsibility to the public, and any general rule sufficiently comprehensive to control and punish every type of deception would also be sufficiently oppressive to obstruct unduly the course of legitimate business. In the second place, no legal rule is an adequate substitute for a buyer's own care. A seller's superior position results largely from his knowledge about both his products and the limits of the law, and the only effective way for the buyer to minimize this advantage is to seek this knowledge for himself. Thirdly, the common law can be, and has been, superseded by statute law in specific areas of abuse. For example, we have considerable legislation to protect the consumer, and will doubtless see more in the future.

Legislation. The one instance of statutory regulation of advertising that we have encountered previously is the prohibition of a materially false misrepresentation to the public about the regular price of an article. The point came up when we discussed the Combines Investigation Act in Chapter 8. In addition, that statute includes the following provision affecting advertising of all types:

(1) Every one who publishes or causes to be published an advertisement containing a statement that purports to be a statement of fact but that is untrue, deceptive or misleading or is intentionally so worded or arranged that it is deceptive or misleading, is guilty of an indictable offence and is liable to imprisonment for five years, if the advertisement is published
   (a) to promote, directly or indirectly, the sale or disposal of property or any interest therein, or
   (b) to promote a business or commercial interest.
(2) Every one who publishes or causes to be published in an advertisement a statement of guarantee of the performance, efficacy or length of life of anything that is not based upon an adequate and proper test of that thing, the proof of which lies upon the accused, is, if the advertisement is published to promote, directly or indirectly, the sale or disposal of that thing, guilty of an offence punishable on summary conviction.[1]

Other federal statutes of general regulation are the Weights and Measures Act[2] and the National Trade Mark and True Labelling Act.[3]

A number of federal statutes not only govern the representations that can be made about particular products, but also provide for inspection of the industry and regulation of the quality of the goods sold. The best known of these statutes is the Food and Drugs Act, which prescribes penalties for the sale of any article of food or any drug that is adulterated or that is manufactured, packaged, or stored under unsanitary conditions. This Act also provides in part that:

No person shall label, package, treat, process, sell or advertise any food in a manner that is false, misleading or deceptive or is likely to create an erroneous impression regarding its character, value, quantity, composition, merit or safety.[4]

---

[1] R.S.C. 1970, c. C-23, s. 37. The Act goes on to provide that the subsections quoted do not apply to a publisher who accepts the advertisement in good faith.

[2] R.S.C. 1970, c. W-7.

[3] R.S.C. 1970, c. N-16.

[4] R.S.C. 1970, c. F-27, s. 5(1).

An identical provision applies to deception in the sale of drugs. There are also separate federal statutes regulating the sale of meat and canned goods, patent medicines, livestock, milk, fruit, vegetables, and honey.[5]

Breach of a Term

Generally, a breach of a term which is a condition entitles the injured party to rescind the contract as well as to sue for damages for any loss suffered. The Sale of Goods Act, however, sets down certain circumstances where a buyer will not be entitled to rescind the contract and return the goods, even though the seller has been guilty of a breach of condition. The Act reads as follows:[6]

> Where a contract of sale is not severable and the buyer has accepted the goods or part thereof, or where the contract is for specific goods the property in which has passed to the buyer, the breach of any condition to be fulfilled by the seller can only be treated as a breach of warranty and not as a ground for rejecting the goods and treating the contract as repudiated, unless there is a term of the contract, express or implied, to that effect.

This section means that the buyer must keep the goods and content himself with damages where the broken contract of sale does not contemplate delivery by instalments (is not severable) and the buyer has indicated his intention to keep the goods or treated them in a way inconsistent with the seller's ownership of them — that he has, in short, "so acted as to induce reasonable men to conclude that the goods satisfy the requirements of the contract".[7] The section seems to contemplate a second situation where rescission would be lost — when the contract is for specific goods, the property in which has passed to the buyer. This statement is misleading, however, because property in the goods would not pass to the buyer where the seller had committed a breach of condition by appropriating improper goods to the contract, unless and until the buyer subsequently waives this breach by accepting the goods.[8]

Illustration:

> A salesman for Agrarian Implements Ltd. calls on Macdonald, a farmer, and shows him a catalogue containing pictures of various types of agricultural equipment that his firm has for sale. The salesman tells Macdonald that they have just taken into stock "one brand new" combine of a type pictured in the catalogue. Macdonald agrees to buy it and signs the necessary papers.

---

[5] Meat and Canned Goods Act, R.S.C. 1970, c. M-6, s. 37; Proprietary or Patent Medicines Act, R.S.C. 1970, c. P-25, s. 8(1)(f); Live Stock and Live Stock Products Act, R.S.C. 1970, c. L-7, ss. 39, 40, 41; Milk Test Act, R.S.C. 1970, c. M-13, ss. 3, 4; Fruit, Vegetables and Honey Act, R.S.C. 1970, c. F-31, s. 15.

[6] See, for example: R.S.B.C. 1960, c. 344, s. 17(3); R.S.O. 1970, c. 421, s. 12(3); R.S.N.S. 1967, c. 274, s. 13(3).

[7] Cheshire and Fifoot *The Law of Contract* (3rd ed.), p. 164. This classic statement seems to have been dropped from subsequent editions.

[8] See: Guest, A. G. (ed.) *Benjamin's Sale of Goods,* pp. 149, 346, 393-5. London: Sweet & Maxwell, 1974.

When the combine is delivered, a neighbour of Macdonald recognizes it as one with which the same salesman had earlier given him an extensive demonstration, and which the salesman had referred to as "a demonstrator model that we could let you have at a bargain". Macdonald at once ships the combine back to Agrarian Implements Ltd. The company then sues him for the price.

The combine was a specific article at the time Macdonald agreed to buy it. Nevertheless, he is entitled to treat the contract as at an end and refuse to take delivery of it. Agrarian Implements Ltd. has been guilty of breach of an implied condition as to description (that the combine was new), and for this reason title did not pass to Macdonald.[9]

If, however, Macdonald took delivery of the combine and used it for his farm work, he could not subsequently, upon learning that it was not new when he bought it, insist upon a right to return it. He must content himself with damages.

Again, even when the goods are specific and title has passed to the buyer at the time of sale, if the seller fails to deliver on time, the buyer may subsequently refuse to take them and may rescind the contract. The section concludes by stating that it does not apply where there is a term of the contract, express or implied, to the effect that the buyer can treat a breach of condition as grounds for rejecting the goods. When the parties specify a time for delivery, they imply such an intention.

In *Leaf v. International Galleries*[10] we can see the possible consequences for the buyer when the seller is guilty of a breach of condition but the buyer has accepted the goods. Leaf purchased a painting of Salisbury Cathedral which the seller, International Galleries, represented to him as a painting by Constable. When Leaf attempted to resell the picture five years later, the error in its origin came to light; it had not been painted by that famous English artist. Leaf sought to return the picture to International Galleries and recover the purchase price. The court held that the Sale of Goods Act section quoted above applied, so that Leaf did not have the right to treat the contract as being at an end. As he did not sue for damages, which he might have obtained, his action failed. It is interesting to note that the court chose to regard the representation as having been incorporated into the contract of sale as a term; its decision leaves to one side the question whether, had the case been treated as one of either innocent misrepresentation or common mistake, the equitable remedy of rescission might have been available at that late date.

Wrongful Withholding or Disposition by the Seller

When the title to goods has already passed to the buyer, a seller who refuses to deliver them according to the terms of their contract is guilty of a tort: the buyer may sue him for damages for *wrongful detention*. Moreover, he may oc-

---

[9] See Varley v. Whipp [1900] 1 K.B. 513.
[10] [1950] 2 K.B. 86.

casionally obtain a court order for their delivery. If, in addition to his failure to deliver, the seller transfers the goods to a third party, he will have disposed of goods which do not belong to him; the buyer may sue him for damages for the tort of *conversion,* that is, for converting the buyer's goods to his own use or purposes.

REMEDIES OF THE BUYER

Rescission

As we have seen, rescission is a remedy available either for misrepresentation or for breach of a condition. It is limited in its application to situations where it is still possible to restore the parties substantially to their positions before the contract was made; the remedy is further restricted by the provision in the Sale of Goods Act which we have considered in the preceding section under "breach of a term". Nevertheless, it remains a valuable right for the buyer when the seller is in breach of a condition by failing to deliver the goods.

Beginning in 1965, all provinces passed various forms of consumer protection legislation purporting to give a buyer the right to rescind certain kinds of contracts of sale.[11] Unfortunately there has been virtually no co-operation among the various governments, and the resulting statutes form a bewildering array with respect to both the extent and the nature of the buyer's remedies. Even the titles of the statutes vary widely. This legislation was inspired by an act in the United Kingdom providing for a "cooling-off period" with respect to door-to-door sales.[12] During the "cooling-off period" after a door-to-door sale, a buyer may rescind the contract by giving written notice to the seller. Upon doing so, he has no further obligation under the contract and may recover any moneys already paid.

In these statutes, the "cooling-off period" varies from two to ten days. In some provinces it is based on the time when the contract is "entered into"; in others, from the date on which a written memorandum of the contract is received by the buyer. In some provinces the legislation does not apply to sales of under 50 dollars. In Ontario and British Columbia, the Act applies to both goods and services.[13] The Nova Scotia legislation, incredibly, may encourage unscrupulous sellers to charge all that the traffic will bear in excess of any limits placed on them by the Act or regulation — the Act states:

> Nothing in this Act shall have the effect of depriving a lender or of interfering with the right of a lender to collect from a borrower,

---

[11] See, for example: Consumer Protection Act, St. of B.C. 1967, c. 14 as amended 1968, c. 10; 1969, c. 5; 1970, c. 8; 1971, c. 11; R.S.O. 1970, c. 82; R.S.N.S. 1967, c. 53 as amended 1970-71, c. 32.

[12] Hire-Purchase Act, 1964, c. 53, s. 4 (U.K.).

[13] R.S.O. 1970, c. 82, s. 30; St. of B.C. 1967, c. 14 as amended by 1968, c. 10, s. 4.

a) the principal of a debt, loan or credit; or
b) the cost of borrowing thereon at the lesser of the sum or rate shown in a statement required by section 15.[14]

A "cooling-off period" is a departure from the common law approach to contracts. As our courts have developed the concept of contract, rights and liabilities of the parties are established as of the time a contract is formed, and thereafter it is too late for one of the parties to change his mind and repudiate without being in breach of contract. This principle is consistent with the view that both parties to a contract should in general be able to rely on its performance from a clearly ascertained point in time. A statutory provision for a cooling-off period is an encroachment on this principle, justified by a need to control the exploitation of consumers by door-to-door salesmen. Some of the provincial securities acts also contain a provision for a cooling-off period in the purchase of new shares and bonds issued by a company. These statutes remain exceptions to the general principle that contracts should be performed by both parties as agreed; they apply only to narrowly defined types of transactions.

Perhaps more important than the cooling-off-period provisions — which apply only to door-to-door sales — these statutes contain disclosure requirements with respect to all consumer credit sales. They require sellers to provide buyers with a detailed written statement of the terms of credit in dollars and cents and in percentage interest rates, as well as any charges for insurance and registration fees. The buyer is not bound by the contract if the seller fails to comply with the requirements.

A new approach to concern over consumer protection has led to a series of statutes and bills, currently before provincial legislatures, to deal with misrepresentations to consumers. They are known by such various names as the Trade Practices Act,[15] the Unfair Trade Practices Act,[16] and the Business Practices Act.[17] They deal with deceptive and misleading representations made to consumers. Generally speaking, they broaden the protection available to the consumer by making the transaction unenforceable or subject to recission at the buyer's option, and they grant administrative agencies broad powers to revoke licences to sell, and to lay charges against sellers for breaches of the statute and regulations passed under it. A second legislative approach, taken by Manitoba, concentrates less on unfair trade practices than on generally improving the remedies available to buyers by making "every oral or written statement made by a seller, or by a person on behalf of the seller regarding the quality, condition, quantity, performance or efficacy of goods or services that is (a) contained in an advertisement; or (b) made to a buyer, . . . an express warranty respecting those goods or services."[18] It is likely within the next few years that all provinces will pass statutes that are a variation on one or the other of these approaches. Since

---

[14] R.S.N.S. 1967, c. 53, s. 16(2).
[15] Statutes of British Columbia, 1974.
[16] Bill 78, Alberta, 1974.
[17] Statutes of Ontario, 1975.
[18] Consumer Protection Act, St. of Man. 1970, c. C200, s. 58(8).

consistency is hardly a hallmark of legislative reform in this area, it is quite possible that some provinces will pass both.

The variations in all these forms of consumer protection are so great as to confuse buyers, especially those who happen to move from one province to another: consumer education is very difficult, if not impossible, under these conditions. In addition, nation-wide firms which are anxious to comply with the laws find the task unnecessarily complicated. So far there has been no attempt to create a uniform system of consumer protection in Canada.

While a substantial number of cases occur under the consumer protection acts (none as yet under the new deceptive practices acts), there is little evidence that injurious trade practices have lessened to a significant degree and that those consumers least able to take care of themselves now receive significantly more protection than before 1965. Indeed, it is unlikely that any significant advance will be made in consumer protection until governments provide adequate funds for administrative agencies to police the regulations and represent consumers properly. Until a unified consumer protection policy is developed, it is unlikely that effective agencies will be established and funded.

Damages

For non-delivery. Generally speaking, failure to deliver is, in time sequence, the first breach that may injure a buyer. The seller may be in breach of other terms, as where he supplies defective goods, but the buyer does not become aware of such a breach until after delivery, even though the seller committed the breach beforehand.

When a seller fails to deliver goods, the buyer is free to turn and purchase the goods elsewhere. Indeed, the buyer is under a duty to mitigate his damages, and he should keep his losses to a minimum by purchasing from another source if that will help matters. If the buyer insists upon delivery after it has been refused him, the damages awarded, if any, will be no greater for the fact that the price may have risen while he continued to insist upon performance by the seller. As we have seen in Chapter 15, the damages are generally assessed at any excess of the market price at the time of breach (that is, the price the buyer would have had to pay another supplier) over the contract price. Where the goods are not readily available elsewhere and the buyer purchases them for the purpose of resale, the court may include the buyer's loss of expected profits in its assessment of damages.

If delivery is delayed through the seller's fault and the buyer accepts the goods, he is entitled to damages equal to the excess of the value the goods would have had for him if they had been delivered on time over their actual value to him when delivered. Often, of course, the actual money loss incurred will not be sufficient to justify an action for damages.

For other types of breach. Other than non-delivery, the types of breach of which a seller may be guilty are breaches of any of the implied terms as to title, description, suitability and quality, or compliance with sample, or breach of an express term inserted at the instance of the buyer as to the quality or capability of the goods. The damages sustained by a buyer from breach of any of these terms may sometimes be greater than the price of the goods; in this event, if he is to recover his loss, the buyer must take the initiative and sue the seller. If, however, the damages are less in amount than the price, he should tender to the seller what he regards as the appropriate part of the price. Should the seller refuse the tender and sue him, the buyer may counterclaim for his damages in reduction of the price. To reduce the risk of a levy of court costs against him, the buyer should pay into court the amount he tendered to the seller before the action was started.

In tort. As explained above, a buyer may sue his seller for damages for the wrongful withholding or disposition of his goods. He may also obtain damages for deceit, if he can establish that the seller made a fraudulent misrepresentation before the contract of sale was formed.

Specific Performance

The Sale of Goods Act gives the court discretion to order specific performance of a contract for the sale of goods, that is, order the seller to deliver the goods to the buyer. Generally the court does not grant this remedy when a seller refuses to deliver, because money damages are nearly always an adequate remedy. Where the goods have a unique value for the buyer, however, the court may exercise its discretion in his favour and order specific performance.

THE BILL OF LADING

Its Purposes

A bill of lading is an essential part of many sales transactions and important to the remedies of the seller, as we shall see in the next section. We can best understand the nature of a bill of lading by considering its purposes:

(a) It is a receipt issued and signed by the carrier, acknowledging that specified goods have been delivered to him for shipment.
(b) It is a contract between the shipper (seller) and the carrier to transport the goods to a stated destination.
(c) It may be evidence of title to the goods.

For the first two of these purposes the bill of lading may be either a *straight* or an *order* bill of lading; to serve the third purpose, it must be an order bill of lading.

Straight Bill of Lading

By the terms of a straight bill of lading the shipment is consigned directly to a designated party. When a seller employs a straight bill, he usually consigns the goods to the buyer.[19]

---

[19] In international transactions the shipment may instead be consigned to a bank that is financing the buyer.

A straight bill of lading specifies the name and address of the person who is to receive an *arrival notice* once the goods reach their destination. Anyone holding the arrival notice and representing the consignee named in the bill of lading is entitled to obtain possession of the merchandise. It is not necessary to present a straight bill of lading to prove title, and a consignee may obtain possession of goods at the point of destination without surrendering such a bill to the carrier.

Order Bill of Lading

An order bill of lading is made out to the order of a specified person who, as a result, has title to the goods in the course of transit. The party thus named in the bill of lading may then transfer title to the goods to someone else by endorsing it. An order bill of lading operates in a manner similar to a negotiable instrument.

The customary practice is for a seller to consign his shipment to the order of himself. By having the bill of lading made out to his own order, a seller can retain the right of disposal during transit. In this way he can withhold title from the buyer until the latter accepts a bill of exchange drawn on him for the price of the goods. The seller, or his agent, then endorses the bill of lading over to the buyer so that the buyer may obtain the goods from the carrier.

Alternatively, the seller may endorse the bill of lading in blank, that is place only his signature on the document, unaccompanied by any words specifying the party who is next to have title. An *endorsement in blank* has the effect of giving any bona-fide bearer of the bill of lading the right to receipt of the goods.

An order bill of lading is a useful device for transferring the ownership in goods independently of their physical possession. The purchase of goods is often financed while the goods are in transit to the buyer — the buyer being unwilling or unable to pay for the goods in advance of their delivery to him, and the seller being unwilling to ship without some assurance of payment. The party financing the transaction (the seller's or buyer's bank, for example) may hold the bill of lading as security for payment by the buyer. This device makes it easier to find persons who will finance purchases of goods. Since the order bill of lading serves this purpose, it is used more often than the straight bill of lading in foreign trade, where the need for security of payment is greater.

REMEDIES OF THE SELLER

Lien

A seller's primary concern is that he should receive the contract price of the goods from the buyer. One of the sanctions he sometimes has at his disposal is withholding delivery until he is paid. In these circumstances we say that the unpaid seller has a *lien* on the goods — that is, while they remain in his possession he has a claim or charge on them for their agreed price, and can refuse to part with them until the debt is satisfied. Once the seller delivers the goods to the buyer, however, he loses this special right to possession except where the buyer obtains them by theft or trickery. The right of lien is based upon possession and is extinguished for all time when possession passes in good faith to the buyer.

Not every contract of sale creates a right of lien for the seller. The remedy exists only in the following situations:

(a) where the contract makes no stipulations that the buyer is to have credit, so that payment may be required upon delivery; or

(b) where the goods have been sold on credit, the term of credit has expired without payment being made, and the seller still has possession of the goods; or

(c) where the buyer becomes insolvent before delivery.

In the third of these situations, a seller who refuses to deliver in the face of his contractual obligation is excused only if he can show that the buyer is insolvent. To avoid liability for breach of his promise to deliver, he should be sure of the facts before he exercises the right of lien; otherwise he takes the risk that the buyer may subsequently sue him for breach. It is not enough simply to hear that the buyer's financial position is questionable — it is necessary to be more specific, and to show that the buyer is definitely unable to meet his current debts as they come due. Otherwise the seller must still deliver as promised, although he becomes an unsecured creditor of the buyer for the price of the goods.

A seller may waive his right of lien in two ways. He may waive it by implication — as he does in the usual credit sale — by agreeing that delivery is to take place before payment is due: he will often have little opportunity to know whether the remedy may be useful until he has parted with the goods. Secondly, he may voluntarily deliver the goods before he need do so. In either event he waives his right of lien on the faith of the buyer's credit.

Stoppage in Transitu

If a buyer becomes insolvent after his unpaid seller has parted with possession of the goods, the seller may still have time to order the carrier to withhold them from the buyer, especially when the goods are shipped a long distance. If given notice in adequate time, the carrier is bound to obey these instructions. If the carrier delivers to the buyer in spite of such a notice, he is liable for damages for conversion.

The right of stoppage in transitu is an extraordinary one because it allows a seller who may have neither title to goods nor possession of them to exercise control over them. Like the right of lien, however, this remedy disappears once the buyer obtains possession.

We have seen that a buyer may resell goods that have not yet reached him if he holds an order bill of lading endorsed in his favour, or in blank, and assigns the bill of lading to someone else. After the seller exercises his right of stoppage in transitu, however, the buyer cannot pass good title to anyone who knows that stoppage in transitu has occurred. On the other hand, the buyer can pass good title to an innocent assignee of the bill of lading who is unaware that the right is likely to have been exercised and who has given value for the instrument.

Illustration:

> Lamb's Woollen Mills Ltd., Lancaster, England, ships a large order of women's sweaters to Byers Importers of Halifax, Nova Scotia. Since Byers is an old customer, Lamb's Woollen Mills forwards to him an order bill of lading for the goods, endorsed in blank. While the goods are still in transit, Lamb's Canadian agent learns that Byers is insolvent and notifies the carrier not to deliver the goods to Byers. In the meantime Byers resells the goods to Premium Department Stores Ltd. by assigning the bill of lading. The officers of Premium Department Stores Ltd. are unaware of the exercise of the right of stoppage in transitu or of Byers' impending bankruptcy.
>
> In these circumstances Premium Department Stores Ltd. obtains the right to possession of the goods from the carrier. Lamb's Woollen Mills Ltd. ranks only as a general creditor of Byers, and in any subsequent bankruptcy proceedings would share in the available assets by receiving a reduced amount of its claim in common with the other general creditors. These available assets would of course include the money paid by Premium Department Stores Ltd. for the sweaters.

In exercising the right of stoppage in transitu, a seller takes the same risk concerning his buyer's insolvency as he does in exercising a right of lien: if his information subsequently proves false, he may be sued for damages for non-delivery.

Resale

After exercising the right of lien or of stoppage in transitu, an unpaid seller may, under a provision in the Sale of Goods Act, give notice to the buyer and resell the goods to a third party; the new purchaser obtains good title to them.[20] This additional right is especially helpful when the goods are perishable, but is not confined to such emergencies. It enables an unpaid seller to look elsewhere for someone who will pay.

The right of resale is not confined to circumstances where it supplements a lien or stoppage in transitu. It also arises whenever a buyer refuses to accept goods delivered according to the terms of the contract.[21] Resale is then the means by which a seller mitigates his loss.

Exercise of this right by a seller does not preclude an action by him against the original buyer for damages for a deficiency, if the seller has made a diligent effort to obtain a good price on resale but obtains a lower one than that in the original contract.

---

[20] See, for example: R.S.B.C. 1960, c. 344, ss. 44(1)(c) and 52(2) and (3); R.S.O. 1970, c. 421, ss. 38(1)(c) and 46(2) and (3); R.S.N.S. 1967, c. 274, ss. 40(1)(c) and 48(2) and (3).

[21] Guest, A. G. (ed.) *Benjamin's Sale of Goods,* p. 542.

Action for the Price

A seller is entitled to his full price if title has passed to the buyer, whether the buyer has taken delivery or not. If a buyer rejects goods after title has passed, he is rejecting what is his own.

Illustration:

Anderson buys a radio displayed on the floor of Burton's Appliance Store. The radio is tagged "sold" with Anderson's name on it, and Anderson signs a form identifying the radio purchased and stating its price. On his way home Anderson sees another radio in the window of Modern Radio Stores Ltd., and decides that he would prefer this radio. When Burton's Appliance Store delivers the first radio, Anderson refuses to take it. Burton's Appliance Store sues Anderson for the full price of the radio.

The action will succeed. At the time Anderson attempted to repudiate the contract of sale, title had passed to him. If Burton's Appliance Store sues for the price, however, it must be willing and able to let Anderson take delivery of the radio.

Some businesses, such as department stores, make it a practice for reasons of goodwill to take goods back, though title may have passed to the buyer. The waiver of the original contract revests title in the seller so that he may then transfer it to another buyer.

Where the seller is not a dealer in the goods and has merely one item to sell, say an oil painting rejected by the buyer, recovery of the price will be reduced by the price the seller obtains in a bona-fide sale to a third party. If the seller has been unable to sell the painting before the action is brought to trial, the court will reduce the amount recovered by placing a value on the item. Valuation may be very difficult, but the court will not likely place a zero value on a rejected item.

Where the seller is a dealer capable of supplying more customers than in fact purchase such goods from him, the effect of a buyer's non-acceptance is to deprive him of the profit from one sales transaction. Although he might agree to rescind the contract and resell the goods to someone else, he would then have sold two such articles had the first buyer not rejected the goods. In these circumstances, the seller may prefer to sue for damages equal to the profit lost on the transaction, rather than maintain an action for the price.[22] The purpose of damages is to put the seller in the same position, as far as possible, as if the buyer had completed the contract.

In addition, any down payment or deposit received by a seller will be deducted from the price he may recover.

Even where title has not passed a seller is entitled to his full price, if that sum was to be paid on a fixed date before the goods are appropriated to the con-

---

[22] Thompson, Ltd. v. Robinson (Gunmakers) Ltd. [1955], Ch. 177; Mason & Risch Ltd. v. Christner (1919) 46 D.L.R. 710; (1920) 54 D.L.R. 653.

tract. For example, on a rising market, goods are often sold at a firm price for future delivery, the price to be paid in advance.

Damages for Non-Acceptance

If title has not passed to a buyer at the time of his breach, the normal seller's remedy is to sue him for damages. As in our oil-painting example in the preceding section, the award may be simply the excess of contract price over the price the seller can get on the market at the time of the buyer's breach. At other times, when the seller has more goods than customers, he will do much better to sue for the loss of profit on the transaction. This is especially so if the first sale was at market price and the only loss is the loss of profit.

Illustration:

> Read examines a used accordion for sale in Crescendo Music Stores Ltd. He agrees to buy it for $200 provided the bellows are repaired and gold monogram initials are affixed to it; he signs a document to that effect. Before the repairs are made, Read advises Crescendo Music Stores that he has decided to take up the saxophone instead and will not require the accordion. Crescendo Music Stores begins legal proceedings against him.
>
> The appropriate action is for damages for non-acceptance because the title has not passed to Read at the time of his repudiation. If the music store does not have an unlimited market for used accordions, it has sustained damages equal to the profit it would have made had Read purchased the instrument as he promised.
>
> If the repairs and changes had been made, but Read had not been notified of this fact before he repudiated the contract, title would still not have passed to him. In these circumstances the seller might have a claim for additional damages equal to its expenses, if the nature of the required changes (for example, Read's monogram) would not enhance the value of the instrument in a sale to anyone else.

As a practical matter, a seller often sues for the price or, in the alternative, for damages for non-acceptance. This strategy is appropriate when the seller would prefer a simple action for the price (as in our oil-painting example), but when it is not clear whether title has passed to the buyer at the time of repudiation. If the court decides that title had passed the seller will recover the price, reduced by the amount of any proceeds realized through the exercise of the right of sale. If the court decides that title had not passed, the seller will still recover damages for non-acceptance.

Retention of Deposit

In a contract of sale, as in any contract, the parties may provide that in the event of breach the party in default shall pay the other a specified sum of money by way of liquidated damages. As we have seen in Chapter 15, the court will enforce such a term if the amount specified is a genuine estimate by the parties of the probable loss. Depending on the circumstances, an amount paid by a buyer as a deposit may be treated as liquidated damages in the event of his default. In many contracts of sale the reason why the seller demands a deposit is to protect himself at least to that extent in the event of the buyer's non-acceptance; here the intention is clear that the deposit shall be forfeited upon breach by the buyer.[23]

We must, however, distinguish between a *deposit* intended primarily to provide a sanction compelling performance of the contract by the buyer, and a *down payment,* agreed upon primarily as a part payment of the purchase price and unrelated to the seller's probable loss in the event of breach by the buyer. If the title to the goods has already passed to the buyer at the time the buyer repudiates, the seller is entitled not only to retain the down payment, but to sue for the balance of the price. If title has not yet passed, the seller is entitled to retain out of the down payment any damages for non-acceptance that he can prove and is in turn accountable to the buyer for any balance of the down payment.[24] If the seller can establish damages that exceed the down payment he may retain it and sue for the balance of his damages.

QUESTIONS FOR REVIEW

1. Compare the remedies of a buyer who is the victim of (a) fraudulent misrepresentation on the part of the seller, and (b) breach of a term by the seller.
2. Is a buyer entitled to consider the contract at an end whenever his seller is guilty of a breach of condition?
3. When does the seller sue the buyer for damages for non-acceptance, and when does he sue for the price of the goods?
4. What use may an order bill of lading have which a straight bill of lading does not have?
5. If a seller tenders delivery of a larger quantity than the contract specifies and the buyer refuses to accept any part of the goods, may the seller sue successfully for damages for non-acceptance?
6. What are the rights of a seller who, just prior to shipping goods that he has agreed to sell, learns that the buyer has a reputation for paying his accounts slowly?
7. *A* makes a contract of sale with *B* to buy goods that have yet to be manufactured. When the goods are finished, *B* consigns them to A under a straight bill of lading. If the goods are damaged in the course of transit, which of *A* or *B* must sustain the loss (or attempt to recover from the carrier)? Why?
8. The contract of sale is the focal point of the manufacture and distribution of goods. What other types of contract are necessary?
9. Describe some of the ways in which the common law and statute law in Canada prevent deceptive advertising. Discuss the social problem of controlling misleading selling practices.

---

[23] See Stockloser v. Johnson [1954] 1 Q.B. 476.
[24] Stevenson v. Colonial Homes Ltd. (1961) 27 D.L.R. (2d) 698.

CASES FOR DISCUSSION

CASE 1

On December 30 Mrs. Watson agreed to buy a set of cooking utensils for $70 from Never-Burn Pots & Pans Ltd. She signed a document and made a required cash payment of $35. The document stated that the set would be delivered "on or about January 15 next" and stated that "this contract is not cancellable." The contract made no reference to the disposition of the cash payment in the event of breach by either party. When the utensils were delivered to Mrs. Watson on February 1, she refused to accept the articles and requested the return of the cash she had paid. In a letter to Mrs. Watson dated February 14, following, Never-Burn Pots & Pans Ltd. stated, "We agree to cancel the contract as you requested, but according to the terms of the contract your failure to accept delivery means that you have automatically forfeited all the moneys paid thereunder." Mrs. Watson then brought an action to recover the $35 which she had paid on December 30.

    Render a decision. (See *Wilkinson v. Rena-Ware Distributors Ltd.* (1955) 16 W.W.R. 376.)

CASE 2

Wilson, a salesman for Edible Meat Packers Ltd., called on Fowler, who operated a large mink ranch, and persuaded Fowler to buy a quantity of Antarctic whale-meat for feeding purposes in place of the Newfoundland whale-meat he was currently using. The meat was from the first cargo of Antarctic whale-meat that Edible Packers had put on the market. When the whale-meat arrived in a refrigerated freight car, Fowler went to the freight yards to inspect it, discovered that it had been shipped in jute bags, and concluded that he did not like its appearance. He thereupon refused to take or pay for it until he should receive a written assurance from Edible Meat Packers Ltd. that it was safe. He received a letter to the effect that Edible Meat Packers had made a series of tests on its make-up and feeding qualities, and that the test feedings had been made with good results.

    Fowler then took delivery of the whale-meat and in the afternoon included the whale-meat in a ration which was placed on top of the cages where the mink could eat it as they required it. Early the next morning Fowler went to his mink ranch and found all the mink dead except one that had escaped from its cage and had not eaten any of the ration.

    Fowler brought an action against Edible Meat Packers for damages in the amount of $25,000, the value of the mink which had been poisoned. It was established by expert evidence at the trial that the whale-meat in question had in fact caused the death of the mink.

    Render a decision. (See *Farmer v. Canada Packers Ltd.* [1956] O.R. 657.)

CASE 3

King, who lived at Niagara-on-the-Lake, read the following advertisement in a Toronto paper:

> Owner moving to California next weekend. Sacrificing 31-ft. cabin cruiser. Very seaworthy. Sleeps 4, 2 cabins. Fantastic buy for cash.

King then made an appointment by telephone with the vendor, Foote, to see the boat in Toronto. He inspected the boat there and asked various questions about the type of construction, age, and whether it was a good family boat. Foote told him that the boat was about twenty years old and that he had used it for three or four years as a family boat. When King inquired about its seaworthiness and how it handled in rough weather, Foote replied he had been out when the waves were ten feet high, and "it came through O.K." Foote told him that the hull tended to be spongy in the water but dried out in the winter, and that the boat was "in good condition in my opinion". King asked further about the hull, and Foote replied that it was made of ash and had been repaired. King took up a few floor boards to check for water in the bilges, and Foote told him that it shipped quite a bit of water when under way but that the pump was ample to take care of it. King said that he was inexperienced about boats and asked Foote for tips on the care of the boat; Foote replied that there was nothing to do except, perhaps, some work on the valves and rings of the engine. The parties then agreed upon a price of $6,700. King asked if Foote would deliver the boat to Niagara-on-the-Lake, and King, Foote, and two of Foote's children took the boat across the lake, encountering some heavy seas en route. On arrival King paid Foote the $6,700.

King left his new boat docked at a marina and on returning three days later learned that the pump had been working continuously. The boat was hauled out of the water, and it was discovered that the hull was in very bad condition due to dry rot; the estimate for necessary repairs or rebuilding was for $3,400.

King then brought an action against Foote for damages for fraudulent misrepresentation or in the alternative for breach of contract. State with reasons whether you think this action should succeed. (See *King v. Foote* (1961) 28 D.L.R. (2d) 337.)

CASE 4

On April 29 Christner agreed with a salesman of Mason & Risch Ltd., piano manufacturers, to buy a piano for $2,700. On May 28 following, Christner telegraphed to Mason & Risch Ltd. as follows:

> Dear Sir: This is to notify you that I hereby cancel my order for Mason & Risch piano ordered through your local agent.

Christner also wrote a letter of the same tenor to Glassford, the agent who sold him the piano.

Mason & Risch Ltd. nevertheless shipped the piano to Christner, and when he refused to accept it, brought an action against him for the full price of $2,700 or in the alternative for damages of non-acceptance. At the trial Christner's lawyer questioned an employee of Mason & Risch Ltd. as follows:

> Q. What did you do about the selection of an instrument, or what did you cause to be done?

A. We took it up immediately with the factory and had an instrument selected for Mr. Christner, and as soon as it was finished it was shipped.

Q. Before it was . . . [finished] did you get anything out of the way or out of the ordinary?

A. I think we got a telegram from Mr. Christner and a telephone message from Mr. Glassford about it.

Other evidence brought out that the manufacturer's profit on the sale of such a piano would be approximately $750.

What should be the court's decision?

CASE 5

In early December, Wayne Coates, the proprietor of the Sartorial Shop, contracted with the *Willowdale Weekly Advertiser* for the insertion of the following advertisements on the dates mentioned:

December 15
Sartorial Shop's Pre-Christmas Clearance of coats, suits and dresses. 25% off. Your opportunity for Real Savings.

December 28
Sartorial Shop's Annual Post-Christmas Clearance Sale. Entire stock of coats, suits and dresses. ½ off. Your opportunity for Real Savings.

Through an error, the *Willowdale Weekly Advertiser* inserted the latter advertisement in the December 15 issue instead of in the December 28 issue. Mr. Coates immediately drew the matter to the attention of James Pressman, the owner of the paper, and insisted that as he was obligated now to sell his stock at a reduction of 50 per cent instead of 25 per cent, Mr. Pressman should be liable in damages for 25 per cent of the selling price of all articles sold out of stock before Christmas. Mr. Pressman offered to correct the mistake by a front-page story explaining the error, window signs, and any other measures available to him. Mr. Coates refused to have the matter corrected, however, stating that such a correction would appear to his customers as an attempt to avoid his liability to sell according to the terms of the advertisement, and that his customer goodwill would be lost and his integrity impugned. He proceeded to sell his stock to record crowds at a 50 per cent reduction in price.

Subsequently, Coates sued Pressman for $6,000 as damages for breach of contract for advertising services. State with reasons whether the action should succeed. (Adapted from *Meridian Star v. Kay* 41 So. 2d 30 Miss. 1948.)

CASE 6

Disillusioned with its performance, Paul Templeton advertised his 30-foot, yawl-rigged sailboat *P.E.T.* for sale "as is" in the Barrie *Examiner*. Stanley Baker was interested in purchasing the vessel. He had had experience in operating a power-driven boat on the Great Lakes, but his experience in non-powered vessels was limited to rowboat operations off Goderich. He therefore took his mother Mrs. Baker along when going to view the *P.E.T.* His mother had crewed in the annual yacht race from Victoria to Hawaii in 1935, and she had been a competent salt-water sailor in her day.

Stanley and his mother went to view the vessel on April 13. His mother took no active part in the discussion except to ask how she handled. Templeton told them that the boat was "one of the finest wooden-hulled vessels on the lakes," and described it as handling well in the strongest gales Lake Simcoe had experienced. It was, he said, "as sound as a bell". Owing to weather conditions no trial was possible, but Templeton insisted he would stand by what he said. No sale was concluded at that time, and Stanley and his mother returned to Toronto.

Eventually, Stanley decided to stick to power-driven boats. However, his mother had been impressed with *P.E.T.* and the price. On April 22 she rang up Templeton and asked if the boat were still for sale. On being told that it was, she offered Templeton $12,000 cash. She declined Templeton's invitation to view the vessel, reminding him that she had already seen it when she accompanied her son Stanley. Some bargaining then took place, during which nothing was said about the state or condition of the boat, and ultimately, Templeton agreed to take $12,000 cash.

On April 26, Templeton and Mrs. Baker shook hands on the deal, and with Mrs. Baker present, Templeton dictated the terms of their agreement to his new secretary. They then both signed a typed memorandum of sale which read, "This memorandum will acknowledge that in consideration of the payment of $15,000 cash, P. E. Templeton agrees to sell to Miss T. G. Baker his 30 foot saleboat *P.E.T.*" Mrs. Baker then gave Templeton her cheque for $12,000.

On May 1, Mrs. Baker took the *P.E.T.* out for a short trip on Lake Simcoe. Owing to the fact that its timbers were waterlogged and rotten, the *P.E.T.* began to take water and sank 200 yards off shore.

On June 15 following, after consultation with her son and her lawyer, Mrs. Baker commenced an action for rescission of the contract and return of her $12,000. Templeton counterclaimed for $3,000 as the balance owing under the memorandum of sale.

Outline the respective arguments Mrs. Baker and Templeton might use, and offer an opinion about the outcome of the action.

CHAPTER 18

Insurance and Guarantee

THE NATURE OF INSURANCE

In its simplest terms, a contract of insurance is a method for shifting a risk of loss; that is, a method of purchasing protection against a possible loss. Not only does insurance *shift* the risk of loss from the person purchasing the protection, it also *spreads* the risk among a number of parties who have agreed to take a share in the risk.

Illustration:

> Fifty farmers in a county agree at a meeting to form a contract of mutual fire insurance with one another: each promises to pay 1/50th of any loss suffered by fire by any other of the 50 in return for the promises of the others to pay collectively the whole of any loss suffered by him through fire (less his own 1/50th). Thus, when farmer A sustains a loss of $10,000, each of the other 49 will pay him $200 for a total of $9,800.
>
> Such an agreement would contain all the usual elements of an insurance contract, but it would have two great disadvantages: (a) it would require the farmer who suffered the loss to go about collecting (or trying to collect) 1/50th from each farmer, an impractical if not impossible task; and (b) the potential loss each farmer could suffer would vary greatly according to the value of his property, and the relative safety of the property because of its construction, use, or proximity to fire-fighting equipment. A farmer whose property consisted of $20,000 worth of fire-resistant buildings would not be happy to exchange his promise with a neighbour who had $50,000 worth of

hazardous buildings; he would be taking a much greater chance of having to pay his neighbour $1,000 in a total loss than of receiving from him only $400 in a less likely total loss of his own buildings.

The two disadvantages in the above illustration may be overcome in the following ways: (a) the money can be collected *in advance* to form a fund available to pay claims for losses suffered, and used for investment until it is required to pay claims; and (b) the *amount* of money collected can be so calculated that it bears a direct relationship to the risk being assumed, that is the total possible amount of loss and the probability of that loss occurring. The insurance business does in fact proceed on these principles. The only remaining difference of importance is that instead of a group of risk-bearers getting together and agreeing on a co-operative basis to insure one another, an insurance company operates independently as a central agency for insuring risks and administering the funds collected. The insurance company calculates the payment required to insure a particular risk on the basis of recorded past experience with the type of risk in question, as summarized in actuarial tables. The amount it charges is also calculated to produce a profit: it aims for an excess of money received for insuring risks over amounts paid out in claims and amounts reserved for possible bad luck in the future (that is, a series of unexpectedly large claims).

We see, then, that insurance achieves a pooling of risks so that a large number of lucky participants subsidize the losses of a relatively few unlucky ones, and that typically, an insurance company acts as intermediary in this process. Indeed, the need to spread the risk operates even among insurance companies themselves. When an insurance company contracts to provide insurance protection for a particularly large single risk — say, accepts a fire-insurance application on a $5,000,000 plant — the insurance company may re-insure a part of this risk with one or more other insurance companies. In the event of a claim, the loss is then spread among a number of insurance companies. Some international financial institutions, notably Swiss concerns, have specialized in providing re-insurance of this kind for smaller insurance companies.

INSURANCE TERMINOLOGY

An *insurance policy* is written evidence of the terms of an insurance contract. The insurance company providing the protection is called the *insurer;* the party contracting for the insurance protection is the *insured.*[1] The *premium* is the price paid by the insured for the insurance coverage specified in the policy.

The four basic aspects of an insurance contract are the nature of the risk covered, the amount for which it is insured, the duration of the protection, and the amount of the premium. The terms of a policy may require the insurer to pay the insurance money, in the event of a claim, either to the insured or to his estate or

---

[1] In life insurance we must distinguish between the *insured* and the *life insured* when the subject of the insurance is the life of someone *other* than the party contracting for insurance.

to some other person designated as *beneficiary*. When an insured requires supplementary coverage, that is, wider protection than is available under the insurer's standard form policy, additional clauses are incorporated in the contract by attaching them to the policy in a separate insertion called a *rider*. When the parties agree to a change in the terms of an existing insurance contract, they may do so without rewriting the entire policy, by attaching a separate paper or *endorsement* to the face of the policy.

An *insurance agent* acts for his principal, the insurer, to arrange insurance contracts with persons seeking protection for themselves or for beneficiaries. In practice the insurance agent often renders a service to the insured as well, by offering advice about the appropriate coverage.

An *insurance broker* generally acts for the insured rather than for the insurer. As we shall see, the types of risk to which a business is exposed are many and varied, and a large business may find it worth while to delegate its insurance problems to a broker who will determine the coverage required, and arrange the insurance with the companies best suited to provide it at a minimum cost to the insured.

An *insurance adjuster* is an expert in the appraisal of property losses and offers his services to insurance companies for a fee. When a claim has been made, the adjuster advises the insurer about whether in his opinion the loss is covered by the insurance contract and, if so, what the amount of the loss is.

Generally speaking, insurance falls into two classes — *personal* insurance and *property* insurance. Personal insurance includes life insurance, hospital and medical insurance, accident and sickness disability insurance, and workmen's compensation. All other types of insurance are property insurance. Life insurance is unique in that the risk insured against is certain to materialize sooner or later.

STATUTE LAW REGULATING INSURANCE

Each of the provinces has one or more statutes regulating the practice of the insurance business within its borders. The main purposes of these statutes are to protect the public by requiring responsible operation on the part of insurance companies and others in the business, to protect both parties by making certain terms mandatory, and to provide a series of implied terms that apply when the parties have not expressly dealt with their subject-matter. Among other matters, the statutes do the following things: authorize the appointment of a superintendent of insurance who oversees the operations and financial responsibility of licensed insurers within the province; specify licensing requirements for insurers, agents, brokers, and adjusters; describe the terms which must be included in insurance policies; outline the nature of risks not covered unless expressly included in an insurance contract; define the extent to which an insurer may limit its liability; state the effect of misrepresentation on the contract, and the effect of suicide on life insurance; set out the conditions for an insurable interest; give formal recognition to the rights of beneficiaries and assignees; and prescribe the nature of the proof to which an insurer is entitled before it must pay a claim.

In addition to these provincial statutes, there are two relevant federal Acts, the Canadian and British Insurance Companies Act[2] and the Foreign Insurance Companies Act.[3] These Acts provide for compulsory registration of federal, British, and foreign insurance companies desiring to carry on insurance business in Canada, and also for voluntary registration of provincial insurance companies. They outline a system designed to expose any financial instability by requiring statements and returns from as well as inspection of these companies. The Acts describe the types of securities in which these companies may invest their funds, the amounts of assets they must maintain in Canada, and the methods of computing minimum required reserves. They also set out the means by which an insurance company may be federally incorporated.

INSURANCE ON BUSINESS PREMISES AND OTHER ASSETS

Fire Insurance and Insurance Against Damage by Natural Elements

While fire insurance affords protection against loss by fire damage to buildings and contents (inventory, fixtures, and equipment) as specified in one or more policies, it is important to understand that the liability of the insurer usually does not extend to a variety of losses incidental to the fire, nor to fires attributable to certain specified causes. Thus, a fire insurance policy often does not cover many of the following types of risk:

> Losses of books of account, business papers, money, stocks and bonds, and patterns;
> Theft of money or merchandise during the fire;
> Loss of property belonging to others, kept on the premises;
> Medical expenses of persons injured by the fire;
> Loss of profits caused by suspended business operations while the property is being restored;
> Increased hazard from a subsequent change in the nature of business operations or from subsequent vacancy of the premises;
> Fire loss resulting from certain types of explosives kept on the property in excess of the very limited quantity ordinarily specified in the policy;
> Damage caused by a fire used for heating or industrial purposes under the control of the insured;
> Damage caused by riots, or invasion, of which the fire may be a part;
> Damage intentionally caused by the insured.

The insured may be able to obtain protection against many of these additional risks by having special terms inserted to that effect in the policy and paying a higher premium.

In most instances an insurer is liable for the replacement value of property

---

[2] R.S.C. 1970, c. I-15 as amended by R.S.C. 1970, 1st Supp., c. 19.

[3] R.S.C. 1970, c. I-16, as amended by R.S.C. 1970, 1st Supp., c. 20.

destroyed, less depreciation. For this purpose, ''depreciation'' consists in a deduction made because the property was not in good condition before its destruction. It is not depreciation in the accounting sense, based on estimated expired life of the property. One may often purchase insurance for full replacement value, new, without any deduction for depreciation, but this higher protection is more expensive. In any event one is wise to review the replacement value from time to time in order to make sure that protection is adequate; rising construction costs or changes in building by-law requirements may quickly cause existing insurance to become inadequate.

When the insured property is mortgaged by the insured as security for a loan, the lender (mortgagee) should see that the policy contains a *mortgage clause*. This clause requires that in the event of a claim the proceeds shall be paid first to the mortgagee ''as his interest may appear,'' with the balance payable to the insured, and that in so far as the mortgagee has an interest, the insurance shall not be invalidated by any act or neglect of the insured.

In addition to fire insurance, an insured may often buy supplementary coverage against loss by water (rain, snow, or flood), wind, and earthquakes. Hail or crop insurance is also available to farmers in separate policies.

Plate-glass Insurance

For display purposes businesses often make extensive use of plate glass, which is costly to replace. Fire insurance covers the cost of replacement if the breakage is caused by a fire, but not otherwise, and the glass may be broken by such occurrences as automobile accidents, burglary, or the concussion of a nearby explosion. Most businesses take out plate-glass insurance to protect against these risks.

Automobile Collision Insurance

A business using vehicles in its operations may insure itself against risk of loss not only to third persons and their property but also to the vehicles themselves. An insurance contract typically contains a *deductible clause* stating that the insured shall pay the first $50 or $100 (or some higher amount) in respect of each claim. A deductible feature gives the insured a greater incentive to take care of the insured property and, by eliminating a large number of small claims, makes the insurance much cheaper.

Credit Insurance

A business may obtain protection against bad debt losses by insuring the collection of its accounts receivable with a commercial credit insurance company. The insurer's assessment of the credit-worthiness of the customer-debtors whose accounts it insures determines the cost of the insurance. The risk of loss may be greater if the debtor resides outside Canada. A government agency, the Export

Development Corporation, sells insurance to Canadian exporting businesses to protect them against the inability to collect the accounts of foreign customers.

A form of credit insurance may also be obtained by selling accounts receivable to a *factor*. A factor often discounts book debts *without recourse* — that is, if the accounts he buys prove uncollectable, he has no recourse against the business that sold them to him.

Marine Insurance

This type of insurance protects against loss of a ship, its cargo, or equipment caused by perils at sea, including sinking, stranding, burning, collision, contact with sea water, and even piracy and mutiny. Marine insurance may be written for a specific voyage or a fixed period of time, depending on the nature of the risk. In contrast with other types of insurance, a marine insurance contract may include a *lost or not lost* clause by which the insurer becomes liable for a loss that, unknown to the parties, may already have occurred at the time the contract is written.

Marine insurance for perils at sea is now often referred to as *wet marine* to distinguish it from *inland marine*. Inland marine insurance covers many hazards to personal property situated on land and not covered by ordinary insurance contracts, such as damage to a contractor's equipment or farm implements from any cause other than natural deterioration.

Fidelity Insurance

Fidelity insurance protects against the risk of defalcation by employees of the insured. The policy is called a *fidelity bond*, and the insurer is usually called a *bonding company*. When an insurer is obliged to make good a defalcation, it acquires the same right to recover the stolen money or other property that the insured himself would have had against his employee. This procedure is known as *subrogation*. Subrogation is the right of an insurer to succeed to the rights of the insured against the party who caused the loss and anyone who aided in the crime.

Robbery, Burglary and Theft Insurance

Each of these types of insurance provides protection against different categories of risks. They are similar to the extent that each consists in the taking of personal property of the insured without his consent, and with the intent to appropriate it for the benefit of the taker. *Robbery* includes the additional element that the taking must be by force or fear. *Burglary,* as a criminal offence, consists in the unlawful entry of premises with or without force, but burglary policies usually require forcible and violent entry of the premises before the insured may successfully claim for a loss; this requirement encourages an insured to keep his premises properly locked. *Theft* requires neither of the added elements of robbery or burglary, but consists simply in the wrongful taking of the insured's personal property. Theft insurance is therefore more comprehensive protection and requires a higher premium. A policy of any of these types usually limits the liability of the insurer to a relatively small amount (well below the total amount of the policy) for losses of cash, negotiable securities, and jewellery — items easily carried off and disposed of by thieves — to encourage their proper safekeeping.

INSURANCE ON THE OPERATION OF THE BUSINESS ENTERPRISE

Business Interruption Insurance

As we have seen, insurance payable for damage caused to business property by a fire does not include compensation for the loss of profits that ensues when a business firm is unable to operate for a period of time following the fire, or for the costs of moving to temporary quarters. Business interruption insurance protects an insured business against these risks by paying compensation as follows: (a) an amount equal to net operating profit before income tax; (b) expenses that necessarily continue even when the business is not operating; (c) money expended to reduce business losses that the insurer would otherwise have to pay under the terms of the policy (for example, the cost of moving to temporary quarters or overtime wages to hasten repairs).

The cost of this insurance varies with the rate of net operating profit estimated by the insured, the variety of expenses he chooses to classify as fixed charges, and the maximum period for which the coverage is sought. The insured may also choose to insure the payment of all employees' wages and salaries for the same period as the business interruption or for some shorter maximum period. The policy may provide that the compensation ceases as soon as the damage caused by the fire has been repaired, or it may extend compensation until business profits return to normal.

Life Insurance on Lives of Key Officers

A business has a considerable investment in the training and development of its management, and in the event of the premature death of one of its officers must often incur further expense in training and developing a replacement. For this reason it has an insurable interest in its executives and may insure their lives. The insurance premiums are a company expense, and the proceeds of the insurance paid on death are a receipt of the company.

The members of a partnership may also carry life insurance on each other's lives to assist in settling with the estate of any one of them who may die while a partner. Each partner's interest in the firm is a part of his estate and becomes payable to his estate after his death. This form of insurance provides a fund out of which the surviving partners may pay to the deceased partner's estate the value of his share in the firm. The partnership may thus avoid the risk of having to liquidate valuable assets to raise the money needed for settlement.

Public Liability and Property Damage Insurance

Businesses are continuously exposed to possible liability for injury to members of the public or their property. The harm may result from defective equipment or the negligent acts of proprietors or employees in the ordinary course of business. We shall discuss the liability of an employer for his employee's torts in Chapter 21.

Examples of this type of risk are the possibility of injuries to customers in an elevator of a retail store; to passengers in a train, bus, ship, or plane operated by a common carrier; to theatre patrons, through panic in a fire or riot; to pedestrians or motorists and their property in accidents with business vehicles. Various forms of insurance are available to indemnify a business for the liability it may incur in these situations. Thus a business using employees to operate its vehicles carries *non-ownership accident insurance* to protect against the consequences of negligent operation of the vehicles by employees. Food manufacturing and distributing companies may also obtain *product insurance* to protect against liability to members of the public who sustain injury in their use of the product sold.

Bailee Insurance

A repairman may protect himself against the theft or destruction of property left with him for repair so that in the event of a loss he will be able to reimburse his customers for the value of their goods.[4] We shall discuss the liability of a repairman in the next chapter.

INSURANCE FOR EMPLOYEES

Hospital and Medical Insurance

The premiums for this type of insurance are sometimes a joint responsibility of employer and employee, with the employee making his contribution through regular payroll deductions. Although the employer may contribute towards the premiums, claims are payable by the insurer to the employee. A plan of this kind may also include group life insurance coverage for employees.

Workmen's Compensation Insurance

As we shall see in Chapter 21, an employer's liability to employees for injuries sustained in the course of employment has now been resolved over a wide area

---

[4] Although a repairman is not liable for every kind of loss, he is nevertheless responsible to the owner for harm caused by negligence while the goods are in his custody. Accordingly he has sufficient liability to constitute an insurable interest. See Browne, *MacGillivray on Insurance Law* (5th ed.), Vol. 1, p. 476. London: Sweet & Maxwell Limited, 1961.

by statutes providing for compulsory workmen's compensation insurance. A provincial government is in effect the insurer, though it delegates the administration of the insurance to a workmen's compensation board. Employers to whom the legislation applies must make payments — in effect, premiums — to the board on behalf of their employees, who are beneficiaries of any claims made.

SPECIAL ASPECTS OF THE CONTRACT OF INSURANCE

Offer and Acceptance

The offer. In the formation of a contract of insurance, solicitation by an insurance agent is usually just an invitation to do business, and not an offer. The eventual offer is made ordinarily by the party seeking the insurance protection — the prospective insured — when he signs the application form. What, then, constitutes acceptance by the insurer? We need to know so that we can tell when the insurance is in force.

Life insurance. With life insurance, the applicant's offer is not accepted until the insurance company delivers the policy to him; moreover it is a condition precedent to delivery of the policy that the first premium shall have been paid by the insured.[5] But it may take some time for the head office of an insurance company to prepare the policy for delivery: is the insured protected in any way in the interval between signing the application form and taking delivery of the policy? The answer depends upon the wording of the application form and related form for acknowledging receipt of the premium. Many life insurance companies include an *interim insurance provision* as a term in the receipt form given for the payment of the first premium. This provision gives the insured protection from the time he signs the application, provided he has accompanied his application with the full first premium and that the results of his medical examination as reported with the application would be acceptable to the company on the terms proposed in the application. Such interim insurance expires once the insurer delivers the policy to the insured.

Property insurance. Agreements for effecting property insurance are typically less formal than for life insurance. With property insurance, the insurance agent may have an agency contract with each of a number of insurers. Each such agency contract gives him authority to sign and deliver policies and renewal certificates and generally to bind the insurer concerned. In these circumstances a person seeking property insurance can obtain the desired protection immediately, before he has paid the premium or received a policy. The agent need only prepare a memorandum or *binder* for his own records as evidence of the time and nature of the request for insurance. If a person requires immediate protection, it is im-

---

[5] See, for example: Insurance Act, St. of B.C. 1962, c. 29, s. 123, as amended by 1969, c. 11; R.S.O. 1970, c. 224, s. 154; R.S.N.S. 1967, c. 148, s. 139. In subsequent footnotes in this chapter, references to B.C., Ont., and N.S. will be to these statutes.

portant for him to ascertain whether the agent has an agency contract with the proposed insurer.

Ratification after loss. Suppose a creditor, without authority or instructions from his debtor, makes a contract of insurance for the debtor in the expectation that he will adopt the contract and pay the premium. This situation may arise when a creditor believes that his debtor is neglecting his insurance program and has inadequate coverage; he has, of course, a continuing interest in his debtor's solvency. No problem arises if the debtor learns of the creditor's act immediately afterwards and advises the insurance company of his intentions. If the debtor advises the insurer that he agrees to the transaction and will pay the premium, a binding contract of insurance exists; or if he advises the insurer that he does not propose to pay the premium, no contract exists. But what happens if a loss occurs before the debtor has communicated with the insurer: may he still ratify to have the benefit of the insurance? As we shall see in Chapter 20 on agency, the general rule is that one cannot ratify a contract made for him by someone else when he cannot himself make such a contract at the time of his attempted ratification; and one can hardly insure his property against loss after the loss has occurred.

This rule has a general application in insurance law apart from marine insurance.[6] A Canadian court has, however, made a special exception to the general rule when: (a) the insurance was placed in the insured's name by a creditor; (b) the insured property served as security for payment of the creditor's claim; and (c) the insurance money was payable in part to the creditor himself. In these circumstances the court permitted the insured (the debtor) to ratify the insurance contract after loss so that the insurance money was payable as the contract required.[7]

Renewal of policy. Property insurance is written for a limited period of time (usually for one year or three years). A common practice is for an insurance agent to prepare a renewal policy or memorandum and send it to the insured shortly before the current policy expires; the agent takes this method of reminding his clients that their insurance protection is about to cease if not renewed. But unless there is evidence of an agreement between the agent and the insured that they intend the mere delivery of a renewal policy or memorandum to create a new contract of insurance, or such an agreement can be inferred from their past dealings with one another, the agent's act of delivering the renewal policy amounts to no more than making an offer to the insured.[8] No contract is formed until the insured communicates his acceptance, and as the offer is open at most for a reasonable length of time, the insured cannot wait indefinitely to express his assent.

---

[6] See Portavon Cinema Co. Ltd. v. Price and Century Insurance Co. Ltd. [1939] 4 All E.R. 601, at 607.

[7] Goulding v. Norwich Union Fire Insurance Society [1947] 4 D.L.R. 236; [1948] 1 D.L.R. 526. In this case the four judges of the Saskatchewan Court of Appeal were equally divided, so that the decision in the lower court, permitting ratification after loss, was in fact upheld.

[8] Luke's Electric Motors & Machinery Ltd. v. Halifax Insurance Co. (1953) 10 W.W.R. (N.S.) 539 at 542-3; de Mezey v. Milwaukee Mechanics' Insurance Co. [1945] 1 W.W.R. 644.

Since an insurance agent normally acts for the insurer and not for the insured, any question of his making a contract of insurance for the insured without his authority, and subject to his ratification, will arise rarely, if ever.

Legality of Object

Wrongful acts of the insured. In our discussion of legality of object in Chapter 8 we noted that a person might insure himself against the consequences of his own negligence. With this exception, the courts refuse on grounds of public policy to enforce a contract of insurance when the claim arises out of a criminal or tortious act of the insured.[9] Before a court will hold that a claim has arisen out of a criminal or tortious act, however, the insurer must show that the loss was the reasonable or probable result of the wrongful act.

Insurable interest. Chapter 8 has also distinguished an insurance contract from a wager by the fact that the insured has an insurable interest, so that the contract shifts a genuine risk of loss from the insured to the insurer. In that chapter, we defined an insurable interest as the measure of loss suffered by the insured from damage to or destruction of the thing insured. We did not say anything, however, about the time at which the insured must have the insurable interest. The answer depends upon whether the insurance is on property or on a life.

When the contract is for property insurance, the insured must not only have an insurable interest at the time the contract was formed but must also have an insurable interest at the time the claim arises; otherwise, the contract will be void.[10] By contrast, when the contract is for life insurance, the person buying the insurance must either (a) obtain the written consent of the person whose life is to be insured, or (b) have an insurable interest *at the time the contract is formed,* though he need not have it at the time of death of the person whose life is insured.[11] Thus, if a creditor has insured the life of his debtor for the amount of his debt and that sum proves to be more than the balance owing at the time of the debtor's death, the policy is valid and the creditor is entitled to the full value of the policy.[12] This arrangement, however, is not as common as where a creditor requires his debtor to insure his own life, pay the premiums, and make the creditor a beneficiary for the amount of the debt. If at the death of the debtor the amount owing is then less than the value of the policy, the balance is paid to the debtor's estate.[13]

---

[9] See Browne, *MacGillivray on Insurance Law* (5th ed.), p. 520.

[10] See Laverty, *The Insurance Law of Canada* (2nd ed.) p. 79. Toronto: The Carswell Co., 1936; Caldwell v. Stadacona Fire & Life Ins. Co. (1883) 11 S.C.R. 212; Aqua-Land Exploration Ltd. v. Guarantee Co. (1963) 36 D.L.R. (2d) 536.

[11] See, for example: B.C., s. 121(2)(b); Ont. s. 152; N.S., s. 137(2)(b).

[12] Dalby v. The India & London Life (1854) 139 E.R. 465.

[13] Laverty, *The Insurance Law of Canada* (2nd ed.), p. 118. Toronto: The Carswell Co., 1936.

Terms of the Contract

Standard form. Chapter 5 referred to an insurance policy as an example of a standard form contract since it is prepared unilaterally in advance by one of the contracting parties (the insurer). To offset this advantage for the insurer, the courts subject the contract to a strict interpretation of the words it contains: they construe words most strongly against the party using them, as we noted in Chapter 12. They take the attitude, for example, that clauses exempting the insurer from liability in specific circumstances must be stated in clear and unambiguous terms in order to be binding.[14]

Utmost good faith. In our discussion of misrepresentation in Chapter 10 we noted that an insurer may avoid its liability if it can show that the insured did not exercise the utmost good faith in his application for insurance. In one respect, the requirement of utmost good faith on the part of the insured is particularly strict: his claim may be defeated even when it has arisen from causes unrelated to facts that he should have disclosed, but did not disclose.[15]

The terms of the insurance contract may extend the obligation of the insured even beyond that imposed by the requirement of utmost good faith. The application form signed by the party seeking insurance may contain a provision that the applicant warrants the *accuracy* — not merely the *truthfulness* — of the declarations he makes. If in these circumstances an applicant for life insurance replies in the negative to the question, "Have you any disease?" and proves later to have had a disease of which he was unaware and which was perhaps not even revealed by a medical examination, the insurer may avoid its liability. Wording of this kind amounts to an abuse of the standard form contract by the insurer, and whenever such wording has been used the courts have insisted on strict proof by the insurer that the question was answered inaccurately.[16] The new Uniform Insurance Act limits to two years the insurer's right to rescind life insurance contracts on grounds of inaccurate statements or non-disclosure by the insured.[17] This limitation does not extend to fraudulent statements made by the insured or to statements erroneous about his age.

Promptness of notice. Insurance contracts other than for life insurance contain a statutory term that the insured shall notify the insurer promptly of any change that is material to the risk and within his control or knowledge — for example, his installation of steam-powered machinery. Such a term then gives the insurer the option of either cancelling the insurance and returning the unexpired portion of the premium, or of advising the insured that the insurance will con-

---

[14] See, for example: Indemnity Insurance Co. v. Excel Cleaning Service [1954] 2 D.L.R. 721, per Estey, J., at 730; Losier v. St. Paul Mercury Indemnity Co. (1957) 6 D.L.R. (2d) 686, per Schroeder, J.A., at 690-1; Givens v. Baloise Marine Insurance Co. (1958) 13 D.L.R. (2d) 416 at 418.

[15] Seaman v. Fonereau (1743) 93 E.R. 1115.

[16] See Cheshire, Fifoot and Furmston, *The Law of Contract* (8th ed.), p. 276.

[17] See, for example: B.C., ss. 126-9; Ont., ss. 157-60; N.S., ss. 142-4.

tinue only on payment of an increased premium. Prompt notice by the insured in these circumstances is a condition precedent, and the insurer is absolved from liability under the policy if it does not receive such notice. The wording of the policy, unless specially altered, usually permits the insured to give the notice to the agent with whom he placed the insurance; he need not give notice directly to the head office of the insurer.[18]

Such insurance contracts also contain a term requiring the insured to notify the insurer promptly of any loss which occurs. Failure to give notice promptly may free the insurer from liability to pay the claim.

Assignment

Life insurance. A life insurance policy of the type that accumulates a cash surrender value is an item of property — a chose in action — which the insured may assign for value. He may, for example, give a conditional assignment of the policy to a bank as security for a loan: if he defaults on the loan, the bank is entitled to the cash surrender value up to the amount due on the loan.

The insurer's consent to an assignment of life insurance is not necessary, although the insurer is entitled to notice. The risk of the insurer is not affected by an assignment of the benefits of a life insurance contract. The consent of the beneficiary, however, is necessary for a valid assignment where the insured has deliberately chosen to make an irrevocable designation of that beneficiary.[19]

Property insurance. As contrasted with life insurance, property insurance is not assignable without the consent of the insurer; in fact novation is necessary. The reason for this rule is that an assignment substitutes a new person as the insured, and the personal qualities of the insured may be pertinent to the risk assumed by the insurer. When a person sells his house or his automobile, he may have unexpired insurance in respect of the property at the time of the sale. It is not possible simply to impose a new owner of the property of the insurer; the new owner may have habits affecting the property that alter the risk of insuring it. A purchaser must therefore renegotiate the insurance with the insurer, possibly at different premium rates. On the other hand, *after* a risk materializes and a claim is established, an insured may assign his claim (say, to his creditors) without the consent of the insurer.

CO-INSURANCE

It is common knowledge that few fires result in a total loss. It is therefore likely to occur to a person applying for fire insurance that he may save premium cost by

---

[18] Lount v. London Mutual Fire Insurance Co. (1905) 9 O.L.R. 699.

[19] See, for example: B.C., ss. 133-4 as amended by 1969, c. 11, s. 29; Ont., ss. 164-5; N.S., ss. 149-50. In some provinces before the Uniform Act was passed, an insured could not make an assignment without the consent of his beneficiary if the beneficiary was a member of a specified "preferred" class under the insurance statute. The new Acts preserve the rights of such beneficiaries existing at the time these new Acts came into force: B.C., s. 115(3); Ont., s. 146(3); N.S., s. 131(3).

insuring his property for only a part of its total value. Accordingly, fire insurance companies often insert a clause in the insurance contract to the effect that if the insured does not purchase coverage of at least a stated percentage of the value of the property (usually 80%), he will become a co-insurer, along with the insurance company, for any fire loss that results. The insured would not then recover the total loss from the fire, even though the loss itself was less than the face value of the fire insurance policy.

The amount of the claim is calculated from the formula:

$$\frac{\text{actual amount of insurance carried}}{\text{minimum coverage required}} \times \text{amount of loss},$$

subject to the proviso that in no circumstances will the insurer pay more than the amount of the loss itself or more than the face value of the policy.

Illustration:

A building owned by *X* Company Ltd. is insured for $30,000, but the insurance contract contains an 80% co-insurance clause. The building is damaged by fire to the amount of $10,000. The depreciated replacement value of the insured property at the date of the fire is $50,000. The insurance company will then pay:

$$\frac{\$30,000}{80\% \text{ of } \$50,000} \times \$10,000 = \qquad \$7,500$$

and *X* Company Ltd., as insured, must absorb	2,500
in a total loss of	$10,000

We can see from the above illustration how a co-insurance clause provides the insured with an incentive to insure his property for an amount greater than he otherwise might be disposed to do. If the amount of the policy does not meet the requirements of the co-insurance clause, the insured must actually share with the insurer any loss that occurs.

THE GUARANTEE

The Nature of a Guarantee

A guarantee usually arises in one of three common business situations. First, a prospective creditor may refuse to advance money, goods, or services solely on the promise of his prospective debtor to pay for them. Second, a creditor may propose starting an action against his debtor for an overdue debt unless the debtor can offer additional security to support a further delay in repayment. Third, a prospective assignee of the rights under a contract may be unwilling to buy these benefits if he has nothing more to rely on than the undertaking of the promisor in the original contract.

In each of these circumstances, further assurance sufficient to satisfy the creditor or assignee is often supplied by a third party who promises to perform the obligation of the debtor if the debtor should default in performance. The debtor is then called the *principal debtor,* and his obligation is known as the *principal* or *primary debt.* The person who promises to answer for the default of the principal debtor is called the *guarantor* or *surety,* and his promise is a *guarantee* or *contract of suretyship.*

Illustrations:

(a) Crown Autos Ltd. agrees to sell a Super-Cyclone sports car to Dobson provided his uncle, Gilmour, will guarantee payment of the instalments. Gilmour agrees to assist his nephew, and both join in signing an instalment-purchase agreement whereby Dobson promises as principal debtor to make all payments promptly, and Gilmour promises as guarantor to pay off the debt if Dobson defaults payment.

(b) Arthurs purchases a delivery truck from Bigtown Trucks Ltd. under an instalment agreement. After Arthurs has made over half his payments, he defaults because of business difficulties. Bigtown Trucks Ltd. threatens to retake possession of the truck. Arthurs states that if Bigtown Trucks Ltd. takes the truck his business will lose all chance of recovery. He asks the company to give him an extra six months to pay if he can obtain a satisfactory guarantor. The company agrees, and Arthur's friend Campbell, an accountant with worthy financial standing, signs a contract of guarantee, promising to pay the balance in six months if Arthurs fails to do so.

(c) Pearson buys a commercial freezer from Quincy and gives his promissory note payable in 60 days for the full purchase price. Quincy is in need of cash and takes the note to his banker who agrees to give him cash for it less a five-per-cent charge. Quincy *endorses* the note in favour of the bank, that is, he places his signature on it when assigning it to the bank, and thereby guarantees payment if Pearson should default.

We may now note three important characteristics of a guarantee. First, a guarantor makes his promise *to the creditor,* not to the principal debtor. A promise made to a debtor to assist him in the event of default is not a guarantee, and since the promise is not made to the creditor, the creditor cannot recover on it. Second, a guarantee is a secondary obligation arising only on default of the primary debt. For this reason it is a *contingent* liability in contrast to the absolute liability of the principal debtor. A creditor has no rights against the guarantor until default by the principal debtor.[20] Third, a guarantor's duty to pay arises immediately upon default by the principal debtor. The creditor need not first sue the debtor. Strictly speaking, the creditor need not even notify the guarantor of the default before he starts an action to enforce the guarantee. As a practical matter, however, the creditor always does make a demand on the guarantor before suing

---

[20] See Chapter 11, for the distinction between a guarantee and an indemnity; an indemnifier promises absolutely to pay the debt of another person.

him. Of course, when he gives his guarantee, a guarantor may stipulate as a condition precedent to his liability that the creditor must first have sued the debtor and have failed to recover, but it is unusual for him to do so.

In Chapter 11 we noted that the Statute of Frauds applies to a contingent promise to answer for the *miscarriage* (that is, the tort) of another. Such promises are generally described as guarantees.

Illustration:

> John Williams requests a launch from Boat Rentals Ltd. but is refused because of his youthful exuberance. Williams's father, a reputable businessman, informs the manager of Boat Rentals Ltd. that if the company will rent the launch to his son he will be responsible for any of his son's negligent acts causing damage to it if his son does not himself reimburse the company for any such damage. Boat Rentals Ltd. accepts his offer.

In the above illustration, the guarantee is rather like a contract of auto collision insurance, in which the father is the counterpart of an insurer and the boat-rental firm of the insured. If Williams's father had undertaken absolutely (without reference to a failure by his son to make good the loss himself) to assume any costs of his son's possible negligence, his promise would have been an indemnity and even more like a contract of auto collision insurance.

The distinction between guarantee and indemnity, apart from the Statute of Frauds, is of importance in only a few circumstances. Since a guarantor guarantees the liability of the principal debtor, if the principal debt ceases to exist, so does the guarantee. Thus, if a person guaranteed the debt of a consumer debtor and the obligation was not binding under consumer protection legislation (for example, for failure to deliver a written statement of the terms of credit) the guarantor will not be bound to pay either. On the other hand, a promise of indemnity is independent of any obligation of the person who benefits from that promise. Thus, if *A* said to a seller, "If you will supply *B* with a 20-inch portable colour television set, I promise to pay the price," *A*'s liability would not depend on whether *B* has contracted a binding debt; so long as the seller carried out *A*'s wishes, *A* would be bound to indemnify him.

Continuing Guarantee

A continuing guarantee is one which covers a series of transactions between a creditor and his principal debtor. A guarantor may, for example, agree to guarantee *X*'s account with supplier *Y* up to an amount of $5,000. In a series of purchases by *X* and payments by him, *X*'s indebtedness to *Y* will fluctuate considerably; at any given date during the currency of the guarantee, the guarantor is contingently liable for the debt owing if it is less than $5,000 and for a maximum of $5,000 if the debt exceeds that sum — as it may well do whenever *X* purchases a large shipment from *Y*. A continuing guarantee is often given for a specific length of time so that debts contracted afterwards, even if below the maximum amount, are not the liability of the guarantor. In any event, the death of the guarantor ends his liability in respect of further transactions, although his estate remains contingently liable for the debt existing at his death.

A guarantor may also limit his liability under a continuing guarantee in the following manner: if the principal debtor has not defaulted by a specified date, or if he has defaulted but the creditor has not yet started an action to enforce the guarantee, then the guarantor's liability terminates for existing obligations as yet unpaid. The variety of terms of a guarantee are virtually limitless, and they depend only upon the ability of the parties to reach agreement.

Consideration

We have said that a guarantee is a promise, and we know that a promise is not enforceable unless it is given either under seal or for a consideration. Occasionally a guarantor does make his promise under seal, but generally he does not. What then constitutes the consideration for a guarantee?

The consideration is most obvious when the guarantor receives an economic benefit — as when he obtains a higher price as an assignor of an account receivable, because he is willing to guarantee payment by the debtor. More frequently the guarantor does not receive any economic benefit for his promise: but as we have already noted (Chapter 6), consideration need confer no economic benefit on a promisor. We should recall that the essential element of our definition of consideration is simply that the promisee pays a price for the promise of the other party. This price may be the doing, or forbearing to do, of some act (or the promise to do so) by the promisee at the request of the promisor, although without any tangible advantage to the promisor. The creditor gives sufficient consideration for the promise of the guarantor, therefore, if he does some act or forbears to do some act at the request of the guarantor. And the guarantor's request need not even be express; it may be implied from the circumstances.

Illustration:

> Creely threatens to sue Dobbs for his past-due debt. Dobbs asks for 60 days more to raise the money, but Creely refuses to give the extra time unless Dobbs obtains a guarantee from his affluent cousin Grant. Dobbs takes a form of guarantee to Grant, explains the situation, and requests Grant's signature. Grant signs the guarantee and mails it to Creely. Creely forbears to sue Dobbs for 60 days. When Dobbs defaults payment again, Creely sues Grant. Grant defends on the ground that he has received no consideration for his guarantee.
>
> Grant's defence will fail. The court will accept the argument that Grant impliedly requested Creely to forbear to sue Dobbs for 60 days, and that he complied with this request. Accordingly, Creely's action will succeed.

In a similar manner, when a person guarantees a contract whereby the debtor obtains goods or services on credit, it is usually quite easy to imply a request by the guarantor to the creditor that the creditor enter into a contract he would otherwise have refused.

A creditor can jeopardize the ease with which he may prove consideration if he requires the guarantor to sign a printed form of guarantee which reserves the creditor's right to do as he pleases. In *Royal Bank of Canada v. Kiska*[21] the defendant had signed a bank form of guarantee including the words, "The Bank may . . . deal with the customer [the principal debtor] and others and with all securities as the Bank may see fit . . ." In a dissenting opinion Mr. Justice Laskin, as he then was, expressed the view that "there is here no promise of forbearance and the fact that the bank may later have held its hand for a time does not help its case."[22]

Discharge of Guarantee by Acts of the Creditor

A guarantee relates to the performance of a specific promise and no other. Sometimes a principal debtor and his creditor agree to a material change in the scope of the debtor's promise without obtaining the consent of the guarantor. If the change is one that might prejudice the position of the guarantor, his liability ceases. For example, where the principal debtor has pledged securities for the repayment of his debt, the guarantor may be released if the creditor agrees to the substitution of a different type of security.

In *Holland-Canada Mortgage Co. v. Hutchings*[23] a group of 15 citizens jointly guaranteed a loan to a charitable organization so that the organization might obtain necessary funds. Subsequently the loan was renewed, and the interest rate increased from 7% to 8% per annum. Some of the guarantors, learning of the change, refused to give their assent and so were released. The remaining guarantors were not advised of these developments, however, and when the loan was defaulted they were sued on their guarantee. The court held that they were not liable, first because of a material change in the terms of the contractual obligation they had guaranteed and, secondly because they had not known of the withdrawal of many of the joint guarantors with whom they had expected to share their liability.

What happens, then, when a creditor agrees to give the principal debtor a longer time in which to pay his account? May such an agreement so prejudice the rights of the guarantor as to release him? The answer is that a guarantor will usually be released when the principal parties agree to an extension of time without his express consent. A creditor can keep a guarantee alive and enforceable, however, if he makes his promise to extend the time in a written memorandum which includes the words, "subject to reserving my rights against the guarantor". It may seem strange that the creditor and debtor, in a contract between themselves, may thus affect the guarantor's rights; but the creditor has in effect made his promise to the debtor contingent upon the guarantor's willingness to let the debt remain outstanding. The creditor is then really saying to the debtor, "I agree not to require payment until (say) May 31, but you must under-

[21] (1967) 63 D.L.R. (2d) 582.
[22] *Ibid.*, at 592.
[23] [1936] 2 D.L.R. 481.

stand that the guarantor may choose to intervene at any time before then, pay off your debt to me, and having thereby become subrogated to my rights, bring an action against you before May 31.''[24]

Rights of the Guarantor upon Default

Defences. A guarantor may generally defend an action by the creditor upon any grounds that would be open to the principal debtor. Thus, if a debtor has a good defence because of the misrepresentation of his creditor in selling him goods, the guarantor may take advantage of this defence. A guarantor may also set off against the creditor, in reduction of the debt, any claim the debtor has against the creditor, as when the debtor has performed services for the creditor for which he has not yet been paid. It is uncertain whether a guarantor can plead the principal debtor's infancy as a defence on the grounds that if, as guarantor, he were to pay the debt to the creditor, he could not himself succeed in an action to recover it from the principal debtor.[25]

Subrogation. We noted earlier in this chapter that an insurer, upon paying a claim made by an insured under a fidelity bond, becomes subrogated to the rights of the insured and may pursue any remedies which the insured would have against the guilty employee. Similarly, when a guarantor pays off the creditor he becomes subrogated to the rights of the creditor against the debtor and the debtor's assets. He may sue the debtor for the amount he has paid the creditor and for any expenses he has incurred because of the debtor's default; and if the creditor holds shares or bonds or other property pledged as security for the debt, the guarantor is entitled to have these assets transferred to him in mitigation of his loss.[26]

A guarantor may choose to pay off the creditor and become subrogated to his rights as soon as the debt falls due: he need not wait for the creditor to make a demand or sue him. The guarantor may wish to do this when the creditor himself is content to wait because he knows the guarantor is financially sound and able to make payment. In these circumstances, the guarantor may wish to take action against a failing debtor before he becomes insolvent — if he waits until the creditor demands payment, it may no longer be worthwhile suing the debtor.

Requirement of Writing

Chapter 11 has shown that a contract of guarantee must be in writing and signed by the guarantor to be enforceable against him; and we noted that this requirement has been retained even in England and British Columbia, where the Statute of Frauds has been largely repealed. The merits of requiring written evidence of a guarantee have been stated cogently by some of the members of the English Law Revision Committee in its *Sixth Interim Report,* 1937, as follows:

---

[24] See Bristol & West of England Mortgage Co. v. Taylor (1893) 24 O.R. 286; Levy Bros. v. Sole [1955] O.W.N. 989.

[25] See *Report on the Age of Majority,* Ontario Law Reform Commission, 1969, pp. 44-6; Stearns, *Law of Suretyship* (5th ed.), p. 522, Elder, ed. Cincinnati: W. H. Anderson & Co., 1951.

[26] See Royal Bank of Canada v. Dickson (1973) 33 D.L.R. (3d) 332 at 343-4.

We realize that most guarantees, such for instance as those given to a Bank, will, whether the act [Statute of Frauds] is repealed or not, always be contained in a written document; but, if oral contracts of guarantee are allowed, we feel that there is a real danger of inexperienced people being led into undertaking obligations that they do not fully understand, and that opportunities will be given to the unscrupulous to assert that credit was given on the faith of a guarantee which in fact the alleged surety had no intention of giving. A guarantee is in any case a special class of contract; it is generally one-sided and disinterested as far as the surety is concerned, and the necessity of writing would at least give the proposed surety an opportunity of pausing and considering, not only the nature of the obligation he is undertaking, but also its terms. The contract often gives rise to many questions, e.g. whether it is to apply to the whole of a debt or to a portion only, and if the former, whether it is to be limited in amount or to a certain period.

QUESTIONS FOR REVIEW

1. What is the consideration received in an insurance contract from the point of view of the insurer? From the point of view of the insured?
2. *X* throws some old papers in his bedroom fireplace and realizes too late that the papers included some correspondence of great value as a collector's item. He claims the value of the destroyed material under his fire insurance policy. Will he succeed?
3. *D* is persuaded to buy an automobile on the assurance of his friend, *E,* that he will be assisted in meeting the payments. *D* fails to pay for the car, and the seller, *S,* sues *E.* Will *S* succeed?
4. What test can we apply to distinguish a wager from an insurance contract?
5. Black purchases a life insurance policy, naming his wife as beneficiary. Afterwards Black is shot and killed while attempting to hold up a bank. Can Mrs. Black collect the insurance money?
6. Which gives the greater protection: theft insurance or burglary insurance?
7. Explain the circumstances in which the following persons may have a right of subrogation: an insurer; a guarantor.
8. Business interruption insurance usually protects against "extraordinary expenses that reduce the loss otherwise payable". Give two examples of these.
9. What kinds of agreements between the creditor and the principal debtor will operate to release the guarantor?
10. *X* learns that he has a serious disease and applies for life insurance without disclosing this information. He is later killed in an automobile accident. Has the insurer grounds for refusing to pay the claim?
11. Explain briefly why the law affecting the assignment of the insured's rights is not the same for a contract of property insurance as for a contract of life insurance.
12. *A* says to *B,* "The recognition of a guarantee in law is only another means of avoiding the privity of contract rule to meet modern business convenience.

Why, a person may guarantee a debt without even talking to the debtor himself." Discuss the validity of *A*'s reasoning.

13. Why do we need legislation to specify terms of the insurance contract and regulate the conduct of companies and individuals engaged in the insurance industry?

14. *A* owns a building worth $25,000 and takes out two fire insurance policies for $20,000 each, one with the Ajax Insurance Company and the other with the Hercules Insurance Company. In the event of a fire, could he collect $20,000 from both companies?

15. What justification has an insurer for including a term requiring notice of a claim within a very short period of time?

16. Is it correct to say that there is no consideration in a contract of guarantee unless the guarantor receives an economic benefit for his promise?

17. The Brown Co. Ltd. purchases business interruption insurance for a period of one year from January 1, 1968. The maximum period of coverage is 12 months. What is the latest date up to which the business may be reimbursed for loss of earnings?

18. Brown Groceterias Limited lost one of its stores in a fire. The actual value of the property at the time of the fire was $50,000, according to the adjuster. The property was insured with the Pyro Fire Insurance Company. The policy contained the following clause: "This company shall not be liable for a greater proportion of any loss or damage to the property described herein than the sum hereby insured bears to eighty per cent (80%) of the actual cash value of said property at the time such loss shall happen." State the correct amount of the fire insurance claim in each of the following circumstances:

(a) The loss amounted to $40,000, and the insurance carried was $45,000.

(b) The loss amounted to $20,000, and the insurance carried was $25,000.

(c) The loss amounted to $25,000, and the insurance carried was $40,000.

(d) The loss amounted to $45,000, and the insurance carried was $25,000.

CASES FOR DISCUSSION

CASE 1

Hastie Jr., aged 17, rented a car from Ryder Rentals Ltd. It was a term of the contract that he should be responsible for any damage caused to the car during the period of its rental. While taking some friends for a drive on the Trans-Canada Highway he missed a curve and demolished the car in collision with a rock-cut.

Hastie Jr. failed to make good the loss to Ryder Rentals Ltd. and that company threatened to commence legal proceedings against him. At this stage the father of Hastie Jr. phoned the manager of Ryder Rentals Ltd. and promised that he would pay the cost of the wrecked vehicle if the company did not proceed to sue his son. The company thereupon advised its lawyer not to take action. Shortly afterwards, Hastie Jr. was killed in another automobile accident, and Hastie Sr.

then refused to pay Ryder Rentals Ltd. The company brought action against Hastie Sr. for damages equal to the value of its automobile.

What arguments, if any, may Hastie Sr. offer in defence? What should be the results of the action? (See *Kirkham v. Marter* (1819) 106 E.R. 490; *Fairgrief v. Ellis* [1935] 2 D.L.R. 806.)

CASE 2

As accountant at a branch of the Crown Bank, Cole misappropriated rent of $3,000 due to the bank. When the bank inspector discovered these facts the bank notified the Flin Flon Fidelity & Guarantee Co., which had previously bonded Cole for the bank, and claimed the $3,000. The bonding company told Cole that it was not its idea to prosecute if it could avoid it, and a possible way out would be for Cole to get his friends to come to his assistance. Cole then prevailed on his friend Smith to sign a promissory note payable 12 months after date in favour of the bonding company. When Smith dishonoured his note at maturity, the bonding company sued him. Should it succeed? Would the result be different if the bonding company had discounted Smith's note at its bank and Smith had refused to pay the bank at its maturity? (See *U.S. Fidelity and Guarantee Co. v. Cruikshank & Simmons* (1919) 49 D.L.R. 674.)

CASE 3

"Some years ago there was a very prosperous manufacturing concern in a western Ontario city engaged in metal work. Their rented premises formed part of a large block. Their policies were placed through their auditor who sold insurance on the side. One day an employee was drawing off a gallon of varsol from a 48-gallon drum. Nearby was a large vat filled with paint through which an endless chain carried metal stampings. It was a warm, humid day and the employee had forgotten to turn off an open gas jet only a few feet away from the varsol. As he stood there he was suddenly paralyzed by the sight of a blue flame creeping towards him along the floor. It reached the open bucket; a tremendous explosion followed which quickly ignited the paint in the open vat. So intense were the flames that the workmen did not bother to use the doors; they got out through the windows. By the time the local brigade brought the fire under control, the place was a shambles. Valuable machinery was destroyed. Stock belonging to others and in process was ruined. The building was seriously damaged, and the fire had spread to the manufacturers on both sides, damaging their stock and equipment and merchandise."[27]

What special types of insurance coverage would be required to reimburse the insured for his maximum loss in the above situation?

---

[27] Edson L. Haines, Q.C., now a Justice of the Supreme Court of Ontario, "Business Risks and Insurance Coverage", from *Counselling the Average Businessman*, p. 240. Special Lectures of the Law Society of Upper Canada. Toronto: Richard De Boo Limited, 1954.

CASE 4

Thomas, a tobacco farmer in southern Ontario, applied to Carter, an insurance agent, to obtain fire insurance protection on his processing barn and contents. The agent prepared a fire policy with the Courtland & Tillsonburg Insurance Company. Thomas's processing barn contained an apparatus called a steamer in which steam was created by natural gas being lighted under a boiler of water, and the fire policy contained the following related clause:

> No steamer will be left operating unattended either day or night . . . and no open fires will be used and no smoking will be permitted in the building.

Before entering into the insurance contract, Thomas discussed the significance of this clause with the agent, Carter, who told him that the clause applied only to coal, wood, or oil steamers and not to gas steamers, and that "all you need do to comply with the contract so far as this gas steamer is concerned is to turn it off at nights and be sure to sweep out the barn."

One winter morning, having started the steamer operating, Thomas left the processing barn for 15 minutes to get some breakfast. While eating, he saw fire coming through the roof of the barn; the building, valued at $17,000, was totally destroyed. The Courtland & Tillsonburg Insurance Co. contested Thomas' claim on the grounds that he had left the building unattended in breach of the condition subsequent stated in the policy. Thomas replied that the clause referred to was subject to the interpretation explained to him by Carter. Thomas sued the insurance company for the amount of the policy.

Should he succeed? (See *Tarr v. Westchester Fire Insurance Co.* [1953] 2 D.L.R. 655.)

CASE 5

On January 2, Oswald Kirkham lent John Lough $10,000 for one year at six per cent interest per annum. Lough signed a promissory note in favour of Kirkham, and Lough's friend William Mahon endorsed the note as guarantor of the loan. In December following, Mahon was called away on urgent business to Australia and could not be reached when the note fell due. Lough defaulted on January 2 and requested a six-month extension from Kirkham. As consideration for the extension, Lough agreed to name Kirkham as beneficiary of a life insurance policy. Although neither Lough nor Kirkham could contact Mahon to get his consent, Kirkham granted the extension. In the agreement of extension he expressly "reserved my rights against Mahon as guarantor"; Kirkham believed that by keeping Mahon bound to the terms of the original agreement, Mahon would not in any way be prejudiced by the extension. On his return several weeks later Mahon was disturbed to learn of the extension, but took no action.

When the extension expired, Lough's business had become insolvent, and Kirkham sued Mahon on his guarantee. In defence, Mahon claimed:

(a) that the original guarantee was void because he had received no consideration for his promise, and

(b) that in any event the subsequent material alteration extending the time for payment without his consent extinguished his liability as guarantor.

In reply Kirkham claimed:

(a) that his making the loan to Lough was good consideration to Mahon, and
(b) that by Kirkham's reserving his rights against Mahon, Mahon's rights continued to be governed by the original agreement and were not affected by the extension, so that on learning of the extension Mahon could have paid the debt off and sued Lough immediately. By waiting, Mahon voluntarily took the risk that Lough would become insolvent, and cannot therefore blame Kirkham for the present state of affairs.

Whose argument is the better? (See *Gorman v. Dixon* (1896) 26 S.C.R. 87.)

CASE 6

While driving home from work, Saunders was in collision with another automobile driven by Randall. Randall was in the wrong but carried the necessary automobile insurance to indemnify him against liability for injury to third persons and damage to their property. Saunders took his car to Wilby's Auto Body Repair Shop for repair, on the understanding that the total cost would be paid by Randall's insurance company. When the repair work was finished, Saunders went to take delivery of his car, and Wilby said to him: "Will you sign this release so I can get my money from the insurance company?" Saunders asked him, "Is it the release for the car — just for the car?" and Wilby replied, "It's a release so I can get my money." Saunders then signed a release form which read,

> In consideration of the undertaking to pay Wilby's Auto Body Repair Shop $539.95 I hereby release and forever discharge Mr. T. O. Randall from any and all actions, causes of actions, claims and demands, for all known or unknown damage, loss or injury, however arising, which heretofore may have been or may hereafter be sustained by me in consequence of an automobile accident on or about April 3, at the corner of Union and Division Streets.
>
> Read Before Signing.
(*signed*) "J. Alfred Saunders"

Immediately after the collision Saunders was aware that he had sustained some personal injuries which he thought amounted to nothing more than a sprained wrist and being shaken up a bit. However, after signing the above release, he became aware of trouble with his neck and back which required extensive medical attention.

Saunders then brought an action against Randall for compensation for his personal injury. In defence, Randall pleaded that by signing the release, Saunders had estopped (prevented) himself from asserting any further claim as a result of the collision, and further pleaded that the payment of the repair bill of

Wilby's Auto Body Repair Shop constituted accord and satisfaction. In reply, Saunders argued that he had signed the release under a total mistake as to its nature and contents and in the bona-fide belief that he was merely acknowledging that he was satisfied with the workmanship on his car. Saunders was 41 years old, with a Grade 8 education.

Examine the validity of Saunders' claim, and state whether you think it should succeed. (See *Stearns v. Ratel* (1961) 29 D.L.R. (2d) 718.)

CASE 7

Premium Motors Ltd. sold Ralston a car on credit under a contract with a term providing that on the purchaser's signed declaration of good health, any balance owing would be paid should the purchaser die before completing the required payments. For this purpose Premium Motors Ltd. had a separate insurance contract with Standard Form Insurance Co. At the same time Ralston signed an application form for the related insurance in which he replied, "No" to the question, "Have you any disease?"

Three months after making this purchase, Ralston died of a heart condition. Mrs. Ralston was the executrix and main beneficiary of his estate. A few weeks later, a salesman for Premium Motors Ltd. called on Mrs. Ralston, and assuring her that by the terms of the contract no further money would be owing on the car, persuaded her to trade it in on a more expensive model. Mrs. Ralston signed a new contract acknowledging this fresh indebtedness.

Standard Form Insurance Co. refused to reimburse Premium Motors Ltd. for the amount of the unpaid balance of the first car on the grounds that Ralston had given inaccurate information in applying for the insurance. Premium Motors Ltd. then requested this additional amount from Mrs. Ralston and, when she refused to pay it, brought an action against her.

Discuss the legal issues raised by these facts and state whether the action should succeed. (See *Patterson Motors (1962) Ltd. v. Riley* (1966) 56 D.L.R. (2d) 278.)

CASE 8

While driving his truck on an icy road, Martin collided with another truck owned by Sawyer. The two trucks became enmeshed and required the services of two tow-trucks to pry them apart. Despite the fact that the tow-trucks were operated with great care, as the metal separated an accidental spark set fire to Martin's truck, causing further extensive damage to it. The damage caused to Martin's truck by the initial collision was $400 and by the subsequent fire, a further $700.

Martin was insured under a standard automobile policy which, in addition to insurance for public liability and property damage, provided coverage against loss of or damage to the vehicle due to collision or upset with $250 deductible in respect to each separate claim for such collision or upset. The policy also included a rider providing comprehensive coverage from any other cause; this comprehensive coverage was not subject to a deductible clause.

The portion of the insurance contract relating to collision read in part as follows:

> The Insurer agrees to indemnify the Insured against direct and accidental loss of or damage to the automobile caused solely by collision with another object, either moving or stationary, or by upset. Each collision or upset covered hereby shall give rise to a separate claim in respect of which the Insurer's liability shall be limited to the amount of loss or damage in excess of $250. Breakage of glass and loss caused by missiles, falling objects, fire, theft, explosion, earthquake, windstorm, hail, water, flood, vandalism, riot, or civil commotion shall not be deemed loss caused by collision or upset.

The rider providing the additional comprehensive coverage stated simply:

> The Insurer agrees to indemnify the Insured against direct and accidental loss of or damage to the automobile from any cause other than collision with another object, either moving or stationary, or upset.

State with reasons what amount, if any, Martin is entitled to recover from the insurance company.

CASE 9

Stanley Motors Ltd. operates a truck assembly plant in Vancouver. Three months ago, it sold three light school buses to the City of Guadalajara, Mexico. The agreed price for each bus was $9,000 f.o.b. Vancouver, with the purchaser to make all arrangements for shipment from Vancouver to Guadalajara. On the advice of Stanley Motors Ltd., the City of Guadalajara then entered into a contract of carriage with Georgia Motorship Lines Ltd. It was a term of this contract that the carrier should not be liable for damages in excess of $1,000 including any damages attributable to the negligence of its employees.

While employees of Georgia Motorship Lines Ltd. were getting the buses ready for loading at dockside in Vancouver, a mast supporting the tackle equipment broke. A bus fell from a great height on to the dock and was demolished. The accident was the result of the operation of the loading equipment by employees of the carrier. Since the bus had not yet been placed on board ship, Stanley Motors Ltd. concluded that under the terms of its contract of sale it could not hold the City of Guadalajara liable for the price.

Stanley Motors Ltd. carries a basic manufacturer's policy with the Western Mercantile Insurance Company. This policy provides coverage against damage or loss to buildings, equipment, parts, materials, work in process and finished-goods inventories, and includes a transportation floater rider that extends the normal coverage to damage to finished products en route to customers while still at the risk of the insured. Stanley Motors Ltd. therefore claimed its loss under this policy.

Western Mercantile Insurance Company has agreed to pay this claim, but has also commenced action in the name of the insured against Georgia Motorship

Lines Ltd. for damages of $9,000. Georgia Motorship Lines Ltd. has offered to settle for $1,000 but denies liability for any amount in excess of that sum, on the grounds that Stanley Motors Ltd. was bound by the term in the contract of carriage with the City of Guadalajara restricting its liability to $1,000.

Offer an opinion about whether this action should succeed, citing any relevant cases.

CASE 10

Calgary Features Limited required additional financing if it was to exploit some apparently attractive opportunities. Its directors decided to assist the company by raising the sum of $100,000 on their own credit. The company then applied for a loan with Merchants' Bank, on the terms that a guarantee would be signed jointly by all the directors. The guarantee was on a standard form provided by Merchants' Bank and included the clause:

> This guarantee shall be binding upon every person signing the same, notwithstanding the non-execution thereof by any other proposed guarantor.

Four directors signed the guarantee in the office of the bank manager in Calgary. Then one of them sent it to Edmonton, where four other directors signed it together. They noted the absence at the time of the signature of D. Fowler, the company's president (also a director), and agreed among themselves that they were signing only on the condition that the guarantee would not be delivered to the bank until Fowler had signed as well.

When the guarantee was returned to the director in Calgary, he gave it to the bank manager with instructions that it was not to be treated as having been delivered to the bank as an operative instrument until Fowler's signature was obtained. In the end, Fowler refused to add his signature because of a concern that he might thereby diminish his own line of credit at the bank. Nevertheless, the bank manager advanced the company $100,000 and the company gave the bank its promissory note for that amount.

Calgary Features Limited subsequently defaulted on this note and Merchants' Bank endeavoured to require those directors who had signed the guarantee to make good the sum owing. They refused to pay on the grounds of their understanding that the guarantee would not operate unless and until all directors had signed. Merchants' Bank brought an action against these directors to enforce the guarantee.

Explain whether this action should succeed.

CASE 11

Lax Co. Ltd. owed the Conservative Bank $76,500, and the company's principal shareholder, Harcourt, met with the assistant manager of the bank to discuss some means of keeping the loan, now due, in good standing. The assistant manager suggested that the matter would be resolved for the time being if Harcourt were prepared to give the bank his personal guarantee for the company's existing indebtedness. The assistant manager pointed out that the guarantee would operate only until the bank received a joint guarantee from all the directors of the company, now in the course of preparation. He then produced a printed guarantee in standard form, which Harcourt signed without reading.

Within the following weeks, the bank received the expected joint guarantee from the company's directors, and at the same time the company repaid its loan of $76,500. The next month, Lax Co. Ltd. obtained a further loan for $50,000, giving its promissory note for that amount.

Six months later, the creditors of Lax Co. Ltd. obtained a receiving order placing it in bankruptcy. The directors appeared to be impecunious. The Conservative Bank then requested payment of the $50,000 from Harcourt, and Harcourt decided to read his copy of the guarantee. It stated in part, "This guarantee covers all debts of Lax. Co. Ltd., present or future, and the undersigned guarantor hereby acknowledges that no representations concerning it have been made to him by any officer of the bank. The guarantor further acknowledges that this guarantee will be binding upon him whether any other guarantee or security has been given to the bank or not."

When Harcourt refused to pay, the bank sued him. Should the action succeed?

CHAPTER 19

Bailment

THE NATURE OF A BAILMENT

Definition

A bailment is a transfer or deposit of personal property on the understanding that the party receiving the property will return it at a later time or dispose of it as directed. The transferor of the property, usually its owner, is called the *bailor* and the person who receives the custody of it, the *bailee*. The concept embraces a wide variety of economic and social activity. The following transactions are familiar examples of bailment: leaving an article with a railway for shipment; giving stocks and bonds to a bank as security for a loan; leaving a radio with a repairman; storing furniture with a warehouseman; lending a lawn-mower to a neighbour.

Compared with Sale

A bailment is different from a sale. A sale effects a change of ownership, and as Chapter 16 has shown, need not require a change in possession. By contrast, a bailment never alters the fact of ownership but does require a change in possession. Furthermore, the subject-matter of a bailment need not be a chattel: it may be important documents representing legal rights, such as share and bond certificates, bills of lading, and title deeds. If one takes diamonds to a jeweller to have them made into a necklace or takes a share certificate in street form to a broker to have it registered in the owner's name, the transaction is a bailment rather than a sale.

Compared with Trust

The arrangement by which property is transferred to a trustee for the benefit of one or more persons does not create a bailment. The creation of a trust involves a change in ownership — the beneficiary acquires, as we have seen, an equitable interest in the subject of the trust. A receiving order, transferring ownership of the assets of a bankrupt debtor to a trustee in bankruptcy for the benefit of creditors, is not a bailment; nor does the transfer of property to an executor under a will constitute a bailment. We should also note that the subject-matter of a trust may be real property as well as personal property, whereas bailment is confined to personal property.

Compared with Debt

A deposit of money in a bank or trust company creates a creditor-debtor rather than a bailor-bailee relationship. However, the deposit of specific items of personal property for safekeeping does create a bailment. The difference has important consequences if the recipient becomes bankrupt. Although in this country a bank failure is highly unlikely, the problem may arise when stocks and bonds are left in safekeeping with a stockbroker or hotel or apartment-house proprietor who becomes insolvent. A bailee has no title to articles entrusted to him: the articles do not form part of his assets available to creditors, and must be returned to the bailor intact. In contrast, a depositor of money in a bank or trust company is a creditor, and in the event of insolvency he must await his share in the available assets along with the other creditors.

Non-Contractual Bailments

We should also note that a bailment need not arise from a contract between a bailor and bailee. The essential elements of bailment are delivery of possession without the intention to transfer title and with the intention that the property shall be returned to the bailor. All these elements may exist without a contract, as when the owner of an article lends it gratuitously to a friend. Thus, a bailment is created when one person lends another his car or his typewriter. The intention that the object shall be returned need not be stated in an express understanding between the parties but may be presumed from the circumstances. When a customer carelessly leaves his hat behind in a restaurant, the restaurateur becomes an involuntary bailee of the hat — he quite obviously is not the owner — and cannot refuse to return it on his customer's request.

General Classes of Bailments

Gratuitous bailments. These bailments may be for the benefit of the bailor or the bailee, or indeed for the benefit of both parties. Examples of those for the benefit of the bailor occur when a pet is left with a neighbour during vacation, a lawn-mower is left with a friend who has offered to repair it in his workshop, or valuables are left in a relative's office safe. Examples of bailments for the benefit of the bailee are the borrowing of a car for a trip, or a movie projector for a home showing. Examples of bailments for the benefit of both parties occur when a car is left with a friend who has permission to use it from time to time, or when a loan of a camera is made in the hope that the borrower will buy it if he is satisfied with its performance.

Bailments for value. By their very nature, bailments for value are of benefit to both parties: one party obtains the service he desires and the other receives payment. Thus, both the rental of a car and the delivery of a camera to a repairman for repairs are bailments for the mutual benefit of bailor and bailee. We may note, however, that in the car rental the bailee receives the benefit from the change in possession of the chattel (he obtains the use of the car), whereas in the delivery of the camera to the repairman, the bailor receives the benefit from the change in possession (the repairman can then make the repairs requested by the bailor).

LIABILITY OF A BAILEE

Comparison of Liability under Contract and Tort

Sometimes bailed goods are lost, damaged, or destroyed while in the possession of the bailee. The question then arises whether the bailee is liable for the loss suffered. When the bailment is the result of a contract, the contract then contains terms, either express or implied by trade custom, setting out the duties and liabilities of the bailee for the goods in his possession. Thus, a warehouseman is not customarily obliged to insure goods stored with him against loss by fire;[1] but when he has expressly contracted to do so and fails, he is liable to his bailor for the insured value of the goods if they are destroyed by fire. As we noted in Chapter 12 in discussing the interpretation of contracts, parties do not and indeed cannot foresee all the possibilities of harm that may arise. All bailees are, however, under a duty by the rules of the law of tort to take care of property bailed to them. Thus, the standard of care required by the law of tort applies in circumstances not covered expressly or impliedly by the bailment contract, and the standard applies also to gratuitous bailment involving no contract at all. The standard of care demanded by the law does vary, however, according to the type of bailment.

The law of contract and tort further intermingle when a contract of bailment includes a term that the bailee shall not be liable for damage to the goods while in his custody, even when the damage is caused by his negligence in performance of the contract. The courts have come to construe this type of exemption clause very strictly against the bailee, just as we have seen they have done against the seller in a contract of sale.[2] If the goods are damaged for any reason not related to the very performance contemplated by the contract, the bailee is not protected by

---

[1] Fagan v. Green and Edwards, Ltd. [1926] 1 K.B. 102.
[2] See Baldry v. Marshall [1925] 1 K.B. 260, as discussed in Chapter 16.

his exemption clause. Thus, in the English case of *Davies v. Collins,*[3] a United States Army officer took his uniform to the defendants to be cleaned. The defendants gave him a receipt in which they disclaimed all liability for damage arising in the course of "necessary handling". The uniform was never returned, and when the officer sued for its value, the defendants pleaded the exemption clause. It was established, however, that the cause of the loss was that the defendants had sent the uniform to someone else for cleaning, and the court found that the wording of the contract required personal performance by the bailee. Thus the damage had not taken place during "necessary handling" as contemplated in the exemption clause; the exemption clause did not apply. Accordingly, the defendants were held liable for the loss.

The Standard of Care

Generally speaking, the standard of care is least exacting upon a bailee when the bailment is both gratuitous and for the benefit of the bailor, as when *A* permits *B* to store his car in *A*'s garage. The standard of care is most exacting on a bailee when the bailment is gratuitous and for the benefit of the bailee himself, as when one borrows a friend's car and obtains its use as a favour. A gratuitous bailment for the benefit of both parties is, at least in part, for the bailee's benefit and it would appear that the higher standard of care applies to him.

The standard of care for bailments of value falls between that of gratuitous bailments for the benefit of the bailee and of those for the benefit of the bailor. In addition, two special classes of bailee are subject to very high standards of care because they deal with the public generally. These are common carriers and hotel- or innkeepers, whom we shall discuss later in this chapter.

The variations in the standard of care as outlined above make good sense. When a bailment is gratuitous and for the benefit of the bailor, the bailee should not be under a particularly high duty towards the bailor for, after all, he is doing the bailor a favour. Thus, when a bailee allows a bailor to store his car in the bailee's garage, the bailee is not under as high a duty of care as he would be if he were a warehouseman being paid to store the bailor's car.

The standard of care required of a bailee when the bailment is the result of a contract varies according to the type of goods bailed and the extent of the promise to look after the goods, whether this promise of the bailee be express or implied from the circumstances. A bailee for value is expected to take the same care of the goods as a prudent and diligent businessman should of goods belonging to those with whom he transacts business — a standard of care that is at least as high and probably higher than he might choose to apply to his own goods.

A bailee who borrows goods for his own benefit is under a very high standard of care in looking after the goods. The bailor receives no valuable consideration for his kindness, and so it is fair that in these circumstances the bailee should compensate the bailor when damage to the goods results from even very slight carelessness on the bailee's part.

---

[3] [1945] 1 All E.R. 247.

The standard of care must be couched in general terms to permit the necessary flexibility in coping with the innumerable situations that may arise. An example of such general statements is found in the judgment of Mr. Justice
Compton when he distinguished the standards of care required in a gratuitous
bailment for the benefit of the bailor, and a bailment for value:

> What is reasonable varies in the case of a gratuitous bailee and that of a
> bailee for hire [value]. From the former is reasonably expected such care
> and diligence as persons ordinarily use in their own affairs and such skill as
> he has. From the latter is reasonably expected care and diligence, such as
> are exercised in the ordinary and proper course of a similar business, and
> such skill as he ought to have, namely, the skill usual and requisite in the
> business for which he receives payment.[4]

We can see here that the guide is very general indeed, and no test for a particular degree of care is definitive. The nature of the goods bailed may be important. If the property is of great value and easily damaged, lost, or stolen, the
standard of care required, even of a gratuitous bailee in a bailment for the benefit
of the bailor, may be quite high: he must take greater care with expensive
jewellery left with him than with his neighbour's bicycle stored in his garage. In
the words of a Canadian judge, "The substantial question must always be,
whether that care has been exhibited which the special circumstances reasonably
demand."[5]

Proof

When goods are damaged or lost while in the hands of a bailee, it is difficult for
the bailor to ascertain exactly how the loss occurred. In these circumstances the
bailee is better able to establish the facts, and accordingly the courts place upon
him the burden of showing that he was not negligent; he must offer some reasonable alternative explanation accounting for the loss.

REMEDIES OF A BAILEE FOR THE VALUE OF HIS SERVICES

Damages and Quantum Meruit

In a contractual bailment the bailee, as a party to a contract, has the usual contractual remedies for breach by the bailor. Because of the character of bailment,
rescission is hardly ever practical or even possible: a contract for storage or safekeeping or for the shipment of goods cannot be rescinded once the bailee has performed his duties, and in most cases a workman cannot undo his repairs without
doing further damage to the goods he has already repaired. A bailee is, therefore,

---

[4] Beal v. South Devon Railway (1864) 159 E.R. 560, per Compton, J., at 562.
[5] Fitzgerald v. Grand Trunk Railway (1880) 4 O.A.R. 601, per Moss, C.J.A., at 624.

much more concerned to receive compensation for his services than to obtain rescission of the contract.

When he has completely performed his part of the bargain, as when he has redelivered goods stored with him, his remedy is an action for the contract price of his services. In some circumstances an action for the contract price may not be possible, as when a bailor has agreed to deliver a certain quantity of goods to a bailee for shipment in several instalments and subsequently he delivers only part of the goods for shipment. The bailee may sue for damages for the services already performed on a *quantum meruit* basis, and he may also obtain damages for loss of profits he would have earned had the bailor delivered all the goods to him for shipment. We have already discussed the remedies of *quantum meruit* and damages for breach of contract in Chapter 15.

Lien

In most classes of bailment, a valuable remedy available to a bailee is the right of lien on goods in his possession for the value of his services. A lien is a right to retain possession of the goods until the bailor pays what is due for the services. This right is obviously a valuable one, for the bailor cannot repossess his goods until he pays the charges that are due. Generally speaking, a right of lien arises only when the services have been performed and payment is already due. If payment is not due when the goods are to be redelivered, no lien exists, and the bailee is under a duty to return the goods.

Illustration:

> Pliable Plastics Ltd. has very little storage space for its manufactured products. It enters into an arrangement with Stately Storage Limited whereby Pliable Plastics delivers its products for storage on a daily charge basis, and when they are sold, picks them up again for delivery to the buyer. Storage charges are billed and become payable every three months.
>
> Stately Storage has no lien upon the goods stored with it until the end of the three-month period and until it has billed Pliable Plastics. If, after two and one-half months have passed, Pliable Plastics sells a portion of the stored goods, Stately Storage must surrender the goods on demand to Pliable Plastics or to a buyer who presents proper documents. When three months have expired and Stately Storage bills Pliable Plastics, Stately Storage has a lien for all the accrued storage charges upon the goods remaining in the warehouse at that time.

The right of lien was originally a common law right and was limited to bailees who performed services in the nature of repairs or improvement to goods bailed with them. A similar right of lien was recognized in the common law for the benefit of innkeepers and common carriers, who are under a duty to accept goods from anyone so long as they have space for them. In addition to the common law liens, various statutes have created liens in other types of bailment. We shall discuss these rights of lien as they arise in the remaining sections of this chapter dealing with specific types of bailment. We should also note that any bailee for value may make it an express term of the contract of bailment that he should have a lien upon goods bailed with him. In fact bailees usually insist upon such a term.

As we noted in Chapter 17 in our discussion of the rights of an unpaid seller, a lien is a possessory remedy: an unpaid bailee loses his lien on the bailed goods as soon as the bailor obtains possession of them without deceit or fraud.

The Right of Sale

As we have noted, the right of lien is valuable to a bailee because it may embarrass or inconvenience the bailor and induce him to pay off charges which are due. If, however, the bailor is unable to pay off the charges, as when he becomes insolvent, the bailee is left with goods he cannot himself use because he has no title to them, and they may become a burden to him because of the problem of storage. Various statutes give bailees who have a lien upon goods stored with them an additional right to sell the goods. Other bailees, who do not have the right to sell bailed goods by statute, may acquire this right as a term of the bailment contract just as they may acquire the right of lien.

The provisions of the statutes vary in detail, but generally speaking they require first, that a certain time must elapse after payment for the services falls due; secondly, that advance notice be given to the bailor of the bailee's intention to sell; thirdly, that the sale be advertised; and fourthly, that it be held by public auction. The proceeds of the sale are used first, to reimburse the bailee for his costs of holding the sale, and secondly, to pay the overdue charges for his services; any surplus belongs to the bailor. We shall note the right of sale as it occurs in the remaining sections of this chapter.

STORAGE AND SAFEKEEPING

Liability

A warehouseman who takes in goods for storage, a parking-lot operator who rents parking space for several hours and retains the car keys, a bank which rents a safety-deposit box — all are bailees for storage or safekeeping, and by the law of tort all are under a duty to take care of the goods stored with them.

The Judicial Committee of the Privy Council has described the liability of a bailee for value who has custody of goods in these terms:

> They [the bailees] were therefore under a legal obligation to exercise the same degree of care, towards the preservation of the goods entrusted to them from injury, which might reasonably be expected from a skilled storekeeper, acquainted with the risks to be apprehended either from the character of the storehouse itself or of its locality; and that obligation included, not only the duty of taking all reasonable precautions to obviate these risks, but

the duty of taking all proper measures for the protection of the goods when such risks were imminent or had actually occurred.[6]

The express or implied authority that a bailment contract gives the bailee for dealing with the bailed goods may affect his liability for them. Thus, a warehouseman may or may not have implied authority to subcontract for the storage of the goods with another warehouseman — the nature of the goods may be a determining factor. The English courts have held that it is implied in a contract for the storage of furniture that the bailee shall perform the contract personally and that a sub-bailment amounts to a breach of contract.[7] On the other hand, a warehouseman's liability may be somewhat reduced when, by the terms of the contract, the bailor overrides the bailee's usual discretion in handling the goods, as for example when the bailor himself directs where the goods are to be placed.

When a bailor stores goods with a warehouseman he receives as evidence of the contract of bailment a document known as a *warehouse receipt*. This document identifies the goods stored and acknowledges that they are being kept in storage and are deliverable to the bailor's order. Ordinarily, a bailee must return to the bailor the exact goods stored. When, however, the goods stored are *fungible* (that is, replaceable with identical goods also in storage), the bailee's liability is discharged when he returns to the bailor goods of the exact description in the warehouse receipt. For example, when a quantity of grain of a specific grade is stored in a grain elevator in bins containing other grain of exactly the same grade, the bailee is bound to deliver not the exact grain that was bailed with him, but an equivalent quantity of the same grade.

A contract for parking an automobile in a parking lot, even when the car owner locks his car and keeps the keys himself, has frequently been regarded as an example of a bailment for storage. This interpretation has been challenged in an Ontario case in which the operator of a parking lot exhibited signs and included terms on his parking receipts to the effect that "charges are for the use of parking space only," and further disclaimed liability for damage to the vehicle or its contents.[8] The court held that the relationship was one of licensor and licensee. It follows that the court regarded the parking-lot operator's disclaimer of liability as a definition of the relationship contracted for, rather than as an exemption clause in a contract of bailment. According to this interpretation, the parking-lot operator was under a much lower standard of care as a mere licensor of space.

Remedies

As we have already noted, at common law a bailee did not obtain a lien upon goods unless he had performed some repair or improvement on them. Thus, a

---

[6] Brabant & Co. v. King [1895] A.C. 632, per Lord Watson at 640.

[7] Edwards v. Newland [1950] 1 All E.R. 1072.

[8] Bata v. City Parking Canada Ltd. (1973) 2 O.R. (2d) 446.

warehouseman did not obtain a right of lien on goods stored with him unless he had specifically bargained for it. This is still the law in England today. In Canada, however, we have a uniform Warehousemen's Lien Act passed by all the common law provinces except Newfoundland, giving a warehouseman a right of lien on goods stored with him for the amount of his charges. These statutes provide that "every warehouseman has a lien on goods deposited with him for storage whether deposited by the owner of the goods or by his authority or by any person entrusted with the possession of the goods by the owner or by his authority."[9] The Act requires the bailee to give the owner notice when the goods are bailed by someone else, as when a seller of goods delivers them (as bailor) to a warehouseman under the terms of the contract of sale as instructed by the buyer (the owner).

The Act further provides that "a warehouseman may sell by public auction in the manner provided in this section any goods on which he has a lien for charges that have become due."[10] He must give notice to the person who is liable as debtor for the charges for which the lien exists, to the owner when the owner is a different person from the person liable to pay the charges, and to any other persons known by the warehouseman to have a claim or an interest in the goods. The notice must contain a statement that unless the charges are paid within the time specified, the goods will be advertised for sale and sold by public auction at a time and place specified in the notice. The Act then sets out the details of the type of advertisement and the way in which the sale is to be held. In short, the statute gives adequate protection to the bailor or owner while giving the bailee a reasonably prompt method of obtaining payment.

WORK ON A CHATTEL

Liability

Bailment is often an incident of contracts made for the maintenance of various kinds of business equipment, as when a car and truck repair company takes possession of delivery trucks in its garage, when an electronics firm receives business machines for servicing, or when a laundry picks up factory uniforms for cleaning. A repairman who attends to these articles on his own premises is a bailee for value. In accepting the work, the repairman undertakes to do it in a workmanlike manner in relation to the skill he professes to have, and also to have it done by the time he promises. Failure to do these things is a breach of contract on his part. Depending on the circumstances, such breach may entitle the bailor to not pay for work already done or to sue for damages. A bailor is also entitled to the return of his chattel. The standard of care required of a workman towards chattels bailed with him is similar to that required of a warehouseman.

---

[9] See, for example: R.S.B.C. 1960, c. 403, s. 3; R.S.O. 1970, c. 488, s. 2; R.S.N.S. 1967, c. 334, s. 2

[10] R.S.B.C. 1960, c. 403, s. 5; R.S.O. 1970, c. 488, s. 4; R.S.N.S. 1967, c. 334, s. 4

Remedies

Ordinarily, in leaving an article for repair, a bailor gives the repairman implied authority to order such parts as are necessary to carry out the repairs and include the cost of such parts in his charges. If a bailor wishes to limit his expenses, he may make it a term of the contract that the repairman shall not make repairs beyond a specified amount; or he may go even further and stipulate that the repairman should not proceed with the repairs at all if parts and labour exceed a specified amount.

If the parties do not expressly agree about the time for payment, the bailor is ordinarily bound to pay for the work on its completion, although the usage in a particular trade may vary this rule. If a bailor fails to pay for the work done under the terms of the contract, a repairman has the usual contractual remedy to sue for the price of his services as agreed upon in the contract. If a bailor instructs his repairman to abandon the work before it is completed, or otherwise repudiates the contract, the repairman may claim his remuneration in an action for *quantum meruit,* to obtain a reasonable price for the service which he has already performed. He may also sue for damages for loss of the profits he would have earned had he completed his work.

As we noted previously in this chapter, the common law gives a repairman a lien for the value of the work done upon goods left with him. The common law right does not extend, however, to the right to sell the goods; the repairman may do no more than withhold them. Five of the provinces give an additional statutory right to the repairman to sell the goods when the repair charges are three months overdue.[11] These statutes apply safeguards similar to those required of a warehouseman in selling bailed goods.

TRANSPORTATION

Classes of Carriers

The law distinguishes three types of person or business engaged in the transportation of goods. A *gratuitous carrier* is anyone who agrees to move goods from one place to another without reward. A *private carrier* is one who undertakes on occasion to carry goods for reward, but who reserves the right to pick and choose his customers and restrict the type of goods he is willing to carry: he is a carrier whose decision whether to accept a request for his services is in each instance "guided . . . by the attractiveness or otherwise of the particular offer and not by his ability or inability to carry, having regard to his other engagements".[12] A *common carrier* is one who holds himself out to the public as a carrier of goods for reward. The essence of the status of a common carrier is that he does not dis-

---

[11] Mechanics' Lien Act, R.S.B.C. 1960, c. 238, s. 42; R.S.S. 1965, c. 277, s. 45; R.S.O. 1970, c. 267, s. 48; R.S.N.S. 1967, c. 178, s. 44; R.S. Nfld. 1970, No. 24, s. 31.

[12] Belfast Ropework Co. v. Bushell [1918] 1 K.B. 210, per Bailhache, J., at 215.

criminate among those who request his services, nor does he reserve the right to refuse an offer of goods for shipment when he has the means of shipping them. He may, however, be a common carrier on the terms that his services are restricted to a certain area and to those kinds of goods that are suitable for carriage by the equipment he has available. Most railway and steamship companies are common carriers, as are some trucking companies and even gas and oil pipeline companies. Airlines often repudiate the status of a common carrier by reserving the right to refuse goods.

A carrier's liability for damage to goods in the course of transit depends upon the type of carrier he is. In every instance a carrier is a bailee who has *some* responsibility for the goods under his control. Even a gratuitous bailee must exercise at least the diligence and care to be expected of a reasonable man in handling his own property. The duty of care required of a private carrier is somewhat greater. He owes a degree of care commensurate with the skill reasonably to be expected of a competent person in his line of business; and any reference to the amount of care that the reasonable man should apply to *his own* property is irrelevant. The liability of a common carrier is still greater, although he may take advantage of certain recognized defences that we shall examine.

Liability of a Common Carrier

A common carrier undertakes to indemnify his shipper (the bailor) against loss whether it occurs through the carrier's fault or not. He is therefore an insurer as well as a bailee. The historical reason for this special liability was to prevent the practice, once frequent in England, of collusion between carriers and highwaymen, whereby the highwayman would "rob" the carrier of the shipper's goods and the carrier would plead that it was not his fault that the goods were taken. Although these reasons seem amusing when applied to the modern railroad, steamship, and trucking companies, nevertheless there is eminent good sense in the rule itself: its practical effect is to relieve the shipper of any burden of producing evidence that it was the common carrier's want of reasonable care that caused the damage to his goods en route. In most circumstances, since the goods have travelled far from the shipper, it is impossible for him to adduce this evidence. The shipper need only prove (1) that the carrier received the goods in good condition, and (2) that the carrier delivered them in bad condition or failed to deliver them at all. The burden is then on the carrier, if he is to avoid liability, to establish that the cause of the loss was within one of the recognized defences available to common carriers. It is not enough for him to show that he was not negligent. His only defences are an act of God, an inherent vice in the goods, or default by the shipper.[13]

---

[13] These defences are discussed in detail by Paton, *Bailment in the Common Law,* pp. 259-65. London: Stevens & Sons Limited, 1952.

Defences Available to a Common Carrier

We encountered the idea of an act of God in Chapter 14, where we identified it as an example of a condition subsequent. This legal concept somewhat unkindly attributes a special class of misfortune to Providence. Lord Mansfield explained the term as follows:

> I consider it to mean something in opposition to the act of man: for *everything* is the act of God that happens by his permission; *everything* by his knowledge. But to prevent litigation, collusion and the necessity of going into circumstances impossible to be unravelled, the law presumes against the carrier unless he shows that it was done by the King's enemies or by such act as could not happen without the intervention of God as storms, lightning or tempest.[14]

It follows, then, that fire is not an act of God unless caused by lightning and that a common carrier, unlike other bailees for value, is liable for damage to goods caused by fire, even when there is no negligence provable against him.

A shipper may challenge a common carrier's defence by showing that the carrier acted irresponsibly in relation to the act of God. In the famous words of Mr. Chief Justice Cockburn:

> If by his default in omitting to take necessary care loss or damage ensues, he [the common carrier] remains responsible, though the so-called act of God may have been the immediate cause of the mischief. If the ship is unseaworthy, and hence perishes from the storm which it otherwise would have weathered; if the carrier by undue deviation or delay exposes himself to the danger which he otherwise would have avoided; or if by his rashness he unnecessarily encounters it, as by putting to sea in a raging storm, the loss cannot be said to be due to the act of God alone, and the carrier cannot have the benefit of the exception.[15]

Nevertheless, there is a wide variety of occurrences that may amount to acts of God and thus absolve the carrier of liability. If the shipper wishes protection againt these risks, he may obtain it by a separate insurance policy.

A common carrier may also avoid liability for damage to goods if he can show that the goods had the seeds of their own destruction within them at the time of shipment; that is they had an *inherent vice*. Thus, goods may have been in a combustible condition or have had latent defects that rendered them more susceptible to breakage than is typical of goods of their category. This defence by the carrier also includes inadequate packing of the goods by the shipper and is a good defence whether the carrier was aware of the inadequate packing or not.[16]

---

[14] Forward v. Pittard (1785) 99 E.R. 953, at 956-7 (authors' italics)
[15] Nugent v. Smith (1875) 1 C.P.D. 423, at 436.
[16] Gould v. South Eastern & Chatham Railway [1920] 2 K.B. 186.

A common carrier can offer a third defence, that the shipper has been guilty of a breach of duty. A contract for the transportation of goods includes an implied promise on the part of the shipper that the goods are safe to carry; the term exists whether the shipper is aware of the danger or not.[17] It is possible, therefore, for the shipper himself to be in breach of contract and so to release the common carrier from his part of the bargain. Indeed, if the goods cause damage to the carrier's equipment, for instance by exploding, the carrier may successfully sue for damages. Another example of default by the shipper arises when he declares less than the full value of the goods to the carrier. He may do this in order to pay a lower freight charge than he would have paid had he declared their true value. In these circumstances, the carrier is not released from his duty, but his liability is limited to the declared value.

Contractual Terms Limiting Liability of Carriers

A common carrier may, and frequently does, limit the amount of his liability when the shipper does not declare the value of the goods. Notice of this limitation in liability is printed prominently across the shipping document and repeated in detail on the reverse side. Thus, a bill of lading commonly states, "Liability limited to $50.00 unless higher value is declared by the shipper and inserted herein." This term requires the shipper to declare a higher value when necessary and to pay a correspondingly higher rate for the greater liability undertaken by the common carrier. Terms of this kind limiting the liability of carriers who operate interprovincial or international routes must be approved by the Canadian Transport Commissioners and thus there is some public control over the extent to which common carriers may contract themselves out of their special liability.[18] Terms limiting liability when subject to public control often make good sense as between the parties: the common carrier bases his freight charges on all the terms of the contract and the other contracting party (the shipper) knows the extent to which he should contract separately for insurance. While these terms are a type of exemption clause, they seek to limit rather than eliminate the carrier's liability.

The courts may restrict the scope of some forms of exemption clauses in contracts of carriage. In *Bontex Knitting Works Ltd. v. St. John's Garage*,[19] a manufacturer obtained the use of a truck and a driver from a private carrier for two and one-half hours for delivering goods to customers. The contract contained a term that the truck owner would not be responsible for loss or damage to the goods while they were on his truck. In the course of delivery, the truck driver left the truck unattended for one hour to have a meal, and the goods were stolen. When sued for the value of the goods, the truck owner pleaded the exemption clause. The court held, however, that the exemption clause could not be so broad as to exclude the truck owner's fundamental obligation to perform the contract: the manufacturer succeeded in his action for the value of the goods. Here again

---

[17] Burley Ltd. v. Stepney Corporation [1947] 1 All E.R. 507, at 510.
[18] The Railway Act, R.S.C. 1970, c. R-2, s. 322.
[19] [1943] 2 All E.R. 690; [1944] 1 All E.R. 381.

we see an example of the court's unwillingness to construe an exemption clause as freeing a party to a contract from liability for default when the default amounts to a total failure to carry the contract out.

Remedies

All carriers, whether common carriers or not, have the usual remedies for breach of contract when a shipper is in default. There is, however, a distinction between common carriers and other carriers with regard to the right of lien. A common carrier, because he is bound to accept goods for shipment so long as he has space available, cannot question the credit of the bailor who tenders the goods to him. Thus, to protect the common carrier, the common law gives him a lien on goods shipped for the amount of unpaid freight or express charges on those goods. Although some doubt exists, the general opinion is that the common law does not give a private carrier a similiar lien.[20] Of course, the private carrier may, and usually does, acquire a right of lien on the goods as a term of the contract of carriage.

Neither the common law nor any statutes of general application give either common carriers or private carriers the right to sell goods retained under a lien. Both types of carriers, however, usually stipulate for an express right to sell the goods in case of default.

HOTELKEEPERS OR INNKEEPERS

Definition of an Innkeeper

A distinction similar to the distinction between private carriers and common carriers exists between hotelkeepers or innkeepers and others who also offer various accommodation to the public. The traditional word "innkeeper", like the more modern term "hotelkeeper", refers to a person who maintains an establishment offering lodging to any member of the public as a transient guest. He differs from a boarding-house keeper, who may pick and choose whom he is willing to accommodate, and he differs also from a restaurant owner, who does not offer lodging to his guests. The proprietor of a tourist home or motel that does not offer restaurant facilities is apparently not an innkeeper.

Liability

Businesses other than hotels or inns offering accommodation to the public are under a duty to take reasonable care of the belongings of their guests and patrons. Like warehousemen, they are liable for damage or loss caused by their negligence or the negligence of their employees. Under the common law, however, innkeepers are under a much higher liability. They are liable as insurers for

---

[20] Paton, *Bailment in The Common Law*, p. 285.

the disappearance by loss or theft of their guests' goods. The historical reason is similar to that for the liability of a common carrier — to prevent collusion between the innkeeper and thieves. There is, however, an important difference between goods bailed to a common carrier and goods left in the room of a guest of an innkeeper: the bailor of goods to a common carrier gives them over completely to the care of the carrier, whereas the guest of an innkeeper shares the responsibility with the innkeeper, since he has control over his own goods from time to time when he is in his room. Accordingly, an innkeeper may avoid liability if he can show that the disappearance was due to the carelessness of the guest. It may be difficult to decide the cause of the loss in any given case. Leaving a door unlocked in a small country hotel may not amount to negligence, and the innkeeper would be liable if the guest's goods were stolen. The same act of leaving a hotel door unlocked in a large metropolitan hotel after flaunting expensive jewellery might well amount to carelessness absolving the innkeeper.

Again, the considerations which make a common carrier an insurer of physical damage to goods bailed with him do not necessarily apply to an innkeeper: the guest may be able to ascertain whether there was negligence on the part of the innkeeper. Accordingly, an innkeeper is liable for injury to the goods of his guests — as distinct from his liability for their disappearance through loss or theft — only if the injury was caused by the negligence of the innkeeper or his employees. What should happen, however, if the goods of the guests are totally destroyed in a fire in the hotel? Surprisingly enough, there appears to be no clear answer to whether the innkeeper is an insurer or, like a warehouseman, liable for loss by fire only if he or his employees were negligent.[21]

The Innkeepers (or Hotelkeepers) Act

An innkeeper may limit his liability as an insurer for the loss or theft of the goods of his guest by complying with the provisions of the Innkeepers' Act or Hotelkeepers' Act in the various provinces. These Acts are largely based on the English Innkeepers' Liability Act, 1863. Depending upon the province, the Act either reduces an innkeeper's liability to a maximum amount varying from $150 to $40, or eliminates his liability as an insurer entirely.[22] The protection does not apply to circumstances "where the goods have been stolen, lost or injured through the wilful act, default or neglect of the innkeeper or a servant in his employ," or "where the goods have been deposited expressly for safe custody with the innkeeper".[23] If the innkeeper refuses to accept the goods of a guest for safe custody, he loses the benefit of the reduced liability under the statute and is subject to the full common law liability of innkeepers.[24]

With the exception of Manitoba, all provinces require the innkeeper to

---

[21] *Ibid.*, p. 200.
[22] See, for example: R.S.B.C. 1960, c. 195, s. 4; R.S.O. 1970, c. 223, s. 4(1); R.S.N.S. 1967, c. 146, s. 3
[23] *Ibid.*
[24] R.S.B.C. 1960, c. 195, s. 5; R.S.O. 1970, c. 223, s. 5; R.S.N.S. 1967, c. 146, s. 4

display conspicuously a copy of the section of the Act which limits liability in order to take advantage of the section. If an innkeeper fails to comply with this requirement, he loses the protection of the Act. Saskatchewan and Newfoundland require that the notice be posted in the hall or entrance, but the remaining provinces require it to be posted in the ''office and public rooms and in every bedroom . . .''[25]

Remedies

An innkeeper, like a common carrier, owes a duty to the public generally. As we have seen, he is restricted in his right to refuse guests. Accordingly, the common law gave him a lien over the goods of his guests for the value of his services. The right was only a lien, however, and did not include the right to sell the goods. Boarding-house keepers and proprietors of restaurants had no such right to a lien.

This appears to be the law today in England. The Innkeepers' Acts of the various provinces, except for Newfoundland, extend the right of lien to boarding-house keepers and lodging-house keepers on the goods of their guests.[26] The Acts also give the right to sell the goods of guests by public auction if their bills remain unpaid for a specified period — one month in the Prairie provinces, six weeks in Newfoundland, and three months in the remaining provinces. The requirements of notice and advertising vary from province to province. There appears to be no right of lien or sale in a restaurant proprietor either by common law or under the Innkeepers' Acts.

PLEDGE OR PAWN

While these two terms have the same legal significance, a pawn has a colloquial usage that restricts it to transactions with a pawnbroker. A pledge or pawn is a bailment of personal property as security for repayment of a loan. The borrower is the *pledgor* and the creditor the *pledgee*. The subject-matter of a pledge may be goods, as when they are left with a pawnbroker, or it may be share or bond certificates, as when they are left with a bank. As with other forms of bailment, the basis of the transaction is that the title to the thing bailed remains with the borrower (bailor), although the possession passes to the lender (bailee).

A pledge is a bailment where the change in possession is for the benefit of the bailee. He requests possession of the pledgor's personal property as security for the loan he has made to the pledgor. In agreeing to lend the money, he gives valuable consideration for the pledge. Accordingly (as we noted above under ''Liability of a Bailee''), as a bailee for value he must exercise such care as is reasonable ''in the ordinary and proper course'' of his business. A banker is expected to store negotiable bonds in his vault and is liable for their loss if they are left out of the vault and stolen.

[25] R.S.B.C. 1960, c. 195, s. 6; R.S.O. 1970, c. 223, s. 6; R.S.N.S. 1967, c. 146, s. 5.
[26] R.S.B.C. 1960, c. 195, s. 3; R.S.O. 1970, c. 223, s. 2; R.S.N.S. 1967, c. 146, s. 2

A pledgee obtains a lien on the personal property pledged with him. The pledgor cannot recover possession of his goods until he has repaid the debt for which they are security. In addition, by pledging his goods, the pledgor gives authority to the pledgee to sell the pledged goods upon default. Such authority to sell is implied if not stated expressly in the contract of pledge. The lender (pledgee) may reimburse himself out of the proceeds of the sale for any costs incurred as a result of the default and for the amount of the unpaid loan. The surplus, if any, belongs to the borrower. If the property does not bring enough in the sale to liquidate the debt, the borrower remains liable as an ordinary debtor for the deficiency.

The rule is different for pawnbrokers, where the legal effect is governed by provincial statute. A pawnbroker may obtain absolute ownership of the pledged goods after he retains them for a specified period, sends notice of a last opportunity to redeem to the pawner and publishes a final notice in a newspaper.[27]

HIRE OR USE OF A CHATTEL

Examples of a bailment for hire or use are renting an autmobile for personal or business use, leasing heavy construction equipment for building purposes, leasing a postage-meter machine or electronic data-processing equipment for office use. Bailments for hire or use of a chattel are bailments in which the change in possession is for the benefit of the bailee; the bailor's benefit is in the form of payment for the use of the property.[28]

The standard of care required of a bailee who hires equipment is that he takes such care of the rented property as a prudent man would exercise in the use of his own property. In the Ontario case of *Reynolds v. Roxburgh*,[29] the defendant had rented a portable steam engine from the plaintiff to power a wood-cutting saw. The engine exploded immediately after it was put into use, and the plaintiff sued the defendant for the value of the destroyed engine and boiler. He alleged that the defendant had not tested the steam gauge and safety valve before commencing to run the machine. The court applied the rule that "the hirer of a chattel is required to use . . . the degree of diligence which prudent men use . . . in keeping their own goods of the same kind."[30] The court held that this standard of care did not require the bailee to test the safety gauge and valve. Accordingly it held that the defendant was not in breach of his duty as a bailee for hire and was not liable to pay for the destroyed steam engine.

In bailments of this kind where the bailee has relied on the skill and judgment of the bailor to supply an article suitable for the bailee's requirement, and where it is the business of the bailor to supply such articles, the bailor impliedly warrants that the equipment is reasonably fit for the purpose for which it was

---

[27] See for example: The Pawnbrokers Act, R.S.O. 1970, c. 341, ss. 19-21.

[28] See Tillings v. Balmain (1892) 8 T.L.R. 517.

[29] (1886) 10 O.R. 649.

[30] *Ibid.*, per Armour, J., at 655.

hired.[31] Some doubt exists whether this liability extends only to defects of which the bailor ought to have been aware; but if a strict analogy is drawn with the corresponding implied term in a contract of sale, a bailor, in common with a seller, should not be able to plead that the offending defect in the chattel is something he could not have detected.[32] We may note that in *Reynolds v. Roxburgh* the explosion of the steam boiler killed one man and severely injured another, so that while the point was not raised in the case, the liability of the bailor as well as the bailee might have been in issue.

If a bailee has contracted to hire a chattel for a given period of time he will be liable for the whole rental, even if he finds that he has overestimated the length of time he requires the use of the equipment. (In the same way, a tenant of a building is liable for rent for the full period of the lease whether he occupies or uses the premises or not.) A bailor may, of course, agree to take equipment back ahead of time and to reduce the rental charges: when he does so, he is consenting to a discharge of the original contract of bailment and to replacing it with a substituted agreement.

A variation in a contract for the hire of a chattel is a contract of hire with an option to purchase. The bailee hires the chattel on the understanding that he has an option to purchase it by instalment payments, and if he does so, the title to the chattel will pass to him when the instalments are completed. Frequently, these arrangements state that rental already paid for the hire of the chattel may be applied against the price if the hirer decides to buy. During the time before the hirer exercises such an option, the contract creates a bailment, and the hirer has no contractual obligation to pay the purchase price. Several decades ago the parlours in many farmhouses across Canada were equipped with pianos under an arrangement of this kind. Today, the "hire-purchase agreement" is widespread in England but not in Canada, although it has reappeared recently in the sale of colour T.V. sets. In Canada, the usual device for purchasing articles "on time" is the conditional sale agreement which, as we shall see in Chapter 30, also creates a type of bailment for value.

Since in contracts for the hire or use of a chattel it is the bailor who requires to be paid for renting out his equipment, his only right of action arising out of the bailment is an action for breach of contract or for the price of the services. He has no security in the form of possession of the chattels of his debtor; accordingly, the remedies of lien and sale do not apply in these circumstances. A bailor has, of course, the right to sue for the return of his property if the bailee retains it beyond the end of the rental period.

FINDERS

A person who finds a valuable object is not bound to take possession of it, but once he does he becomes a bailee for the owner, and must exercise the degree of

---

[31] Fowler v. Lock (1872) L.R. 7 C.P. 272 at 280; Griffith S.S. Co. v. Western Plywood Co. [1953] 3 D.L.R. 29.

[32] For a discussion of the bailor's duty see Paton, *Bailment in The Common Law*, pp. 289-99.

care to be expected of a bailee where the bailment is gratuitous and for the benefit of the bailor (the owner).

Sometimes, of course, the identity of the owner of the object cannot be ascertained: the question then arises whether the finder is entitled to keep or sell it. Is there then simply a bailment, or has ownership been acquired along with possession? In these circumstances, a finder generally acquires a good title against everyone except the owner; but the rule has been qualified so that it applies only to goods found in what the court, in its wisdom, chooses to regard as a "public place". The result is that in many instances a finder will not be entitled to keep the object as against a person who owns or controls the "private" property within which the object was found, even though that person may have been unaware of its existence.

Although the question of the rights of a finder arises frequently, it is fraught with conceptual difficulties that tend to make the facts of each case more decisive than the legal rules themselves. The court may have to decide whether the area within which the object is found can fairly be described as a "public place", or it may have to decide whether the property within which a person finds an object can be said to have been within the "control" or "custody" of someone else. One or two examples will serve to illustrate these difficulties. Suppose someone finds a $100 banknote on the floor of a retail shop: is a store where the public is invited a "public place", and if so, are some parts of the store more "public" than others?[33] Or again, suppose the owner of a piece of furniture gives temporary possession of it to a repairman, who finds valuable items in a secret compartment that is unknown to the owner: can the finder be said to "control" or to "have custody of" the property within which the object was discovered?[34]

The rights of a finder of a valuable object on another's land have been stated as follows: "The possession of land carries with it in general, by our law, possession of everything which is attached to or under that land, and, in the absence of a better title elsewhere, the right to possess it also. And it makes no difference that the possessor is unaware of the thing's existence."[35]

QUESTIONS FOR REVIEW

1. How does a bailment differ from a sale?
2. What important statutory rights does a warehouseman obtain?
3. Why does a common carrier require a shipper to state the value of goods delivered for shipment?
4. Distinguish a private carrier from a common carrier.
5. What is a hire-purchase agreement?

---

[33] See Bridges v. Hawkesworth (1851) 21 L.J. Q.B. 75, where a customer was held to be entitled, as against the shopkeeper, to banknotes dropped on the main floor of the shop by some unknown person and found there by the customer.

[34] See Cartwright v. Green (1803) 32 E.R. 412, where the court decided in the negative.

[35] Pollock and Wright, *Essay on Possession in the Common Law,* p. 41, cited by Vaines, *Personal Property* (3rd ed.), p. 333. Chapter 16 in the latter book is recommended as general reading on the subject of "finding".

6. What does the defence of *inherent vice* mean?
7. State whether there is a bailment in each of the following circumstances and if so, what standard of care is required of the bailee:
   (a) *A* takes his friend *B,* and *B*'s family, on a motor trip. *B* insists on paying for the gasoline.
   (b) *C* finds an old wallet lying on the sidewalk. He picks it up, sees that it contains no money, and throws it back on the sidewalk.
   (c) *F,* on his way to the theatre, takes his car to a parking lot, the attendant asks him for the keys, and *F* leaves to the attendant the task of finding a space for the vehicle.
   (d) *G,* a student, borrows a book from the university library. Would it make a difference if *G* were instead an alumnus?
   (e) On a warm winter day *H* goes to the *J* Restaurant for a meal. On leaving the restaurant afterwards, he inadvertently leaves his hat and overcoat behind.
8. Give an example of a condition subsequent in a contract of bailment.
9. In which type of bailment does the bailee owe the greater duty of care: a gratuitous bailment for the benefit of the bailor, or a gratuitous bailment for the benefit of the bailee?
10. In what respect is the liability of a common carrier greater than the liability of a warehouseman?
11. Under what circumstances does a bailor owe a duty of care to a bailee?
12. Assuming that there is no term in the contract of bailment requiring the bailee to insure the goods against loss by fire: (a) is a warehouseman liable if such loss occurs; (b) is a common carrier liable?
13. Why is a pledge a more valuable right than a lien?
14. (a) For what type of harm does an innkeeper have the liability of an insurer towards his guests?
    (b) To what extent does the statute of your province limit this liability?
15. Jones took his 75-horsepower outboard motor to Martin's Marina and Repair Centre for annual overhaul and storage. Since considerable repairs and parts were needed, Jones left a deposit of $100 with Martin. Shortly afterwards, before making any repairs, Martin went bankrupt. What are Jones's rights in the bankruptcy proceedings?
16. The rule that a man is presumed to be innocent until proved guilty has its application in criminal proceedings. It does not always follow in private disputes brought before the courts that the defendant will be presumed to be innocent of the complaint made against him. Give one or two examples of situations in which the onus is on a defendant to establish his lack of fault.
17. What types of bailee have an obligation that is in conflict with their freedom of contract?
18. Is there a special reason for giving a common carrier a lien on goods shipped?
19. How does the history of the common law help to explain the special liability of a common carrier or a hotelkeeper?
20. How may an exemption clause arise in a contract of bailment?

CASES FOR DISCUSSION

CASE 1

Walcot arrived at the Red Lantern Hotel on a Saturday afternoon, checked in, and handed the bellhop a bag containing negotiable securities worth $2,000. He said nothing to the bellhop, who placed the bag under a counter at the bar, as he had often done on Walcot's previous visits. Walcot then conducted some business with others whom he had arranged to meet in the bar of the hotel and once or twice called for the bag and either deposited in it, or withdrew from it, some business papers.

When Walcot returned that evening to pick up the bag and take it to his room, he discovered that it had been stolen and another one substituted. Walcot sued the hotel proprietors for $2,000. Should the action succeed? Are there any other facts you would like to know before deciding? (See *Whitehouse v. Pickett* [1908] A.C. 357.)

CASE 2

Rowan drove his car on to a parking lot operated by Lee. When he turned his car over to Lee's employee, he received a parking receipt in return for a deposit of $1.50. The ticket contained on its face the following clause:

> Charges are for the use of parking space only. The company assumes no responsibility for loss through fire, theft, collision or otherwise to the car or its contents, whether due to negligence or otherwise. CARS PARKED AT OWNER'S RISK.

The parking-lot employee then volunteered to park the car for Rowan: in attempting to do so, and before the car ever reached the parking space, he ran it at relatively high speed into the side of another car already parked, causing considerable damage to both cars.

Rowan brought an action against Lee for damages for negligence or, in the alternative, for breach of the contract of bailment. Offer an opinion about whether his action should succeed.

CASE 3

Mrs. Hubbard inherited a number of valuable pieces of furniture, *objets d'art,* bric-a-brac, china, and glassware. Not having room in her home for them, she had the Bailey Storage Co. pack the articles in steel-banded boxes and take them to its warehouse. Subsequently, her family suffered financial reverses, and the storage charges got into arrears to the extent of $400. Bailey Storage Co. sent Mrs. Hubbard notice of its intention to sell the goods at public auction if the charges were not paid by a specified date. At the last moment Mrs. Hubbard persuaded the manager of Bailey Storage Co. not to dispose of the goods in this way, but to deliver them to Scrawley, an antique dealer and auctioneer to whom she promised she would give authority to sell the goods; she urged that Scrawley's experience in handling such articles would make it possible to realize much more from their sale. As soon as the goods were delivered to the auctioneer, however, Mrs. Hubbard claimed personal possession of them, asserting that Bailey Storage Co. had thereby forfeited its warehouseman's lien. At the same time the Bailey Storage Co. claimed possession of the goods. The auctioneer, fearful of his liability for delivering the goods to the wrong person, kept them in custody and insisted that the matter be resolved by reference to the court. Before any court action commenced, the goods were stolen from Scrawley's premises one night when an employee inadvertently left a door unlocked. Is Scrawley liable and, if so, to whom? (For reference, see *Heriteau v. Morris Realty Ltd.* [1944] 1 D.L.R. 28.

CASE 4

In January Mrs. Bradshaw acquired a new, silver-blue mink jacket which cost her husband $2,500. In April she took it to Collier Fur Co. for storage during the summer months. The proprietor said that although he did not have his own storage facilities, he had arrangements with another firm that had a good vault. Mrs. Bradshaw replied that it was immaterial to her where the jacket was stored as long as it was properly looked after. Collier Fur Co. then gave her a document setting out the transaction and sent the jacket to Tidy Cleaners & Dyers Ltd. where it was stored. The document read in part as follows:

> In consideration of the payment of $25.00 insurance and storage charges, Collier Fur Co. agrees to accept the garment described above for storage and further agrees to insure same against loss or damage by fire, theft or moths for the season of 1975. Unless advised within five days from the date of this receipt, valuation of the garment as shown here will be accepted by both parties as correct and just and not subject to further alterations. Liability of Collier Fur Co. in any event is not to exceed the valuation of the garment as stated in this receipt.

For the purpose of determining the insurance and storage charge Mrs. Bradshaw set a valuation of $1,200 on the jacket, and this valuation was inserted in the above agreement.

When Mrs. Bradshaw requested the jacket in the fall, Tidy Cleaners & Dyers Ltd. could not produce it, and it became apparent that it had been either lost or given to another customer by mistake. Mrs. Bradshaw sued Collier Fur Co. for damages of $2,500 for negligence. Collier Fur Co. admitted liability for only $1,200 and tendered that sum in settlement by depositing it with a court official. What should the court's decision be? (See *Banks v. Dennis* (1956) 2 D.L.R. (2d) 441; *Davies v. Collins* [1945] 1 All E.R. 247.)

CASE 5

Shaw, an automobile dealer, arranged with a Dr. DiLemma, a customer of long standing, to exchange the doctor's 1973 Mercury for a 1976 Lincoln over the Thanksgiving weekend, with a view to a possible trade-in if the doctor was satisfied with the new car.

Dr. DiLemma drove the Mercury into the garage operated by Shaw and left it there. Over the holiday one of the employees of Shaw's business, an apprentice mechanic, came back to work on his own stock car. Normal procedure when employees wished to work in the garage for their own purposes was for them to obtain specific permission; the mechanic had attempted to telephone Shaw for permission but kept getting a busy signal. Nevertheless, he went to the garage and parked his car next to Dr. DiLemma's Mercury. While working on his car, the apprentice put a five-gallon can of gasoline in the trunk. He then noticed a piece of sheet metal hanging down from the back and undertook to cut it off with an oxyacetylene torch; a tremendous explosion followed.

On returning from his cottage with the 1976 Lincoln the following day Dr. DiLemma saw the burned-out shell of his Mercury in the main building of the garage. (Shaw had also left his own car in the garage, but it survived with some minor damage.) Shaw refused to accept responsibility for the damage done to the 1973 Mercury or to allow a reasonable amount on its trade-in for the 1976 Lincoln. He contended that as no sale had been effected, the Mercury belonged to the doctor at the time of the explosion and had been left on his premises voluntarily. Dr. DiLemma then brought an action against Shaw for damages. Should he succeed?

CASE 6

The general manager of Maritime Steel Ltd. telephoned Fundy Towing Co. Ltd. and requested that a cargo of steel bars be picked up at Sydney and delivered to the company's plant in Saint John. On previous occasions these parties had contracted by an exchange of letters, all of which included clauses to say that the Fundy Towing Co. Ltd. was not liable for any loss of or damage to cargo as long as its tugboat was kept in seaworthy condition. On this occasion, they said nothing about such a term in their telephone conversation. They did, however, undertake to confirm in writing the terms agreed to in their conversation, though both neglected to do so.

Fundy Towing Co. Ltd. loaded the steel on a scow at Sydney. The scow was then linked by a tow-line with three others and towed as the rearmost scow behind a new tugboat. It was not possible for the master of the tug to keep the last scow in view. Going under a bridge in Saint John harbour, the last scow collided with the pier of the bridge. The load of steel was spilled: some was lost and much of what was recovered was so twisted that Maritime Steel Ltd. incurred considerable expense in restoring it to a usable condition.

Maritime Steel Ltd. sued Fundy Towing Co. Ltd. for damages for breach of contract, claiming the value of the steel lost, depreciation in the value of the steel recovered, salvage expenses, and loss of profit. Evidence was produced to show that the master of the tug, a person of considerable experience, had not followed a course in the centre of the opening under the bridge, and that the accident had been caused by a tow-line between the scows that was rather longer than usual.

What are the issues in this case? Should the action succeed? (For reference, see *A.I.M. Steel Ltd. v. Gulf of Georgia Towing Co. Ltd.* (1965) 50 W.W.R. 476.)

CHAPTER 20

Principal and Agent

THE NATURE OF AGENCY

As we shall use the term, *agency* is a relationship in which one person, known as an *agent,* is authorized to bring another person for whom he acts, known as a *principal,* into contractual relations with third parties. Agency is created by a special type of employment contract in which a principal delegates to an agent the task of negotiating for him and making some or all of his contracts. A person may also volunteer gratuitously to act as an agent. His promise to do so is not binding upon him, but once he undertakes to act as agent in a particular transaction for his principal he is bound by all the duties of an agent under contract.

Sometimes *agency* is given the larger connotation of a general representative capacity and encompasses a wider variety of activities than entering into contracts on behalf of a principal. It is in this larger sense of the term that an auditor is sometimes spoken of as an "agent" for the shareholders of a company: his function is to review the accounts and report to its shareholders on the fairness of the company's financial statements, but he is in fact appointed by the company (his client) at the annual general meeting and has no authority to enter into contracts for either the company or its shareholders. Similarly, the so-called real estate "agent" does not have authority, as such, to sell the property of his client — his role is to introduce prospective purchasers, and his client contracts directly with the purchaser. In this chapter, most of our references will be to instances in which the agent's role is to enter into contracts for his principal.

To understand the law relating to principal and agent we must distinguish two levels of contract: (a) the contract between the principal and the agent, known as the *agency agreement,* and (b) the contracts which the agent makes with third parties for his principal. The contract between the principal and his agent should clearly define the limit of the agent's authority: how far he can go in making a contract with a third party without obtaining further instructions from his principal. The agency agreement may confer upon the agent a very wide and general authority to make contracts, or a highly restricted authority, or any degree of authority between these extremes.

The agency relationship is ubiquitous in business affairs. A limited company can only enter into contractual relations when its officers and employees act as agents on its behalf, whether the contracts be for hiring employees, purchasing goods and services, or selling its product. In partnership, too, agency plays an important role. Each partner is presumed by law to be an agent with very wide authority to act on behalf of the partnership; often the partnership agreement concerns itself with the limits to be placed on this authority. Lawyers act as agents for their clients in the purchase or sale of land and buildings. A stockbroker is an agent for clients who place orders with him to buy or sell shares for them. An insurance agent acts on behalf of his principal, the insurance company, to negotiate contracts of insurance. The auctioneer and the commission merchant have authority to make sales contracts for their principals and also have possession of the goods they are to sell. A *del credere* agent, as we have seen in Chapter 11, not only makes contracts for his principal but guarantees performance by the third party.

Any person who has the capacity to contract may as a principal engage an agent to contract on his behalf. An agent reflects the same capacity to contract that his principal shines upon him. Accordingly, if a minor engages an agent, the contracts made by the agent for him are as voidable at his option as if he had made them personally.

While the principal must be competent to contract, the agent need not be capable of contracting in his own right. An agent may be a minor and yet bind his principal in contracts with third parties. However, as between his principal and him the agency agreement is voidable at his option.

THE WAYS IN WHICH AN AGENCY RELATIONSHIP CAN BE ESTABLISHED

By Express Agreement

An agency agreement may be oral, written, or in writing under seal; as long as there is a definite understanding between the principal and agent, whatever its form, the agency relationship has been created by an express agreement. If an agency agreement is to extend beyond one year, it must be in writing to be enforceable in provinces where the relevant section of the Statute of Frauds continues to apply; as we have seen, it does not apply in British Columbia. In any event, it is desirable for each party to have a copy of the agency agreement in writing and signed by both of them in order to minimize future misunderstanding about the scope of the agent's authority and other terms of the arrangement.

An agent should always have his authorization in writing if he wishes to make promissory notes, accept drafts, and draw cheques in the name of his principal, and he should sign in a way which makes it clear that he is acting in a representative capacity; otherwise he may be personally liable on the instrument.[1]

A *power of attorney* is a special type of express agency agreement. In the usual and strict sense of the term it refers to a grant of authority under the seal of the principal. An agent who does not receive his authority under seal can be authorized to do all acts on behalf of his principal except sign documents under seal for him. Accordingly, whenever the parties envisage that the agent may need to sign and seal documents in the course of his service, he receives his authorization under seal in a power of attorney. Sometimes an agent's written authority is called a power of attorney although it is not under seal, but this description is not strictly accurate. A power of attorney, for example, is given to an agent if he is expected to carry through a real estate transaction to its completion, including giving a grant of land under seal.

A contract of agency, like any other contract, may contain implied terms; these terms may supplement the express authority in the contract. Thus, when a principal expressly authorizes his agent to make a purchase, say, of Irish linen in Belfast, the agent would also have implied authority to make a contract for shipment of the goods to Canada.

By Ratification

Sometimes a person purports to act as an agent knowing he has no authority but hoping that the proposed principal will later adopt the contract. This subsequent adoption by the principal is called *ratification*. The need for ratification may arise for either of two reasons: first, because the person purporting to act as agent is not an agent at all for the principal whom he identifies; or, secondly because he has only a limited authority and has exceeded it. If the principal does not ratify, no agency relationship is formed, and the person who intended to act merely as an agent becomes personally liable to the third party for any loss which follows from his misrepresentation.

When a principal does ratify, the effect of his ratification is to establish the contract with the third party retroactively, as if the agent had been truly his agent at the time he made the contract. The principal, agent, and third party are then in the same position with regard to the contract, as if the agency agreement had existed from the beginning.

The named principal need not state his ratification expressly. It may be implied from the fact of his assuming the benefits of the contract made for him. Moreover, his ratification cannot be partial: he cannot accept the benefits without also reimbursing the agent for his costs, nor can he ratify only those aspects of the transaction which prove to be to his advantage and refuse to ratify the balance of the contract. A principal must also ratify within a reasonable time to be able to claim the benefit of the contract.[2]

---

[1] See Bills of Exchange Act, R.S.C. 1970, c. B-5, s. 52(1).

[2] Metropolitan Asylums Board Managers v. Kingham & Sons (1890) 6 T.L.R. 217.

Not all contracts made by an agent without authority may be ratified by the principal, however; in some circumstances the court will not recognize the ratification. In the first place, when an agent purports to accept an offer "subject to the ratification of my principal," the later ratification will not be retroactive. This apparent exception is simply an application of the rules of offer and acceptance: a conditional acceptance by the agent is not acceptance at all. The offeror may revoke his offer at any time before acceptance. In these circumstances the eventual "ratification" of the principal is really only an acceptance of the original offer. At most, an attempt by an agent to accept subject to ratification is merely an inducement to the offeror to hold his offer open.

Secondly, in jurisdictions that have not revised their companies legislation to overrule the common law, a company, after it comes into existence, will be unable to ratify contracts made for it by agents or promoters before it was incorporated. The reasoning given for this rule is that an agent cannot make a contract on behalf of a principal if at the time the principal could not make the contract on its own behalf. In these circumstances, even if the firm after coming into existence acquiesces and acts under the contract, it cannot obtain any rights against the third party or be liable to him.

Illustration:

A and *B*, promoters of the *C* Co. Ltd., enter into a contract for the supply of office equipment before the company is incorporated. After its incorporation, *C* Co. Ltd. uses the office equipment but fails to pay the suppliers. If the suppliers sue *C* Co. Ltd., it may defend successfully on the grounds that it was impossible for it to ratify the contract, not having been in existence when the contract was made for it. The suppliers may, however, sue *A* and *B* for damages for having warranted they had authority to act when they did not.[3] In addition, since no contract was formed, title to the office equipment did not pass and the suppliers may now repossess it.

This result can be avoided if, after incorporation, *C* Co. Ltd. expressly contracts with the suppliers for the purchase of the office equipment; but such a contract is necessary to relieve the promoters of liability and to make the company liable. In certain jurisdictions outside Canada, notably in some of the United States, the inconvenience of the rule for business purposes has been recognized: the courts there may find that the conduct of a company following its incorporation implies that the company has "adopted" the contracts made for it by its promoters. The common law rule has been changed by statute in some Canadian jurisdictions. For a fuller discussion see Chapter 29: "The Management and Operation of a Corporation".

Thirdly, a principal cannot ratify a contract made for him if at the time he purports to ratify the act he could not himself have made that contract.

---

[3] Kelner v. Baxter (1866) L.R. 2 C.P. 174. For a criticism of this decision see: *Interim Report of the Select Committee on Company Law, 1967* (Ontario), pp. 10-12; Nugan, "Pre-Incorporation Contracts", in *Studies in Canadian Company Law*, Ziegel (ed.), Vol. I, Ch. 6.

Illustration:

A arranges on behalf of *P,* but without *P*'s authority, to insure *P*'s buildings against fire loss with the entire insurance payable to *P*. The buildings burn down, and *P* announces his ratification of the contract of insurance. The ratification will not be effective because at the time *P* attempts it, the buildings are destroyed, and it would be impossible for him to insure them himself.[4]

Another aspect of this third point is that a principal cannot ratify when the rights of an outsider are affected.

Illustration:

A, without authority from *P,* purports to accept *T*'s offer to sell a large quantity of canned goods to *P*. Subsequently, before the delivery date, *T* learns that *A* had no authority. Because the market is uncertain, he is afraid to wait for *P*'s ratification and makes a contract to sell the same goods to *X*. Ratification by *P* will now be ineffective because an outsider, *X,* has acquired rights to the goods.

This illustration raises a further problem. Suppose the market value of the goods is rising rapidly at the time *T* learns *A* was without authority to buy them. Can *T* effectively revoke his offer to sell and retain the goods for later sale to someone else at a higher profit? In these circumstances the rights of an outsider are not in question. The solution turns upon the legal significance of *A*'s acceptance. If *A*'s acceptance is a nullity until ratification by *P,* then *T* can revoke his offer before that time because it will not have been accepted. If, on the other hand, *A*'s acceptance creates a binding contract, we are confronted with the paradox that *T* will be bound while *P,* not yet having ratified, has a choice to bind himself or not. This situation arose in *Bolton Partners v. Lambert*[5] where *T*'s offer was accepted by *A* on behalf of *P* but without authority, and *T* then attempted to withdraw his offer with the full knowledge of *P* and before *P*'s ratification. In that case the court held that *T* was bound by *P*'s subsequent ratification.

The decision has been followed in a few English cases although it has been criticized by English jurists and restricted in recent English texts.[6] In *Fleming v. Bank of New Zealand*[7] Lord Lindley noted that the decision in the *Bolton* case "presents difficulties," and the court reserved liberty to reconsider the authority of the case in the future. These misgivings are reflected in the position taken by courts

---

[4] See Portavon Cinema Co. Ltd. v. Price and Century Insurance Co. Ltd. [1939] 4 All E.R. 601, at 607. One Canadian case questions this rule: Goulding v. Norwich Union Fire Insurance Society [1948] 1 D.L.R. 526. In that case, however, the agent was a mortgagee who had an insurable interest in the property himself. See also Chapter 18.

[5] (1889) 41 Ch. D. 295.

[6] See Fridman, *The Law of Agency* (3rd ed.) pp. 55-7, London: Butterworth & Co. Ltd., 1971; Powell, *The Law of Agency* (2nd ed.), pp. 141-7. London: Pitman & Sons, 1961.

[7] [1900] A.C. 577.

in the United States where revocation is held to be effective if it precedes ratification. The point has not often come before the Canadian courts, but in one case the court referred to Lord Lindley's statement and impliedly disapproved of the decision in the *Bolton* case.[8] As a result it is questionable whether the *Bolton* decision applies in Canada. Certainly if it does apply, it is subject to the important qualifications that ratification must not have the effect of prejudicing the rights of an outsider, and that the principal must ratify within a reasonable time.

Finally, a principal cannot ratify if at the time the agent made the contract, he failed to name his intended principal or at least mention the existence of a principal whose identity can then be ascertained. This rule makes it impossible for a person to enter into a contract simply in the hope that he may subsequently find a principal to ratify and so relieve him of his rights and duties. An undisclosed principal is denied a right later to ratify and enforce a contract made without his authority. On the other hand, as we shall see, when a contract is made *with* the authority of an undisclosed principal, he may intervene and enforce it personally, or he may be held liable on it should the third party learn of his existence and identity in time.

By Estoppel

When a person allows another to believe that a certain state of affairs exists, with the result that the other relies upon such belief, he will be prevented from afterwards stating that the true state of affairs was different. This rule of law is called *estoppel*: a person is *estopped* from stating the actual facts when he has induced another to rely on an entirely different version. The rule has relevance to the law of agency when a principal acquiesces in a person's acting as his agent in a matter where he has not actually given him authority.

The creation of an agency by estoppel, therefore, awaits a situation in which the agent's authority is merely apparent, and not real. An agent may acquire apparent authority from a past manner of transacting business by the principal or from trade custom. Such circumstances may make it appear to third parties that the agent has authority for the contract in hand. In fact, however, he does not have any real authority for the purpose: there exists no understanding between him and his principal, express or implied, to grant him this authority.

While conceivably a person may appear to have authority though he is not an agent at all, the more common occurrence is that he is an agent whose apparent authority exceeds his real authority. An agent may exceed his real authority by venturing into tempting sidelines; adjoining fields sometimes look more interesting. Alternatively, the agent may have acted within the limits usually ascribed to agents of his type but in violation of a special restriction placed by the principal on his activities. In either of these situations the principal may well be unhappy about a contract made for him. Indeed, he may object to performing it. We have

---

[8] Goodison Thresher Co. v. Doyle (1925) 57 O.L.R. 300.

now to decide when the principal can legally refuse to perform and when he will be bound by the contract.

The test is whether the third party should have been on notice about the agent's abuse of authority or whether he could reasonably assume from the kind of business in which the agent is engaged that the agent had authority for the contract in question. A third party has a responsibility to follow up indications that the agent does not have the necessary authority. The law cannot spell out in detail what these indications are: instead, it credits all third parties with a measure of business acumen, experience, and common sense to be exercised according to the circumstances. Presumably a third party should first check with the named principal about the agent's authority if the proposed contract is not within an area ordinarily attributable to such agents, or if its consequences are of relatively great importance for the principal and the third party. An agent does not, for example, usually have authority to borrow money in his principal's name or sell his business for him. Further, an agent authorized to sell goods is not necessarily authorized to accept the purchase money, particularly where payment to the agent is not customary trade practice or where the principal has sent an invoice to the third party requesting payment. If the third party pays the money to the agent and the agent absconds, the third party may have to pay the money over again to the principal.[9]

On the other hand, it would be impractical or inconvenient in day-to-day business for third parties to check an agent's authority in every instance. A presumption of authority is established by trade usage for various types of agency. The principal who seeks to restrict abnormally his agent's authority takes the risk that his agent will have, in the eyes of third parties, an apparent authority exceeding his real authority and make contracts in excess of his real authority. Such a principal will be estopped (prevented) from denying liability on contracts made for him within the range of this apparent authority. It is sometimes said that a principal "clothes" his agent with apparent authority: what frequently happens is that the principal provides the material and the agent cuts the cloth according to a somewhat more daring style than the principal had specified for him. In any event, third parties are entitled to judge by appearances — the clothes will make the man.

The moral for the principal who especially restricts his agent's authority is to be sure that the third parties with whom the agent is likely to deal have a direct notice of the restriction.

A principal may also be estopped from denying liability on contracts with third parties because of conduct known as *holding out*. If the principal has represented someone to be his agent, either by words suggestive of that relationship or by acquiescing in similar contracts made for him by that person in the past, he will not be permitted to deny the existence of an agency. If he holds someone out as his agent, it will avail him nothing to allege that no express agency agreement with that person exists.

---

[9] Butwick v. Grant [1924] 2 K.B. 483.

Pickering v. Busk[10] is a leading case illustrating agency by estoppel. Pickering authorized a broker, Swallow, to buy hemp for him, and after the purchase Pickering left the hemp on deposit at a wharf in Swallow's name. Then Swallow sold the hemp (which he had no real authority to do). As a result of the sale, the hemp was delivered to a concern which became bankrupt, and was then transferred to Busk, a trustee acting for the bankrupt concern. Pickering claimed that the contract with the purchasing concern should not be binding on him so that he might recover the hemp from Busk. The court held that Pickering's conduct in leaving the hemp in the broker's name had given the broker apparent authority to sell as well as to buy. Accordingly, Pickering failed to recover the hemp from Busk and could only claim as a creditor of the bankrupt concern. As we shall see, he might also have had a claim against his agent for breach of their contract of agency.

The question of apparent authority may also arise on the termination of the agency agreement. If the agent continues to enter into contracts for the principal and third parties have had no notice of the termination, the principal is bound by the contracts. The matter is of practical importance, as we shall see, when a partner retires from a partnership firm, since partners customarily act as agents for the partnership in contracts with outside parties, such as suppliers.

The transaction known as a *consignment* may also for some purposes create an agency by estoppel. As we noted in Chapter 16, the effect of a consignment is to transfer physical possession of goods from their owner, the consignor, to another person, the consignee. The consignor may continue to own the goods even when he gives the consignee the appearance of ownership. The intention underlying this type of consignment is to give the consignee authority to sell the goods as agent for the consignor. The Factors Act states that a mercantile agent (for example, a retail shopkeeper or commission merchant) who holds articles for sale on consignment may effectively sell the goods or use them as security for a loan even when he exceeds his authority.[11] As a result, the third party (the buyer or lender) obtains good title to the goods against the consignor. The third party must, however, have accepted the goods innocently and in good faith, that is, without knowledge that the owner had forbidden their sale or pledge to him.

A presumption of agency for certain purposes is created by the relationship known as *cohabitation*: the fact that a man and woman are living together (whether married or not) gives the woman an authority to make binding contracts in the man's name for household necessaries which are suitable to their accustomed style of living. The courts have distinguished this type of agency from agency by estoppel by permitting private financial arrangements between the

---

[10] (1812) 104 E.R. 758.
[11] See, for example: Sale of Goods Act, R.S.B.C. 1960, c. 344, s. 59; Factors Act, R.S.O. 1970, c. 156, s. 2; R.S.N.S. 1967, c. 97, s. 2. Note that the Factors Act retains a now obsolete definition of *factoring*. When the act was passed a *factor* was one who sold merchandise shipped to him on consignment by the owner and, generally, received a commission based on the amount received from sales. In recent years factors have abandoned their selling and merchandising function and have concentrated on credit and collection activities.

man and woman to rebut the presumption of agency, *even though these arrangements are not known to the suppliers*. Thus, the man may avoid liability on contracts made in his name if he can show that he forbade the woman to pledge his credit, or that he has provided her with a sufficient allowance to buy the articles without pledging his credit.

A man's liability on these grounds is narrow because of the defences available to him, and cohabitation is a perilous argument for merchants who would recover their claims at law. Agency by estoppel, if it can be proved, will add more substance to their claims: if a husband has honoured contracts made in the past by his wife, even for luxuries, he will have held her out as his agent to the particular merchants who supplied the goods and will be liable on further such contracts until he expressly notifies those suppliers. A man may always avoid liability to specific merchants by advising them directly not to supply further articles on his credit.

By Necessity

As a general rule, English law does not recognize agency by necessity. It is easy to think of circumstances where one person enters into a contract on behalf of another without authority and where the party receiving the benefit of the contract has a moral duty to ratify. But no system of law provides a complete compendium of moral sentiments. The law does not make the party benefited liable against his will. "Liabilities are not to be forced upon people behind their backs any more than you can confer a benefit upon a man against his will."[12] No agency by necessity is created when a man orders the repair of the roof of a neighbour's house though the neighbour is on holidays and in his absence the roof has been severely damaged by a gale. The party requesting the repair of the roof will be personally liable if, after the owner of the repaired property returns from his holidays, he refuses to pay for the work: the owner may have preferred another type of shingle, or the work done may have been more extensive or costly than he thought necessary.

The courts have recognized only a few exceptions to the general rule which denies the validity of agency by necessity. The owner of a barge salvaged at sea is bound to compensate the rescuer.[13] A carrier of goods usually has authority as an agent by necessity to dispose of them at a reasonable price if an emergency arises and the goods are perishable and he is unable to communicate with their owner for instruction.[14]

Agency by necessity is also established by the fact that a husband fails to provide for the maintenance of his wife and family. The legal fact of marriage, not cohabitation, creates the possibility of an agency by necessity. Accordingly, a wife may render her husband liable for necessaries by making contracts in his

---

[12] Falcke v. Scottish Imperial Insurance Co. (1886) 34 Ch. D. 234 per Bowen, L.J., at 248.
[13] The Five Steel Barges (1890) 15 P.D. 142 at 146.
[14] Couturier v. Hastie (1856) 10 E.R. 1065.

name when they are not living together and pending an order for maintenance from the court, provided the separation is not her fault. The goods purchased must be essential for the sustenance of the wife and family at a level suitable to the style of living maintained by the husband, and the husband will not be liable if the wife has adequate means of her own for the purpose — it must be necessary for her to make the purchases.

In those instances in which an agency by necessity can be established, it differs from an agency by ratification because the consent of the principal is not required to make him liable and to relieve the agent of liability. Though the principal may protest, he is liable. Even his express notice to the third party that he does not intend to pay will not avail.

THE DUTIES OF AN AGENT TO HIS PRINCIPAL

Obedience

As in so many other special types of contract, custom and trade usage have imported a series of rights and duties for both agent and principal as implied terms of the agency agreement. Any of these implied terms may, of course, be incorporated expressly in the agency agreement; or it may be excluded by an express term or even by the special circumstances surrounding the particular agency agreement. The breach of any term concerning duties, whether express or implied, gives the aggrieved party his usual remedies against the other for breach of contract. For example, an agent may have private instructions restricting his authority and in disobedience exceed that authority. While his principal will be bound by the resulting contract if the agent has acted within his apparent authority, the principal will be able to recover from the agent if a loss follows from his breach of duty.

When an agent acting within his apparent authority is guilty of fraudulent misrepresentation in making a contract for his principal, the third party may rescind the contract though the principal did not authorize the misrepresentation and may even have forbidden it. Furthermore, in these circumstances the third party may successfully sue the principal as well as his agent for the tort of deceit.[15] Thus the principal may suffer a loss because the contract will not be performed or because he must pay damages, or for both these reasons. If the principal was innocent of the fraud, he may in turn successfully sue his agent for damages to compensate him for his loss, but if he participated in the misrepresentation he is a co-conspirator and has no rights against his agent.

The law regards notice to an agent as being notice to his principal: what an agent knows his principal is deemed to know. The agent, therefore, has a duty to

---

[15] Lloyd v. Grace, Smith & Co. Ltd. [1912] A.C. 716. See Fridman, *The Law of Agency* (3rd ed.), pp. 240-2; Fleming, *The Law of Torts* (4th ed.), pp. 315-27. Sydney: Law Book Co. of Australasia, 1971.

keep his principal informed about all important developments affecting his service. Keeping in close touch with his principal will also give the agent the advantage of learning any new information that may have come to the principal and will assist him in carrying out his duties. For example, a principal may learn that certain creditors have a charge upon land that his agent is trying to purchase for him. If the agent were to complete the purchase without knowledge of the claim, the principal would suffer a loss that might have been avoided had his agent kept in touch with him.

Competence

An agent may promise to act for his principal without receiving payment for his services. Such a promise is a gratuitous promise from which the agent may withdraw before he performs. Nevertheless, if he does proceed to act on behalf of the principal, he is bound to use reasonable care, skill, and diligence.

Illustration:

> P purchases a piece of land by instalment payments and leaves the agreement for the purchase with his friend, A, who undertakes to make the payments while P is out of town. P also gives A the money needed to make the payments. A negligently pays the money to the wrong person. P may hold A liable for the loss. Since, however, there is no consideration for A's promise to perform the services, P must sue A in tort for negligence and not for breach of contract.

In other agency relationships in which the agent is to be paid for his services, the amount of skill which the principal can expect depends on the nature of the engagement and the known competence of the agent for the purpose. An agent ought not to agree to represent his principal in complicated and technical transactions for which he is not qualified, but he has a better chance of avoiding liability for the consequences if he can show that the principal was fully aware of his modest qualifications.

Personal Performance

The general rule is that an agent cannot delegate his duties because of the high degree of confidence and trust implicit in an agency relationship. An agent's usual terms of reference include the personal exercise of his judgment, skill, and discretion on his principal's behalf. For this reason, there are relatively few situations in which an agency agreement can properly be performed vicariously by a sub-agent. Moreover the agent who wrongfully delegates his responsibilities is guilty of a breach of duty to his principal.

There are circumstances, however, in which the nature of the agency relationship or trade usage will give the agent an implied authority to delegate all or part of his duties. Thus, if one engages a stockbroker to buy or sell shares for him, the broker will have implied authority to effect the actual purchase or sale through a sub-agent on the floor of the stock exchange. Again, when a bank acts as agent for its customers, it may sometimes require the services of other banks which represent it in countries where it has no branches itself. Indeed, whenever a limited company is appointed as an agent, it must perform through sub-agents, its employees. Finally, a principal may give his express consent to performance by a sub-agent, or he may subsequently ratify that type of performance.

In those instances in which the agent has implied authority to perform through a sub-agent, there is generally privity of contract only (a) between the principal and the agent, and (b) between the agent and the sub-agent: in other words, no privity of contract exists between the principal and the sub-agent. Accordingly, the principal may recover from his agent for the consequences of an improper performance by the sub-agent, but he has no claim in contract against the sub-agent himself.

We must next consider whether contracts made by a sub-agent will make the principal liable to the third party. The third party may enforce the contract against the principal if the sub-agent has express authority to act for him, or undertakes contracts which the principal subsequently ratifies, or acts in circumstances where the principal is estopped from denying his authority. Of course, the circumstances in which an estoppel will arise are more limited in view of the general rule against delegation discussed in the first paragraph of this section. If a sub-agent fails to bind his principal, the third party may sue the sub-agent for breach of warranty of authority.

Good Faith

The duty of good faith arises from the fact that parties are in a special relationship of trust, a *fiduciary* relationship, of which principal and agent is only one example. The law also imposes a duty of the same high degree of good faith and loyalty on members of a partnership and participants in joint business ventures,[16] as well as on members of professions in their relations with clients and patients.

An agent receives a fee or commission for his services. Any money which comes into his possession in respect of contracts made for his principal belongs to the principal. He must keep separate records so that he can account to the principal for this money. It is important that the money should be put in a separate bank account. If the agent becomes bankrupt, property in his possession belonging to his principal cannot then be confused with assets available for the claims of the agent's creditors.

A stockbroker is both an agent and a trustee for his client (his principal) when he holds money and securities for the client with authority to buy and sell stocks and bonds for his account. Any book profit the broker realizes from selling securities at a higher price than their cost, or any advantage he secures from buying stocks or bonds at an especially favourable price, accrues to his

---

[16] See Jirna Limited v. Mister Donut of Canada Ltd. [1970] 3 O.R. 629.

client. He must account to him for such profits: his remuneration is limited to a broker's fee.

Good faith requires that the agent place the interest of his principal above all else except the law. He should inform his principal of any information coming to his attention that might influence the principal's decisions. If he has been authorized to buy property at a certain price and learns that it can be obtained for a lesser sum, he is bound to impart that information to the principal. He cannot buy the property at the lower price and expect reimbursement at the price indicated by the principal. The duties of a patent attorney to his client also illustrate the rule. A patent attorney undertakes for a fee to make applications on behalf of an inventor for patent protection for his invention. If the patent attorney's work in this connection suggests to him further refinements or improvements in the invention, he has a recognized duty to give his client (the inventor) the benefit of his ideas: he must not try to exploit these ideas to his own advantage by an independent application for a patent in his own name.

An agent is not acting in good faith when he serves two principals in respect of the same transaction. The two principals in a business transaction will have conflicting interests, as each will want to get the best possible bargain for his own business. The most common breach of faith by agents consists in their accepting commissions also from third parties as well as from their principals. Such conduct is tantamount to taking bribes to secure something less than the best possible bargains for their principals.

In a section entitled Secret Commissions,[17] the Criminal Code (Canada) provides that an agent commits a criminal offence when he corruptly demands or accepts any remuneration from a third party in the conduct of his principal's business affairs. The third party who offers such a bribe or kickback is equally culpable. The section applies when the double agency proceeds "corruptly". We may assume that an agent can act legally for both parties if they are aware of the arrangement and have given their consent. Ordinary business prudence dictates, however, that a principal should have a separate agent of his own to represent him in business transactions.

In *Andrews v. Ramsay*,[18] a real estate agent had been engaged to assist in selling property on a commission basis. In addition, he accepted a commission from the purchaser. The court held that he was liable to his principal not only for the return of his regular selling commission but also for the commission he had received from the third party. Probably, had he chosen, the principal might also have avoided the resulting contract with the third party on grounds of fraud: the third party who offers a payment in these circumstances is as guilty as the agent and is a party to the fraud.

Occasionally a stockbroker may receive independently, from different clients, an offer to buy and an offer to sell the same shares. If he is a member of a recognized stock exchange, he will be subject to the rule that before he can match

---

[17] R.S.C. 1970, c. C-34, s. 383.
[18] [1903] 2 K.B. 635.

this sale, or any part of it, he must first make the offer to buy and the offer to sell available to all other members of the exchange. Only in the event that there is no response will he have the opportunity of selling one client's shares directly to the other. The rule was devised to prevent the manipulation of stock prices by contrived transactions, but it serves also to ensure that the broker will get the best available prices for his clients.

In *Salomons v. Pender,* [19] a real estate agent arranged a sale of land for the owner to a company in which the agent was a director and shareholder. The court held that he was not entitled to a commission because he had also an interest in the business of the other contracting party.

An agent's loyalty to his principal is also compromised when he makes himself the other party to the contract without prior notice to, and approval of, the principal. When he acts as the other contracting party and not as an agent, he places his own interest in conflict with that of his principal. He will be concerned to get the best of the bargain for himself and not for his principal. In *Robinson v. Mollett* [20] a client gave a broker an order to buy tallow for him. The broker already held some tallow on his own account, and he simply sent this tallow to his client. The court held that the client did not have to accept or pay for it. There was no evidence that the broker had obtained either the best tallow or the best price for his principal. Indeed, there is a presumption in these circumstances that the broker would obtain as much personal profit as he could. Again, in *McPherson v. Watt* [21] a solicitor was engaged to sell property and found that he would like to own it himself. He bought it ostensibly in the name of someone else. The court held that he could not enforce the purchase.

THE DUTIES OF THE PRINCIPAL TO HIS AGENT

Commission

The fee or commission which an agent is to receive for his services, and the method of determining it, comprise an important term in the agency agreement. If there is no express understanding about the agent's remuneration, he is entitled to a reasonable fee to be determined by reference to the fees of an agent who performs comparable services. A request by a principal for services of a kind for which an agent would normally expect to be paid implies a promise on his part to pay a reasonable fee, if none has been agreed upon expressly. These circumstances are simply another example of *quantum meruit*.

The terms on which a principal retains a *real estate agent* raise special

---

[19] (1865) 195 E.R. 682. It is, however, more precise to say that a director owes certain specific duties to the company than to say he is an agent of the company, as such. See Chapter 29, under "Duties of Directors". See also Farrar v. Farrars Ltd. (1889) 40 Ch. D. 395.

[20] (1874) L.R. 7 H.L. 802.

[21] (1877) 3 App. Cas. 254.

problems about his liability to pay a commission. Placing property for sale with a real estate agent is essentially an offer to pay a fee to the agent in return for a strictly defined service. The prospective seller's offer to pay a commission will only ripen into a contract when the agent does what he has been engaged to do. Many real estate agreements state that the agent is entitled to his commission when he introduces a prospective purchaser who is "ready, willing, and able to purchase" — the fact that the sale is not completed by reason of the seller's refusal to perform will not deprive the agent of this right.[22] The seller may, however, withdraw his offer at any time before a satisfactory purchaser is introduced, and he will not be liable to pay commission. He might even sell the property on his own, and he will not be liable to pay the real estate agent a commission unless the real estate agent was instrumental in introducing the purchaser to him. Real estate agents do, however, often urge their clients to sign an *exclusive listing agreement* which is to operate for a stated period of time. In such an agreement the client undertakes to pay a commission on any sale of his property during the period whether it is sold by him, the agent in question, or any other real estate agent. A client is not, of course, obliged to enter into such a contract, but if he does he will be bound by its terms.

Sometimes a prospective seller insists that the listing agreement contain a term that the agent is not entitled to his commission unless and until a sale is completed. Such a term governs the rights of the agent; he is not entitled to his commission even when he introduces a suitable purchaser whose offer the seller refuses.

Each of the provinces of Alberta, New Brunswick, Nova Scotia, Ontario and Saskatchewan has a statute rendering a contract to pay commission to a real estate agent unenforceable unless it is in writing and signed by the prospective seller of the property. In these provinces, when the agreement for the agent's services is in oral form only, the agent will not have acquired an enforceable right even though he may have introduced a willing and able purchaser to his client.[23]

Costs

If an agency agreement does not say so directly, there will in any event be an implied term in it that the principal will reimburse the agent for all reasonable outlays he makes within the scope of his real authority. The principal is under no obligation to reimburse the agent for unauthorized acts unless he ratifies them. An agent's ability to claim reimbursement in a court action may, as a practical matter, depend upon his having kept proper accounts and records to substantiate the claim.

---

[22] Columbia Caterers & Sherlock Co. v. Famous Restaurants Ltd. (1956) 4 D.L.R. (2d) 601.
[23] Real Estate and Business Brokers Act, R.S.O. 1970, c. 401, s. 34; Real Estate Agents' Licensing Act, R.S.A. 1970, c. 311, s. 22; Real Estate Brokers Act, St. of Sask., 1968, c. 58, s. 41; Statute of Frauds, R.S.N.B. 1973, c. S-14, s. 6; Real Estate Brokers' Licensing Act, R.S.N.S. 1967, c. 260, s. 17.

THE RIGHTS AND LIABILITIES OF THE THIRD PARTY

The Principal Alone Is Liable on the Contract

An agent will incur no liability on contracts he makes for his principal when the agency relationship is functioning as intended. Having brought the contract into being, the agent steps out of the picture: his principal will be liable for performance and will be the one able to enforce it against the third party. To ensure this result, the agent must describe himself to the third party as an agent and identify his principal. An agent will not have any liability to the third party even when he acts outside his real authority but within his apparent authority and has bound his principal; but he may, as we have seen, be liable to the principal for breach of the agency agreement.

To be sure that he has no liability in contracts made for his principal, an agent in acting for his principal should eliminate any doubt about his status or the identity of the principal.[24] The following are examples of signatures that will accomplish this purpose:

> "The Smith Company Limited
> per W.A. Jones"
> or
> "W.A. Jones
> for The Smith Company Limited."

The identification of his principal is a part of the process by which an agent can make it clear to the third party that he is acting only as agent. If an agent does not name his principal, it may be more difficult for him to prove that the third party regarded him as merely an agent: he adds to the risk that the third party may be entitled to look to him for the actual performance of the contract.

Conceivably, however, an agent can persuade a third party to enter into a contract with an unidentified principal. He may describe himself as agent for a party who does not wish for the time being to disclose his name. If the third party is prepared to contract on these terms, he is waiving his recourse against the agent and limiting it to someone whose identity he does not know. Sometimes, options for the purchase of individual pieces of property intended for land assembly into a large block — required for example for a plant site — are negotiated by an agent on such terms. The reasoning is that if the prospective purchaser is a very large company, the disclosure of its identity might induce owners to hold out for excessive prices.

Let us think for a moment of a contract requiring the payment of a sum of money by the principal to the third party. Let us assume further that the third party was well aware that the person who negotiated the contract with him was

---

[24] See Hills v. Swift Canadian Co. [1923] 3 D.L.R. 997, cited in Lawson v. Kenney (1957) 9 D.L.R. (2d) 714, by Danis, J., at 718.

acting as an agent only. The principal will not be freed of his liability to the third party merely by transferring the necessary money to his agent. The principal will remain liable to the third party until the third party actually receives the money:[25]

Illustration:

> *A* buys goods on credit from *T*, advising *T* that he is doing so as agent. *P* transfers the purchase money to *A*. *A* absconds. *P* still owes *T* the price of the goods.

If, however, the third party conducts himself in such a way as to lead the principal to think that his agent has already settled the obligation to the third party, that is, that the agent has already paid the third party on his principal's behalf, the principal might well be induced to recompense his agent. In these circumstances the third party will be estopped from claiming that he has not been paid, and the principal will have discharged his obligation by payment to his agent.

Illustration:

> *A*, acting as agent for *P*, purchases goods from *T* on credit. *T* mistakenly sends an invoice with the goods marked "Terms: cash." *A* then presents the invoice to *P* saying that he has already paid *T* for the goods, and *P* pays *A* an equivalent sum. *A* absconds. *T* will not succeed in an action for the price of the goods against *P*: his conduct in wording the invoice played an important role in inducing *P* to pay *A*.[26]

The Agent Alone is Liable on the Contract

When an agent categorically describes himself as a principal though he is in reality acting for an undisclosed principal, the agent alone will have rights and liabilities relative to the third party. The principal can neither sue nor be sued on the contract. If the agent describes himself (incorrectly) as the "owner" of a house or a ship, the third party will be entitled to regard the operation of the contract as confined to himself and the agent.[27] The agent must, however, do something more than merely fail to disclose the existence of a principal; he must also contract on terms that he himself is the real principal.

In some circumstances, when an agent makes a contract for his principal *under seal*, a special problem may arise: the agent alone may be able to enforce the contract against the third party or be sued by the third party; the principal has no rights or obligations under the contract.[28]

---

[25] Irvine & Co. v. Watson & Sons (1880) 5 Q.B.D. 414.

[26] Heald v. Kenworthy (1855) 24 L.J. Ex. 76; Fridman, *The Law of Agency*, pp. 146-7; Powell, *The Law of Agency* (2nd ed.), pp. 167-9.

[27] Humble v. Hunter (1848) 116 E.R. 885.

[28] Harmer v. Armstrong [1934] 1 Ch. 65; Margolius v. Kellner [1937] 2 D.L.R. 145. See Fridman, *The Law of Agency*, pp. 144-6.

Either the Principal or the Agent May Be Held Liable on the Contract

Sometimes a person who is in fact an agent makes no mention of his status, and deals with a third person without representing himself as either principal or agent. The third person very probably is influenced by the personal credit and character of the agent. What are his rights when he discovers the existence and identity of the principal? He will have the option of holding either principal or agent liable for performance of the contract. If he elects to take action against either one, he cannot afterwards sue the other. If he has already obtained judgment against the agent when he learns of the real principal, he has no recourse against the principal. If, however, the fact of agency emerges in the course of litigation, the action may be discontinued and fresh proceedings taken against the principal.

Once the third party elects to sue the principal, the principal may treat the contract as being made with him and has all of the defences of a contracting party.

Illustration:

> *A* buys goods on credit from *T* without disclosing that he is acting for *P*. Upon default in payment *T* learns that *A* was in fact *P*'s agent, and sues *P* for the price. *P* is entitled to counterclaim if the goods are not according to the contract or if *T* has been guilty of breach of any other term in the contract of sale.

Alternatively, the third party may choose to hold the agent liable on the contract even when he learns of the existence and identity of a principal. To escape liability to the third party, the agent should therefore be sure the third party understands from the outset that he is acting *as agent*. Merely writing the word "broker" after his signature may be insufficient: a signature like "Wm. A. Jones, broker" does not necessarily imply the existence of a principal, because brokers (so called) sometimes deal as principals on their own account. Similarly, a signature followed by the word "agent" may be taken as a form of advertising rather than as an intimation of an agent's status for the contract in question.

An undisclosed principal has contractual rights as well as liabilities: he may intervene and enforce the contract against the third party. To succeed, however, he must show that the contract was made with his authority; as we have seen, an undisclosed principal cannot ratify an unauthorized contract. Further, when the principal attempts to exercise his rights, the third party is entitled to deduct from his obligation any amount owing to him personally by the agent (that is, to exercise a right of set-off).[29]

Illustration:

> *A* sells goods on credit to *T* without disclosing that he is doing so on behalf of a principal, *P*. The contract price for the goods is $500. At the time of the

---

[29] Isberg v. Bowden (1853) 155 E.R. 1599.

sale *A* owes *T* $325 in respect of an entirely separate transaction. In due course *T* receives a statement of account from *P* requesting payment of the $500 to *P*. Until this time *T* supposed that he had been dealing with *A* as principal. *T* is entitled to his set-off against *A* and need remit only $175 to *P*. (If *A* had made it clear to *T* that he was acting as agent, *T* would have had to pay *P* the full $500.)

The Agent Is Liable for Fraud or for Breach of Warranty of Authority

There can be no contract when a person holds himself out to be an agent but has no authority and the named principal does not ratify.

The situation may arise because of fraud on the part of the alleged agent. One may give the name of a reputable person as his principal for the purpose of obtaining goods on credit — circumstances in which the seller would do well to ask the agent to produce his credentials. The unfortunate seller may not be able to recover his goods if the false agent has absconded with them. The seller will have an action in tort for deceit against the fraudulent agent, but for him to realize it the culprit must be apprehended and have personal resources available to satisfy the court judgment.

Another way in which an agent may act without any real authority arises when, unknown to the agent, his principal is dead or insane or bankrupt. No contract between a third party and the principal can be formed after the principal has ceased to exist or has lost his contractual capacity. And no contract is formed between the agent and the third party either, because the agent will have acted *as agent*. The recourse of the third party lies not on the ineffectual contract, but in an action against the agent for *breach of warranty of authority*. It will not matter that the agent is unaware of the demise or misfortune of his principal at the time he acts for him. It is incumbent on the agent to communicate with his principal frequently enough to be assured of his continued well-being.

Jurists have not always agreed on whether breach of warranty of authority is a tort or a wrong to be redressed within the law of contract. If the remedy is contractual, it is not related to the abortive contract between the third party and the principal: it is a breach of a separate *implied* contract between the agent and the third party consisting of a single implied promise by the agent that he has authority to act.

We have seen that an agent may be liable if he acts in anticipation of ratification which he never receives, or if as a promoter he contracts on behalf of a company as yet unincorporated. These are two further instances of breach of warranty of authority.

We must be careful to distinguish breach of warranty of authority from breach of the agency agreement. *Breach of warranty of authority* is a wrong for which a third party may sue an agent. *Breach of the agency agreement* is a wrong for which a principal may sue his agent, or the agent sue the principal, as the case may be.

An agent may be liable to a third party for negligent misrepresentation as well as fraudulent misrepresentation and breach of warranty of authority. The Canadian courts have held that a real estate agent, though engaged and paid by the vendor, also owes a duty of care in statements he makes to the purchaser.[30]

THE END OF AN AGENCY RELATIONSHIP

Frequently an agent performs services for his principal, or at least keeps his time available to act as agent and is to that extent unavailable for employment. In this respect, he is akin to an employee. Courts are increasingly willing to infer that a principal-agent relationship contains elements of an employer-employee relationship as well. When such an inference is drawn each party will be entitled to reasonable notice before termination becomes effective,[31] as discussed in the next chapter.

In the absence of evidence of an employment relationship, an agent's authority may be terminated on any of the following occasions:

(1) at the end of a time specified in the agency agreement;
(2) at the completion of the particular project for which the agency was formed;
(3) upon notice by either the principal or the agent to the other that he wishes to end the agency;
(4) upon the death or insanity of either the principal or the agent;
(5) upon the bankruptcy of the principal;
(6) upon an event which makes performance of the agency agreement impossible.

Where no specific duration is fixed for the agency relationship, it is an implied term of the agency agreement that either party may bring the relationship to an end by notice to the other. In other words, an option clause is implied which, when availed of, will discharge the contract by agreement and without breach. If, however, the agreement specifies a period of time, a premature withdrawal by either principal or agent without the consent of the other constitutes a breach of contract.

Occasionally, an agency agreement may be discharged by frustration. An example of an agency that becomes impossible to perform occurs when the owner of goods has engaged an auctioneer to sell them for him and the goods are destroyed by fire, while still in the agent's possession pending their sale.

When an agency is terminated for any reason other than the death, insanity, or bankruptcy of the principal, the principal may be bound by his former agent's continuing to act within his apparent authority. In his own interest, the principal ought to bring the termination to the attention of all third parties likely to be affected.

---

[30] See Avery et al. v. Salie et al. (1972) 25 D.L.R. (3d) 495.
[31] See Martin-Baker Aircraft Co. v. Canadian Flight Equipment [1955] 2 Q.B. 556.

QUESTIONS FOR REVIEW

1. Give examples of common business relationships to which the law of principal and agent applies.
2. In what four ways can an agency relationship be established?
3. Does an express agreement for agency have to be in writing? In what circumstances is the *form* of the agency agreement important?
4. How does the need for ratification arise?
5. In what circumstances may a principal be unable to ratify a contract made earlier for him?
6. What is the meaning of the rule of *estoppel*? Whose interest is protected by the legal recognition of agency by estoppel?
7. What is the test for determining whether a third party can enforce against a principal a contract made by an agent who has exceeded his real authority?
8. When a principal acquiesces in a series of misrepresentations by his agent and has then to pay damages to the third party for the tort of deceit, may the principal recoup his loss by suing his agent? Explain.
9. A merchant sues a man for a debt contracted in the man's name by a woman with whom he has been living. If the merchant sues on grounds of cohabitation, the man has some defences not available to him if the merchant had instead been able to allege agency by estoppel. What are those defences?
10. When an agency by necessity has been established, need the third party prove the consent of the principal in order to succeed? In what situations does the law recognize the possibility of an agency by necessity?
11. In what way may an agent disobey his principal so that the principal will suffer a loss? What is the nature of the principal's remedy against the agent?
12. Is vicarious performance generally permissible in agency agreements?
13. In what ways may an agent act in bad faith?
14. In what respect does the authority usually given to a real estate agent differ from the authority given to most other types of agent?
15. Is it possible for an agent to avoid liability to the third party even when he has not identified his principal?
16. The right of the undisclosed principal to intervene and enforce the contract against the third party is in apparent conflict with a general principle of law which we have considered in an earlier chapter. What is this principle?
17. What requirement must be satisfied before the undisclosed principal can sue the third party?
18. How may an agent become liable to a third party for not having kept in touch with his principal?
19. What is the difference between breach of warranty of authority and breach of the agency agreement?
20. In what respect may a consignee act within his apparent authority but beyond his real authority?

CASES FOR DISCUSSION

CASE 1

Roberts, a real estate agent acting for Smith in the sale of a house, knowingly made a false representation to a prospective purchaser, Young, that a second kitchen in the house had been installed in conformity with city regulations. In fact, Smith had received a letter from the city building inspector stating that no building or plumbing permit had been obtained for the installation of the second kitchen, and that the installation constituted a violation of a city zoning by-law because the building was situated in a one-family-dwelling district; the letter further advised Smith that all stoves and sinks must be removed within 30 days. Smith had given a copy of this letter to Roberts and in no way authorized the false representation which Roberts subsequently made to Young. The sale to Young was completed, and when Young later learned the facts concerning the kitchen he refused to proceed with the contract. Smith brought an action against Young for specific performance, claiming that he had not authorized the false assertion made by Roberts. Young counterclaimed for a rescission of the contract and damages for deceit. Who should succeed and why? (See *Toll v. Rogers and Richey* (1959) 29 W.W.R. 84 (B.C.); *Lash and Moneta Builders v. Miller* (1956) 5 D.L.R. (2d) 469.)

CASE 2

On July 2, two salesman for the Bright Lighting Company secured a written order from Watts for a generator and appliances suitable for his farmhouse. A few hours later when Watts was working in the fields, the salesmen drove past, and Watts called to them. One came to the fence, and Watts told him: "I've been thinking about the generator. You'll have to countermand that order. I can't afford it. We have to shingle the barn and other things, and we can't meet it."

The salesman then told Watts that they were just returning from the village where they had mailed Watt's written order to the offices of the Bright Lighting Company, and insisted that it was now too late for Watts to do anything about it. Watts replied that he did not care what they said; as far as he was concerned, "The deal is off."

On July 10, the copy of Watts' purchase order was stamped "O.K. for shipment" in the offices of the Bright Lighting Company, and on July 12 Bright Lighting Company wrote to Watts acknowledging receipt of his order. The lighting equipment was shipped to Watts on July 30, and refused by him. It was afterwards sold by the railroad company for storage.

Bright Lighting Company then sued Watts on the contract they claimed to have with him. Discuss the main arguments that could be made by each side and the probable result.

CASE 3

A young people's group at a Toronto church decided to include a sleighing party in their winter program of social activities. The secretary consulted the yellow pages of the telephone directory and under "Sleigh Rides" found an advertisement for Kelly's Pavilion on the outskirts of the city. He then made the necessary arrangements with a booking office in the city, as designated in the advertisement. These arrangements included payment of a ten-dollar deposit at the booking office, the balance to be paid at the time of the party.

On the evening of the sleigh ride the group turned up at Kelly's Pavilion but could not locate anyone on the premises. After some searching they found a barn on adjacent property and encountered Dinsmore, the person who was to conduct the sleigh ride. Each member of the group paid his fee to Dinsmore, who then backed out a two-ton Chevrolet truck and fastened the sleigh to it. The surface was very slippery, and several of the male members of the party had to push to get the truck going. Once the truck was moving, the driver was reluctant to have it stuck again, and he took the party around the field at about 15 to 20 miles per hour. As the sleigh went around a turn at high speed one of the group, Miss Lambert, fell off, and the runner went over her foot. She had to receive medical attention and lost wages as a result of being unable to go to work for some weeks.

Miss Lambert brought an action against Kelly's Pavilion for damages for breach of the implied contractual term to carry her safely. In defence, the owner of Kelly's Pavilion claimed that Dinsmore was not his employee; that the property from which Dinsmore operated had formerly been used by the Pavilion but had since been leased by it to Dinsmore; and that Kelly's Pavilion continued to operate as booking agent for his sleighing parties only as a convenience. The booking office applied the deposits it received for sleigh rides against the rent due from Dinsmore.

Should this action succeed? (See *Lawson v. Kenney* (1957) 9 D.L.R. (2d) 714.)

CASE 4

In February the Wholesome Doughnut Co. offered to buy from Superior Egg Products Ltd. 50,000 pounds of Grade-A, spray-powdered egg yolk at 90¢ a pound to be delivered in July following. Superior Egg Products Ltd. replied as follows on an acknowledgment stub attached to the purchase-order form received from Wholesome Doughnut Co.:

Gentlemen:

We have received the above order and will ship according to your instructions on or about July 15.

> Superior Egg Products Ltd.
> per Francis Bacon [signed]
> Sales Manager.

Soon after, eggs became in very short supply, and Superior Egg Products Ltd. approached Wholesome Doughnut Co. to cancel the contract before it had delivered any of the spray-powdered egg yolk. Wholesome Doughnut Co. refused to accede to this request, claiming that it was relying upon the supply of egg yolk for the manufacture of doughnuts in performance of its contracts with its own customers. Superior Egg Products Ltd. then claimed that the contract was not binding. It alleged that the contract had been made for it by an employee who had failed to obtain the required approval of its senior officers before accepting and that the contract contained an implied condition that Superior Egg Products Ltd. would be able to obtain sufficient eggs at the usual price for the purpose of performing it. In April the Wholesome Doughnut Co. purchased the egg yolk it required from another source at $1.10 a pound, and at once brought an action against Superior Egg Products Ltd. for damages for breach of contract.

Should it succeed? (For a similar case, see *Canadian Egg Products Ltd. v. Canadian Doughnut Co.* [1954] 2 D.L.R. 77, and [1955] 3 D.L.R. 1.)

CASE 5

On January 10, Abbott signed an exclusive listing agreement with York Realty Ltd., real estate agents, for the sale of his residence in Toronto. The agreement gave exclusive authority to York Realty Ltd. until the following July 10 to sell the property at a price of $87,000. It read in part:

1. If an offer to purchase the said property is obtained from a purchaser in accordance with the price and terms of payment thereof, herein set out, I hereby agree to pay you a commission of 6% of the price set out in such offer whether or not I accept such offer.
2. If any sale is effected during the currency of this authority from any source whatsoever and at any price, I agree to pay you the above commission on the price agreed upon in such sale.
3. All inquiries from any source whatsoever shall be referred to you and all offers submitted to me shall be brought to your attention before accepting or rejecting same.

York Realty Ltd. made efforts to sell the property but had not succeeded when Abbott received a notice of expropriation of the property by the Municipality of Metropolitan Toronto pursuant to By-Law No. 5905, passed May 3. The purpose of the expropriation was to acquire land necessary for construction of a new expressway. A price of $80,000 was determined by arbitration, and Abbott then delivered to the Municipality the deed to the property, as required by the law.

York Realty Ltd. claimed commission of $4,800 (6% of $80,000) and when Abbott refused to pay, sued him. Discuss the defence or defences available to Abbott, and state whether you think the action should succeed.

CASE 6

The firm of Howard & Scott, engineers, was retained by Hopeful Gold Mines Ltd. as its mining and engineering consultant. For a monthly fee of $500 plus any related travelling expenses, Hopeful Gold Mines Ltd. was entitled to three days per month of the services of either Howard or Scott, on request. These services were to take the form of a professional opinion on the quality of ore samples submitted to Howard & Scott from time to time, and on the engineering feasibility of economically extracting ore from any particular property designated by Hopeful Gold Mines Ltd. Howard & Scott had, in all, about twenty-five clients for whom they would do varying amounts of consulting work during the course of a month. Scott was also a director of Hopeful Gold Mines Ltd.

Two months after this agreement was made, Howard was informed by a prospector, Watkins, of the latter's discovery of some mining claims, and after assaying samples of ore from these claims the firm of Howard & Scott concluded that the claims merited further investigation. Howard arranged to make a trip into the area. Before leaving, he phoned the president of Hopeful Gold Mines Ltd. and informed him that he would be going into the area in question "for other clients" and would "if possible, try and get some claims staked in the same approximate area" for Hopeful Gold Mines Ltd. The president of Hopeful Gold Mines Ltd. agreed, and authorized Howard to undertake the necessary investigation of the area on behalf of Hopeful Gold Mines Ltd.

No claims were staked for Hopeful Gold Mines as a result of this trip, but Howard & Scott did proceed on their own to incorporate a new company, Yellow Gold Mines Ltd., to purchase from Watkins his rights in the claims he had discovered and exploit the property. In addition to the usual monthly bill for $500 retainer, Howard charged Hopeful Gold Mines Ltd. with one-half his travelling expenses on the trip.

When these facts came to light, Hopeful Gold Mines Ltd. brought an action for damages against Howard and Scott. Evidence was adduced to show that Howard had not in fact been retained by "other clients" for the purpose of making the trip in question. State whether such an action would succeed. (See *Tombill Gold Mines Ltd. v. Hamilton et al.* [1955] 5 D.L.R. 708.)

CASE 7

In late 1974, Jickles entered into a franchising agreement with Snacks Unlimited, Ltd., to operate three shops in Winnipeg. Under the contract, each shop was to make and sell milk-shakes, hot dogs and hamburgers, the ingredients to be of a specified high quality and the products made to uniform standards. The premises were also to be equipped and maintained according to a prescribed format and the shops would have the decor and distinctive sign of "Snacks Unlimited". The concept anticipated large sales to the public since persons entering any of the stores would already be acquainted with the merits of the products by the national and local advertising programs of Snacks Unlimited, and familiar with other franchised stores operating in exactly the same manner.

It was a part of the franchising agreement that Jickles buy his store equipment from Snacks Unlimited, on which both parties understood there was to be a profit for the latter; that Jickles would take a sub-lease from Snacks Unlimited for the three shops, on which a mark-up on the rent would accrue to Snacks Unlimited; that Jickles would deposit in advance the sum of $40,000 interest-free as prepaid rent; that Jickles would pay a franchise fee of 2% on gross sales, of which 1% would be allocated to advertising by Snacks Unlimited; and that wherever possible Jickles would buy his supplies from sources indicated by Snacks Unlimited. Jickles was persuaded by representations made to him that these terms were a reasonable price to pay for the lower costs of his supplies owing to the mass purchasing power of the franchising organization.

As was typical with such contracts, every aspect of the relationship was to be developed by the franchisor, Snacks Unlimited, which would find the real estate, negotiate the lease, arrange the purchase of equipment, select the personnel, arrange the advertising and supervise the operation. Snacks Unlimited undertook not to enfranchise any other shop within two miles in any direction from any of Jickles' shops. Jickles was supplied with a *Confidential Manual of Operating Procedure* which specified the standards of cleanliness, lighting, maintenance, repairs, employee uniforms and demeanour required in each shop. The agreement concluded with the words, ''The relationship between the parties is only that of independent contractors. No partnership, joint venture or relationship of principal and agent is intended.''

Jickles operated his three shops successfully during 1975, showing a net profit of $35,000 on gross sales of $500,000. In the fall of 1975 Jickles was made aware, quite by accident, that the companies from whom he was required to purchase his supplies were paying a rebate of between 5% and 20% to Snacks Unlimited, Ltd. On the question of whether he was thereby obliged to pay a price higher than the prevailing market price for comparable supplies, it was difficult to generalize: for some materials this was true; for others he paid much the same price and in some instances even a somewhat lower price. In any event, Snacks Unlimited, Ltd. had instructed all the suppliers to have no dealings or negotiations with its franchisees which might indicate the true nature of the arrangements made with them for rebates.

Jickles brought an action against Snacks Unlimited, Ltd. for an accounting of these undisclosed profits and rebates and an order requiring them to be paid over to him.

Discuss the merits of Jickles' case and indicate with reasons whether his action should succeed.

CHAPTER 21

The Contract of Employment

DEVELOPMENT OF THE LAW GOVERNING EMPLOYMENT

Before the middle of the 19th century, the law relating to employment was almost entirely represented by a body of common law rules defining *the relationship of master and servant*. This law developed in an early business environment where the employer (master) always had a separate contract with each of his employees (servants); welfare legislation and trade unions were unknown. The individual contract of employment is still commonplace today, and the law of master and servant continues to have an important application. Nevertheless, the economic and social changes of the last hundred or more years have qualified the common law in two significant respects. First, statutes have been passed to prescribe minimum standards of working conditions; we shall refer to this branch of the law as *employee welfare legislation*. Secondly, the emergence of trade unions has produced the phenomenon of the collective agreement and a whole separate body of law, which we may call *the law of collective bargaining*, to govern the relationship between employers and trade unions. In this chapter, therefore, we shall discuss the master-servant relationship at common law, employee welfare legislation, and collective bargaining, in that sequence.

Before beginning, a note of caution is in order. In our treatment of welfare legislation and collective bargaining we cannot cite all the relevant statutes in the space available, and in any event it might even be dangerous to do so: this part of the law frequently changes and statutes may soon become obsolete. The purpose of the chapter is simply to acquaint the reader with the general approach of the law in another main area of business administration. The chapter cannot be regarded as a reference to aid in solving specific labour problems; for this purpose the reader should consult the works that have been specially prepared in this field, and which we shall cite from time to time in footnotes.

RELATIONSHIP OF MASTER AND SERVANT

Compared with Agency

The relation of master and servant, or, in modern terms, that of employer and employee, is established by a contract that gives one party (the employer) authority to direct and control the work of the other party (the employee). Thus, an employee is one who holds himself available to his employer during his hours of employment to perform services for which he is hired. These services may or may not include making contracts with third parties as agent for his employer.

The distinction between agent and employee, then, is one of function. The same person is often both an employee and an agent. In some instances, the terms of employment may be such that an employee's chief duty is to make contracts with third parties on behalf of his employer: a purchasing agent for a company has a duty to order goods on the credit of his company and authority to do so within the limits of his agency. He is nonetheless also a company employee and subject to the direction of its senior officers. Other employees have very limited duties as agents of their employer. For example, the driver of a delivery truck is an employee who may act as an agent when he takes his truck into a garage for servicing, thereby binding his employer to pay the charges. In many types of employment, an employee has no occasion to enter into contracts on behalf of his employer and no authority, express or implied, to do so — a stenographer or lathe operator, for instance.

On the other hand, the functions of agency and employment may be completely separate: an agent may not be an employee at all. Thus, a person may be a commission agent, that is, one who receives a commission on the sale price of the goods that he sells for his principal to third persons. He may be under no duty to sell these goods, nor bound to keep himself available for his principal, but may simply receive remuneration in the form of commissions for whatever contracts he makes on behalf of his principal.

The difference between an agent and an employee, when these two functions are entirely separate, may be important upon the termination of the relationship. We have seen in the last chapter that when an agency agreement is of indefinite duration, an agent may have no recourse against a principal who terminates it without notice. An employee, as we shall see, often has a right of action for damages for wrongful dismissal in similar circumstances.

We have noted that a principal may be liable for the torts of his agent in a rather restricted area. The liability of an employer for the torts of his employee is much wider. Accordingly, it may be important for an injured third party to establish that the wrongdoer who caused him harm was acting as an employee of a company, rather than as its agent.

Compared with an Independent Contractor

An independent contractor undertakes to do a specified piece of work such as building a house. The contract between the parties does not create an employer-employee relationship because the contractor is not subject to the supervision of the person engaging him. His job is to produce a specified result, and the means he employs are his own affair.

It is not always easy to distinguish between an independent contractor and an employee. Occasionally the two functions are combined in a single person: the owner of a building may hire a building contractor to do certain repairs for a fixed price, but the agreement may also stipulate that the repairs are to be made under the supervision of the owner. Such circumstances may make it difficult to decide whether the person doing the work is primarily an independent contractor or an employee.

When a person who undertakes work is clearly an independent contractor, liabilities incurred by him in the course of accomplishing his task are almost entirely his own.

Illustration:

> Parkinson engages Imperial Contractors to erect an administration building on a downtown lot. In the course of the construction work, Miss Chance, a passerby on the sidewalk far below, is injured by a falling brick. The accident is attributable to the inadequate protection for pedestrians provided by Imperial Contractors. Imperial Contractors and not Parkinson would generally be liable for the injury so caused.
>
> On the other hand, Parkinson does have the limited duty to take reasonable care to hire a competent contractor; also, if the nature of the work undertaken is such that the possibility of damage to adjoining property is apparent — for example, blasting with dynamite[1] — or if the work is inherently dangerous to third parties, Parkinson has an obligation to satisfy himself that the contractor takes reasonable precautions to avoid such damage.

As we shall see in Chapter 31, the person engaging a building contractor may have to follow certain procedures in paying the contractor in order to avoid having his land and buildings become subject to suppliers' and wage-earners' liens. Apart from this complication, a person engaging an independent contractor is not generally responsible for the contractor's obligations.

The Relationship at Common Law

In defining the relationship of master and servant, the courts have developed rules about the employer's liability to third persons, the required notice to terminate the relationship, grounds for dismissal, and assessment of damages for

---

[1] Aikman v. Mills & Co. [1934] 4 D.L.R. 264.

wrongful dismissal. These rules are part of the common law as it continues to apply to individual employment contracts, and we shall now deal with them in turn.

THE EMPLOYER'S LIABILITY

Liability in Contract

A promisor remains liable to perform his obligations under a contract, and is relieved of liability only by mutual agreement or legal frustration of the contract. As we noted in Chapter 13, this liability remains even when the parties contemplate that the promisor will not perform personally, but that someone else, either an employee or an independent contractor, will perform on his behalf. Thus, when a construction company undertakes to erect a building, it remains liable for the proper performance of the contract according to the specifications, although it hires a subcontractor to put up the structural steel and this subcontractor does defective work. So too will it be liable for breach of contract should its own employee do improper work.

Liability in Tort

In our discussion of vicarious liability in Chapter 4, we noted that an employer is liable for a tort his employee committed in the course of employment. An employer need not have authorized the wrongful act: he is liable even though he has forbidden the particular act. All the injured party need establish is that the employee caused the damage while engaged in his employer's work. If, however, the harm results while the employee is not engaged in his employer's work, as when he takes time off from his duties to attend to some personal matter, the employer is not liable: the employee alone is liable. Nor is the employer liable if the employee delegates the work to someone else without the employer's consent.

Illustration:

(a) Hotspur is employed by Henry's Dairy to drive a milk truck. While proceeding on his appointed rounds, he negligently collides with another vehicle. He has committed a tort in the course of his employment; the owner of the damaged car may sue both Henry's Dairy and Hotspur.

(b) Hotspur injures a pedestrian as a result of negligent driving while taking his family to the theatre in the milk truck after hours, and without permission or knowledge of his employer. In the words of a Nova Scotia judgment in a similar case, Hotspur has "departed from the course of his employment and . . . embarked upon an independent enterprise — 'a frolic of his own' — for purposes wholly unconnected with his master's business."[2] He alone is liable: Henry's Dairy is not.

---

[2] Hall v. Halifax Transfer Co. Ltd. (1959) 18 D.L.R. (2d) 115, per MacDonald, J., at 120.

(c) While delivering milk, Hotspur becomes embroiled in an argument with a customer about the quality of the milk and assaults the customer. Is Henry's Dairy vicariously liable to the customer for the assault?

Of the three illustrations, this last is the most difficult to resolve. As one judge put it, "Before the employer can be held liable the blow complained of must be closely connected with a duty being carried out in the authorized course of employment and not delivered at a time when the servant has divested himself of his character as a servant."[3] We must ask whether the unauthorized and wrongful act of the employee is "so connected with the authorized act as to be a mode of doing it" or whether it is "an independent act."[4]

If engaging in conversations about his employer's product is an authorized incident of Hotspur's employment so as to be a mode of doing it, his employer is also liable for the assault; but if his conversation is an independent act, Hotspur alone is liable. The court will therefore entertain evidence of trade practice in this matter before reaching its decision.

We may note that when an employer has been held liable for the negligence of his employee, the employer has a right to be indemnified by his employee;[5] he may, if he deems it worth his while, sue the employee.

One must not confuse the vicarious liability of an employer with the liability of a principal on contracts made for him by his agent, as discussed in the previous chapter. Vicarious liability relates to the tortious conduct of an employee acting within his duties under an employment contract: the liability of a principal relates to a different kind of conduct, namely the agent's act of entering into contracts for the principal. The doctrine of vicarious liability means that *both* the employer and employee are liable for the tort: the law of agency relieves the agent of any liability and makes the principal solely liable, assuming the agent has acted within his authority.

NOTICE OF TERMINATION OF INDIVIDUAL EMPLOYMENT CONTRACTS

When an employee has been hired for a stated period of time and that time has elapsed, no notice is necessary on the part of either employer or employee. Neither party has any right to expect anything more than the cessation of employment at the end of the specified time: each has been, as it were, on notice ever since the employment contract was formed.[6]

---

[3] Wenz v. Royal Trust Co. [1953] O.W.N. 798, per Aylen, J., at 800.
[4] Salmond, *The Law of Torts* (16th ed.), p. 474, Heuston, ed. London: Sweet & Maxwell Limited, 1973.
[5] Finnegan v. Riley [1939] 4 D.L.R. 434.
[6] See, for example, Employment Standards Act, R.S.O. 1970, c. 147, s. 13(3)(a).

Employers and employees often make no agreement about when the employment relationship is to end, and do not expressly stipulate what length of notice is required to terminate employment. They may intend the hiring to be by the week, the month, or some other length of time, renewable for successive periods and possibly lasting for many years; or as often happens, they may simply regard the employment as a general or indefinite hiring.

In the absence of an express term about notice in a contract of employment, the common law implies a term that reasonable notice shall be given. Sometimes a court can determine the length of reasonable notice from evidence of an established customary practice followed by the particular employer for the type of employee in question. In other circumstances, the court must ask what type of hiring the parties intended when they made the employment contract. Reasonable notice for a weekly hiring is one clear work week, and for a monthly hiring, one clear work month.[7] If the hiring is a general or indefinite hiring, reasonable notice depends on all the circumstances of the employment, but usually varies between three and six months; it may be as long as one year.[8] In most provinces and at the federal level as well, the length of required notice is specifically set down by statute.[9] These statutory provisions are minimum requirements only: customary provisions in a particular trade or express contractual terms may require longer periods of notice.

When no other evidence about the intention of the parties is available, the court may infer a weekly or a monthly hiring from the mere fact that the employee receives his pay by the week or the month. A court is, however, perfectly free to find other considerations that outweigh any inferences one might draw from the length of the pay period. The court may, for example, rule that a hiring is indefinite even though the employee is paid by the week. As stated in *Lazarowicz v. Orenda Engines Ltd.*:

> Upon all the circumstances of this case I have come to the conclusion that the plaintiff, despite the fact that his wages were stated to be a weekly sum only, was employed upon a general or indefinite hiring only, and for these reasons: Firstly, the plaintiff was a graduate engineer. . . . At the time he was employed by the defendant corporation [he] had been employed . . . at a monthly salary of $450. He was secure in that position and there seems little reason to conclude that he would have left that position to accept one with the defendant company if he were to be merely a weekly servant. A more important circumstance is the actual work performed by the plaintiff.

---

[7] The notice required to terminate a weekly or monthly hiring is similar to the notice required to terminate a weekly or monthly tenancy. For a fuller explanation see Chapter 24 under "Termination and Renewal of a Tenancy".

[8] See Bardal v. The Globe and Mail Ltd. (1960) 24 D.L.R. (2d) 140; Duncan v. Cockshutt Farm Equipment Ltd. (1956) 19 W.W.R. 554; Campbell v. Business Fleets Ltd. [1954] 2 D.L.R. 263.

[9] See, for example: Employment Standards Act, R.S.O. 1970, c. 147, s. 13; Labour Standards Act, 1969, St. of Sask. 1969, c. 24, ss. 24-5; R.S.N.S. 1967, c. 186, s. 14.

. . . The evidence . . . shows that he was in a position of some considerable importance, requiring a great deal of mechanical and technical experience.[10]

An employer is not in breach of the employment contract if in dismissing the employee without notice he tenders an additional amount of pay for a period equal to the length of time required for reasonable notice. In the *Lazarowicz* case, the court held that reasonable notice in the circumstances was three months; and since the employee had been given only one week's salary in lieu of notice, it held that the employee was additionally entitled to the balance of three months' salary.

When an employee proposes to leave of his own accord, he has a contractual obligation to give his employer the same amount of notice as he would be entitled to receive himself. If he does not do so the employer may, if he thinks it worth while, sue the employee for damages equal to the loss caused by this breach of contract.

An employee is justified in leaving without giving the usual notice if he can show that he was obliged to work under dangerous conditions that the employer refused to correct. Here the employer has broken the contract, freeing the employee from his obligations, for it is an implied term in the contract that the employer will maintain a safe place to work. Again, an employee has grounds for leaving immediately if he is ordered to do an illegal act.

GROUNDS FOR DISMISSAL WITHOUT NOTICE

The Contractual Basis

The requirement of notice does not apply to an employer if he can show that he has dismissed the employee *for cause*. Dismissal for cause is a concept that derives from the general law of contract; when an employee's conduct amounts to a breach of his contract of employment, his employer may be entitled to consider himself discharged from any further obligations and to terminate the contract at once. Of course, in contract law generally, not every petty breach would have this result.[11] However, in view of the frequently unequal bargaining power between an employer and an individual employee, there is a danger that an employer can impose his idea of what an important breach is. In response to this problem, the common law has tended to classify the kinds of breach that are grounds for dismissal without notice, and the collective bargaining process has developed the idea further. In some jurisdictions, employees have gained additional protection by statute.[12]

---

[10] (1960) 22 D.L.R. (2d) 568, per Robertson, C.J.O., at 573. (Affirmed on appeal: (1962) 26 D.L.R. (2d) 433.)

[11] See Chapter 15, "Implications of Breach".

[12] See, for example, Employment Standards Act, R.S.O. 1970, c. 147, s. 13(3)(c).

Misconduct

In the times of Henry VIII and Elizabeth I the law treated any violence by a servant against the person of his master as a minor form of treason, and visited the employee with the grisly methods of execution reserved for that most heinous of offences.[13] Even wishful thinking by an employee was hazardous while witchcraft remained an offence. This attitude of the law, demanding of employees the utmost in subjection and loyalty, has lingered long: until comparatively recent times, a strike was regarded as a form of conspiracy.

Today, misconduct against an employer, while it may be grounds for a dismissal, is not a crime in itself. An employee guilty of grossly immoral conduct such as might bring his employer's business into public disrepute, disturb the morale of other employees, or cause the employer direct financial loss, may be summarily dismissed by the indignant employer. Conviction for a crime, especially when it involves moral turpitude such as stealing or embezzlement, is also grounds for summary dismissal.

An employer is entitled to repose confidence in his employee, and, depending upon the nature of the employment, evidence of a lack of integrity is often grounds for instant dismissal. An employee's deception need cause no pecuniary loss to his employer: it is enough that the employer can no longer trust him.

Disobedience

Wilful disobedience of a reasonable and lawful order from an employer is always grounds for immediate dismissal without notice. The offence is broad enough to include situations where the employee does not directly disobey but acts in a manner inconsistent with the usual devotion to duty expected of employees of his kind. In the old case of *Ridgway v. Hungerford Market Co.*[14] a clerk entered in a company minute book a protest, in his own handwriting, against a resolution of the directors calling a meeting to appoint his successor. He was dismissed at once and forfeited the right to any reasonable notice that would have been implied in the directors' resolution.

Incompetence

The degree of skill an employer may demand depends partly on the representations of the employee when seeking the position and partly on the degree of skill ordinarily to be expected of an employee of his category and rate of pay. If an employee accepts a position on the understanding that he is capable of doing a particular kind of work and it becomes apparent that he cannot in fact do this

---

[13] See Smith, *The Law of Master and Servant* (6th ed.), p. 390, E. M. Smith, ed. London: Sweet & Maxwell Limited, 1906. We have followed the classification of grounds for dismissal outlined by Smith at pp. 102-15.

[14] (1835) 111 E.R. 378.

work satisfactorily, his employer may then dismiss him without notice. The strict application of this principle is found in the words of an English judge:

> It appears to us that there is no material difference between a servant who will not, and a servant who cannot, perform the duty for which he was hired.[15]

On the other hand, incompetence as a cause for dismissal becomes more difficult to justify the longer an employee has been retained.[16]

Illness

Permanent disability or constantly recurring illness entitles an employer to consider the contract at an end, independently of any terms in the contract requiring notice. An employer cannot, however, recover from his employee for damages for breach of contract in these circumstances: the contract has been discharged by frustration, and not by breach.

Effect of Dismissal

Any of the four grounds for dismissal set out in the preceding subsections illustrating "dismissal for cause" permits an employer to treat the contract of employment as being discharged. Misconduct, disobedience, or incompetence amount to discharge by the employee's breach, whereas illness discharges the contract by frustration. Discharge for any one of these personal failures of performance by an employee relieves his employer of the duty to give notice.

Adverse Economic Conditions

Ordinarily, an employer does not have the right to dismiss his employees without notice because of adverse economic conditions. As we have noted, reasonable terms of notice are implied by law. An employee might expressly agree to give his employer the right to dismiss him in adverse economic conditions without notice, and an agreement to this effect would exclude an implied requirement for such notice. However, where a right to notice is provided by statute, even an express agreement to give it up would be ineffective and the statute would take precedence, requiring the employer to give notice or wages in lieu of notice.

Neither does an employer have the right to temporarily lay off employees without notice, for economic reasons. Some statutes now permit an employer to do so for periods as long as three months, under conditions prescribed by regulation.[17]

---

[15] Harmer v. Cornelius (1858) 141 E.R. 94, per Willes, J., at 99.

[16] See Duncan v. Cockshutt Farm Equipment Ltd. (1956) 19 W.W.R. 554; Bardal v. The Globe and Mail Ltd. (1960) 24 D.L.R. (2d) 140.

[17] Canada Labour Code, R.S.C. 1970, c. L-1 and Regulation 30; Employment Standards Act, 1974, St. of Ont. 1974, c. 112, s. 40(3)(b) and Rev. Reg. of Ont. 1970, Reg. 244 as amended.

DAMAGES FOR WRONGFUL DISMISSAL

For an employee to succeed in an action against his employer for damages for wrongful dismissal, he must show that the employer has broken the contract. The employer will have broken the contract if he has failed to give his employee the notice to which he was entitled. An employer often defends an action of this kind either by showing that he did not have to give notice because the employee was dismissed for cause, or that adequate notice was in fact given. If the employer's defence fails, the court is left with the task of assessing damages.

The measure of damages for wrongful dismissal is merely a special application of the rules for determining the amounts of damages in contracts generally. In Chapter 15, we saw that the purpose of an award of damages is to place an injured party in the same position as if the contract had been completed. In the context of an employment contract, we must ask what amount of damages will compensate the employee for his failure to receive the required notice of termination.

In assessing damages, the first task for the court is to decide what length of time would have been reasonable notice in the circumstances. As we have noted, the court has considerable discretion when the contract is for a general or indefinite hiring. Mr. Chief Justice McRuer of the Ontario High Court said:

> There can be no catalogue laid down as to what is reasonable notice in particular classes of cases. The reasonableness of the notice must be decided with reference to each particular case, having regard to the character of the employment, the length of service of the servant, the age of the servant and the availability of similar employment, having regard to the experience, training and qualifications of the servant.[18]

The next step in assessing damages for wrongful dismissal is to multiply the employee's rate of pay by the length of reasonable notice. A party injured by breach of contract, however, is under a duty to act reasonably in order to mitigate his loss. Accordingly, we must then ask whether the employee has made a serious attempt following his dismissal to obtain reasonably comparable work elsewhere. If the employer shows that the employee had such an opportunity to work elsewhere but declined it, the court will reduce the award of damages by the amount the employee might have earned during the required term of notice.

Finally, we must ask whether the damages that flow naturally from the employer's breach may include any losses other than salary. The employee may have incurred travelling expenses in seeking other employment, or lost pension benefits that would have accrued to him had he been retained for the additional period represented by reasonable notice. We noted in Chapter 15, however, that the common law does not give damages for injured feelings caused by breach of contract. This principle applies to employment contracts as well. Although a wrongfully dismissed employee may suffer a devastating blow to his morale, he

---

[18] Bardal v. The Globe and Mail Ltd., per McRuer, C.J.H.C., at 145.

must content himself with a declaration by the court that he was wrongfully dismissed, and with money damages limited to his pecuniary loss.

Sometimes an employer has such a general dissatisfaction with or mistrust of an employee that he dismisses him apparently without cause. If the employer should later discover that there were in fact specific grounds for dismissing the employee without notice, he may use these grounds to defeat an action by the employee for wrongful dismissal.[19]

EMPLOYEE WELFARE LEGISLATION

History

In the social upheaval that followed the industrial revolution and before the emergence of trade unions, the employer had nearly all the advantage in bargaining power: often, the worker had either to accept the proposed terms of employment or see his family starve. The movement for reform in working conditions stressed the economic inequality between employer and employee. Reformers urged that society had a duty to protect the weaker contracting party. The arguments of the reformers, however, went directly against 19th century ideas on freedom of contract as a pillar of a larger political philosophy of *laissez faire*. The freedom of contract doctrine asserted that society functions most efficiently when contracting parties are left free to exact whatever terms their bargaining power will command, and that a society will come closest to realizing its economic potential when individuals are left to their own resources in resolving their conflicts of interest without the intervention of any outside arbiter.

The reform movement therefore had to proceed against formidable opposition by the proponents of freedom of contract. Nevertheless, the pressures of a changing society were irresistible: they resulted in a series of acts of Parliament commencing a little before the middle of the 19th century. These statutes marked a new role for the state — active intervention on the side of the employees.

Initially, the reform found expression in statutes specifying the minimum age of workers, maximum hours of work, the presence of safety devices for machinery, the maintenance of safe premises in which to work, and the definition of the liability of employers when an employee was injured in the course of employment. These statutes were only a beginning. A review of the statute law we are to consider briefly in this section illustrates the degree to which our legislatures have qualified freedom of contract between individual employers and employees.

To the extent that employees are now represented by trade unions, the

---

[19] The courts admit such evidence even if it comes to light after the action has been started. See, for example: Lake Ontario Portland Cement v. Groner (1961) 28 D.L.R. (2d) 589; Aspinall v. Mid-West Collieries Ltd. [1926] 3 D.L.R. 362.

disparity in bargaining power between an employer and his employees has been largely redressed: contracts bargained for by trade unions protect the interests of the employees. There remain, however, important categories of work in which employees typically are not unionized. In these types of work, the employee still negotiates his contract of employment on an individual basis with the employer. Accordingly, legislation enacted for the welfare and protection of employees continues to afford a minimum standard of working conditions for many people.

Legislative Jurisdiction

In Canada, a comparatively small but very important group of businesses is engaged in activities of a kind which bring them under federal jurisdiction, and for these the rights and duties of employers and employees are governed by federal labour legislation. These industries include shipping, air transport, interprovincial transportation systems, telegraphs, radio, banking, and the operations of federal crown companies.[20] The remainder of our economic activity, comprising the bulk of what we think of as industrial and commercial enterprise, is subject to provincial rather than federal legislation.

Regulation of Working Conditions

Each of the provinces has enacted a variety of statutes prohibiting child labour, regulating the hours of work of women and young persons, and providing for the safety and health of employees while at work. The provinces may appoint inspectors to determine that these requirements are complied with. Other statutes specify a minimum age at which children may leave school and accept full-time employment.

All provinces as well as the federal government provide by statute for minimum-wage rates, and grant discretionary power to a designated government agency to fix a minimum wage that varies with the industry. The legislation provides for limited working hours, with some exceptions, of eight hours a day and a maximum of 44 or 48 hours a week. These statutes also require overtime rates if the number of hours worked exceeds the specified maximum.

All but two provinces have given formal statutory sanction to agreements among employers and employees in a particular trade or industry by which all agree to minimum rates of wages, and maximum hours of work and days of labour within a specified zone.[21] This sanction is subject to the provisions of other statutes dealing with hours of work, minimum wages, and working conditions. The agreements must be reached at a properly convened conference of the employers and employees affected. Recognition of agreements of this kind is an important qualification of the usual attitude of the law towards restraint of trade.

---

[20] British North America Act, 1867, 30 & 31 Vict., c. 3, s. 91.
[21] See, for example: Municipal Act, R.S.B.C. 1960, c. 355, ss. 857-65; Industrial Standards Act, R.S.O. 1970, c. 221; R.S.N.S. 1967, c. 142.

All provinces now provide for annual vacations with pay. The most frequent requirement is for employers to grant their employees one week's paid vacation after one year of work. Some provinces also provide for public holidays with pay.

A federal act prohibits discrimination in employment based on race, colour, religion, or national origin, whether practised by employers or trade unions.[22] Some of the provinces have enacted comparable legislation in respect of industries coming within their jurisdiction. Provincial and federal statutes may also prohibit an employer from discriminating between his male and female employees by paying female employees less for the same work.

Unemployment Insurance

In 1941, the Canadian Parliament passed the Unemployment Insurance Act.[23] This Act established an unemployment insurance fund to which employers and employees must contribute according to a published schedule of rates. Coverage is very wide, with only such limited exceptions as persons over 65 years of age, or those receiving retirement pensions, employed by a spouse, employed by provincial governments, foreign governments, and international organizations.[24] Employees contribute to the fund through payroll deductions made by their employer. The employer has the task of accounting for the employees' contributions and remitting them regularly along with his own. Unemployment insurance benefits are payable out of the fund to workers who have contributed in the past and are currently unemployed. These benefits are not available in a number of circumstances, one of which is loss of work caused by a labour dispute in which the employee is on strike. Other employees, not on strike but "locked out" because a plant or business is shut down by a strike, remain eligible for benefits.

Workmen's Compensation

While the common law recognized that an employer could be liable to an employee for injury sustained by that employee in the course of performing his duties, it was notoriously difficult for the employee to recover damages. In particular, the employer might defend the action successfully if he could show that the injury resulted from the contributory negligence of the employee, the negligence of a fellow employee, or the fact that the employee had assumed a risk of injury as a customary incident of the type of work he had contracted to do.

The doctrine of *contributory negligence* prevented an employee from succeeding if the evidence showed that he himself was partly responsible for the accident, even in a small degree. Nor was an employer liable for injury to an

---

[22] Canada Labour Code, R.S.C. 1970, c. L-1, s. 5.
[23] Unemployment Insurance Act, 1971, St. of Can. 1971-2, c. 48.
[24] *Ibid.*, s. 3(2).

employee caused by the negligence of a fellow employee, provided the employer took reasonable care to hire competent workmen: the usual result was that the employer escaped liability for negligence by one employee that caused injury to another. In addition, the meaning of *fellow servant* (or fellow employee) proved to be difficult for the courts to interpret: they held that a hod-carrier and a carpenter's helper were fellow servants, whereas motormen on different street cars were not. Finally, the defence of *assumed risk,* broadly interpreted, might itself defeat almost any action by an employee, for it could be argued that every risk is a risk an employee assumes in accepting his particular employment.

An action at common law also suffered from the fact that the burden lay with the employee to prove negligence on the part of his employer; he might find it exceedingly difficult to do so, especially if he suffered shock from his injury. In addition, the dependants of a deceased employee who had been killed rather than injured in the course of employment had no cause of action — the right to sue for personal injury caused by a tort died with the injured person at common law. Legislation was enacted in England in the latter part of the last century to permit action against an employer by the relatives of an employee killed while on the job. The legislation also clarified and extended the liability of the employer; but the burden of proof remained with the employee or his dependants to prove negligence on the part of the employer. Similar statutes were passed in the Canadian provinces.

The final step was the enactment of the Workmen's Compensation Act. This statute made substantial improvement in the rights of injured employees, or of their immediate dependants in the event of death caused by accident while at work. The Act was passed in England in 1906 and later enacted in each of the provinces of Canada with various modifications.[25] Each of these Acts creates a Workmen's Compensation Board to hear employees' claims. They also establish a fund to which employers subject to the Act must contribute regularly and out of which claims are paid. Payment out of the fund is in lieu of a personal action against the employer. To succeed, an employee need only show that the injury was caused by an accident in the course of employment. The defences of contributory negligence, negligence of a fellow servant, and assumed risk no longer apply. An employee's claim will fail only if it is shown that the accident was caused substantially by his own wilful misconduct. Even then, the employee or his dependants will recover if the accident has caused death or serious disablement. The requirement of proving negligence on the part of the employer, so long a barrier to compensation for injury, no longer exists. Also important, the costs and hazards of litigation are avoided. Since an employee makes his claim against a compensation board and does not start a personal action against his employer, the employee need have no fear of prejudicing his future with his employer by making his claim.

Coverage varies somewhat among the provinces. Generally included are

---

[25] See, for example: Workmen's Compensation Act, St. of B.C. 1968, c. 59; R.S.O. 1970, c. 505; R.S.N.S. 1967, c. 343.

workmen engaged in construction, mining, manufacturing, lumbering, fishing, transportation and communications industries, and in public utilities. Industries are classified according to the degree of hazard. Exemptions include casual employees and employees of small businesses employing fewer than a stated number of workmen. For employees excluded from the usual workmen's compensation benefits, several provinces have added a second part to the Workmen's Compensation Act defining the employer's liability for injuries caused by defective plant and equipment and negligence of other employees, and granting the employee a right to damages in spite of contributory negligence on his part. In other jurisdictions, the common law rules still apply to casual employees and to those in small businesses.

COLLECTIVE BARGAINING

The process of establishing the conditions of employment by negotiations between an employer and the bargaining agent for his employees is known as *collective bargaining*. For those industries within federal jurisdiction, a federal statute regulates the subject of collective bargaining.[26] Statutes passed by each of the provinces regulate all other industries.[27] These acts state that all employees are free to belong to trade unions and that membership in a trade union by an employee does not provide his employer with grounds for dismissing him. The acts also require employers to recognize the representative union as the bargaining agent for employees for the purpose of determining the general terms of their employment.

If an employer is unwilling to recognize a trade union voluntarily, as often happens, the union may have to apply to be certified before it can proceed to bargain for the employees. *Certification* is an acknowledgment by an administrative tribunal (called in some provinces a labour relations board) that a particular union commands sufficient support in terms of membership to justify its role as exclusive bargaining agent for the employees. The arrangement has the practical advantages of confining the negotiations to a single representative of the employees and avoiding the confusion of rival unions claiming the right to act as bargaining agents of the employees in question. We must distinguish between a bargaining agent and a bargaining unit: a *bargaining agent* is a union which has the exclusive right to bargain with the employer on behalf of the bargaining unit: the *bargaining unit* includes a specified group of employees eligible to join the union, whether they join or not.

When employer and union conclude their bargaining, they place the terms agreed upon in a contract called a *collective agreement*. The terms usually include a definition of the employees covered, an acknowledgment by the employer that the union contracting is their recognized bargaining agent, an outline of the steps which both parties must take in settling grievances, seniority

---

[26] The Canada Labour Code, R.S.C. 1970, c. L-1.

[27] See, for example: Labour Code, St. of B.C. 1973, c. 122; Labour Relations Act, R.S.O. 1970, c. 232; Trade Union Act, St. of N.S. 1972, c. 19.

provisions in the promoting and laying off of employees, wage rates, hours, vacation periods, the duration of the collective agreement, and the means by which it may be amended or renewed. Often there is a clause acknowledging that the maintenance of discipline and efficiency of employees is the sole function of the management of the company, subject to the right of an employee to lodge a grievance. The agreement almost invariably forbids strikes or lockouts as long as it continues to operate; indeed, most provinces require that such a term be included. The employees covered do not generally include those employed in a confidential capacity, those who have authority to hire or discharge others, or those employed as guards or security police in the protection of business property. A number of provinces also exclude certain professional groups such as engineers, although the tendency in recent years has been to include more of the professions.

The terms of a collective agreement generally prescribe in detail the procedure for dismissing employees, so that the common law rules for notice of dismissal and grounds for dismissal are superseded. To the extent also that the collective agreement prescribes working conditions above the level required by existing legislation, it replaces employee welfare legislation as a protection for the interests of workers.

LABOUR DISPUTES

Types of Disputes

We may identify four major types of disputes affecting trade unions: jurisdictional disputes; recognition disputes; interest disputes; and rights disputes.

A *jurisdictional dispute* is a disagreement between competing unions for the right to represent a particular group of employees; the type of work they do may have two attributes, each of which seems to bring it within the terms of reference of a different trade union. Such a simple operation as drilling a hole through both metal and wood might raise a question whether the worker should belong to the metalworkers' or the woodworkers' union.

A *recognition dispute* arises between an employer and a union when the employer insists on negotiating employment contracts directly with his employees and resists a union demand that it be recognized as the employees' bargaining agent.

An *interest dispute* is a disagreement between an employer and a union about the particular terms to be included in a collective agreement.

A *rights dispute* is a difference of opinion between employer and union on the interpretation of terms in a collective agreement already in existence.

Legislative Regulation

As we noted at the outset, the regulation of labour disputes is a whole field of study in its own right, and we cannot do more than indicate a few of the basic methods used. For an adequate treatment of the law, one must consult recognized works in the field.[28]

Statutes have now provided machinery which either eliminates or minimizes the need to resort to strike action in each of the four main types of dispute mentioned above. Certification procedure, briefly considered in the preceding section, has done much to resolve jurisdictional disputes and is the only legal means of settling recognition disputes.

Our provincial statutes require both employer and employees to follow a series of procedures designed to aid in the settlement of interest disputes: first, they require a genuine attempt over a specified period of time to bargain in order to reach agreement;[29] secondly, if the parties fail to agree, they must submit to *conciliation procedure,* that is, bargain further with the help of a conciliation officer or board; finally, if the parties still fail to agree, the employer cannot declare a lockout or the union begin strike action until a further specified *cooling-off period* has elapsed.

For the fourth type of dispute, a rights dispute, the law imposes *arbitration procedure:* the parties are bound to accept the interpretation placed on the collective agreement by an arbitrator. In conciliation procedure the parties are not bound to accept the solution proposed by the conciliation officer, but in arbitration procedure the decision of the arbitrator is binding.

In summary, we can see that only in interest disputes does the possibility of lawful strike action exist, and then only after the prescribed conciliation procedure and cooling-off period. A strike is "illegal" if the preliminary grievance procedures set down by statute have not been followed or, even when they have been followed, the strike is not conducted according to carefully defined rules. The means by which a strike is implemented must be free of compulsion, intimidation, or threat. Furthermore, a strike may become unlawful if undertaken with intent to injure another and not with the intent of furthering the trade interest of the strikers.

Although strikers are entitled to picket at or near the place of the employer's business, they must do so peaceably and for the purpose only of obtaining or communicating information. Statements made on placards or in literature distributed at the scene of the picketing must be correct and factual. Mr. Chief Justice McRuer of the Ontario Supreme Court outlined the scope of these rights as follows:

> It is one thing to exercise all the lawful rights to strike and the lawful rights to picket; that is a freedom that should be preserved and its preservation has advanced the interests of the labouring man and the community as a whole

---

[28] Carrothers, *Collective Bargaining Law in Canada,* Toronto: Butterworths, 1965; *Labour Relations Law* (2nd ed.), (The Labour Relations Law Casebook Group ed.), Kingston, Queen's University, 1974.

[29] In Canada, an employer need not bargain with a union that has not been certified and with which he has not previously made a collective agreement. In the United States, an employer must bargain with a union representing the majority of his employees, whether it is certified or not.

to an untold degree over the last half-century. But it is another thing to recognize a conspiracy to injure so that benefits to any particular person or class may be realized. Further, if what any person or group of persons does amounts to a common law nuisance to another what is being done may be restrained by injunction.[30]

IMPLICATIONS OF THE COLLECTIVE AGREEMENT FOR THE INDIVIDUAL EMPLOYEE

A collective agreement is entered into by an employer and a representative union: generally, each party is a large organization or institution and the individual employee does not actively negotiate the terms of his employment directly with his employer. His bargaining is undertaken for him by his union, and comparatively little ground is left for him to negotiate with his employer at the time of making a contract of employment.

The trade union has, of course, been a means by which workers collectively have achieved a bargaining power that they cannot have individually, and there is no gainsaying the improvement in working conditions that they have secured in this way. On the other hand, to gain this advantage the individual has surrendered some of his freedom of contract in the process: his individual wishes are necessarily subordinated to the collective objectives of the organization which represents him. He has the benefit of the collective agreement by virtue of his status as a member of the bargaining unit rather than by virtue of his personal contracting prowess. The authors Eells and Walton have made the point this way:

. . . contract becomes largely the technique of group manipulation and use. Professional managements speak for the large corporation, and professional labor leaders speak for workers; the contract thus arrived at becomes a contribution to a code of administrative behavior by which the individual's personal right to contract is considerably diminished. As a working proposition, then, we are prepared to assert that contract is meaningful today more in terms of its use by organizations and less in terms of its use by individuals.[31]

The Province of Quebec has a unique piece of legislation that takes this process a stage further: the terms of a collective agreement may apply even to workers who are not members of the bargaining unit for which the union was entitled to negotiate.[32] The legislation provides that when a union has bargained for a certain rate of pay with one or more large employers within the industry, the

---

[30] General Dry Batteries of Canada Ltd. v. Brigenshaw [1951] O.R. 522, per McRuer, C.J.H.C., at 528.

[31] Eells and Walton, *Conceptual Foundations of Business,* pp. 207-8. Homewood, Ill.: Richard D. Irwin Inc., 1961.

[32] Collective Agreement Decrees Act, R.S.Q. 1964.

parties may apply to the Minister of Labour for a decree extending the provisions of the collective agreement to all other employers and employees within the industry or trade in the province or a region of the province. To succeed, the application must establish that the collective agreements already written have acquired a preponderant significance and importance for establishing conditions of labour within the industry or region. The effect is to establish a minimum wage law within the area covered by the decree, and extend the terms of the collective agreement to workers not represented in the formation of the contract.

Not only does the union have the dominant role in bargaining on behalf of the individual worker; often the worker may not have the freedom to choose whether to belong to the union. In *Bonsor v. Musicians' Union*[33] the plaintiff, who had been wrongfully expelled from the union and found it impossible to earn a livelihood as a musician without being a member, testified as follows:

> I would like to tell his lordship that if I could earn my living forthwith without being a member of this so-called Musicians' Union I would not want to join it, but I have got to join it in order to work because it is a closed shop. I will always pay my subscriptions, but I will not take any active part in union matters. I will be a member by force because I am forced to be a member.[34]

After quoting the above statement of the plaintiff, Lord Justice Denning commented:

> When one remembers that the rules are applied to a man in that state of mind, it will be appreciated that they are not so much a contract as we used to understand a contract, but they are much more a legislative code laid down by some members of the union to be imposed on all members of the union. They are more like by-laws than a contract.[35]

Trade unions are, of course, only one of the modern institutions that are having this effect on contract. Contracts between existing businesses which restrict competition by fixing prices or output effectively diminish the freedom of contract of the consuming public; we have considered the law dealing with this problem in Chapter 8. In addition, as we have seen, many financial institutions (insurance companies and finance companies, for example) present those to whom they sell their services with a standard form contract containing the printed terms of the agreement set down in advance on a take-it-or-leave-it basis, thereby diminishing the opportunity for the other contracting party to bargain for terms that are satisfactory to him.

---

[33] [1954] Ch. 479. (The dissenting judgment of Denning, L.J., was approved on appeal to the House of Lords: [1956] A.C. 105.)

[34] *Ibid.*, at 485.

[35] *Ibid.*

THE LEGAL STATUS OF TRADE UNIONS

We touched briefly on the legal status of trade unions when discussing capacity to contract in Chapter 7. We noted there that trade unions are accorded a recognized status before labour relations boards for the purpose of rendering them amenable to the board's rulings; but this recognition is for a limited purpose, and we must not infer from the fact that unions have a separate existence before an administrative tribunal that they necessarily have comparable standing before the courts. We noted also that the technique of representative action provides a possible means by which unions may sue or be sued in the courts.

For various reasons, our legislatures have eschewed the otherwise obvious course of requiring trade unions to come within existing companies legislation, and so conferring on them a corporate existence comparable with that of other business organizations. Nevertheless, the legislatures seem to be moving in that direction and when there is no decisive statutory authority, the courts are able to cite the reasoning in the famous *Taff Vale* case, a decision handed down by the House of Lords in 1901.[36] In that case, a trade union was held to be a "quasi-corporate" body that could be sued. The decision held the union liable in damages for the company's loss as a result of a strike in which two agents of the union "put themselves in charge . . . and   illegally watched and beset men to prevent them from working for the company, and illegally ordered men to break their contracts." On these facts the court interpreted the strike as a conspiracy in restraint of trade in relation to the then existing law of England. It next preoccupied itself with the question whether, even given an admitted wrong, the union as such could be sued for damages. It decided in the affirmative. Although the result of the *Taff Vale* case was nullified shortly afterwards by an act of Parliament,[37] and although this act was adopted by the provinces of Canada, the *judicial reasoning* concerning the legal personality of trade unions survived and persisted. Recently it has grown in importance.

The Supreme Court of Canada in 1960 made extensive use of the *Taff Vale* decision in the case of *International Brotherhood of Teamsters. v. Thérien.*[38] Thérien was the owner of a Vancouver trucking business and had been engaged by City Construction Company for some years when the company entered into a collective agreement with the Teamsters' Union requiring, as one of its terms, that all employees should be union members (*a closed-shop agreement*). Thérien agreed then to hire only union members for the operation of his trucks, but declined to join the union personally because he wished to maintain his relationship of an independent contractor in dealings with City Construction Company, and because in the capacity of an employer in his own right he was

---

[36] Taff Vale Railway Co. v. Amalgamated Society of Railway Servants [1901] A.C. 426.

[37] See Trade Disputes Act, 1906, 6 Ed., c. 47, s. 1, declaring that actions of a trade union in furtherance of its interests would not thenceforth be interpreted as a restraint of trade.

[38] (1960) 22 D.L.R. (2d) 1. This decision has been followed in a Manitoba case: Dusessoy's Supermarket St. James Ltd. v. Retail Clerks Union Local No. 832 (1961) 34 W.W.R. 577.

forbidden by the Labour Relations Act of British Columbia from participating in union activities. The union took a different view, however, and as a result of union threats to picket City Construction Company, the general manager of that company advised Thérien that the company must dispense with his services. Thérien suffered a significant loss of business as a result, and brought action against the union claiming damages for the wrongful conduct of the union. The union defended on the grounds that it was not a legal entity and so could not be sued and, secondly, that in any case it had not been guilty of conduct that might constitute a tort.

On the first argument of the union the court noted that the union had been certified as a bargaining agent under the terms of the Labour Relations Act, and that:

> It is necessary for the exercise of the [statutory] powers given that such unions should have officers or other agents to act in their names and on their behalf. The Legislature, by giving the right to act as agent for others and to contract on their behalf, has given them two of the essential qualities of a corporation in respect of liability for tort since a corporation can only act by its agents.[39]

The court quoted with approval the remarks of Lord Halsbury in the *Taff Vale* case:

> If the Legislature has created a thing which can own property, which can employ servants, and which can inflict injury, it must be taken, I think, to have impliedly given the power to make it suable in a Court of Law for injuries purposely done by its authority and procurement.[40]

Having identified the union as a suable legal entity, the court then found that the union had threatened to resort to picketing instead of following the grievance procedure set out in the collective agreement, and that the consequence of this conduct was the injurious termination of Thérien's arrangement with City Construction Company. It awarded damages to Thérien and ordered an injunction restraining the union from interfering with him in the operation of his business.

At the time of writing, the *Thérien* decision is only one of a succession of Canadian cases developing the common law on the subject of the legal status of trade unions. It does not apply, of course, in provinces whose statutes specifically define the circumstances in which trade unions may be sued. In particular, Ontario and Saskatchewan have statutes that restrict the possibility of an action against a trade union for torts.[41]

---

[39] International Brotherhood of Teamsters v. Thérien, per Locke, J., at 11.
[40] Taff Vale Railway Co. v. Amalgamated Society of Railway Servants [1901] A.C. 426, per Halsbury, L.C., at 436.
[41] Rights of Labour Act, R.S.O. 1970, c. 416; Trade Unions Act, R.S.S. 1965, c. 287, ss. 25-6. For legislation expressly making unions suable entities, see: Labour Code, St. of B.C. 1973, c. 122, s. 147; Labour Act, St. of Man. 1972, c. 75, s. 127; Industrial Relations Act, R.S.N.B. 1973, c. I-4, s. 114(2).

QUESTIONS FOR REVIEW

1. Explain the following terms: collective agreement, vicarious liability, independent contractor, arbitration, assumed risk, conciliation, certification, "illegal" strike.
2. Give two reasons why it may be important to ascertain whether an agent may also be an employee.
3. What are the essentials of tort liability?
4. What are some of the torts an employee might be guilty of in the course of his employment?
5. What conditions must be satisfied before an employer is liable for a tort committed by an employee against a third person?
6. An employee is laid off because there has been a sharp decline in the market for his employer's products. Is the employee entitled to notice?
7. On what grounds is an employer justified in dismissing his employee without notice?
8. An employee leaves his position without giving notice to his employer. What factors should the employer consider before commencing legal action against the employee?
9. Quality Meat Packers Ltd. have major factories and warehouses from coast to coast. How does this fact complicate the company's collective bargaining with its employees?
10. In what respects has the freedom of contract of an employee with his employer been qualified by modern developments in the law?
11. Why was it difficult, before the passing of the Workmen's Compensation Act, for an employee injured at work to obtain redress?
12. How has the Workmen's Compensation Act removed these difficulties?
13. What is collective bargaining? What are some of the usual terms of a collective agreement?
14. What kind of labour disputes are there?
15. Under what circumstances may the *form* of an employment contract affect its enforceability? What statute is relevant?
16. Discuss the social justification for the doctrine of vicarious liability.
17. In Victorian times Sir Henry Maine, a legal historian, stated that as society progressed, human relationships changed from a basis of status to that of contract. Many modern writers see in recent developments a return to a condition of status, such as that evolving for employees. It can be argued that a return to status is a return to a more rigid class society, with all its implications of a lower class akin to medieval serfdom. To what extent is this gloomy picture accurate? Comment on the validity of the argument.

CASES FOR DISCUSSION

CASE 1

Rushmore operates a fleet of trucks under the name of Supersonic Delivery Service. His business consists in picking up parcels on request from small shops and delivering the parcels to customers of the shops. One day Rushmore received a request from Jones Tool & Die Co., to deliver 20 iron pipes, six feet long and six inches in diameter, to Wilson at 149 Restful Vista Drive. He thereupon despatched one of his drivers, Hastie, to pick up the pipes and take them there. Hastie delivered the pipes in error to 149 Wistful Vista, the residence of McGee. Not finding anyone home there, Hastie left the pipes in an unlocked garage at the back of the house.

When McGee returned home at night, he opened the garage door to put his car inside, and groping for the light switch, tripped over the pipes and sustained a serious back injury. What, if anything, is the nature of McGee's recourse? (See *Turner v. Thorne* (1960) 21 D.L.R. (2d) 29; *Cook v. Lewis* [1952] 1 D.L.R. 1; *Tillander v. Gosselin* [1967] 1 O.R. 303; *Dahlberg v. Nadiuk* (1970) 10 D.L.R. (3d) 319.)

CASE 2

In 1959 Able was engaged by Cranbrook Collieries Ltd. as mine manager. In addition to his monthly salary he was given an allowance of $15 a month for coal to heat his house, since the house was not in the vicinity of the mine. About two years later Able was dismissed, on the grounds that he was often absent from his work and did not give proper supervision to the mining operation. Able argued that it was an incident of his position that he should be away from the mine from time to time for the purpose of consulting equipment suppliers and seeking new employees. Able brought an action against Cranbrook Collieries Ltd. for damages for wrongful dismissal.

In the course of the trial, one of the teamsters employed by the mine testified that Able had instructed him to take coal to his house secretly, and that he had done so regularly without knowledge of any other employee of the mine. This fact was unknown to the directors of Cranbrook Collieries at the time they dismissed Able.

Should Able's action succeed? (See *Aspinall v. Mid-West Collieries, Ltd.* [1926] 3 D.L.R. 362; *Lake Ontario Portland Cement v. Groner* (1961) 28 D.L.R. (2d) 589.)

CASE 3

Darwin operated a retail food supermarket which obtained 60% of its merchandise from Prairie Wholesale Grocers Limited. As a result of a wage dispute the employees of Prairie Wholesale Grocers Ltd., who were members of the Office & Shop Clerks Union, went on strike. An official of that union then telephoned Darwin to enlist his support and apply economic pressure on Prairie Wholesale Grocers Ltd. by reducing purchases from it. When Darwin refused, members of the union picketed Darwin's supermarket. They stopped cars on their way into the parking lot of the supermarket to distribute leaflets, intimating, inaccurately, that Darwin's store was controlled by Prairie Wholesale Grocers Ltd. The placards used while picketing contained the words "Darwin's Supermarket" and "Strike" in large letters, although none of Darwin's own employees were on strike. As a result, Darwin lost customers and brought an action against the union for damages and an injunction to restrain the picketing of his premises. Discuss the defences available to the union and state whether they would succeed. (See *Dusessoy's Supermarkets St. James Ltd. v. Retail Clerks Union Local No. 832* (1961) 34 W.W.R. 577.)

CASE 4

In August 1948 the directors of Universal Printing Co., publishers of an evening newspaper of large circulation, approached Bell with a view to interesting him in becoming their assistant advertising manager. They explained to Bell that if he accepted he would probably succeed the present advertising manager upon his retirement. At the time Bell held a responsible position with a Toronto advertising agency and was 43. During the discussions Bell emphasized that his present position was a very satisfactory one, that it was important at his age that his employment should be permanent, and that he would not consider a change that did not offer the prospect of a position lasting for the balance of his working life.

After careful consideration Bell accepted the position offered at a salary of $12,000 a year. He was promoted to advertising manager in 1956, and in the period from August, 1948, to July, 1962, his salary was increased regularly until it reached $2,000 a month. In addition, every year he received a discretionary Christmas bonus of two weeks' salary approved by the directors plus a special distribution pursuant to a profit-sharing plan confined to selected employees and made under the sole direction of the principal shareholder of Universal Printing Co. Ltd. Bell's receipts under the profit-sharing plan were $6,800 in 1960, $6,200 in 1961, and $5,000 in 1962.

In August, 1962, the President of the Universal Printing Co. Ltd., T. G. Dodds, called Bell into his office and after some opening pleasantries about Bell's prowess in golf, told Bell that he thought another advertising manager he had in mind could produce better results for the company. Dodds told Bell that if he could see his way clear to resigning forthwith he might have three months' salary in lieu of notice. Bell replied that he could not afford at this stage in his career to admit the incompetence implied in a resignation, and refused. Later in the afternoon his secretary brought him the following letter:

> August 8, 1962.
>
> Dear Mr. Bell:
> This is to confirm the notice given to you today of the termination of your employment with Universal Printing Co. Ltd. as of this date. Enclosed is a cheque for your salary to date. Your past contributions to our pension plan have been commuted to a paid-up basis that will pay you $85 a week commencing at age 65.
>
> T. G. Dodds.

Bell at once made efforts to secure other employment, and by December 8, 1962, secured a position with an advertising agency at a salary of $18,000 a year. If he had remained a further year with Universal Printing Co. Ltd., the paid-up value of his pension would have increased by $1,500.

Bell brought an action against Universal Printing Co. Ltd. for damages for wrongful dismissal. What amount of damages, if any, should he recover?

CASE 5

Smith delivered milk on one of the routes of Farmers' Dairy. The dairy had the following notice to its drivers posted in its general office:

> To comply with a request from the insurance company our drivers are not permitted to take a rider or helper on their trucks unless authorized by the company. If these instructions are disobeyed Farmers' Dairy Ltd. will not accept responsibility in case of accident.

One Saturday morning Smith asked a customer, Mrs. Brown, if her son Teddy would like to help him deliver milk. The youngster prevailed upon his mother to let him go, as he had helped Smith once before and had a good time, and Smith had given him a drink of chocolate milk.

At one of the stops on the route the boy was getting into the truck with his hand on the door and one foot on the running-board when Smith started the truck suddenly. The boy was thrown to the ground and injured by the truck. His parents sued Farmers' Dairy Ltd. for damages equal to the medical expenses incurred. Should they succeed? (See *Hamilton v. Farmers' Ltd.* [1953] 3 D.L.R. 382.)

CASE 6

Walker was hired as a chemist by the Plastic Toy Co. The contract of employment contained a term that Walker would not work for competitors nor disclose to anyone any information about secret processes used by Plastic Toy Co. Walker worked in the laboratory of the company for a period of about three years when he was given three months' notice of his dismissal.

After his discharge Walker endeavoured to earn a living as a consulting chemist and by promoting the sale of paint. It then appeared that Walker was disclosing certain information about manufacturing processes to the chief competitors of Plastic Toy Co. Specifically, he disclosed secret processes related to the production of equipment used in the colouring of the products of Plastic Toy Co., processes that were of value to that business.

Plastic Toy Co. brought an action against Walker for damages and for an injunction restraining Walker from disclosing further information. One of Walker's defences was that no injunction could be granted to deprive him of his right to practise his profession as a chemist. Discuss. Should Plastic Toy Co. succeed in its action? (See *Reliable Toy Co. and Reliable Plastics Co. v. Collins* [1950] 4 D.L.R. 499.)

CASE 7

Jones was a porter employed by the Great East-West Railway Company. The passenger train on which he was working had discharged its passengers and was standing in a railway station. It was struck by another train as a result of the negligent operation of the railway and Jones was severely injured. He brought an action against the Great East-West Railway Company for damages for negligence.

In defence, the railway company produced its copy of an employment contract signed by Jones. The contract included the following clause:

> The employee, C. W. Jones, agrees that in consideration of employment and wages by the Great East-West Railway Company, he will assume all risks of accident or casualty incident to such employment and service whether caused by the negligence of the Company or of its employees or otherwise, and will forever release, acquit, and discharge the said Company from all liability therefor. The said employee waives all rights to workmen's compensation that might otherwise arise under this contract.

Without rendering a decision, discuss the various public policy considerations inherent in a legal dispute of this kind. (For a similar case, see *Pittsburgh, Cincinnati, Chicago, and St. Louis Railway Company v. Kinney,* 95 Ohio St. 64, 115 N.E. 505 (1916) cited by Zelermyer, *Introduction to Business Law: A Conceptual Approach,* p. 144.)

CHAPTER 22

Negotiable Instruments: Their Nature and Uses

DEVELOPMENT

The ancestry of the negotiable instrument can be traced back to an ancient form of the bill of exchange, a document by which a merchant or "banker" in one city instructed a colleague elsewhere to make a payment to a certain person (or to the bearer) on or after a certain date. Such bills were probably used by the merchants of ancient Greece and Rome, from whom the practice was passed on to the medieval Islamic world. Negotiable instruments came into wide use to meet the needs of merchants in the great age of discovery and trade.

> So soon as commerce between distant nations began to be developed, it became clear that some system of adjusting accounts was a far safer and easier way of making payments in distant places than the primitive method of handing over the actual money due. And, by the end of the twelfth and the beginning of the thirteenth centuries, the various parts of the machinery needed for making these adjustments were at hand. The lawyers and the merchants soon showed that they had sufficient ingenuity to assemble them.[1]

By means of a bill of exchange a merchant in London, for instance, who had bought goods from a merchant coming from Hamburg could arrange for these goods to be paid for in Hamburg, thereby making it unnecessary for the Hamburg merchant to take coins or bullion back with him. The London merchant could

---

[1] Holdsworth, *A History of English Law,* (2nd ed.), p. 128. London: Methuen & Co. Ltd., 1937.

464

pay an appropriate sum to a London firm dealing in bills of exchange, and this firm would draw a bill on its agent in Hamburg instructing him to pay the Hamburg merchant in local currency on a certain date. The Hamburg merchant would exchange his goods for the bill.

With trade taking place in both directions, the credits collecting in Hamburg would be set off by similar credits in London through goods sold by English merchants in Hamburg. The money-changing firms and merchants then learned to set off credits on a multilateral basis among several of the great trading cities, in place of purely bilateral settlements. At regular intervals, usually at annual fairs held in the trading cities, they would get together and tally the paper they had honoured and settle the differences by payment to those with a favourable balance. In return for the money merchants could save in not having to transport gold back and forth, the money-changers were able to charge a handsome fee.

If the London money-changing firm had promised to pay either the Hamburg merchant *or* any person to whom the merchant assigned it in writing, the written promise or instrument could be a valuable aid to commerce in yet another way. The Hamburg merchant might well have creditors of his own: he could then use the written promise of the London firm to satisfy a debt he himself owed in London or elsewhere. If, however, the Hamburg merchant's creditor was in Bristol, it would be difficult for the Bristol merchant to check with the promisor in London to assure himself that the promise being transferred to him arose from a proper transaction and was valid. Accordingly, the custom grew that, provided the document was not a forgery (or suffered from one or two other defects that we shall discuss later), the promisor must honour any instrument presented for payment by a bona-fide transferee of it. In our example the London firm, having promised in an instrument to pay either the merchant in Hamburg *or* the merchant's assignee, must now pay the Bristol merchant; the London firm has in effect waived any right to object, as against the Bristol merchant, that some aspect of the initial transaction has been unsatisfactory. Thus, most defences that a promisor could raise to resist payment to an ordinary contractual assignee were ignored in favour of the great convenience in trade over long distances; such convenience could only be realized by a custom that entitled a prospective holder to rely on the validity of a commercial instrument if it seemed valid on its face. An assignment of this kind became known as *negotiation* and the written promise to pay became known as a negotiable instrument.

GOVERNING LEGISLATION

While it is a great business convenience to have a privileged class of assignable contracts that are almost instantly transferable, rules are needed to define carefully the type of promises covered and the limitations on their use. Initially, these rules were a major component of the Law Merchant,[2] but as a growing

---

[2] *Supra*, Ch. 3, "The Sources of Law".

proportion of economic activity came to take place outside the jurisdiction of the merchant guilds, the ordinary courts adopted the rules in reaching their decisions. Eventually, a very large body of case law developed around the subject. In the latter part of the 19th century, a major effort in England consolidated the rules in a single statement of the law, which was passed after Parliamentary debate as the Bills of Exchange Act (1882).

In Canada, the subject of negotiable instruments is within federal jurisdiction. The Bills of Exchange Act[3] follows the English act closely, even to the point of retaining references to the English practice of "crossing" cheques and ignoring our practice of "certifying" them.

When one observes how smoothly negotiable instruments function as an accepted technique in business affairs, he is likely to overlook the complex legal foundation supporting the practice. In relation to the huge volume of business transacted by means of this device, the amount of litigation concerning negotiable instruments is astonishingly small. And yet the law itself is rather technical. To cover every aspect of it in a book of this kind would be to assign to this branch of law an emphasis out of all proportion to its practical importance for business administration. What we need to know in broad outline is what the law aims to do and how it accomplishes its purpose.

NEGOTIABLE INSTRUMENTS AS PERSONAL PROPERTY

Negotiable instruments are part of that class of personal property we have called *choses in action*. We encountered this concept in earlier chapters (particularly Chapter 13) and in this chapter will consider the characteristics that distinguish negotiable instruments from other types of choses in action.

We should observe at the outset that the fact that a chose in action may lend itself to transfer by endorsement does not mean it is necessarily a negotiable instrument. For one thing, an owner can sometimes transfer a negotiable instrument to another person without endorsement. Further, businessmen frequently use an endorsement to transfer ownership in choses in action other than negotiable instruments, as where they transfer their rights in order bills of lading and (in some jurisdictions), in bond and share certificates.

A negotiable instrument usually arises out of an earlier contract in which the consideration on one side is a promise to pay a sum of money. The promisor's delivery of it is a tender of performance on his part: however he is only conditionally discharged, because if he dishonours the instrument the promisee's rights revive under the original contract. The promisee may choose to sue, however, using the negotiable instrument rather than the original contract as his basis of action. Every negotiable instrument contains an express or implied promise made by one or more parties to pay its amount. In the absence of evidence to the contrary, the promisee is presumed to have given good consideration for it.

---

[3] The Bills of Exchange Act, R.S.C. 1970, c. B-5. In this and the following chapter, when a footnote mentions a section only, the reference will be to this Act.

Thus, a negotiable instrument is normally a self-contained contract with all the necessary written evidence of its terms stated on its face, and an "action on the instrument" is generally a simpler legal undertaking than an action on other types of contract.

TYPES AND USES OF NEGOTIABLE INSTRUMENTS

The Bills of Exchange Act governs the usual types of negotiable instruments: bills of exchange (or drafts), promissory notes and cheques. The fact that the Act confines itself to these three types does not mean that other kinds of instruments possessing the special quality of negotiability may not exist, but disputes concerning them would have to be resolved by reference to the common law and not to the statute. In point of fact, bearer bonds have been held also to be negotiable instruments.[4]

Following U.S. practice, there has been a growing custom in the securities market to treat share certificates as negotiable instruments[5]. Ontario has impliedly recognized share certificates as negotiable instruments[6] and the new Canada Business Corporations Act states expressly that a share certificate whose transfer is not restricted by words printed on its face is a negotiable instrument.[7] Ontario certificates may be subject to principles developed by common law, but the province has no jurisdiction to bring them under the federal Bills of Exchange Act. On the other hand, the federal government has made share certificates of federally-incorporated companies expressly subject to that Act.

In this and the succeeding chapter we shall confine our discussion to the three common forms of negotiable instruments governed by the Bills of Exchange Act.

Bill of Exchange

The essence of a bill of exchange is a written order by one person, the *drawer,* addressed to another person, the *drawee,* to pay a specified sum of money to a named person, the *payee,* or to bearer at a fixed or determinable future time or on demand. The initiative for a bill of exchange lies with the creditor, who calls upon his debtor to acknowledge his indebtedness and agree to pay according to the terms stated in the instrument. A drawer sometimes designates himself as a payee; at other times he may direct that some other person or business to whom he himself owes money shall be the payee instead. A mere order to pay, properly phrased, is a bill of exchange in itself, but the drawer expects that the drawee will

---

[4] Bechuanaland Exploration Co. v. London Trading Bank (1898) 2 Q.B. 658; Goodwin v. Robarts (1875), L.R. 10 Exch. 337; Edelstein v. Schuler [1902], 2 K.B. 144.
[5] Ontario, *Interim Report of the Select Committee on Company Law,* pp. 40-48. Toronto: Legislative Assembly, 1967.
[6] Business Corporations Act, R.S.O. 1970, c. 53, s. 77(2).
[7] Canada Business Corporations Act, St. of Can. 1975, c. 33, s. 44(3).

respond by consenting to his terms. When a drawee chooses to comply with a demand for future payment he expresses his consent by signing the instrument in conjunction with the word "accepted" and the date. In this way the drawee becomes an *acceptor*.

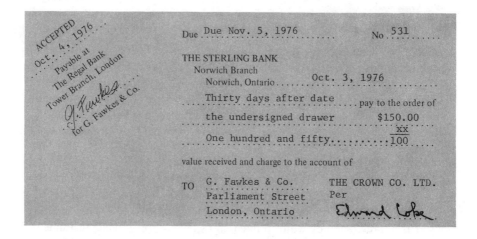

FIGURE 1: A Bill of Exchange (Accepted Time Draft)

A bill of exchange may circulate among a number of holders as an item of valuable personal property even before it has been accepted. In these circumstances it has value for the holder because, by drawing and delivering it, the drawer has made an implied promise guaranteeing its payment.[8] Its acceptance, when it comes, adds the express promise of the acceptor.

It is possible for a debtor on whom a bill of exchange has been drawn to accept it, payable out of his current account at the bank. The drawer (or a subsequent holder) may then leave the instrument with his own bank for collection and deposit it in his account; that bank will present it to the acceptor's bank for payment out of the acceptor's account. After its amount is deducted from his account, the cancelled bill of exchange may be returned to the acceptor as a voucher evidencing payment in the same way that his cancelled cheques may be returned to him.

There are three types of bills of exchange, depending upon the time at which they are to be paid:

> *Demand drafts,* payable immediately upon presentation without the addition of any days of grace. The cheque is the leading example of a demand draft, and we treat it separately below.
>
> *Sight drafts,* in which the drawee is ordered to pay "at sight". In

___
[8] S. 130.

Canada, three days of grace for making payment are allowed after presentment for acceptance.

Time drafts, payable a stipulated number of days, months or other period "after date" (after the date stated on the instrument) or "after sight" (after presentment for acceptance). Three days of grace should be added in fixing the maturity of a time draft. A bill payable at a given time after sight is a time draft, not a sight draft.

Presentment for acceptance is necessary whenever the bill is payable at sight or after sight, so that the time at which payment is due may be determined.[9]

Sight drafts can be used as a collection device. Instead of employing a collection agency to recover its slow accounts, a business may draw sight drafts on recalcitrant customers and have the drafts presented for acceptance and payment through its bank. The drawees will have a new incentive to accept and pay, not wishing to become known to the bank as poor credit risks.

Time drafts can be used as a means of finance for the business drawing them. By discounting them at a bank or by pledging them as security for a bank loan, the drawer can obtain cash in advance of the time when payment is due from the customer. Thus, instead of having to wait until the credit term of its sales expires to realize cash from them, a business may draw a time draft on each customer immediately following a sale, and discount or pledge these drafts. As we see in Chapter 30, however, there are other means of achieving this result without the use of drafts. It may be possible, for example, for the business to borrow from a bank by conditionally assigning its accounts receivable, to sell its accounts to a factor, or to assign them to a finance company.

Drafts and bills of lading often complement one another when goods sold on credit have to be shipped to the buyer by common carrier. Their joint use permits the seller to withhold possession of the goods from the purchaser when they reach their destination until he accepts a draft drawn on him for the price. The purchaser may examine the goods but will not be able to obtain possession from the carrier until the seller transfers the bill of lading to him.

Promissory Note

The essence of a promissory note is a written promise by one person, the *maker,* to pay a specified sum of money to another person, the *payee,* at a fixed or determinable future time or on demand. In business affairs, the maker is usually a debtor of the payee. It is he who takes the initiative in preparing the instrument, though he may of course do so at the urging of the payee.

Unlike a bill of exchange, a promissory note never undergoes presentment for acceptance. It contains an express promise to pay from the outset. From the point of view of a subsequent holder, a promissory note that has been endorsed by the payee is identical in its effect to an accepted bill of exchange. Indeed, the

---

[9] S. 75.

Bills of Exchange Act applies equally to both bills and notes except in its provisions relating to the acceptance of bills of exchange.

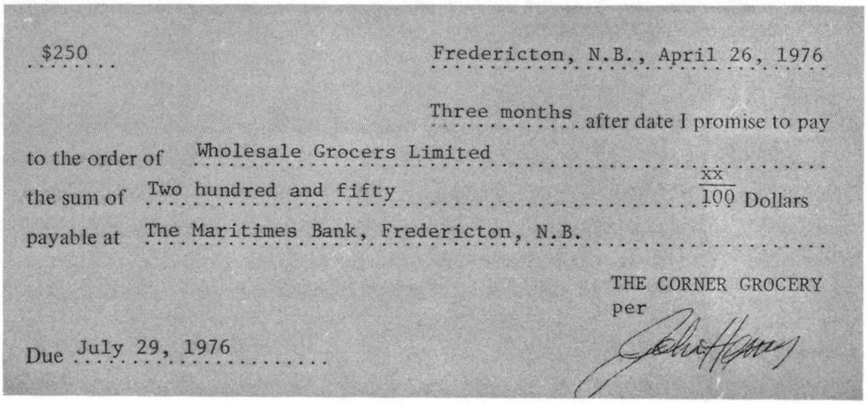

FIGURE 2: A Promissory Note

A maker of a note may word it so that it will be payable out of his current bank account at maturity, and it will then be paid through his bank, and returned cancelled to him.

Cheque

A cheque is a bill of exchange drawn against a bank and payable on demand. From the point of view of the holder, a cheque contains the implied promise of its drawer that he has funds on deposit at the bank sufficient to meet its amount, or that the amount is within the terms of a line of credit granted by the bank. For this reason it is sometimes convenient to think of the drawer of a cheque as a "promisor". The bank on which the cheque is drawn is called the *drawee bank*.

Since a cheque is payable on demand, its separate presentment to a bank for acceptance, when payment can be had at once, would in most instances be superfluous. The Bills of Exchange Act nowhere expressly authorizes the acceptance of cheques, nor does it refer specifically to the current banking practice of "certifying" cheques.[10] *Certification* amounts to an undertaking by the bank to pay the amount of the cheque to its holder when later presented for payment and, to ensure this result, the bank forthwith deducts the amount of the cheque from the drawer's account. Certification takes the form of the bank's stamped acknowledgment, with date, on the face of the cheque.

---

[10] See Falconbridge, *The Law of Negotiable Instruments in Canada*, p. 43. Toronto: The Ryerson Press, 1955.

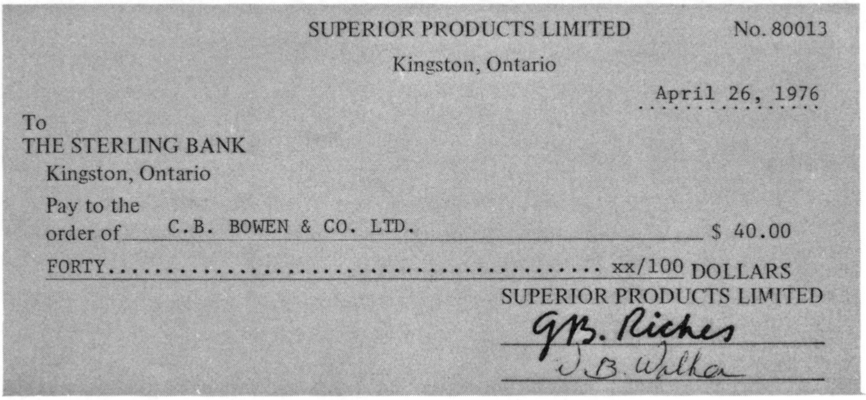

SUPERIOR PRODUCTS LIMITED	No. 80013

Kingston, Ontario

April 26, 1976

To
THE STERLING BANK
  Kingston, Ontario

Pay to the
order of _____ C.B. BOWEN & CO. LTD. _____ $ 40.00

FORTY.. xx/100 DOLLARS

SUPERIOR PRODUCTS LIMITED

G.B. Riches
J.B. Walker

FIGURE 3: A Cheque

Occasionally a supplier will refuse to release goods until paid by certified cheque. The purchaser must then prepare the cheque payable to the supplier and have the drawee bank certify it before he delivers it. Perhaps less frequently, it may be the payee rather than the drawer who requests the bank to certify a cheque: a cheque certified in this way is assured of collection and safer to hold than cash—a thief would have to forge an endorsement before he could realize its amount. Certification at the request of the holder also forestalls any attempt by the drawer to stop payment on the cheque in the inverval before it would normally be charged to his account, without the necessity of cashing the cheque at the drawee bank.

For most practical purposes, certification of a cheque is comparable to the acceptance of other types of bills of exchange.[11] The bank concerned is the drawee to whom the instrument is addressed, and once having undertaken certification it assumes a definite liability to the holder for the amount of the cheque.

The drawer of a cheque may postdate it by giving it a date after the time it is delivered to the payee. A cheque is an order addressed to a bank, and the bank must follow the instructions given to it on the face of the cheque: the bank is therefore not entitled to pay the instrument before its date. While a cheque is by definition payable "on demand," a holder's right to demand payment is not effective until its date arrives; in the meantime the instrument operates like a time draft, though without the benefit for the drawer of three days of grace.[12] Post-

---

[11] The difference between certification and acceptance is confined to the circumstance where the drawee bank fails, and even then relates only to certification at the request of the holder (rather than of the drawer). When a cheque is certified at the request of the holder, the drawer is entirely discharged of his implied promise that the bank will honour the cheque. "It is as if the holder takes a deposit receipt of the bank for the amount of the cheque." (Falconbridge, *op. cit.*, p. 45.)

[12] If, instead, the cheque were dated January 15 and had the words, "Payable on January 31," written on it, three days of grace would be added. (Falconbridge, *op. cit.*, p. 26.)

dating is sometimes a convenience for a drawer who expects to be unavailable at the time a present liability matures and who does not wish to pay in advance.

Having delivered his cheque, a drawer may have cause to regret his act before the cheque has had time to be charged against his account. In these circumstances the drawer may countermand or "stop payment" by advising his bank not to pay the cheque. The countermand amounts to a cancellation by the drawer of the directions he has formerly given to the bank on the face of the cheque. A bank recognizes countermands of cheques as an accommodation for its customers, and may require the drawer to agree that he will not hold the bank responsible if, through its inadvertence, the cheque is paid out of his account in spite of the countermand.

A postdated cheque can be countermanded at any time before it is paid by the bank. A cheque which has been certified at the request of its drawer and not yet delivered to the payee may be countermanded and the amount added back to the drawer's account at the bank. Since the bank has a liability on the certified cheque, the bank will not countermand it unless it is surrendered by the drawer for cancellation or the drawer agrees to indemnify the bank should it be presented for payment.

As we have seen, payments can also be made from current bank accounts by means of sight drafts, time drafts, and promissory notes. In recent years, however, the cheque has come largely to supersede these other means of payment. This development is doubtless related to the practice of paying accounts once each month. Suppliers who once relied heavily upon the acceptance of a draft as immediate acknowledgment of indebtedness have learned to depend upon the contractual basis of the transaction and the credit-worthiness of their buyers. The business community has been slowly gaining experience in the considerable lengths to which its members may trust one another, and in applying that knowledge in the use of the banking facilities at its disposal. It is a result dictated by self-interest, for a good credit reputation is a prized business resource, and a great stigma attaches to a business that issues cheques which prove to be "n.s.f." (not sufficient funds). The comparative simplicity of payment by cheque has therefore been found to be justified in all but the smallest minority of instances. There are still a few trades in which the routine use of sight and time drafts persists by tradition, and in the field of international trade, where the parties are often unknown to one another and have to deal at great distance, drafts retain an advantage.[13] The promissory note, particularly the demand note, survives as the common method by which a borrower provides evidence of his indebtedness for a bank loan.

Creditors of all kinds, including employees, have become accustomed to expect payment by cheque. In place of individual pay envelopes for each employee containing the exact currency of his weekly wages, the general practice is now to issue pay cheques: even these may be deposited by the employer directly

---

[13]See Howard, "Is the Bill of Exchange Outmoded?", *The Canadian Banker,* Summer, 1959.

in the employee's personal bank account, so that the employee quite literally never sees his pay. As a result, the risks inherent in handling large amounts of cash are eliminated. For the same reason, the use of cheques affords an easy and relatively safe method of making payments by mail.

We should recall that a cheque, even certified by a bank, is not legal tender. Strictly speaking, a creditor is entitled to payment in Bank of Canada notes and in coins up to the designated amounts for each denomination. A supplier who insisted upon the letter of the law in this respect would, however, find himself at a serious competitive disadvantage. Furthermore, if he refused a *reasonable* tender of payment and the matter came to court, the court costs could be charged against him.

PREREQUISITES FOR LIABILITY

Until an instrument is delivered, the drawer, acceptor, or maker, as the case may be, has no liability. Even after he has signed it he may change his mind and tear it up before delivering it.

Delivery may be "actual", the instrument being issued personally by the promisor to the payee, or it may be "constructive". Constructive delivery can take the form of issue to an agent of the payee, or simply of notice to the payee that the instrument is complete and ready for him.[14] Once an instrument has been delivered, the term "negotiation" becomes the usual description for any subsequent transfer of it by the payee to a new holder and for any later transfers between successive holders.

A drawee has no liability in respect of a bill of exchange until he accepts and delivers it. This result follows simply because until acceptance he has done nothing to assume liability for it. Only when and if he becomes an acceptor does he assume liability.

MEANING OF NEGOTIABILITY

Negotiability is the quality possessed by a class of promises in writing that allows a transferor to assign his right to payment without having to notify the promisor and that may put the transferee in a better legal position to enforce the right than the transferor enjoyed. A negotiable instrument is, therefore, a special type of assignable contract. As we noted in Chapter 13, its transfer is distinguishable by three features not common to the ordinary assignment of contractual rights:

(a) Notice of the assignment need not be given to the promisor. In other words, a negotiable instrument may be transferred (or assigned) from one holder to another without advising the promisor about each new holder and the promisor becomes liable to each successive holder in turn.

---

[14] S. 39.

(b) The assignee may sometimes acquire a better right to sue on the instrument than his predecessor (assignor) had. Chapter 23 examines this aspect of negotiable instruments.

(c) A holder may sue in his own name any other party liable on the instrument without joining any of the remaining parties.

ESSENTIALS FOR NEGOTIABILITY

If an instrument is to fulfil the purposes mentioned above, it must possess a very high degree of transferability. Nothing in its wording should cause an outside party to hesitate to take it in the course of trade. In the first place, the promise or order must be set out in writing. Otherwise the transferee would hold no evidence of the promise to present for payment.

Secondly, the obligation must be for a money payment. An obligation in terms of money avoids special inquiry about the value of the subject-matter of the promise. Other forms of obligation — to render services, to transfer ownership of a chattel — would require a prospective assignee to investigate the value of what he is being promised.

Thirdly, the money promised must be a "sum certain". The amount may be repayable in instalments or with interest and still be a "sum certain".[15] To promise to pay "the balance owing to you for services rendered" is to deprive the promise of the status of a negotiable instrument. A prospective holder could not ascertain from the face of the instrument the scope of the contractual right being offered.

Fourthly, the promise or order must be unconditional, so that a prospective holder need not look outside the instrument to learn all the implications of some qualifying phrase. Promises to pay "if the goods are delivered in good condition," "subject to an allowance for poor material," or "if at maturity date I can afford to do so," are conditional promises. The resulting contract, though valid between the immediate parties, lacks the special quality needed for negotiability: any attempt to transfer the rights under it would be a mere assignment lacking the advantages of negotiability.

Fifthly, the negotiable instrument must be payable at a fixed or determinable future time or on demand.[16] The value of a contractual right being offered for transfer can only be appraised when that right contains an indication of the time at which the promise is to be performed.

Sixthly, negotiation must be of the whole instrument, not for part of the amount.

---

[15] Ss. 28 and 186.

[16] In this respect it is hard to justify the element of uncertainty introduced by the definition of "determinable future time" in s. 24(b), *viz.*, "on or at a fixed period after the occurrence of a specified event which is certain to happen *though the time of happening is uncertain*" (italics added). Thus it seems a promissory note payable "at my death" would be a valid negotiable instrument. The proviso must be of little practical importance in business.

Finally, the negotiable instrument must be signed by the drawer if it is a draft or cheque or by the maker if a promissory note. Wherever written evidence is required as a condition of enforcing a contract, the signature of the promisor is an indispensable aspect of the writing.

A cheque or other negotiable instrument can be dated on a Sunday or other legal holiday without affecting its validity. The instrument may be impeached only by showing that the consideration for it was illegal because the transaction out of which it arose was in violation of some statute such as the Lord's Day Act.[17] Nevertheless, it is common practice not to give a negotiable instrument a date which is a Sunday.

THE LEGAL SIGNIFICANCE OF AN INSTRUMENT THAT IS NOT NEGOTIABLE

An interesting question arises when A draws a bill on B payable to C, and B refuses to accept. Does drawing the bill nevertheless serve as notice to B that he must now pay C instead of A? The Bills of Exchange Act provides the answer. Even when the instrument satisfies all the prerequisites for negotiability, the act of presenting it for acceptance will not of itself amount to notice of an assignment of the debt it describes.[18] Accordingly, B is not affected by the instrument if he refuses to accept, and he owes nothing to C.

Although a document may not amount to a negotiable instrument (where, for example, the order or promise is conditional or the sum to be paid is uncertain), it may still transfer contractual rights enforceable between the parties and still be capable of assignment as an ordinary contractual right. When a court rules that a document is not a negotiable instrument, the result is that the Bills of Exchange Act cannot operate to liberate any transfer of it from the inconvenient rules that apply to ordinary contractual assignments. Accordingly, when a promise expressed in an instrument is made subject to the satisfaction of some stated condition, no holder of the instrument can enforce the promise until the condition is met.

METHODS OF NEGOTIATION

By Endorsement and Delivery

An order instrument is one expressed to be payable "to A," "to A or order," or "to the order of A". The condition for its negotiation by A is that it be endorsed by A as well as delivered by him. Endorsement may take a number of forms which we shall examine below, but the essential element for our present purposes

---

[17] See Falconbridge, *op. cit.*, p. 26.
[18] S. 127

is a subscription (traditionally on the reverse side of the instrument) of the signature of the person to whose order the instrument is then payable.

Anyone who purchases an order instrument without requiring the proper endorsement acquires a legal right of very limited value. He is probably confined to recourse against the person who transferred it to him and has no rights against any prior parties.[19] In any event, when the instrument is payable "to order," a new holder can never acquire a better legal right than his predecessors until he has obtained the endorsement on the instrument of the designated person. He has a right to demand the necessary endorsement.[20]

By Delivery Only

Endorsement is not necessary if the instrument is a "bearer" instrument. An instrument is in bearer form when it is made payable in the first instance "to bearer," or "to *A* or bearer," or when no payee has been named and a space is left blank for the insertion of a name. It is also in bearer form when it is payable to an abstraction (for example, "Pay to Petty Cash") or to a fictitious or nonexisting person, as there is no one capable of endorsing. An instrument payable to the order of a specified person becomes a bearer instrument if he endorses it by signing his name without further words or instructions; until it is later endorsed payable to order, it may be negotiated by delivery alone.

An important safeguard gained in using an order instrument is that its dishonest negotiation amounts to the offence of forgery under the Criminal Code.[21] In addition, as we shall see again, the Bills of Exchange Act makes forgery one of the exceptions to the rule that a holder may acquire a better right than the transferor had, and thus affords an extra protection (the defence of forgery) to the parties liable on an order instrument. Because a bearer instrument may be negotiated by delivery only, a thief may successfully negotiate it without resorting to forgery. For this reason, if a bearer instrument proves to have been lost or stolen at some previous time, its holder may still require the party liable to pay provided he can show that he acquired the instrument without knowledge of the loss or theft.[22]

The effect is that businessmen rarely prepare their negotiable instruments in bearer form. Occasionally, however, order instruments are converted into bearer form by their holders. Employees, for example, frequently endorse their pay cheques before taking them to the bank for cash or deposit. If their endorsement consists in nothing but their signature they have converted the cheques into bearer instruments.

Until comparatively recent times, Bank of Canada banknotes bore on their faces a promise by the Bank to pay the designated amount "on demand to bearer".

---

[19] See Falconbridge, *op. cit.*, p. 55.
[20] S. 61.
[21] The Criminal Code, R.S.C. 1970, c. C-34, s. 332.
[22] Megrah and Ryder (eds), *Byles on Bills of Exchange,* pp. 193 and 367. London: Sweet & Maxwell, 1972.

These notes circulated like promissory notes in bearer form, acquiring their ready transferability from the unquestioned credit of their maker, the Bank of Canada. Their wording has now been changed to delete any form of promise and substitute the simple assertion that "This note is legal tender," in recognition of their statutory origin.[23] These banknotes continue to circulate in the same way as bearer instruments, however, not requiring their holder's endorsement each time they are tendered in payment. The old Canadian banknotes, if stolen, could not be traced through successive transactions and recovered from an innocent holder.[24] It is probably true that this rule applies to legal tender generally, even when not in the form of a promissory note, and therefore applies to Bank of Canada notes with the new wording.[25]

TYPES OF ENDORSEMENT

Endorsement in blank. The party entitled to payment on an order instrument signs his name — and nothing else — by way of endorsement, thus making it payable to bearer.

Special endorsement. The party entitled to payment on an order instrument specifies the next person to whom payment is to be made. For example:

Pay to Prometheus

(signed) "I. Zeus."

Restrictive endorsement. The party entitled to payment on an order instrument renders it henceforth non-negotiable by specifying how payment by the party primarily liable shall be made, as by endorsing it, "for deposit only," or, "pay to Prometheus only." If the payee to whom an instrument has been delivered wishes to be sure that it will not be stolen from him, his endorsement forged, and the instrument sold to a new holder (for example, cashed at a bank), he should endorse it, "for deposit only," over his signature. It can then only be deposited to the credit of his account at the bank. The English practice of crossing cheques (drawing two straight parallel lines across the face of the cheque and writing, "for account of payee" between the lines) accomplishes the same purpose.

---

[23] The Bank of Canada Act, R.S.C. 1970, c. B-2, s. 21 authorizes the use of Bank of Canada notes as legal tender. The Currency and Exchange Act, R.S.C. 1970, c. C-39, s. 7, specifies the coins that are legal tender.

[24] "Bills and notes payable to bearer circulate as money, and are considered as such. The bona fide possessor is, therefore, the true owner, for it is essential to the currency of money that property and possession should be inseparable." (*Byles on Bills of Exchange*, p. 199.)

[25] See Atiyah, *The Sale of Goods* (4th ed.), p. 5. London: Pitman, 1971. However, see *Bank of Montreal v. Bay Bus Terminal (North Bay) Ltd.* [1972] 3 O.R. 881, for a change in effect caused by the new wording. The court there held that a Bank of Canada note bearing the statement that the Bank would pay the face amount "to the bearer on demand," entitled the holder under s. 156 of the Bills of Exchange Act to require the Bank of Canada to give him another note of the same denomination when the original note had been lost (or destroyed by fire). The new wording would appear to preclude recovery from the Bank since, no longer being in the form of a promissory note, new banknotes are not governed by the provisions of the Bills of Exchange Act.

Conditional endorsement. The party entitled to payment specifies a person to whom payment is next to be made, provided he has lived up to the terms of a contract between them as, for example, "pay to the order of Bacchus if sober." A condition thus included in the wording of an endorsement differs in its effect from a condition written into the instrument by a drawer, acceptor or maker because it does not make the original promise in the instrument conditional. The party primarily liable may disregard a conditional endorsement in making payment, but the endorser may recover from the endorsee (Bacchus) if the condition was not satisfied.

Qualified endorsement. The person entitled to payment transfers his rights in such a way as to deny his liability as an endorser, for example, "James Bond, without recourse". Anyone giving value for such an instrument is on notice that he has no remedy against the particular person who has endorsed in this fashion, should the party primarily liable default: as we shall see, in the absence of a qualified endorsement, an endorser normally has a liability to subsequent endorsees. Manufacturers or wholesalers who "factor" their accounts receivable sometimes use a qualified endorsement. A factor may be willing to purchase drafts drawn on customers and endorsed over to him "without recourse"; the result is that the factor bears the ultimate risk of collection, without recourse to his client (the manufacturer or wholesaler).

Anomalous endorsement. A person with a recognized credit standing places his signature on a negotiable instrument with the sole object of adding his liability, as endorser, to that of the party primarily liable (drawer, acceptor, or maker). The endorsement is "anomalous" or exceptional because it is not added for the purpose of negotiating the instrument, and the endorser will never have been a holder in his own right.

An instrument may be negotiable in the technical sense of satisfying the conditions for negotiability, and yet not be negotiable in the practical sense of attracting prospective holders who are willing to buy it. The quality of an instrument depends upon the credit of the parties who have accepted liability in respect of it; an anomalous endorser can contribute to negotiability in this way. It can also be a convenient means of guaranteeing a debt, as we are to see.

PURPOSES OF ENDORSEMENT

An endorsement may be the means of:
(a) transferring title to an instrument payable to order;
(b) giving increased security to the payee (or subsequent holder);
(c) identifying the party entitled to payment, or
(d) acknowledging a partial payment.

We examined the first of these purposes above when we looked at the methods of negotiation and the types of endorsement. By far the majority of endorsements serve simply as the method of transferring ownership in the instrument.

We have also seen that an endorsement can be a means of providing increased security by adding one's name as an anomalous endorsement. Whenever one subscribes his signature as endorser without any words qualifying liability, he becomes liable for payment if the party of primary liability (the acceptor, maker or drawer) defaults. This result follows though the endorser has never owned the instrument and is not in the act of negotiating it to someone else.[26] For this reason an anomalous endorsement is a means of guaranteeing a debt, with the endorser in the role of guarantor.[27]

A bank may occasionally require an endorsement for the purpose of identifying someone seeking to cash a cheque. As the holder of a negotiable instrument, a bank has no right to charge the amount against its customer's account if the instrument includes an endorsement forged by the person cashing it. To protect itself the bank may therefore require an endorsement of the form:

> T. Smith is hereby identified
> *(signed)* "R. Jones."

As endorser, Jones is not liable for payment as are other endorsers should the party primarily liable default. His liability is limited to the loss which would follow from having identified someone as T. Smith who later proved not to be that person.

If the maker of a note is to pay his debt by instalments, it is up to him to see that every time he makes a partial payment he secures on the instrument an endorsement by its holder for the amount paid. Otherwise he remains liable for the full face amount of the instrument if it is subsequently negotiated to a holder who is unaware of the partial payments. An example of this type of endorsement is:

> May 14, 19 . . . . .
> Received in part payment, $75.00
> *(signed)* "B. Brown."

An alternative arrangement that avoids the need for such endorsements is for the debtor to make a series of separate notes bearing the dates of the various instalments and to require the surrender of the related note on the occasion of paying each instalment.

THE LIABILITY OF AN ENDORSER

We have already noted that an endorser is liable to any holder for the amount of the instrument, should the party primarily liable dishonour it, but the idea needs elaboration. An endorser is entitled to very prompt notice of the dishonour from the holder, or he will be freed from this liability. Dishonour is the failure by the party primarily liable to pay the instrument according to its terms. If the instrument is a draft, dishonour may take the form of either the drawee's refusal to accept or, if he accepts, of his later refusal to pay as acceptor:[28]

---

[26] S. 131. The endorser is liable to the payee even though the payee has not himself endorsed. Robinson v. Mann (1901), 31 S.C.R. 484. Also, *Byles on Bills of Exchange,* pp. 173-4.

[27] The same effect may be had without endorsement if both the guarantor and debtor sign in the first instance as joint makers of a promissory note.

[28] S. 133(a).

In the rather unusual event that an order instrument is negotiated several times, a particular endorser's liability extends not only to the present holder but to any other endorsers after the time of his own endorsement and before its final negotiation to the present holder. He has no liability to any fellow endorser whose signature was already on the instrument at the time he endorsed. In these circumstances, a holder has a choice of endorsers to require payment from when the instrument is dishonoured, provided each of them has received the necessary notice of dishonour.[29] In this game of musical chairs an endorser who is held liable has recourse against any prior endorser but not against any subsequent one.[30] The ultimate loser will be the first endorser (or the drawer if the instrument is a draft) — assuming he cannot recover from the party primarily liable.

An endorser may also be liable when the reason for non-payment by the party primarily liable is either the forgery of a prior endorsement to the endorser's or, if the instrument is a draft or cheque, the forgery of the drawer's signature.[31] The only holder who can recover from an endorser in these circumstances is one who has satisfied the conditions for qualifying as a "holder in due course," as explained in the next chapter. The result is that when a loss arises from a forged endorsement or the forged signature of the drawer, it must ultimately be borne by the person who acquires the instrument immediately following the forgery.

Illustration:

A knew that C maintained an account at the B Bank. A drew a cheque on the B Bank payable to himself, forging C's signature as drawer. A then endorsed the cheque and "cashed" it at a hotel operated by D. D endorsed the cheque and deposited it in the hotel account at the X Bank. The X Bank presented the cheque for payment to the B Bank through the bank clearing system. The B Bank recognized the forgery and refused to pay the cheque out of C's account. The cheque was then returned to the X Bank.

The X Bank is entitled to recover the amount which it had previously credited to D's account in respect of the cheque. The X bank is the holder (in fact, a holder in due course) and D, as the endorser immediately after the forgery, is liable.[32] In this illustration there is no other endorser between D and A, the perpetrator of the fraud, and the loss must fall upon D unless A can be apprehended and the funds recovered from him.

An endorser also warrants to any later party to whom the instrument may be negotiated by endorsement that he had a good title to it.[33] Finally, the holder must "duly present" the instrument for payment or endorsers will not have any

---

[29] Alternatively, the holder may sue all the endorsers as co-defendants in a single action and leave them to work out their individual liability among themselves.

[30] S. 101. Each endorser has, after receiving notice of dishonour, the same period of time for giving notice to earlier endorsers that the holder had after dishonour.

[31] S. 133(b).

[32] S. 50(1) and (2).

[33] S. 133(c).

liability to him. For this purpose, an instrument payable on demand must be presented for payment within a reasonable time after its endorsement, and an instrument which is not payable on demand must be presented on the day it falls due.[34]

THE LIABILITY OF A DRAWER

The drawer of a draft undertakes that on due presentment it shall be accepted and paid according to its terms, and that if it is dishonoured he will compensate the holder or any endorser who is compelled to pay it and who takes the necessary proceedings on dishonour.[35] The drawer of a cheque undertakes that the cheque will be paid from his account on demand: if there are insufficient funds for the purpose in his account, he is liable to the holder or to any endorser from whom the holder may recover. Because the parties to a cheque do not ordinarily contemplate a formal acceptance of it by the drawee bank, the drawer of the cheque becomes for practical purposes "the party primarily liable" comparable to the acceptor of a draft or the maker of a note.

A bank is subject to the instructions of its customer in the disposition of the funds he maintains on deposit with it. The duty and authority of a bank to pay a cheque end when its customer countermands payment or when it receives notice of the customer's death.[36] While the holder cannot then realize the amount of the cheque through the offices of the bank, the liability represented in the cheque does continue. The drawer of a cheque who stops payment on it is in fact dishonouring his instrument, and may be sued by the holder. The death of the drawer makes the amount of the cheque a charge against his estate, and it becomes one of the debts his personal representative (executor or administrator) must settle.

NOTICE OF DISHONOUR

We have noted that the contingent liability of both an endorser and a drawer depends upon a prompt notice of dishonour from the holder. This notice must be given to the endorsers and drawer not later than the business day next following the dishonour.[37] It may be mailed, and if it is, the time limit applies to the time of depositing it in the post office and not to the time it is received.[38] An endorser or drawer is entitled to *express* notice of dishonour from the holder except where he waives his right to notice.[39] It is not enough for the holder to show that the endorser or drawer heard about the dishonour from some other source.[40]

---

[34] S. 86.
[35] S. 130.
[36] S. 167.
[37] S. 97. Under some circumstances, a delay in giving notice may be excused (s. 105).
[38] S. 103(2).
[39] S. 106(1)(b).
[40] S. 99. See also Falconbridge, *op. cit.,* p. 92.

For many purposes the form in which the communication is made may vary as long as it conveys the essential message. In two instances, however, a special form of notice of dishonour known as *protest* is prescribed. Protest is required if the instrument is drawn or payable or accepted in Quebec[41] or outside Canada.[42] It consists in engaging the services of a notary public, or justice of the peace where no notary public is available, to confirm the dishonour personally and make a note of the fact. The notary public must also prepare a notice of his protest in prescribed form[43] and deliver it to the endorsers and drawer within the same time as for a notice of dishonour generally.[44]

It is the holder who contacts the notary public for the purpose of protesting the instrument. The holder may pay the notary public his fee, but he is entitled to be reimbursed by the endorser or drawer to whom the notice of protest is delivered.[45] To avoid the possibility of this expense an endorser may waive his right to any notice of dishonour by including the words, "No Protest" in his endorsement.[46]

LIABILITY OF THE TRANSFEROR BY DELIVERY

The term "transferor by delivery" describes anyone who negotiates an instrument in bearer form. Since no endorsement is required, a transferor by delivery is not liable on the instrument as would be an endorser.[47] The only liability he does have is confined to the one person to whom he negotiates the instrument, called his *immediate transferee*: the liability is only for such loss as the immediate transferee would sustain if the instrument were not genuine. The transferor by delivery has no liability if the party primarily liable proves financially incapable of paying it. The only action that may be brought against him is one by his immediate transferee on the grounds that the instrument is not what it purported to be, that he had no right to transfer it, or that at the time of transfer he was aware it was valueless.[48] Since the most common bearer instrument is a banknote, a person who incurs a loss for having received valueless counterfeit money has therefore a legal recourse against the person who transferred it to him.

LIABILITY OF THE ACCEPTOR AND MAKER

The acceptor of a bill, by accepting it, undertakes to pay it according to the terms of his acceptance.[49] Similarly, the maker of a promissory note undertakes to pay

---

[41] S. 114.
[42] S. 112.
[43] The prescribed forms are set out at the end of the Act.
[44] S. 126
[45] S. 124
[46] S. 106(1)(b).
[47] S. 137(2).
[48] S. 138.
[49] S. 128.

it according to its terms.[50] On the death of either the maker or acceptor, his liability passes to his personal representative.

THE STATUTE OF LIMITATIONS

We have seen that the holder of a negotiable instrument must duly present the instrument for payment and, when necessary, give the required notice of dishonour if he is to establish his legal rights against all prior parties to the instrument. He must then also prosecute his legal rights, by court action if necessary, within six years (five in Quebec) because thereafter an action on a negotiable instrument is barred by the Statute of Limitations.[51] The period of six years dates from the maturity of the instrument, the time of the most recent payment made in respect of it, or the date of any written acknowledgment from which a promise to pay may be implied, whichever date is the latest. The lapse of this period of time does not, however, extinguish the liability of the parties completely. A discussion of how such a liability may be revived will be found in Chapter 31.

QUESTIONS FOR REVIEW

1. A student insists that a cheque cannot be a form of draft because it originates with a debtor and not with a creditor. Is his reasoning correct?
2. Describe briefly the respective uses of demand drafts, sight drafts, and time drafts in commercial practice.
3. We sometimes refer to negotiable instruments as "a special class of promises in writing," yet a bill of exchange and a cheque take the form of an *order* to pay. Can these two views be reconciled?
4. Explain why a promise cannot take the form of a negotiable instrument if it is conditional.
5. What is meant by the "negotiation" of a negotiable instrument? In what ways may it take place?
6. "The act of endorsing and delivering a negotiable instrument payable to order differs from an ordinary assignment of contractual rights in three important respects." Explain this statement.
7. Allen drew a draft on James ordering him to pay Thomas "the amount of my account furnished". James accepted, writing, "Correct for, say, $750." Is this a negotiable instrument?
8. Gower has drawn a time draft on Cohen payable three months after sight to Jenkins. The draft is complete and regular with the possible exception of a clause that Cohen, the drawee, is "to pay the amount of this draft out of money due me on December 31 for professional services rendered". If

---

[50] S. 185. If the party seeking payment is a "holder in due course" as defined in the following chapter, the maker of a note cannot refuse to pay on the grounds that the payee whom he has named in his note either does not exist or lacks capacity to endorse.

[51] See, for example: R.S.B.C. 1960, c. 370, ss. 3 and 4; R.S.O. 1970, c. 246, s. 45(1)(g); R.S.N.S. 1967, c. 168, s. 2(1)(e).

Cohen refuses to accept the draft, does he owe its amount in future to Gower or to Jenkins?

9. Under what circumstances does an instrument, negotiable in its origin, cease to be negotiable?

10. You are the maker of a note in which you undertake to pay $500 to a moneylender on demand. Subsequently you pay an instalment of $200 to the moneylender in respect of this liability. What steps should you take to ensure that you will not have to pay the full $500 at some later time?

11. Contrast the liability of an ordinary endorser and a transferor by delivery as to: (a) the parties to whom each is liable; and (b) the scope of his liability.

12. What liability, if any, would a person incur in the process of paying an account, unwittingly, with counterfeit bank notes?

13. You are a holder of a bill of exchange drawn by Richardson on Ward, payable to MacDonald or order, accepted by Ward, and endorsed in blank by MacDonald. Upon presentment by you to Ward for payment, payment is refused. What is your legal position? What steps should you take to protect your rights?

14. The endorsements appearing on the back of each of three negotiable instruments are reproduced below. An asterisk following a name indicates an actual signature. Identify each of the endorsements by type and explain its effect for the parties concerned:

    (i) Pay to John Factor, Without Recourse
        The Synthetic Textile Co. Ltd.
        per Terry Lean,*/ Manager.
        John Factor*

    (ii) Pay to James Hawkins,
         S. Trelawney*
         For deposit only,
         James Hawkins*

    (iii) Pay to Archibald Grosvenor only
          No Protest
          Reginald Bunthorne*
          Archibald Grosvenor*
          Archibald Grosvenor is hereby identified,
          Ralph Rackstraw*

15. In negotiating a loan from Hi-Rise Bank, Martin was required to provide a guarantor. Martin's good friend Roberts agreed to guarantee the bank loan. Martin made a promissory note, payable on demand, to the order of Hi-Rise Bank; Roberts placed his signature on the bank as endorser. Martin was subsequently unable to pay when the bank made a demand for payment; it then called on Roberts to pay the amount. Roberts defended by claiming that he had received no consideration for his endorsement. Examine the validity of this argument.

CASES FOR DISCUSSION

CASE 1

On April 28, the University of Ontario made a note payable to the Baroque Construction Co. Ltd., three months after date. The amount of the note was expressed simply as "the balance due to you for construction of our Arts Building". On May 2 following, the Baroque Construction Co. Ltd sold the note to a private financier, R. Jay, for $4,750, having shown him accounts and vouchers indicating a balance of $5,000 due from the university. On July 31, R. Jay presented the note to the treasurer of the university for payment and was advised by him that the construction contract with the Baroque Construction Co. Ltd. contained a guarantee clause and that serious defects had developed in the foundation of the Arts Building. He stated that the university was not prepared to pay the note for this reason. R. Jay countered with the argument that the defective work was not the slightest concern of his, and that the proper officer of the university had signed the note. He then sued the University of Ontario on its note. Should he succeed? Give reasons.

CASE 2

Jordan received a shipment of linen from Bale. Bale, who resided in another city, delivered the shipment personally and obtained a cheque in full payment from Jordan. Bale immediately went to Jordan's bank, but rather than cash the cheque simply had it certified so that it would be much simpler to take the amount home. The following day Jordan discovered that there was a substantial shortage in the shipment. He telephoned his bank at once to stop payment. The bank refused because Bale had certified the cheque. Jordan insisted that the bank must accept his order to stop payment regardless of certification. Is he right? Explain. What other remedies are available to him?

CASE 3

Elston owned all the issued common shares of Ham Ltd., a company incorporated in Ontario. In addition, Elston lent the company $160,000 of his personal funds and obtained in return a promissory note of the company payable to his order.

For personal reasons Elston had subsequently to borrow money on his own account from the Atlas Bank. To secure this loan he transferred the Ham Ltd. promissory note to the bank, but without endorsing it.

The Atlas Bank gave no notice to Ham Ltd. that it was the transferee. Two months after the bank acquired the note, Elston sold his shares in Ham Ltd. to new owners who had no knowledge of the existence of the note. At the same time Elston gave Ham Ltd. a general release of all claims he had against it in terms wide enough to include the company's obligation to him on the $160,000 note.

Elston defaulted on his personal loan from the Atlas Bank and the bank then demanded payment of the note from Ham Ltd. Ham Ltd. refused to pay, and the Atlas Bank brought an action against it for $160,000.

Give reasons whether or not this action should succeed. (See *Aldercrest v. Hamilton* [1970] 3 O.R. 529.)

CHAPTER 23

Negotiable Instruments: Their Enforcement

THE HOLDER IN DUE COURSE

We have already noted an important quality of negotiable instruments: a transferee is sometimes able to enforce payment of the debt when the transferor himself could not do so. The idea of an item of property gaining something from the mere fact of its transfer is not unique to negotiable instruments — we examined this question in Chapter 9, when we learned that an innocent purchaser of goods can often retain them even when his transferor, who had obtained them fraudulently, would himself have had to surrender them to the original vendor. Similar results may occur in the registration of ownership in land, as we shall see in Chapter 24. By and large, however, this possibility has not existed for choses in action; the general principle applied by our courts has been that an assignee of a chose in action takes no greater rights than the assignor had. Accordingly, negotiable instruments are a special exception to the principles governing the assignment of choses in action, and in this one respect negotiation more closely resembles a transfer of title to goods than an assignment of a chose in action.

A negotiable instrument does not become more valuable on transfer in the sense that the amount payable increases: what does happen is that in the course of transfer it bypasses certain arguments which a party liable might have used as a successful defence against the transferor, had the transferor chosen to try to collect its amount instead of negotiating it further. The new holder's (transferee's) chances of success, if he tries to enforce the instrument against a prior party, are better than were those of the transferor.

The essence of the modern concept of negotiability is that an innocent third-party holder shall not be subject to many defences and shall have a very high probability of realizing his claim. By the middle of the 17th century, the concept had been developed to the point where the law recognized the validity of the transfer of a bill of exchange by endorsement and the holder's right to sue on the instrument. However the holder could still have his claim defeated by the party liable showing, for example, that he had received no consideration or that the instrument had arisen out of an illegal transaction. It was not until the end of the 17th century that the implications of negotiability were fully realized in the law.[1] In 1697, the English Court of Chancery upheld the claim of a holder who had taken a bill in satisfaction of "an honest debt" when the drawer (the defendant) had argued that the bill had, in the first instance, been given without consideration.[2] Again, in 1699, the court held that a person who had lost a bill payable to himself or bearer could not recover from a holder who had given consideration to a stranger who had found the bill.[3] Chief Justice Holt held that in the circumstances the course of trade "creates a property in the assignee or bearer". In commenting on the case, Holden has written:

> Here for the first time in history the Common Law Courts and the Court of Chancery recognized the claim of the *bona fide* holder for value of a bill. A chariot had been driven through the hitherto impregnable lines of the common law maxim *nemo dat quod non habet* [no one can give what he does not have].[4]

The possibility that one may acquire something more than the transferor himself had is restricted in that the holder of the negotiable instrument must satisfy a number of rather strict conditions which ensure that his cause is virtuous and worthwhile.[5] Only then can he succeed to a better right than the transferor had. These conditions are as follows:[6]

(a) He must have taken the instrument complete and regular on the face of it.

(b) He must have acquired it before it was overdue and without notice that it had been previously dishonoured if such was the fact.

---

[1] See Kempin, *Legal History, Law and Social Change*, Ch. 12, especially pp. 95-6.

[2] Anon., (1697) 92 E.R. 950; 1 Comyns 43.

[3] Anon., (1699) 91 E.R. 118; 91 E.R. 698; 91 E.R. 1393. See also, Miller v. Race (1699) 97 E.R. 398.

[4] Holden, *The History of Negotiable Instruments in English Law*, p. 64. London: The Athlone Press, 1955.

[5] In point of fact it is only necessary that in the negotiation of the instrument there shall have been a holder in due course prior to the present holder. The present holder will then succeed to the rights of a holder in due course whether or not he himself satisfies all the essential conditions, provided he was not a party to any fraud or illegality affecting the instrument. The Bills of Exchange Act, s. 57. (Subsequent references to this Act in this chapter will be by section only.)

[6] S. 56.

(c) He, or someone through whom he claims, must have given consideration ("value") for the instrument. [7]

(d) He must have taken the instrument in good faith and without notice of any defect in the title of the person who negotiated it.

The holder who satisfies these conditions is known as a *holder in due course*.

We can understand this part of the law better when we see how it operates to the advantage of business. Over the years, business experience has shown that the concept of negotiability has a convenience far outweighing the probable total cost of its abuse, particularly when the law can be designed to inhibit abuse. By confining the legal advantage to a holder in due course, the possibility of abuse is greatly reduced.

The provisions that one cannot be a holder in due course if he has taken the instrument with a knowledge of its previous dishonour, or in bad faith, or with notice of a defect of title in the transferor, all have a common purpose. They deprive a holder of any advantage in conspiring with someone to take the instrument from him as transferee with a view to outflanking the defences of the party liable. The transferee will not qualify as a holder in due course and will therefore still be subject to all the defences which the party liable might have used against the transferor: he will gain nothing by the maneuver.

When the instrument is a time draft or note, a prospective holder of it can tell at a glance whether it is overdue or not. If it is already due, an obvious question for him to ask is why the present holder is trying to negotiate it instead of presenting it for payment. A prospective holder will have more difficulty, however, deciding whether a demand draft is overdue. If it has already been outstanding an "unreasonable" length of time (which varies with the circumstances), it is deemed to be overdue. [8] A new holder does not then become a holder in due course.

An outstanding demand note may have a different signficance from a demand draft. A demand note is sometimes given as evidence of long-term indebtedness. As such, it may remain outstanding a long time without necessarily raising doubts about its collectability. Consequently, the criterion of an unreasonable length of time used in other areas of the law may be unsuitable in determining whether it is overdue. [9] The time may well be much longer.

One important practical effect of the legal concept of a holder in due course is that banks are willing to discount drafts and cash cheques drawn on other banks with relatively little delay and at much reduced risk to themselves, since they acquire these instruments in the capacity of a holder in due course. If the law recognized no such concept, banks would be reluctant to purchase negotiable instruments and hold them as assets, because they would first have to make

---

[7] S. 57 requires that he shall have taken the instrument "for value" but s. 54 provides that where value has been given at any time for a bill, the holder is *deemed* to be a holder for value as regards the acceptor and all parties who became parties prior to such time.

[8] S. 70(2).

[9] S. 182. See also Falconbridge, *The Law of Negotiable Instruments in Canada*, p. 110.

exhaustive inquiries into the circumstances in which each was issued to ascertain that there was valuable consideration in the underlying transaction and that it was free of fraud, illegality, duress or undue influence. They could not afford to acquire instruments which would be subject to defences such as these when the time came to collect from the party primarily liable.[10]

THE MEANING OF DEFENCES

The term ''defences'' is a legal description for the various arguments that a party liable on an instrument may put up against a holder who is demanding payment. There are two variables to consider: (a) the status of the holder relative to the party liable, and (b) the nature of the defence of the party liable. To understand the meaning of a defence, we have to keep in mind a legal action in which the plaintiff is the holder of the instrument and the defendant an acceptor, maker, drawer or endorser.

TYPES OF HOLDERS

As a first step we must identify the relationship between the holder and the party liable as either that of immediate parties or of remote parties. When a holder has had direct dealings with the party from whom he proposes to collect the amount of the instrument, the two of them are *immediate parties*. If they have not had direct dealings with one another and yet are parties to the same instrument, they are *remote parties*. A holder in due course must acquire the instrument by negotiation from the payee or other endorser subsequent to the payee; accordingly he is *always* a remote party relative to the acceptor of a draft, maker of a note, or drawer of a cheque.

Illustration:

> *A* draws a cheque in favour of *B*. *B* endorses it to the order of *C*. *C* endorses it to the order of *D*. *D* is the present holder of the cheque.

> *A* (Drawer)——→*B* (Payee)   ↗*C* (Endorsee) ↗*D* (Endorsee)
>   (Endorser)↗   (Endorser)↗   (Holder)

> *A* and *B*, *B* and *C*, and *D* are immediate parties. The remote partes are *A* and *C*, *A* and *D*, and *B* and *D*. Whether the present holder, *D*, is a holder in due course will depend upon whether he satisfies the essential conditions specified above.

---

[10] As an additional protection a bank will require the endorsement of the person from whom it acquires the instrument; but recourse against endorsers is at best a second resort, and a digression banks naturally wish to avoid.

TYPES OF DEFENCES

Apart from the value of an instrument as evidence, a holder's chance of success in collecting from an immediate party is no better than his contractual rights under the agreement between them. The negotiable instrument does not change the holder's position in substance. From the point of view of a defendant, the party liable has a greater panoply of defences with which to thwart a holder who is an immediate party than he has to confront any other type of holder. He can use against him not only the defences he has available against remote parties but also a line of *mere personal defences*.

At the other extreme, a holder who is a holder in due course has the best possible chance of success in his demand for payment. The party liable has a greatly reduced list of possible defences with which to resist the demands of a holder in due course, although the defences still available to him are impregnable and good against all holders. Defences of this kind are termed *real defences*.

A holder may be a remote party who fails to measure up to the standards of a holder in due course. He is then in a position between an immediate party and a holder in due course, and subject not only to real defences but also to *defect of title defences*. (He is not, however, subject to mere personal defences.)

We may now examine each of these types of defences in detail.

MERE PERSONAL DEFENCES

All the defences — real, defect of title, and mere personal — are available to the defendant when the contestants are immediate parties, but some of these (the mere personal defences) are generally available *only* when they are immediate parties. The defences that are good only against an immediate party are (a) lack of consideration, and (b) the right of set-off.

If a negotiable instrument is given as a gift, it represents a promise as yet unperformed. As with any gratuitous promise, the promisor may plead a lack of consideration if he chooses to repudiate and is sued. The peculiar nature of negotiable instruments as a readily assignable class of promise requires some slight elaboration in the law, however. While it is unlikely that a negotiable instrument would change hands more than once without consideration being given during at least some stage in its negotiation, if nevertheless it is negotiated without either the holder or any prior party's having given "value" for it, the party liable can continue to plead a lack of consideration, even when the plaintiff is a remote party. Thus, it is a condition for the enforcement of a negotiable instrument that the holder *or someone through whom he claims* (that is, a prior party) must have given value for the instrument. To this extent a lack of consideration, as we shall see again later, may be more than a mere personal defence.

As between immediate parties, the defence of lack of consideration may also cover deficiencies in the underlying contract out of which the delivery or negotiation arose. In these circumstances, the instrument is given as a means of paying the price stipulated in the contract. If the underlying contract proves void or voidable for reasons of mistake, provisions in a statute (as with wagers), or public policy, the promisor may argue that he has received no legal consideration for his instrument.[11]

The argument that a negotiable instrument given in discharge of an already existing contractual obligation is given for past consideration is precluded by the Bills of Exchange Act. The Act states than an antecedent debt or liability constitutes valuable consideration for the instrument.[12]

The idea of set-off emerged briefly in Chapter 13, where we considered what happens when an assignor of an account receivable at the same time owes his debtor money on a different transaction; we saw that the assignee of the account receivable acquires no better right than the assignor had at the time the debtor received notice of the assignment. In addition, set-off frequently arises as a result of the transaction creating the account receivable, as when a supplier delivers goods that are deficient from the point of view of quality or quantity and then assigns the account. What is the effect when the buyer has paid for the goods with a negotiable instrument?

Illustration:

May Dental Supplies Ltd. sells $500 worth of supplies to Dr. Nichols and receives a cheque in payment. Shortly afterwards, Dr. Nichols discovers that the shipment is short of several valuable items worth $225, so that the dental supply company is in default.[13]

Dr. Nichols then advises May Dental Supplies Ltd. that he has countermanded payment of the cheque at his bank. May Dental Supplies Ltd. sues him on the instrument. Dr. Nichols can use the defence of set-off and May Dental Supplies Ltd. can recover only $275 by court action. Here the principals in the legal action are immediate parties.

Suppose instead that May Dental Supplies Ltd. deposits Dr. Nichols' cheque and the cheque is charged against Dr. Nichols' account at his bank. The defence of set-off is henceforth lost to Dr. Nichols. The bank where Dr. Nichols keeps his account is entitled to keep the full $500 it has taken from his account. The dentist and the bank are remote parties in respect of the transaction. By his act of drawing and delivering his cheque, the dentist has "cast his instrument upon the world" and has become accountable to any

---

[11] Lack of consideration is a reason for refusing to honour a negotiable instrument. It is a different matter if the promisor has already honoured his instrument and then seeks to recover its amount in a separate action. Thus, if one pays a wager or makes a gift of money by cheque, he cannot recover the amount by court action unless he can offer additional reasons such as duress or undue influence.

[12] S. 53. See also English Law Revision Committee, *Sixth Annual Report*, pp. 17-18.

[13] Strictly speaking, there is no distinction between default (nonfeasance) and breach (misfeasance), except that in legal actions the defendant usually claims by way of set-off where the plaintiff has been guilty of some default and by way of counterclaim where the plaintiff was himself guilty of breach. Thus, a seller is in default if his shipment is short of the quantity ordered, and in breach if the goods do not meet the specifications of the contract.

subsequent holder for its full amount should the payee succeed in negotiating it for value to a third party.[14]

The defence of set-off provides a convenient illustration of the difference between the effect of an ordinary assignment of a debt and the negotiation of a negotiable instrument. In the law of negotiable instruments the defence is good between immediate parties but is lost when the party seeking to enforce the instrument is a remote party with respect to the defendant. In an ordinary assignment, the defence of set-off remains available against an assignee.

DEFECT OF TITLE DEFENCES

Knowledge

We have seen that a holder in due course must by definition have taken the instrument without knowledge of any defect in title and, when he has done so, these defences will not avail against him. Therefore, if he takes the instrument *with* knowledge of one or more of these defects, he is not a holder in due course and a defence based on any of these defects will be successful.[15] Such defects are:

    (a) fraud, duress, undue influence, illegality;
    (b) incapacity to contract as a result of drunkenness or insanity;[16]
    (c) absence of delivery when the instrument was complete at the time;
    (d) want of authority in an agent to complete the instrument on behalf of the party primarily liable;
    (e) discharge of the instrument by payment before its maturity date;
    (f) renunciation of a holder's rights in the instrument before its maturity date.

We are already familiar with the concepts in the first two defects of title defences as they relate to the law of contract.

Illustration:

Conn advised Mark that Mark's family would probably come to personal harm unless Mark subscribed to Conn's "family insurance protection plan". Mark drew a cheque in favour of Conn for $100 as the premium cost for one year's family protection. *X,* an underworld leader who was fa-

---

[14] In practice, the bank where May Dental Supplies Ltd. deposited the cheque would not sue Dr. Nichols if it found he had countermanded the cheque at his own bank. It is much easier for this bank to charge the amount back to May Dental Supplies Ltd., as it is entitled to do on the strength of the dental-supply company's endorsement at the time of deposit.

[15] Ss. 56 and 58(2).

[16] Depending upon the circumstances, insanity might instead be interpreted as a real defence. See Falconbridge, *op. cit.,* p. 134.

miliar with Conn's means of livelihood, cashed the cheque for Conn. Before X managed to take it to the bank, however, Mark, on advice from the police, had directed his bank to refuse payment.

X is a remote party relative to Mark but he is not a holder in due course because he has taken the instrument with notice of the defect of title (in this instance, duress). Mark is, therefore, justified in refusing payment to X. In other words, Mark has a good defence against the holder, X.

Incapacity as a defect of title defence is confined to drunkenness and insanity; incapacity of a minor is discussed separately in the next section.

We have seen that delivery is a necessary step in establishing the liability of the acceptor of a draft, the maker of a note or the drawer of a cheque. For reasons of convenience, a businessman may sign a completed negotiable instrument in advance of the time it is to be delivered to the payee. He may, for example, be going on a business trip and anticipate that an account will have to be paid while he is away; he may wish merely to withhold delivery of the instrument until the liability is definitely established. In these circumstances, absence of delivery would amount to an unauthorized acquisition by the payee in advance of the intended time of delivery. The defence of "absence of delivery" also includes circumstances where a negotiable instrument is actually delivered to the payee, but subject to a condition which must be satisfied by the payee before the undertaking set out in the instrument will become operative.[17] If the condition is not satisfied, neither the payee nor any holder who acquires the instrument from him with a knowledge of this defect of title can enforce payment of it. However, one who acquires the instrument without notice of this absence of delivery may qualify as a holder in due course and be able to enforce payment.

Want of authority is another defect of title defence which may arise when a party has assumed liability by signing an instrument in which some of the details are still left blank, and has delivered the instrument to someone else in this form. No problem arises if the person to whom the instrument has been delivered completes it in strict compliance with the terms of the authority granted to him for the purpose; the instrument then has the same effect in law as though the party liable had personally completed it. Any abuse of such authority, however, creates a defect of title, and the party liable may refuse payment to the party guilty of the abuse and to any holder who takes the instrument with notice of this defect (or, for that matter, to anyone who is not a holder in due course). On the other hand, the party liable will have to pay if the holder acquires the instrument as a holder in due course, and he will be liable for it in whatever form it was actually completed.[18] There is always a risk, therefore, in leaving it to someone else to fill in the detail of a negotiable instrument.

The payment of an instrument on or after its maturity is an absolute discharge of the instrument,[19] but the instrument must have been clearly can-

---

[17] S. 40(1)(b).
[18] S. 32.
[19] S. 139.

celled at the time of payment. If it is regular on its face and does not appear to be overdue (as with a draft or time note) or outstanding for an unreasonable length of time (as with a cheque), a holder in due course can enforce the instrument even when it has been discharged by payment.[20] The reason is that a party paying the instrument has the responsibility for cancelling it: otherwise he takes the risk that it will find its way into the hands of a holder in due course and he will be liable to pay it a second time. Of course, if the holder takes the instrument with knowledge that it has already been paid, he is not a holder in due course but merely a remote party, and cannot enforce the instrument. Cancellation usually is effected by writing or stamping the word ''paid'' (with the date) across the face of the instrument.

For similar reasons, a holder's simple renunciation of his right to payment operates as a discharge of the instrument.[21] Needless to say, such a holder creates a problem if he chooses to disregard his renunciation and negotiates the instrument to someone else. His renunciation does not affect the rights of a holder in due course, but by definition, a holder in due course has an instrument that on its face does not disclose that it is overdue nor does he know of the prior renunciation. Accordingly, any remote party who takes an instrument with notice of its renunciation cannot enforce it.

Value

The proviso that lack of consideration is a defence against a remote party if value has never been given for the instrument means that the remote party cannot be a holder in due course: by definition, a holder in due course, or someone through whom he claims, must have given value.[22]

Illustration:

Boone gives his son a cheque for $100 to buy a new suit. Boone Jr. endorses it to Tweed, a tailor, in payment for a suit; Tweed endorses the cheque to his brother as a wedding gift. Tweed's brother can successfully sue Boone Sr., because at one stage value has been given for the cheque.

REAL DEFENCES

The following defences are good against any holder, even a holder in due course:

(a) incapacity to contract because of infancy;
(b) a forged signature on the instrument;
(c) want of authority, in someone who has represented himself as an agent, to sign on behalf of the party liable;

---

[20] There cannot be a holder in due course of an instrument paid before its maturity if it has been plainly cancelled. By definition, a holder in due course must take the instrument ''complete and regular on the face of it''.

[21] S. 142.

[22] See *Byles on Bills of Exchange,* (23rd ed.), pp. 190-1 (Megrah and Ryder, eds.)

    (d) absence of delivery where the instrument is incomplete when taken;

    (e) fraud as to the nature of the instrument;

    (f) alteration of the instrument;

    (g) cancellation of the instrument.

The incapacity to contract of a person under age is a real defence even when the instrument is given in payment for necessaries. A minor cannot be sued successfully on his negotiable instrument. The supplier may sue the minor for a reasonable price of the necessary goods, but this remedy has to be distinguished from an action on the instrument itself. While no holder will have any recourse against a minor who is a prior party on the instrument, his recourse against other parties is not affected.[23]

A forged signature may be that of either the party primarily liable or an endorser. Either type of forgery is a real defence for persons who have assumed liability on the instrument prior to the forgery. The real defence of forgery therefore provides the drawer of a cheque with grounds for refusing to honour his instrument, apart from estoppel as discussed below. Since the funds out of which his cheque is to be paid are on deposit at the bank named as drawee on the cheque, the bank is necessarily involved as a result of the forgery.

Insofar as the *drawer's* signature is concerned, a bank is supposed to know the signatures of all its customers[24] and for this purpose keeps their specimen signatures on file. It therefore has an obligation to detect a forgery of the drawer's signature and restore any amount it mistakenly pays out of his account for this reason.

In Canada, a bank's liability extends also to the payment of instruments bearing forged *endorsements*.[25] To understand a bank's liability in this respect we must distinguish between a "drawee bank" and a "presenting bank". Let us suppose, for example, that X of Winnipeg draws a cheque on the Bank of Montreal, Winnipeg main branch, and mails it to Y of Vancouver. Y cashes or deposits it at a local branch of the Royal Bank of Canada. The Royal Bank is the presenting bank; the Bank of Montreal, the drawee bank. With a forged endorsement, the presenting bank and not the drawee bank has the primary obligation to detect the forgery. For this reason a bank will take special precautions when asked to cash a cheque for a person who is not known to it or who has no account there. If the drawer of a cheque proposes to recover the amount when it proves to have been paid out of his account on a forged endorsement, he must advise his bank of the forgery within a reasonable time which must not exceed one year from the time he learned of it.[26]

The Bills of Exchange Act does not specify a similar time limit for notice when the signature of the party primarily liable has been forged. Nevertheless, a

---

[23] See Falconbridge, *op. cit.*, p. 135. But see Soon v. Watson (1962) 33 D.L.R. (2d) 429, where an infant was held liable on a note. No authority is cited in the judgment and it is unlikely to be followed.

[24] Bank of Montreal v. The King (1908) 38 S.C.R. 258.

[25] S. 49(1) and (3).

[26] S. 49.

person who, through forgery of his signature, is alleged to be a party to an instrument when in fact he is not, has a duty to apprise any holder or prospective holder of the facts as soon as he learns of them. If he does not do so, he may be estopped from using the real defence of forgery of his signature in an action brought against him for the amount of the instrument.[27] While not in fact a party to the instrument, he must take reasonable steps to avoid a loss for those who would be deceived by the forgery of his signature.

Illustration:

(a) *A* drew a cheque on the Merchants Bank payable to the order of *B* and delivered the cheque to *B*. *X* stole the cheque from *B* and presented it for payment at a branch of the Crown Bank. At that time *X* forged *B*'s signature as the necessary endorsement of the payee.

The Crown Bank would refuse to cash the instrument for *X* unless *X* could produce identification papers purporting to show that he is the payee, *B*. If the Crown Bank were to cash the cheque for *X*, the loss would fall upon it and would probably come to light along the following lines: the Crown Bank would stamp its name and the date on the cheque and clear it to the Merchants Bank branch against which it is drawn; the Merchants Bank would charge the amount against *A*'s account there; *B*, discovering the loss of the cheque, would ask *A* for a duplicate; *A* would then ascertain that the cheque charged against his account bore the forged endorsement of *B*; *A* (because of his real defence) would require the Merchants Bank to restore the amount to his account; the Merchants Bank would recover the amount from the Crown Bank because the Crown Bank's stamp on the cheque acts as its implied guarantee of the authenticity of prior endorsements, such as *X*'s forgery of *B*'s signature.[28]

(b) The circumstances are the same as in (a) except that, instead of taking the cheque to the Crown Bank, *X* persuaded a druggist, *C*, to cash it for him. *C* then deposited the cheque in his account at the Crown Bank after endorsing it as required by the bank.

The Crown Bank, when all the facts are ascertained, may recover the amount from *C* on the strength of his liability as endorser.[29] It would normally recover the amount by charging it against *C*'s account if the balance is sufficient.

When someone purporting to be an agent signs a negotiable instrument on

---

[27] S. 49, which establishes forgery as a real defence, also recognizes by its wording that a party liable may be estopped from using that defence.

[28] See clause (f) of Article 24 of the by-laws of the Canadian Bankers Association quoted by Falconbridge, *op. cit.*, p. 61.

[29] Banks normally require their customers to endorse the cheques they present for cash or deposit, even if the cheques are in bearer form. However, even if *C* had not endorsed, he would, as a transferor by delivery, have warranted to the Crown Bank (his immediate transferee) that he had a right to transfer the cheque: it can be argued that he would not have this right because of *X*'s forgery.

behalf of another, though without any authority real or apparent, his act is simply a specific type of forgery and the effect is the same. In each instance, the party to whom the instrument ascribes liability can deny such a liability on the grounds that the instrument is not his. In other words he has a real defence, good against all possible holders. As with agency law in general, the defence of want of authority will not avail if, in the eyes of prospective holders, the agent has an apparent authority to sign on behalf of his principal.[30] We must distinguish want of authority to *sign* from want of authority to *complete* an already signed instrument (for example, to fill in the amount on behalf of the party liable). As we have seen, an instrument which has been completed in an unauthorized manner can be negotiated to a holder in due course who may then require the party liable to pay the instrument.

We have noted that absence of delivery when an instrument is complete at the time is a mere defect of title defence and of no avail against a holder in due course. If the instrument is incomplete and undelivered when it is intercepted by the wrongdoer, the signer will have a real defence good against all holders. The term "absence of delivery" requires a careful interpretation, however. It includes a failure to satisfy a condition to which the delivery of the instrument was subject (for example, a failure to supply specified goods in return for the instrument), and it includes misuse of a signature or incomplete document supplied by the signer for a special purpose only. It does not, on the other hand, include an abuse of authority by an agent of the signer to whom the instrument has been delivered only for the purpose of completing it and transferring the property in it to someone else.[31]

Illustration:

> *X*, a new employee, advised *Y*, the proprietor of the business, that the bank had asked him to procure a new specimen of his employer's signature for its files. *X* persuaded *Y* to give him his signature on a blank piece of paper. *X* completed the paper in the form of a demand note payable to the order of himself with *Y*'s signature in the space for the maker of the note. *X* then told an acquaintance, *Z*, that *Y* was away on a trip and that he (*X*) needed money at once for a family emergency. *Z* discounted the note for *X* and shortly afterwards presented it for payment to *Y*, who refused to pay it.
>
> There has been an absence of delivery; the instrument was incomplete at the time, consisting of nothing but a signature on a piece of paper. The note was not delivered by *Y* to *Z* through the agency of *X* because *Y* had given his signature to *X* for the special purpose of supplying the bank with a specimen of his signature, and without any authority to convert the paper into a complete negotiable instrument. In the result, *Y* has a real defence, good against any holder, even a holder in due course such as *Z*. *Z*'s only

---

[30] See "By Estoppel," *infra*, Ch. 20.
[31] S. 40(1)(b).

recourse is to sue *X* (if he can be apprehended and has sufficient property to satisfy a court judgment). In addition to his fraud, *X* would be liable to *Z* on the strength of his endorsement.

Fraud is usually a defect of title defence, and the victim will have no protection against a holder in due course. In only one instance does fraud provide the party liable on a negotiable instrument with a real defence. That circumstance arises when the party liable can plead that he has had the nature of the instrument misrepresented to him. The leading case, insofar as negotiable instruments are concerned, is *Foster v. Mackinnon*.[32] We have discussed the case in Chapter 9, but it will be helpful to review it briefly here. The defendant Mackinnon, was an aged gentleman who had been induced to place his signature on a bill of exchange on the assurance that he was merely signing a guarantee. The plaintiff was a holder in due course to whom the bill had been negotiated. The court stated that if Mackinnon was negligent in signing the document he would be bound by it, but if he was not negligent he would not be bound. The case remains authority for the rules (a) that the signer of a negotiable instrument owes a duty of care to prospective third parties (holders), and (b) the age of the signer may be such an extenuating circumstance as to save him from the claim that he was negligent in signing and so to permit him to use the defence of *non est factum*.

An alteration of a negotiable instrument must be apparent to the naked eye to provide a good defence. No holder who takes an instrument bearing an apparent alteration can expect to enforce it against any party prior to the alteration on any terms. If, however, the alteration is not apparent, the instrument may be negotiated to a holder in due course who can sue parties prior to the alteration according to the original terms of the instrument.[33] He may also sue anyone who has endorsed the instrument subsequent to the alteration for the balance of the altered amount.

The drawer of a cheque owes a duty to his bank to prepare the instrument in such a way as to render its alteration difficult, and if he leaves spaces blank or otherwise invites alteration, he and not the bank must absorb the loss attributable to such an alteration.[34]

In the same way, if the cancellation of an instrument is apparent, the party liable has a good defence against every possible plaintiff.[35] If the cancellation is made before maturity and is not apparent, an artful and dishonest holder may seize the opportunity so gratuitously provided to negotiate the instrument for value. If so, the party liable may have the disconcerting experience of having to honour his instrument a second time, this time in favour of a holder in due course.

---

[32] Foster v. Mackinnon (1869) L.R. 4 C.P. 704. See reference to defence of *non est factum* in Chapter 9.

[33] S. 145.

[34] Falconbridge, *op. cit.,* p. 139.

[35] S. 143.

CONSUMER BILLS AND NOTES

The modern concept of negotiability is a highly refined one, the combination of a long historical process in which the law has been adapted to the convenience of business. The advantages of negotiability have had to be restricted, however, because of abuses that have become increasingly the subject of complaint. A select committee of the Ontario Legislature described this abuse in part as follows:

> Cases were brought to the Committee's attention where the seller in an instalment sales transaction misrepresented to the purchaser, in some cases dishonestly and fraudulently, the terms of the contract. Yet the purchaser was compelled to pay the whole debt because the discounter of the promissory note (the finance company) which formed part of the contract was a holder in due course with no knowledge, or provable knowledge of the representations made.
>
> The promissory note is a statement of obligation by which the signer promises to pay the holder an amount of money, but there is nothing in the note to the effect that there is any contractual obligation which must be fulfilled by the vendor of the goods or services before the money is payable
> . . . .
>
> If the paper was negotiated and had been bought by a finance company, a dissatisfied customer's refusal to pay because of the dealer's failure to fulfil his promise was no defence in an action on the note. Even if the dissatisfied customer went to court, the court, if it held that the finance company was a holder in due course, had to find in favour of the finance company and the disillusioned customer had to pay not only the purchase price but court and legal costs. The customer had a right of action against the dealer for non-performance, but this remedy was valueless with "fly-by-night dealers."[36]

In limited circumstances, the courts managed to hold that a finance company and dealer were so closely related as to preclude the finance company from claiming to be a holder in due course.[37] The courts found it impossible, however, to change a fundamental concept recognized under The Bills of Exchange Act in the majority of cases where no special relationship existed between conditional seller and finance company. Accordingly, Parliament amended the Bills of Exchange Act to remove the protection afforded the holder in due course in consumer credit arrangements where a finance company acts in concert with a seller of goods on the instalment plan.[38] After defining a consumer transaction, the statute states:

---

[36] Ontario, *Final Report of the Select Committee of the Ontario Legislature on Consumer Credit*, Sessional Paper No. 85, pp. 19-21.

[37] See Federal Discount Corporation Ltd. v. St. Pierre (1962) 32 D.L.R. (2d) 86, and Range v. Corporation de Finance Belvédère (1969) 5 D.L.R. (3d) 257.

[38] R.S.C. 1970 (1st Supp.) c. 4.

Every consumer bill or consumer note shall be prominently and legibly marked on its face with the words "consumer purchase" before or at the time the instrument is signed by the purchaser or by anyone signing to accommodate the purchaser [that is, a guarantor].[39]

The penalties for failure to comply with this section are severe: the instrument is void in the hands of either the seller or the finance company (although they might negotiate it to an innocent holder in due course).[40] In addition, everyone who normally participates in obtaining such an instrument without the appropriate marking is guilty of an offence and subject to a fine.[41] Most important, even when the instrument is properly marked on its face,

the right of the holder of a consumer bill or consumer note . . . to have the whole or any part thereof paid by the purchaser or . . . [a guarantor] is subject to any defence or right of set-off, other than counterclaim, that the purchaser would have had in an action by the seller on the consumer bill or consumer note.[42]

Thus, a buyer on consumer credit can now raise against a finance company that sues him as holder of his promissory note, all the defences formerly available only against the seller.

FUTURE DEVELOPMENTS

Probably the greatest revolution in the use of negotiable instruments awaits the full application of computer techniques now beginning to come into operation. The ability to make almost instantaneous adjustments to individual account balances by "on-line" connections with a centrally-located computer could eliminate the necessity for drawing cheques as a method of payment in many transactions: possibly only a standard form of authorization will suffice. In any event, it seems likely that the actual physical transfer of paper representing written promises will be significantly reduced, and the holder in due course will become a less common phenomenon.[43]

QUESTIONS FOR REVIEW

1. An infant is a party to a negotiable instrument given by him in payment for necessary goods. What is his liability on the instrument?
2. In what circumstances may a remote holder of a negotiable instrument *not* be a holder in due course?
3. You have drawn a cheque against your bank account payable to a friend, Guron. Later, your friend tells you he does not propose to cash it. He offers

---

[39] *Ibid.*, s. 190(1).
[40] *Ibid.*, s. 190(2).
[41] *Ibid.*, s. 192.
[42] *Ibid.*, s. 191.
[43] See Baxter, I.F.G., "The Simple Payment of Money", 24 *U. of T. Law Journal*, p. 63 (1974).

either (a) to give you a signed memorandum to that effect, or (b) to return the cheque to you. State which alternative you would prefer.

4. Describe the liability to the present holder of a ''n.s.f.'' cheque, of a person who has negotiated it to him in bearer form, without endorsing.

5. *P* drew a cheque for $100 in favour of *Q*. *P* has his account at the *R* Bank. In drawing this cheque, *P* left a blank space before the words ''one hundred'' and *Q* added the words ''two thousand and''. The *R* Bank paid *Q* $2,100 and the latter left the country with the proceeds. May *P* insist that the *R* Bank make good his loss of $2,000? Why or why not?

6. Ayer drew a draft on Coole with the drawer named as payee. Coole accepted it, and Ayer then endorsed it to the order of Winter. Before Winter had endorsed it, the instrument was stolen and Winter's signature was forged by way of endorsement. The party guilty of the forgery succeeded in negotiating the bill to Frost who took it innocently and who in turn negotiated it to Holder. Examine the position of each of the parties to the instrument with respect to its enforceability.

7. *X* delivered $50,000 worth of goods to *Y* and drew a draft on him for that amount payable in 90 days. *Y* accepted and *X* then discounted the draft at his bank for the sum of $49,200 credited to his account. *Y* dishonoured the draft at maturity. Describe *X*'s liability.

8. On October 1, S. W. Martin made a note for $125 payable to the order of his son, Martin, Jr., as a birthday present. The note was due October 31, following. Martin Jr. misplaced the note and his father refused to pay its amount until it was found. Martin, Jr. did not locate the note until January 2, by which time his father had died. Martin, Jr. presented the note for payment to the executor of his father's estate, who refused to honour it. Give reasons why he should or should not be entitled to payment.

CASES FOR DISCUSSION

CASE 1

On January 12, Waters was advised by the St. Lawrence Bank, at which he maintained a current account, that a note for $3,150 signed by him and made payable out of his account was due January 19 following. Waters knew that he had never made such a note but did not notify the bank to that effect, taking the position that there must have been some mistake which was no concern of his.

Subsequently the note was paid, as it appeared, on Waters' forged signature and Waters insisted that the bank should add the $3,150 back to his account. The bank refused and Waters sued it.

Outline the legal argument which Waters would use, and the defence of the St. Lawrence Bank. Explain also how your decision can be justified in terms of business practice.

CASE 2

Jones drew a cheque payable to Lockhart, but retained it with a view to determining first whether the goods which he had purchased from Lockhart were satisfactory. Jones' clerk Anderson gave the cheque to Lockhart without authority to do so. (Anderson normally had nothing to do with the preparation or delivery of Jones' negotiable instruments.) Lockhart endorsed the cheque for value to Smith, who took it without notice of the circumstances. When Smith attempted to cash the cheque, he discovered that Jones had countermanded it by requesting his bank to stop payment. Smith sued both Jones and Lockhart for the amount. State with reasons the rights of the respective parties and the probable result of the action.

CASE 3

In January, the business of Langley and Sons was adjudged bankrupt on a petition of its creditors. The following month, while the bankruptcy proceedings were still under way, Langley illegally sold Martin some property which should have been included in his estate for the purpose of settling with his business creditors. Martin was unaware of Langley's bankruptcy and gave Langley a 90-day promissory note for $1,000. Before the note fell due, Langley endorsed it as a gift to his father-in-law, G. Scott, who was aware of Langley's financial condition and the circumstances under which the note had been obtained.

Subsequently, the trustee in bankruptcy recovered the property from Martin, as he was entitled to do under the Bankruptcy Act. Martin then refused to pay the note, and Scott sued him on the instrument. Should Scott succeed? Would the result be different if Scott had paid Langley $600 for the note?

CASE 4

Andrews, a clerk, set before Barton, his employer, a number of mimeographed circular letters which required the employer's signature at the foot. He arranged the letters so that, in respect to all but the first copy, no more was visible than the blank space for the signature at the bottom. One sheet in the pile was not a copy of the letter but a completed form of promissory note for $1,000 payable to the order of Andrews. Having by this ruse secured Barton's signature as maker of the note, Andrews negotiated it to Carter, who paid $995 for it (since 30 days remained until its maturity date) and took it without notice of the means employed to obtain it. When Carter later presented the note for payment, Barton refused to pay it. Carter then sued Barton on the note. Who should succeed? Give reasons for your decision.

CASE 5

Taylor mentioned to Gilbert, a real estate broker, that he was thinking of selling his house if he could get $85,000 for it. Gilbert suggested that Taylor sign an exclusive selling agreement but Taylor refused, saying that he would gladly pay Gilbert a commission if he produced a purchaser. Gilbert then proceeded to expend considerable time and money in advertising Taylor's house and showing it to prospective buyers. Two weeks later, when Gilbert telephoned Taylor to ask whether he could bring a prospective buyer to the house, Taylor said he had changed his mind about selling and not to bother. Angered by what he considered to be unfair treatment, Gilbert threatened to sue Taylor for his expenditures unless Taylor would pay him $200. Taylor said, "All right, just to get rid of you I'll put a cheque in the mail today." He mailed the cheque. The following day he had second thoughts and requested his bank to stop payment. Gilbert sued Taylor on the cheque. Should he succeed?

PART FOUR
Real Property

CHAPTER 24

Interests in Land and Their Transfer

THE NATURE OF INTERESTS IN LAND

The Meaning of Real Property

Since land is commonly referred to as *real property,* it will be helpful to inquire into the meaning of the term. The word *property* itself has two meanings which are closely related. The more common definition of property is "everything which is the subject of ownership . . . everything that has exchangeable value or which goes to make up wealth . . . ."[1] By this definition, property means *the thing itself,* whether it be a piece of land, a piece of cheese, or a bill of lading, a share certificate, or the tangible things these documents represent. The lesser-known meaning of property is not the thing itself but the legal interest in the thing — the right or rights in the thing which the law will recognize and protect. Property in this sense has been called "the highest right a man can have to anything . . . ."[2] and "ownership, the unrestricted and exclusive right to a thing; the right to dispose of a thing in every legal way, to possess it, to use it, and to exclude everyone else from interfering with it".[3] A common synonym for the term "property" in the sense of ownership is the word *title:* the expressions, "ownership of a thing" and, "title to a thing" are used interchangeably. Although the

---

[1] Black, *Law Dictionary* (revised 4th ed.), p. 1382. St. Paul: West Publishing Co., 1968.
[2] Earl Jowitt, *Dictionary of English Law,* p. 1426. London: Sweet & Maxwell Limited, 1959.
[3] Black, *Law Dictionary.*

first meaning of property — the thing itself — is of general importance in law, it is in the second sense that we use the word in the present chapter.

Historically, the word ''real'' referred to the kind of remedy a party could get in court when his property rights were interfered with. Certain types of interests in land gave the owner a remedy by way of *real action* — a right to repossess the interest interfered with — rather than a remedy by way of *personal action* — a right to money damages but not a right to have the interest back again. Real actions were available only when one of a carefully defined class of interests was interfered with; but in time the term ''real property'' came to refer to interests in land generally, whether or not a real action would lie for the recovery of the interest, and we shall so use the term.

The law of real property has special concepts and terms of its own, and we must take great care to use the terms accurately. The reasons for this special terminology are partly historical and partly attributable to the peculiar qualities of land. Land is permanent except on the rare occasion when a piece of it slides into the sea and is lost, or is permanently flooded by a large hydro development, such as occurred along the St. Lawrence Seaway. Otherwise a given piece of land exists perpetually: it remains long after its temporary owners are gone, and it has a fixed location. An interest in land recognized by law may affect that land and the people concerned with it long after the temporary owner who created the interest has died. Thus, if the owner of land grants a city the right to lay watermains across his land and maintain and repair them, this right could affect a subsequent owner who would like to tear up the pipes and erect a building. If over many years successive owners of the land were to grant away more of their rights, eventually there would be a complex bundle of rights held by various persons. Each subsequent owner would own the land minus the rights granted away. In this manner, land may easily be the subject of many complicated interests.

The Definition of Land

The word *land* has a special meaning in the law of real property. Ordinarily, when we think of land, we think of the surface and its contours. For everyday usage this concept is sufficient, but when a purchaser buys land he must know more accurately what the term includes. In law, land includes not only the surface but all that is under the surface, including the minerals, oil, or whatever else is present within the boundaries of the lot, and everything above the surface including the buildings on the land and the column of air as well. It used to be said that land included all the earth to the centre of the globe and all the air up to the heavens. For all practical purposes, the owner of land today does have his ownership extending below the surface as far as man can penetrate with mine shafts and oil wells. But it is a different matter with the column of air above the land: various statutes, international treaties concerning air travel, and municipal by-laws limiting the use of land have cut down ownership of the column of air considerably. Aircraft may pass freely over the land at a safe height, and the owner is often restricted in the height of buildings he may erect.

Perhaps most important to remember is that land includes all things permanently affixed to it — trees, buildings, fences. Thus, when *A* transfers his house and lot to *B,* the document describes the land only, according to its location and dimensions, but it is nevertheless presumed that everything affixed to the land goes with it. Lawyers do not draw a distinction between lands and buildings as do businessmen and accountants. Although for business purposes we report the depreciation of buildings but not of land, the two are lumped together in law when ascertaining ownership or transferring the title to land.

The Use of Land

Land, as we have noted, has special qualities distinguishing it from goods and chattels: it is virtually indestructible and has a fixed location. The owner of a chattel may do as he pleases with it — he may even destroy it, and no one has the legal right to interfere. Land has never been regarded in this manner when it is situated in a community where people reside in reasonable proximity to one another. If a landowner sets off explosives or lights fires which spread sparks on to his neighbour's lands, the danger is obvious. From very early times, communal governments assumed the power to regulate and prohibit dangerous activities in populous areas. Community regulations thus limit a landowner's right to use his land for dangerous activities.

There are further restrictions on the use of land which seriously affect the owner's freedom of activity. The courts have long recognized that a user of land may be restrained from committing the tort of *nuisance*. A nuisance is any activity that interferes with the ordinary comfort and enjoyment of land of other persons in the vicinity. It may take the form of smoke, noxious vapours, noise, polluted water, or other harmful liquids flowing in streams or percolating through the earth — things which escape from the land of the user and interfere with other persons' lands. A person who has sustained injury from a nuisance may obtain money damages for his loss and also obtain an injunction from the court restraining the offender from continuing the conduct responsible for the nuisance.

Community regulation has grown rapidly in recent years. Early regulations covered only such damages as fire and health hazards, but increased density and size of urban centres and the complexities of city life generally have forced municipal governments into large-scale regulation of the use of land. Zoning by-laws prescribe the use and type of buildings that may be erected in various districts of a municipality; building regulations prescribe minimum standards of quality of materials and size of all parts of structures erected within the area; planning by-laws set out the requirements for roadways and water and sewage services, and often also prescribe the amounts of land to be given by a land developer to the municipality for use as school and park areas. A large body of public law, steadily growing even larger, sets limits on the use owners may make of their land in urban and suburban areas.

The Development of Strict Rules in Land Law

In feudal times land was the most valuable asset, the source of almost all wealth, because it included crops, animals, timber, and serfs. Without industry or merchant trade, land represented the wealth of the country. In England, the king learned early to utilize the feudal system of landholding to consolidate his strength. In feudal England no one *owned* land except the Crown. A lord *held* land from the Crown, subject to certain rights and duties. So long as the lord performed his duties, he and his heirs continued to hold the land. In turn, each lord granted portions of his estate to vassals, who held the land from the lord subject to various rights and duties. The vassals often granted their land to sub-vassals subject to further rights and duties. In later feudal times these relationships became extremely intricate and technical. The king objected to the complexities because they made it difficult for him to enforce his own feudal rights and collect taxes. Parliament passed statutes and the courts handed down decisions to cut down the number of interests in land. Gradually, a strict set of legal rules grew up for recognizing a limited number of interests in land. If a holder of land tried to create a type of interest not already recognized by the courts, the interest would be void. In contrast with the law of contract where, generally speaking, rules grew up to meet business convenience and fairness, the rules for recognition of classes of interests in land often had no relation to convenience or fairness: rather, they were intended to limit arbitrarily the number of interests and keep them within manageable proportions. Even so, the variety of interests that can arise in relation to just one piece of land is great. Many if not most of the old rules have been repealed or modernized by various statutes, but comparatively speaking, the old concepts have been very slow to die in this field of the law.

The strictness of the courts is more understandable when we consider how imaginative and resourceful were the medieval landowners and their lawyers in developing concepts of ownership of land. They carved up ownership in two main ways: (a) according to the duration of time the holder of the interest would have the right to exclusive possession of the land — interests called *estates in time,* and (b) according to the kind of use permitted or restricted upon the land — called *interests less than estates.* We shall discuss these interests in the following two sections.

ESTATES IN TIME

Freehold Estates

The fee simple estate. This estate, usually referred to as the fee simple, is the greatest interest a man can own in land. It comes closest to the idea of complete ownership in English law. Thus, when we speak of a person as owning land, we mean that he holds the fee simple in it. The holder of the fee simple holds it for all time present and future, subject only to its return to the government in the event of his dying without having relatives to inherit it and without having made a will giving it to some person. He may grant the whole of the fee simple away, he may grant away a lesser interest keeping the rest for himself, or he may grant the whole of it in various portions to different persons.

Illustrations:

(a) *A*, the holder of the fee simple in Blackacre, may grant it to his older brother *B* for the rest of *B*'s life. At *B*'s death it returns to *A*, or to *A*'s heirs if he had died before *B*.

(b) *A* may grant Blackacre to his brother for life with the rest of the fee simple going to a nephew *C* at the brother's death.

There are further ways in which the holder of a fee simple may carve up his estate into portions and grant them to other persons; the above illustrations serve merely as examples.

The life estate. The second freehold estate is the life estate. It is an estate in land for the life of one person — usually for the life of the person who holds the estate, but not necessarily: a person may hold a life estate to be measured by the life of another person. Thus *A* may grant Blackacre to *B* for the rest of *A*'s own life — if *A* dies within a few months, the life estate ends, and *B* loses his interest. This type of life estate, however, is quite rare. The more usual life estate, for the life of the person to whom the interest is given, often arises under the terms of a will. Thus, the owner of a fee simple may by the terms of his will give a life estate in the family home to his wife; or if he is a widower, give a life estate to his eldest child. In either of these situations he may also direct that the rest of the fee simple pass, let us say, to his grandchildren.

The balance of a fee simple, after a life estate has been carved out, is called either a *reversion* or a *remainder*. It is called a reversion when the grantor of the life estate reserves the balance of the fee simple for himself and his heirs (that is, it *reverts* to the grantor or his heirs after the life estate ends). It is called a remainder when it goes to some third person. The balance of the estate in illustration (a) above is a reversion and in illustration (b) a remainder.

Unfortunately the life estate creates many problems. First, it is very difficult to sell land subject to a life estate: very few people will buy only the remaining years of the life tenant's interest, an uncertain period of time; similarly, they will rarely buy the reversion or remainder, because it is impossible to tell how long the life tenant will live, thereby delaying the purchaser's right to the land. Thus, both the *life tenant* and the *remainderman* must be persuaded to join in the sale and together grant the whole of the fee simple. Secondly, the life tenant is limited in the changes he can make on the land without the consent of the remainderman: he cannot tear down buildings or cut down trees without the permission of the remainderman even if he wishes to replace them with something more valuable; he must leave the land to the remainderman substantially as he received it. On the other hand, he is under no duty to make repairs, and may let the buildings decay. Thirdly, he cannot compel the remainderman to contribute anything to the cost of substantial repairs and maintenance needed on the land even though they will ultimately be of great benefit to the remainderman in preserving its value.

The life estate was much more common until the beginning of this century when land was still a very important measure of wealth. In our society today, land is no longer a major portion of a person's wealth. His assets are mainly in the form of shares and bonds, bank accounts, life insurance, jewellery, and automobiles. This change in the form of wealth has led to a different method of providing a life income for a surviving dependant.

Instead of creating a *life estate in land* a person may give a *life interest* in a sum of money. He directs in his will that a portion of his assets be liquidated into a fund of money and invested, and the income to be paid to the dependant for life. On the dependant's death, the principal sum is paid to those who would formerly have been remaindermen of real property.

Dower and homestead rights. Dower is a special type of life interest, a vestige of ancient property law which remains in force in New Brunswick, Nova Scotia, Ontario and Prince Edward Island. It is the wife's right to a life interest in one-third of the real property held by her husband in fee simple during their married life. Although the wife has no right to possession of the land unless and until her husband dies, dower attaches to it the moment the husband takes title to it.[4] If he subsequently sells it without her consent, her dower remains with the land when it is transferred to the purchaser, and on the death of her husband, she may maintain her right to dower against the purchaser.

The fact that the widow obtains only a one-third life interest appears to contradict the statement that the holder of an estate has *exclusive* possession. As we shall see, however, an estate may be held jointly by two or more persons, and although one holder cannot exclude a co-holder of the estate, he can exclude all other persons.

Dower was a valuable right of the family dowager in the Middle Ages. With her dower interest she could not be forced from the family estate, and her right to one third of the income from the estate maintained her for the rest of her life. Today a man of considerable wealth may have no other real property than his own home. A large portion of his wealth is probably invested in business — as capital in a partnership or as shares in a limited company. Either of these assets is deemed to be personal property even though the partnership or company owns land. The balance of his assets may be invested in other forms of securities or in a bank account. All these things are personal property to which dower does not attach. Suppose the family home is worth $80,000 when the husband dies. If he were to leave his wife nothing in his will, she would still be entitled to dower, but she could not afford to run the house unless she had a private source of income. On the other hand, if she should consent to the sale of the house by the court and

---

[4] This statement is a simplification of the problem: if the land is subject to a mortgage, difficult technical questions arise, and in some circumstances the husband may sell it and defeat the wife's dower interest. See Falconbridge, *The Law of Mortgages* (3rd ed.), pp. 312-27. Toronto: Canada Law Book Company Limited, 1942.

receive her one-third share of income from the $80,000 (she is not entitled to the capital sum but only to the interest on it), the amount invested at nine per cent will be no more than $2,400 annually for the remainder of her life, hardly a sum on which she could live. We can see that dower in most cases has ceased to be a practical benefit to the wife: it remains only as a nuisance and a complication in property transactions.

A more adequate form of protection is given by six of the provinces. The four western provinces, Nova Scotia, and Ontario have statutes permitting dependants of a testator to apply to the court for an order that part of the estate be given for their maintenance notwithstanding that the testator gave most or all of his estate to other persons. These statutes give the court a wide discretion in deciding what portion, if any, should be given to the testator's dependants for their maintenance.[5]

The obsolescence of dower has been recognized by most common law jurisdictions, including England, Australia, New Zealand, many of the United States and the four western provinces and has accordingly been abolished by them. It remains in force in the Maritime provinces and Ontario. Newfoundland abolished dower indirectly: in 1834 it passed a unique statute changing all real property interests into personal property interests. Since dower attaches only to real property interests, an effect of the statute was to destroy dower.

The western provinces abolished dower but replaced it with *homestead rights*.[6] These rights vary substantially from province to province, but their general characteristics may be described together. A family may have occupied several residences over the years, but at a given moment only *one* of them can be the homestead. If a husband and wife occupy a house for several years and then by mutual agreement give up the house and move to another, only the second house will be the homestead — and so on with subsequent changes by mutual consent. Rights in the homestead include the right to refuse consent to a change of homestead or to its sale (sales made without consent are void), a life estate in the *whole* of the homestead to the surviving spouse, and certain immunity from seizure of the homestead by creditors. In British Columbia, homestead rights do not arise until the wife registers her claim in the land registry office, but in Alberta, Manitoba and Saskatchewan they arise as soon as husband and wife establish a home within the meaning of the statute. Homestead rights accrue to either spouse in Alberta and Manitoba, to the wife only in British Columbia and Saskatchewan.

Homestead rights give the wife somewhat better protection than dower: during her husband's lifetime she can prevent the sale of the homestead completely, and if she survives him she has an exclusive life interest in the whole of the homestead rather than the one-third interest of dower. Homestead rights are less cumbersome than dower — they do not affect other real property of the spouse.

---

5 Testator's Family Maintenance Act, R.S.B.C. 1960, c. 378, as amended by St. of B.C. 1971, c. 64; R.S.M. 1970, c. T 50; R.S.N.S. 1967, c. 303; Dependants' Relief Act, R.S.O. 1970, c. 126; R.S.S. 1965, c. 128 as amended by St. of Sask. 1970, c. 8; Family Relief Act, R.S.A. 1970, c. 134.

6 Homestead rights are often referred to as ''dower'' in the western provinces.

In contrast with usage in jurisdictions retaining dower, a husband in one of the western provinces may freely dispose of lands and buildings used for business without worrying about homestead rights, and his purchaser need not search to discover outstanding homestead interests. On the other hand, in a number of cases the court has had to decide which of two or more homes retained by the family was the homestead. We might add, of course, that dower rights would have attached to all of them.

In a judgment that attracted a good deal of controversy, the Supreme Court of Canada decided that, following separation from her husband, a wife who had made no monetary contribution to the acquisition of her husband's ranch in Alberta but who had performed substantial services over a long period of time in the maintenance and improvement of the ranch, had not acquired any interest in that property.[7]

Leasehold Estates

A leasehold estate is an interest in land for a definite period of time — a week, a month, a year, a hundred years, or any other specific period. Here we find the great distinction between a freehold and a leasehold estate: the freehold estate is either for an *infinite* time (the fee simple) or an *indefinite* time (the life estate), whereas the leasehold is for a *definite* time. In a leasehold estate, the person to whom the interest is granted is called the *lessee* or *tenant* and the grantor of the interest is called the *lessor* or *landlord*.

Historically, leaseholds have always been considered lesser estates than freeholds. This was so even though it was obvious that leases for one hundred years would almost invariably last longer than a life tenancy, a freehold estate. A leasehold interest must be derived from a freehold interest and cannot last longer than the freehold from which it is derived.

Illustration:

By will *T* gives *A* a life estate in Blackacre with the remainder after *A*'s death to *X* in fee simple. *A* leases Blackacre to *B* Co. Ltd. for one hundred years. Several months later *A* dies. *X*, the remainderman, can take possession of Blackacre and put *B* Co. Ltd. out. *X* is not bound by the lease because *A* could not create a leasehold interest in Blackacre to last longer than his own life estate.

The above result is an application of the rule that a person cannot grant to another a greater interest than he himself holds.[8]

---

[7] Murdoch v. Murdoch (1974) 41 D.L.R. (3d) 367.
[8] In 1877 England passed the Settled Estates Act creating an important exception to the rule. The statute was later enacted only in British Columbia and Ontario. Under the statute a life tenant may lease his estate for a term not exceeding 21 years, and the lease will be valid against the remainderman. If the life tenant dies, the lessee pays the rent to the remainderman for the balance of the lease, and he may stay in possession. The statute also provides that the rent bargained for by the life tenant must be the best reasonably obtainable.

Leasehold interests share an important characteristic in common with freehold interests: they give the lessee a right to exclusive possession of the land comprised in the lease. Thus the lessee has the right to keep all persons off the leased land including the lessor himself, unless the lessor has reserved the right to enter the property for inspection and repairs. The law concerning leasehold interests is the meeting-place of the strict concepts of real property and the flexible concepts of contract. Leases play an important role in commerce and industry, and they have recently assumed a new role in finance as an alternative to the traditional method of borrowing money on the security of mortgages. Leaseholds are discussed more fully in Chapter 25, under the better-known heading of "Landlord and Tenant".

Concurrent Interests in Estates

Two or more persons may become owners of the same estate in land at the same time. They are concurrent holders of the estate whether it be a fee simple, a life estate, or a leasehold estate. In the absence of any special agreement between them or of special terms set out in the grant by which they acquired the interest, concurrent holders are deemed to be *tenants in common*. Tenants in common hold equal shares in the estate, that is, each is entitled to the same rights over the property and an equal share of the income. Each interest is an *undivided* interest: one tenant cannot fence off a portion of the property for his exclusive use — each is entitled to the use of the whole property. However, tenants in common may agree expressly to hold unequal shares, transfer the share of one to another, or divide and fence the property into exclusive lots. In addition a tenant in common may transfer his interest to any third party without the consent of the others: the transferee becomes a tenant in common with them. When a tenant in common dies, his interest goes to his heirs, who continue to hold the interest with the other tenants in common.

Another form of concurrent interest is the *joint tenancy*. A joint tenancy arises only when expressly created in the grant of the estate or afterwards by an express agreement between the holders of the estate. The feature which distinguishes the joint tenancy from the tenancy in common is the *right of survivorship*. Under the right of survivorship the interest of a deceased joint tenant passes immediately on his death to the surviving tenant or tenants instead of to the heirs of the deceased tenant. Thus, if *A*, *B*, and *C* own Blackacre in joint tenancy, upon *C*'s death his interest will pass to *A* and *B*, who will continue to own Blackacre in joint tenancy between them. *C*'s interest does not go to his heirs, nor does his wife have a dower interest.

A joint tenant may destroy the right of survivorship at any time before his death without the consent of the other joint tenants. This process, called *severance*, turns his joint tenancy into a tenancy in common with the other tenant or tenants. Even after such an act, if there are two or more other tenants remaining, they still remain joint tenants with each other but are tenants in common with the person who has severed his joint tenancy. The most common method of severance is by a joint tenant's granting his interest to a third party; the grant automatically turns the interest transferred into a tenancy in common with the remaining interests. There are other methods of accomplishing severance, such as by giving a mortgage on one's share of a joint tenancy, but a joint tenant cannot sever his share by disposing of it in his will. The courts have held that a will speaks only at the moment the testator has died, and at that moment his share has already passed to the surviving joint tenant or tenants.

Husband and wife often obtain title to the family home in joint tenancy. On the death of either spouse the survivor automatically receives full title to the property. The joint tenancy is an advantage to the wife when her husband dies because the house does not form part of the husband's estate, thus becoming entangled in problems of *probate* (administration and settling of the husband's estate). Unfortunately, much of the convenience of this method is lost where an estate is large enough to attract estate tax. Very often, especially if the house was purchased with the husband's money, the tax authorities decide that the house is part of the husband's estate for tax purposes. As a result the house may be seized to pay death duties, or at the very least the widow will need to obtain a release from the tax authorities before the property can be sold. In small and medium-sized estates, where the family home is the main asset and tax releases may be easily obtained, joint tenancy still offers an advantage.

Condominiums

The condominium is a modern response to a shortage of housing and recreational areas in large urban centres, and purports to provide the occupiers with the satisfaction of home ownership and communal access to recreational areas that they could not hope to purchase for their own exclusive use.

Nearly all the common law provinces have enacted legislation permitting the granting of an estate in fee simple in individual units of multiple-unit developments, such as high-rise apartments, row housing or groups of single-family semi-detached, or duplex, or similar residences.[9] The legislation is not restricted to residential housing and applies equally to the development of commercial and industrial buildings. The owner of a unit is entitled to exclusive possession of his unit and also obtains an undivided part ownership, in common with other unit owners, of *common elements* including structures and areas external to the unit such as entrances, stairs and elevators, and communal facilities such as laundries, recreation rooms, garages, swimming pools, tennis courts, playgrounds and so forth. The purchaser acquires his unit subject to several important conditions: in a multiple-unit building he must, like a tenant in such a building, allow entry to make necessary repairs to services; he must contribute to the operation, upkeep and in some degree to the restoration of the common property, and he must insure his own unit. In addition, he becomes a member of the *con-*

---

[9] See, for example: St. of B.C. 1966, c. 46 (where condominiums are called "strata titles"); R.S.O. 1970, c. 77; St. of N.S. 1968, c. 4.

dominium corporation charged with responsibility for management of the condominium development as a whole and given statutory powers for that purpose. He is subject to the rules and regulations governing the development. Although the corporation is not the owner of the common elements, it may own one or more units and thus share in that ownership. For example, it may own units rented to janitorial and supervisory staff as well as for its own use. Each unit can be bought and sold, mortgaged and passed to successors on death. It is separately assessed and taxed and may be sold for unpaid taxes. Such transfers do not affect the ownership of other units.

The legislation has done away with the technical difficulties in the common law by granting ownership of a freehold entirely separated from the ground by other units of freehold. However it does leave a number of practical problems that necessarily arise in complex high-rise buildings. For example, the definition of a unit is a matter of critical importance: does the unit-owner's property extend beyond the surface of the walls of the rooms? If a piece of plaster an inch thick is knocked out of the wall, is the damage to the property of the unit-owner or to the common elements, and thus the corporation's responsibility to repair? If the description of the unit included ownership of, let us say, the space three inches beyond the surface of the wall, and wiring or plumbing in the space immediately behind the plaster within that three inches failed, would the unit-owner be responsible for repairs even if these services were destined for a unit other than his own? In most circumstances it is a serious disadvantage to own much of the area beyond the surface of the inner walls. Responsibility for repairs and maintenance are generally in the hands of the corporation, but where services are within the unit, it is important to set out clearly where responsibility lies.

The equivalent of condominium ownership has long existed in many parts of the world, especially where buildings are expected to have a very long life, often calculated in hundreds of years. A modern apartment building of low quality, constructed for rental accommodation, may have an expected life of only 40 to 50 years. Its conversion to a condominium may have pitfalls for an unwary buyer who purchases a rapidly deteriorating asset. For example, if such an apartment building, already 15 years old, were converted to a condominium and the purchaser bought a unit with an instalment mortgage over a 25-year period, the building might well be in a state of great disrepair by the time he had paid the mortgage off. Instead of acquiring an appreciating asset, as is usually the case with the purchase of a residential home, the condominium unit-owner might find his unit had lost a substantial part of its value. Accordingly, it is important for a prospective purchaser of a unit to take great care in assessing the quality of construction in a condominium building.

In a good-quality rental apartment building, a competent landlord is interested in maintaining his asset in good condition. He will have the necessary management and technical expertise to do so. In a condominium, when the last unit has been sold off the purchasers of condominium units become the owners of the complex. If the entrepreneur who built the condominium retains no further interest, the tasks of maintaining the condominium in a good state of repair, paying its bills and having generally efficient management become the collective responsibility of unit-owners through the condominium corporation. Ordinarily, it would not be possible for individual owners to run a large development, and they would authorize the corporation to engage an expert to oversee the operation. Frequently the entrepreneur, while he still controls the condominium corporation as the owner of the unsold units, will arrange a management contract for, let us say, five years. Thus, even after selling off the last unit, the entrepreneur may stay on as manager at a substantial fee. In these circumstances, it is important for the unit-owner to assess the reputation of the entrepreneur and the quality of management he is likely to provide for the condominium development. Even when management is in competent hands, the unit-owner cannot sit back as a house-owner ordinarily can and attend to his own property. He must remain concerned about the sound management of the condominium corporation on a continuing long-term basis.

The financing and sale of condominium units are more complicated than that of a privately-owned residence because of the continuing obligations of a unit-owner to pay charges levied by the condominium corporation and because of the relationship between a master mortgage of all the common elements, including the ground on which the condominium development is located, and the mortgages of the individual units. So too, the nature and amount of insurance required for a condominium presents special problems. In event of the destruction of high-rise apartment buildings, the apportionment of loss between each unit and common elements and the responsibility for subsequent reconstruction present considerable difficulty. Thus, while there are many attractive features in the development of condominiums, there are also new problems confronting a prospective purchaser that must be weighed against the advantages.

An alternative to condominiums is co-operative housing. In a co-operative housing development a member merely buys a share in the co-operative organization and, by virtue of his equity in it, becomes entitled to occupy one of the units in the development. A risk attendant on this type of home ownership, however, is a possibility that the whole co-operative venture may flounder because of bad management and insolvency: all members are affected equally in the failure, and may lose their equity investment even though they may personally have been honouring their obligations and required contributions for taxes and upkeep. Financing a share in co-operative housing presents difficulties of its own. A member buys an equity share and has rights to occupy a unit that are similar to a leasehold interest. The method of borrowing money on the value of a share in a co-operative, combined with the right to occupy a unit, is more complicated than a straight loan by way of mortgage on a private residence. On the other hand, a co-operative venture usually connotes a high degree of commitment to a community project, and more direct involvement in management than is typical of condominium ownership. A high level of involvement in the management of the co-operative is probably the best assurance of sound management and survival.

INTERESTS LESS THAN ESTATES

Easements

In addition to estates in land divided according to time, there are other interests distinguished by the use or benefit they confer upon the holder. None of these interests gives the right of exclusive possession as do freehold and leasehold estates.

At the beginning of this chapter we referred to an example of a landowner's granting a right to a city to lay water-mains over his land and to maintain and repair them. This right belongs to the class of interests called easements. An *easement* is a right enjoyed by one landowner over the land of another and is obtained for a special purpose rather than for the general use and occupation of land. The most common type of easement is a *right of way:* the holder of a right of way may pass back and forth over the land of another in order to get to and from his own land. He does not have the right to remain on the other's land or bring things on the land and leave them there or to obstruct others from using the land, but he can maintain an action against anyone who interferes with his right to pass. Other examples of easements are the right to string wires and cables across land, to hang eaves of a building over another's land, to drain water or waste materials from one piece of land over a watercourse on another's land. Once granted, an easement attaches to the land and binds subsequent owners — they cannot interfere with the exercise of the easement. Similarly, purchasers from the owner of the land benefiting from the easement succeed to his rights.

An essential requirement of an easement is that there must be a *dominant tenement* (a piece of land which is to benefit from the easement) and a *servient tenement* (the land subject to the easement). The location of the dominant tenement has presented difficulties. It has long been decided that the dominant tenement need not directly adjoin the servient tenement, but it must be reasonably close to it. This qualification is vague, but the law has not been able to devise a more exact definition. It is highly unlikely that if Blackacre is twenty miles from Whiteacre, the owner of Blackacre can acquire a right of way over Whiteacre; but it is not clear what the answer would be if half a mile separated the lands and if it were shown that the proposed easement would be of great benefit to the use and enjoyment of Blackacre.

The term "easement" is sometimes used to describe certain statutory rights such as the right granted a telephone company to run wires and cables either underground or overhead on poles. The telephone company has the right to leave wires where they have been installed and to inspect and repair them when necessary — rights very similar to easements. But often the telephone company owns no land in the area. The nearest land that could be considered a dominant tenement may be many miles away. Strictly speaking, the right is not an easement: it owes its existence to a statute. If a telephone company were to attempt to create an easement to lay cables over long distances by contract without the aid of a statute, no easement would come into existence because there would be no dominant tenement reasonably close by. Although it might have contractual rights against the promisor, the company would have no real property interest in the cables. A subsequent purchaser of the lands would not be bound to let the company use the land or even to let it take the cables away.

An adjoining landowner may acquire an easement without a written grant by the owner of the servient tenement. The method by which he may do so is called *prescription*. In medieval England, a custom grew that if a man habitually exercised a right over the land of another for a very long time and if that right *could* have been granted to him as an easement, it was presumed that he had received a grant of easement at one time but had subsequently lost the grant. This fiction was merely a convenient way of permitting a man to rely on a right he had exercised for a very long time. From this fiction developed a rule that if a man continuously exercised a right, openly, notoriously, without fraud or deceit, without using force or threats against the owner of the land, and at no time acknowledged the right of the owner in writing or paid for the use of the land, he would acquire an easement by prescription after 20 years. The right had to be exercised continuously, that is without interruption by the owner's exerting his rights of ownership through exacting a fee or keeping the prospective easement holder off the land.

An easement by prescription is as valid as an easement by grant and is fully recognized in the four Atlantic provinces and in parts of Manitoba and Ontario. Easements by prescription are not recognized in the three most western provinces or in those parts of Manitoba and Ontario covered by *land titles* registration, a system of recording interests in land to be discussed in the last section of this chapter. In areas where easements by prescription may arise, a landowner must guard against the establishment of easements which he does not desire. One great danger is that a former owner of the land may have permitted the exercise of a right for many years. The time continues to run from the moment that the right was exercised regardless of a transfer of ownership of the land. Thus, there may be considerably less than 20 years to go when the current owner obtains title. A serious consequence may be that while the prospective easement may seen inoffensive to the current owner who does not foresee the future use of the land, when the easement has been created it may later destroy the market value of the land.

Illustration:

X obtains an easement by prescription over a ten-foot strip of Blackacre by using it as a right of way to his garage on Whiteacre for over 20 years. During this period Blackacre contains only a single family dwelling. Later it becomes suitable for erecting a large apartment building, but municipal building regulations for the construction of apartments require that the ten-foot strip be used for the creation of a parking area. Without the ten-foot strip there will be insufficient parking area to comply with the regulations. The owner of Blackacre will be unable to develop the property or sell it to another party interested in developing it unless and until he can buy a release of the easement from the owner of Whiteacre.

Covenants

Often an owner of a large piece of land wishes to sell part of it yet control or restrict the use of that part he proposes to sell. His motives are understandable enough: he may wish to see the property kept in good repair so that the area does not deteriorate; he may wish to prevent the carrying on of a noisy business that would interfere with his privacy; he may wish the purchaser to improve the land by planting trees and shrubs, thus enhancing the beauty of the area. He may, of course, extract a promise from the purchaser to do any or all of these things as part of the consideration for the sale of the land. If the purchaser does not abide by his promise, the vendor has his normal contractual remedies for breach. But if the purchaser resells the land to a third party, there is no privity of contract between the vendor and the third party, and the third party need not fear a contractual action by the vendor if he chooses to ignore his predecessor's promise. The vendor has a remedy only if the purchaser's promise has created an interest in land that the law recognizes as binding upon all subsequent holders. Recognition of such interests would create further complexities.

Illustration:

> *V*, owner of Blackacre and Whiteacre, sells Whiteacre to *P*. As part of the consideration he obtains a promise that *P* and all subsequent owners of Whiteacre will keep in repair all buildings on both Whiteacre and Blackacre. So long as *P* owns Whiteacre, he is bound by his promise. Subsequently *P* sells Whiteacre to *A*, who is aware of that promise. *A* refuses to carry out the promise made by *P*, and *V* sues him for breach. The court would have no difficulty disposing of the promise to repair buildings on Blackacre: *A* has no connection with *P*'s promise concerning Blackacre—he has no interest in that land nor was he a party to the contract between *V* and *P*. Thus, he is not bound to repair the buildings on Blackacre.
>
> The promise concerning Whiteacre is more troublesome. It may seem reasonable for *V*, who still owns adjoining lands, to require Whiteacre to be kept in good repair so that the area will remain at high market value. The courts have held, however, that it is too onerous to subject subsequent owners to such positive duties, and that as a matter of public policy it would be dangerous to permit the creation of interests in land requiring the owner to personally perform promises in perpetuity. Lands might eventually be tied up by an interminable series of such promises or covenants for the benefit of surrounding lands.

In spite of discouragement from the courts, vendors continued to extract promises from purchasers, some highly desirable and some injurious and spiteful. In the middle of the last century one of these covenants was questioned in the English Court of Chancery in the famous case of *Tulk v. Moxhay*.[10] The court

---

[10] (1848) 41 E.R. 1143.

decided that it was too onerous to require a subsequent holder to act *positively* in order to carry out the covenants (as in the above illustration), but if the covenant were purely *negative, that is, if he were required to refrain from certain conduct* or certain use of the land, then the court would hold the covenant valid and enforceable. These negative covenants became known as *covenants running with the land,* or *restrictive covenants.* Restrictive covenants are subject to a rule similar to that concerning easements — there must be a piece of land subject to the covenant and another piece which receives the benefit of the covenant. A covenant that the courts recognize as running with the land is enforceable by any subsequent holder of the land benefiting from it against any subsequent holder of the land subject to it.

There are a number of rules governing the types of conduct that may be regulated by restrictive covenants, how the benefits of the covenants may be transferred, and how they may be enforced.[11] Covenants which are highly unreasonable or against public policy will not be enforced by the courts against subsequent holders.[12]

Suppose the owner of land subject to a restrictive covenant acts in defiance of it before an aggrieved adjacent owner manages to obtain an injunction, by erecting a high wall, for example, or cutting a doorway through an existing wall. Is the adjacent owner without remedy? The court may exercise its discretion, especially in case of deliberately provocative breaches of a covenant, to grant a *mandatory injunction* requiring the wrongdoer to tear down the prohibited wall, or block the doorway and restore the wall. If it is too late to restore the damage, as when the wrongdoer has cut down a row of hundred-year-old oak trees, the court may award damages in lieu of an injunction.

Restrictive covenants are widely used in residential areas to regulate the uses to which land may be put. Typical restrictive covenants prohibit the use of land for other than residential purposes, limit building on the land to one-family dwellings, require minimum frontage per house, and specify minimum distances at which buildings may be erected from the sidelines of the lot or from the street line.

If over the years the character of the area has changed and a once reasonable covenant has become unduly restrictive, the affected landowner may apply to the court to have the covenant terminated. The court will require that the owner of the land for whose benefit the covenant was made be served with notice and given an opportunity to defend the covenant.

---

[11] See Preston and Newsome, *Restrictive Covenants* (5th ed.). London: Sweet & Maxwell Limited, 1971. An Ontario court has held that for a restrictive covenant to be enforceable, the party seeking to enforce it (the covenantee) must not only own land to be benefited by the covenant but his land must also be identified in the instrument creating the covenant. Re Sekretov and City of Toronto (1973) 33 D.L.R. (3d) 257. For statutory authority to modify or discharge a restrictive covenant see, for example, Conveyancing and Law of Property Act, R.S.O. 1970, c. 85, s. 62(1).

[12] The Conveyancing and Law of Property Act, R.S.O. 1970, c. 85, s. 22, states, for example, "Every covenant made after the 24th day of March 1950 that but for this section would be annexed to and run with land and that restricts the sale, ownership, occupation or use of land because of the race, creed, colour, nationality, ancestry or place of origin of any person is void and of no effect."

Restrictive covenants to regulate land use over an entire neighbourhood are referred to as *building-scheme covenants*. In a building scheme each owner mutually agrees with all other owners to be bound by the covenant in return for the promise of all neighbouring owners to be similarly bound. In order to have the court remove the covenant for the benefit of one owner, all the adjoining owners must be served with notice and given a chance to state their opinions. As a result, it may be very difficult to have a restrictive covenant under a building scheme terminated.

Covenants are gradually being replaced by municipal regulations in the form of zoning and building by-laws, especially in newly developed areas. Nevertheless, covenants still play an important role in older settled parts of our cities and towns; sometimes they unduly restrict the development of an area.

Other Interests

There are several other interests in land that are less than estates, but they warrant description only in a treatise on real property. One of these interests has become increasingly important and deserves special mention — the right to take minerals, oil, and gas from under the surface of land occupied by others. The right to remove these materials is usually embodied in an agreement commonly referred to as a *lease*. An oil, gas, or mineral lease bears little if any similarity to a true leasehold interest. Rather, it comprises several interests in land combined in one agreement between the parties. To the extent that the agreement permits the lessee to occupy a portion of the surface area of the land (often only a very small proportion of the area from which the oil, gas, or mineral is taken) it is similar to a true lease. To the extent that it grants the right to travel back and forth over the owner's land, lay pipes, and move equipment and also the materials taken from the ground, it is similar to an easement. To the extent that it permits the removal of these materials which were previously the real property of the owner and have now become the personal property of the lessee, it is similar to an ancient interest in land known as a *profit à prendre*. The law concerning these mineral, oil, and gas leases has become highly specialized in recent years. It will suffice to know that these agreements are more than mere leases and that they form a highly developed field of study of their own.

ADVERSE POSSESSION

Suppose that twenty years ago *A* stole ten dollars from a corner store. Had he been caught at the time, he might well have been sentenced to jail. But if twenty years later this fact is discovered and throughout that time *A* has been a law-abiding person, almost everyone will feel that it would be morally, if not legally, wrong to pursue the matter. Similarly, if a man had left several pieces of furniture with a friend while he travelled around the world, the friend would probably return them without question a few months later. But if the owner did not ask for their return until a dozen years later, his friend would probably have come to think of the pieces of furniture as his own and resent having to part with them. This desire to leave things undisturbed, as they have been for a very long time, finds its expression in the law of *limitations*. The policy of the law is that a person who has a right of action against another must pursue it within a definite period of time or lose his right: he must not keep the other party in indefinite jeopardy of being sued.[13] In Chapter 31, we shall discuss when a creditor who does not sue his debtor within the time permitted will lose the right to sue. Limitation statutes are not concerned with the merits of the plaintiff's claim: they require only that he prosecute his claim within a definite time or abandon it.

Rules of limitation apply to interests in land. They might arise as an issue, for example, in the following circumstances:

(a) *A* occupies land owned by *B*. He treats it as his own and improves it. His family continues to occupy the land for many years after his death. After several generations, the heirs of *B* try to dispossess the heirs of *A*.

(b) *A* mistakenly puts up a fence which encloses not only his own land but part of *B*'s land. He erects a costly building covering a portion of *B*'s land that he had enclosed. Years later the mistake comes to light, and *B* insists on the destruction of the building so that he may get his land back.

These circumstances present difficult problems for the court. Clearly in each case *B* owned the land; but to dispossess *A* or his successors would work hardship and injustice. In medieval times, when there were many large estates and absentee landlords, squatters who entered and stayed on their lands for long periods were very common. In recent times, with speedy means of transport and communication and with accurate surveys available, the number of squatters has become smaller. Even so, disputes frequently occur, and modern statutes in England and the five eastern common law provinces set out limitation periods beyond which an owner loses his right to regain possession of his land.[14] By adverse possession an occupier of land can extinguish the title of the owner; the possessor becomes in effect the owner of the land himself.

The three most western provinces and parts of Manitoba and Ontario have in force a modern land titles system governing the recording of interests in land. In the belief that this advanced system of registration, combined with modern methods of surveying, can eliminate almost all errors, and with a policy of having all interests in land recorded exclusively in the official registry, all these jurisdictions have provided by statute that the title of the registered owner cannot be extinguished by adverse possession.[15] But the attitude of people towards

---

[13] In matters of criminal law, in theory at least, a person should be prosecuted and punished regardless of the time that has elapsed since he committed an offence. The state is the prosecutor, and limitation statutes generally do not apply to it.

[14] See, for example: Limitations Act, R.S.O. 1970, c. 246, s. 4 (ten years); Limitations of Actions Act, R.S.N.S. 1967, c. 168, s. 9 (20 years).

[15] See, for example: Land Titles Act, R.S.A. 1970, c. 198, s. 63(1); Real Property Act, R.S.M. 1970, c. R30, s. 61(2).

reviving long-dormant claims, as we have discussed above, has caused resistance to the new rules. There have been cases where the courts of some of these jurisdictions were unwilling to accept the full implications of the statutory provisions. In some cases they have avoided the provisions, and in effect recognized possessory interests.[16]

Of course, not every possession of the land of another is *adverse* possession against him. The most common example of one person in possession of the land of another is that of a tenant in possession under a lease. The terms of the lease govern the relations between landlord and tenant: though the lease may run many years longer than the time needed for adverse possession to destroy an owner's title to land, the lease will govern their relations, not the statutory rules on limitation periods. But if the tenant were to stop paying rent due under the lease and ignore his other obligations, treating the land as if it were his own, he would then be in adverse possession, and the limitation period would begin to run from the time of his breach. The landlord could, of course, sue the tenant for breach of the lease and have him evicted; but if he failed to pursue his remedies within the time set out in the statute, he would lose all his rights. In these circumstances we see the elements needed for adverse possession: the possessor stays in exclusive possession; he treats the land as his own, and ignores the claims of other persons including the owner.

A further element of adverse possession is that it must be *open and notorious* — a man who furtively creeps into a deserted house each night and sleeps there for a period equal to the limitation period would not thereby extinguish the title of the owner. A court takes various facts into account in deciding whether a person has established possession that is both exclusive, and open and notorious. By showing that he has paid the municipal taxes, made improvements to the property, fenced the property, or performed other acts normally done by an owner, the possessor may strengthen his claim of adverse possession.

Adverse possession ceases to be effective if it is interrupted by the owner before the limitation period has elapsed. Thus, if the owner demands and receives rent from the possessor in acknowledgment of the owner's superior rights to the land, the adverse possession ceases until the period covered by the rent expires. If the possessor remains in possession after the rent period expires, the limitation period will begin to run again; but it begins anew and must run the full duration to extinguish the owner's title — it is not added to the previous period. Assuming the owner has not interrupted possession, the possessor may pass on his possession to another person, and the limitation period still runs against the owner from the time of the entry into adverse possession by the first possessor.

The law regards the owner of land to be in possession until another person establishes adverse possession. The consequences of this rule are twofold: first, an owner's title is not prejudiced merely by the fact that he has not occupied the land or leased it to a tenant — land abandoned for an indefinite period nonetheless remains the property of the owner; secondly, when an adverse pos-

---

[16] See Sinclair v. McLellan [1919] 2 W.W.R. 782; Boyczuk v. Perry [1948] 1 W.W.R. 495.

sessor abandons land before the limitation period has expired, the law regards possession as returned to the owner — the limitation period must start afresh if the possessor returns, or if a third person goes into adverse possession.

THE TRANSFER OF INTERESTS IN LAND

An interest in land may be transferred in any one of several ways. On death, if the holder of the interest dies *intestate* (without leaving a will), his interest will pass according to statutory rules of inheritance to his heir or heirs; that is, the interest will pass automatically to his closest relatives. If, for example, a widower holds a fee simple in Blackacre and at his death he is survived by two sons, his sons will become the owners of the fee simple. A man need not allow his wealth to go automatically according to these rules of succession. He may make provision by will to dispose of his property according to his wishes and the claims he feels he should satisfy. A second way that land may be transferred is therefore by the terms of a will.

A person may also dispose of an interest in land during his lifetime. Indeed, transfers between living persons are the most common way of disposing of interests in land. The methods used to transfer land have developed over hundreds of years; by the middle of the 19th century, a comparatively uniform method had been evolved in the use of a *grant*. The document effecting a grant contains a description of the grantor, the grantee, and the interest being transferred, and is signed and sealed by the grantor before a witness. Since the document is under seal, it is often called a *deed of conveyance* — frequently shortened to *deed*. We should recall, however, that every document under seal is a deed, and many deeds are not concerned with transfers of land at all. The equivalent of a grant under the land titles system, used in some areas as described in the next section, is called a *transfer* and is effective without being made under seal.

The holder of an interest in land may be compelled to transfer it against his will. A creditor may obtain judgment against him in court and eventually have the land sold in order to satisfy the debt. An increasingly common type of compulsory transfer of land is *expropriation*. When a public body such as the federal government or a local school board requires land for its activities, it may proceed under statute to force the transfer of land to itself. It must of course, pay compensation for taking the land, and if the parties cannot agree upon a price the statute provides for arbitration or judicial proceedings to determine the price to be paid.

The most important of the above methods of transfer is by voluntary grant in performance of a contract for the sale of land. The holder of an interest may grant the whole of it or only part, reserving the rest of it to himself. When he grants only part of it, the balance remains his. For example, when a landlord grants a lease for five years he retains the reversion, and possession returns to him at the end of the lease. Again, if the holder of a fee simple grants a life estate, the reversion stays with the holder and his heirs. When a person grants an easement over his land, he retains his interest in the land (the servient tenement).

Often the transferor of an interest wishes to transfer almost all his interest, retaining only a small part for himself. In these circumstances the *form* of the grant changes: he conveys away his whole interest except that he expressly *reserves* the part he wishes to keep. Thus, if *A* owns both Blackacre and White-acre and wishes to sell Whiteacre but retain an easement over it in order to get to and from Blackacre, he will grant Whiteacre reserving to himself a right of way over it. Such *reservations* are quite common in grants of land.

We may conclude that a transfer of an interest in land can have two results: first, if it is a transfer of the *whole interest,* then the interest remains unaltered but is in the hands of another person; secondly, if it is a transfer of only *part of an interest,* the interest is divided into two parts and there are two holders — the grantee with the interest he has obtained under the grant, and the grantor with the interest he has retained because he did not transfer it by the grant.

THE RECORDING OF INTERESTS IN LAND

It is evident from our discussion of interests in land that these interests are varied and complex and also that they may be transferred in a variety of ways. How is a prospective purchaser to discover what interest a vendor really holds in the land he proposes to sell? How may he discover what claims others have? Ordinarily, under the terms of a contract to sell land, the vendor sets out the interest he is selling and gives the purchaser the right to examine all the title documents in order to ascertain whether the vendor really has the interest claimed. In England, until recent times, the owner of land kept all the title documents to his land going back many years, often centuries. The system worked quite well, but it placed a very high value on these title documents as evidence of the owner's interest. Thus an accidental loss or destruction of the documents could create serious problems of proving ownership. And, of course, such documents deteriorated through much handling over the years.

In Canada and the United States a more reliable method of ascertaining title has developed. Each transfer of an interest in land is recorded in a public registry office. The usual practice is for the grantor to deliver to the grantee the original document and a duplicate copy. The grantee in turn files both of them with the registrar. The original is then recorded (formerly by hand or typewriter, but now usually on microfilm), assigned a number, and filed away. The duplicate is stamped and certified by the registrar, and the number of the original is recorded on it. It is then returned to the grantee. The registry office records are stored in a fireproof structure — both the original document and the photocopy of it — and in addition the purchaser has the duplicate copy of the original. Thus the danger of loss or destruction of the record of transfer is virtually eliminated. This method has now come into use in many parts of England also.

Generally, there is one registry office for each regional political division within a province or state. For example, each county or district within a province usually has a land registry office located in the county or district town, the seat of regional government. Under the protection of provincial statutes, the purchaser need *search* (examine) the title to the particular piece of land he is buying only in the registry office. Everyone who has an interest in the land must register it to protect himself. Otherwise he takes the risk that a *bona-fide purchaser,* that is, a purchaser who buys the land without knowledge of an unregistered claim, will buy free of that claim. Before the introduction of the registry system, if *V* granted his fee simple in Blackacre to *X* and subsequently *V* made a second grant of the same interest to *P* who did not know of the first grant, *X* would have title to Blackacre and *P* would have nothing. For when *V* granted Blackacre to *X,* he gave away all that he had — he had nothing more to give to *P.* Accordingly, the grant to *P* was a nullity. But under the registry system, if *P* registers his deed before *X* registers his, *P* will effectively cut out *X* and obtain title to Blackacre. The result of such provision is of course that purchasers register their grants immediately on receiving them. Prospective purchasers rely on records in the registry office: they buy interests according to these records and need not worry about other interests which may have been granted but not recorded.

Reflecting the rules of the statutes of limitations, some registry systems limit to forty years the period in the records that a purchaser must search for evidence of good title.[17]

Illustration:

X is considering the purchase of Red Oaks from *Y.* The records in the registry office show that *A* sold Red Oaks to *B* in 1890, but *B*'s name does not appear again. The next entry on the record is a grant in 1913 by *M* to *N,* and from then on there is a continuous chain of title to the present holder, *Y.*

X need not worry about the transfer from *A* to *B.* In all probability *B* transferred title to *M,* and *M* neglected to register the grant, but it is not necessary to establish this link. The fact that *M* conveyed the land to *N* more than forty years ago and that there is no subsequent difficulty with the title establishes a title upon which *X,* as an intending purchaser, can rely.

Searching the title to a piece of land under the registry system can be a laborious and sometimes a hazardous task. An error in one of the documents which has gone undetected may later be discovered and disclose an outstanding interest, creating serious consequences for the current owner. If harm results through the negligence of a lawyer, he must compensate his client. Lawyers take out liability insurance to compensate clients in case of such error.

The risks inherent in this system of registration encouraged the adoption of a newer system in the mid-19th century. The new system is called the *land titles* or the *Torrens* system, named after an officer in the Australian marine shipping-registry department. He adopted the system of ship registration directly for land registration. The distinctive feature of the system is that as each new transaction concerning a piece of land is submitted for registration, it is carefully examined and approved before being actually recorded. At the time of recording, all out-

---

[17] The Registry Act, R.S.O. 1970, c. 409, ss. 111-2; Limitations of Actions Act, R.S.N.S. 1967, c. 168, s. 19.

standing interests in the piece of land are brought up to date and certified as being correct by the land titles office. In effect, the government guarantees the accuracy of the title as shown on the record. There are variations from jurisdiction to jurisdiction in the methods of recording and in the type of guarantee given by the government. The great advantage of the system is that the purchaser need not search through forty or more years of records to discover the state of the title. The land titles office will give him a complete statement, valid to the moment the statement is issued.

As we have seen, the land titles system attempts to do away with the risks of adverse possession and to give absolute and concise information on the state of the title. The older registry system makes no attempt to do this: its purpose is simply to give a complete record of all title documents and let the searcher judge their validity for himself. The registry system exists in the older settled parts of Canada — the four Atlantic provinces and throughout most of southern Ontario and parts of Manitoba. The land titles system is used in the three westernmost provinces, most of Manitoba, throughout most of northern Ontario, and in a few southern Ontario districts.

We must not conclude that a careful search of the recorded documents will assure a purchaser that his land is free from *all* claims that may later prejudice him. We have noted that in those provinces using the registry system, a purchaser cannot rely on the records because the vendor's title may have been extinguished by adverse possession. The purchaser should personally inspect the property to see if there is evidence of a third party who appears to be asserting a right of exclusive possession over the whole or any part of the lands. Nor is adverse possession the only possible source of trouble: there are other claims against lands not ordinarily recorded under either the registry or the land titles system. Two such claims are arrears of municipal tax on the land and, in some provinces, arrears of tax against corporations accruing while they hold the land. If any of these claims comes to light after the purchaser has paid for the land, he must satisfy them in order to protect his interest in it. Thus, a prospective purchaser should obtain evidence from the municipality of any taxes outstanding and evidence from the provincial government of any arrears of corporation taxes. This information cannot be obtained from the registry or land titles office but only from the government concerned.

A further claim may arise if the vendor is a judgment debtor. When a creditor has sued and obtained a judgment against his debtor, and has registered this judgment with the sheriff for the county or district, the creditor may subsequently require the sheriff to *levy execution,* that is, seize and hold a sale of the debtor's lands in order to realize funds to pay the debt. A judgment creditor may levy execution against the land even after the debtor has sold it, unless the purchaser pays the debt. Accordingly, a purchaser should make a search for executions in the sheriff's office to ensure that there are none before completing the sale. In order to facilitate this search the sheriff's office and the land registry office are often in the same building, or special facilities are provided in the registry office to search the execution records.

Another hazard to the purchaser may be created by a tenant in possession of the land. In most jurisdictions, short-term leases, usually for three years or less, need not be registered or even in writing and are valid against purchasers who buy the interest of the landlord. Thus, the purchaser must inspect the property to see if there are any tenants, and if there are, he should obtain an acknowledgment from them of the type of tenancy they claim to hold. If the vendor assures the purchaser that the tenant is only a monthly tenant who can be given one month's notice to vacate, the purchaser may later discover that the tenant has a two-year lease. He would be unable to put the tenant out even though he had bought the premises for the purpose of obtaining possession for himself and carrying on business there. But if the purchaser obtains a signed acknowledgment from the tenant that he is a monthly tenant only, the court would not permit the tenant to claim later that he had a lease for two years. A purchaser may thus rely upon a signed statement of the tenant.

In summary, the sale of an interest in land is a complex transaction requiring careful examination of the records at the local registry or land titles office, the offices of municipal and provincial governments, the local sheriff's office, and an inspection of the land itself. We should remember, however, that a sale of land is completed and title passes to a purchaser when he obtains delivery of the deed. The purchaser becomes full owner of his newly acquired property at that moment in time. Registration or recording of land titles gives protection against subsequent fraudulent acts by an unscrupulous vendor.

QUESTIONS FOR REVIEW

1. What is property?
2. What is real property?
3. What is title?
4. What is included in the term ''land''?
5. Distinguish between a remainder and a reversion.
6. What is a deed?
7. What is a grantor? A grantee?
8. In whose interest is it to register a grant of land? Why?
9. Jones' neighbours are having a party and making noise at night. What rights has Jones?
10. In what ways may title to land be acquired?
11. Doe planted a weeping willow tree near the boundary of his lot. The tree has grown and is now weeping on Smith's adjoining lot. Has Smith any rights? Would the age of the tree make any difference?
12. What are homestead rights? In what provinces do they apply?
13. Describe the basic distinction between the land titles system and the registry system.
14. Is a purchaser sufficiently assured of obtaining a good title to land by searching in the registry office? Why?
15. What is a building-scheme covenant?
16. What is a reservation in a grant?
17. In what respects does the existence of a life estate hamper the sale of land?

18. Why is a telephone company's use of land for its cable often not an ease-ment? What is the significance of the fact that no easement is created?

19. ". . . we conceive of the land as property, something that is specifically owned. But such ownership expresses only a practical relationship among men: the land itself is common to everyone. What we think of as property we actually hold in trust." (From *Survival Day Bulletin,* 1971.)

  (a) Discuss some of the respects in which the law recognizes an obligation to others in the use of property (both real and personal) that we own.

  (b) Explain also the basis of the argument that individual owners should re-tain considerable discretion in the use of their property free from restric-tion.

  (c) Outline briefly the nature of the dilemma encountered in the attempt to devise laws that will control or restrain economic activity causing pollu-tion.

CASES FOR DISCUSSION

CASE 1

John Carter purchased a house in the city of Ottawa. He then called on his widowed daughter-in-law for whom he had high regard and said: "Mary, I want you to look at the house I have bought for you. You won't have to worry about rent any more." Mary was very pleased. She moved into the house with her children within a few days. She paid the taxes and looked after the house but paid no rent to her father-in-law. John Carter paid the fire insurance premiums on the house throughout the period of his daughter-in-law's occupancy. He lived with his daughter-in-law and grandchildren for a year and a half.

Twelve years later John Carter died, and his executor found the duplicate copy of the deed to the house among his papers. The deed was in John Carter's name. The executor then claimed the house from Mary as part of the Carter estate to be given to other beneficiaries under the will. Mary knew little of matters of law; she could only state that she believed the house had been bought in her name and that she had lived in it continuously from the time of the purchase until the dispute with the executor.

Who has the right to the house, Mary or the executor? Why? (See *Casey v. Canada Trust Co.* (1961) 25 D.L.R. (2d) 764.)

CASE 2

Arthurs owned a row of a dozen retail stores in a new shopping district. He took great pride in the fact that they were all designed with colonial-style façades for their full three storeys. He occupied one store himself and ran a profitable an-tique business. He rented the other eleven stores. A friend interested him in a development scheme to build a large office building, but to raise the necessary capital for his share of the venture, Arthurs found it necessary to sell all the stores and lease back the one he occupied himself. The shopping district was prosper-ous, and he had no trouble selling them. From each purchaser he obtained the following covenant inserted in each grant: ''The Grantee covenants on behalf of himself and his assignees not to erect neon or other lighted signs either on the face of the building or at right angles to it, and further covenants not to let the facade fall into disrepair or to become unsightly.''

Three of the stores adjacent to each other were purchased by Brown, Crawford, and Dugan respectively. Several years later each received an offer to purchase his store from Super Duper Discount Stores Ltd. The price was very high, and all three accepted the offers. A few days after completion of the sales, Super Duper moved into possession and began to erect a large neon sign over the stores and to remove the colonial façade. Arthurs arrived and was horrified. He demanded that the work stop at once. The manager of Super Duper refused, and Arthurs immediately brought an action for an injunction to restrain both the erection of the neon sign and the removal of the colonial façade, and for an order to restore the façade and to obey the terms of the covenant, and for damages. At the trial Super Duper admitted that it was aware of the covenant when it bought the stores but claimed that there was no privity of contract with Arthurs and accordingly that no part of the covenant was binding.

Who should succeed? Why? (See *Haywood v. Brunswick Building Society* (1881) 8 Q.B.D. 403; *Clegg v. Hands* (1890) 44 Ch. D. 503.)

CASE 3

Fox owned a summer cottage near Fredericton, New Brunswick. He sold it and delivered a grant to Simpson in exchange for $19,000 cash on June 10. On June 11, Simpson received a telephone call to return home to Newfoundland where his mother was seriously ill; he left without registering his grant to the cottage. When Fox learned that Simpson had left the area he called an acquaintance, Entwistle, and asked him whether he was interested in buying the cottage at a bargain price of $16,000. Entwistle had offered Fox that amount several months before and Fox had refused. Entwistle eagerly accepted the offer on June 20 and paid Fox. On the same day, Entwistle received a grant to the cottage and registered it without knowlege of its prior sale to Simpson. Fox then absconded with the money from both sales.

Several weeks later, Simpson returned to find Entwistle occupying the cottage. When Entwistle refused to move, Simpson brought an action to have Entwistle put out and himself declared the owner.

The Registry Act, R.S.N.B. 1973, c. R-6, contains the following provision:

19. All instruments may be registered in the registry office in the county where the lands lie, and if not so registered, shall . . . be deemed fraudulent and void against subsequent purchasers for valuable consideration whose conveyances are previously registered.

Will Simpson succeed in his action? Would the result be different if Entwistle had heard that Simpson had purchased the cottage before he paid Fox the $16,000? Give reasons.

CASE 4

Peter Green owned and operated Green's General Hardwares and also owned the lands and buildings where the business was carried on. His younger brother John worked for him as manager, as did his son Edward. Peter died leaving a will in which he gave the business and real property to John for life, with the remainder to Edward at John's death. John and Edward could not agree on how to run the business: John wanted to push sales and expansion as quickly as possible; Edward feared that such action would make the business unstable — he preferred to build more slowly, consolidating the gains of the business. The dispute became heated, and John fired Edward. Within several years the business was in serious financial difficulty, and John had allowed several buildings, including a warehouse, to fall into disrepair. Edward sought by court action to force John to keep the buildings in good repair. Should he succeed? Why?

John died and left a will giving his whole estate including the business and buildings to his wife. Who is entitled to the business and why?

CASE 5

Broum and Vulkan were joint tenants of a large property, Homicide Heights, until Broum shot and killed Vulkan while they were hunting together on the property. Broum was subsequently convicted of criminal negligence as a result of this "accident". Later, when he sought to sell the whole property for $500,000 to a firm of real estate speculators, Mrs. Vulkan protested. Explain briefly whether she would have legal grounds for complaining. (See *Shobelt v. Barber* (1967) 60 D.L.R. (2d) 519.)

CASE 6

For over thirty years Montgomery owned two farms: Green Gables, on which he lived, and Wildwood. The two were separated by a farm owned by Cavendish. Montgomery continuously used a road across the Cavendish farm to go to and from Green Gables and Wildwood. The access to the road was through a gate on the boundary of the Cavendish property. During most of these years Montgomery gave Cavendish a large turkey for New Year's, presumably as a gesture of good will and appreciation for the use of the road.

Three years ago Montgomery sold Wildwood to Newcombe. Newcombe made relatively little use of the road over the Cavendish property (going across twice yearly to visit Montgomery with mortgage payments) until last year, when he also acquired Green Gables. The old road then became valuable to Newcombe as the most convenient access between his two properties. In the meantime, however, the Cavendish family had extended their lawn across the roadway and Newcombe's suddenly increased use of the road led to a dispute about his rights.

Cavendish sought a court injunction to restrain Newcombe's use of the alleged right-of-way. Indicate whether the court would grant the injunction.

CASE 7

Running southerly from Halifax along the Atlantic is a provincial highway approximately a thousand feet from the shoreline, where Essex Oil Ltd. has owned
a service station on the east side of the road since 1953. The Essex Oil property
extends about 900 feet along the east side of the highway and 300 feet east to a
right-of-way owned by the province for a proposed scenic highway that would
run closer to the seacoast parallel to the existing highway. The oil company's
land was unfenced except along the existing highway, beside the station. On the
other side of the right-of-way and running down to the Atlantic shore is the
Webster Trailer Court and Campsite, a business that was operating there for some
years before Essex Oil opened its station.

The province continuously deferred construction of the new road, and the
right-of-way, a strip about 150 feet wide, lay vacant. The trailer court obtained a
licence from the province to use the right-of-way but made no request of Essex
Oil Ltd. to use that portion of its land not occupied for the business of the service
station. Beginning in 1954, without any communication with Essex Oil, Webster's employees cut the grass on both the provincial right-of-way and the oil
company's land, cleared litter, planted flowers, and painted the fence on the far
side of the oil company's land, adjacent to the existing road. The employees converted the whole of this land into a playground for guests, putting up tennis
courts and a baseball diamond.

Finally, in 1973, some 19 years after the trailer court had begun to make use
of this land, the province announced that it had abandoned all plans to build a road
on the proposed site. Essex Oil Ltd. then decided to dispose of its unused land. It
therefore wrote to Webster Trailer Court and Campsite, offering to sell it the strip
of land for $25,000.

Mr. Webster, owner of the trailer court, consulted his solicitor, who
checked the title deed and confirmed that the disputed land belonged to Essex Oil
Ltd. The solicitor also advised him, however, that if the trailer court were to
remain in possession for another two months it would have been using the land for
20 years and would then, under Nova Scotia law, have obtained title by adverse
possession and without any payment to Essex Oil Ltd.

The Webster Trailer Court and Campsite did not reply to Essex Oil's offer and
continued to make use of the land for the enjoyment of its guests. Essex Oil Ltd.
wrote again in three weeks and received no reply. A week later, the local manager
of Essex Oil Ltd. attempted to reach Mr. Webster by telephone. His secretary
advised that he was out of town for another four weeks, but had left word that on his
return he would be glad to discuss the offer in the oil company's first letter.

The full 20-year period had only elapsed by two or three days when the
management of Essex Oil Ltd. became suspicious of what was going on and immediately had a fence constructed around the unfenced sides of its strip of land,
right across a number of tennis courts and through the baseball diamond. It had
no sooner done so than it received a letter from the Webster Trailer Court and
Campsite solicitor stating that his client had a "possessory title" to the disputed

land. Webster Trailer Court and Campsite then brought an action against Essex Oil Ltd. for a court order to the effect that it had acquired title to the land.

Discuss the validity of the plaintiff's case and the nature of the argument, if any, that might be offered by the defendant. (For reference, see *Wallis's Ltd. v. Shell-Mex and BP* [1974] 3 All E.R. 575.)

CHAPTER 25

Landlord and Tenant

THE NATURE OF THE RELATIONSHIP

Definition of a Tenancy

A leasehold interest is created when a landlord (lessor) grants a term to a tenant (lessee). A *term* is an interest in land for a definite period of time. The landlord thus divides the interest in the land between himself and the tenant by giving a term to the tenant and retaining the reversion. At the end of the term, the tenant must give up the land: the right to possession reverts to the landlord. The word *lease* is used both as a short form for leasehold interest, and to refer to the agreement between landlord and tenant creating the leasehold.

As we have seen in the preceding chapter, a leasehold interest is an estate in land. When a leasehold has been validly created, certain rights and duties automatically accrue to both the landlord and the tenant. But the requirements of land law for the creation of an estate are strict, and do not take into account the intentions of the parties; even if the parties clearly intend to create a leasehold interest, but fail to fulfil these requirements, no estate in the land comes into being, and the usual rights and duties between landlord and tenant do not arise. The consequences may be serious for either party but especially for the would-be tenant: he may be evicted by the owner at once; he has no right himself to evict strangers; he cannot acquire further interests in land such as easements, which may only be annexed to a freehold or a leasehold estate. For these reasons the essentials for the creation of a leasehold interest deserve emphasis. They are, first, that the tenant must obtain the right to exclusive possession, and second, that the tenancy must be for a definite or ascertainable period of time.

535

Most provinces have now distinguished *residential tenancies* as a special class of tenancy in their landlord and tenant legislation. They have done so in an effort to recognize the special importance of basic shelter for individuals who lease apartments and houses as their place of residence. We shall deal separately with these amendments in a later section of this chapter. The discussion below will therefore apply to *commercial tenancies:* its relevance to residential tenancies must be read in relation to the specific statutory amendments.

Exclusive Possession

Exclusive possession denotes the historic distinction between estates in land and lesser interests in land. It distinguishes control over the land from a mere right to use the land in common with others. A man who has a right to use land in common with others may have an easement, as we have discussed in the preceding chapter, or he may be merely a *licensee*. A licensee enters upon land with the consent of the owner, as for example when he goes fishing in a farmer's stream; he is on the land lawfully, not as a trespasser, but he has no interest in the land. He does not have the right to put others off the land or to object if the activity of others interferes with his use and enjoyment of it. Moreover, in some circumstances the owner may put him off the land even when the owner has given him a contractual right to be there. The rights of a contractual licensee can be quite complicated and are better left for a treatise on land law.[1] A tenant's right to exclusive possession gives him far greater power than a contractual licensee. He may keep anyone off his land, and his landlord has no right to put him off the land until the term ends. The tenant may keep even his landlord from entering the land unless he has given the landlord the right to enter for a specific purpose, such as to view the state of repair of the property and to make repairs. The right to exclusive possession of land gives the tenant the ability to acquire other lesser rights — a tenant may acquire an easement over adjoining land for the duration of his tenancy in the same manner as the holder of a fee simple may acquire an easement.

There have been numerous cases about what constitutes exclusive possession. The main problem is whether a person has exclusive possession when under the terms of his lease he gives others limited rights of use or access over the land. Thus, if a businessman contemplates obtaining a lease that reserves to the landlord or other persons the right to make special use of the premises at the same time, he exposes himself to serious risk. He should obtain legal advice about the matter. Generally speaking, it is wise not to grant any right for the use of the premises either to a third person or to the landlord under the terms of the lease, except that it is quite permissible for the landlord to be given the right to enter for the purpose of inspecting the premises and making repairs.

---

[1] Burn (ed.) *Cheshire's Modern Law of Property* (11th ed.), pp. 567-70. London: Butterworths, 1972.

Definite or Ascertainable Period

A lease must begin on a fixed date, and it must end on a fixed or ascertainable date; the final date need not be specified if the period itself is definite. Thus, a lease that is to begin on March 1 of a certain year to run for a week, a month, a year, five years, or 500 years will be a valid leasehold interest because the date of expiry can always be worked out accurately. If the parties attempt to create a term for an uncertain period, the term is void and no leasehold interest comes into existence. It has been held that a lease "for the duration of the war" or "until the tenant becomes insolvent" is void. If, however, the parties wish to have a lease of such a nature, they can accomplish their purpose by a comparatively simple change in the wording. The requirement of certainty will be satisfied if a lease must end *at the latest* upon a certain date, but may be brought to an end *at an earlier date* through the happening of a particular event. Thus we may have a valid lease from *A* to *B* for 100 years to be terminated earlier if and when "hostilities between country *X* and country *Y* should formally come to an end," or "should *B* become insolvent".

CLASSES OF TENANCIES

Term Certain

A term certain is a tenancy which expires on a specific day ending the term without any further act by either the landlord or the tenant. A lease of a summer cottage "from June 1 to August 31" of a particular year, or a long-term lease of a cold-storage plant "from March 1, 1973 to February 28, 1985," are examples of typical leases for a term certain. The tenant is expected to vacate before the end of the last day of the tenancy unless he has made new arrangements with the landlord. If he stays on without making any arrangements, he becomes an *overholding tenant* and may be put out by the landlord. If, however, the landlord accepts further rent without protesting, a new tenancy may be created, as explained below.

Periodic Tenancy

A periodic tenancy is a leasehold interest which renews itself automatically on the last day of the term for a further term of the same duration, unless either the landlord or the tenant serves notice to bring the tenancy to an end. A periodic tenancy may be created by a formal agreement, but in Canada it arises more often in an informal way when a tenant moves into possession and pays an agreed rent to the landlord at regular intervals as agreed between them, either in writing or orally. If, for example, he pays rent on the first day of each month, as each month ends the tenancy renews itself for another month without further agreement between the parties. A periodic tenancy also comes into existence when a tenant remains in possession after his tenancy for a term certain has expired, and pays further rent to the landlord. The most common type of periodic tenancies are weekly, monthly, and yearly. The yearly tenancy is often called a *tenancy from year to year*.

We may note here the contrast between a term certain and a periodic tenancy: a term certain *ends* automatically unless the parties make an arrangement to continue it; a periodic tenancy *renews* automatically unless either of the parties serves notice to end it. We shall discuss the requirements of notice below, under "Termination and Renewal of a Tenancy".

Tenancy at Will

A tenancy at will is not a true leasehold interest because it does not last for a definite period, nor does the tenant have any right to exclude the landlord and remain on the premises. He is there merely at the landlord's will, and the landlord may demand possession at any time without notice. The tenant does, however, have a reasonable time to gather up his possessions and leave.

On the other hand, a tenant at will is under no obligation to remain in possession and pay rent. He may vacate possession at any time without notice. Such a tenancy may exist when the owner of real property allows a prospective purchaser to occupy it pending the conveyance of title to him, or when a landlord permits a tenant to remain on a day-to-day basis pending the wrecking of the building to make way for new construction. A tenancy at will may be gratuitous, or the landlord may exact a payment without turning the arrangement into a leasehold.

Tenancy at Sufferance

A tenancy at sufferance is not a tenancy at all. The typical example is that of an overholding tenant. He entered into possession rightfully under his lease but now stays in possession wrongfully after his term has expired. Since he came into possession lawfully, he is not treated as a *trespasser* unless the landlord orders him to leave and he refuses. (Ordinarily, a trespasser is one who enters without consent or lawful right on the lands of another or who, having entered lawfully, refuses to leave when ordered to do so by the owner.) We should contrast the position of a tenant at sufferance with that of a tenant at will. Although a tenant at will has no estate in the land and can be put out by the landlord, he is nonetheless there lawfully, by agreement. A tenant at sufferance has no agreement with the landlord: his occupation of the land is merely suffered by the landlord until the landlord acts to put him out.

COVENANTS

Payment of Rent

The covenant to pay rent is more easily understood if we remember the nature of a leasehold interest. A leasehold is quite literally a specific period of time carved out of the fee simple and sold for a fixed sum. Very often this fact is recognized in leases by stating the total rent to be paid during the whole of the lease, before setting out how this sum is to be paid. In this respect the transaction is similar to an instalment purchase of a chattel. For example, the tenant may promise to pay the sum of $12,000 to lease a suite of offices for five years in 60 monthly instalments of $200 per month. Thus, when the leasehold is transferred to the tenant, he becomes the holder or owner of that period of five years somewhat like the purchaser of a car on instalments becomes the owner of an interest in the car; each is to pay for his purchase over the succeeding few years.[2] We may carry the analogy further: if the car is destroyed, the buyer must still pay for it. Similarly, if leased premises are destroyed, the tenant is still liable for the rent — he has purchased a leasehold interest consisting of a certain geographically defined area, and he must pay for it whether or not the building and amenities continue to exist for the full term. It appears, then, that the doctrine of frustration has no application to leaseholds, with perhaps the exception of leasehold interests above the ground floor in a multi-storey building. If, for example, a ten-storey building burns down, can the landlord insist that a ninth-floor tenant continue to be liable for rent because the tenant may employ a surveyor to show him exactly where his office suite used to be and may still use the space if he wishes? To the present time, there are no decisions on this problem, but probably the tenant would be released from his obligation to pay rent. A leading treatise states:

> If the subject-matter [of a lease] is destroyed entirely, it is submitted that the lease comes automatically to an end. . . . There being no such thing in law as a [lease] . . . of a volume of space above the surface of the earth . . . it is submitted that no [lease] . . . of part of a building without any of the soil upon which the building stands, can survive such a destruction of the building as leaves no physically defined subject matter . . .[3]

In addition, it is generally the duty of the landlord to provide access to leased premises on upper floors by means of staircases or elevators, and his failure to do so might in itself relieve the tenant from liability to pay rent.

When a tenant leases only a portion of his landlord's building, the landlord usually retains control over heating and repairs and maintenance. In these circumstances it is very common to provide in the lease that liability to pay rent shall be suspended if the leased premises are substantially destroyed by fire or other cause, other than the tenant's own negligence. Such a provision is not implied, however, and unless it is expressly stated in the lease, the tenant remains liable for the rent — subject to our discussion above concerning leases of premises above the ground floor.

The tenant's covenant to pay rent is independent of any express promise by

---

[2] We shall discuss the nature of a purchaser's interest in an instalment plan purchase in detail in Chapter 30.

[3] Woodfall, *Landlord and Tenant* (27th ed.), pp. 966-7. London: Sweet & Maxwell Limited, 1968.

the landlord to make repairs to the property, and the tenant is not excused from paying rent on the grounds that the landlord has not performed his part of the bargain. A tenant is not, however, liable for further rent when the acts of his landlord amount to an eviction, as we shall see when we consider the covenants of "repairs" and "quiet enjoyment" below.

The terms of the covenant to pay rent are binding on both parties. During the term, the landlord cannot increase the rent unless specific provision has been made, as where the parties agree that the landlord may increase the rent by an amount equal to any increase in property taxes. If the landlord wishes to increase the rent, he cannot do so until the term expires: he may, of course, bargain for an increase in any subsequent lease.

Assignment and Subletting

A tenant may wish to assign the balance of his term for a wide variety of reasons. He may for example have been so successful that he requires larger premises before the lease expires, or he may be offered a large sum as goodwill for the sale of his business, the sale necessarily entailing the assignment of his lease to the purchaser. A tenant, as owner of his term, has the right to assign it just as the owner of a fee simple or a chattel has the right to sell and transfer his property. A tenant cannot terminate his contractual obligations to his landlord by assigning; if the assignee of the term does not fulfil these obligations after the assignment, the landlord may still successfully sue the tenant. For this reason, the tenant always makes it a term of the assignment of his tenancy that the assignee shall carry out all of the covenants of the tenant in the lease and indemnify the tenant for any loss caused by the assignee's default. Thus, while remaining liable on his covenants to the landlord, a tenant may none the less assign his interest to whomever he pleases.

A landlord leasing his premises, however, is often as much concerned with the character and reputation of the tenant as he is with his ability to pay the rent: it may be a matter of prestige, for instance, to have the head office of a large Canadian corporation as a tenant in a new building in order to encourage other prospective tenants of good quality. A landlord may also be concerned about the type of business to be carried on for one or more of several reasons: the prestige or reputation of the building; unprofitable competition with the business of other tenants of the landlord or with that of the landlord himself — a problem often arising in large business blocks and shopping centres; noise, fumes, or traffic interfering with other tenants; the wear and tear certain businesses may inflict upon the premises. Various combinations of these reasons may determine whether or not a landlord will accept a particular tenant. Yet if the tenant were free to assign to whomever he pleased he would, by assigning, defeat the landlord's objectives. For this reason, a landlord almost invariably requires his tenant to covenant that he will not assign the lease without leave (permission) from the landlord.

Now, if the landlord may grant leave or withhold it as he chooses, the tenant in turn will be in a difficult position. Circumstances may arise that not only make assignment by the tenant reasonable and in no way harmful to the landlord but also make refusal by the landlord an extreme hardship upon the tenant. Accordingly, tenants often stipulate that the words "but such consent shall not be unreasonably withheld" be added to the covenant. In the provinces of Manitoba, New Brunswick, Ontario, Prince Edward Island, and Saskatchewan, these words are implied by statute as part of the covenant unless they are expressly excluded. It is both harsh and unusual for them to be expressly excluded; a tenant should be cautious about entering into a lease where in the provinces mentioned above the landlord excludes the implied words, or in the other provinces refuses to permit the addition of these words to the covenant requiring his consent to an assignment.

A sublease differs from an assignment as follows: an assignment is a transfer of the *whole* of the tenant's term to the assignee; so long as the assignee performs all his covenants, the tenant has no further right or interest in the lease. A sublease is a transfer of *part only* of the tenant's term to the subtenant. If the term given the subtenant expires just one day before the expiration of the main lease (thereby leaving the tenant with a reversion of one day), the tenancy of the subtenant is created not by an assignment but by a sublease, and the tenant becomes the landlord of his subtenant. The sublease may differ materially from the main lease in the rent payable, in any of the covenants given by either party, and in the extent of the premises sublet (the subtenant may hold only a portion of the premises leased to the tenant). In a sublease, just as in an assignment, the tenant remains liable to his landlord to perform all the covenants under the main lease. The discussion concerning the requirement of consent of the landlord for assignment applies equally to subleases — the covenant usually refers to subletting as well as assignment.

Restriction on Use of Premises

As we have noted, a landlord is usually concerned with both the character of his tenant and the use to which the premises are to be put. Once the landlord has accepted the tenant, he can do nothing about the tenant's particular personality or character. He may, however, exercise control over the uses which the tenant may make of the premises by exacting a covenant restricting the use to particular trades, or even prohibiting all trades by restricting use for residential purposes. Such covenants are enforceable against the tenant's assignees and subtenants.

A tenant may, of course, be equally interested that his landlord should not rent adjoining premises to a competing business. He will often obtain a covenant from his landlord to that effect. If, however, the landlord should commit a breach by renting adjoining premises to an innocent third party unaware of the covenant, the tenant will not be able to take action against the third party. His remedy will be limited to an action for damages against the landlord.

Even in the absence of an express covenant, there is an implied covenant by the tenant to treat the premises in a tenant-like manner, that is, use them only for those purposes for which they are reasonably intended. Thus he could not turn a cold-storage plant into a glue factory, or a private residence into a hotel. In other words, a tenant may be prevented from carrying on activities for which the premises were not intended and which would cause excessive wear and tear.

Fitness for Occupancy

A leading writer on the subject of landlord and tenant, in commenting upon the existence of implied covenants of fitness of the leased premises, has said: "One is reminded here of the chapter on the subject of snakes in the treatise on Iceland referred to by Dr. Johnson. Speaking generally, there is no covenant for fitness at all on the part of the lessor. The lessee takes the . . . premises as he finds them and at his own risk."[4] Unless he is given an express covenant in the lease concerning the fitness of the premises for his particular use, or unless the landlord has made a misrepresentation, thereby giving the tenant the usual remedies in contract and tort for misrepresentation, the tenant is responsible for his own investigation of the premises and must take them as he finds them. There is one exception to this common law rule: when a landlord rents premises as a furnished house or furnished apartment, he gives an implied warranty that they will be in a habitable state at the beginning of the lease.

As we noted in Chapter 13, a landlord is not liable to his tenant or his tenant's family or guests for injuries caused by the unsafe condition of the premises unless the landlord was, or ought to have been, aware of the dangerous condition when the lease was entered into and failed to warn the tenant who was unaware of the danger until the mishap occurred. If, however, the landlord covenants to make repairs and the tenant sustains a loss because the landlord fails to do so after receiving notice of the danger, the landlord will be liable for the loss. In all other circumstances the tenant, as the party in exclusive possession of the property, will bear any responsibility which arises from injuries caused to persons on the property.

Repairs

As a general rule, a landlord is not liable to make repairs to the property unless he expressly covenants to do so. Quite apart from law, of course, the landlord has an economic incentive to maintain his property in rentable condition. In some circumstances, he may be liable to repair structural defects which develop, particularly if his failure to repair would amount to an indirect eviction of the tenant and consequently a breach of the covenant for quiet enjoyment, as we shall see in the next subsection. For example, if the failure of a landlord to repair a leak in the roof of an office building results in the soaking and eventual crumbling of the

---

[4] Foa, *Outline of the Law of Landlord and Tenant* (4th ed.), p. 71. London: The "Law Times" Office, 1928. (In the book to which Dr. Johnson referred, the chapter on snakes contained one brief sentence: "There are no snakes in Iceland.")

ceiling and walls in an office suite, the tenant has an action against his landlord even where there is no covenant to repair. If the rented premises are in a large building, the landlord is responsible to his tenants for the maintenance of corridors, stairways, and elevators.

The tenant also is not liable to make repairs to his premises unless he has expressly covenanted to do so. This rule is, however, subject to two exceptions. First, he must not make such use of the premises as will cause excessive wear, as we have already noted. Secondly, he is liable if he commits *waste*. Waste may be either *voluntary* — as when a tenant pulls down part of a building or otherwise damages it, or makes alterations which reduce its value — or *permissive,* that is negligent, as when a tenant is aware of some small damage such as a leak in the roof and realizes that more serious harm will result if he does not repair it, and yet neglects to do so. The law concerning permissive waste is complex and rather uncertain, but fortunately also of little consequence today, since parties to a lease generally make an express agreement about which of them shall keep the leased premises in good repair.

When a tenant leases an entire building or property, the landlord frequently obtains a covenant from him to keep the property in good repair, reasonable wear and tear excepted. The tenant thereby agrees that he will make such repairs as are necessary to keep the property in the same condition as when the lease began, except for normal depreciation. The tenant will not be liable for rot caused by faulty construction or for deterioration in the property due to a normal and progressive action of the forces of nature. Unless the lease expresses a different intention, however, the covenant to repair includes liability of the tenant to make good any loss by fire or storm. Often the tenant will limit his liability in this respect by qualifying the covenant to repair with the words "loss by fire, lightning, and tempest excepted".

When a tenant leases only part of a building, the landlord usually undertakes to provide various services such as heat, water, and elevator service and also to keep the premises in good repair. We should note that there is an important difference between a covenant to repair on the part of the tenant and on the part of the landlord: the tenant is in possession of his premises and should be aware of their falling into disrepair — he is in breach of his covenant the moment he permits the premises to fall into disrepair, and it is not up to the landlord to remind him about it. The landlord, not being in possession of the tenant's premises, is not presumed to be aware of any state of disrepair in them and his duty to repair does not arise until the tenant serves notice to repair upon him. A landlord who undertakes to repair the premises will often reserve to himself the right to go on the premises at reasonable hours and inspect and view the state of repair. Reserving this right, however, does not place any duty upon him to make inspections or to repair until he has received notice from the tenant.

Quiet Enjoyment

The whole purpose of a tenant in acquiring a lease is to obtain possession and to "enjoy" the premises during the term of the lease. Accordingly, the landlord covenants to give quiet enjoyment either impliedly, simply by granting the lease, or expressly, in a specific covenant for that purpose. The covenant has two aspects: first, it is an assurance against the consequences of the landlord's having a defective title *at the time he gives the lease,* and second, it is a covenant that the landlord will not *subsequent to the making of the lease* himself interfere, or permit anyone obtaining an interest in land from him to interfere with the tenant's enjoyment of the premises.

Illustrations:

(a) Greer owns a large tract of land including certain warehouses. A mining company survey shows valuable ore deposits; Greer grants the company a long-term mining lease, and the company undertakes extensive mining excavations. Subsequently Greer leases the warehouses to Atkins, who wishes to use them to store heavy machinery manufactured elsewhere. Atkins discovers that the mining operations have undermined the foundations of the warehouses, making them unsafe for use. Since the mining company is carrying on its activities properly, and Greer cannot prevent its operations because he had validly granted it a mining lease before he granted Atkins his lease, Greer's title was defective; therefore, he committed a breach of his covenant for quiet enjoyment.

(b) Muggins leases a suite of offices to McAdam and McCollum, a firm of practising accountants. Subsequently he leases the area on the floor directly above to a machine shop. The machine-shop operations create noise and heavy vibrations, making it impossible for the accountants to carry on any aspect of their practice with adequate care. Muggins is in breach of his covenant.

The courts have held that breach of the covenant of quiet enjoyment requires physical interference with the enjoyment of the premises, and that mere interference with the comfort of the lessee through some personal annoyance is not in itself sufficient. In a recent unreported Ontario appeal case[5] a tenant argued that his liability for rent had been abrogated by the landlord's default in the covenant for quiet enjoyment because the latter had undertaken to reroof the apartment, causing considerable temporary disruption to the tenant, and a large pet snake apparently owned by another tenant was allowed to roam over the lawns. The court ruled that at most the tenant would have been entitled to claim for damages, but not to treat this contract as a breach of the covenant for quiet enjoyment.

Insurance

In the absence of an express provision, neither the landlord nor the tenant is under a duty to insure the premises for the benefit of the other. In most cases, of course, the landlord will insure the premises to protect his own investment. If the

---

[5] Greenbranch Investments Ltd. v. Goulborn and Goulborn (November 20, 1972).

leased property consists of an entire building or group of buildings that pass into the complete control of one tenant, especially if the lease is for a very long term, the rent may be set on the understanding that complete responsibility for the premises passes to the tenant and that he will insure them. The question of insurance is closely tied to the problem of what should happen to the tenancy in case of complete destruction of the premises by fire, flood, or storm. Unfortunately, parties often fail to consider these possibilities very carefully. Failure to make proper provision can lead to great hardship, particularly for the tenant. A lease providing that if the premises are substantially destroyed, the liability to pay rent is suspended until the building is repaired, may not be a benefit to the tenant; indeed, it may place him at the mercy of a capricious or simply undecided landlord. While the landlord decides what to do, the tenant, although not paying rent, is temporarily out of business. If he leases premises elsewhere, he may find when the building is repaired that he is liable to pay rent for both locations. A fair term of a lease should state that the repairs must be made within a certain time and that if they are not made within that time, the tenant then has the option of terminating the lease rather than waiting until the premises are restored. A further variation gives the tenant the right to make the repairs himself and deduct the costs from future rent.

Provision of Services and Payment of Taxes

The division here is, again, between tenancies for the whole building and those for a suite or a portion of a building. When the tenancy is for a portion of a building only and the landlord retains control over the building as a whole, it is usual for him to covenant to provide a reasonable amount of heat during the colder months of the year, water, sometimes electric power, and occasionally even telephone service. When the tenancy is for the whole of the building, it is usual for the tenant to provide all these things for himself.

Generally, property taxes are paid by the landlord when the tenant leases only a portion of the building. If he leases the whole of the building, the taxes may be paid by either party. As long as the agreement is clear, it is not important who pays them: if the landlord pays them, the rent is that much higher; if the tenant pays them, it is that much lower. In the absence of an agreement it is the duty of the landlord to pay the taxes.

REMEDIES FOR BREACH OF COVENANT

Remedies of the Landlord

Damages and rent. A landlord may sue for damages caused by his tenant's breach of any covenant other than the covenant to pay rent. The right to recover rent requires some explanation. Suppose, without such legal justification as a serious breach of the covenant of quiet enjoyment by the landlord, the tenant abandons the premises and pays no further rent. The landlord is then in a predicament. If he leaves the premises vacant and insists on his rights under the lease, he will have an action for the rent due under it. (In land law, apart from any statutory provisions to the contrary, there is no duty to mitigate damages as there is in contract law.) But the tenant may be impecunious at the time and unable to pay the full amount due. On the other hand, if the landlord occupies the premises or rents them to another tenant at a lower rent in order to reduce his loss, by the rules of the law he will be presumed to have accepted the surrender by the tenant, and all further obligations to pay rent will cease.

While a lease creates an interest in land, it is also a contract between the parties. The courts could look to the principles of contract law for solution, but it was not until recently that they conceded this possibility: they gave a way out to the landlord by stating that if he desired to resume possession and continue to hold the tenant liable for rent, he must advise the tenant that any such reletting is on the tenant's account and any deficiency would still be owing by the tenant. While this approach assists the landlord, the tenant remains at his mercy if the landlord chooses not to attempt to mitigate damages. This position was affirmed as late as 1963 in an Ontario Court of Appeal decision.[6] Subsequently, Ontario and several other provinces amended their landlord and tenant laws with respect only to residential tenancies, as follows:

> Where a tenant abandons the premises in breach of the tenancy agreement, the landlord's right to damages is subject to the same obligation to mitigate his damages as applies generally under the rule of law relating to breaches of contract.[7]

Does this amendment lead to the implication that no similar rule exists for commercial tenancies? It would appear so. The Supreme Court of Canada has affirmed the rule that a landlord of a commercial tenant may choose to mitigate damages but he has no duty to do so.[8] It is essential, however, that the landlord advise the tenant that he will hold him liable for any loss sustained, notwithstanding that the landlord relets the premises.

Under the Bankruptcy Act, in the event of the tenant's bankruptcy the landlord has priority over other creditors to the amount of three months' rent in arrears.[9] For rents due in excess of this sum, he ranks only as a general creditor. Provincial landlord and tenant acts recognize the right of a trustee in bankruptcy to repudiate an outstanding lease without further liability or, with proper notice, to continue to use the premises for so long as may serve the purposes of liquidation and pay rent at the rate specified in the lease.[10]

Eviction. This remedy is sometimes called the landlord's right of re-entry.

---

[6] Goldhar v. Universal Sections and Mouldings Ltd. (1963) 36 D.L.R. (2d) 450.

[7] St. of B.C. 1970, c. 18, s. 2; R.S.M. 1970, c. L70 as amended by St. of Man. 1970, c. 106, s. 3; R.S.O. 1970, c. 236, s. 92; St. of P.E.I. 1972, c. 25, s. 3.

[8] Highway Properties Ltd. v. Kelly, Douglas & Co. Ltd. (1971) 17 D.L.R. (3d) 710.

[9] R.S.C. 1970, c. B-3, s. 107(1)(f).

[10] See, for example: R.S.B.C. 1960, c. 207, s. 33; R.S.O. 1970, c. 236, s. 37(2) and 38(1); R.S.M. 1970, c. L70, ss. 46(2) and 47(1).

The right of re-entry for failure to pay rent is a term implied by statute if not expressly included in the lease. The period for which rent must be in arrears before the landlord is entitled to re-enter and evict the tenant varies from province to province. It is as short as seven days in British Columbia and as long as six months in Newfoundland.[11] The landlord must first serve the tenant with a written demand to either pay the rent or give up possession. He may then evict the tenant by following the procedure laid down in the landlord and tenant legislation of the particular province.

Leases often provide that the landlord may re-enter and evict his tenant for breach of any of the other covenants in the lease. Since eviction amounts to a forfeiture, that is, to the penalty against the tenant of forfeiting his term to the landlord, the court is very reluctant to permit eviction for breach of any covenant other than one relating to payment of rent, use of the property, or assignment of the lease. The court grants relief against forfeitures either under the general principles of equity or under various statutory reliefs found in provincial legislation.[12] Generally speaking, so long as the tenant subsequently makes good his breach, the court will restrain the landlord from evicting him and will declare the lease to be valid under its original terms.

Distress. The landlord has a power of distress or the right to *distrain* for rent; that is, he may seize assets of the tenant found on the premises and sell them to realize arrears of rent. Usually, the landlord authorizes a bailiff to distrain on the property of the tenant. The right to distrain does not arise until *the day after* the rent is due and a demand for payment has been made. A landlord cannot prevent his tenant from removing goods from the premises even as late as the day the rent is due: he may, however, object if the tenant is clearly removing the goods in order to avoid the landlord's power of distress. If the goods are removed in spite of the landlord's objection or if they are later removed fraudulently to prevent the landlord from asserting his rights, after the right has arisen, the landlord may follow the goods and have them seized in another location, provided that they have not been sold in the meantime to an innocent purchaser. The time limit within which a landlord may seize goods in this fashion varies from province to province.

Certain personal property is exempt from seizure: necessary household furniture, a limited supply of food and fuel, and mechanic's tools. Apart from these, goods found on the premises which belong to the tenant or to his wife, children or near relatives (provided the relatives live on the premises as part of the tenant's family) are subject to seizure. If the goods of third parties such as boarders are seized by mistake, they must be released later on proof of ownership. The landlord may also seize goods purchased on the instalment plan and not fully paid for, but before he can sell these goods to realize on them, he must first

---

[11] Tenements (Recovery of Possession) Act, R.S. Nfld. 1970, c. 372, s. 2; Landlord and Tenant Act, R.S.B.C. 1960, c. 207, ss. 29, 30. The period is 15 days in Ontario: R.S.O. 1970, c. 236, s. 17.

[12] Judicature Act, R.S.O. 1970, c. 228, s. 22; R.S.B.C. 1960, c. 213, s. 2(14).

pay the balance owing to the seller. A lease may contain a term by which the tenant "contracts out" of his right to exemptions should the landlord distrain for rent; the result, in the words of the Ontario Law Reform Commission, is that "a successful seizure can leave the tenant with nothing but the clothes on his back."[13]

Injunction. If the tenant proposes or has undertaken a use of the premises which would be in breach of a covenant restricting use, the landlord may obtain an injunction ordering the tenant to cease the prohibited use. The landlord may obtain an injunction against certain types of use even when these were not prohibited under the terms of the lease, if they are inconsistent with the general design and ordinary use to which the property would be put. Thus, a landlord could obtain an injunction to prevent a house ordinarily used as residential property from being turned into a hospital.[14]

Generally speaking, wherever a landlord could obtain an injunction, he also has the right to re-enter the property and evict the tenant. Which of these remedies he chooses depends largely on the circumstances, and in particular, whether the lease is an otherwise desirable one from the point of view of the landlord.

Remedies of the Tenant

Damages. A tenant may recover from his landlord for damages arising from the breach by the landlord of any of his covenants. The landlord may, in pursuing his remedies when he believes the tenant has committed a breach, infringe the tenant's rights. He may, for instance, evict the tenant in the erroneous belief that the tenant, being in arrears of rent, has been served with notice, or that the tenant has broken his covenant restricting the use of the premises, or made an assignment of the lease without consent. Such wrongful eviction by the landlord is a breach of the covenant for quiet enjoyment. Similarly, if the landlord distrains upon more goods than were reasonably necessary to satisfy a claim for arrears of rent, the tenant may recover damages from him. The landlord or his bailiff, in attempting to distrain upon the goods of the tenant, must not enter the premises illegally, that is by use of force, or the landlord will subject himself to an action for damages for trespass. A tenant may thus prevent an exercise of the power of distress by keeping his premises continually locked; but, of course, in these circumstances the threat of distress is a continuing harassment to the tenant.

Although a landlord has no liability to replace premises destroyed by fire, lightning, or tempest, if he has expressly covenanted to keep the premises in good repair or rebuild if they are destroyed, his failure to do so will be a breach not only of the covenant to repair but also of the covenant for quiet enjoyment.

---

[13] Ontario, *Interim Report on Landlord and Tenant Law Applicable to Residential Tenancies,* 1968, p. 14 (Ontario Law Reform Commission). We shall see in our discussion below that many of the provinces have now abolished the remedy of distress for residential (though not for commercial) tenancies.

[14] McCuaig v. Lalonde (1911) 23 O.L.R. 312.

Injunction. A tenant may also obtain an injunction to restrain a landlord from further breach of the covenant of quiet enjoyment. The court will not grant an injunction, however, where it would be futile to do so. Thus, while a court will grant an injunction against the landlord for interfering with quiet enjoyment by a continuing nuisance, such as vibrations, noise, or fumes escaping from the landlord's premises, it would not grant an injunction to prevent an activity which had already destroyed the usefulness of the tenant's premises, as where vibration had so damaged the structure that it was condemned as unsafe for occupation. The tenant's remedy would be in damages and in vacating the premises.

Termination of the lease. If the landlord in breach of the covenant of quiet enjoyment has rendered premises unfit for normal use and occupation by the tenant, the tenant, in addition to any other remedy which he may have, may terminate the lease and vacate the premises. Upon so doing, he ceases to have any further liability to the landlord under his covenants. The breach of the covenant for quiet enjoyment must amount to the total eviction of the tenant before he obtains this option. If the landlord's interference is only with part of the premises or only a nuisance or inconvenience, rather than amounting to a total eviction, the tenant is still bound to pay the rent and cannot terminate his lease. His remedies are then an action for damages for the injury suffered and an injunction to restrain further breach. For example, even in residential tenancies where tenants have been given greater rights than in commercial tenancies, the courts have not supported tenants who collaborated to withhold rent in the face of the landlord's neglect to complete the promised amenities in a new apartment building (elevators, garage, parking lots, pool, sauna, laundry room, landscaping and so forth).[15]

TERMINATION AND RENEWAL OF A TENANCY

Surrender

As we noted under "Classes of Tenancies" above, a tenancy for a term certain expires automatically without notice. Although not necessary, a landlord sometimes serves a reminder on his tenant that his lease is about to expire and that he must vacate on the date of expiry. Upon vacating the premises, the tenant surrenders them to the landlord.

A surrender may also take place during the term of a tenancy by agreement between the landlord and tenant. The agreement may be express, as when the tenant pays the landlord a sum of money to release him from the obligations for the balance of the term because the premises have become unsuitable for the tenant. Alternatively, the landlord may bargain for the tenant's surrender of the remainder of his term when the landlord needs vacant possession in order to sell

---

[15] C. Jowell, "Comments — Landlord and tenant relations — rent-withholding in Ontario", 48 *Can. B. Rev.* 323 at p. 328 (1970), and reference to *In the Matter of Vivene Developments Ltd. v. Jack K. Tsuji,* an unreported case, transcript, County Court Reporters, Toronto, March, 1969, cited by Jowell.

the property or wishes to make substantial alterations or demolish the building. At other times, tenants for various motives may abandon the premises without making an agreement to surrender to the landlord. As we have seen, a landlord may, by his conduct, be presumed to have accepted a surrender of the premises, as when he re-rents to another tenant or takes possession of the premises himself and proceeds to make use of them for his own purposes. In theory, it may often be difficult to decide from the circumstances whether the landlord has accepted a surrender and thereby released the tenant from any further obligation to pay rent. Since abandonment is usually committed by an impecunious tenant, the landlord's right of action against him has little practical value.

Forfeiture

We have noted that a tenant may forfeit his term by breach of one of his covenants. Once forfeiture takes place, the relationship of landlord and tenant is terminated. The tenant has no further obligations under the lease, although he may still be liable in damages for injury suffered by the landlord by his breach of a covenant before forfeiture. Similarly, if a landlord has attempted to effect a forfeiture by improperly evicting his tenant, thereby entitling the tenant to consider his obligations under the lease at an end, the relationship of landlord and tenant is terminated, but the tenant may still maintain an action for damages based upon the landlord's breach of his covenants.

Termination by Notice to Quit

A periodic tenancy renews itself automatically unless either the landlord or the tenant serves *notice to quit* on the other party, that is, serves notice that he intends to bring the tenancy to an end. Notice to quit served by a tenant is sometimes called notice of intention to vacate. In weekly, monthly, or quarter-yearly tenancies, the length of notice required to bring the tenancy to an end is *one clear period of tenancy*. In other words, one party must give the other notice *on or before the last day of one tenancy period* for the tenancy to come to an end *on the last day of the next period*.

Illustration:

(a) Burns rents a house from Green on a monthly basis commencing on March 1 at a rent of $150 per month. The following September, he receives notice from his employer that he will be transferred to another location in November. Burns must serve Green with notice to quit on or before September 30 if he wishes to terminate the tenancy on October 31. October will then be a clear month. If, however, he does not serve notice until after September 30, October will no longer be a clear month, and Burns will not be able to terminate the tenancy until November 30, by serving notice to quit any time in October. In these circumstances, November will be the clear month.

(b) Giles rents an apartment on a weekly basis while he is in town temporarily to supervise the installation of some heavy equipment in a local manufacturing plant. His weekly tenancy begins on Saturday and ends the following Friday. In order to terminate the tenancy on any particular Friday, he must serve notice on or before the previous Friday so that the following week will be a clear week. If he gives notice on Saturday, a clear week cannot begin until the following Saturday, and he cannot terminate the tenancy until the Friday after that.

The English rule that six clear months' notice is necessary to terminate a yearly tenancy at the end of the first year or any succeeding year of the tenancy applies in all provinces except New Brunswick, Nova Scotia and Prince Edward Island. In these provinces only three clear months' notice is required.

Illustration:

Billings leases the Greenbrier summer hotel, located in the Muskoka district of Ontario, from O'Brien at a yearly rental of $6,000 per year, commencing April 1, 1970. The yearly tenancy will renew itself automatically each April 1 unless either party gives six clear months' notice before April 1, that is, on or before September 30 of the preceding year. If Billings wishes to vacate the property by March 31, 1977, he must serve notice on or before September 30, 1976. If he serves notice on October 1, 1976, it is too late; the tenancy will automatically renew itself on April 1, 1977, and continue to March 31, 1978. Thus, the maximum time that may elapse between giving notice and terminating the tenancy may be 18 months less a day, that is from October 1, 1976, to March 31, 1978.

We have already noted that if a tenant remains in possession after the expiration of a term certain, he becomes a tenant at sufferance and may be evicted by the landlord at any time on demand. If, however, the landlord accepts further rent from the tenant, a periodic tenancy then arises on all the terms of the original lease except those repugnant to a periodic tenancy. An example of a repugnant term would be a covenant by the landlord to redecorate the premises every three years during a term certain of 12 years. This covenant would not become part of a subsequent periodic tenancy.

Generally speaking, if a periodic tenancy arises after the expiry of a *term certain expressed in years* (for example, a lease for five years at an annual rental of $2,400 payable in instalments of $200 per month), then the periodic tenancy created will be a *yearly tenancy*. If instead the term certain is stated as a *term of months* (say, a lease for eight months at a monthly rent of $200), then the periodic tenancy created will be a *monthly* one; similarly, if the term certain is expressed in terms of weeks or quarter-years, a succeeding periodic tenancy will be weekly or quarter-yearly respectively. The wording used to describe the term in the original lease may be ambiguous and can result in a difficult question of interpretation about whether a succeeding periodic tenancy created by the payment of rent is a yearly, monthly, or weekly tenancy. Suppose, for example, in the original lease a term certain is granted for one and a half *years* at a *monthly* rent of $200. Is the term thereby created one expressed in years or months? There has been conflict in the Canadian cases.[16] If such a problem should arise, it is best to seek legal advice at once: if the periodic tenancy following the original lease is held to be a yearly one, it may be impossible for either party unilaterally to bring the tenancy to an end for a period of up to 18 months; whereas, if the periodic tenancy is a monthly one, the maximum period of notice would be just under two months.

The above requirements for a valid notice to quit are those which ordinarily apply, but the parties to a lease may agree to vary them to suit their own needs. Thus, landlord and tenant may agree that some period less than six months, say two months, is sufficient notice for either party to terminate a yearly tenancy. Similar variations may be agreed upon for any type of tenancy.

Renewal

A lease for a term certain, particularly a lease of premises for a retail store, often provides for a renewal at the option of the tenant. The reason why a prospective tenant will often ask for such an option is good business sense: if he is taking the risk of opening a retail outlet in the area, he does not want to be burdened with a long-term lease if the venture proves unprofitable. On the other hand, if he takes only a short-term lease and the venture proves to be a success, he has no assurance that he will be able to negotiate successfully for a new lease at the expiry of the original lease. An option gives him the opportunity to terminate the tenancy at the end of the original lease if he does not wish to continue, yet he has the security of exercising the option if business proves successful. A typical option arrangement would be an initial lease for three or perhaps five years, with an option for perhaps a further five or ten years. Landlords are usually quite willing to grant such options provided they receive some protection against inflation and sufficient notice to obtain a new tenant if the option is not exercised.

The various forms of protection a landlord may seek are numerous. In general, a landlord will require that the rent in the renewal be increased by the amount of any increase in taxes which occurs during the original lease, and sometimes also he will require either a fixed increase in rent or a series of percentage increases at various intervals during the term of the renewal. A landlord will usually require at least three months' notice on the part of the tenant that he intends to exercise the option, and probably six months' notice if the renewal is for a long period, such as ten years.

RESIDENTIAL TENANCIES

Beginning in 1969, most provinces have enacted legislation that reflects the changing social attitude in Canada with respect to housing. Because of rapid urbanization in the past two decades, the size of Canadian cities increased very

---

[16] See Williams, *The Canadian Law of Landlord and Tenant* (3rd ed.), pp. 122-4. Toronto: The Carswell Company Limited, 1957.

quickly, attracting the vast majority of immigrants as well as depleting the rural areas of the country. Much of this influx has been met by rental accommodation, especially in high-rise apartment buildings, as the newcomers to the cities have not had adequate capital to invest in the purchase of private homes, the costs of which have risen at a substantially higher rate than the general level of inflation. The typical city tenant now lives in a large apartment complex, knows few of his neighbours and is remote from his corporate landlord. He has come to regard himself as a part of the consumer movement and to think of his relation with his landlord as originating in a contract for services rather than an acquisition of an estate in land. The new legislation reflects this view by repealing a number of rules of the law of landlord and tenant that differ from rules of contract law. It does so, however, only for residential tenancies, and does not affect the leasing of premises for business purposes. We shall briefly review major changes in residential tenancy law.

The landlord in a residential tenancy is prohibited from requiring any security deposit in excess of one month's rent, and even that sum may only be applied to the payment of rent for the last rent period under the tenancy agreement; the landlord must also pay interest on the amount of the deposit at a specified rate.[17] Formerly, landlords used security deposits to reimburse themselves for damage to the premises during a tenancy agreement; and if a landlord refused to return any or all of the deposit the burden lay with the tenant to sue him for it. While the abolition of security deposits removes the landlord's advantage, the benefit may be illusory in a time of chronic housing shortages. Landlords may simply raise their rent by an amount adequate to cover the risks met formerly by security deposits.

The amending legislation has abolished the landlord's remedy of distress.[18] This change was made in response to criticism by the Ontario Law Reform Commission, which described distress as "an extra-judicial remedy for the recovery of rent," and complained that, in many leases a tenant was required to waive his usual rights to retain necessary goods against an exercise of this remedy.[19]

The doctrine of frustration is now declared to apply to residential tenancies.[20] It replaces the common law rule that a contract for a leasehold estate in land contains an absolute promise by the tenant to pay rent and keep the property in repair; as we noted in Chapter 14, a tenant is normally liable to pay rent for the balance of the term even when the premises become uninhabitable through no fault of his own, and also to restore the property if it is destroyed for any reason during

---

[17] The Landlord and Tenant Act, R.S.O. 1970, c. 236, s. 84. The protection afforded tenants with respect to security deposits varies considerably from province to province. See for example: St. of B.C. 1970, c. 18, s. 2 (new ss. 37 and 38); St. of N.S. 1970, c. 13, s. 9.

[18] St. of B.C. 1970, c. 18, s. 2 (new s. 39); St. of Man. 1970, c. 106, s. 3 (new s. 88). R.S.O. 1970, c. 236, s. 86.

[19] See Ontario Law Reform Commission, *Interim Report on Landlord and Tenant Law Applicable to Residential Tenancies,* 1968, Chapter 2, and preceding discussion in this chapter under "Remedies of the Landlord".

[20] St. of B.C. 1970, c. 18, s. 2; St. of Man. c. 106, s. 3; R.S.O. 1970, c. 236, s. 88.

the tenancy. It should be noted, however, that this requirement for restoration of the property has customarily been expressly excluded in leases in multi-storey buildings.

Several other changes complement the recognition of the possibility of frustration. Formerly, the failure of a landlord to perform his own covenants, even if they were major terms, did not release the tenant from his obligation to pay rent unless the landlord's breach amounted to an eviction of his tenant. The new legislation makes a number of promises or covenants in a residential lease interdependent, so that breach by one party of a condition entitles the other to regard himself as freed from his own obligations.[21] We have already noted that when a tenant wrongfully breaks his lease by abandoning his residence and failing to pay the rent, his landlord's right to damages is subject to his obligation to mitigate damages by re-renting the property as quickly as he reasonably can. In addition, a landlord may not arbitrarily or unreasonably withhold his consent to an assignment or subletting.[22]

The legislation makes the landlord liable for maintaining residential premises in a good state of repair fit for habitation, and states that the tenant's knowledge of the lack of repair before the lease is irrelevant.[23] Formerly, a tenant would have been deemed to accept the property in its state at the time of entering into the lease. The landlord had no liability for repairs or injury caused even by hidden dangers about which the tenant could not reasonably have known: he was liable for repairs only when renting furnished premises.

The legislation also makes provision for the establishment by any local municipality of a landlord and tenant advisory bureau to receive complaints and mediate disputes between landlords and tenants in respect of residential tenancies.[24]

FIXTURES

As we noted in Chapter 24 in our introduction to real property, land includes everything fixed to it. Trees, fences, and buildings form part of the land, but they are distinguished from the land itself in that they are called fixtures. Technically, then, an oil derrick, a grain elevator, a stand of timber, and a large office building are all fixtures. Although they are not commonly called fixtures, legally and indisputably they belong to that class. An object which is affixed to a fixture (such as a furnace installed in a building) is itself a fixture. It is in this more restricted sense that the word is commonly used, and where the possibility of disagreement arises.

---

[21] St. of B.C. 1970, c. 18, s. 2 (new ss. 42 and 49); St. of Man. 1970, c. 106, s. 3 (new ss. 91 and 98); R.S.O. 1970, c. 236, s. 89 and 96.

[22] St. of B.C. 1970, c. 18, s. 2 (new ss. 34(2) and 44); St. of Man. 1970, c. 106, s. 3 (new ss. 82 and 93), R.S.O. 1970, c. 236, s. 91.

[23] St. of B.C. 1970, c. 18, s. 2 (new s. 49); St. of Man. 1970, c. 106, s. 3 (new s. 98); R.S.O. 1970, c. 236, s. 96.

[24] St. of B.C. 1970, c. 18, s. 2 (new ss. 66); R.S.M. 1970, c. L70, s. 85; R.S.O. 1970, c. 236, s. 110.

Whether an object is held to be a fixture may determine who is its owner. Generally, an object permanently affixed to a building becomes a part of the building and of the real property itself. In a sale of land the vendor cannot remove fixtures which were attached at the time of the contract of sale; they belong to the purchaser. Similarly, a tenant cannot remove fixtures because they belong to the landlord. The question of what is or is not a fixture does not often arise in a sale of land: usually the purchaser and the vendor agree between them what fixtures remain with the land; if the vendor wishes to take certain fixtures away with him, he stipulates expressly for that right in the agreement of sale. The problem may be more difficult in the law of landlord and tenant, however, for after the lease begins the tenant may bring certain objects onto the premises for his own benefit without any agreement with the landlord. The question then arises whether he may take them away with him when he vacates the premises.

The result would be exceedingly harsh if a tenant temporarily attached very valuable objects to the building, unaware of the consequences of so doing, and later discovered he could not remove them under any circumstances; and the landlord might well reap an unjust benefit. Understandably, the law has developed more flexible rules in these circumstances than in a sale of land. To apply these rules we must decide, first, whether the object has become a fixture and, second, if it has become a fixture, whether it belongs to certain classes of fixtures which may be removed by a tenant.

To determine whether the object has become a fixture, we may ask a number of questions. Has the object been fastened to the building with the intention that it shall become a fixture? What use is to be made of it? How securely and permanently is it attached to the building? How much damage, if any, will be caused to the building by its removal? A picture hanging on a hook in the wall is quite obviously not attached. A partition nailed and bolted to the walls of the building is quite clearly a fixture. But what would we conclude about a table that has been bolted to the floor to prevent delicate machinery on it from being jarred, machinery bolted to the floor to prevent vibration, a display stand tacked to a wall so that it will not topple over, a neon sign held in place by guy wires bolted to the roof of the building? Generally speaking, objects not bolted or anchored in any way but merely resting on their own weight are presumed not to be fixtures. Objects affixed even comparatively flimsily create a presumption that they are fixtures, although this presumption may be rebutted by asking what a reasonable man would intend when he attached the object, as for instance in affixing the display stand mentioned above. Objects which are held not to be fixtures may be removed by the tenant at any time. If he should inadvertently forget to remove them from the premises when the lease expires, they still remain his property, and he may claim them afterwards.

Even if it is decided that an object was affixed in such a manner that it has become a fixture, the tenant may still have the right to remove it if he can show either (a) that it was attached for the personal convenience of the tenant or for the better enjoyment of the object, as when it is purely ornamental, or (b) that it was a *trade fixture,* that is, an article brought on to the premises for the purpose of carrying on some trade or business, including manufacturing. Both these classes of fixtures are commonly called *tenant's fixtures*. A tenant may remove them before the end of his tenancy, provided that in doing so he does not do permanent damage to the structure of the building and repairs what damage he does. If, however, the tenant leaves without removing his fixtures and the term expires, the fixtures will be presumed to become part of the premises and accordingly the property of the landlord. We might add that tenant's fixtures include only those fixtures brought on to the premises by the tenant himself. Fixtures installed by the landlord or left by preceding tenants are the landlord's property from the beginning of the tenancy, and may not be removed.

From the above discussion, we should conclude that it is difficult to state precise and predictable tests to determine in every circumstance whether objects brought on to the premises and attached to them remain the property of the tenant or become a part of the building. The problem can often be avoided by recognizing in advance that the risk of disagreement at the expiry of the term exists, and by making an express agreement concerning fixtures. If the parties expressly agree that a particular object, which would otherwise undoubtedly be a fixture, is to remain the property of the tenant, severable by him and removable at the end of the tenancy, such an agreement is conclusive of the matter: a difficult decision based on implications arising from the facts will never have to be made. It would, of course, be wise to make such an agreement in writing.

TRANSFER OF THE LANDLORD'S INTEREST

As we noted at the beginning of this chapter, a landlord grants away a present right to possession in his land for a term and reserves to himself the right to possession at the end of that term — that is, the reversion. He also receives the benefit of the tenant's covenants. When a landlord sells his land subject to a lease, he parts with both his reversion and the benefits of the covenants given by his tenant. Accordingly, the purchaser acquires the whole interest in the land subject to the outstanding lease, but he succeeds not only to the rights of the former landlord but also to his duties. We may well ask, "How can the purchaser receive both the rights and duties of the landlord when the tenant was not a party to the sale and there is no privity of contract between the purchaser and the tenant?" The answer is that as between the tenant and his present landlord — even one who has become a landlord by purchasing a reversion — there is *privity of estate*. The doctrine of privity of estate is much older than the doctrine of privity of contract. It dates from feudal times, from the relationship between a lord and his vassal. Although the archaic aspects of this doctrine have been abolished, privity of estate between a new landlord and his tenant has been retained and is eminently sensible: neither the landlord nor his tenant can destroy the stability of the relationship by claiming that the original contract of lease does not bind them.

The creation of privity of estate with a new landlord does not bring to an end privity of contract with the former landlord. Although a landlord may sell his reversion, he still remains personally liable on his covenants to his tenant, in particular the covenant for quiet enjoyment. Thus, if the new landlord should interfere with the covenant for quiet enjoyment in an irreparable manner, the tenant, if he chose, could sue the original landlord in contract. He might well have to do this if the new landlord had subsequently become insolvent or had little in the way of assets. The doctrine of privity of estate is a concept of real property and does not apply to personal property, with the possible exception of ships.[25]

The leasehold estate acquired by a tenant, like other interests in real property, is valid against other persons who subsequently acquire an interest in the land. Thus, if after leasing his land the landlord borrows against it under a mortgage, the mortgagee's (that is, the creditor's) title will be subject to the rights of the tenant. In the event of default by the mortgagor (the landlord-borrower) the mortgagee may claim the reversion, but he is not entitled to evict the tenant. As long as the tenant observes the terms of the lease, the mortgagee is bound by it and cannot obtain possession other than as provided under the lease. On the other hand, if the tenant obtains a leasehold interest in property already mortgaged, he is, in theory at least, at the mercy of the mortgagee in the event that the mortgagor defaults, unless the mortgagee concurred in the lease at the time it was given. The danger is not very real, however, for the best interest of the mortgagee will almost always be to collect the rent rather than put the tenant out and try to obtain a new tenant. The danger is more real if the lease is a long-term one, and the value of the premises for leasing purposes has increased greatly over the rent being charged the present tenant. For this reason, it is wise to have the concurrence of the mortgagee when a tenant contemplates a long-term lease.

To protect his interest, a tenant should register a long-term lease in the land registry office. Otherwise his interest may be destroyed if the landlord fraudulently sells to a bona fide purchaser who has no notice of the tenancy. The need for registration varies from province to province. In some provinces, leases as short as three years must be registered, while in others, only leases over seven years need be. Leases under three years need not be registered in any province.

ORAL LEASES

When a tenant is in possession under a short-term lease of three years or less, his lease need not be in writing in order to satisfy the Statute of Frauds in most jurisdictions, although, of course, a written lease is wise in any event.[26] Leases of longer than three years are generally speaking unenforceable if not in writing. If, for example, a tenant enters into an oral lease for five years and the landlord later

---

[25] See: Lord Strathcona Steamship Co. v. Dominion Coal Co. [1926] A.C. 108; Port Line Ltd. v. Ben Line Steamers Ltd. [1958] 2 Q.B. 146. See also Chapter 13 under "Exceptions to the Privity of Contract Rule" (Contracts Concerning Land).

[26] The enforceability of oral short-term leases may depend upon the amount of rent to be paid. See for example, Statute of Frauds, R.S.O. 1970, C. 444, s. 3, and R.S.N.S. 1967, c. 290, s. 2; Carter v. Irving Oil Co. [1952] 4 D.L.R. 128, per MacDonald, J., at 131; Williams, *The Canadian Law of Landlord and Tenant* (3rd ed.), pp. 51-2.

changes his mind and refuses to let the tenant into possession, the tenant is without remedy. If, however, the tenant is already in possession and has paid rent, the doctrine of part performance as discussed in Chapter 11 under the Statute of Frauds will apply; under the rules of equity the court will order the landlord to give the tenant his lease in the terms originally agreed between them. The landlord too may obtain specific performance and hold the tenant bound to a long-term oral lease if, after taking possession, the tenant should wish to avoid the lease and vacate the premises.

LEASEBACKS

In Great Britain, it has long been common practice for the owner of a fee simple to grant a long-term lease and retain the reversion, whereas in similar circumstances in North America he would sell the fee simple outright. Several factors have contributed to this difference, but perhaps the main one is the strictly limited amount of land available in Great Britain and the significance accordingly attached to retaining the ultimate reversion. In North America, where until recently land has been relatively cheap and almost unlimited, it has not been valued so highly. In England, leases for 21 years, 49 years, or 99 years are very common, and sometimes leases for as long as 999 years are granted. For practical purposes, the longer the term of the lease, the more the position of the tenant approximates that of an owner in fee simple: only the remote reversionary interest of the landlord or his heirs and the regular payment of rent serve to remind the tenant of his status.

In North America, the supply of land no longer appears limitless; particularly is this so in and around large cities. A lease is a flexible and adaptable tool of finance, especially to the investor who desires a secure, long-term income. For these reasons, the use of relatively long-term leases of commercial properties has grown rapidly throughout North America. An established company with a good record of earnings is often able to arrange with a financial institution, usually an insurance company, to finance its acquisition of a new building by a long-term leasing device known as a *leaseback* which forms part of a larger transaction. The business and insurance company arrange the entire transaction in advance. First, the business obtains a short-term loan, usually from a bank, to finance construction of the building. As soon as the building is completed, the business sells it to the insurance company and pays off its bank loan. The insurance company then leases the building back to the business. The lease is usually for a period of 20 or 25 years, with the lessee business receiving an option to renew for two or three additional five-year periods. The lessee business acts very much as the owner of the property rather than as a tenant, paying for all repairs, maintenance, insurance, and property taxes during the currency of the lease.

The leaseback device has several advantages for the lessee business. First, the business need not go through the relatively more expensive and elaborate procedure of issuing securities in the capital market as a means of financing its expansion. The arrangements for a leaseback are relatively simple, once a willing financial institution is found to undertake the project. Secondly, the leaseback may be more advantageous than buying the property and mortgaging it, because a mortgagee will not generally provide the full value of the project, leaving the company to raise the balance, whereas under a leaseback a financial institution provides the whole amount required. Thirdly, the lessee business may be able to claim a larger deduction for rent expenses in computing its taxable income than it could claim as capital cost allowance and interest on borrowed funds, had it purchased the building instead and financed it by a bond issue or a mortgage.

From the point of view of the lessor financial institution, the rented property represents an investment of funds which, in addition to providing regular rental revenue including amortization of the cost of the property, also gives the lessor the reversionary interest and possession of the entire property at the expiration of the lease. In addition, if the lessee business gets into financial difficulty, the legal formalities in evicting it are simpler and quicker than for a mortgagee foreclosing on a mortgage. This latter consideration is of comparatively little consequence, since leasebacks are confined in practice to large businesses with good earning records. Under leasebacks, any improvements in the building constructed by the tenant and any inflation in land values inure to the benefit of the landlord at the expiration of the lease.

Sometimes a leaseback includes an option to the lessee business to purchase the premises at the end of the term or the last renewal of the term. The price at which the option may be exercised by the lessee may be determined in a variety of ways; it may be simply a specified sum of money, or it may be calculated by a formula taking into account, for example, whether the option is exercised at the end of the original term or the end of a renewal.

The leaseback, as compared with other leases, is a relatively long, detailed, and complex document, often very carefully setting out the rights a tenant has in making alterations and adding fixtures to the building, as well as in the types of trade he may carry on. Sometimes the lessor may impose restrictions on the future borrowing of the lessee business, as a means of insuring that it will not enter into obligations so great as to impair its ability to pay the rent.

QUESTIONS FOR REVIEW

1. Define: lessor; leasehold estate; reversion; power of distress; fixture; overholding tenant; leaseback; forfeiture.
2. What is the significance of the statement that a landlord's promise to make repairs is *independent* of the tenant's promise to pay rent?
3. Should a leasehold interest be shown as an asset (with an equal and offsetting liability) on the balance sheet of a business? If so, at what amount?
4. What are the two elements of the landlord's covenant to provide his tenant with quiet enjoyment of the premises?
5. Give an example of a tenancy for a term certain and of a periodic tenancy.
6. What is the importance of determining whether a periodic tenancy is weekly, monthly, or yearly?

7. Distinguish between an assignment and a subletting.

8. By what term do we describe the relationship between a purchaser of the landlord's interest and the tenant?

9. Jones obtains a lease of a warehouse for a term certain of five years. During the term of the lease the landlord, Brown, mortgages the land to Sweetwater Mortgage Company. At the expiration of the lease Jones and Brown enter into a further lease for another five years. Is there any difference in the position of Jones during the first term and the second term in so far as the mortgage is concerned?

10. What remedies may a landlord have when his tenant is in breach of a covenant to restrict the use of the premises?

11. In what way may a tenant be in a difficult position when the premises burn down, even if the lease provides for the suspension of rent until the premises are rebuilt?

12. What difference usually occurs in a covenant to provide services when a tenant rents the whole of a building rather than only a portion of it?

13. What alternatives are available to a tenant under lease for a term certain when he finds he is not able to use the premises for the full term?

14. Which of the covenants usually found in a lease are given exclusively by the tenant? exclusively by the landlord? by either party?

15. What two essentials must be satisfied for the successful creation of a leasehold interest? In what ways may a would-be tenant be prejudiced if he does not succeed in acquiring a leasehold interest?

16. What incident in the relation of landlord and tenant distinguishes a tenancy at sufferance from a periodic tenancy?

17. If a tenant wrongfully vacates before the expiration of the lease, is he always liable for rent for the balance of the term? Does it matter whether the tenancy is residential or commercial?

18. Outline the arguments for and against the landlord's right to distrain for rent.

19. What public policy underlies a distinction between residential and commercial tenancies?

CASES FOR DISCUSSION

CASE 1

Three years ago, Tilbury leased a farm from Barnsworthy under a 15-year lease. In the course of tilling a new field which he had just brought under cultivation with a great deal of hard work, Tilbury's plough struck an object which, on examination and careful extraction, proved to be an ancient boat built by early men, of considerable archeological interest and value. A large metropolitan museum offered him $5,000 for it. At this point Barnsworthy intervened, insisting he was entitled to the money, and the museum refused to proceed with the purchase until the two parties could settle the matter. Which of them should be entitled to the purchase money, and why?

CASE 2

Bone, the owner of a downtown block of stores, rented one of them to Bull, who opened a retail china shop on the premises. Bull had a number of display cases built with glass doors to keep their fragile contents out of the reach of curious customers. The cases were secured to the wall by one-inch nails. Bull also purchased and installed heavy-duty air-conditioning equipment which was connected to the water supply and anchored to the floor.

Several years later, Bull was adjudged bankrupt on a petition of his trade creditors. At the time he owed Bone $420 for three months' rent. The trustee in bankruptcy claimed the display cases and air conditioner for the benefit of Bull's general creditors, but Bone claimed them as lessor of the store. Discuss the respective rights of Bone and of the trustee in bankruptcy.

CASE 3

Horner rented a store from Saxe under an oral lease at a rent of $200 per month. The only terms discussed by the parties were the rent and the date upon which Horner would take possession, namely May 1. When Horner first inspected the store, he commented that the plaster on the ceiling appeared to be in a dangerous condition. Saxe assured him that it had been that way for some time "without anything happening".

In September of the same year, a customer in Horner's store was injured by falling plaster. He sued Horner and was awarded damages of $2,000. Horner refused to pay further rent to Saxe until the damages of $2,000 were made up to him, claiming that the store had been in a dangerous condition at the time he rented it. Two months later Saxe sued Horner for $400 arrears of rent. Horner counterclaimed for damages of $2,000. Who should succeed and why?

CASE 4

Kruger leased a warehouse to Pool for a term certain of eight months at a rent of $400 per month, commencing January 1 and expiring August 31. Pool did not move out on August 31 and tendered his cheque for $400 in payment of rent for September. It was accepted by Kruger. On October 1, Pool appeared at Kruger's office with another cheque for $400. Kruger said he had inspected the warehouse and was disappointed by the rough treatment the building was receiving from Pool's employees. When Pool replied that he could hardly expect otherwise in a busy operation, Kruger stated it was not worth his while to rent it under those conditions unless he received at least $500 per month. Pool refused to pay that much and tendered his cheque for $400. Kruger refused the cheque and ordered Pool to "clear out of the warehouse at once". Pool left and mailed the cheque to Kruger, who simply held it and did not cash it. On November 1, Kruger called Pool by telephone and asked if he would pay $500. Pool said "No." Kruger replied that he was at the end of his patience and had given Pool a full month to change his mind. He sent a bailiff to evict Pool that very day, cashed Pool's cheque for the previous month, and sent Pool a demand for "the $100 still owing".

Pool was forced to move his stock to a more expensive warehouse at once and suffered some damage to his goods when they were moved into the street by the bailiff. He sued Kruger for his losses of $1,000 caused by the eviction. Should he succeed? Give reasons for your opinion.

CASE 5

Frost Investments Limited owned three adjoining buildings downtown which it rented to various tenants as office space. All three buildings were heated centrally from a single heating plant in Building No. 1. The Generous Loan Company occupied offices in Building No. 3 under a lease in which the lessor (Frost Investments) convenanted to maintain the heat continuously above 60 degrees from October 1 to May 24, except for weekends. In January a serious fire occurred in Building No. 2 with the result that the heating connections between Buildings No. 1 and No. 3 were severed. The damage was so serious that Frost Investments Limited decided to complete the demolition of Building No. 2 and rebuild. In the meantime, Generous Loan Company suffered a significant drop in business because of the temperatures (or absence of them) in its offices. It eventually vacated the premises and leased other quarters at a higher rent. It then brought action against Frost Investments Limited claiming damages of $700 for the additional amount of rent it had to pay the new landlord for what otherwise would have been the balance of the term of its lease with Frost Investments, and $3,000 for its estimated loss of profits. Frost Investments Limited counterclaimed for rent for the balance of the term of the lease, seven months at $250 per month. What do you think the decision should be? (See *Head v. Community Estates and Building Co. Ltd.* [1944] 3 D.L.R. 189; *Johnston v. Givens* [1941] 4 D.L.R. 634.)

CASE 6

Robertson rented a service station from Imperial Oil Limited under a lease for a term of 12 months commencing July 1, at a rent of $275 per month payable on the first day of each month. The lease contained the following clause:

> If the lessee shall hold over after the term . . . the resulting tenancy shall be a tenancy from month to month and not a tenancy from year to year, subject to all the terms, conditions and agreements herein contained insofar as same may be applicable to a tenancy from month to month.

On May 28 of the following year, Imperial Oil sent Robertson a notice stating that he must deliver up vacant possession on the expiry of the lease. On June 30, Imperial Oil representatives visited Robertson and asked him what he intended to do. He replied that he would not leave the premises "peacefully". Robertson remained in possession on July 1, and sent a cheque by registered mail to Imperial Oil as rent for that month. Although the area superintendent had given instructions to the accounting department not to accept any rent from Robertson, a junior clerk deposited it in the company bank account. Soon afterwards, a senior officer discovered the error, informed Robertson that the act of the clerk in accepting the cheque was inadvertent and against instructions, and delivered a new cheque from the company to Robertson for $275. Robertson returned the cheque.

Was a new tenancy created or could Imperial Oil obtain a court order for immediate possession? (*Imperial Oil Ltd. v. Robertson* (1960) 21 D.L.R. (2d) 535.)

CASE 7

Upp and Adam, the owners of a chain of variety stores, submitted to Carnival Shopping Centre Ltd. a signed offer to lease space in the latter's shopping centre. The offer stated that the lease should contain a clause protecting the variety store against competition in the shopping centre, should provide for expansion of its warehouse, and should contain all those clauses "to be found in the usual form of shopping centre leases". By way of acceptance, the general manager of Carnival Shopping Centre Ltd. added his signature to the paper containing the offer.

In the months following the signing of this agreement, the parties had many discussions about the amount of warehouse space to be made available and the rent that would be charged for it. Finally, some six months after the offer was signed, the solicitor for Carnival Shopping Centre Ltd. sent a form of lease to Upp and Adam for them to sign. They replied that they did not wish to proceed with the lease. Carnival Shopping Centre Ltd. brought an action against them for breach of contract.

Should this action succeed? (See *Causeway Shopping Centre Ltd. v. Thompson & Sutherland Ltd.* (1965) 50 D.L.R. (2d) 362; *Friesen v. Braun* [1950] 2 D.L.R. 250.)

CHAPTER 26

Mortgages of Land

THE CONCEPT OF THE MORTGAGE

The history of the word ''mortgage'' helps us to understand its meaning. Mortgage is derived from the Norman French words *mort,* meaning dead or passive, and *gage,* meaning pledge. In the Middle Ages the Church condemned the lending of money for interest as the sin of usury. Nevertheless, even in a primitive economy some form of credit was often needed, and men simply would not lend money and assume the risk that it might not be repaid unless they received some benefit for taking the risk. To evade the usury laws a man would lend money on the condition that the borrower would pledge his land as security. The lender would actually take possession of the borrower's land (a *live* gage rather than a mortgage) and retain it until the loan was repaid. Meanwhile he would be entitled to keep any of the crops or rents earned from the land. These benefits derived from the land would be the equivalent of interest, but since the lender was in possession he was considered to be entitled to the benefits: the courts did not consider the transaction usurious. If the borrower did not repay the debt on the appointed day, he lost all right to claim his land — it became the land of the lender absolutely.

This ancient form of live gage was very cumbersome, first because it meant that the borrower had to give up possession of his land (the best means he might have of earning the money for repayment) and secondly because the lender had to take possession in order to obtain the benefits (an arrangement that might be inconvenient or impossible for him). As England grew commercially, so did the need for more sophisticated means of obtaining credit; the law changed to meet

these needs. Eventually, the lender was permitted to exact interest on his loan
without going into possession, that is, he was permitted to take his security as a
mort gage.[1] He had a right to the interest as well as to the principal sum as a debt
owed by the borrower. The lender retained the right to go into possession and take
the land absolutely upon default by the borrower. This latter right, the right to take
the land absolutely, was the cause of the main development in the law of
mortgages.

THE DEVELOPMENT OF MORTGAGE LAW

Harshness of the Common Law

Under the common law, a mortgage is a conveyance of an interest in land
(usually the fee simple) by the *mortgagor* (the borrower) to the *mortgagee* (the
lender) as security for a debt, with a condition that if the debt is repaid by an appointed day the conveyance becomes void and the interest in the land reverts to
the mortgagor. If the appointed day passes without the debt being repaid, the
condition then expires, and the mortgagee owns the interest absolutely. The
common law courts construed the condition strictly: if the mortgagor was
delayed by a storm or by illness and arrived with the money the day after the final
day for payment, it was too late — the mortgagee could keep the land. Moreover, the mortgagee was still entitled to repayment of the debt: he could sue the
unfortunate mortgagor and collect the debt even while retaining the land. The
gross unfairness of this position was soon remedied by the court of equity. If the
mortgagor appealed to the court of equity, it would restrain the mortgagee from
suing for the debt unless he agreed to reconvey the land to the mortgagor on
payment of the full sum owing. At this point in the development of the law the
mortgagor did not, at least, lose his money as well as his land. He could keep one
or the other, depending on whether the mortgagee chose to keep the land and not
sue for the debt, or to sue for the debt on condition that he would reconvey the
land.

The Mortgagor's Right to Redeem

The mortgagor was still in an unfair position, because the choice lay with the
mortgagee. If the mortgagor had borrowed only a small sum of money on the security of land worth many times as much, it would be small comfort to know that
he would not be sued but that the mortgagee would keep his land instead. Thus if
a mortgagor, delayed by a severe storm, arrived the morning after the last day to
pay off his mortgage, he could not demand the return of his estate worth many
thousands of pounds even though he had borrowed only a few hundred pounds

---

[1] For a more detailed history of mortgages, see Falconbridge, *The Law of Mortgages of Land* (3rd
ed.), pp. 1-6. Toronto: Canada Law Book Company Limited, 1942. This book is the leading treatise on the law of mortgages in Canada.

and now tendered payment. The court of equity eventually granted a remedy in these cases of hardship as well. If the mortgagor petitioned the court and pleaded hardship and also tendered payment of the debt in full, the court would acknowledge his interest in the land and permit him to *redeem* it; it would order the mortgagee to reconvey the land to him. This right of redemption obtained by the mortgagor from a court of equity has become known as the *equity of redemption;* it is often called simply the *equity*. We see here the derivation of the modern business term "equity" meaning the interest of the proprietors of a business in its total assets after allowing for creditors' claims.

The Mortgagee's Right to Foreclose

Gradually, over a long period, the chancery courts entertained petitions of hardship based on weaker and weaker excuses, longer and longer after the day for payment had passed, until finally they accepted almost any excuse provided full payment was tendered. The scales were then tipped in favour of the mortgagor. A mortgagee who was quite willing to accept payment for a long time after the due date might finally despair of ever obtaining payment and begin to improve the land, treating it as his own. Years later, the mortgagor could appear and force him to reconvey upon tender of satisfaction of the debt. In a turnabout, mortgagees now began to appeal to the chancery courts for a declaration that the mortgagor had had every reasonable opportunity to redeem and that if he did not do so within a fixed time set by the court his right to redeem would be forever foreclosed. The mortgagee could then safely treat the land as his own. By the 19th century, this period was generally accepted as six months from the date of the hearing of the case.

In practice, a mortgagee rarely takes possession until after he has obtained foreclosure, unless he believes that the mortgagor has no intention of trying to redeem and will allow the premises to become dilapidated. There are three main reasons for not going into possession: first, a mortgagee generally wants his money rather than the mortgagor's property — he would prefer to encourage the mortgagor to pay off the debt; secondly, his occupation would be uncertain — the mortgagor might at any moment tender payment and demand possession; thirdly, he must account for any benefits he receives from his occupation of the land and deduct it from the amount owing if the mortgagor tenders payment — thus, he loses any material advantage of taking possession.

The Consequences of These Developments

In summary, then, a mortgage is a conveyance of an interest in land as security for a debt. If the debt is repaid as promised, the mortgage is discharged and the mortgagor has the title to the land returned to him. If he defaults, the land becomes the property of the mortgagee subject to the right of the mortgagor to redeem. Most mortgages today call for repayment, not in a lump sum on the last day, but in a series of instalment payments of principal and accrued interest.

These mortgages almost always contain an *acceleration clause* which states that upon default of any instalment, the whole of the principal sum of the mortgage and accrued interest immediately falls due; default accelerates the maturity date, and the mortgagee may pursue all his remedies.

Upon default the mortgagee may put the mortgagor out and take possession himself. He may also ask the court for an order of foreclosure. The mortgagor may repay the loan at any time before the deadline specified in the court order and obtain the return of his land, but if he does not do so, the land becomes the mortgagee's absolutely.

Even after the final day for redemption the mortgagee may successfully sue the mortgagor for the debt until the period prescribed by the Statute of Limitations runs out,[2] provided of course he can still reconvey the land to the mortgagor.[3] Once the mortgagee has sold the land to a third party he loses his right to sue for any deficiency, even though the mortgagor may subsequently become very wealthy. The courts presume that by selling the land the mortgagee has accepted the receipts of the sale in full satisfaction of the debt. On this basis he may also retain any profit made on the sale.

Under the land titles system (covering the areas discussed in Chapter 24 above) mortgages are called *charges.* Charges are not, strictly speaking, conveyances of the legal title. Rather, they are liens upon the land, and the ordinary remedy available is to force a sale of the land and to realize upon the proceeds, as we shall see below when we discuss the mortgagee's remedy of sale.

RIGHTS OF THE MORTGAGEE AND MORTGAGOR
UNDER COMMON LAW AND EQUITY

Although the courts of common law and equity are merged, the interests of the mortgagee and mortgagor are still interpreted according to the remedies available before the merger. As a result, the mortgagee is considered to be the holder of the *legal* title, and the mortgagor to have the *equitable* title, that is, his interest is recognized by equity and will be enforced against the mortgagee under the circumstances we have already described. The remedies of the mortgagee upon default by the mortgagor are as follows: (a) he may sue the mortgagor on his personal covenant to repay, just as a creditor may sue any debtor who is in default; (b) he may dispossess the mortgagor and occupy the land himself (or put in a tenant); (c) he may sell the land, as explained below; (d) he may proceed with an action for foreclosure and eventually destroy the mortgagor's right to redeem;

---

[2] The limitations periods vary from six to 30 years in different provinces. The matter is complicated by the number of parties who may be involved in a mortgage transaction and the variety of problems that may arise.

[3] Except in Manitoba and Saskatchewan, where a final order of foreclosure extinguishes the right to sue on the personal covenant of the mortgagor: Mortgage Act, R.S.M. 1970, c. M200, s. 16; Limitation of Civil Rights Act, R.S.S. 1965, c. 103, s. 6.

and (e), subsequent to foreclosure he may again sue on the covenant to pay the debt, always provided he is willing and able to reconvey the land.

The remedies of the mortgagor after default are as follows: (a) he may repay the mortgage loan together with interest and all expenses incurred by the mortgagee up to and including the date of the order of foreclosure and obtain a reconveyance of his land; (b) he may obtain an accounting for any benefits received by the mortgagee and deduct these from the amount owing on redemption; (c) if sued on his covenant to repay after foreclosure, he may require the mortgagee to prove that he is ready and able to reconvey the land upon repayment.

THE MORTGAGEE'S REMEDY OF SALE UPON DEFAULT

As we have seen, once the mortgagee forecloses and disposes of the land, he no longer has any right to demand payment. Two alternative remedies have developed, however, whereby the land may be sold and the mortgagee still maintain an action to recover the *balance* of the debt if the sale has not produced a sufficient price to satisfy it completely. These two remedies may be described as follows.

Sale by the Court

The mortgagee may request to have the land sold under the supervision of the court (or in some of the western provinces, under the supervision of the registrar of titles), the sale to be either by tender or by auction. Some jurisdictions permit the mortgagee himself or his agent to bid — others prohibit such bidding. The sale must be duly advertised for a specified period and carried out according to provincial statutes and regulations. In some jurisdictions the court or registrar sets a reserve price below which no tenders will be accepted. This reserve price is not disclosed. When the tenders are opened, the highest one is accepted if it is over the reserve price. If no bid is above the reserve price, then the land remains unsold and the mortgagee may resort to his other remedies.

When a sale produces a successful bid, the mortgagee is entitled to recover his principal and accrued interest and expenses of the court action and the sale. If the sale produces a smaller sum than the total amount of the above items, the mortgagee may obtain judgment against the mortgagor for the deficiency. If the sale is for a larger sum, the surplus is returned to the mortgagor.

In some jurisdictions, when a mortgagee starts a foreclosure action and the mortgagor believes that the land is worth more than his mortgage debt, the mortgagor may himself request the court to hold a sale. We shall return to this topic when we discuss provincial variations later in this chapter.

Sale by the Mortgagee

Many mortgages, and in some jurisdictions the statutes governing mortgages, give the mortgagee a contractual *power of sale* that may be exercised privately without court action or supervision, although advance notice to the mortgagor is generally required. The mortgagee may exercise his power of sale at any time after default. By executing a proper grant and declaring that the grant is made in pursuance of his power of sale, he may validly transfer the title to the land to any third person. The sale must, however, be a genuine sale and not amount to a fraud upon the mortgagor. The mortgagee may not sell to himself, or to himself through an agent, or partly to himself and partly to another person or persons. He may sell to a company of which he is a shareholder and officer, but such sales will be jealously scrutinized by the court and may be easily upset if there is any evidence of taking unfair advantage by selling at an unreasonably low price. Whenever a mortgagee exercises his power of sale, he is under a duty to take reasonable steps to obtain a fair price for the land. If the mortgagor can show that the mortgagee sold for an unreasonably low price, the court will reduce the deficiency accordingly or give the mortgagor judgment for any surplus he should have received.

The same rules concerning the proceeds of the sale apply here as in a sale by the court: if there is a deficiency, the mortgagee may still sue the mortgagor for it; if there is a surplus, he must return it to the mortgagor.

SALE BY A MORTGAGOR OF HIS INTEREST

Financial Arrangements

The mortgage transaction is, as we can see, a sophisticated credit arrangement. When it concerns but two parties, it is reasonably straightforward. The transaction becomes more complex, however, with the addition of a third party to the relationship.

Illustration

> *A*, the owner of Blackacre, mortgages it to *B* for $50,000. Subsequently he sells Blackacre to *X* for $80,000. How is the price to be paid by *X*? There are three possibilities. First, *X* may pay *A* the full $80,000 and obtain an undertaking from *A* that he will pay off the mortgage to *B*. Second, *X* may pay $30,000 to *A* for *A*'s equity of redemption and a further $50,000 to *B* in full payment of the mortgage. Third, *X* may pay *A* $30,000 as above, and accept Blackacre *subject to the mortgage;* that is, he will himself assume responsibility for paying off the mortgage. We can see that the third possibility is really a variation of the second — instead of paying the mortgage off at once, *X* simply pays it off as it falls due.

In facts similar to the above illustration the first possibility rarely occurs, because *X* takes the risk that *A*'s creditors might obtain the purchase money through court action or *A* might abscond so that the funds never reach *B*, leaving *X* to pay *B* in order to redeem the mortgage. He might end up paying $130,000 for Blackacre instead of $80,000. The second possibility does not occur very frequently either, for two reasons: first, because by the terms of the mortgage the mortgagor may not have the right to pay off the mortgage before the due date; secondly, because purchasers rarely pay the full purchase price for land. Land transactions are almost invariably financed by a credit arrangement, usually in the form of a mortgage. Therefore, it is often most convenient for X simply to pay $30,000 to obtain Blackacre and to assume liability for making payments on the mortgage.

In some circumstances, especially where the mortgagor has significantly reduced the first mortgage by instalment payments, the purchaser may arrange for a new mortgage for a larger sum of money. He would use the proceeds of the new mortgage to pay off the existing mortgage and use the balance towards the cash portion of the purchase price.

Effect of Default by the Purchaser

What would happen if X should then default on payment? Obviously the fact that A has sold to X does not affect B's rights as mortgagee holding the legal title to Blackacre; he retains all his rights against the land. He may also recover from A, the mortgagor, on his covenant to repay the debt. If he sues A, what rights does A have upon paying off the mortgage? A may successfully sue X for the full sum of money he was required to pay to B. The reason for this result is that as part of his purchase price for Blackacre, X assumed the mortgage and agreed to pay it off. The law implies that the promise to pay off the mortgage includes a promise to indemnify A, that is save A from any liability under it. Also, by paying off the mortgage A has in effect purchased the mortgagee's rights. He becomes *subrogated* to the mortgagee's rights and is in effect a mortgagee to whom X is now a mortgagor. At this point A may invoke all the remedies against X that B might himself have utilized against the land and the mortgagor.

Instead of suing A, may the mortgagee B sue the purchaser X directly? There is no contract between B and X giving B this right. Nor do the courts recognize any privity of estate between a mortgagee and the purchaser of the equity as they do in landlord and tenant. He may successfully sue X only if he can obtain an assignment of A's right to indemnity discussed in the preceding paragraph. As a practical matter A will often agree to assign his right to avoid having the mortgagee sue him on his covenant in the mortgage. In Ontario, a statutory provision in the Mortgages Act gives the mortgagee the right to sue the purchaser X directly, without obtaining an assignment from A, the mortgagor.[4] Under the statute X is liable only while he holds the equity. If he sells it to yet another purchaser Y, then Y becomes liable to pay the mortgage, and X is released from his obligation to the mortgagee B.

SECOND MORTGAGES

A prospective purchaser often finds he does not have sufficient money to buy the

---

[4] Mortgages Act, R.S.O. 1970, c. 279, s. 19(2), (3).

equity in land already subject to a mortgage, or the owner of land already subject to a mortgage may wish to make improvements on it by raising an additional sum and using his equity as security. There is only one legal title to the land and that is already held by the mortgagee. Nevertheless, the mortgagor or his successor may mortgage the equity and still retain an equity of redemption; equitable title may be divided up as many times as the holder of the equity wishes to do so and can find creditors willing to take an interest in the equity as security for the debts owed to them. Second mortgages (that is, mortgages of the equity of redemption) are quite common. Less common are third or fourth mortgages (further mortgages of the equity of redemption).

Illustration:

> *V* offers Hillcroft for sale for $23,000, subject to a mortgage for $12,000 to *M* Co. Ltd. *P* would like to buy Hillcroft, but he has only $7,000 in cash, and he needs $11,000. He arranges to borrow $4,000 from his business associate M_2 and to give M_2 a second mortgage on Hillcroft. Having made these arrangements *P* accepts *V*'s offer to sell, and they arrange a *closing date* (a date for completing the transaction).
>
> On the closing day the following transactions take place: (a) *V* delivers a transfer of Hillcroft to *P*. (b) *P* delivers a mortgage of Hillcroft to M_2. (c) M_2 gives *P* $4,000. (d) *P* gives *V* the total sum of $11,000 and also assumes the first mortgage made by *V* with *M* Co. Ltd. These transactions usually take place simultaneously in the office of one lawyer or in the registry office; each party trades the necessary documents and sums of money and immediately registers the transfer and mortgage. The net result of the transaction is as follows: *P* holds the equity in Hillcroft subject to the first mortgage to *M* Co. Ltd. for $12,000 and the second mortgage to M_2 for $4,000. He is indebted in the sum of $16,000.

The second mortgagee has rights similar to those of the first mortgagee except that his interest is the equity of redemption, not the legal title, and he ranks behind the first mortgagee in priority of payment. Thus, if *P* defaults payment on both mortgages, the first mortgagee may start an action for foreclosure. The second mortgagee may decide to stand by and do nothing. If the first mortgagee completes the foreclosure against the equity in Hillcroft, the interest of both *P* and the second mortgagee is destroyed. The second mortgagee loses his security in Hillcroft and is left with only a right of action for debt against *P* who may be insolvent. If the first mortgagee proceeds with a sale under power of sale or sale by the court, the proceeds will be paid, first, to satisfy the first mortgage debt and expenses of the sale, and second, to satisfy the second mortgage debt. The second mortgagee will be paid only to the extent that there is any surplus after paying off the first mortgagee. Of course, the sale may bring in more money than the total amount owed on both mortgages, and the excess will go to *P*.

When the first mortgagee begins a foreclosure action, the second mortgagee may redeem, that is, pay off the first mortgage himself and receive an assignment of it. But then he will have invested an additional sum in the land: in our illustration above, he would have to pay out about $12,000. With P insolvent, he would have little hope of collecting by suing for the debt. He may in turn commence a foreclosure action, and will in effect have bought Hillcroft for about $16,000 (which may or may not be a good buy depending on the current real estate market); or he may proceed with either of the forms of sale, taking the risk that the sale may not bring in enough to pay off the sums he has invested.

A second mortgage invariably provides that default on the first mortgage is also immediate default on the second mortgage. Otherwise the second mortgagee might find himself in the following position: payment of his second mortgage is not yet due and thus there is no default, but the first mortgage is in default (having an earlier due date); the first mortgagee then pursues one of his remedies against the land — foreclosure, sale by court, or exercise of the power of sale. The result of foreclosure would be to destroy the second mortgagee's interest in the land. Similarly, a sale either by the court or by the first mortgagee would destroy his interest as well although he would receive compensation to the extent that the sale brought in more than the debt due on the first mortgage. The second mortgagee may treat default on the first mortgage as a breach of the mortgagor's obligation to protect the second mortgagee's interest in the land, and he may immediately act upon his usual remedies.

A mortgagor may place successive mortgages upon his equity, and each will rank in priority according to their creation in time. Each subsequent mortgage will give all the usual remedies to the mortgagee, subject to the prior rights of any earlier mortgagee. Each subsequent mortgage presents a greater risk to the creditor for several reasons: first, the land is subject to a greater financial debt and any drop in price will injure the security of the latest mortgagee first; secondly, a succession of mortgages on one piece of land usually indicates financial instability in the borrower and poor management on his part; thirdly, a failure to act reasonably promptly in case of default may result in the destruction of the secured interest in the land, if a prior mortgagee exercises his power of sale; fourthly, the cost of redeeming prior mortgages may be too high — in order to prevent foreclosure of his interest he may have to lay out more money than he can afford.

Sometimes the mortgagor defaults on only the second mortgage, or if he has defaulted on the first as well, the first mortgagee may be quite satisfied with the adequacy of his security and is willing to "sit tight" and see what the subsequent mortgagees and creditors intend to do. He need not worry since he has the prime interest in the land and no one can affect his position. In this situation, the second mortgagee may still proceed with foreclosure or a sale, and the effect of either remedy is to destroy the interest of the mortgagor in the equity of redemption without affecting the first mortgagee. If the second mortgagee forecloses, he becomes the sole holder of the equity of redemption subject to the prior interest of the first mortgagee. When the second mortgagee proceeds by sale, the purchaser obtains the whole of the equity of redemption clear of the mortgagor's interest, though of course still subject to the first mortgage. In either case the new holder of the equity of redemption must make satisfactory arrangements with the first mortgagee; he may redeem the first mortgage or else assume the obligations under the first mortgage by agreement with the first mortgagee.

THE MORTGAGEE'S RIGHTS COMPARED WITH RIGHTS OF OTHER CREDITORS

A creditor who has no security other than the promise of his debtor is a *general creditor,* and his claim ranks as a general claim; a creditor who has one or more forms of collateral security is a *secured creditor* and has a prior claim against one or more of the assets of the debtor. If the debtor becomes insolvent, the general creditors must wait until the claims of the secured creditors have been satisfied out of the assets over which they have their claims. Sometimes the sale of a security brings in more than the amount owing the secured creditor, and the excess becomes available for the settlement of general claims. Here we may see the relation of the mortgagee's remedy of sale to other creditors' claims: as we noted previously in this chapter, after a sale of the mortgaged land by the mortgagee any surplus is returned to the mortgagor; if he is insolvent, the surplus goes to his creditors. At other times the particular security realizes less than the amount of the secured creditor's claim, and he will then rank as a general creditor along with all the general creditors for the amount by which his security falls short of covering his claim.

Illustration:

(a) Harper is the proprietor of a successful small retail business. When his place of business is expropriated to make way for a new parking garage, he decides to take the big step of building a new and much larger store. He arranges the financing of a new building worth about $120,000 and obtains a mortgage for $80,000 from Commerce Mortgage Co. Unfortunately his area suffers a serious recession when a large local industry closes. Harper has meagre working capital and cannot weather the indefinite loss in sales. He becomes insolvent and is declared bankrupt. A trustee is appointed, and in due course the building is sold; the remainder of Harper's assets are also sold. The following is a statement of Harper's financial position after all the assets are liquidated:

Assets		*Liabilities*	
Bank balance from:		Commerce Mortgage	
sale of building	$102,000	Co.	$78,000
sale of other assets	38,000	General Creditors	85,000
TOTAL	$140,000	TOTAL	$163,000

The assets would be distributed as follows:

Commerce Mortgage Co.	$78,000
General Creditors	62,000
	$140,000

We see that the mortgagee receives 100 cents on the dollar of debt owed to it from the sale of the building. In addition the sale produces a surplus of $24,000. This sum is added to the $38,000 realized from all other assets, and is paid out rateably to the general creditors. Here they receive $\frac{62,000}{85,000}$ of each dollar of indebtedness — about 73 cents on each dollar.

(b) Suppose, however, that the sale of the building brings a much smaller sum because of the depressed market — say $60,000. The assets and liabilities are now as follows:

Assets		*Liabilities*	
Bank balance from:		Commerce Mortgage	
sale of building	$60,000	Co.	$78,000
sale of other assets	38,000	General Creditors	85,000
TOTAL	$98,000	TOTAL	$163,000

The assets would now be distributed as follows:

	Creditors		
	Secured	*General*	*Total*
Commerce Mortgage Co.	$60,000		
plus $\frac{18,000}{103,000}$ x 38,000		$6,640	$66,640
General creditors			
$\frac{85,000}{103,000}$ x 38,000		31,360	31,360
	$60,000	$38,000	$98,000

Note: We obtain the figure of $103,000 by adding the deficiency of $18,000 on the mortgage debt to the total unsecured debt. In these circumstances the mortgagee receives a total of almost $67,000 from a debt of $78,000 — about 85 cents on each dollar of debt. On the other hand the general creditors suffer much more severely: they receive about $\frac{31,000}{85,000}$ of each dollar of indebtedness — about 37 cents on each dollar. We may note that their position is somewhat worsened by the fact that the mortgagee ranked as a general creditor for that portion of his debt unsatisfied by the sale of the building, thus dividing the assets among a larger group of claims.

THE MORTGAGE AS A CONTRACT AND AS A TRANSFER OF AN INTEREST IN LAND

The Mortgage as a Contract

The mortgage document is a contract containing a number of important terms, the most important being the personal covenants of the mortgagor to pay off the debt and of the mortgagee to discharge his interest in the land upon repayment. It is useful to set out the more important covenants of each party. The mortgagor covenants:

(a) to pay the debt and accrued interest, either at maturity date or in instalments as agreed by the parties;[5]
(b) to keep the property adequately insured in the name of the mortgagee;
(c) to pay taxes on the land and buildings;
(d) to keep the premises in a reasonable state of repair.

The mortgagee covenants:

(a) to execute the necessary discharge of the mortgage upon repayment in full;
(b) to leave the mortgagor in possession and not interfere with his use and enjoyment of the mortgaged premises so long as the mortgagor observes all his covenants.

We may note that the mortgagor signs the mortgage, and the mortgagee merely accepts without joining as a signer of the document. His promises are set out as provisos — some are simply implied by the principles of mortgage law — and his acceptance of the document binds him to the terms. It is apparent that the contractual obligations form a large part of the mortgage transaction.

The Mortgage as a Transfer of an Interest in Land

We have seen that a mortgage is a transfer of an interest in land in the same way as a grant is, but the transfer is subject to the terms of the mortgage contract. Since a mortgage is basically a transfer, it must comply with the usual requirements for a transfer, adequately describing the parties and the land being transferred, and must be in the proper form required for registration in the registry office of the jurisdiction. Our discussion in the preceding chapter concerning the recording of interests in land applies equally to interests created by way of mortgage. Thus, if a mortgagee fails to register his mortgage, a subsequent purchaser from the mortgagor, unaware of the mortgage, will acquire title free from it upon registering his grant. Similarly a subsequent mortgagee, unaware of the first mortgage, will establish priority over it if he registers first. We are concerned here only with establishing the mortgagee's interest in the land: failure to register does not wipe out his other rights as a creditor of the mortgagor. Failure to register may result in the complete loss of the land as security where there is a transfer to an innocent purchaser, or to loss of priority against another secured creditor of the mortgagor who registers his claim first.

---

[5] Except in Alberta and Saskatchewan, where a mortgagor cannot be sued personally for the mortgage debt. See the section dealing with provincial variations, below.

Assignment

Often a mortgagee may wish to obtain cash by selling the mortgage rather than by waiting for the mortgage debt to fall due in order to collect. The mortgage may be a sound investment, having good security and a reliable debtor, or it may be a risky investment. In either case, the mortgagee may sell his mortgage at the best price he can get for it. The sale of a mortgage is a transaction involving both the contractual and real property aspects of the mortgage. The mortgagee *assigns* his rights to the covenants made by the mortgagor, and *grants* or transfers his interest in the land to the purchaser (assignee). Sometimes, in order to obtain a higher price for the mortgage, the mortgagee will guarantee payment — that is, if the mortgagor defaults in payment, the mortgagee on the demand of his assignee will pay off the mortgage and take back an assignment. In most sales, however, the mortgagee sells the mortgage outright, and the purchaser takes the risk of default together with all the usual remedies of a mortgagee.

A purchaser of a mortgage, as an assignee of contractual rights, is bound by the usual rules of assignment in contract. As we have seen in Chapter 13, the debtor, in this case the mortgagor, is not bound by the assignment until he receives notice of it, and the assignee takes subject to the equities and the state of the mortgage account between the mortgagor and mortgagee.

Discharge of Mortgages

When a mortgagor, or a subsequent purchaser of his equity, pays off the whole of the mortgage debt at maturity of the loan, he is entitled to a discharge from the mortgagee. A discharge operates both as an acknowledgment that the debt has been paid in full and as a reconveyance of the legal title from the mortgagee to the holder of the equity. To protect himself, the holder of the equity of redemption registers the discharge in the land registry office; by registration he conclusively becomes the holder of the legal title. A fraudulent mortgagee cannot then successfully exercise his power of sale and grant the legal title to an innocent purchaser on the pretence that the mortgage is unpaid and in arrears. A fraudulent mortgagee has been known to do just that and to deprive a mortgagor of his land when the mortgagor has neglected to obtain a discharge and register it.[6] In areas under the land titles system, a discharge from the mortgagee operates to dissolve the charge upon the mortgagor's land.

A mortgage usually contains a contractual term permitting the mortgagor to repay the mortgage and to obtain a discharge even before the debt matures. The term permitting such repayment may have various conditions attached to it. Often the mortgagee requires a period of notice, usually three months, before he need accept the money; such a requirement gives him time to find a new borrower so that the money received does not lie idle earning no interest until he finds a new investment. A mortgagee often requires payment of a bonus, for ex-

---

[6] Dicker v. Angerstein (1876) 3 Ch. D. 395.

ample three months interest, in lieu of notice, or he may require both notice and a bonus. Certain types of mortgages, particularly second mortgages and short-term mortgages, permit repayment "at any time without notice or bonus". Mortgages containing such a term are frequently called *open mortgages.*

These flexible mortgage-prepayment clauses often contain various other prepayment possibilities. The mortgagor may be able to prepay part of the debt rather than all of it, simply to make good use of extra earnings and to reduce his interest payable on the mortgage loan. The mortgage may also permit the mortgagor to prepay a specified portion of the mortgage debt and to obtain a *partial discharge,* that is, a discharge of a definite portion of the mortgaged lands. Partial discharges are common when the mortgagor is a land developer. He may own a large piece of undeveloped land and wish to sell off a part of it free from any encumbrance, or he may himself wish to erect a large building on a particular part of the land and require finance in the form of a large new mortgage which he cannot obtain except as a first mortgage. These various methods of prepaying part or all of a mortgage debt play an important role in the credit financing of land development.

PROVINCIAL VARIATIONS

The remedies available to mortgagees and mortgagors developed, as we have seen, over a long period of time. The various provinces of Canada adopted the English law existing at the date each province obtained its first legislative body; the dates range from 1756 in Nova Scotia to 1870 in Alberta and Saskatchewan. Accordingly, the variations in the mortgage law received by each province may be considerable. Subsequent to its adoption of the English law, each province developed its own procedures and made statutory amendments to meet its own needs. These needs differed widely according to the economy of the province and the character of business within it. The result is a rather confused and sometimes inconsistent pattern of remedies for both mortgagee and mortgagor. We present here a brief summary of the main variations in these remedies.

Except in Alberta and Saskatchewan, a mortgagee may sue on the covenant to repay the mortgage. In all provinces, he may also request the court or registrar to hold a sale of mortgaged land, and except in Nova Scotia, he may sell under a power of sale if it is provided for either by statute or under the terms of the mortgage. In British Columbia, in that portion of Manitoba under the registry system, and in Ontario, New Brunswick, Prince Edward Island, and Newfoundland, the mortgagee may foreclose the equity of redemption in the manner we have already discussed. In Alberta, Saskatchewan, and that portion of Manitoba under the land titles system, the usual remedy is sale by the court: if the sale does not produce any satisfactory bids then the mortgagee may proceed to foreclose, but foreclosure appears to be a rare remedy in practice. In Nova Scotia, although the court issues an order of "foreclosure and sale," foreclosure is not really permitted: the court must hold a sale.

With the exception of New Brunswick, in those provinces permitting the mortgagee to start an action for foreclosure the mortgagor may request the court to hold a sale provided he deposits a sum of money (usually under $100) as security for the costs of the sale in the event of its producing no acceptable bids. He may thus prevent the mortgagee from foreclosing his interest in land worth considerably more than the mortgage debt. We should remember, however, that if the market value of the land does exceed the mortgage debt, the mortgagor, unless he is considered a bad personal credit risk, should be able to refinance the land by obtaining an extension of his mortgage or arranging for a new mortgage and paying off his old mortgagee to whom he has defaulted. In all jurisdictions the mortgagor has the right to redeem the land by paying off the entire debt before foreclosure or sale.

A TYPICAL REAL ESTATE TRANSACTION

The Circumstances

A real estate transaction can best be understood by following a typical sale in some detail from start to finish. We shall use for an example a fictional piece of land in Oshawa, Ontario. John Vincent owns the land and building on Main Street described in his grant as Lot 27, Plan 7654 in the City of Oshawa. The building fronting on Main Street consists of a large store at ground level and three suites of offices on the second floor. Vincent occupies the store himself and runs a men's-wear shop. The offices are rented to three tenants, one to Dr. A. McAvity, dentist, the second to Happy Auto Insurance Company, and the third to C. McCollum, chartered accountant. Business has been poor; Vincent is 70 years old and wishes to retire. He has advertised without success to find a buyer of his business. He has received many inquiries about purchasing the building, a prime location, but no one is interested in buying his rather old-fashioned stock and fixtures. He has finally decided to run a selling-out sale and then sell the building.

The Offer to Purchase

Hi-Style Centres Ltd., a firm selling women's wear, operates a chain of stores and is anxious to have an outlet in Oshawa. They approach Vincent with the proposal that he rent the store to them. Vincent has decided to leave Oshawa and retire to Victoria, B.C., and wishes to break all business connections in the East. He says he would consider an offer to purchase but not to rent. Hi-Style makes two offers to purchase, both rejected by Vincent as too low. It now makes a third offer which Vincent is considering seriously. The essential terms are as follows:[7]

---

[7] The offer to purchase may also include other terms, the importance of which varies according to the circumstances, in particular the nature of the property. For example the vendor might be required to give a warranty that the heating plant conforms to regulations; to produce a certificate of inspection of boiler or gas installations; to warrant that the premises do not violate existing zoning by-laws; to identify all encroachments or easements in respect of which the property is either a servient or a dominant tenement; and to allow the prospective purchaser access to the premises for the purpose of checking the land survey.

(a) Hi-Style offers to buy the premises for $145,000, payable as follows: $5,000 as a deposit by certified cheque attached to the offer; assume the first mortgage of about $69,000 held by the Grimm Mortgage Company; give back to Vincent a second mortgage of $30,000 [interest and other terms set out in detail]; pay the balance on closing date.

(b) The sale is to be closed 60 days after the date of the offer.

(c) Hi-Style may search the title and submit *requisitions* (questions concerning claims against Vincent's title) within 20 days of acceptance of the offer. Vincent promises to deliver a copy of the survey of the lot which he has in his possession for examination by Hi-Style. If serious claims against Vincent's title are raised and Vincent cannot answer them satisfactorily, the contract will be terminated and the deposit returned to Hi-Style. If no requisitions are submitted within 20 days, it is presumed that Hi-Style accepts Vincent's title as satisfactory.

(d) Vincent is to remain in possession and the building is to remain at his risk until closing. He promises to keep the building insured to its full insurable value. He also undertakes to give possession of the building in substantially the same condition as it was at the time of making the contract. If the building is destroyed or seriously damaged, Hi-Style may elect to take over the premises and to receive the proceeds of all insurance, or it may elect to terminate the contract, with Vincent to suffer the loss, if any.

(e) Vincent is to pay all taxes and insurance until closing and deduct from the amount due at closing all outstanding current expenses, such as accrued water and electric bills, unpaid taxes, and insurance. He will transfer all insurance policies to Hi-Style, provided the insurance companies are willing to accept Hi-Style as a satisfactory risk, and Hi-Style will pay for the prepaid unexpired portion of such policies.

(f) Vincent warrants that his three suites of offices are leased to tenants as stated at rents of $275 monthly per suite under leases expiring two years after date of closing for Suite No. 1, two years four months after closing for Suite No. 2, and Suite 3 as a monthly tenancy only. He will deliver the original of the two leases and assignments of the leases on closing, an acknowledgment from the third tenant that he is only a monthly tenant, and signed notices to the tenants that Hi-Style is the new landlord to whom they are to pay their rent.

(g) The offer is open for two days and acceptance must be communicated to the office of the lawyer for Hi-Style in Oshawa before 5:00 p.m. on the second day.

Preparations for Completing the Transaction

Vincent has two copies of the offer. He decides to accept it and sends one signed copy to Hi-Style's lawyer, Harmon, retaining the other copy for his own lawyer, Vale. He also sends a copy of the survey of his lot to Harmon. The manager of Hi-Style has taken the careful step of having Harmon draw up the offer in the first place. Thus Harmon is familiar with its terms; in particular, he has made a special note in his file of the last day to submit requisitions concerning title to the land, as well as the date of closing the transaction.

Harmon now takes the following steps. (1) He sends a junior member of his law firm to the registry office to search the title to the lot and also compare the survey he has received from Vincent with the plan of the whole area as filed in the registry office, to make sure there are no discrepancies in the boundaries of the lot. (2) He writes to the city tax department asking for a certificate showing the state of real property taxes, both arrears and current, and encloses the small fee usually required for the certificate. (3) He writes to the Grimm Mortgage Company and asks them to prepare and forward a *mortgage statement* showing what the exact amount outstanding on the mortgage, including accrued interest, will be on the date of closing. (4) When his junior employee returns with the completed data from the search of title, Harmon examines them to discover whether a limited company has held the land at any time since the last day of December, 1967. If so, he will write to the office of the provincial government which keeps these records (in Ontario it is the office of the Ministry of Revenue), ask for a certificate showing the state of corporation taxes on the land, and enclose whatever fee is charged. (5) He asks his client to examine the premises carefully to confirm that the building is occupied by the tenants and by Vincent as stated in the contract and that there are no other persons who appear to be exercising an adverse claim over any part of the premises. In the case of valuable commercial property on main streets, the boundaries are very important, especially if demolition and reconstruction are even remotely contemplated. Harmon advises Hi-Style to hire a surveyor to make a new survey and compare it with the old, thus checking whether adjacent owners are in possession of any part of the lot and have perhaps extinguished Vincent's title to portions they have occupied.

Within a few days Vincent's lawyer, Vale, prepares a *draft deed,* that is, a copy of the grant which Vincent will later sign for delivery on closing. He sends a copy to Harmon, who examines it and approves of its content. Harmon prepares a draft copy of the second mortgage to be given by Hi-Style to Vincent on closing and sends it to Vale. To avoid any confusion about names or initials and about description of the land to be conveyed, both lawyers check very closely to see that all details are described in identical terms in the following documents: the grant received by Vincent when he originally bought the land; the first mortgage by Vincent to Grimm Mortgage Company; the draft deed by Vincent to Hi-Style; and the draft second mortgage from Hi-Style to Vincent.

Harmon finds that Vincent's title to the land is in good order and that there are no outstanding corporation taxes or municipal taxes except for the current year. He receives a mortgage statement from Grimm Mortgage Company, and it agrees with the statement made by Vincent concerning the amount outstanding. A few weeks before the date of closing, Vale prepares a document called a *statement of adjustments* (see below) setting out all the items, both credits and debits, that must be adjusted between the parties to arrive at the correct amount to be paid by Hi-Style to Vincent on the date of closing. The closing date is to be April 15.

Re: Lot 27, Plan 7654, in the City of Oshawa
Hi-Style Centres Ltd. purchase from Vincent

STATEMENT OF ADJUSTMENTS

1. SALE PRICE			$145,000.00
2. Deposit paid by purchaser		$ 5,000.00	
3. First mortgage to Grimm Mortgage Company to be assumed by purchaser	$ 69,283.54		
Plus interest, April 1 to 15 at 9%	259.81		
		69,543.35	
4. Second mortgage back to vendor		30,000.00	
5. Unpaid taxes for current year, $2,295.00, charged to vendor to April 15 — 3½ months		669.38	
6. Rent received in advance:			
Suite # 1: 1½ months	412.50		
Suite #2: 1½ months	412.50		
Suite #3: ½ month	137.50		
		962.50	
7. Union Hartford Fire Insurance Policy no. 8953744, three years, expires Nov. 1, current year. Amount: $10,000 Premium: $570. Unexpired portion: 6½ months			102.92
8. Full tank of furnace oil — 400 gallons at 36.4¢.			145.60
9. BALANCE DUE ON CLOSING		39,073.29	
		$145,248.52	$145,248.52

The Closing

On the morning of April 15, Vale and Harmon meet at the registry office. Harmon checks with the sheriff's office to search for executions and finds none. He also brings his search of the title up to date to make sure no new documents have been registered against it. He gives Vale the properly executed mortgage for $30,000 made out in duplicate, and a certified cheque for $39,073.29. On behalf of the vendor Vale delivers the following documents to Harmon:

(a) properly executed grant in duplicate;

(b) original copy of leases to Suites No. 1 and No. 2;

(c) properly executed assignments of each lease;

(d) acknowledgment of tenant in Suite No. 3 that he is a monthly tenant at a rent of $275 payable in advance;

(e) notice signed by Vincent to each tenant of Suites No. 1, No. 2, and No. 3 informing them of the change of ownership and requesting them to pay all future rent to Hi-Style;

(f) current tax bill.

He also hands to Harmon, for the purpose of inspection, a certified copy of the insurance policy on the building and a transfer noting both the interest of Hi-Style as purchaser and Vincent as second mortgagee. Vale will subsequently send these to the insurance company himself. After trading documents, Harmon registers the grant from Vincent to Hi-Style, and Vale registers the second mortgage from Hi-Style to Vincent.

Vale agrees not to release the funds he has received until Vincent delivers possession to Hi-Style. The mechanics of delivering possession to the purchaser sometimes cause great friction and even court action. To avoid such friction the vendor should arrange to be completely out of the premises by the time the deal is closed and deliver the keys to the purchaser. If this is not done, the purchaser may understandably be very upset and demand that the money not be released. Once anger replaces common sense both vendor and purchaser may become obstinate, and the vendor's lawyer holding the cheque is caught between them. In the present case, however, all goes smoothly: Vincent vacates the premises the day before and delivers the keys to Vale who now hands them over to Harmon. On returning to his office, Harmon calls the manager of Hi-Style to tell him the keys are available. The manager picks up the keys, goes to the building, and finds the store vacant. He calls Harmon and informs him that Hi-Style is now in possession. Harmon calls Vale and tells him that he may release the cheque to Vincent. The sale has now been effected.

After the Closing

Each lawyer, however, has several things to do besides submitting his bill. Vale will write to Grimm Mortgage Company to inform them of the sale and name the purchaser. He will also write to the city tax office to inform them of the change of ownership. He will write to the insurance company enclosing the copy of the policy and the transfer, and request the return of the policy with an endorsement noting the change of ownership and the interest of the second mortgagee in the property. He will also request that a copy of the policy be sent to the purchaser.

Harmon will communicate with Vale to see that all these things have been completed. He will also write to Grimm Mortgage Company and to the city tax office asking each of them to send all further notices to the head office of Hi-Style. He will write to each of the tenants to inform them of the change of ownership, enclosing Vincent's notice and giving them the address at which Hi-Style would like the rent to be paid.

Only after all these things have been done, when each lawyer is able to return all the documents to his client and to make the full report of all details, will the transaction be complete.

It is important to stress that each sale of land is a separate and distinctive transaction: the terms should be tailored to meet the specific requirements of the parties in the circumstances. Perhaps we see the greatest degree of standardization in contracts for the sale of similar houses in a subdivision. Even there, however, significant variations are made in credit arrangements, extra features installed by the builder, or special agreement for completion of the house after possession. In the sale of commercial property, the variations are far greater: often, possession does not pass on closing, as where the whole premises are already rented to tenants and are purchased for their investment value, or where the vendor remains on as a tenant himself. Sometimes where the sale of a business is involved, the purchaser covenants to buy goods from the vendor, or the vendor covenants to refrain from opening a competing business in the same neighbourhood. Our fictional illustration set out above is not a model for other transactions, nor does it deal with every detail which might arise in the circumstances. Rather it is intended to give a picture and an understanding of a typical real estate transaction.

QUESTIONS FOR REVIEW

1. How did equity first mitigate the harsh common law rule by which the mortgagor lost his land and still owed the debt?
2. Describe the equity of redemption.
3. What is foreclosure? How does it protect the mortgagee?
4. Describe the two possible types of sale on default of the mortgagor.
5. Who receives the surplus after a sale?
6. What is a second mortgage? Under what circumstances does it commonly arise?
7. State two reasons why we rarely find a mortgagee in possession before foreclosure.
8. What is a closing date?
9. Distinguish between a general creditor and a secured creditor.
10. What is priority of payment?
11. Name two duties of the mortgagor in addition to his obligation to pay off the mortgage debt.
12. Name two duties of the mortgagee.
13. In what circumstances would a mortgagor ask the court to sell his land rather than permit the mortgagee to foreclose?
14. Why should the lawyer for a purchaser of real property search for executions in the sheriff's office?
15. What interest does a mortgagee have in seeing that the mortgaged property is adequately insured? What constitutes adequate insurance from his point of view?
16. What possible financial arrangements may a purchaser make when he acquires land subject to an existing mortgage?

CASES FOR DISCUSSION

CASE 1

Burton owned the premises and business of Burton's Hardware, subject to a mortgage he had given to Milton as security for a loan of $10,000. Burton suffered severe business losses and finally became insolvent. Milton foreclosed and took possession of the property which had been left in a severely dilapidated condition by Burton. The municipal tax department served Milton with a demand to pay tax arrears of $2,400; otherwise the premises would be sold at a tax sale. Milton was undecided whether it was worthwhile paying the tax arrears and delayed making a decision. Meanwhile he became occupied with another large business transaction. The municipality finally proceeded with the sale after giving Milton adequate notice. At the sale Ponsby bought the premises for $2,400.

Several years later Burton re-established himself in business and became very successful. Milton sued Burton on his personal covenant for the mortgage debt. In argument before the court Burton claimed that Milton must return the mortgaged premises before he would be entitled to payment of the debt. In reply Milton stated that the premises were lost because of the arrears of taxes that accrued while Burton was in possession, and thus it was Burton's failure to perform his covenant to pay taxes that caused the property to be lost. Burton conceded that this argument might well have been sound if the property had been sold while he was in possession, but not after foreclosure.

Discuss the merits of each argument, and state whether the mortgagee should succeed. (See *Dowker v. Thompson* [1941] 2 D.L.R. 141.)

CASE 2

Walters, a wealthy businessman, bought Sunnydell Acres, a rather rundown farm, with a view to making it into a model dairy farm. He arranged a mortgage with Farm Mortgage Corp. for $20,000 and proceeded to renovate the farm. He found it difficult to run the farm because of a farm-labour shortage and decided finally to buy additional automatic equipment. For this purpose he arranged a second mortgage on Sunnydell with Meekins for $6,000.

A short time afterwards, Walters suffered the misfortune of having his entire herd fall ill with a fatal cattle disease. He abandoned Sunnydell and returned to the city. Farm Mortgage Corp. foreclosed and sold the farm to Jones. Meekins, the second mortgagee, then sued Walters on his personal covenant for the second mortgage debt. In defence Walters claimed that Meekins could not sue unless he could reconvey Sunnydell to him in return for payment.

Should Meekins succeed? What difference, if any, is there between the position of Milton in Case 1 and Meekins in the present case? (See *Brown v. Weil* (1923) 53 O.L.R. 27.)

CASE 3

Allan purchased a 200-acre farm on the St. John River in New Brunswick for $30,000. He paid $6,000 cash and gave back a mortgage of $24,000 to his vendor, Bowes. The mortgage was payable over a 15-year period with interest at 9½% in instalments of about $200 per month. Within a year, Bowes fell ill and decided to retire to a warm climate. He sold the mortgage to Manor Mortgage Co. with only a slight discount on the amount then outstanding because he personally guaranteed payment by Allan.

A year later Allan received an offer to purchase his frontage on the St. John River, an area of about 10 acres, for $12,000. He visited the offices of Manor Mortgage Co. and asked if they would be interested in giving a discharge of the mortgage over the 10 acres. Manor Mortgage Co. agreed to do so provided Allan would give a $1,000 bonus and a further $7,000 in reduction of the mortgage debt. The arrangement was carried out, and the 10 acres was discharged from the mortgage, leaving the mortgage on the remainder of the farm. Subsequently, Allan defaulted on the mortgage, having also let the farm fall into disrepair. Manor Mortgage Co. sued Bowes as guarantor of the mortgage debt for the balance of $16,000 then outstanding.

Should Manor Mortgage Co. succeed? (See *Farmers' Loan Co. v. Patchett* (1903) 6 O.L.R. 255, and *Molson's Bank v. Heilig* (1895) 26 O.R. 276.)

CASE 4

Four years ago Azoic Wholesalers Ltd. purchased a warehouse building for $243,000. To finance the purchase the company paid $39,000 in cash, gave a 7% first mortgage to the Reliable Insurance Company for $162,000, and an 8% second mortgage of $42,000 to the vendor. The vendor subsequently sold the second mortgage to Sharpe Retailers Ltd. for $35,000. All documents were duly registered. For the next few years Azoic Wholesalers Ltd. managed to pay interest on both mortgages and somewhat reduce the principal.

Azoic Wholesalers Ltd. has become insolvent and declared bankrupt. A trustee in bankruptcy has been appointed, and all the assets of the company sold. The following statement shows its financial condition after all assets were liquidated:

Azoic Wholesalers Ltd.

STATEMENT OF CONDITION AT DATE OF DISTRIBUTION

Assets		*Liabilities*	
Bank balance from:		Reliable Insurance Co.	
		(first mortgage) $156,000	
sale of building $171,000			
sale of all other assets 48,000		Sharpe Realties Ltd.	
		(second mortgage) 39,000	
Total available cash 219,000			
		General creditors 96,000	
Deficiency of assets 72,000			
$291,000		$291,000	

Required: Calculate how the available cash will be distributed to the various creditors.

CASE 5

Lawlor purchased a small house from Albee at a price of $50,000. He paid $10,000 in cash and gave Albee a first mortgage for the balance. A year later, when Lawlor had reduced the principal amount of the mortgage to $33,000, he encountered financial reverses which made it impossible for him to continue to repay further mortgage principal as required. Albee brought an action against Lawlor and obtained an order for foreclosure.

Soon after, the insurance of $30,000 on the house expired and Lawlor renewed it while he was seeking to refinance with a new mortgagee. A few weeks later the house was seriously damaged by fire; the insurance adjuster appraised the loss at $25,000.

Both Albee and Lawlor immediately claimed the insurance money. The insurance company refused to pay Albee on the grounds that the insurance policy contained no mortgage clause which would have assigned to him rights in any claim "in so far as his interest may appear". The insurance company also refused to pay any part of the loss to Lawlor on the grounds that he had no insurable interest in the property.

Discuss the validity of the claims of Albee and Lawlor. Assume that there is no evidence to show that the fire was other than accidental in its origin. (For reference, see *Hanson v. Queensland Insurance Company, Limited* (1966) 56 W.W.R. 215.)

CASE 6

Three years ago, the Lister Company Ltd. borrowed $100,000 from the Hi-Rise Bank. Lister Company Ltd. was engaged in the textile business and gave a real estate mortgage on one of its buildings as collateral security for the bank loan: the mortgage provided security in the land, building, and fixtures in the building.

The company was later adjudged bankrupt on a petition of its creditors. A question arose about whether certain expensive machinery in the mortgaged building was in fact a fixture against which the bank would retain priority in liquidation. The trustee in bankruptcy, representing the general creditors, claimed it was not a fixture, so that the proceeds from its sale would be applied to all creditors' claims and not solely to that of the bank as mortgagee.

An officer of the bank and the trustee in bankruptcy went personally to inspect the machine, but were unable to agree whether it could be described as being "permanently" affixed. The bank then commenced legal proceedings to have its claim as mortgagee of the machine confirmed. At this point, the trustee offered by way of compromise to recognize the bank's priority to the extent of $10,000, a sum much less than the probable resale value of the machine; the bank accepted his offer and withdrew its action.

A few days later it came to the bank's attention that at the time it took the mortgage on the building the machine in question had been affixed to a cement floor in the plant in a permanent way, but that the building had since been renovated and the machine thereafter left much less securely affixed to the new floor. This was clearly information that neither the bank nor the trustee had had when they contracted to substitute $10,000 in cash for the mortgage claim. The trustee refused to waive this agreement, however, and the Hi-Rise Bank brought an action asking the court for rescission of that contract and an order acknowledging its claim as a secured creditor with respect to the machine.

Discuss the nature of the argument on which the bank would base its claim and indicate whether its action should succeed. (For reference see *Huddersfield Banking Co. v. Henry Lister & Son, Ltd.* [1895] 2 Ch. 273; *Fairgrief v. Ellis* [1935] 2 D.L.R. 806.)

PART FIVE

Forms of Business Organization

CHAPTER 27

Partnership

THE PARTNERSHIP ACT

Until the mid-19th century, there was no generally available procedure for incorporation of companies. Up to that time corporations had been created only for special purposes involving large projects such as railways or public utilities. Even after the convenience of incorporation became generally available, the procedure was rather expensive and cumbersome until the introduction of the private company at the beginning of the present century. During the preceding century and a half the chief mode of carrying on business other than as a sole trader was by way of partnership.

Since partnership was the accepted mode of carrying on an enterprise, problems concerning almost every aspect of partnership arose and became the subject of legal decision starting about the middle of the 18th century. By the 1880s, there was a virtually complete body of rules which were well settled, but the maze of decisions on detailed points made it difficult to discover the broader principles. To remedy this situation, the British Parliament in 1890 passed the Partnership Act,[1] which brought together the multitude of cases under more general principles and codified the law as the experts in the field then believed it to be. The English Act has been adopted in substantially the same form by all the common law provinces.

The Act has remained virtually unchanged from its original form for several reasons: first, this area of the law had reached maturity, and its principles were

---

[1] 1890, 53 & 54 Vict., c. 39 (United Kingdom).

highly developed by the time the Act was passed; secondly the Act, which was substantially the work of Sir Frederick Pollock, the recognized authority in the field of partnership law, was well drawn, and with few exceptions its sections are models of clarity, readily comprehensible to the intelligent businessman; thirdly, the corporation was rapidly emerging as the dominant form of business organization, thus relieving any pressure to adapt the partnership form to changing business requirements. These factors probably account for the fact that there have been comparatively few cases on the interpretation of the Act. The Act itself is an accurate representation of the state of partnership law today. Two of the leading textbooks on the subject are rather slim volumes, yet are quite adequate as commentaries on the statute.[2]

THE NATURE OF PARTNERSHIP

Advantages and Disadvantages

There are obvious advantages in carrying on a venture, whether a business venture or any other kind, as a joint undertaking by two or more persons rather than as one person alone. Working together, members of a group may pool their knowledge and wisdom, physical and financial resources. There are also obvious disadvantages: disagreements may lead to stalemates or ineffective activity by the group; dishonesty or incompetence of one member of a group may lead to heavy losses suffered by other members; when the group wishes to make important decisions, it may lose valuable time in arranging a meeting. None of these problems exists where a person acts solely on his or her own behalf. Generally speaking, however, the advantages of group activity outweigh the disadvantages, at least in the minds of people who contemplate a joint undertaking. As a result, they often undertake to carry out common goals in partnership with each other. Under our system of law, the word *partnership* refers exclusively to joint business enterprises carried on for profit. It does not refer to other joint ventures, such as charitable enterprises, joint trustees of an estate, or public boards.

We shall briefly discuss the development of the joint venture or consortium, which has much in common with partnership, in the next chapter.

The Partnership Concept of Business

"Partnership is the relation which subsists between persons carrying on a business in common with a view of profit."[3] To the businessman this definition of

---

[2] Drake, C. D., *Law of Partnership*. London, Sweet & Maxwell, 1972 (based on 15th ed. of *Pollock on the Law of Partnership* by Gower); Underhill, *The Principles of the Law of Partnership* (9th ed.), Hesketh, ed. London: Butterworth & Co. Ltd., 1971.

[3] The Partnership Act, 1890, s. 1(1). The same wording is used in Canadian versions of the statute. See, for example: R.S.B.C. 1960, c. 277, s. 3; R.S.O. 1970, c. 309, s. 2; R.S.N.S. 1967, c. 224, s. 3. In subsequent footnotes in this chapter, references to B.C., Ontario, and N.S. will be to these statutes.

partnership, as contained in the various partnerships acts, is extremely important because of the consequences which may follow from a finding that he is a partner. We shall discuss these consequences in a later subsection. Whether two or more persons are partners within the meaning of the definition depends upon all the circumstances of a case; businessmen may be found to be partners in carrying on a business even though they have not so agreed. Naturally the element of agreement is a very important one, and if two persons expressly agree to form a partnership, this is ordinarily conclusive of the question; but in the absence of an agreement they may still be held to be partners if they have acted as such. In any event, the courts will insist upon looking at the substance of the relationship, and not necessarily be guided by what the parties may themselves choose to call it.

Since the term *partnership* applies only to business, it is important too to discover whether the activity carried on amounts to a business. The term is a nebulous one. Business may be said to include "every trade, occupation, or profession," but does not include every activity carried on for a profit. For instance, owning property and collecting rent from tenants need not amount to carrying on a business. Hence the joint ownership of property does not of itself make the owners partners. Similarly, if a group of investors forms a syndicate to hold a portfolio of securities, this arrangement does not amount to carrying on a business unless the investors engage in the trade of buying and selling shares, rather than merely retaining them for investment income.

The Fact of Partnership

Not every business relationship makes the parties to the relationship partners with each other. In the first place, isolated or even intermittent transactions carried on jointly do not by themselves establish the parties as partners. Thus if two merchants in the Atlantic provinces pooled an order of goods purchased in Montreal so that they could fill one freight car and thus obtain a lower freight rate, such an arrangement would not make them partners. Businessmen may carry on a venture with common interests in its success, yet even when these interests are of a substantial and continuing nature the venture may not be a partnership. Generally speaking, the sharing of *gross receipts* does not create a partnership: if an owner of a theatre were to rent it to a drama group and one of the terms of the contract of rental was that he would receive ten per cent of the gross receipts, such an arrangement would not make the owner a partner in the venture of producing a play.

On the other hand, a receipt of *a share of the profits* of the business is evidence tending to establish a partnership. Without other facts tending to show that a partnership exists, the mere sharing of profits alone is not sufficient evidence; and in particular it is insufficient evidence if the sharing of profits is part of an arrangement to (a) repay a debt owed, (b) pay an employee or agent of the business as part of his remuneration, (c) pay a widow, widower or child of a deceased partner an annuity, (d) repay an advance of money made as a loan by which the lender is to receive a rate of interest varying with the profits, (e) pay the seller of a business an amount for goodwill varying with the profits. None of the above payments makes the recipient of the payment a partner in the business.[4]

In the absence of one of the above specific situations, it is virtually impossible to imagine circumstances in which the only evidence available would be the fact that a person is sharing in the profits of a business. A person receiving a share of profits has usually contributed property or money to the business. Even though partners often share profits in a ratio other than one based on capital contribution, nonetheless the courts consider profit-sharing which coincides with this ratio strong evidence of partnership. Another important factor is whether the person receiving the profits has taken part in the management of the business. Evidence showing that he has taken some active role in the business, particularly in making decisions on important matters, when added to the fact that he has shared in the profits of the business, will usually suffice to establish him as a partner. A person may also find himself liable as a partner by estoppel if he allows a third party to rely on a representation made by him or by anyone else that he is a partner in the firm and as a result of that representation the third party advances credit to the firm. The situations that may arise are, of course, limitless: the above discussion is intended to illustrate only some of the questions that arise most frequently.

The Liability of a Partner

What is the significance of deciding that a particular venture is a partnership and identifying a person as a partner in the venture? The significance lies primarily in the partner's unlimited liability to outsiders who have dealt with the partnership. Generally speaking, a person who is held to be a partner becomes personally responsible together with the other partners for the debts and liabilities of the partnership. In particular: (a) "every partner in a firm is liable jointly with the other partners for all the debts and obligations of the firm incurred while he is a partner;" (b) he is liable for "any wrongful act or omission of any partners acting in the ordinary course of the business of the firm," in other words, he is liable for their negligence or other torts; (c) a partner is liable for a misapplication of any trust funds which have been placed in the care of the partnership.[5]

Probably the greatest risk of liability to which a partner subjects himself results from the possible contractual obligations of the partnership. "Every partner is an agent of the firm and his other partners for the purpose of the business of the partnership, and the acts of every partner who does any act for carrying on in the usual way business of the kind carried on by the firm of which he is a member, bind the firm and its partners,"[6] unless the authority of the partner has been restricted by agreement with the other partners and the third party knows of this restriction. Any acts done by a partner within his usual authority

---

[4] B.C., s. 4; Ont., s. 3; N.S., s. 4.
[5] B.C., ss. 11 to 14; Ont., ss. 10 to 13; N.S., ss. 11 to 14.
[6] B.C., s. 8; Ont., s. 6; N.S., s. 7.

and relied upon by an outsider will bind the firm and all the partners. Thus, a restriction placed upon the authority of a partner has the same effect as a restriction placed upon the authority of an agent by his principal: it does not affect outsiders who do not have knowledge of the restriction.

If, as the result of a contractual obligation, the commission of a tort, or the misapplication of trust funds, the liabilities of a partnership exceed its assets, then a creditor or injured party, having obtained judgment against the partnership and exhausted its assets in trying to satisfy the judgment, may seize the personal assets of any partner or partners until the judgment has been satisfied. Thus, serious misconduct or negligence on the part of one partner can easily create so large a liability on the part of the partnership that it drains the assets of even the wealthiest partner in the firm. Hence we can see the great importance of learning whether, as a question of fact, a partnership has been created.

In principle, a person is liable only for the obligations of a partnership created while he is a member of the firm. Hence, "a person who is admitted as a partner into an existing firm does not thereby become liable to the creditors of the firm for anything done before he became a partner," and "a partner who retires from a firm does not thereby cease to be liable for partnership debts or obligations incurred before his retirement."[7] The only way he may free himself from his obligations is by novation between the partners remaining in the firm, its creditors, and himself.[8] Even after retiring from a partnership, a partner may be liable by estoppel to third parties who reasonably believe he is still a member of the firm and advance credit to the firm in reliance on his membership. A retiring partner may free himself from this liability by carrying out the requirements of the Partnership Act.[9] Thus, an advertisement in the official gazette of the province is notice to persons generally who had not dealt with the firm before the retiring partner left the firm, but all persons who have dealt with the firm on a fairly regular basis before the partner's retirement must receive actual notice of the retirement if the retiring partner is to be fully protected. It is customary, therefore, to send notices to all those persons who have dealt with the firm more or less recently, depending on the nature of the business. Estoppel does not apply when a partner dies. His estate is not liable for credit extended to the firm after his death, even though the creditors do not know he has died.[10]

Does a Partnership Have a Separate Personality?

In the next chapter, on corporation law, we shall discuss in considerably more detail the significance of the separate personality of a group. It has been established as a matter of law that a corporation does have a separate personality of its own. In the law of partnership the position is somewhat confused and doubtful. Perhaps the most widely-held view is a strict one that a partnership has no in-

---

[7] B.C., s. 20; Ont., s. 18; N.S., s. 19.
[8] See Chapter 14 under "Discharge by Agreement" (Substituted Agreement).
[9] B.C., s. 39; Ont., s. 36; N.S., s. 38.
[10] *Ibid*.

dependent existence and merely represents the collective rights and duties of all the partners.

In actual practice, however, and in some of its legal implications, a partnership does have a semi-separate existence of its own. For example, *partnership creditors* have first call against partnership assets before the *personal creditors* of an individual partner. This is so because until the creditors of the partnership have been paid, it is impossible to distribute the share of an individual partner. If, after these creditors are paid, no assets remain, then the partner has no share for his personal creditors to seize.

Another instance of this separation occurs in the rule that a deceased partner's personal creditors have first call against the personal assets of his estate.[11] Thus, if the partnership assets are insufficient to pay off the partnership creditors, they must wait for the personal creditors to be paid out of the personal estate of the deceased partner before they can take what is left in order to satisfy their debt. Under the Bankruptcy Act, this rule applies also to the estate of a living partner who becomes bankrupt.[12]

Again, real property held by a partnership is treated according to the usual rules governing real property as far as a partnership is concerned, but in so far as the individual partners are concerned, their interest in the real property is considered personal property. Thus, neither dower rights nor homestead rights apply to partnership property.

Fourthly, a partnership may bring an action in the name of the partnership without naming all the partners as plaintiffs, and a third party may sue a partnership in its partnership name without naming all the partners as defendants. Thus, for the purposes of court action, the partnership may be treated as a separate entity. It is, in fact, desirable to sue a partnership in the firm name rather than in the names of the individual partners: all the provincial acts have incorporated a rather anomalous rule, developed in the case law prior to the acts, that partners are liable only *jointly* for debts and obligations of the firm. The significance of this rule is that only one cause of action arises from the obligation. If by inadvertence or ignorance of the facts a plaintiff brings action against some of the partners and obtains judgment against them, his rights will be exhausted, and if he later discovers that there were other partners, he will not be able to sue them. This risk is eliminated if he sues the defendants in the firm name, as all provinces now permit him to do. Once the assets of the firm are exhausted, he may go against the assets of any of the partners. We should note that the rule concerning joint liability does not apply to actions based upon tort or breach of trust; in either of these cases a plaintiff may bring a subsequent action against partners who were not parties to the original action. Such liability is called *joint and several liability*.

Finally, as an accounting matter, a partnership is treated as a separate entity with its own assets, liabilities, and financial statements.

---

[11] B.C., s. 11; Ont., s. 10; N.S., s. 11.
[12] R.S.C. 1970, c. B-3, s. 113.

THE RELATION OF PARTNERS TO ONE ANOTHER

In the event that certain matters are not expressly covered in a partnership agreement, the Partnership Act sets out a number of implied terms that will apply. Unfortunately, although all the provinces have adopted the English Act, they have rearranged the sections to conform to their customary way of setting down statutes. The result is that the numbering of no provincial Partnership Act conforms either to the English Act or to the Act of another province. Generally speaking, the sections concerned with the relations of partners to one another start at about section 20 and embrace the succeeding dozen sections. For convenience we shall use the numbering of the Manitoba Act as representative of the general scheme.[13] The main implied terms are summarized below, with explanatory comment where necessary.

S. 23(1). "All property and rights and interests in property originally brought into the partnership stock or acquired, whether by purchase or otherwise, on account of the firm or for the purposes or in the course of the partnership's business are called . . . 'partnership property' and must be held and applied by the partners exclusively for the purposes of the partnership, and in accordance with the partnership agreement." A partner is therefore not entitled to use the property for his private purposes. All property bought with money belonging to the firm is deemed to have been bought on account of the firm and is available only for the use of the firm.

S. 27(a). "All partners are entitled to share equally in the capital and profits of the business and must contribute equally towards the losses . . . ''

S. 27(b). If a partner incurs expenses or personal liabilities "in the ordinary and proper conduct of the business of the firm," or in doing anything to preserve the business or property of the firm, the firm must indemnify him for these expenses or liabilities.

S. 27(c). If a partner contributes to the partnership a sum of money or other valuable consideration in excess of what he has agreed to subscribe under the partnership agreement, he is entitled to interest at the rate of five per cent on the value of the excess contribution while it remains with the firm.

S. 27(e). "Every partner may take part in the management of the partnership business." In small partnerships, this implied term is occasionally varied. For example, a father who takes a son into partnership may wish to reserve the management of the firm to himself. Very large partnerships, such as large law firms, often have two or three classes of partners, and it may be that only the senior partners may take part in the management of the firm.

S. 27(f). "No partner shall be entitled to remuneration for acting in the partnership business." This term is often varied according to the circumstances of the partnership arrangement. If one partner is the managing partner who hopes to derive his livelihood from the partnership business, whereas the other partner or partners are merely investing partners, the partnership agreement will often

---

[13] R.S.M. 1970, c. P30.

provide that he will be "paid" a weekly salary. Sometimes the payment of this salary will be considered merely an advance on his share of the partnership profits, that is, as drawings. It will be calculated as part of the profits at the end of the financial year and deducted from his share. In other instances, he will be entitled to this salary as his fee for managing the partnership, and only profits in excess of his salary will be divided among all the partners.

S. 27(g). "No person may be introduced as a partner without the consent of all existing partners."

S. 27(h). "Any difference arising as to ordinary matters connected with the partnership business may be decided by a majority of the partners, but no change may be made in the nature of the partnership business without the consent of all existing partners." In case of a serious deadlock this provision can be troublesome. The minority may insist that the particular decision did not concern an ordinary matter but affected the *nature* of the partnership business.

S. 27(i). "The partnership books are to be kept at the place of business of the partnership or the principal place if there is more than one and every partner may, when he thinks fit, have access to and inspect and copy any of them."

S. 31. "Partners are bound to render true accounts and full information of all things affecting the partnership to any partner or his legal representative." The only circumstances under which this term and the previous one might be varied would be in a partnership having several classes of partners. It is possible that by express agreement the most junior group of partners might not have access to all the books and records of the partnership. Even such a reservation, however, would be restricted to a narrow class of information.

S. 32(1). "Every partner must account to the firm for any benefit derived by him without the consent of the other partners from any transaction concerning the partnership or from any use by him of the partnership property, name or business connection."

S. 33. "Where a partner without the consent of the other partners carries on any business of the same nature as and competing with that of the firm, he must account for and pay over to the firm all profits made by him in that business." These terms are varied occasionally according to the nature and requirements of the partnership. For example, a businessman might be carrying on a retail business in the downtown area and subsequently enter into a partnership to carry on a similar business in a suburban shopping centre. These two businesses might be considered "of the same nature and competing with" each other. As a term of the partnership agreement, the partner owning the downtown business would require the partners in the suburban business to consent to his continuing in business at his downtown location.

S. 34(1). A partnership is, by its very nature, a personal relationship between the partners. A person enters into a partnership with another in the belief that the other person has the desired qualities for the business venture. As one would expect, therefore, no partner may assign his share in the partnership, either absolutely or by way of mortgage, so as to permit the assignees to take over his duties or "to interfere in the management or administration of the partnership business or affairs, or to require any accounts of the partnership transactions, or to inspect the partnership books''. An assignee may, however, "receive the share of profits to which the assigning partner would otherwise be entitled and the assignee must accept the account of profits agreed to by the partners.''

TERMINATION OF PARTNERSHIP

Implied Statutory Rules

The dozen sections of the Partnership Acts following those just discussed provide a further series of implied terms dealing with the dissolution of the firm. In addition, two sections found in the earlier group are relevant to dissolution and are discussed briefly below:

S. 29. "Where no fixed term is agreed upon for the duration of the partnership, any partner may determine the partnership at any time on giving notice of his intention so to do to all other partners.'' The notice so given may be oral or in writing. If the partnership was originally constituted by deed, however, a notice in writing signed by the partner giving it is necessary.

S. 30. "Where a partnership entered into for a fixed term is continued after the term has expired and without any express new agreement, the rights and duties of the partners remain the same as they were at the expiration of the term so far as is consistent with the incidence of a partnership at will.'' A *partnership at will* is one having no fixed term. Thus, if the partners continue to act in the same manner as they acted during the term of the agreement, it is presumed that the partnership continues, except for the fixed term. Without such continuing conduct, however, the partnership is dissolved by the expiration of a fixed term. Similarly, if it was entered into for a single venture or undertaking, it expires by the termination of that venture or undertaking.

S. 36(1). "Subject to any agreement between the partners, every partnership is dissolved as regards all the partners by the death or bankruptcy or insolvency of any partner.'' This term, perhaps more than any other, is varied by the partnership agreement. Even in a simple partnership between two persons, their agreement should provide for some means of ascertaining the value of the partnership upon the death or insolvency of either of them so that the remaining partner may save the business from collapse and may buy out the share of the deceased or insolvent partner. In partnerships having large assets and many members, the operation of this implied term dissolving the partnership could be disastrous. Accordingly the partnership agreement usually provides that the partnership will continue in existence upon the death or insolvency of any partner. Varying kinds of arrangements may form a part of the partnership agreement to provide for buying out the share of a deceased partner, usually by the use of life insurance schemes. The problems involved are primarily financial rather than legal or technical. These arrangements must take into account the ability of the remaining partners to pay for the share of the deceased or insolvent partner, methods for ascertaining the value of that share, and the tax consequences of a particular method.

S. *36(2).* "A partnership may, at the option of the other partners, be dissolved if any partner suffers his share of the partnership property to be charged under this act for his separate debts." Thus, if one of the partners does assign or charge his interest in the partnership to his creditors, the remaining partners may dissolve the partnership if they choose to do so.

Dissolution by Law

A partnership is essentially a contractual arrangement, and is accordingly dissolved by any event which makes it unlawful for the business of the firm to be carried on or for members of the firm to carry it on in partnership. The results here are in keeping with the general law of contract concerning illegality.

Even when there is disagreement amongst the partners concerning dissolution, or where dissolution at a specific time would be contrary to the terms of the partnership agreement, nevertheless, on the application by one or more partners the court may order the partnership dissolved under the following circumstances:

S. *38(a).* "Where a partner is found . . . [mentally incompetent] . . . or is shown to the satisfaction of the court to be of permanently unsound mind . . ." In these circumstances, the application may be made on behalf of the incompetent partner as well as by any other partner.

S. *38(b).* "Where a partner, other than the partner suing, becomes in any other way permanently incapable of performing his part in the partnership contract."

S. *38(c).* "Where a partner, other than the partner suing, has been guilty of such conduct as, in the opinion of the court, regard being had to the nature of the business, is calculated to prejudicially affect the carrying on of the business." For example, if a partner in a brokerage firm was convicted of theft, his partner could apply successfully to the court to have the partnership dissolved even though the partnership was by agreement to continue for a fixed term.

S. *38(d).* "Where a partner, other than the partner suing, wilfully or persistently commits a breach of the partnership agreement, or otherwise so conducts himself in matters relating to the partnership business that it is not reasonably practicable for the other partner or partners to carry on the business in partnership with him."

S. *38(e).* "Where in any case circumstances have arisen which in the opinion of the court, render it just and equitable that the partnership is dissolved." This latter provision is a general catch-all clause, giving courts a wide discretion to prevent serious injustice to partners when unforeseen circumstances arise.

S. *40.* "Where a partnership has been dissolved or a partner has retired, and where, if applicable, a declaration of the dissolution has been registered under the Business Names Registration Act, any partner may publicly give notice of the dissolution or retirement and may require the other partner or partners to concur for that purpose in all necessary or proper acts, if any, which cannot be done without his or their concurrence." Thus, if one partner brings about the dissolution of a partnership, either under the provisions of the agreement or by order of the court, he may require the other partners to do all necessary acts to make the dissolution effective. For example, he could require other signing partners to sign cheques or any other documents necessary to discharge liabilities to creditors and to free the assets of the partnership so that they might be liquidated and divided amongst the partners.

S. 42. "On the dissolution of a partnership every partner is entitled as against the other partners in the firm and all persons claiming through them in respect of their interest as partners, to have the property of the partnership applied in payment of the debts and liabilities of the firm and to have the surplus assets after such payment applied in payment of what may be due the partners respectively . . .''

S. 47. "In settling accounts between the partners after a dissolution of partnership the following rules shall, subject to any agreement, be observed:

(a) Losses including losses and deficiencies of capital are to be paid first out of profits, next out of capital, and lastly, if necessary, by the partners individually in the proportion in which they were entitled to share in the profits.

(b) The assets of the firm including the sums if any contributed by the partners to make up losses and deficiencies of capital, are to be applied in the following manner and order:

(i) in paying the debts and liabilities of the firm to persons who are not partners therein.

(ii) in paying to each partner rateably what is due from the firm to him for advances as distinguished from capital.

(iii) in paying to each partner rateably what is due from the firm to him in respect to capital.

(iv) the ultimate residue, if any, is to be divided among the partners in the proportion in which profits are divisible.''

The above provisions are usually strictly adhered to. In some special circumstances where, let us say, a relatively poor partner has invested the whole of his assets in a rather risky partnership venture, the partners might possibly provide between themselves that if liabilities exceeded the assets of the partnership itself upon dissolution, the balance would be borne wholly by the wealthier partner. With this rather limited exception, however, the above rules would apply in almost all cases.[14]

---

[14] See Garner v. Murray [1904] 1 Ch. 57 for an interpretation of this section when partners make unequal capital contributions or share losses unequally and one of them with a deficiency of capital is insolvent. See also Smails, *Accounting Principles and Practice* (5th ed.), pp. 256-60. Toronto: The Ryerson Press, 1954.

THE PARTNERSHIP AGREEMENT

As we have seen, parties may be held by the courts to be partners simply by their conduct. As a result, third parties have little interest in the terms of a partnership agreement: unless a third party is made aware of the internal arrangements of the partnership, he is entitled to assume that the usual rules as codified in the Partnership Act apply. The partnership is bound by a contract made with the third party provided it was within the usual authority of the partner making the contract, and it is liable for torts committed against third parties within the usual rules of agency and master and servant.

The significance of the partnership agreement lies in the relations of the partners among themselves. A partnership agreement may be wholly oral and yet be valid and enforceable provided it does not come within one of the sections of the Statute of Frauds. The Statute of Frauds affects a contract of partnership only if by its terms it extends beyond one year and performance has not commenced. Once the partnership begins to operate, the statute has no effect.[15] As we know, however, an oral agreement is subject to the flaws of memory of the parties to that agreement, and if only for certainty it is worthwhile to have a written record of the partnership agreement. Of course, we may ask the question, "Why have an agreement at all, whether oral or written?" If we refer briefly to the law of marriage, which concerns another and older form of "partnership", we find that the state takes a definite interest in marriage and lays down as a matter of law certain rights and duties of the spouses. Within comparatively narrow limits, the parties to a marriage can vary the usual rights and duties. If they wish to do so, however, they must be very clear about these variations. Such variations are rare when young, previously unmarried persons wed. They are more common between elderly people, a widow and a widower, let us say, who decide to marry for companionship in old age. Often they will wish their separate estates to go to their own children and not to the children of the spouse. Accordingly, they will enter into an ante-nuptial agreement, setting out specifically what will happen to their respective estates on the death of each of them.

The law of business partnerships sets down far fewer restrictions upon the agreements or the relations among the partners. They may agree to whatever terms they wish, provided the terms are not illegal and do not offend public policy. Business partnerships, like marriages, can be perilous ventures, and probably because dissolution of the partnership is somewhat easier, a higher proportion of partnerships break up after a very short time. Estimates vary, but it is reasonably safe to say that only one partnership in three survives the first two years. The reasons for dissolution are extremely varied. Many are dissolved because the business venture has proved unprofitable. Others are dissolved because the venture has proved very profitable and the partners have gone on to form a limited company. Still others dissolve because of an inevitable conflict of

---

[15] Burdon v. Barkus (1862) 45 E.R. 1098. In British Columbia this requirement has been abolished: Statute Law Amendment Act, St. of B.C. 1958, c. 52, s. 17.

personalities which the parties cannot resolve. A large portion of profitable partnerships are destroyed by misunderstanding or mistrust. The failure to decide important issues in advance often leads to the kind of misunderstanding and
mistrust which creates an eventually irreparable breach between the parties.

The main purpose of a partnership agreement is therefore to set out, as
carefully and as clearly as possible, the objects of the partnership, the responsibilities of each of the partners, the capital contributions of each to the firm, the
time and energy that each will devote to the business of the firm, the respective
shares of profits and losses that each partner will take, procedures for settling disagreements (usually by arbitration), and provisions for dissolution or for one or
more of the partners to buy out the other partners.

In order to draft an effective partnership agreement, the parties must be candid with each other at the very outset and they must deal with the most probable
events that might upset the partnership or change its course of action. A well-
drafted, carefully-thought-out partnership agreement is of itself no guarantee of a
successful partnership. The other elements of a sound business idea, reasonably
good luck, mutual trust and good faith, and diligence of application must be
present for a partnership to succeed: a well-drawn agreement simply minimizes
one of the hazards.

If only for the reason of subjective bias, it is virtually impossible for
partners to draft their own agreement. The usual problems of ambiguous words
and unconscious interpretations favourable to the individuals concerned can
create the same misunderstandings that arise in the law of contract. In addition,
individual partners are unaware of many of the pitfalls that accumulated experience and learning in the field may avoid. For these reasons a partnership
agreement is, perhaps more than any other type of agreement, one that should be
drafted with expert advice and assistance. If the parties to the agreement are investing large sums in the venture, then each should have his own legal counsel to
help protect his investment.

REGISTRATION OF PARTNERSHIPS

Almost all provincial jurisdictions require the filing in a local registry office of a
declaration under the terms of the Act giving such essential information as the
names and addresses of each partner and the name under which they intend to
carry on business, the time during which the partnership has existed, and an acknowledgment that the persons named in the declaration are the only members of
the partnership. Similarly, declarations must be filed in case of any change in the
membership of the partnership or in the name of the partnership. Further, the Act
requires a declaration of the dissolution of the partnership.

The penalties for failure to carry out the requirements of the statute vary
from province to province. In Ontario and Nova Scotia they are particularly
severe; for example, the Ontario Act states, ''no partnership in respect of which a
declaration has not been filed as required by this Act and no member thereof is
capable of maintaining any action or other proceeding in any court in Ontario in

respect of any contract made in connection with the business carried on by the partnership.''[16] In addition, the Acts usually provide that failure to comply with the requirements is an offence, subject to a fine. The records of the declaration of partnership are open to the public and may be examined upon payment of a small fee.

The purposes of this registration system are quite clear. It provides the minimum of essential information about the partnership and particularly about the names of partners in the partnership firm, thus enabling a plaintiff to serve each partner with notice of an action where he deems it wise to do so. It is also helpful to prospective creditors or other suppliers in checking the accuracy of information given by a member of the partnership concerning the membership of the firm.

LIMITED PARTNERSHIP

All provinces except Nova Scotia and Prince Edward Island have either a Limited Partnership Act or a set of provisions in their Partnership Act permitting the carrying on of business under certain very restricted conditions, with limited liability. These Acts came into force about the same time that the private limited company form (discussed in the next chapter) became available for general use. In the great majority of cases, the limited company is a more useful method for obtaining limited liability. As a result, very little use has been made of limited partnerships.

The major requirement for the formation of a limited partnership is that there must be one or more general partners, that is, partners with unlimited liability. The remaining partners may have a liability limited to the amount paid in cash by each of them as a sum of capital to the limited partnership. The name of one or more of the general partners must be part of the partnership name. Some provinces permit the use of the name of a limited partner, but he must be clearly designated as such in a line immediately beneath the name of the partnership upon letterheads, confirmations to customers, and statements of account. Otherwise, he is deemed to be a general partner. In the other provinces, the names of the limited partners may not be used at all: if they are used, they become general partners immediately.

All the Acts prohibit a limited partner from taking an active part in the management of the partnership. The penalty for taking an active part is, again, liability as a general partner. The words of prohibition vary considerably in each of the statutes.[17] A limited partner would be "taking an active part" if he were personally to transact any business on account of the firm or be employed for that purpose as an agent or as a lawyer; but he can examine the records of the firm, inquire as to its progress and advise as to its management without incurring the

---

[16] Partnerships Registration Act, R.S.O. 1970, c. 340, s. 9(1). See also R.S.N.S. 1967, c. 225, s. 19.
[17] See, for example, Partnership Act, R.S.M. 1970, c. P30, s. 63(1).

liability of a general partner. The result is that a limited partner who attempts to take part in the management of the firm does so at a considerable personal risk. He may find himself in the dilemma that if he does not interfere, the business may fail completely; yet if he chooses to exercise some control in order to save the business, he will incur unlimited liability. For this reason more than any other, limited partnerships have been rarely used.

The limited partnership provisions set out more stringent regulations for registration than are demanded of ordinary partnerships. Failure to comply with requirements of detailed essential information also results in the loss of limited liability.

QUESTIONS FOR REVIEW

1. What purpose did the codification of partnership law serve? Why has the statute remained unchanged?
2. In what sense is a partner an agent?
3. What is the main value of the partnership agreement?
4. What are two main characteristics that make a joint undertaking a partnership?
5. Why might a person be anxious to disclaim being a partner in a firm?
6. A partner's duty of good faith is similar to that of an agent. State two situations where a duty would arise.
7. Jones and Smith enter into a partnership agreement written on the back of a postcard. Does this document constitute the whole of the agreement between them?
8. What is partnership by estoppel?
9. Fry, a partner in the firm of Potter, Skillet, and Fry, assigns his interest in the firm to Cook without the consent of his partners. What are Cook's rights? What are the partners' rights?
10. Why is it advantageous to sue a partnership in the firm name?
11. Grey and Burton have formed a limited partnership. Burton is a limited partner. Describe Grey's position. What types of conduct should Burton avoid if he is to continue to enjoy limited liability?
12. Name two important instances of joint undertakings for profit that are not partnerships.
13. In what circumstances will unanimous approval rather than a simple majority be required in a business decision of a partnership?
14. What type of partnership results when a group of partners continue to carry on business together after their agreement has expired?

CASES FOR DISCUSSION

CASE 1

Kuli owned a tobacco farm and entered into an agreement with Magory whereby Magory would:

(1) work the land for Kuli for one year;

(2) obtain possession of a house on the land during that period;

(3) obtain from Kuli half the necessary supplies for the land and provide the other half himself;

(4) market the crop and give half the proceeds to Kuli.

Were Kuli and Magory partners? (See *Re Imperial Leaf Tobacco Co. Ltd. and Kuli* [1940] O.W.N. 503.)

CASE 2

Hallvorson and Bowes agreed to form a partnership to carry on a restaurant business. Hallvorson agreed to pay in $1,500 as his capital contribution. The parties started operation of the restaurant before Hallvorson paid in his $1,500. Both parties worked diligently at the business for several months, all the while arguing about the respective capital contribution of each. During this period only Bowes had contributed capital. Finally Bowes ordered Hallvorson to leave. Hallvorson sued for a declaration that he was a partner even though he had not contributed his capital share.

What should be the result? (See *Hallvorson v. Bowes* (1913) 2 W.W.R. 586.)

CASE 3

A, B, and *C* carried on the business of building contractors in partnership without a written agreement. *A* was the founder of the business and still managed it. The success of the firm had been due throughout its existence to the capacity and personal qualities of *A,* who financed it and skilfully ran it. By oral agreement, each partner had the right to periodically draw such sums from profits of the firm as were necessary for his living expenses — such withdrawals to approximate the proportionate interest of each partner. There was no express agreement concerning the sharing of profits.

A, without the knowledge of *B* and *C,* invested excess funds of the firm in property entirely unrelated to the business of the firm, the profits of which he claimed for himself. These investments in no way interfered with the operations of the firm's business, and he eventually replaced the funds he had taken.

What are *B*'s and *C*'s rights? (See *Kelly v. Kelly* (1913) 3 W.W.R. 799.)

CASE 4

Wright carried on business as a stockbroker in Toronto. By agreement with Randolph, a New York broker, Randolph transacted on the New York Stock Exchange such business as in his discretion he saw fit to accept for Wright's clients and charged rates agreed upon by the parties. The parties shared the fees realized from these transactions equally. Ryckman, a creditor of Randolph, started an action against him and joined Wright as his partner.

What is the position of Wright? (See *Ryckman v. Randolph* (1910) 20 O.L.R. 1.)

CHAPTER 28

The Nature of a Corporation and its Composition

THE NATURE OF A CORPORATION

The business corporation or limited company is the dominant feature of the modern business world. Not only is it the main instrument of big business, it also rivals partnership as a means of carrying on smaller enterprises.

A corporation is a *person* in the eyes of the law, that is, it is a *legal person*. To understand the nature of a corporation we must first comprehend the idea of a legal person. A legal person is an entity recognized by the legal system as having rights and duties under that system. At first glance it might seem obvious that each human being is a legal person and that only human beings can have rights and obligations. But this is an oversimplification. The law need not recognize every *natural* person as a *legal* person: when slavery existed, a slave was not considered a legal person but a chattel with no rights or duties. He had no right to complain about mistreatment; he could not sue either his master or anyone else. Nor could his master sue him if he disobeyed. The master could physically punish him, even kill him, just as he could punish or kill his dog. Today all human beings are recognized as legal persons in civilized countries, but we do assign varying statuses and capacities to them, sometimes virtually removing legal personality, as with a person who has been judged insane.

We have said that legal personality need not coincide with human personality. Not only may it be withheld from human beings, but it may also be granted to other than human beings. It has been granted to inanimate objects, such as *idols* (in India) and *funds* (in European countries). These objects have rights and duties under the law, but, of course, they can neither insist on these rights nor carry out their duties except through human agents.

The most important non-human legal person is the corporation. The corporation evolved from the need to look after the common interests of a *group* of natural persons. Men argued about whether the group, be it a group of monks in a monastery or merchants carrying on a business, could have a "personality" distinct from each of the individual members, a *group personality* with a separate existence of its own. Scholars from the Middle Ages onward engaged in deep philosophical and political controversy about the nature of the state as a group personality and about the nature of lesser groups within the state. The political controversy still continues today, but the legal principle is firmly established, both in common law and civil law countries, that a corporation may be created as a separate and distinct legal person apart from its members. To distinguish the corporate legal person from a human legal person the corporation is sometimes called a legal *entity* rather than a legal person.[1]

There are numerous types of corporations: government corporations created to carry on special governmental activities — the Bank of Canada, the Canadian Broadcasting Corporation, Central Mortgage and Housing Corporation, Air Canada; municipal corporations to run local government; charitable corporations — the Red Cross, the Heart Foundation, the Ford Foundation; educational institutions; and business corporations, the most numerous type of all. For the purposes of this book, we are concerned only with the business corporation.

THE SIGNIFICANCE OF A SEPARATE CORPORATE EXISTENCE

The significance of the separate legal personality of a business corporation can best be understood when compared with partnership under the following subheadings:

Limited Liability

As we have seen, each partner is liable for the debts of the partnership to the limit of his personal assets. A corporation is liable for its own debts, but its shareholders are liable only to the amount of the price of the shares they have purchased from the corporation. If, as is usual, a shareholder has paid the full price, he can lose no more in the event that creditors seize the corporation's assets: if he still owes the corporation part of the purchase price, his liability is *limited* to the payment of the balance of the price. It is for this reason, the limited liability of their shareholders, that business corporations are referred to as limited companies.

Transfer of Ownership

A partner cannot retire from a partnership and release himself from his liabilities

---

[1] See Bonham and Soberman, "The Nature of Corporate Personality", in *Studies in Canadian Company Law* (Ziegel, ed.) Vol. I, Ch. 1.

unilaterally. He must bargain for his release both with his partners and his creditors; he may even be liable for debts contracted *after* his retirement, unless he has given notice to persons who habitually deal with the partnership and has fulfilled the requirements of the Partnership Act. Since a shareholder has no liability for corporate debts even while he retains his shares, creditors of the corporation have no interest and no say in what he does with his shares. The shareholder may sever all connections with the company simply by transferring his shares to another person.[2] Consequently, anyone may buy the shares and is entitled to all the rights of a shareholder upon registration of the transfer at the company's office.

Management

A partnership is unsuitable for a venture involving a large number of investors. Each partner, as agent of the partnership, poses a danger of binding a partnership to an unwise and perhaps ruinous contract, and as the number of partners increases the risk is correspondingly greater. This state of affairs would discourage many prospective investors, especially when added to the perils of unlimited liability for partnership debts. In contrast, shareholders have no authority to bind their company to contractual obligations — only officers of the company may do so. A partnership usually requires unanimity on major business decisions, a requirement that could stalemate a firm with a large number of partners. In a company, management is delegated to an elected board of directors that reaches decisions by simple majority votes. Major decisions referred back to the shareholders do not require unanimity but at most, a two-thirds or three-quarters majority, depending on the issue for decision and also on the requirements of the corporation law statutes in the jurisdiction.

Continuous Existence

We have seen that the death or bankruptcy of a partner in the absence of special provisions in the partnership agreement dissolves a partnership. Even when provisions are made in advance to continue the partnership and to pay off the share of the deceased or bankrupt partner, the procedure is often cumbersome and expensive. A corporation exists independently of any of its shareholders. A person's shares may be transferred by gift or by sale, by seizure by his creditors, or by statute transmitting them to his personal representative on his death, yet none of these events affects the existence of the corporation. The corporation continues in existence perpetually unless it is dissolved by order of a court, by failure to comply with statutory regulations, or by voluntary surrender of its legal status to the government.

Loyalty

A partner owes a strong duty of loyalty to the partnership, usually making it im-

---

[2] Subject to restrictions placed on transfer of shares in private or closely held corporations. See the section, ''Broadly Held and Closely Held Corporations'' below.

possible for him to carry on another business independently and on his own behalf without the consent of all the other partners, or to enter into contracts with the partnership on his own behalf. A shareholder owes no such duty to the corporation: he may carry on any independent business himself and may trade freely with the corporation as if he were a stranger.

Separation of Ownership and Management

The separation of ownership and management ranks with limited liability as a most important feature of the business corporation. These two features permit the raising of large amounts of capital: they enable the investor to invest a specific sum of money and receive a regular return on it, without either taking any additional risk beyond the sum invested or having to take an active part in management of business affairs. Of course, the investor may choose to take an active role in the corporation by running for office, or he may sell his interest if he becomes dissatisfied with the operation of the company; but it is primarily the possibility that he may limit his risk and take no active part that has made corporate investment so attractive to the investor generally.

Although at one time the leading shareholders in a corporation were usually its managers as well, since World War I there has been a steadily increasing separation between those who invest and those who manage. The most distinctive development of the large corporation on this continent is this separation of management and ownership.[3] The separation is, however, less pronounced in Canada than in the United States becuase many large Canadian corporations are wholly-owned subsidiaries of foreign parent corporations.

LIMITATIONS ON SEPARATE CORPORATION EXISTENCE

Convenience and Abuse

One can easily fall into the habit of thinking of a corporation as a real creature *independent of the law,* but it is a mistake to do so. We must remember that a corporation, in so far as it may enter into legal relations, must be considered a creature of the legal system with no existence apart from that system. A legal system which has granted recognition to a corporation may just as easily withdraw it whenever necessary to protect interests considered more important. Thus, while the corporate form with its limited liability may be a tempting instrument for sharp dealing and fraud, the law does not assist such activity; when necessary it ignores separate corporate existence and goes behind the "corporate veil" to hold the individuals controlling the corporation responsible for their acts. On the other hand, if the law were to ignore corporate personality on very slight pretext, it would be perilous to rely upon the advantages of incorporation,

---

[3] For a detailed study of this subject see Berle and Means, *The Modern Corporation and Private Property.* New York: The Macmillan Company, 1932.

and this most useful tool of commerce would become ineffective. We are confronted here by conflicting interests of society: the desire for a reliable and useful tool of business and the desire to do justice and prevent the tool from being improperly employed. In the main, the attitude of the courts has been to accept corporate personality at face value and to go behind it only as a last resort. The courts have proceeded cautiously — many would say timidly — treating each case on its own particular merits. As a result, it is difficult to state consistent general principles about when the courts will look behind the corporate veil and when they will refuse to do so. We shall examine the basic position taken and discuss several areas where the courts have gone beyond the corporate entity to deal directly with the controllers of the enterprise.

Salomon's Case

The classic case on the inviolability of the corporation as a separate entity came before the House of Lords in 1897 in *Salomon v. Salomon & Co. Ltd.*:[4]

> Salomon had carried on the successful business of shoe manufacturer for many years. In 1892 he formed a corporation in which he held almost all the shares (the few remaining shares being held by members of his family) and sold his business to the corporation. As part of the purchase price he took back bonds as a secured creditor of the corporation. Unfortunately a series of strikes in the shoe industry eventually drove the corporation into insolvency, and a trustee was appointed to wind it up. Salomon tried to enforce his rights as a secured creditor, but was resisted by the trustee for the general creditors. The trustee claimed that the corporation was merely a sham for Salomon, that he was the true owner of the business and the true debtor — as such he should not be permitted to act as a creditor and take priority over his own creditors but should surrender the bonds to them and pay off all debts owed by the corporation. The lower courts supported the trustee's position, but the House of Lords decided in favour of Salomon. The Lords said that either the corporation was a true legal entity or it was not. Since there was no fraud nor any intention to deceive, since all transactions had been fully disclosed to all parties and the statutory regulations complied with, the corporation was duly created and had validly granted the bonds to Salomon. Accordingly, he ranked as a secured creditor of the corporation.

The decision came as a surprise to the commercial and legal worlds of the day. Many writers believed (and some still do) that the court had gone too far in giving an independent existence to the corporation. Nevertheless, as a leading writer on the subject has said, "Since the *Salomon* case, the complete separation of the company and its members has never been doubted."[5] Lest it be thought that Salomon was a shrewd profiteer, we should note that he did his best to save

---

[4] [1897] A.C. 22.
[5] Gower, *Modern Company Law* (3rd ed.) p. 71. London: Stevens & Sons Ltd. 1969.

the company, even to the extent of pledging the bonds to raise money which he put back into the company. The action was first started by the pledgee of the bonds, who demanded that the bonds be honoured.

Undoubtedly some later cases have carried the logic of *Salomon's* case to absurd lengths. For example, it has been held that the owner of a business who transferred all its assets to a corporation of which he was the sole owner, but neglected to transfer the benefit of the fire insurance policy on the assets as well, could recover nothing when these assets were destroyed by fire.[6] The scholastic logic, worthy of medieval philosophers, stated that the assets were owned by the corporation (true) and a shareholder has no direct ownership in these assets, but only in the corporation itself (also true), and therefore has no insurable interest in the assets! How it follows from *Salomon's* case that a shareholder has no insurable *interest* (as distinguished from ownership) in the assets of a wholly-owned corporation is beyond the writers' comprehension. Unfortunate decisions such as this have led to a dislike of *Salomon's* case, although it is generally admitted that the principle in the case has worked well in the commercial world. When the application of the *Salomon* decision leads to absurd results, courts should refuse to follow it: the sections below illustrate the movement away from "strict logic" in the application of the rule.

Taxation

The corporate entity bestows certain legitimate tax advantages, the details of which are better dealt with in a book on taxation. To prevent tax evasion, the income tax acts of almost every country including Canada have provisions that disregard the "separateness" of the corporation from its controlling shareholders and related companies. Under Canadian tax law, a corporation is charged a lower rate of tax on its first $100,000 of taxable income[7] than on taxable income exceeding that amount. Since the owners of a corporation might be tempted to incorporate several more companies, split the assets and the profits among them, and thus multiply the number of times they could take advantage of the low rate on the first $100,000, our tax law permits the $100,000 to be claimed just once on behalf of a whole group of "associated corporations" however many there may be.[8] It is interesting to note some of the descriptions of associated corporations: where one of the corporations controls the other; where both of the corporations are controlled by the same person or group of persons; where the persons in control of two corporations are "related" (within the wide meaning given by the Act) to each other.[9] For taxation purposes, then, the fact that the shareholders of two corporations are "related" makes the two corporations "associated" for the purpose of the low tax rate on the first $100,000 of taxable income. Similarly, the

---

[6] Macaura v. Northern Assurance Co. [1925] A.C. 619.
[7] Income Tax Act. St. of Can. 1970-71-72, c. 63, s. 125(1) and (2), as amended.
[8] *Ibid.*, s. 125(3).
[9] *Ibid.*, s. 256(1).

Income Tax Act may disregard corporate separateness in a sale of assets between a controlling shareholder and a corporation, or between two related corporations, in order to prevent tax evasion by manipulation of the sale price.[10]

Residence

It is often important to ascertain where a corporation "resides" in order to decide whether a particular rule or statute applies to it. The concept of corporate residence has not been clearly developed; in fact, the criteria for determining the issue may vary according to the type of problem concerned. Thus, a corporation may be held to reside in state A under one statute and in state B under another.

Neither the place of incorporation nor the place of its head office necessarily determines a corporation's place of residence, although both may be important. We may look behind these formal attributes to examine such matters as the principal place of operations, of management, and the residence of the controlling shareholders — in other words, consider the human factors behind the corporate facade. These elements are frequently contradictory and do not easily lead to a clear decision about a corporation's place of residence. Generally speaking, however, when the place of incorporation and head office coincide, the presumption is that a corporation is resident in that place.

The place of residence is important in matters of taxation: generally speaking, a non-resident corporation pays taxes only on income earned within the jurisdiction, whereas a resident corporation pays taxes on its whole income wherever earned. Residence may also be crucial in determining whether a corporation is an enemy alien. In the leading case of *Daimler v. Continental Tyre*,[11] a company incorporated and carrying on business mainly in England was declared to be an enemy alien and therefore unable to bring an action in the English court because almost all of its shareholders were German nationals residing in Germany. Thus, it was the residence of the controlling shareholders that determined the residence and therefore the enemy character of the company. We may note that the company was still recognized as a legal entity — it was not considered a sham — but because of its enemy character, it lost its rights during hostilities as would a natural person who was an enemy alien.

Agency

Just as a company employs agents, it may in turn act as an agent for others. Some companies regularly engage in the business of acting as agents for others: investment dealers, shipping agents, auctioneers, foreign buying agents, and many others may be corporations. The question arises whether a company may be said to act as agent for its own shareholders, that is, to carry on a business transaction directly on behalf of its shareholders rather than for its own benefit. An

---

[10] *Ibid.*, s. 69, and ss. 251 and 252.
[11] [1916] 2 A.C. 307.

express agreement making the company an agent for its shareholders is perfectly valid, for in such cases the shareholders clearly wish the company to act for them.

It is more difficult to establish such an agency relationship when it has to be implied from the circumstances. We should note that it is sometimes the shareholders who hope to benefit from the claim that the company acted as their agent[12]; at other times the government or another outsider wishes to hold the shareholders liable as principals. *Salomon's* case was an example of the latter situation, and there the court rejected a claim by the creditors that even if the company did exist independently, it acted not for itself but as Salomon's agent. Sometimes the courts have accepted the claim and at other times have rejected it. Although it is difficult to extract a clear principle from the subsequent decisions, it seems fair to say that when the transactions very clearly indicate that the company was acting as an agent for the shareholders, the court will so hold.[13] Perhaps the most striking example of how far the courts will go occurred in *Re F. G. (Films) Ltd.*:[14]

A British film company was incorporated with a very small capital, no employees, and no business offices. Its principal shareholder was an American citizen who held 90% of the shares. It proceeded to "hire" an American film-producing company, of which the American was president, to produce a film in India. The U.S. company provided all the capital, cast, and management. The British company then attempted to register the film as one made by a British company to obtain certain tax advantages. Not only did the court refuse to hold that the U.S. company was the agent of the British company, but, looking at all the surrounding circumstances of the British company, its incorporators, its capital, and its operations, the court declared that in fact the reverse was true: the British company was acting as agent of its American shareholder and the American film company for purposes of registering the film. Accordingly, the court decided that the film was produced by the American company.

Fraud

A court will not lightly impute fraud in any transaction, for to do so is to place a serious stigma on the person so accused and perhaps induce a criminal prosecution against him. Once the court believes that fraud has been demonstrated, however, it will disregard all formal blocks in its way to hold the defrauder liable. The court will not permit the technical objection that the company as a separate entity, rather than its shareholders, has committed the fraud. One such instance occurred in *Patton v. Yukon Consolidated Gold Co.*:[15]

---

[12] Smith, Stone & Knight Ltd. v. Birmingham Corporation [1939] 4 All E.R. 116.
[13] *Ibid.*
[14] [1953] 1 W.L.R. 483.
[15] [1934] 3 D.L.R. 400.

The defendant, Treadgold, while acting as agent for a company he had helped promote, the Yukon company, bought the assets of the North Fork company for it at a high price. Treadgold owned virtually all the shares in North Fork, but did not disclose this interest to the directors of the Yukon company. In a subsequent action against him by the Yukon company for breach of his duty as an agent, he defended by stating that the North Fork company was an entirely separate entity from himself, that it was North Fork, not Treadgold, that sold its assets to the Yukon company, and that he was therefore under no duty to disclose his position as shareholder in that company. The court dismissed his contention, held that the whole scheme was one devoted "to make a secret profit for himself," and accordingly held him liable to repay all the profits made by North Fork.

There are other areas where the courts disregard the corporate entity. The above examples serve only to illustrate some of the more important instances.

METHODS OF INCORPORATION[16]

Royal Charter

The oldest method of incorporation is by royal charter granted by the King as part of his prerogative. The first companies were incorporated by this method in 16th-century England. The charter, when issued by the Crown, signified the birth of the company — from the moment of issue the corporation was in existence. Until the 19th century, all companies were created by charter, including many famous names in the development of England's empire. Some of these are still in existence, the best known to Canadians being the Hudson's Bay Company founded in 1670. A few royal charters are still issued today to universities, learned societies, and charitable institutions, but none to business corporations.

Special Acts

At the end of the 18th century, Parliament began to pass special statutes to incorporate companies for large projects which were virtually impossible to finance in any other way. These projects were usually of a semi-public nature — railroads, canals, waterworks, and other public utilities. Today, special acts are still used to incorporate such companies as the Bell Telephone Company and the Canadian Pacific Railway, and also to create special government corporations like Central Mortgage and Housing Corporation, the Canadian Broadcasting Corporation and Air Canada.

Parliament and the provincial legislatures have also passed statutes setting out procedures for the incorporation of businesses in which the public has a

---

[16] See Neuman, "Letters Patent and Memorandum of Association Companies", in *Studies in Canadian Company Law*, (Ziegel, ed.) Vol. I, Ch. 3.

special interest. In those fields where it is desirable that specific safeguards and procedures be required for the protection of the public, no one may carry on business unless he complies with the statutory provisions. Thus, all banks must be incorporated under the federal Bank Act, and trust and loan companies under the federal acts regulating these businesses or the relevant provincial statutes.

General Acts

The English system of registration. Today, almost all business corporations are incorporated under the provisions of a statute of general application. Under a statute of this type any group of persons who comply with its requirements may form a corporation. In Canada we have had a unique development, in that different types of general acts have evolved. The first type of incorporation, based on the English Companies Act, depends on Parliament rather than the royal prerogative. It is often referred to as the *registration system,* and has been adopted by the three westernmost and the two easternmost provinces. The Act requires the applicants to register a document that sets out the fundamental terms of their agreement, called a *memorandum of association.* It is the "birth certificate" of the company, the counterpart of the charter of a royal charter company. As soon as the applicants register the memorandum with the appropriate government office, the company comes into existence. We shall call companies incorporated in this manner *memorandum companies.*

The letters patent system. The provinces of Manitoba, Quebec, New Brunswick and Prince Edward Island (and the federal government, until 1976), employ a different system under their general acts. In all these jurisdictions, the incorporating document is called the *letters patent,* a direct offspring of the royal charter except that it is issued under the authority of the Crown's representative in each jurisdiction rather than directly by the Crown. Ontario used this system until the end of 1970, when it made major changes in its corporation law, to be discussed below. The federal government adopted the new Ontario procedures in 1975, but with substantial differences.

Under the letters patent system, a general statute regulates the conditions under which the Crown representative — a government agency — may issue letters patent. In procedure, the steps taken by applicants do not differ greatly from those for registering a memorandum under the English system, but there are some important differences in the result of incorporation by letters patent, as well as in terminology. Since the great majority of corporations operating in Canada have been incorporated by letters patent under either federal, Ontario or Quebec acts, and since their business operations and the sale of their securities extend throughout the country, one encounters these corporations frequently even in provinces using the registration system for incorporation within the province. In the remaining jurisdictions one encounters corporations incorporated by memorandum perhaps less frequently, but references are often drawn from and comparisons made with English law on the subject.

The certificate of incorporation system. In 1970, Ontario passed a new

Business Corporations Act.[17] This statute made a number of important changes in the constitution of business corporations, their operation, and the labels applying to corporate documents. Under the Act, incorporators sign and deliver *articles of incorporation* to the government office, but the charter obtained from the government is called a *certificate of incorporation*. Unfortunately, the terminology chosen by the Ontario government is unnecessarily confusing in the Canadian business and legal context: Ontario has adopted terms used in various parts of the United States, in particular the word "articles", which has a different current meaning in Canada. We shall note the changes in Ontario law in the appropriate sections of this and the following chapter. The many thousands of companies incorporated before the new Ontario Act came into force continue their existence under their old charters until they apply for new documents. Most of them are likely to continue for many years under their old letters patent. The changes in the law made by the 1970 Act apply to all these corporations, however, just as they do to newly incorporated businesses.

The new Canada Business Corporations Act[18] adopts the Ontario method of incorporation as well as the same terminology. For up to a five-year period, however, federally incorporated companies may remain under the old act and are governed by all its provisions.[19] Before the five-year period expires they must apply for a "certificate of continuance" under the new Act or be dissolved for failure to do so.[20]

In discussing business corporations in Canada, one must keep in mind this variety of methods of incorporation. Wherever the differences have important consequences we shall point them out.

BROADLY HELD AND CLOSELY HELD CORPORATIONS

When the first general statutes permitting incorporation of business enterprises were passed both in England and Canada in the mid 19th century, the legislators believed limited companies would be used primarily for large undertakings having many shareholders. These acts required at least seven incorporators who signed the original application to establish the company. By the turn of the century it had become evident that incorporation was also a useful and fully effective tool for family businesses — as in *Salomon's* case — and partnerships. It had further become evident that the big publicly-held corporations needed to be restrained from misleading investors. Various statutory requirements had been created to ensure disclosure and publication of a corporation's financial position, both in soliciting prospective investors and in reporting to shareholders. These regulations seemed inappropriate for the small family business, as did the requirement for seven shareholders, the latter being merely a technical require-

---

[17] R.S.O. 1970, c. 53.
[18] St. of Can. 1974-75, c. 33.
[19] *Ibid.*, s. 261(3).
[20] *Ibid.*, s. 261(8).

ment that could be satisfied by giving one share each to six employees or relatives while the true controlling shareholder held all the remaining shares.

These facts were recognized in 1908 when the British Parliament enacted provisions to permit the formation of *private companies,* distinguished from all other companies, which we shall call broadly held corporations, by the following characteristics:

(a) the right to transfer shares must be restricted in some manner;
(b) the number of shareholders is limited to 50;
(c) any invitation to the public to buy shares is prohibited.

In addition, the number of shareholders required was reduced to three. In most jurisdictions today, the minimum number of shareholders required for a company, whether broadly or closely held, is three, two or even one.[21]

Provisions for the incorporation of private companies exist in substantially the same form as in the English act in the acts of British Columbia, Alberta, Saskatchewan, Prince Edward Island and Nova Scotia.[22] New Brunswick has a somewhat similar provision, permitting a company to be a close corporation (another expression for closely held corporation) and premitting restrictions to be placed upon the transfer of shares. Ontario until 1971 and the federal government until 1976 also incorporated private companies: however the new acts no longer maintain a formal distinction between public and private corporations, although a corporation may still restrict the right to transfer shares[23]. None of these acts specifies the type of restriction, which can take almost any form. In practice, the most common restriction is to require the consent of the board of directors, but there are other varieties such as giving the right of first refusal to existing shareholders or directors before a shareholder can sell to an outsider, or giving a major shareholder the right of veto. The restriction requiring the consent of directors gives them the discretion to approve or reject a proposed member of the company, much as partners can determine whether they will admit a person as one of them. Thus, a restriction on the transfer of shares frequently represents the wishes of the majority of businessmen who want to be able to choose their fellow members in a small enterprise on the basis of competence and trust as they could in partnership.

In those jurisdictions maintaining the distinction between public and private companies, a limit of 50 members represents the mathematical separation between the two categories. Although the figure is arbitrary, it is probably a reasonable point at which the members of a company must make the choice to restrict their numbers or convert the company into a public company. The limit of 50 does not handicap a private company that wishes to give its employees a profit-sharing

---

[21] See, for example, R.S.O. 1970, c. 53, s. 4(1): "One or more persons . . . may incorporate a corporation . . ."; St. of B.C. 1973, c. 18, s. 7(1): ". . . one or more natural persons may form a company . . ."

[22] Nova Scotia's recognition of private companies, oddly, is found in The Securities Act, R.S.N.S. 1967, c. 280, s. 1(2). This section simply defines a private company. The Companies Act does not refer to private companies.

[23] R.S.O. 1970, c. 53, s. 47; St. of Can. 1974-75, c. 33, s. 6(1)(d).

scheme: there is no restriction on the number of employees who may be shareholders in a private company. Because of the prohibition against inviting the
public to subscribe and the restrictions on transfer of shares, shares in private
companies are never quoted on stock exchanges or traded by brokers.

As suggested, the main use of the closely held corporation is to incorporate
small and medium-sized business enterprises where the number of investors is
small. Closely held companies have often been described as incorporated partnerships. Although the description is apt, we must not be misled by it: a closely
held corporation is a true limited company with the same legal significance and
corporate independence as the broadly held corporation. In fact, when a large
corporation creates a subsidiary or branch, it often does so by incorporating a
closely held company. Many large English and American corporations operate
wholly-owned subsidiaries in Canada that are closely held corporations: all the
shares are held by the parent company abroad, except for a few that may be held
here by corporate officers. A number of these subsidiaries rival our own large
public companies in size, but with this important exception, broadly held corporations are generally much larger than closely held ones.

The vast majority of companies are incorporated as closely held corporations — probably over 90% in Canada: the closely held corporation is of importance in a wide cross-section of economic activity. It may therefore seem
surprising that the topic is largely neglected as a subject of study in business administration. The literature of economics, finance, accounting and management
directs its attention to the broadly held corporation in the securities market and
the related need for financial disclosure. This type of corporation has come to
typify bureaucracy in a business setting, and as a result, there is a popularly-held
image of the large corporation operating in a world of efficient capital markets,
proxy battles, take-over bids, conglomerates, intercorporate directorships, professional organization men and classic organization charts. Until recently, at
least, the closely held corporation has been permitted the luxury of operating in
an atmosphere of relative privacy. This may explain why much less is known and
written about it. In the closely held corporation, as we have noted, the owners or
a significant proportion of them are usually the managers as well, thus focusing
questions of management and ultimate decision making within a small group.
We shall examine the legal implications of this characteristic of closely held corporations in the next chapter.

THE JOINT VENTURE OR CONSORTIUM

The joint venture or consortium is an arrangement whereby two or more parties
(often corporations) enter into an agreement to contribute a part of their respective resources (particular assets and expertise) to a specific project. Sometimes
the project requires a greater capital outlay than any one company, even a large
one, may be prepared to put at risk (for example, the Alberta Tar Sands and the
Mackenzie Valley Pipeline proposal). A joint venture spreads the risk among the
participants. In the oil and gas industry, large companies have found it practical

to undertake exploration expenditures jointly to discover oil and gas reserves. Inevitably most of their efforts result in dry holes, but a single wildcat discovery may result in the location of very large recoverable reserves and provide a handsome return to each of the participants. Rather than devote their exploration budgets individually to a few projects with a high probability of failure in each, the companies have preferred to spread the risk in this way.

The status of a joint venture in law is rather vague. In many respects, it is like a partnership and may have a semi-separate existence of its own for the purpose of suing and being sued. As in a partnership, it is normal for a joint venture to establish a separate accounting entity for the allocation of contributions and the distribution of revenues. Sometimes joint ventures are incorporated and each participating company holds shares in the venture, but they are more often formed simply by agreement among the participating parties.

Participants do not typically regard the joint venture as being so much a separate business as an extension of their own operations and collaboration with other parties. The venture is for a specific project or series of explorations, and of limited duration. Profits are not retained jointly for investment in other projects, but are distributed to each of the participants in proportions set down in the joint-venture agreement. The parties may also try to limit their liability by providing that their only contribution will be those things specifically set out in the agreement, that the agreement shall not be construed as a partnership, and that their liability will not be joint and several. As we have seen in Chapter 27, such restrictions may not be effective if it is subsequently determined that the venture was as a matter of fact in the nature of a partnership.

Participants may also try to limit the authority of members to act as agents for one another in the operation of a joint venture and may identify one of themselves (or an independent party) as the "operator" of the joint venture. Whether such an arrangement will be effective to limit the agency of each participating member remains a question of fact to be determined by the court if a dispute arises with an outside third party.

Co-venturers in a joint venture or consortium are in a fiduciary relationship with each other with respect to the purposes of the undertaking. They are much like partners with a continuing duty of utmost good faith in the conduct of the affairs of their joint enterprise.

THE CONSTITUTION OF A CORPORATION

The Charter

Almost all commercial corporations are incorporated under a general act. In Canada, we now find three forms of charters in use — memorandum of association, letters patent and certificate of incorporation. These documents set out essential information about the corporation — its name, objects, and authorized capital, whether it is a private company, and any restrictions on the transfer of shares. These essential facts are required under all the corporation acts. In addition, some jurisdictions require the terms and conditions governing the various classes of shareholders to be set out in the charter itself. In those provinces using the memorandum of association, these terms are not usually set out in the incorporating documents but are found in the *articles of association,* discussed below.

Occasionally to suit the special requirements of the closely held corporation, matters not usually found in an incorporating document will be placed there: they are often included when a compromise arrangement has been made between two groups. For example if two companies merge, the shareholders of the smaller company may wish to have some special privileges entrenched in the document incorporating the new company. Matters directly dealt with in a charter are comparatively difficult to alter. They give considerable protection to the shareholders who benefit from them, but tend to tie the company down. In order to change the rights given in the incorporating document, a special amending procedure must be followed resulting in the issue of *supplementary letters patent* or in the filing of an *alteration of the memorandum of association* or *articles of amendment*. These amendments form part of the constitutional document of the company just as did the original charter. In most circumstances, the charter is an unsuitable instrument for reflecting special arrangements among the shareholders. Instead, shareholders enter into a separate shareholders' agreement outside the corporate constitution, setting out how they will exercise their powers. This topic will be discussed further in the following chapter.

By-Laws or Articles

Incorporators generally keep the incorporating documents as short as possible to gain flexibility in the operation of the company. The company still needs detailed operating rules for its day-to-day affairs; the skeleton provided by the incorporating document must be filled out and given muscle in order to act. In a memorandum company, these rules are called *articles of association*. In a letters patent company or certificate of incorporation company they are called *by-laws*. Since the vast majority of companies are incorporated under the letters patent or certificate of incorporation system, we shall refer to these written rules as by-laws.

What we say about by-laws generally applies to articles of memorandum companies as well, but with this important exception: all such articles are specially entrenched; that is, they require confirmation by more than a simple majority at a shareholders' meeting (specifically, by a three-quarters majority). To avoid this procedure, memorandum companies make many decisions in the normal course of business by passing ordinary resolutions requiring only a simple majority to ratify them. By-laws are somewhat more flexible, many types requiring confirmation by only a simple majority of shareholders, although corporation acts do specify some matters which must be dealt with by special by-laws requiring an increased majority. Another difference is that in a letters patent company, the power to originate by-laws is the prerogative of the directors; in memorandum companies an article, and under the Canada Corporations Act a by-law, may in certain circumstances originate with the shareholders at a general meeting.[24] In Ontario the position appears to be a half-way house: ordinarily, directors originate all by-laws, but there is an extraordinary procedure whereby shareholders may, after serving notice, pass a by-law at a separate meeting[25].

By-laws fall into three main categories. The first category provides general operating rules for carrying on the business of a company. These rules are found in the first by-laws of general application, which are usually passed at the first meeting of the shareholders. The first by-laws are often quite long and elaborate, dealing with such matters as the number and qualification of directors; their term of office; the place and required notice for meetings of directors; the *quorum* necessary (that is, the minimum number of directors who must be present) before a meeting can act on behalf of the company; the categories of executive officers; provisions for voting by proxy, for the allotment of shares, and for the declaration of dividends; general authorization of the directors to borrow funds. The following brief excerpts from general by-laws will illustrate the matters usually looked after:

The affairs of the Company shall be managed by a board of five (5) directors.

The qualifications of a director shall be the holding of at least one share in the capital stock of the Company provided, however, that any person who is an officer or director of any other company which is a shareholder of the Company may hold office as a director of the Company.

Three of the directors shall form a quorum for the transaction of business.

Questions arising at any meeting of directors shall be decided by a majority of votes. In the event of an equality of votes the Chairman of the meeting in addition to this original vote shall have a second or casting vote.

The remuneration to be paid to the directors shall be such as the board of directors shall from time to time determine and such remuneration shall be in addition to the salary paid to any officer or employee of the Company who is a member of the board of directors.

Shares in the Company's capital stock shall be allotted by resolution of the board of directors on such terms and conditions and to such persons as the directors shall deem advisable.

The directors may from time to time by resolution declare dividends and pay the same out of the funds of the Company available for that purpose, subject to the provisions (if any) of the letters patent or any supplementary letters patent of the Company.

The requirements vary somewhat between jurisdictions, but a general by-law of this type may be passed by the directors in advance of the first shareholders' meeting, and it will have force until the next annual meeting of shareholders, when it must be confirmed. An advantage in having detail relegated to a general

---

[24] St. of Can. 1974-75, c. 33, ss. 98(5) and 131(1).
[25] R.S.O. 1970, c. 53, s. 101.

by-law and separated from the charter is that the detail may later be altered on approval of the shareholders without the formality of having the charter changed.

A second purpose of by-laws is to authorize a change in the incorporating document itself, such as a change in the name, objects, or authorized capital, or the conversion from a private to a public company, or vice versa. In order to make application for a change, the directors must first pass a by-law setting out the change, and a general meeting of the shareholders must confirm the by-law by the majority required under the particular statute. After confirmation, the by-law and evidence of its proper approval are sent to the appropriate government authority. In a letters patent company, the amendment does not become effective until the government authority issues supplementary letters patent. In a memorandum company, the formal change becomes effective as soon as the proper documents are registered; the act of registering amounts to the alteration of the memorandum. Neither the Ontario Act nor the new federal Act is clear about when either an original certificate of incorporation or a subsequent amendment becomes effective.[26]

A third purpose of by-laws is to give the directors express authority from the shareholders to carry out specific transactions requiring approval by by-law, either because of the provisions of the statute in the jurisdiction, or the provisions of the company charter, or simply because no authority has been given in the general by-laws. The particular matters requiring this type of approval vary somewhat from province to province, but the directors usually require the authority of a special by-law before they can validly lend money to company employees to enable the employees to purchase shares in the company; approve contracts in which a director or directors have a personal interest; elect an executive committee from among themselves; or authorize their own remuneration. Although directors usually have the authority to borrow money on the security of the company's assets under a general borrowing by-law, they may nevertheless ask the shareholders to confirm a major loan transaction. Often creditors will insist upon such a confirmation in the form of a by-law.

Capital

The word ''capital'' has different meanings in different contexts. In all provincial jurisdictions, when a company is incorporated, its charter places an upper limit on the number and money value of shares it may issue. This limit is called the ''authorized capital,'' and forms the basis on which the government levies its fees for incorporation. The government charges a minimum fee for incorporation, plus a scale of fees which increase as the authorized capital increases. A corporation need not issue all its share capital: many retain a portion of their authorized capital and never issue it to shareholders. The *issued and paid-up capi-*

---

[26] See R.S.O. 1970, c. 53, ss. 4(1) and 5(1) and (2), and St. of Can. 1974-75, c. 33, ss. 8 and 255(3). Neither act states that the Minister *shall* date the certificate with the same date as that on which the articles are filed by the incorporator.

tal of a corporation is that part which has been subscribed and paid for by the shareholders.

At the federal level, the Canada Business Corporations Act has done away with the concept of authorized capital. A corporation may state the maximum number of shares that can be issued if it so wishes, or it can leave matters open-ended.[27] The fee for incorporation is a flat fee unrelated to the amount of capital investment.[28] A federal corporation must, however, still keep a "stated capital account" disclosing the consideration received for each share issued.[29]

The issued capital of a company is the result of a series of contracts — contracts of subscription — between the company and its shareholders. We should bear in mind that there are several ways of becoming a shareholder: by being one of the original applicants for incorporation; by buying additional shares issued by a company subsequent to its incorporation; or by acquiring shares already issued to another shareholder, either by gift or by purchase. The first two ways are the results of contracts between the shareholder and the company; the transaction causes an increase in the issued capital as shown in the accounts of the company. The third way is the result of a transfer to which the company is not a party at all; the terms, including the price, are arrived at independently of the company and do not affect its accounts.

Until the early part of the 20th century, all shares had a nominal or *par value* — that is, a fixed value placed upon them like a bank note or a bond. Usually, these shares were in large denominations such as $100, $500, or $1,000. Generally speaking, they were issued by the company at their par value. Within a short time after issue, however, a share rarely had a market price identical with its par value. If the company had fared well and was declaring large dividends, or had excellent prospects, its shares would be in high demand and command a premium price on the market, often several times their par value; if the company had suffered losses or was a poor earner, its shares might bring only a fraction of their par value on the market. Accordingly, par value provides little or no indication of a fair price for shares. In addition, par value creates a hardship. As we shall see in the next chapter, a company is prohibited from issuing its shares at a discount other than for the payment of commission. If a company's shares are selling on the market at, say, half their par value and the company requires additional capital in order to improve its position, investors will not purchase a new issue at par. In order to make a more successful issue, the company must reduce the par value of the shares to a more realistic figure and reduce its capital accordingly by obtaining an amendment to its charter.

The idea was evolved in the United States of issuing *no par value* shares, that is, shares which represent a specific proportion of the issued capital of the company rather than a fixed sum of money.

---

[27] St. of Can. 1974-75, c. 33, s. 6(1)(c).
[28] Draft Regulations and the Canada Corporations Act, PART 10, Schedule of Fees, s. 2(a).
[29] St. of Can. 1974-75, c. 33, s. 26(1).

Illustration:

> Pliable Plastics Limited is incorporated with an authorized share capital of
> 20,000 no par value shares. It has paid the provincial government fees
> enabling it to issue these shares at a maximum total price of $1,000,000 or,
> in other words, $50 per share. In its initial share issue, the company offers
> 12,000 shares for sale at a price of $40 per share. All these shares are sold,
> giving the company an issued and paid-up capital of $480,000. Sub-
> sequently, Pliable Plastics Limited suffers losses and its stock sells on the
> market at $30 per share. The directors deem it advisable to raise further cap-
> ital. It would be quite proper for them to issue the remaining 8,000 shares
> at whatever price the market will pay without any amendment to the com-
> pany charter.

The advantages of no par value shares, in particular the fact that they may
be issued from time to time at prices that correspond with the current appraisal of
their worth by investors, resulted in their adoption by all the jurisdictions in the
United States and soon after in Canada. The English still permit only the use of
par value shares, although considerable support exists for adopting the use of no
par value shares as well. The new federal Act goes to the other extreme in
abolishing par value shares entirely.[30]

Par value shares are still in common use. At present, virtually all preferred
shares have a par value and pay a preferred dividend based on that value, and
many are redeemable by the company at par.

THE CAPACITY OF A CORPORATION

We have discussed the nature and significance of corporate personality as separate and distinct from shareholders, and examined the various ways in which a
corporation may be created. We have now to discuss the capacity of a corporation to perform acts and enter into binding obligations on its own behalf. In
Chapter 7 we noted that the capacity of a natural person may vary considerably
according to his status, as for example, the capacity of an infant, lunatic, alien or
soldier; in some instances his capacity to enter into obligations by contract or to
incur liability for negligent or other acts is more limited than that of the normal
adult citizen.

The capacity of a corporation could conceivably be identical with the capacity of a normal adult person, but in fact it is not. In Chapter 7 we also stated that
the corporation presents special difficulties because it cannot act on its own voli-
tion, but only through its agents or organs. Whenever practical, the courts do
treat corporations as having the same capacity as a human being, but there are
many exceptions to this principle. In addition, not all corporations have the same
capacity; as we are about to see, there are different statuses among corporations

---

[30] *Ibid.*, s. 24(1).

as there are among human beings. We also noted in Chapter 7 that municipal corporations are usually quite strictly limited in their capacity. Any attempt to act outside that capacity is *ultra vires*, that is, a nullity, and has no legal effect. Corporations formed by memorandum of association have somewhat similar limitations on their capacity (except in British Columbia, where the doctrine of *ultra vires* has been abolished by statute). These corporations are considered creatures of the general statute which permits their creation. As a matter of interpretation, the courts have adopted strict rules in defining the capacity of such corporations. Judges have traditionally made the assumption that the common law is a complete body of law and that statutes changing the common law must be strictly construed and limited to the words of the statute, so as to leave the common law rules as little affected as possible. Since memorandum companies are statutory creations with no existence at common law, the courts have strictly limited their powers to those given by statute. Further, the courts have assumed that the memorandum of association forms a part of the statute; accordingly, they construe its terms equally strictly. Thus in the famous case of *Ashbury Rwy. & Carriage Co. v. Riche*,[31] the House of Lords held that an English corporation did not exist outside the sphere of the objects set down for it in its memorandum:

> The company's object was to carry on the business of *building contractors* and to construct railways and railway equipment. The company undertook to purchase an interest in a railway, that is, to *invest in and operate* a railway. The court held that the contract for that purpose was a complete nullity, that the corporation did not exist for that purpose, and that the contract created no rights and liabilities for the company or against it. Accordingly the vendor of the interest in the railway failed in his action against the company for its refusal to perform the contract.

To avoid the possibility of similar situations arising, incorporators ever since have stated the objects as found in the memorandum of association as widely as possible by putting them in very broad terms and sometimes making a long enumeration of the various powers of the company. For the most part, by skilful drafting they have avoided the unhappy consequences of the *Ashbury* case, but the danger still exists today in several jurisdictions that an unwary person in contracting with such a company may find himself without remedy if the company should repudiate the contract.

As we have noted earlier in this chapter, letters patent companies are the descendants of the old royal charter corporations created by the Crown. The royal charter corporations derived their validity from the traditional prerogative of the king, and this prerogative was considered a part of the common law of England. Thus it was that corporations created by royal prerogative were considered analogous to human beings, and their capacity was much more liberally construed by the courts.[32] They were considered to have the ability to perform any act which a

---

[31] (1875) L.R. 7 H.L. 653. See also Re Jon Beauforte (London) Ltd. [1953] Ch. 131, and Gower, *Modern Company Law* (3rd ed.), p. 90.
[32] British South Africa Company v. De Beers Consolidated Mines, Ltd. [1910] 1 Ch. 354.

human being was capable of performing except those things obviously beyond its factual powers, for example, to make a contract of marriage or commit bigamy, suicide, or assault. Until 1916 it was unclear whether a letters patent company had the capacity of a royal charter company or was restricted in much the same way as a memorandum company. In that year, however, the Privy Council decided, in the case of *Bonanza Creek v. Rex*,[33] that letters patent companies were truly children of the old royal prerogative and accordingly had the wide capacity ascribed to royal charter companies. Hence the narrow rule of interpretation concerning *ultra vires* acts in the *Ashbury* case does not apply to letters patent companies.

In the 19th century, rather lame attempts were occasionally made to justify the *ultra vires* rule as protecting shareholders from the management's engaging in unauthorized activities. Whatever credence was placed in this argument at the time, it now appears to be totally discredited. The unfair risk to the innocent outside contractor far outweighs any imagined benefit to shareholders. We should note, too, that lawyers and judges have never doubted the power of Parliament or provincial legislatures to abolish the *ultra vires* rule simply by declaring that corporations have the capacity of a natural person. It is strange, then, that the unfortunate rule has survived so long without statutory reform. One explanation is that until recently there was no procedure for systematic law reform in either England or Canada. Rules like the *ultra vires* rule, though clearly harmful, affect only a small number of people and tend to be ignored by legislatures in the face of larger public issues. With the recent development of law reform commissions in numerous jurisdictions, systematic improvement of many technical areas as well as social reforms are now being recommended by these commissions. British Columbia, which remains a memorandum jurisdiction, has declared in its new Companies Act that a "company has the power and capacity of a natural person of full capacity".[34] Ontario, when it changed in 1971 from the letters patent system to a certificate of incorporation system, was aware that the new statutory system might revive the doctrine of *ultra vires* in Ontario. Accordingly, Ontario included the following provision in the Business Corporation Act: "No act of a corporation . . . is invalid by reason of the fact that the corporation was without capacity or power to do such act . . ."[35] Although these words probably accomplish the same purpose as the words of the new British Columbia Act, the straightforward approach of the British Columbia provision is more easily understood and therefore preferable. It should be noted that the new section of the Ontario Act also applies to corporations originally incorporated by letters patent. The new federal Act has also taken into account the change from incorporation by letters patent to incorporation by certificate, and states, "A corporation has the capacity and, subject to this Act, the rights, powers and privileges of a natural person."[36]

---

[33] [1916] 1 A.C. 566.
[34] St. of B.C. 1973, c. 103, s. 23(1). The United Kingdom restricted but did not entirely abolish the *ultra vires* doctrine on entering the Common Market. See European Communities Act, 1972 (U.K.) c. 68, s. 9(1).
[35] R.S.O. 1970, c. 53, s. 16.
[36] St. of Can. 1974-75, c. 33, s. 15(1).

In summary, then, the strict approach of the *Ashbury* case concerning *ultra vires* applies to companies formed under the acts of Alberta, Saskatchewan, Nova Scotia and Newfoundland. It does not apply to companies formed under the federal Act or the Acts of the four letters patent provinces, nor does it apply to British Columbia and Ontario. However, we should note further that all corporations statutes except the new federal Act still require charters to contain a clause setting out a corporation's objects. An objects clause has the following significance: whether or not a contract by which the corporation exceeds its objects is void, the making of such a contract is misconduct; a shareholder may bring an action against the officers of the company responsible for the breach of its objects, and where possible ask for an injunction to restrain their misconduct. (In the case of a very great breach, he may ask to have the company wound up.) The results are far more sensible than under the *ultra vires* rule, for innocent outsiders contracting with the company are not left without remedy.

NATURE OF CORPORATE SECURITIES

From the Point of View of their Holders

The classic distinction between shares and bonds or debentures has long been that the holder of the share is an investor and owner of an interest in the company and that the holder of a bond or debenture is a creditor. In the business world today, there is no such clear-cut distinction between the shareholder and the bondholder. In the language of modern business the true "equity" owner of the business, the man who takes the greatest risk, is the common shareholder. From this end of the scale, we proceed by degrees to the man who is purely a mortgagee or bondholder at the other end of the scale, where the holder's risk is least. In between we may have varying types of preferred shareholders, unsecured creditors, and debenture holders and other secured creditors. Often when he decides to invest in the bonds of a company rather than its preferred stock, a business man does not believe that he has made the choice between becoming a creditor and becoming an investor. He believes in both instances that he is an investor, but that he enjoys a higher security in the one form of investment than in the other. His investment considerations are primarily determined by economic considerations, or perhaps by convenience. For example, he may choose to buy bonds instead of shares because they have a maturity date and he will not have to worry about selling them on the market; or because the bonds promise a more certain return than dividends and "growth". Alternatively, he may choose preferred shares because he can still claim a dividend tax credit while realizing something like an interest form of return.

We have seen (in Chapter 13) that share and bond certificates are a type of personal property subject to different rules of transfer and ownership from those that apply to sales of goods. We noted further in Chapter 22 that these choses in action may in some circumstances be treated as negotiable instruments. Thus, bond certificates in bearer form may be considered as a type of negotiable instrument at common law. The Corporations Act of Ontario by implication, and the federal Act expressly, treat share certificates in bearer form as a type of negotiable instrument. These developments have followed stock market custom in Canada and current practices in the United States.

In theory, if bonds and shares are to serve the purposes of a capital market they should be readily transferable (that is, ''liquid'') and this purpose is promoted when the hazards of owning them are minimal. When bonds and shares are treated as negotiable instruments, an innocent holder for value may often acquire a better title than his predecessor had, as for example when he purchases bonds or share certificates that have been stolen.

In practice, giving bond and share certificates negotiability has aggravated a major problem with respect to forged and stolen certificates, particularly in recent years in the United States. Since an innocent holder for value can obtain good title to a stolen certificate, looser practice has developed in accepting these certificates. Two unfortunate results have flowed from this development: first, there has been an increased temptation to indulge in theft as it is easy to sell stolen certificates; secondly, it has become easier to pass off forged (and therefore worthless) certificates on purchasers. The innocent holder of a forged negotiable instrument, as we have seen, obtains no title, being subject to the real defence of forgery.

At this point it is very difficult to foresee where future developments with respect to negotiability will lead.

From the Point of View of the Corporation

The line between the shareholder and the bondholder is nonetheless a distinct and important one in its legal consequences for the company. First of all, since a bondholder is a creditor, the interest paid to him is a debt of the corporation. It must be paid whether the company has earned profits for the year or not. A shareholder is not a creditor, and receives dividends only when the directors declare them. A consequence, especially important for taxation, is that interest payments are an expense of doing business and are deducted before income can be calculated; dividends, on the other hand, are payable from profits after income tax has been calculated. Secondly, bonds are usually secured by a mortgage on the real property of the corporation (debentures, by a floating charge on the assets in general). If the corporation becomes insolvent, the bondholders receive their money back not only before the shareholders but also before the general creditors: they are secured creditors, and the trustee acting for them can sell the company's assets to satisfy the debt owed to them. Thirdly, bond or debenture holders do not have a direct voice in the management of the company unless it is in breach of the terms of the *trust deed* or *indenture* under which the securities were created. Only when the corporation gets into financial difficulty or is in breach of the trust deed may the trustee, acting on behalf of the bond or debenture holders, step in and take part in management. It is true, however, that bondholders do exert an indirect form of control over management in the restrictive clauses written into bond indentures as a means of making bond issues sufficiently attractive to be saleable at the yield offered. While it is probably unwise for bondholders to place extensive restrictions on the future decisions of management in this way, bond indentures may include formulae placing a ceiling on the further long-term borrowing and leasing in which the company may engage, on the amount of dividends it may pay, and even, in smaller companies, on the salaries of officers.

Preferred shareholders are in an intermediate category. Depending on the rights provided for them in the description of preferred shares in the company's charter, they do not normally have the right to vote unless the payment of dividends to them has fallen in arrears. In this respect they are more like creditors than investors. Nevertheless, the payment of preferred dividends is not a contractual commitment of the company, as is bond interest. Furthermore, a preferred shareholder must enforce his rights as an individual and is not dependent upon a trustee for their realization, as a bondholder normally is.

In the latter part of the 19th century, the capital structures of corporations tended to become complex. Often they included three or more kinds of shares and several priorities of bonds. The related securities were in large denominations, that is, of a relatively high par value. The tendency since the turn of the century has been towards a simplification of capital structures. Today, most companies have, in addition to an issue of common shares, one or two types of bonds or debentures and possibly a single class of preferred share; and a large proportion of their financing will have been achieved by retained earnings.

The Rights and Privileges of Security Holders

The various combinations of rights and privileges that may attach to either preferred or common shares are extensive. They depend on the financial position of the company, the advice of the investment house acting as its underwriter, and to some extent on the bias of the incorporators or of management. Among companies already in operation and requiring further financing, managers will differ in their assessment of the risk to the corporation and their own tenure that a particular balance of financing in the capital structure will create: some have a greater aversion to debt than others, and some dislike equity financing because of its potential, real or imagined, for disturbing the present balance in voting power. All these factors influence not only the method of financing chosen, but also the rights that may attach to the various securities issued. In itself, modern company legislation places few constraints on the financing of companies, and leaves it to incorporators or management to set out clearly the rights and privileges of each class of security in the charter or by-laws.

Problems of interpretation arise in the drafting of rights for various classes of shareholders just as they do in the drafting of statutes, contracts and wills. The courts have decided some important questions in only comparatively recent times, but they have gradually worked out a more or less consistent set of interpretations to look after most omissions by the draftsmen of shareholder rights in company constitutions. Thus problems are less likely to arise in recently incorporated companies because the draftsmen, aware of the court decisions, take pains to set out explicitly the various priorities and rights pertaining to shareholders of various classes. Many companies still exist, however, with constitutions drawn up without the benefit of this case law. For example, if the charter or by-laws of a company state that the preferred shareholders shall have a return of capital and accumulated arrears of dividends upon winding up, do they share in a surplus sum of money left after the common shareholders have also had their capital returned to them, or does this surplus sum belong exclusively to the common shareholders? As late as 1947 the Supreme Court of Canada held, with some assistance from the specific wording of the federal Companies Act, that the preferred shareholders shared in the surplus with the common shareholders, pro rata.[37] But in 1949 the House of Lords, in the *Scottish Insurance* case,[38] decided that the statement of rights of the preferred shareholders was exhaustive and that any surplus fund remaining after the preferred shareholders had received what was their due under the statement belonged to the common shareholders. In 1950 the Supreme Court of Canada became our final court of appeal. There has been no decision in Canada subsequent to the *Scottish Insurance* case, and it is almost impossible to predict which way the courts may go in a future case on the winding up of some corporation which has not stated expressly what should happen to the surplus fund.

QUESTIONS FOR REVIEW

1. Distinguish a legal person from a natural person.
2. Describe the effect of a finding that companies are ''associated'' for taxation purposes.
3. What is a royal charter?
4. What kinds of companies are incorporated by special act?
5. From whom does a letters patent company derive its existence? How does a memorandum company differ?
6. Is a certificate of incorporation more like letters patent or a memorandum of association? Why?
7. What arguments did the creditors use in attempting to show that Salomon should be held liable?
8. Distinguish between a charter and by-laws.
9. What are the three main purposes of by-laws?
10. What did the *Ashbury* case decide? How was the result of this case qualified by the *Bonanza Creek* case? What recent statutory developments have superseded the common law in this area?
11. What are the main characteristics of a closely held corporation?
12. Under what circumstances might a company require an amendment to its charter?

---

[37] International Power Co. Ltd. v. McMaster University et al. [1946] 2 D.L.R. 81.
[38] Scottish Insurance Corporation, Ltd. v. Wilsons & Clyde Coal Company Ltd. [1949] A.C. 462.

CASES FOR DISCUSSION

CASE 1

Parliament passes a statute declaring that it is against the public interest for any railway company to transport coal mined by itself because such activity tends to restrict competition. Rocky Mountain Railway Company subsequently purchases all the shares of Albert Collieries Limited. Albert Collieries has always shipped its coal on the Rocky Mountain line and continues to do so. The Department of Justice has started an action to obtain an injunction against further shipments of Albert coal on the Rocky Mountain line.

Summarize the arguments for each side. Who should win? (See *U.S. v. Lehigh Valley Railroad Co.* 220 U.S. 257 (1910) (United States Supreme Court).) Court).)

CASE 2

Arthurs, Barton, and Coombes were the directors and sole shareholders of Driftwood Products Limited. After several years of hard work and considerable success all three decided to take a vacation together and leave their office manager in charge. They flew to the Bahamas for three weeks of sun and fishing. While they were away, the company manager instructed its lawyer to sue a debtor who was long overdue in payment of his account. Several days after the action was started, it was learned that all three shareholders had been killed when their fishing boat overturned in a storm. The debtor has suggested defending the action by claiming that the creditor company ceased to exist when all three shareholders were killed.

Explain the ways in which this contention may be answered. (See Gower, *Modern Company Law* (3rd ed., 1969), pp. 75-7; *Hague v. Cancer Relief Institute* [1939] 4 D.L.R. 191.)

CASE 3

Consolidated Apple Corp. Ltd. is a Nova Scotia company. Its objects as stated in its memorandum of association are as follows: "To carry on the business of growing, processing and marketing apples and other fruits and vegetables; to finance and assist farmers and other growers by extending credit and providing expert advice on raising produce in consideration for receiving exclusive marketing rights; and to carry on all related and ancillary business activities."

Consolidated Apple made an offer to purchase a timber lease together with a lumber mill and all accessory equipment for $1,300,000 from Rising Sun Pulp Company. The offer was accepted. Consolidated Apple made a down payment of $200,000 and took possession of the timber tract and the mill. After several months' operation Consolidated Apple decided it had made a bad buy; it abandoned the lumber mill, defaulted on the first payment when it fell due shortly afterwards, and subsequently started an action for the return of the $200,000 down payment.

Would it succeed? Why? Would the results be different if all the circumstances, including the incorporation of Consolidated Apple, had occurred in New Brunswick? in British Columbia? (See *Ashbury Rwy. & Carriage Co. v. Riche* (1875) L.R. 7 H.L. 653, and *Bonanza Creek Gold Mining Company, Limited v. The King* [1916] 1 A.C. 566.)

CASE 4

Macbeth, the owner of 50 acres located on the outskirts of Niagara Falls, decided to sell, and on January 2 signed an exclusive listing agreement with Ross, a real-estate broker. Macbeth agreed to pay Ross a commission of 5% on the sale of the property, which he listed at $350,000.

On January 19, Ross filed articles of incorporation for a new company, Burnam Wood Properties Ltd., of which he was the sole shareholder. He appointed his friend Lennox as general manager.

Several weeks later, on March 2, Ross introduced Macbeth to Lennox as general manager of Burnam Wood Properties Ltd. but said nothing to suggest that he, Ross, had any interest in the company. Within a few days Lennox submitted an offer on behalf of the company to purchase Macbeth's property for $240,000. Macbeth rejected the offer but made a counter-offer to sell at $290,000, of which half was to be paid on closing the transaction and the balance as a first mortgage with interest at 10% per annum. This offer was accepted by Burnam Wood Properties Ltd. The deal was closed on March 15, when Macbeth received a certified cheque for $145,000 and took back a first mortgage for $145,000 from Burnam Wood Properties Ltd. Macbeth paid Ross his commission of $14,500.

Shortly afterwards, Burnam Wood Properties Ltd. entered into negotiations with another company, Castle Hall Developments Ltd., and sold the 50 acres to it for $450,000, realizing a quick profit of $160,000.

On April 24 following, Macbeth learned of the resale by Burnam Wood Properties Ltd. and, incensed about the poor deal he seemed to have made, undertook inquiries about the company. It was then that he learned about Ross's share ownership in the Burnam Wood Company. Macbeth immediately sued Ross and Burnam Wood Properties Ltd., jointly, for recovery of the real-estate commission of $14,500 and for the $160,000 profit realized on the second sale by Burnam Wood Properties Ltd. to Castle Hall Developments Ltd.

Examine the validity of Macbeth's claim and offer an opinion about its chances for success. In particular, examine the nature of Macbeth's rights, if any, against Burnam Wood Properties Ltd. (For reference, see *Christie v. McCann* [1972] 3 O.R. 125.)

CHAPTER 29

Management and Operation of a Corporation

LIABILITY FOR ACTS OF ITS AGENTS

Effect of Publicly-filed Documents

Generally speaking, a corporation is liable for the acts of its agents under the ordinary rules of agency. An officer of a corporation acting within his usual authority but without express authority may bind it to contracts made with third parties. A corporation may ratify acts made by unauthorized agents on its behalf. The duties of agent to principal and principal to agent also remain the same.

There are, however, some rather subtle and more elaborate implications of the ordinary rules of liability for agents' acts when corporations are involved. In the first place, certain corporate documents are registered in a public office and available for examination on payment of a small fee, in a manner similar to the registration of title documents concerning land. In most jurisdictions, the public is deemed to have notice of the contents of these documents whether they have read them or not. Hence, if the documents contain a prohibition against either the corporation's or one of its officers' carrying out certain acts, a third party cannot rely upon what otherwise might be the officer's apparent authority to perform those acts. The basic incorporating document is filed in the appropriate office in Ottawa or in the capital of its province of incorporation.

Illustration:

The Churchill Company Ltd., incorporated under the Companies Act of Manitoba with its head office in Winnipeg, operates a chain of department

633

stores. Because of the personal convictions of its incorporators, the letters patent of the company contain a provision that the company cannot deal in any tobacco products with a view to their resale to the public. A branch manager of the company store in Sackville, N.B., decides to introduce a line of cigarettes, and on his requisition the purchasing department orders a quantity of cigarettes from the Pure Tobacco Co., Sackville, whose management have no knowledge of any prohibition in the letters patent of the purchasing concern. A majority shareholder of the Churchill Company Ltd. learns of the transaction and insists that it be rescinded.

The Pure Tobacco Co. will not succeed if it sues the Churchill Company Limited for damages for non-acceptance or for the price. The management of the tobacco company is not entitled to rely on the usual authority of the purchasing department of the Churchill Company Ltd. because they are presumed to have notice of the prohibition in its letters patent, however impractical or unusual it would be for them to examine the copy of the corporate documents filed in a government office in Winnipeg or the copy retained in its head office there. If, however, the cigarettes had been delivered and then partly sold, the Churchill Company would be deemed to have accepted the benefit, to the extent that it did not redeliver the cigarettes in their original packing within a reasonable time, and would be liable to pay a proportionate part of the price.

What happens if the restriction is in a by-law or article, rather than in the charter itself? Here we should note an important difference between letters patent and certificate of incorporation companies on the one hand and memorandum companies on the other. The corporations acts of the various provinces using incorporation by registration have copied the English Act in requiring not only the memorandum but all articles in it to be registered. Accordingly, anyone dealing with companies incorporated in those jurisdictions (except British Columbia) is bound by restrictions in their articles as well as in their memorandum. In contrast, the by-laws of a letters patent or certificate of incorporation company are not registered in any public office, and persons dealing with the company are not bound by the contents of these by-laws. Thus, a prohibition in the articles of a memorandum company *would* prevent a third party from relying on the otherwise apparent authority of an officer of that company, while the same prohibition in the by-laws of the other two types of companies would not prevent a third party from relying on the apparent authority of one of their officers.

Whatever merit there may be in the theory that third-party contractors in a small country like England ought to read publicly-filed documents, the application of such a rule in Canada — where there are 11 incorporating jurisdictions, and contracting parties are frequently several thousand miles from the head office of the corporation or the city in which the documents are filed — may create a wholly unfair burden, and lead to substantial injustice. The rule is merely a snare for the innocent and unwary. There is no reason why a corporation should be able to avoid contractual commitments when a natural person under the usual rules of apparent authority would be bound. After all, a corporation already has the benefit of limited liability not available to the natural person. Two provinces and the federal government have now chosen to abolish the rule about notice in registered documents entirely. In Ontario, the section of the Business Corporation Act that does away with the doctrine of *ultra vires* is believed to have the same effect with respect to notice to third parties of documents registered in a public office.[1] The words of the Ontario statute do not easily appear to lead to this result: one must take the word of specialists who understand the law of New York State, where this provision originated, to come to the desired result — an unfortunate way to develop the law of Ontario. The new British Columbia Act has also done away with the rule in a direct statement that ''in any proceeding by or against a company no person shall be affected by or shall be deemed to have notice or knowledge of the contents of the document or record concerning the company by reason only that the document or record has been filed with the Registrar or is available for inspection at an office of the company.''[2] The Federal Act[3] uses almost the same words as the British Columbia Act. Of course, if a contracting third party actually has read or knows the contents of a restriction he will be bound by it, but in saying this we are merely restating the common law rule of agency: if a third party knows of an express restriction between the principal and agent, he cannot claim to rely on an apparent authority that ignores the restriction.

Indoor Management Rule

A second agency problem which is peculiar to companies arises from requirements in the company's constitution and governing act that it must perform certain acts in a specific manner if they are to be valid. What is the effect upon an innocent third party if the act has been performed in an irregular manner — if, for instance, the confirmation of a by-law by the shareholders requires a minimum period of notice to the shareholders in advance of the meeting, and a lesser period was actually given? In the leading English case of *Royal British Bank v. Turquand*,[4] it was held that in the absence of notice of the irregularity or of suspicious circumstances (or of a prohibition in the public documents), everything which appears regular on its face may be relied upon by an outsider and will bind the company. This question of the propriety of the internal processes of a company is often referred to as *indoor management*,[5] and is simply a variation of the question of apparent authority in agency law generally: an innocent third party may rely on the regularity of a corporate act, just as he may rely on the apparent authority of an agent, if it is reasonable for him to do so in the circumstances.

---

[1] R.S.O. 1970, c. 53, s. 16.
[2] St. of B.C. 1973, c. 18, s. 28.
[3] St. of Can. 1974-75, c. 33, s. 17.
[4] (1856) 119 E.R. 886.
[5] See Prentice, ''The Indoor Management Rule'', in *Studies in Canadian Company Law*, (Ziegel, ed.), Ch. 10.

Pre-incorporation Contracts

We have noted in Chapter 20 that, at common law and apart from statute, a corporation cannot ratify a contract made on its behalf before it came into existence. For this purpose the date on which the memorandum is registered or the letters patent or certificate are issued is crucial; if the contract is made any time after the corporation came into existence, then the law of agency as discussed earlier in this chapter and in Chapter 20 applies. On the other hand, if the contract was just made the day before the corporation was created, at common law the corporation cannot ratify and bind either itself or the third party. A new contract must be negotiated between the parties to carry out their original intent. It may be possible for a third party to sue the person who represented himself as agent of the corporation for breach of warranty of authority, but even this limited remedy is uncertain.

Ontario and the federal government appear to be the only jurisdictions so far to have remedied the deficiencies of the common law. Section 20(a) of the Ontario Business Corporations Act[6] provides that a corporation may adopt a pre-incorporation contract and thereupon "is entitled to the benefits and is subject to the liabilities that were contracted in its name or on its behalf and the *contractor* [the person who made the contract on behalf of the corporation] ceases to be entitled to such benefits or to be subject to such liabilities." If the corporation does not adopt the pre-incorporation contract, the Act expressly makes the contractor entitled to the benefits and subject to the liabilities under it. In neither event, then, can the contract be considered a nullity. Section 20 also seeks to prevent unfair manipulation by a corporation and a contractor. For example, a contractor may make a contract on behalf of a corporation which he himself will subsequently incorporate and control and to which he plans to give virtually no assets. If, after incorporation, he decides that the contract is a bad bargain, under section 20(2) he might cause the corporation to adopt the contract and thereby escape any personal liability as its agent-contractor. To prevent this abuse, section 20(4) goes on to state: "Whether or not the pre-incorporation contract is adopted by the corporation, the other party may apply to the court which may . . . make an order fixing or apportioning liability as between the contractor and the corporation in any manner the court considers just and equitable under the circumstances." The unfortunate consequences of the common law position have been overcome by the Ontario Business Corporations Act. The new Canada Business Corporations Act contains a similar reform, and also provides that a promoter acting on behalf of a corporation before it comes into existence may avoid personal liability and waive any benefits under the contract where the contract is in writing and includes an express term that he will not be bound by the agreement.[7] Unfortunately, in its new Companies Act British Columbia did not see fit to reform the law in this area.

---

[6] R.S.O. 1970, c. 53.
[7] St. of Can. 1974-75, c. 33, s. 14(4).

DUTIES OF DIRECTORS[8]

To the Shareholders

Business corporations differ from one another as much in their size and composition as municipalities, trade unions and governments. These variations are necessary if corporations are to perform their widely differing functions in our society; corporations should not all be cast in the same mould. Modern legislation tries to take these needs into account and is reasonably flexible in permitting widely differing corporate structures, although, as we shall see, flexibility is restricted by a belief that certain elements are essential to all corporations.

The two basic organs common to all corporations are the body of shareholders and a much smaller body called a *board of directors,* elected by the shareholders. In very large corporations the board of directors may have as many as fifteen or twenty members. Generally speaking, when the board is larger than a dozen, it appoints from among its members a *management committee* or *executive committee,* usually numbering five or six, which directs the affairs of the company and refers only the more important matters to the less frequent meetings of the full board of directors. In turn, the board of directors usually calls no more than the required annual meeting of the shareholders, at which the board reports to the shareholders on the state of the company's affairs and holds elections for the coming year. Thus, we see that the directors function throughout the year very much as the cabinet of a government functions, with very wide powers.[9]

As in public office, the concentration of such great power in the hands of a few persons may tempt them to use it for their own interests and against the interests of those for whom they should be acting. One might conclude that their first duty is to those shareholders who have elected them. This is not so, however. Just as a member of Parliament, once elected, owes his first duty to the country as a whole rather than to his constituency, so, the courts have stated, does a director owe his first duty to the company as a whole. This statement raises again, of course, the philosophic argument about whether the company is entirely separate from the shareholders.

To the present time, both English and Canadian courts have tended to treat the shareholders and the company as entirely separate entities, and state that the duties of the directors are owed almost exclusively to the company itself. Hence, no general duty is owed by the board of directors to the shareholders. In the absence of statutory provisions, if the directors of a company receive a takeover bid whereby the proposed purchaser makes an offer to buy all the shares in the company at a particular price, the directors are under no legal duty to forward

---

[8] See Palmer, "Directors' Powers and Duties", in *Studies in Canadian Company Law,* (Ziegel, ed.), Vol. 1, Ch. 12.

[9] Directors of closely held corporations do function in the way described. As we shall see below under the heading "Sources of Shareholders' Rights", large corporations are frequently run by "management" — senior executive officers who are employees of the corporation — and the board of directors itself is remote from day to day operations of the business.

this offer to the shareholders for their consideration.[10] They may reject the offer out of hand or they may accept it on behalf of their own share interest and not communicate the offer to the other shareholders. Only if the directors offer to act on behalf of the other shareholders, thereby creating an agency relationship, will they be under the duties of an agent.[11] Under the securities legislation enacted in several of the provinces since 1966, if the directors choose to advise the shareholders to either accept or reject a takeover bid, they are required to issue a *directors' circular* to the shareholders setting out, among other things, their own interests, their own intentions with respect to the offer, and details of any arrangements made with the offeror company concerning their continuance in office or compensation for loss of office. American courts have been willing to employ equitable principles to place a duty upon the board of directors towards the general body of shareholders, and have held that when negotiating about the sale of a controlling block of shares, the directors are dealing in the assets of the corporation:[12] in these circumstances, they are under a duty to act in the best interests of the shareholders generally. Thus, in the United States, if directors obtain higher than the market price for their own block of shares because it represents control, they must apportion the excess among *all* the shareholders.

To the Corporation

Contrasted with the paucity of decisions concerning the directors' duties towards shareholders, their duties towards the corporation itself have produced a large body of case law. Although the judgments are complicated by the inherent complexity of corporate relations, some fairly clear general principles have evolved. These may be conveniently broken down in three groups: (1) the duties of care and skill; (2) the duty to disclose an interest in contracts with the company; and (3) the duty to refrain from abuse of corporate opportunity.

Care and skill. The duties of care and skill required of a director towards a corporation are minimal. We have not as yet developed standards for a professional class of directors; it is therefore difficult to assign to them any special degree of skill, competence, or expertise such as we demand of a doctor, accountant, lawyer, or engineer. A director is bound to exercise reasonable care, that is, not to be negligent in carrying out his duties. In this respect no greater diligence is required of him than is required of the average man; he is placed under no higher standard.[13] Also, a director is always safe in his ignorance, at least as long as he is not deliberately ignorant. Accordingly, if he fails to attend a meeting at which something occurs that may amount to a breach of duty by the directors

---

[10] Percival v. Wright [1902] 2 Ch. 421.
[11] Allen v. Hyatt (1914) 17 D.L.R. 7.
[12] Perlman v. Feldman 219 F. 2d 173 (1955).
[13] But see, R.S.O. 1970, c. 53, s. 144: "Every director and officer of a corporation shall exercise the powers and discharge the duties of his office honestly, in good faith and in the best interests of the corporation, and in connection therewith shall exercise the degree of care, diligence and skill that a reasonably prudent person would exercise in comparable circumstances." It is uncertain whether this section, which first appeared in 1970, may have the effect of raising the standard.

who do attend, he will not incur any liability himself. There is no duty upon him to attend the meetings of the directors regularly, nor to examine the books of the corporation, nor to search carefully into its financial position. He is entitled to rely on the information he receives from the officers of the company, such as its president and treasurer, and on professional advice from accountants and lawyers.[14] He may not, however, wilfully close his eyes to mistakes and misconduct. If he acquiesces in such matters, he may be liable in damages to the company for any losses which result.

To disclose an interest in contracts with the company. In contrast to the standards of care and skill, the duty of good faith towards the company, as disclosed in this and the following subsection, requires a high standard of conduct by a director. In many ways, perhaps his most important duty is to disclose his interest in contracts made with the company. His interest may arise by direct ownership of an asset being sold to the company, or it may arise in more indirect ways: a director may be a shareholder in another company that is selling to or buying from his company, or the person making a contract with his company may be acting as agent or trustee for him or for a member of his family. The problem arises very frequently with related companies. They may not necessarily be in the relationship of parent and subsidiary. It may merely be that one or more directors of one company are shareholders and perhaps directors of a second company.

Illustration:

> Brown holds a large number of shares in each of World Electric and Universal Shipbuilding, and he is a director of each of these companies. Universal Shipbuilding requires expensive turbo-generator sets for two large ships under construction. World Electric is one of several manufacturers of turbo-generators. Now Brown is faced with an obvious conflict of interest: can he encourage or even support a contract between the two companies? On one side, it is in Brown's interest to see Universal Shipbuilding obtain the equipment at the lowest possible price. On the other side, it is in his interest to see World Electric get the contract and obtain the highest possible price.

The courts have evolved a set of rules to look after the situation. In virtually every jurisdiction these rules have been codified and form a part of corporation legislation. Generally speaking, a director who has an interest in a contract must disclose this fact at a meeting of the board of directors considering the contract, and he must not vote on the matter. If after learning of this interest, the remaining independent members of the board still wish to go through with the contract, then a binding contract will be created by a subsequent vote of these independent members of the board. Failure by a director to disclose his interest gives the company the right to rescind the contract upon learning of his interest in it. Alternatively, it may affirm the contract on the terms in which it was made.

---

[14] Dovey v. Cory [1901] A.C. 477.

Sometimes almost all the directors of a company are interested in a contract, and the remaining independent directors are not enough to form a quorum. In these circumstances, the contract should be presented to a general meeting of the shareholders for their ratification after full disclosure has been made to them. This practice is generally followed, although there are no decided cases on the point, for without this subsequent ratification, the contract probably remains subject to rescission.

To refrain from abuse of corporate opportunity. In the preceding paragraphs we discussed the duty that arises when a director has an interest in a contract proposed to be made with the company. In this section we shall discuss primarily his duty to the company in a transaction he makes *with a third person* as a means of acquiring an interest in a property or venture. In other words, we are dealing here with contracts he makes with persons other than the company. If it appears in the particular circumstances that it was a director's duty to acquire property for the company or at least to give the company the chance of first refusal, and if instead he acquires title to the property for himself, then he has intercepted an opportunity belonging to the company and committed a breach of duty. Under the principles of equity, he is regarded as a trustee of the property; that is, he holds the formal legal title in trust for the true beneficial owner in equity, the company. We shall discuss the ways in which this duty may arise and the remedies available to the company in case of breach.

The duty of a director to acquire property on behalf of a company may arise in two main situations. The first situation occurs when he has received a mandate to act as agent either in the purchase of a specific piece of property or in the purchase of a class of property generally. In these circumstances he is under a duty ordinarily placed upon any agent to acquire property for his principal. If a director buys property for himself after he has received an express mandate to acquire such property for the company, there is no difficulty in finding him guilty of a breach. In the absence of an express mandate it may become a difficult question, to be decided from all the circumstances of the case, whether the director received an implied mandate to act as agent.

The second situation occurs when a director receives information about a profitable venture or an opportunity to buy property at an advantageous price. If this opportunity has arisen because of his corporate office, that is, if he has received the information as a director of the company, then it is his duty to give the company first chance at acquiring an interest in the venture or property. If the company decides not to acquire the property, the director is probably free to do so. But he makes a dangerous decision if he assumes that the company would not want the property anyway, or that it would be disadvantageous for the company to acquire the property, and then acquires it in his own name without consulting the company. Here again, it may be very difficult for a court to decide whether in the circumstances the information came to him personally, because he is a man with expert knowledge in a particular field, or came to him in his role as a director of the corporation. Nevertheless, once the court decides that the opportunity belonged to the corporation, the result is quite clear: purchasing on his own behalf is a breach of duty.

The courts have held that a subsequent sale to the company of property held by a director, without disclosure of his interest in it (as when his interest is indirect, through a second company or a trustee who ostensibly sells to the company), is strong evidence of a scheme to sell that property to the company from the very date of its acquisition. The courts have held that purchasing property with the intention of reselling it to the company is tantamount to acquiring it as an agent of the company in the first place; thus, the director is under a duty to buy as agent for the company.

The position of a director who acquires an interest in property or a venture while he is under a duty to act for the company is the same as that of any agent who acquires an interest on behalf of his principal: although he may have formal or legal ownership of the property, he holds it for the benefit of his principal, the beneficial or equitable owner. On discovery of the transaction the company may force him to transfer the interest to it while reimbursing him for his cost of acquiring the interest; he is not entitled to any profit. If, when the company discovers the transaction, the director has already sold the property to a bona fide purchaser or to the company itself, then he must disgorge to the company any profits that he made as a result of the transactions.[15] If in subsequently selling to the company he did not disclose his interest in the property, the company may choose the remedy of rescission for non-disclosure as discussed in the preceding subsection. In these circumstances, then, the company may elect either to rescind the contract, if that is possible, and obtain the full purchase price back, or to accept the property and obtain the profits made by the director.

Professor Beck has specified the standard that ought to be applied by directors in governing their conduct vis-a-vis the company, as follows:

> The modern doctrine of corporate opportunity is simply an extension of Equity's old rule that a fiduciary must not use his position to appropriate for himself benefits which he ought to have acquired, if at all, for his principal. In corporate terms, the test should be whether the opportunity was so closely associated with the existing and prospective activities of the corporation that the directors should fairly have acquired it for, or made it available to the corporation. If an affirmative answer is given to the question posed, a showing of good faith should, as in all cases of fiduciary duty, be no defence. . . . It is a standard which no Anglo-Canadian court has explicitly formulated but it is one which is implicit in the early cases and it is a natural extension of Equity's guardianship to protect the corporation and its shareholders.[16]

DUTIES OF PROMOTERS

The term "promoter of a company" is a vague one. Nowhere, either in the stat-

---

[15] Canada Safeway Ltd. v. Thompson [1951] 3 D.L.R. 295, and [1952] 2 D.L.R. 591.
[16] Beck, S.M., "The Saga of Peso Silver Mines: Corporate Opportunity Reconsidered", 49 *Can. B. Rev.* p. 92 (1971).

utes concerning company law or the issue of securities, or in the decided cases, is the term comprehensively defined. Perhaps one of the best definitions is that given by Chief Justice Cockburn in a comparatively early case when he defined a promoter as ''one who undertakes to form a company with reference to a given project and to set it going, and who takes the necessary steps to accomplish that purpose''.[17] As Professor Gower has pointed out, he may play a comparatively minor role in the process.[18] In addition, he may be a promoter *after* the company has been formed if he assists in the subsequent public issue of securities. The definition of promoter does not, however, include persons employed in a professional capacity, such as accountants, engineers, and lawyers. It becomes a question to be decided in the particular circumstances whether a person is a promoter of a company. The courts have taken a wide view of the persons who may be considered promoters of a company. They are justified in doing so, for the duties placed upon promoters are neither morally nor legally onerous: they consist of disclosure and good faith towards the company.

Like a director, a promoter may have acquired property on his own behalf when he was under no duty to acquire it for the benefit of the company nor had any intention of doing so. If he subsequently sells the property to a company he has assisted in promoting, he is under the same duty to disclose his interest in the sale as if he were a director, and the company has available the same remedy of rescission for failure to disclose. Because of the nature of a newly-formed company, often the promoter and his colleagues are the only ones having an interest in the company at the time the contract is made. For example, a company may be formed with only three shares issued to the three incorporators. If the promoter discloses to them his interest in a contract under which the company is to acquire its principal asset, and if the incorporators, being all the existing shareholders, approve the sale, it could be argued that disclosure has been made to all who have an interest in the company and nothing more need be done. Yet obviously, if the company were to make a public issue of its securities soon afterwards without disclosure of the promoter's interest, the company would avoid providing prospective investors with essential information. Accordingly, it has been held that a promoter must disclose his interest in a contract with the company either to an entirely independent board of directors concerned with the welfare of the company or, if one does not yet exist, then to all the shareholders and potential shareholders of the company as a whole.[19] In other words, he must make a disclosure in the prospectus, advertisement, or other circular being used to encourage investment in the company.

We have seen that a director may be under a duty to acquire property on behalf of his company, and even when he acquires it in his own name he may be presumed to hold it as trustee for the company. A promoter is under a similar duty, but in one sense the duty is even more extensive for him. He may, for ex-

---

[17] Twycross v. Grant (1877) 2 C.P.D. 469 at 541.
[18] Gower, *Modern Company Law* (3rd ed.), p. 271, and Chapter 13 generally.
[19] Erlanger v. New Sombrero Phosphate Co. (1878) 3 App. Cas. 1218.

ample, buy an interest in property before the company has come into existence, with the intention of promoting a company and selling his interest to it at a profit without full disclosure and consent. In these circumstances, he is presumed to have purchased the property in trust for the company even though at the time of his purchase the company is non-existent. Accordingly, the company, after purchasing the property, may compel him to disgorge any secret profits he has made on the transaction if it can bring his scheme to light.[20]

Generally speaking, then, the duties of the promoter in acting on behalf of the company are disclosure and good faith, and are essentially similar to the duties owed by a director.

RIGHTS OF SHAREHOLDERS

Sources of Shareholders' Rights

In large, broadly held corporations, shareholdings are widely distributed, frequently with no single shareholder or group holding more than five per cent of the voting stock. No majority or even controlling group of shareholders can be discerned; only in exceptional, almost catastrophic circumstances can a group be mobilized to try to save the company from its faltering managers. In these corporations management is largely self-perpetuating, even when it is inefficient and perhaps incompetent. It should be noted too that in large corporations management — the senior executive officers — operates almost entirely independently of the board of directors. The chief executive officer, the general manager, is often a director and president of the company, but he provides only a tenuous link between senior management and the board. Those decisions that are referred to the board are usually rubber-stamped when the president speaks in their favour.

Paradoxically, such managers are probably supported in their lofty position by a sage piece of practical advice to individual investors: "If you don't like the management, sell!" In other words, "Do not get into costly corporate struggles; cut your losses by getting out and re-investing in a company more to your liking." This advice is a guiding principle that leaves poor managers in control until their corporation's misfortunes become manifestly public knowledge — at which time it may be too late to salvage one's investment.

In closely held corporations, the problem is radically different. The usual problem is serious disagreement among the principal shareholders, the "corporate partners," who are usually directors and senior employees of the company. In the absence of careful contractual arrangements to provide him with safeguards, a minority shareholder in a closely held corporation may find himself "locked in" and "frozen out" at the same time.

The minority shareholder is "locked in" in the sense that he probably can-

---

[20] In re Olympia Ltd.: Gluckstein v. Barnes [1900] A.C. 240.

not sell his shares except at a small fraction of what he honestly believes they should be worth. There are two reasons for this unhappy state of affairs. (1) In most closely held corporations the sale of shares is restricted, usually requiring the consent of the board of directors. And it is the dominating majority on the board who have made the minority shareholder's life miserable. They are unlikely to consent freely to the transfer of minority shares. (2) Even if the minority shareholder is free to sell his shares, he will have great difficulty in finding a willing buyer. In the best of times his market would be restricted to prospective buyers who would consider acquiring his interest as if it were a share in a partnership; how much more difficult it is, then, to sell to a buyer who would only have the prospect of occupying the minority shareholder's unhappy position.

The minority shareholder may be "frozen out" in the following manner: (1) the majority directors may fire him from his job with the company, or at the very least refuse to renew his employment contract when it expires; (2) they may remove him from the board of directors, or re-elect someone else in his place at the next election; (3) they may increase salaries to themselves or pay large year-end employee bonuses, so that the company itself earns no apparent profit. Even if a profit is shown, it may be retained by the company, since dividends are payable only at the discretion of the board of directors. Thus, it can happen that a minority shareholder with his life savings invested in a corporation may find himself deprived of his salary-earning position, his directorship, and his prospect of any dividends on his investment; and he may also be without a marketable security — even though he has a substantial share interest in the corporation.

In these circumstances the majority shareholders have not broken any law, and no remedy exists at common law. Canadian courts have shown far less willingness to wind a company up at the request of a minority shareholder than they have in similar circumstances with respect to a partnership. Only British Columbia and the federal government have attempted to remedy the situation by statute. We shall discuss the British Columbia and federal provisions, and ways of avoiding the problem by use of shareholders' agreements, under "Rescuing the 'Locked-in' Shareholder", below.

During the late 19th and early 20th centuries, judges were able to work out remedies on a case-to-case basis for a few of the abuses suffered by minority shareholders, but on the whole they have been unable to devise legal principles to assist minorities unless the controlling group can be proven guilty of fraud. As a result, most developments protecting the rights of shareholders have occurred in legislation. However, the main concern of legislative reform has been with the broadly held corporation. Some of these reforms have been helpful to the minority shareholder in the closely held corporation as well, but by and large the only real protection for minority shareholders is through carefully-drafted contractual arrangements made *before* the minority shareholder buys into a company. Notable exceptions are the British Columbia and federal provisions referred to above, which are designed especially to help minority shareholders.[21]

---

[21] St. of B.C. 1973, c. 18, s. 221; St. of Can. 1974-75, c. 33, s. 234.

The protection given under the various statutes breaks down into two main categories: disclosure of the company's affairs, and the right to a voice in the company's affairs. A third category, financial rights to profits and assets on winding up, has developed from two sources: interpretation of the incorporating statute and interpretation of the corporate documents of record.

Statutory Safeguards: Disclosure

The financial statement. The importance of disclosure derives from the assumptions that the cold light of publicity offers investors an opportunity to evaluate the effectiveness of management and that in extreme cases publicity is an effective deterrent to high-handed behaviour or misconduct in management.[22]

Of the several types of disclosure, perhaps the most important takes the form of the annual financial statement of the corporation, which must be sent to shareholders of broadly held corporations before the annual general meeting. All corporations acts require certain minimum information to form part of the financial statement, though requirements vary significantly. Generally speaking, the basic items for the purpose of such disclosure are the income statement, showing the results of operations for the financial year; the balance sheet, showing the company's assets and sources of assets as of the financial year-end (including details of changes in share capital during the year); a statement of changes in financial position, analyzing changes in working capital; a statement of retained earnings showing changes during the year, including the declaration of dividends; and a statement of contributed surplus. The annual financial statement should be in comparative form, showing corresponding data for the preceding financial year. In addition, some statutes require that shareholders be sent a comparative interim financial statement for the six-month period following the last financial year.

To assist in the analysis and evaluation of the financial statement, all the acts except those of New Brunswick, Newfoundland and Prince Edward Island provide for the appointment of an independent auditor by the shareholders of all broadly held companies (but not private or closely held companies). The auditor must be an independent person not in the employ of the corporation, and he represents the shareholders' interests. He has the duty to investigate all the records and accounts of the corporation so that he may check on the fairness of the financial statement well in advance of the annual general meeting of shareholders. His task is to present to the shareholders his opinion of the financial statement issued by the directors. He must state whether in his opinion the statement fairly presents the financial position and results of operations of the company.[23] Both the auditor's report and the financial statement must be issued to all shareholders well before the company's annual general meeting; the period usually specified is

---

[22] See Harris, "Access to Corporate Information", in *Studies in Canadian Company Law*, (Ziegel, ed.) Vol. 1, Ch. 16.

[23] See section 5500, *CICA Handbook* (The Canadian Institute of Chartered Accountants) for a complete statement of the form and content of the auditors' report.

at least ten days before the meeting. These items are included in the company's *annual report* to shareholders.

The financial statement is prepared from the *books of account*. Only the auditor, as representative of the shareholders, and the directors have the right to examine these books; shareholders as such do not have access to them. If a shareholder suspects that something is wrong, he may communicate his information to the auditor in the hope that the auditor will make use of it, but the auditor has no duty to undertake a special examination at the request of a shareholder. Or again, a shareholder may communicate with a director who would be sympathetic to his point of view and who may be willing to check the information against the books of account. As a last resort, a shareholder may, in all jurisdictions except Prince Edward Island, apply to a court for the appointment of an inspector.

Appointment of inspector. All the jurisdictions (except Prince Edward Island) have statutory provisions for applying to the courts to appoint an inspector to investigate the affairs of the company and to audit its books. The statutes give inspectors sweeping powers of inquiry, and the remedy could be a very effective one were it not for two difficulties. First, most of the jurisdictions require a rather large percentage of the shareholders to join in the application. The percentage varies from 5 per cent to 25 per cent among the provinces; in a large public corporation, this requirement could easily be prohibitive. At present, only the Ontario and federal acts permit a sole shareholder to apply for the appointment of an inspector.[24] Secondly, almost all the statutes require either that the applicant give security to cover the probable costs of the investigation, or at least permit the court or investigating body in its discretion to require security for costs. In the past it has been customary to require security for costs from the complainant, and in a full-scale investigation of a big corporation, the costs are so large as to discourage any but the wealthiest minority shareholders.

The authors suggest that the right of inspection would be more effective if the acts provided for a preliminary enquiry at which the shareholder need only make out a *prima facie* case, that is, produce sufficient evidence of the probability of serious mismanagement to warrant further investigation. If so, the court should be prohibited from requiring security for costs by the applicant. This is the approach taken in the Business Corporations Act of Ontario and the federal Act with respect to shareholders' derivative actions.[25] We shall return to a discussion of these actions later in the chapter.

Documents of record. The second major requirement of disclosure is the statutory provision that a company must maintain certain *documents of record* at its head office for the inspection of any shareholder during the usual business hours of the company. The documents of record to which the shareholders have access include minute books of the proceedings at meetings of the shareholders; a register of all transfers of shares, including the date and other particulars of each transfer; a copy of the company charter; a copy of all by-laws (or articles) and

---

[24] R.S.O. 1970, c. 53, s. 186(1); St. of Can. 1974-75, c. 33, s. 222(1).
[25] R.S.O. 1970, c. 53, s. 99(3); St. of Can. 1974-75, c. 33, s. 235(3).

special resolutions; a register of shareholders stating their names and addresses; and a register of the directors setting out their names, addresses and occupations and the dates of their holding office. These documents may often be of use to a minority group of shareholders attempting to collect evidence to support a claim of misconduct or ineffectiveness on the part of the directors. In addition, the share register permits a dissentient group to obtain the addresses of all other shareholders so that they may communicate with them and explain their complaints.

Another document of record is the minute book of the proceedings at meetings of the board of directors. Unlike the other documents of record, however, directors alone, not the shareholders, have a right of access to it.

Record of insider trading. Since the early 1930s, United States federal securities legislation[26] has required directors and officers to report their own trading in their company's securities, so that shareholders may learn whether they are making use of confidential information in order to traffic profitably in the shares of the company (for example, selling short before an unfavourable financial report is issued, or buying in before the announcement of a profitable transaction).

Until 1966, disclosure requirements for directors and officers of Canadian companies were minimal. Only the Ontario and federal acts required directors to disclose information and this was of a very limited scope and usefulness.[27] In 1966, Ontario substantially amended the disclosure requirements of the Corporations Act[28] and passed a new Securities Act[29] requiring detailed information on insider trading to be filed with the provincial Securities Commission, which publishes details each month. At the time of writing, British Columbia, Alberta and Saskatchewan[30] have enacted new securities acts similar to the Ontario statute, to be discussed later in this chapter, and the Canada Business Corporations Act has been similarly revised.[31]

Statutory Safeguards: a Voice in the Affairs of the Company

Notice and attendance at meetings. Disclosure alone, of course, is not a sufficient safeguard for the shareholder. Shareholders must be able to do something about unsatisfactory management. If they wish to voice their objections, they need a forum to do so. The forum provided under all the statutes is the annual general meeting of shareholders. The company may hold other general meetings of shareholders in the course of the year, but it is required by statute to hold at least one annual general meeting. Shareholders are entitled to advance notice of all general meetings, and, as we have seen, they are entitled to receive copies of

---

[26] Securities Exchange Act of 1934, s. 16 (U.S.).

[27] R.S.O. 1960, c. 71, s. 71; R.S.C. 1952, c. 53, s. 98.

[28] St. of Ont. 1966, c. 28, s. 3, now found in Business Corporations Act, R.S.O. 1970, c. 53, ss. 148, 149.

[29] St. of Ont. 1966, c. 142, ss. 109, 110, now R.S.O. 1970, c. 426, ss. 109 to 111.

[30] St. of B.C. 1967, c. 45; R.S.A. 1970, c. 333; St. of Sask. 1967, c. 81.

[31] St. of Can. 1974-75, c. 33, ss. 121-125.

the financial statement before the annual general meeting. They may attend the meetings, question the directors, and make criticisms of the management of the corporation.

The right to requisition meetings. Occasions may arise where the shareholders wish to call a meeting and the board of directors refuses to do so. All the provinces except Newfoundland provide in their statutes that the shareholders themselves may call the meeting. Unfortunately, these provisions require a comparatively large proportion of the shareholders to petition in order to compel the calling of the meeting, a requirement virtually impossible to meet in large corporations where even a comparatively large group of shareholders may hold a very small percentage of the total shares. The lowest percentage required by these provisions is 5 per cent in the British Columbia, Saskatchewan and federal acts; the highest, the almost impossible figure of 25 per cent demanded in Prince Edward Island. The right to requisition a special meeting is therefore rather limited, but is available in at least some cases.

The right to vote. The right to attend meetings and to criticize must ultimately be backed by some form of sanction in the hands of the shareholders. This sanction is found in the right to vote. As we have seen, certain important actions by directors must be confirmed by the shareholders at a general meeting. The shareholders may refuse to confirm the actions of the directors and may materially alter by-laws put before them. Common shares almost invariably carry the right to vote and preferred shares usually carry a right to vote in specified circumstances, such as when preferred dividends are in arrears. The founders of a company can create several classes of shares and weight the voting heavily in favour of a small group of shares held by themselves. For example, they could give class A shares one hundred votes per share and class B, which they issue to the public, only one vote per share. It would, however, be virtually impossible to float an issue of such shares today: securities commissions, stock exchanges and underwriters would very probably refuse such an issue, and without their concurrence a public offering is impossible. Virtually all common stock offered on the market today carries one vote per share. Once these votes on a per-share basis have been assigned, shareholders are protected by statute from any variation in these rights. Thus, no share of a given class can be given a different voting power from other shares of the same class.

Elections and proxies. We have noted that shareholders may vote in the confirmation of by-laws and may appoint their own auditor, but perhaps the most important right to vote is in the election of directors, or in the most extreme cases, the removal of directors. In most broadly held companies, only a small proportion of shareholders manage to attend the annual general meeting at which elections are held. All company law statutes permit a shareholder who will not be present to assign his voting right to any shareholder who will be present at the annual meeting. He does this by signing a *proxy form* in the name of the person to whom he wishes to assign his vote. In a proxy fight between two groups of shareholders, usually the board of directors and a dissentient group, each group solicits all the shareholders by mail in order to persuade them to give their proxy forms to the group making the solicitation. The dissentient group may go to the company head office to copy out lists of all the shareholders from the share register in order to make their solicitations. Here the board of directors has a great advantage: as a matter of practice, they include proxy forms, designating one of themselves as the proposed proxy, with the mailed notice of the annual general meeting.[32] In this manner, all the costs of compiling the list and addressing and mailing the notices are borne by the company, whereas a group of dissentient shareholders, in order to solicit proxy forms, must bear all these costs themselves. In very large corporations, the costs may be prohibitive for a dissentient group. The larger the corporation, the more difficult it is to dislodge an incumbent board of directors, but there have been quite a few instances of dissatisfied shareholders' turning out the entire board of directors and in turn, senior management of a large company.

Cumulative voting. In the United States, many of the jurisdictions have long provided an additional protection to minority-group shareholders by requiring cumulative voting for directors. Ordinarily, where there is no cumulative voting, for each share held each shareholder has one vote for each place to be filled on the board of directors: thus, if the board of directors is composed of nine persons, he will have nine votes for each share held. If 15 candidates were contesting the nine positions, a shareholder holding five shares could give five votes for each of nine candidates. Under cumulative voting he could still give five votes to each of nine persons, or all 45 votes to one person, or any intermediate degree of concentration, such as giving 25 votes to candidate *A* and 20 votes to candidate *B*. In this way, a reasonably significant minority may accumulate all their votes in favour of one or two candidates and thus assure their election to the board, giving the minority an effective voice in the management of the company. Cumulative voting is more helpful to minority groups when a large number of directors is to be elected. If the number of directors is small or if only a small proportion of them is elected each year, cumulative voting is less effective in assisting the minority to elect a member to the board. There has been adverse criticism of cumulative voting because it sometimes permits a minority troublemaker to obtain a seat on the board and stall proceedings of the company. On balance, however, cumulative voting does seem to offer minority shareholder groups some added protection. Ontario has permitted cumulative voting since 1953; Manitoba and the federal government now permit it as well. The acts enable incorporators of a company to provide for cumulative voting, but do not make cumulative voting mandatory.[33] So far as can be gathered, the provision has been rarely if ever incorporated into the charter of an Ontario company as an entrenched right, but it has occasionally been provided for in the by-laws.

---

[32] This advantage is only partly offset by disclosure requirements and by compelling management to provide shareholders with a means to nominate an alternate proxy. See, for example, R.S.O. 1970, c. 53, s. 120(g).

[33] R.S.O. 1970, c. 53, s. 127; R.S.M. 1970, C160, s. 78; St. of Can. 1974-75, c. 33, s. 102.

Pre-emptive Rights

American courts have for many years been concerned with the proportionate holdings of shares of various shareholders. They have declared that at common law a shareholder has a *pre-emptive* right to retain his proportionate holdings in a company. Accordingly, when a company proposes to issue more shares it must offer him a proportion of the new issue equal to the proportion he holds in the already issued shares of the company. A shareholder who has three per cent of the issued shares of a company is entitled to purchase a further three per cent of any further issue of the company. Of course, he may give up this right of pre-emption and not bother to buy the shares. Or he may buy more than the pre-empted number of shares by accepting shares rejected by other shareholders. Such a general principle of pre-emption has not been recognized by either the British or the Canadian courts. In small or medium-sized companies, a right of pre-emption can be very important in retaining the balance of power in control of the company. It ceases to be of very great importance in the largest corporations.

In limited circumstances, however, the Canadian and English courts have recognized rights somewhat similar to pre-emptive rights. Thus, although Canadian directors have the right to issue authorized share capital of the company at their discretion for the capital requirements of the corporation, they must issue shares *only* for the purpose of raising capital. If they have a bona fide intention to raise capital, they may distribute the shares to whomever they wish upon payment of a fair price. But if directors issue shares not for the benefit of the corporation but to affect the voting control in the corporation, they may be restrained from making the issue, or it may subsequently be declared void. For example, if directors were to issue shares to themselves for the purpose of outvoting at a general meeting shareholders who, up to that point, had a majority of the issued shares, the directors could be prevented from carrying out their issue. This rule has been stated in a Canadian decision by Mr. Justice Rose:

> . . . No one would think of saying that directors may never allot shares of an authorized issue without first offering to the existing shareholders the shares which they propose to allot; but the allotment here proposed differs radically from the usual allotment from time to time, as opportunity offers, of the shares of an issue which has been determined upon as a means of providing the company with the requisite working capital. . . . [Here] no shares had been issued for a long time; the company had been carrying on a successful business with the capital which it had; the readily saleable assets were apparently worth three or four times the par value of the issued shares; each shareholder was justified in considering that he had an interest in those assets proportionate to his holding of the issued shares; to do something which would alter those proportions, to do it without giving to each shareholder an opportunity of protecting his interest and to do it not in the usual course of the company's business, but for the purpose of shifting from one body of shareholders to another the power of electing directors and so of

controlling the company's policy, was, I think, beyond the power of the directors.[34]

In practice, many large corporations voluntarily recognize their shareholders' pre-emptive right. Whenever they propose a new issue of shares, they issue subscription rights (pre-emptive rights, or more colloquially, "share rights") to all their present shareholders. Subscription rights are contained in a document from the company giving a shareholder a right for each share held, that is, the option to purchase a new share at a specified price for, let us say, every five subscription rights held in the company. Such subscription rights are transferrable. A shareholder owning 50 shares will then receive 50 rights entitling him to buy 10 shares at a specified price per share. If the market value of the shares exceeds the specified price by a significant sum, the rights themselves will have a market value and may be sold to anyone who wishes to purchase them and exercise the option. Share rights have an expiry date and must be exercised before that date or they become void.

Although the practice of issuing subscription rights is by no means universal, it is considered a fair and businesslike way to raise further capital — so much so that financial circles may be quite critical of a large corporation that issues further shares without issuing subscription rights to its existing shareholders.

Financial Rights to Dividends and Return of Capital[35]

The general purpose of any investment is to obtain a total return greater than the capital sum invested. The total return may include either or both of two elements: an increase in the market value of the shares, and earnings distributed regularly to the investor. Investors in common stock are often concerned with more than the annual distribution of profits. They may be satisfied with smaller dividends if there is a capital appreciation in the company's assets or if a significant part of the profits is retained within the business and has the effect of increasing the value of the shares. Preferred shares, however, are in a different category. Except in rare cases, they are preferred as to capital and are worth no more than the par value of the share plus a small premium, regardless of the increase in the net assets of the company. The preferred shareholder is, therefore, primarily interested in the regular distribution of profits in the form of dividends. Whether dividends are declared is a matter entirely within the discretion of the board of directors. There can be no discrimination, however, in the payment of dividends among shareholders of the same class; each is entitled to such dividends as are declared in proportion to the number of shares of that class held. In addition,

---

[34] Bonisteel v. Collis Leather Co. Ltd. (1919) 45 O.L.R. 195 at 200. But for a recent broadening of directors' discretion see Teck Corporation Ltd. v. Millar et al. (1973) 33 D.L.R. (3d) 288, esp. pp. 328-331.

[35] See Bryden, "The Law of Dividends", in *Studies in Canadian Company Law*, (Ziegel, ed.), Vol. 1, Ch. 9.

directors are bound to pay dividends in the order of preferences assigned to the classes of shareholders. Thus, they could not pay the common shareholders a dividend without first paying the whole of any preferred dividend owing to preference shareholders. Most preferred shares carry *cumulative* rights to dividends; that is, before common shareholders may receive dividends, the company must pay the preferred shareholders any arrears of unpaid dividends for prior years, as well as dividends for the current year.

On the dissolution of a company, provided the company has assets remaining after paying off all its creditors, shareholders are entitled to a proportionate share of the remaining net assets. The distribution of these net assets as between the various classes of shareholders has been the subject of considerable litigation. The rights of various shareholders on dissolution have been discussed in the preceding chapter, in the section "Nature of Corporate Securities".

THE PROTECTION OF MINORITY SHAREHOLDERS[36]

Duties of Directors and Shareholders Contrasted

We have seen that directors of corporations are under high duties of good faith with respect to their actions as officers of a corporation. In contrast, a shareholder owes no positive duty to act for either the welfare of the corporation itself or the welfare of his fellow shareholders. His obligation ends when he has paid the full purchase price for his shares. He may leave his share certificates lying in some forgotten corner, and never trouble to attend meetings or to return proxy forms. In this respect he is much like a property owner. Unless a statute places an obligation upon him to comply with some public duty — for example, filing income tax returns concerning his dividends — he is free to do nothing about his interest in the company. If he attends shareholders' meetings and votes he is free, generally speaking, to exercise his vote in whatever way he pleases and for whatever purposes he desires. By voting in favour of or against a particular resolution, he may cause the company to suffer a loss or may even harm his fellow shareholders; the attitude of the courts is that as a part owner of the corporation he may take into account whatever factors he wishes and vote his shares accordingly.

Possible Oppression of Minority Rights

At the very least, the above statement of a shareholder's freedom to use his vote means that the courts will not substitute their judgment for his when his actions are based upon business considerations. The courts' presumption is in favour of the shareholder from the beginning: it will not interfere even when it thinks that

---

[36] See MacKinnon, "The Protection of Dissenting Shareholders", in *Studies in Canadian Company Law,* (Ziegel, ed.), Vol. 1, Ch. 17.

the shareholder's decision is rather irresponsible or silly. Carried to an extreme, this view would permit completely unreasonable decisions that are deliberately intended to injure other shareholders. The power of the majority shareholders to oppress the minority has not been allowed to go so far. For example, the directors of a company might recommend that the company buy a particular asset at ten times the market price. If the shareholders were to confirm such an absurd contract, the company's assets would be depleted, and the value of its shares would be reduced accordingly. Yet the controlling shareholders might be tempted to confirm such a transaction if they themselves were the vendors of the asset to the company. Thus, if the company paid $100,000 for an asset worth only $10,000, upon completion of the transaction the company would be $90,000 poorer. If the controlling group held two thirds of the shares, the value of their holdings would be reduced by $60,000 as against the $90,000 profit they would make as vendors. Their $30,000 net gain would be at the expense of the minority shareholders, whose shares would be reduced in value to that extent. The controlling group need not, of course, hold an absolute majority: in many large corporations under 10 per cent of the voting shares will assure control. In these circumstances their profits are even greater, for the controlling group distributes the reduction in the total value of share holdings among a very large body of shareholders.

Again, suppose a board of directors has intercepted a corporate opportunity to make a large profit belonging rightfully to the corporation. The majority shareholders might then confirm a resolution stating that the corporation had no interest in the profits made by these directors. The majority would be particularly prone to do this if they were also the directors or business associates of the directors.

The two examples above illustrate gross misuse of corporate assets and opportunities by a controlling group of shareholders. We should note that the wrong in each case has been done to the corporation itself, and only indirectly to the shareholders by the proportionate diminution of the value of their shares. This fact has important implications for the remedies available to a complaining shareholder, as we shall see below.

A third example illustrates a different type of oppression. Suppose the directors and majority shareholders in a company became aware that the company was about to make a huge capital gain, perhaps doubling the value of their shares. The directors might pass a by-law requiring all shareholders who held less than 5 per cent of the company's shares to sell their holdings immediately at current market price to members who held more than 5 per cent of the company's shares. The majority shareholders, all holding more than 5 per cent, might confirm such a by-law. They could then acquire the shares of the minority group and obtain the whole of the capital gain for their own benefit, thus excluding the minority shareholders from the windfall. Here, the harm has been done directly to the minority shareholders; the corporation is not injured. The shareholders may sue the wrongdoers and the corporation for a declaration that the by-law is void and that they are still members of the corporation.

The three examples above illustrate various types of gross abuse of the interests of minority shareholders. They are discussed more fully by Professor Gower in his book *Modern Company Law* under the heading of "Fraud on the Minority".[37] The examples illustrate, respectively: (1) expropriation of the property of the company; (2) ratification of directors' breach of good faith; (3) expropriation of the property rights of minority shareholders. Possibly, these three examples do not cover all varieties of oppression that an ingenious controlling group might devise. There appears to be a power in the court to exercise its discretion and give a remedy to the minority whenever the acts of the controlling group are oppressive and unreasonable. If their acts appear to be spiteful and malicious, so as to harm the minority, if they appear to be discriminatory so as to give the majority an unjustified advantage, or if they appear to be wholly unreasonable so that the only conclusion possible is that their actions are motivated either by malice or by intentional discrimination, the court may come to the assistance of the complaining minority shareholders. From the point of view of a minority shareholder, however, an appeal to the court to exercise its discretion in his favour remains an uncertain and tenuous remedy.

Remedies of Minority Shareholders for Wrongs Done to the Corporation

When a corporation has suffered an injury, as in our first two examples above, it may sue a wrongdoer in the same manner as may a natural person. Ordinarily, an action must be started by its officers or board of directors. If, however, the directors are the wrongdoers they are hardly likely to commence such an action against themselves. Unless an aggrieved minority shareholder is permitted to bring an action in the name of the company, the wrong will go unremedied and the controlling directors will get away with their ill-gotten gain. No legal system can permit such oppressive conduct to continue without a remedy — at least in theory. Thus, a minority shareholder may start an action on behalf of the corporation in the name of himself and all other aggrieved shareholders — a representative or class action *derived from* the injury to the company, and frequently called a *derivative action*.

Unfortunately, at common law the courts have great difficulty with the concept of an outsider, a mere shareholder, suing in the name of the company. They have surrounded this right with procedural requirements that have the effect of almost stifling any theoretical right to a remedy. For example, the minority shareholder must satisfy the court that he has exhausted all internal remedies by showing that he has made formal demands for a company meeting to discuss the alleged misconduct and that all reasonable demands by him have been refused by the company. This procedure can be time-consuming and costly. Secondly, he must establish that the wrong is unlawful and has actually injured the company, frequently a difficult thing to do without access to corporate files and accounts.

Even worse, if the court does agree to proceed with the case, it almost

---

[37] (3rd ed. 1969), Chapter 24, pp. 561 ff.

always accedes to the claim of the corporation that the investigation of its affairs is a very expensive matter, and that the complaining shareholder should be required to deposit a substantial sum of money with the court as security for costs in the event that he loses the case.

Despite these barriers, there is a rich literature of corporate oppression uncovered and remedied by the courts. It is certain, however, that larger numbers of minority shareholders with just grievances have been defeated by the procedural difficulties.

Three legislative attempts have been made in Canada thus far to overcome these procedural barriers. The Ontario,[38] British Columbia[39] and federal acts[40] permit a shareholder to obtain leave from the court to bring a derivative action and thereby gain better access to a remedy. In the first place, he need not exhaust every possible avenue of internal remedy within the corporation. He need only establish that he has "made reasonable efforts to cause the corporation to commence or prosecute diligently the action on its own behalf," and that he "is acting in good faith and it is *prima facie* in the interests of the corporation or its shareholders that the action be commenced." If he establishes these things, then the court may make an order to commence the action. The Ontario and federal acts prohibit the court from requiring the shareholder to give security for costs.[41] Indeed, the court is informed that "at any time or from time to time while an action commenced under this section is pending, the plaintiff may apply to the court for an order for the payment *to the plaintiff* by the corporation of reasonable interim costs, including solicitors' and counsel fees and disbursements . . ."[42] In other words, the court is directed to look to the welfare and ability of the shareholder to continue with the action. It remains to be seen how successful these provisions will be in permitting minority shareholders to vindicate their rights before a court.

Rescuing the "Locked-in" Shareholder

We have briefly described the plight of the locked-in minority shareholder: his former business associates have frozen him out of the company but have been scrupulously careful not to break any rules or to be guilty of harming the corporation itself. No doubt they justify their harsh treatment by recounting his many sins as a partner in the enterprise. But which side is the guilty one is irrelevant: the majority have used their power to make him an outcast. In a partnership, the rules of equity give considerable protection to a minority member: he is entitled to an accounting of profits and to receive his share of them regularly; if the impasse is total between the partners he can insist on a dissolution and sale of the

---

[38] R.S.O. 1970, c. 53, s. 99.
[39] St. of B.C. 1973, c. 18, s. 222.
[40] St. of Can. 1974-75, c. 33, s. 232.
[41] R.S.O. 1970, c. 53, s. 99(3); St. of Can. 1974-75, c. 33, s. 235(3).
[42] R.S.O. 1970, c. 53, s. 99(4). The federal act has a similar provision: St. of Can. 1974-75, c. 33, s. 235(4).

assets and receipt of his proportionate part of the proceeds. Since the other partners cannot continue to use the partnership assets for their sole benefit, they must either face dissolution and sale or else offer him a reasonable settlement. Not so in a closely held corporation: in the absence of contractual protection through a private agreement among the shareholders, a minority shareholder has none of the remedies of a partner.

English legislation first recognized the unfairness of this shareholder position in s. 210 of the Companies Act (1948).[43] MacKinnon describes the effect of the section as follows:

> . . . the right to petition the court is given to any shareholder 'who complains that the affairs of the company are being conducted in a manner oppressive to some part of the members (including himself)'. In order to give relief the court must satisfy itself of two things: first, that the company's affairs are being conducted in an oppressive manner and, second, that the facts justify a winding-up order on the ground that it would be just and equitable to do so but that to wind up the company would unfairly prejudice the oppressed minority. If these two conditions are met then the court may 'make such order as it thinks fit'. This might include regulating the conduct of the company's affairs in future, or ordering the purchase of the shares of any members of the company by other members of the company.[44]

There have been several cases where s. 210 has been successfully invoked to help an oppressed shareholder, but its greatest significance has been to invoke it "as a weapon in negotiation". After all, that is what is needed. The entrapped minority shareholder does not wish usually to force the company to be wound up, just as his opposite number in a partnership is hardly likely to insist on dissolution: he is satisfied to use the threat of dissolution to get a fair deal. So far, British Columbia and the federal government have followed the English lead. British Columbia first passed a section that was substantially the same as the English section in 1960. Its 1973 Act contains a revised and seemingly more effective version of the English section,[45] based on the proposal for a new section in the federal act, now adopted federally.[46]

Shareholder Agreements

Their difficulties and advantages. In the absence of a sensible reform by statute, can a group of, let us say, three equal partners safely transform their business into a corporation? It may make good business sense to incorporate because of

---

[43] 11 & 12 Geo. 6, c. 38 (U.K.).
[44] "The Protection of Dissenting Shareholders", in *Studies in Canadian Company Law*, (Ziegel, ed.), Vol. 1, p. 511, Toronto: Butterworths, 1967.
[45] St. of B.C. 1973, c. 18, s. 221.
[46] St. of Can. 1974-75, c. 33, s. 234.

the nature of the business, its growth and tax position. Yet each of the three partners, if he were aware of the dangers of being a minority shareholder at odds with his other two partners, might well hesitate to give up the protection of partnership law. Fortunately it is possible to devise an employment contract with the corporation and a concurrent agreement among the shareholders themselves — outside the constitution of the corporation — that approximates the protection available to partners. The process is not simple because the concept of the corporation guarded by the courts is that of the broadly held company with shares traded the market. Within this concept, we must remember, directors owe their primary duty to the corporation: they must not fetter their duty to exercise their discretion "bona fide in the best interests of the corporation," however inappropriate that duty may be when applied to a closely held corporation in which the directors themselves hold all the shares.[47] Thus any agreement among shareholders must be restricted to their role as shareholders and must not impinge on their role as directors.[48] Business lawyers are aware of this danger and can avoid it in a well-drafted shareholder agreement. Each set of employment and shareholder agreements must be custom-tailored to the needs of an individual business, just as in partnership. Nevertheless, we may briefly examine the chief elements normally used to protect minority shareholders.

Right to employment. Each shareholder may enter into a long-term employment contract with the corporation with a salary subject to increases at an agreed rate. There may be a provision that after a preliminary financial statement each year, he will receive an employee's profit sharing bonus equal to a specified proportion of the corporate profits before taxes.

Right to participate in management. The shareholders mutually promise to elect each other to the board of directors at each annual meeting and not to nominate or vote for any other person. They may agree not to sell their shares to an outsider without giving the right of first refusal proportionately to the remaining shareholders. They may agree not to vote for any major change in the corporation's capital structure or in the nature of its business except by unanimous agreement.

The right to a fair price for a share interest. The shareholders may agree to a regular method of revaluation of their shares (usually on an annual basis), so that in case of major breach of the shareholder agreement by one of them who remains unwilling to remedy his breach, he will on notice be required to sell his interest to the other two at the appraised value. Finally, any shareholder who is wrongfully expelled or dismissed by the other two, who remain unwilling to reinstate him, may require them to buy out his interest at the appraised value. This provision may also state that in the event of a dispute about appraisal (for example, if through neglect or inadvertence there has been no appraisal for some

---

[47] For example, a majority of the directors may dismiss a minority shareholder from his position as an employee of the company because they honestly believe it to be in the best interests of the company, despite the fact that they had agreed in their role as shareholders to keep him employed.

[48] Motherwell v. Schoof [1949] 4 D.L.R. 812.

time) a named person, usually the auditor, will arbitrate and assess the value of the interest.

There can be many refinements to shareholder agreements; the above provisions are intended to illustrate their general tenor. Any businessman who finds that his would-be fellow shareholders balk at the suggestion of having their lawyer prepare a suitable agreement of this type ought to consider seriously whether it is wise to proceed further in the proposed venture.

Unanimous Shareholder Agreement

The Canada Business Corporations Act has formally recognized shareholder agreements and expressly permits them to govern relationships among shareholders in a closely held corporation in much the same manner as in a partnership. Although these agreements have yet to be interpreted by the courts, it is probable that the courts will apply equitable principles used in partnership in the place of those principles of corporation law that have proven to be inappropriate. For example, the Act permits a shareholder agreement to override, by express agreement, the duty of directors to exercise unfettered discretion solely in the best interests of the company. It states that "an . . . agreement among all the shareholders . . . that restricts in whole or in part the powers of the directors to manage the business and affairs of the corporation is valid,"[49] and that "a shareholder who is party to a[n] . . . agreement has all the rights, powers and duties of a director . . . to the extent that the agreement restricts the discretion or powers of the directors, . . . and *the directors are thereby relieved of their duties and liabilities* to the same extent.[50]

The Act also states that "a transferee of shares subject to an unanimous shareholder agreement is deemed to be a party to the agreement."[51] Thus, on the sale of a share interest in a closely held corporation that is subject to a shareholder agreement, the statutory equivalent of novation takes place: a transferee not only receives an assignment of rights as a shareholder but is also bound to carry out the duties of his transferor. A unanimous shareholder agreement must be "noted conspicuously" on the face of a share certificate in order to bind subsequent transferees.[52]

Only unanimous agreements are recognized by the Act: if all shareholders are not a party to the agreement, the special status granted them by the Act will not come about. Accordingly, these agreements cannot be utilized in companies using employee profit-sharing schemes where employees receive a share interest unless the employees also are made parties to the agreement.

The Act refers to unanimous shareholder agreements at more than a dozen places and treats them almost as if they are part of the corporate constitution,

---

[49] St. of Can. 1974-75, c. 33, s. 140(2).
[50] *Ibid.*, s. 140(4) (author's italics).
[51] *Ibid.*, s. 140(3).
[52] *Ibid.*, s. 45(8).

rather like by-laws.[53] It appears that the new federal Act has created the opportunity to develop a new flexible device for business planning in closely held corporations.

PROTECTION OF CREDITORS

Implications of Limited Liability

We have seen that when a sole trader or partnership firm becomes insolvent, the creditors may seize whatever assets are available, and that if a deficiency remains they may seize the personal assets of the sole trader or partners. In these forms of business organization, a debtor's liability is not limited to his business assets: his personal assets may be seized as well. In addition, unless he eventually receives a discharge from the courts in bankruptcy proceedings, any property he acquires for many years to come may also be seized, and judgment creditors may garnishee his salary or wages.

In a limited company, however, a creditor's rights are limited to the assets held by the corporation. If these assets are inadequate, he has no further remedy against the shareholders of the company. Accordingly, a creditor's only protection is the fund of assets owned by the corporation itself. For this reason, legislatures and courts have tried to evolve rules to assure creditors that these assets will not be impaired by actions of the directors. As we shall see, this task is not an easy one.

Except for such financial institutions as banks, insurance companies and trust and loan companies, the law requires no minimum of issued capital for corporations. Legally, a corporation may carry on business with a share capital of one dollar. Of course, a company would find it exceedingly difficult to obtain credit with only a nominal equity investment. As a practical matter, therefore, companies formed with small capital investments do not pose serious problems for creditors. It is of course possible that such a corporation might have a judgment creditor for a large sum of money as a result, let us say, of the negligent operation of a company truck. Legislatures have attempted to meet this problem through compulsory insurance plans related to highway traffic. The primary concern of the law with respect to capital is with corporations which once had a capital (or "equity") base substantial enough to persuade creditors to extend large amounts of credit; when subsequently such corporations suffer a substantial impairment of that capital, it may be important to know how that impairment took place.

It is not possible to devise legal rules that are capable of protecting creditors from the risk of extending credit to a company whose management runs it badly and impairs its capital through business losses. The rules that have evolved are

---

[53] See, for example: s. 98(1) "Unless the articles, by-laws *or a unanimous shareholder agreement* [italics ours] otherwise provide, the directors may, by resolution, make, amend, or repeal any by-laws that regulate the business affairs of the corporation."

designed rather to prevent the kinds of decisions that will deliberately impair a corporation's ability to meet its obligations. These rules are essentially of two kinds: rules prohibiting, and making directors personally liable for approving, any payment by the company to its shareholders that renders the company's liquid assets insufficient to pay the then outstanding claims of creditors, or any such payment when the company is already insolvent; and rules prohibiting ''return of capital'' to shareholders (for example, by declaring excessive dividends) even when the company might still be left with sufficient liquid assets to pay its creditors. We will consider these two types of rules briefly in turn.

The Solvency Test

After a company has received assets from shareholders by an issue of share capital, its further transactions with those shareholders will be confined largely to payments of dividends, and in certain circumstances to the redemption or purchase back by the company of its own shares. If payments by the company in either of these instances were to have the effect of rendering the company insolvent — of depleting its liquid assets below what was required to pay its then outstanding debts — the directors might become personally liable to the company for the deficiency. They would be equally liable, of course, for authorizing such transactions after the company had become insolvent. Their liability in this respect is, in many Canadian jurisdictions, set out specifically in a provision of the corporations act.[54]

It is questionable to what extent this test protects creditors since, for example, a large payment of dividends might not render the company insolvent as of the time it is made, but might nevertheless be very unwise. In relation to the flow of receipts and pattern of payments to which the company is already committed, the payment might foreseeably contribute to insolvency in the following months. Thus, a simple ''balance-sheet'' test of solvency applied at the time of a transaction may not be enough in marginal situations.[55]

The Maintenance of Capital Test

The creditors of a limited company have a second line of defence, albeit one to which less importance is now attached than formerly. This protection consists in a number of provisions in the corporations acts designed to ensure that the origi-

---

[54] See, for example: St. of B.C. 1973, c. 18, s. 150; R.S.O. 1970, c. 53, s. 136. However in Nova Scotia, the Companies Act, R.S.N.S. 1967, c. 42 does not provide that directors have any liability in respect of dividend payments, but if the company adopts the regulations in Table A appended to the Act, it will be subject to regulation 136 which provides, ''No dividend shall be paid otherwise than out of profits.''

[55] The federal Bankruptcy Act provides, additionally, an ''after the fact'' test which permits a trustee in bankruptcy to apply for a court inquiry in respect of dividends paid within 12 months preceding bankruptcy to determine whether the dividend rendered the company insolvent, and which authorizes the court to give judgment to the trustee against the directors, jointly and severally, in the amount of such dividend. R.S.C. 1970, c. B-3, s. 79.

nal and subsequent infusions of assets in the form of shareholder "capital" will be preserved — or at least not deliberately depleted. (As we have noted, no corporations act can insist that this "contributed capital" be preserved in the face of losses from operations.)

The theory underlying provisions for the maintenance of capital requires more than a solvency test; it requires that assets paid into the company by shareholders be preserved as far as possible within the company as a "capital fund". It recognizes that the assets provided to a business by its creditors may, as part of a total package of resources available to management, be depleted by business losses and thus become inadequate to pay creditors in full. Hence, the theory requires that the additional amount of assets provided by shareholders be as far as possible maintained and available for absorbing business reverses so that creditors may still be paid in full. The maintenance of capital test therefore goes beyond the solvency test.

Putting it another way: a business might, depending on the composition of its assets, have assets just equal to its liabilities and be able to pay its creditors as their claims fall due. It could have reached that precarious financial condition by having deliberately paid back to shareholders money they had invested in the company; it would still satisfy the solvency test but would have violated the maintenance of capital test. Suppose, on the other hand, it had reached that condition because of unavoidable business losses: while it would not have deliberately impaired its capital fund, the prior existence of the fund (now exhausted) has at least avoided insolvency to date. The case for a maintenance of capital requirement was succinctly explained by Adam Smith:

> Traders and other undertakers may, no doubt, with great propriety, carry on a very considerable part of their projects with borrowed money. In justice to their creditors, however, their own capital ought, in this case, to be sufficient to ensure, if I may say so, the capital of those creditors; or to render it extremely improbable that those creditors should incur any loss, even though the success of the project should fall very much short of the expectation of the projectors.[56]

His argument applies to all forms of business organization but seems particularly cogent when the business is a corporation that confronts its creditors with limited liability.

The accounting system, for all its deficiencies, especially in periods of rapidly-changing prices, is designed to provide a signal whenever a transaction results in an impairment of capital. Thus, a dividend payment that has the effect of creating a negative balance in retained earnings account — indicating disbursements to shareholders of more assets than have accrued to date in the form of profits — would impair the capital fund. Similarly, a reduction in share capital account, recording a redemption or purchase by the company of its own shares,

---

[56] Smith, A., *The Wealth of Nations*, pp. 291-3 (as reprinted, New York: Random House, 1937).

is a signal indicating a possible impairment of the capital fund (depending upon whether the reduction exceeds accumulated retained earnings).

Needless to say, this accounting test assumes a particular meaning of "capital fund." We are not here thinking of particular assets or classes of assets; we are thinking of the capital fund as a source of assets. If we translate all types of assets into dollar amounts, add them together and then deduct from that total the dollar amount of all liabilities and retained earnings to date, we necessarily come to a dollar figure that is an abstract idea — the capital fund. Once a company begins operations, capital of this kind can no longer be related directly to the very assets contributed by shareholders in exchange for their shares or to any specific assets into which those original assets have since been converted in the course of business. The closest we can come to describing this concept of capital is as an *equity* or *interest* in an aggregate of business assets: capital in a financial sense. It is capital in the context of the right-hand side of a balance sheet, not of the left-hand side.

We can see that the attempt to protect the capital fund as a form of security for creditors has drawn on both legal and accounting theory. The resulting "model", however, has been subject to considerable erosion and as we are about to see, has become something of a patchwork. Practical considerations have, as discussed below, compromised the strict principle against impairment of the capital fund.

Implications of the Maintenance of Capital Test

Dividends. Suppose a corporation had an issued capital of $5,000,000. After several years of operations it has wiped out all its retained earnings by payments of dividends, leaving the shareholders' interest at $5,000,000 again. If it were now to declare and pay a further dividend to its shareholders, the result would be as much a reduction of the capital fund as if it had returned part of its capital to its shareholders directly by buying in their shares: the directors would declare such a dividend at their peril. On the other hand, if the company had suffered successive losses over several years, resulting in the reduction of its net assets to an amount well below the capital paid in by shareholders, the same rule would prevent the company from paying any dividends until it had earned enough profits to restore the deficiency in its capital fund. If the rule were applied in these circumstances, the company's shares might become virtually unmarketable, for it might be many years before the company could again declare dividends. The very few reported Canadian decisions in which the payment of dividends has been an issue do not provide any clear guidance on this question, although some English decisions seem to support the view that a company with an accumulated past deficit may nonetheless be permitted to pay dividends to its shareholders out of the current year's earnings.[57] From the point of view of directors who may have a statutory

---

[57] See Fraser and Stewart, *Canadian Company Law* (5th ed.), pp. 538-42. Toronto: The Carswell Company Ltd., 1962.

liability for approving such a dividend payment, the proposition is risky: "It appears, however, that on the present state of the authorities it would be unwise to assume that previous or current losses in capital . . . may be ignored unless specifically so provided by statute."[58] The one instance in which some of our corporations acts have specifically authorized the payment of dividends out of capital is the payment of dividends by a corporation with wasting assets (for example, a mine) out of funds derived from the operations of the company.[59] For other companies, it has always been possible to take the formal step of amending the company's charter so as to "reduce" the share capital by writing an existing deficit off against it; the company would then start with a clean slate, and could pay dividends out of current earnings.

Purchase of a corporation's own shares. The Business Corporations Act of Ontario (1970), and the Canada Business Corporations Act (1975) have adopted the U.S. practice of permitting companies to purchase their own outstanding common shares. The Canada Business Corporations Act authorizes this practice subject to two conditions: that the company is neither already nor is by the transaction rendered insolvent (the solvency test); and that "the realizable value of the corporation's assets after the payment" be not less than "the aggregate of its liabilities and stated capital of all classes" (the maintenance of capital test).[60] This development was not, however, a complete innovation: for many years, most jurisdictions have permitted the issue of redeemable preferred shares, though the proportion of financing by preferred shares relative to common shares has typically been small. Formerly, it had been possible to reduce common share capital only by following the formalities required for an amendment of the company's charter and obtaining the consent of creditors; except for Ontario and federally-incorporated companies, this continues to be the law in Canada.

Issue of par value shares at a discount. Corporations statutes usually contain two other provisions designed to maintain the capital fund. These are general prohibitions against issuing par value shares at a discount and against lending company funds to shareholders, directors and employees.

The original rationale underlying the prohibition against issuing par value shares at a discount appears to have been that creditors would be assured that an amount of assets at least equal to the declared par value would be paid into the company. This protection is illusory, however. In the first place, there has long been an important variation to this rule in order to permit the payment of a com-

---

[58] R. M. Bryden, "The Law of Dividends," in Ziegel (ed.), *Studies in Canadian Company Law,* Vol. I, p. 299. Toronto: Butterworths, 1967. At p. 277, Prof. Bryden observes, "The most difficult area of the law relating to dividends is that dealing with determination of the maximum sum that may lawfully be distributed. If it can be said that absence of litigation indicates a clear state of the law, Canadian law in this area should be regarded as a paragon of clarity. In the century that this country has existed there has not been a single reported decision in which the limitations upon the funds from which a company may declare dividends have been analyzed."

[59] See for example: R.S.O. 1970, c. 53, s. 154. The Acts of British Columbia and Nova Scotia do not contain any comparable provision.

[60] St. of Can. 1974-75, c. 33, s. 32. The corresponding section in the Ontario Act proposes a solvency test only. R.S.O. 1970, c. 53, s. 39(3).

mission to underwriters who handle the distribution of shares. When an underwriter deducts his commission from the proceeds of the sale of par value shares and remits the balance to the issuing company, the effect is to issue par value shares at a discount. Even when there is no underwriter in the picture, companies, especially small ones, may and do issue shares directly to subscribers and deduct a commission from the sale price — really a discount — in consideration for subscribing for the shares. Statutes usually specify a maximum percentage discount that can be given by a company, whether the sale is by underwriter or directly to a shareholder. We can see, therefore, that there is no magic in par value as a protection for creditors.

Still more important, legislation cannot prevent shares initially issued by a company at par value from subsequently trading in the stock market at prices below that par value. If the company were to seek additional financing by a further issue of shares, it would have to issue them at or near the market price of the shares of that class already outstanding — but that transaction may be prohibited as constituting an issue of par value shares at a discount greater than that permitted by statute. With this possibility in mind, many companies choose to do the bulk of their share financing by means of shares without par value.

The principle that a company should have $100,000 in net assets for every $100,000 of share capital it has issued becomes especially difficult to apply whenever shares are issued for a consideration other than cash. The value to be placed on assets other than money is likely to be very much a matter of opinion. It is therefore difficult in practice to interfere with the valuations placed by a company's board of directors upon such consideration as land, buildings and equipment, oil and mineral rights, patents and copyrights that have been acquired in exchange for an issue of shares.

We have already noted that the new Canada Business Corporations Act no longer permits the issue of par value shares. It will therefore eliminate the discount problem entirely for federally incorporated companies.

Loans to shareholders, directors and employees. The idea behind the prohibition of loans to shareholders is that such loans, especially if not collected promptly, would have the practical effect of an indirect return of capital to shareholders. At the very least, the company would be deprived of valuable liquidity. The prohibition is usually extended to loans to directors and employees of the company. It is difficult to apply normal credit standards to such loans, and their existence also deprives the company of liquidity. Again, exceptions have had to be made to permit loans to employees with a view to enabling them to purchase houses for their own use and encouraging them to purchase shares in the company.

Reduction of stated share capital. Occasionally a company may wish to "reduce" its stated share capital for the valid reason that it no longer reflects tangible net assets; the company may have a large deficit on its books caused by losses in previous years. It can reorganize its capital and make a fresh start by writing off its stated share capital. To do so, it needs to obtain an amendment to its charter in respect of the description of its shares and then make the appropriate accounting entry: it makes no payment of money or other assets to shareholders, but it removes the stigma of a deficit from its balance sheet. In these circumstances, the actual *fund of assets* remaining for the payment of creditors' claims is not diminished by the reduction in share capital. We mentioned earlier that a specific reason for a company's choosing to reduce its share capital in this way would be to remove any doubt about the legality of dividend payments out of current earnings.

SECURITIES LEGISLATION

In Canada, securities legislation is substantially within provincial jurisdiction[61], as contrasted with the United States where the related controls are divided between federal and state jurisdictions. Each Canadian province has a Securities Act or Securities Fraud Prevention Act, under which a government board, known as a securities commission in most of the provinces, is created. The securities commission operates as the enforcing agency, charged with ensuring that the requirements of the Act are complied with.

Two main objectives of securities legislation are common to all provinces: to prevent and punish fraudulent practices in the securities trading business; and to require full disclosure of financial information to prospective buyers of shares and bonds offered for the first time to the public. These objectives are consistent with a policy of increasing the efficiency of the capital market, first by maintaining the confidence of investors and second, by providing sufficient information for rational investment decisions. A basic purpose of securities legislation is to make the capital market an efficient medium for allocating available funds among competing investment opportunities; improving the investor's ability to make an intelligent choice gives the most deserving projects a priority. However, until the recent developments in legislative reform discussed below, very little attention had been given in Canada to the formation of a clear public policy in securities law.

Traditionally, our securities legislation has used two devices for achieving the objectives described above: registering or licensing those engaged in various aspects of the securities business; and requiring the issuer of securities to the public to file a prospectus with the securities commission.

The registering of persons engaged in the securities business is an important device for ensuring a reasonable measure of ethical conduct. Licensing is on an annual basis, and each securities commission has authority under its provincial statute to revoke, suspend or refuse to renew the licence of anyone when in its opinion such action is in the public interest. Operating without a licence is a

---

[61] Federally incorporated companies, in addition to being subject to provincial securities acts, must file any prospectus with the federal government; St. of Can. 1973-74, c. 33, s. 186. In 1971, the securities regulatory authorities in the provinces of Alberta, British Columbia, Manitoba, New Brunswick, Ontario, Prince Edward Island, Quebec, and Saskatchewan agreed to a number of "National Policies" which include, for example, an agreed procedure by which an underwriter may clear a prospectus in more than one province. In addition, the five most western provinces from British Columbia to Ontario agreed upon a further number of "Uniform Act Policies".

criminal offence. Depending upon the jurisdiction, a licence may be required of persons engaged in a wide variety of activities. Those affected include brokers (who buy and sell securities as agents), investment dealers (who buy and sell securities as principals), broker-dealers (who may act as either principal or agent in the promotion of mining companies), securities issuers (companies issuing their securities directly to the public without the intermediate services of investment dealers), salesmen employed by any of these businesses, and investment counsel and securities advisers.

The "filing" of a prospectus with a securities commission is not merely a formality. The commission will refuse to file a prospectus if, after a thorough review of the contents, its staff concludes that the prospectus is misleading or omits required data, and no one may issue securities to the public unless and until the prospectus has been filed. The prospectus requirements are an attempt to ensure that prospective investors have access to the pertinent facts about the company before deciding whether or not to invest in it. In many instances, the investor is entitled to a copy of the prospectus before buying the securities and may rescind the contract of subscription if he does not receive the prospectus and acts to repudiate the contract within a specified period. The minimum detail required in the prospectus is prescribed by statute (possibly in regulations appended to the act) and is too comprehensive to set out here in full. It will be sufficient to note that the prospectus must, among other things, include a full description of the securities to be offered (either shares or bonds) with a statement of their voting rights, preference, conversion privileges, and rights on liquidation, if any; the nature of the business carried on; the names, addresses and occupations of the directors; the proposed use of the proceeds from the issue of securities; details of any share options to be given by the company[62]; the remuneration of the underwriter; the dividend record of the company; and the particulars of property and services to be paid for out of the proceeds of the issue.

The enactment of revised securities acts in the various provinces, commencing in 1966, has ushered in a new era of public control over the securities industry in Canada. In addition to licensing and prospectus provisions, the new legislation has introduced important forms of control largely inspired by experience in the United States since the establishment of the Securities and Exchange Commission in 1934.[63] One of the most important innovations gives the securities commission control over the stock exchanges within the province (in On-

---

[62] A share option is a right to subscribe for shares in the company at a fixed price within a specified time, given by a company as consideration for the payment of money, the rendering of services (often the services of directors), or any other valuable consideration. The option becomes valuable at any time before expiry that the market price exceeds the option price. The English Companies Act (1967), c. 81, s. 25, makes it illegal for directors to deal in stock options.

[63] It is not possible to do justice to this important area in the present chapter. For a complete discussion of the changes in Ontario see: Bray, "Recent Developments in Securities Administration in Ontario: The Securities Act, 1966", in *Studies in Canadian Company Law*, (Ziegel, ed.), Vol. 1, Ch. 14; Carscallen, *Ontario Securities and Companies Legislation*, 1966, (The Institute of Chartered Accountants of Ontario); Beck and Johnston, *Cases & Materials on Securities Regulation* (Toronto: Osgoode Hall Law School, York University, 1973-74).

tario, for example, over the Toronto Stock Exchange.[64]) The significance of the provision is that control by the regulatory body now extends not only to issues of new securities but also to trading in already outstanding securities: the act specifies the minimum of financial information that must be disclosed to share-holders of all companies whose shares are traded on the stock exchange.[65] In ad-dition, the new legislation contains provisions designed to make the proxy a more effective means of registering shareholders' opinions[66] and to give share-holders who have received a takeover bid for their shares sufficient information and time to assess the merits of the bid.[67] The takeover provisions include a requirement for disclosure of the number of shares in the offeree company held by the offeror company and its officers, details of recent trading in those shares, and terms of any agreement between the offeror and the officers of the offeree company.[68] As we noted above, this legislation also requires publication of in-siders' transactions in their company's shares.[69]

CORPORATE REORGANIZATION, MERGERS, AND WINDING UP

The fields of corporation law subsumed under this heading are complex, often technical, and always difficult. They are fields requiring the talents of experts, both financial and legal. Needless to say, no one faced with the problem of mak-ing a decision in one of the above areas should undertake a course of action without expert assistance from beginning to end of the project. The problems in-volved usually concern creditors' rights, the effects of taxation, the relevance of combines legislation, and the rights of various classes of shareholders, in addi-tion to the general economic consequences for the corporations involved and the adaptability of the legal devices available under the statute law of the jurisdic-tion.

QUESTIONS FOR REVIEW

1. Is the public considered in law to have notice of the by-laws of a letters pat-ent company? of the articles of a registered company? of the provisions of the Corporations Act under which any company is incorporated?
2. What is the significance for a company of the rule that part of its constitution is deemed to be public knowledge?
3. Do the directors owe their duties to the shareholders or to the company? Why is it possible to distinguish between the shareholders and the company?
4. What types of duties do directors have? What are the remedies of the com-pany for breach of each of these duties?

---

[64] The Securities Act, R.S.O. 1970, c. 426, s. 140.
[65] *Ibid.*, s. 120.
[66] *Ibid.*, ss. 103 and 105.
[67] *Ibid.*, s. 82.
[68] The contents of the takeover bid circular are prescribed in full in s. 91 (Ontario Act).
[69] *Ibid.*, s. 110.

5. What type of transaction is most likely to put a promoter in breach of his duty to the company?
6. What main categories of shareholders' rights does this chapter discuss?
7. Distinguish between the books of account and the documents of record in relation to (a) content; (b) shareholders' rights.
8. What is the point of a statutory requirement that directors must disclose their transactions in shares of the company?
9. What practical difficulties stand in the way of a shareholder who has reason to believe that the affairs of the company warrant a special investigation?
10. What is the value of a shareholders' right to attend a general meeting?
11. What is a proxy? Why is the proxy important to shareholders? What is a proxy battle? How may a group of dissentient shareholders utilize the proxy system? In what respect do the directors have an advantage over minority shareholders in a proxy battle?
12. How might the existing directors contrive to minimize the effect of cumulative voting if introduced?
13. In what ways might a majority group of shareholders act to the detriment of the remaining shareholders? What recourse does the minority group have?
14. What statutory provisions have as their purpose the maintenance of capital?
15. Describe two main ways in which the rights of shareholders differ from the rights of bondholders.
16. What are the purposes of securities legislation? What are the legal devices for achieving these purposes?

CASES FOR DISCUSSION

CASE 1

Messrs. Forrest, Moss, and Pine jointly purchased a valuable piece of land conveniently located in Calgary for $60,000, with a view to erecting a large apartment building financed by public subscription. They then incorporated Forest Park Apartments Ltd. with an authorized capital of $1,000,000 composed of 10,000 shares of $100 par value. They made a public offering of 7,000 of the shares at par value and alloted all of them. As provisional directors they called the first general meeting of the shareholders, at which they were duly elected, and all other formalities, including confirming the first articles of association, were carried out.

A subsequent meeting of the directors passed a resolution to purchase the land from Messrs. Forrest, Moss, and Pine by allotting to them 1,200 shares in the company. Shortly after the transaction was completed, Foley, who had purchased 500 shares in the company, learned the details and complained to the directors. They informed him that in their opinion the land was worth at least $150,000 and that the company had obtained it at a bargain price. Foley was still dissatisfied and threatened to start an action against them. What would be the substance of his complaint, and what remedies would he request? Would he succeed? (*Erlanger v. The New Sombrero Phosphate Company* (1878) L.R. 3 App. Cas. 1218, and *In re Olympia Ltd.: Gluckstein v. Barnes* [1900] A.C. 240.)

CASE 2

(a) Igor Gilbert carried on business in Winnipeg as sole proprietor manufacturing precision nylon gears. His products were of very high quality and attracted the attention of Corbin Industries Limited, a large manufacturer of precision tools. Corbin Industries negotiated with Gilbert and finally arranged that Gilbert incorporate a company, Gilbert Gears Limited, and sell 90 per cent of the shares to Corbin Industries for $180,000. Gilbert retained ten per cent of the stock and stayed on as a director and general manager of the new company on a salary-plus-share-of-profits basis.

Gilbert Gears Limited was incorporated under the Companies Act of Manitoba. Its by-laws provide that two directors must sign any contract in which the value of goods and services exceeds $10,000. It is customary in the trade for contracts of much larger amounts to be made with the signature of the general manager alone.

Gilbert continued to run the business as a one-man show, much to the chagrin of Corbin Industries. Finally he signed a contract to provide $150,000 worth of gears within two months to Eager Instrument Company, a competitor of Corbin Industries. The contract, if performed, would have tied up the entire production of Gilbert Gears and prevented them from filling emergency orders for Corbin Industries, which was the parent company's prime reason for buying into the enterprise. On the instructions of Corbin Industries, Gilbert Gears Limited called a special meeting of its board of directors, and passed a by-law dismissing Gilbert as general manager and declaring the contract with Eager Instrument Company invalid on the grounds that the by-laws prohibited such a contract unless signed by two directors. Eager Instrument Company sued Gilbert Gears Limited for breach of contract. Who would succeed?

(b) Suppose instead that Gilbert Gears Limited were incorporated in Alberta by memorandum of association. All other facts remain the same. Would this change affect the result of the action? (See *Biggerstaff v. Rowatt's Wharf Limited* [1896] 2 Ch. 93, and *Ernest v. Nicholls* (1857) 10 E.R. 1351.)

CASE 3

Collins Co. Ltd. is a private company incorporated in Ontario with an authorized capital of $100,000 composed of 1,000 shares having a par value of $100. The company has five directors who among them hold all 700 of the issued shares, 360 being held by one of them named Bonner.

Abel, the treasurer and one of the directors of the company, reported to a directors' meeting that he had received several requests from other directors for more shares to be issued. He stated that in his opinion the company could make use of additional capital and that the shares should be issued at $150, which would represent a fair price. All the directors agreed. The chairman then asked each director to state how many shares he would like. All except Bonner asked for varying amounts from 60 to 100 shares. Bonner stated he did not care how many shares he received just so long as he received the same proportion of the new issue as his present holdings represented in the issued shares; and if all 300 were to be issued, he wanted:

$$\frac{360}{700} \times 300 \text{ shares,}$$

that is, 154 shares. Abel then introduced a motion that since it was impossible to meet all these requests, each director should be permitted to buy 60 shares. Bonner objected that he would then hold only 420 out of 1,000 issued shares and would lose voting control, a primary object of his initial investment. Notwithstanding these objections, the resolution was passed, four to one, authorizing the issue of 60 shares to each director.

Bonner brought an action to restrain the board from making the issue on the grounds that it deprived him of his controlling interest. Discuss. (See *Bonisteel v. Collis Leather Co. Ltd.* (1919) 45 O.L.R. 195; *Martin v. Gibson* (1907) 15 O.L.R. 623. For an extraordinary struggle for control see the account in Gower, *Modern Company Law* (3rd ed., 1969), pp. 571-4, concerning *Greenhalgh v. Arderne Cinemas Ltd.* [1951] Ch. 286. See also, *Teck Corporation Ltd. v. Millar* (1973) 33 D.L.R. (3d) 288 at 328-331.)

CASE 4

As of last summer, Mr. C. Chaplin was a director and vice-president of Pan Metal Mines Ltd. A new group had acquired majority control in the company in January; prior to that time Chaplin had been in effective control, serving both as general manager in charge of exploration policy and as chief financial officer. In the latter capacity, he had raised $750,000 for the company last year. After control changed hands, he remained as vice-president, and was paid a salary at the annual rate of $40,000.

At each meeting of its directors Pan Metal Mines Ltd. entertains several offers from prospectors who wish to sell their claims. At a meeting of the board of directors on March 10 last, the directors discussed at some length an offer from a prospector known as Lucky Longfellow, who was prepared to sell a group of claims about five miles from the company's own property for $40,000 cash and shares in a new company that would be formed to take over the property. The members of the board eventually decided to reject Longfellow's offer by a vote of four against the proposal and three in favour. Chaplin was one of those who voted against accepting the offer. In arguing against acceptance, he had noted that the company did not as of that time, have the required $40,000 in cash; its bank balance stood at $29,000.

On April 21 following, Chaplin was approached personally by Longfellow and a geologist, McGee, who persuaded him to join a group of three others to acquire the same claims from Longfellow. A new company, Hiawatha Mines

Ltd., was incorporated in June and Chaplin and the others each purchased 50,000 new shares at 35¢. each from the company. Mr. Longfellow received $40,000 in cash out of the proceeds of this issue of shares, plus an additional 50,000 new shares, as consideration for transferring his claims. Shortly thereafter, Hiawatha Mines made a public issue of a further 200,000 shares. When the company was formed, the parties had no more information about the prospect of finding ore on the property in sufficient quantity to justify a mining operation than they had had when Longfellow presented his proposal to Pan Metal's board of directors. However, as a result of encouraging tests of ore taken from the property in late July, the market price of Hiawatha shares rose to $1.25.

On August 16, the newly-appointed president of Pan Metal Mines, O.R. Murrow, sent Chaplin a memorandum stating, "It is imperative that all officers of this company make full disclosure of their interest in any other mining companies." At the next meeting of the board of directors on August 20, Mr. Chaplin disclosed his interest in Hiawatha Mines Ltd. Mr. Murrow asked him if he was prepared to turn over to Pan Metal Mines his interest in Hiawatha, at cost. Mr. Chaplin demurred and after a heated debate refused. The board of directors then passed a motion on a 6 to 1 vote rescinding Chaplin's appointment as vice-president, to take effect immediately, with no further salary to be paid.

Chaplin sought other employment and three months later managed to secure a position at $2,000 a month; in the process he learned to his sorrow that his reputation among mining men had been seriously damaged as a result of his dismissal by Pan Metal Mines Ltd. He brought an action against that company for damages of $50,000 for wrongful dismissal, and the company counterclaimed for the profit of $52,500 he had made on his shares in Hiawatha, then selling for $1.40 (50,000 shares at $1.05 = $52,500).

Discuss the nature of the issues raised by these facts and offer a decision. (For references see *Regal (Hastings) Ltd. v. Gulliver* [1942] 1 All E.R. 378; *Midcon Oil & Gas Ltd. v. New British Dominion Oil Co. Ltd.* (1958) 12 D.L.R. (2d) 705; *Peso Silver Mines Ltd. (N.P.L.) v. Cropper* (1966) 56 D.L.R. (2d) 117, affirmed S.C.C. 58 D.L.R. (2d) 1; *Canadian Aero Service Ltd. v. O'Malley* (1974) 40 D.L.R. (3d) 371.)

CASE 6

O'Mara and Zimmerman had each been for about twenty years president and vice-president respectively, as well as directors, of Dominion Air Surveys Ltd. The company is engaged in the business of topographical mapping and geophysical exploration and O'Mara and Zimmerman were each professionally-qualified geophysicists enjoying widely-respected reputations.

Five years ago, a controlling interest in Dominion Air Surveys Ltd. was acquired by Eagle Air Services Ltd. of Boston. With the change in ownership, O'Mara and Zimmerman began to feel less secure in their positions, and their misgivings were enhanced as it became increasingly evident that their former authority to make independent decisions for the company was being eroded by head office. As a hedge against loss of their positions, they incorporated another company, Blue Sky Photogrammetry Ltd., with objects almost identical to those of their present employer, Dominion Air Surveys Ltd.

In 1972, the Canadian government invited tenders on some extensive aerial survey work to be undertaken in the Caribbean area as a project of the Canadian International Development Agency. So that Dominion Air Surveys could make an expert submission of a tender, O'Mara recommended the purchase of an aerodist (an airborne electronic distance-measuring device) for $75,000 and when the purchase was approved by head office, he and Zimmerman proceeded to use the device to gain a clear idea of the work that would be involved in the C.I.D.A. project. They then submitted a well-documented tender on behalf of Dominion Air Surveys Ltd. Two other companies also submitted tenders at this time.

About three weeks later, and before any tender had been accepted, O'Mara and Zimmerman resigned their positions as officers and directors of Dominion Air Surveys Ltd. and devoted their time to the preparation of another tender, this one to be submitted by their newly incorporated company, Blue Sky Photogrammetry Ltd. This proved to be the successful tender, the Canadian government being impressed with the professional qualifications of O'Mara and Zimmerman and also being anxious to avoid political criticism for awarding the contract to any company owned outside Canada (as were the three other companies submitting tenders). O'Mara and Zimmerman then undertook the work for their new company, earning a substantial profit for it, as well as acquiring a basis for obtaining other new business.

Dominion Air Surveys Ltd. brought an action against O'Mara and Zimmerman alleging breach of their fiduciary duty as directors and asking damages of $150,000, the amount estimated to be the profit made on the C.I.D.A. contract.

Offer, with specific legal reasons, an opinion about the outcome of this action. (References: *Cook v. Deeks* [1916] 1 A.C. 554; *Peso Silver Mines Ltd. (N.P.L.) v. Cropper* (1966), 58 D.L.R. (2d) 1, [1966] S.C.R. 673, 56 W.W.R. 641; *Canadian Aero Service Ltd. v. O'Malley* (1974) 40 D.L.R. (3d) 371.

CASE 7

The general manager and president of Vanguard Corp. Ltd., J. B. Leeder, engaged Andrews, a real-estate agent specializing in the sale of industrial property, to sell its large warehouse in Regina. The terms of the written agreement included a promise by Vanguard Corp. Ltd. to pay Andrews a commission of $20,000 on completion of the sale if a price of $350,000 were obtained.

Andrews obtained an offer to purchase the warehouse at $350,000 signed for Powell Industries Ltd. by its president. The offer had been prepared on an ordinary residential offer to purchase form. Leeder accepted on behalf of Vanguard Corp. Ltd., but inserted the following: "Subject to negotiation of final details and preparation of a formal contract in consultation with our respective solicitors."

At this stage, two directors of Vanguard Corp. Ltd. learned of the transaction and protested that under the by-laws of that company a transaction involving this amount of money must be approved by the board of directors. At a meeting called to consider the matter, the directors refused to approve the transaction and after further discussion with Powell Industries the parties mutually agreed to call the deal off.

When Vanguard Corp. Ltd. refused to pay Andrews the commission he brought an action against it for $20,000. He alleged first that the acceptance of the offer to purchase entitled him to his commission, and second, that in any event his agency agreement with Vanguard Corp. Ltd. contained an implied term that Vanguard would do nothing to prevent the satisfactory completion of a transaction at the required price so as to deprive him of the agreed commission.

Evaluate these arguments and indicate whether the action should succeed. (For references, see: *Shirlaw v. Southern Foundries* [1939] 2 K.B. 206; *Friesen v. Braun* [1950] 2 D.L.R. 250; *Luxor (Eastbourne) Ltd. v. Cooper* [1941] 1 All E.R. 33.)

CASE 8

The General Wolfe Hotel Company Ltd. was incorporated in 1956 to operate a hotel property in downtown Vancouver. At the outset, 60,000 of its common shares of $10 par value each were purchased and paid for by Anglo-Canadian Bus Lines Ltd. A further 40,000 shares were purchased by the public and they were listed for trading on the Toronto, Montreal and Vancouver stock exchanges.

In 1959, General Wolfe Hotel Company Ltd. issued $600,000 of 8½% mortgage bonds, secured by a first mortgage on the hotel property and maturing November 30, 1974. These mortgage bonds were held chiefly by two large insurance companies.

General Wolfe Hotel Company Ltd. sustained operating losses through the 1960s and, with a view to reducing its fixed charges, entered into negotiations in late 1969 with its bondholders and its principal shareholder, Anglo-Canadian Bus Lines Ltd. It was able to persuade the bondholders to accept a reduction in the interest rate on the bonds from 8½% to 6¾% in return for a guarantee by Anglo-Canadian Bus Lines Ltd. that the interest and principal would be paid. In turn, the hotel company gave Anglo-Canadian Bus Lines Ltd. a second mortgage on the hotel property in which it undertook to pay the principal sum of $25,000 to the bus line, due November 1, 1980 with interest in the meantime at 7%, payable only in years in which the operating profits of the hotel company would cover its total interest obligations. This second mortgage was given solely in consideration for the assistance of the bus line in guaranteeing the hotel company's first mortgage bonds, and no money changed hands at the time.

The hotel company continued to experience financial difficulties, and at the annual general meeting of its shareholders in April, 1973, its treasurer reported that a cash-flow forecast showed that the company would be able to generate sufficient cash from operations to repay, at the most, $400,000 of the $600,000 mortgage bonds maturing November 30, 1974. Alarmed by the prospect of imminent default on the repayment of the principal amount of these bonds, the shareholders passed a resolution authorizing the directors "to take whatever steps may be necessary to refinance the bonds maturing next year".

J. P. Stillwell, president and chairman of the board of General Wolfe Hotel Company Ltd. then entered into further negotiations, on behalf of the board, with the company's bondholders and principal shareholder. A senior officer of Anglo-Canadian Bus Lines Ltd. advised Stillwell that on the expiration of its guarantee the bus line would take no further part in financing the hotel, and that if the hotel company directors could devise a plan that would assure the bus line that it would not incur any loss on its guarantee, the bus line was prepared to donate to the directors its interest as principal shareholder in the hotel company. He stated that the bus line was no longer interested in protecting its investment in the hotel company and that it had already written off most of the second mortgage on the hotel property in 1969.

Anglo-Canadian Bus Lines Ltd. transferred all of its 60,000 shares in General Wolfe Hotel Company Ltd. to Stillwell for himself and fellow directors on the understanding that the shares would have to be returned if they could not come up with a satisfactory overall plan of refinancing. Three of the directors, including Stillwell, then purchased for their personal account outstanding bonds of the hotel company of a face value of $250,000; the insurance companies holding these bonds sold them for $220,000 cash. The directors divided the shares received from the bus line equally among themselves. Stillwell himself purchased the second mortgage on the hotel property from the bus line for $15,000 cash. (The latter transaction amounted to an assignment of rights by the bus line to Stillwell and the liability of General Wolfe Hotel Company, as mortgagor, remained unaltered at $25,000.)

The directors then called a special general meeting of shareholders to ratify this plan of refinancing. As a part of the plan, the directors personally owning $250,000 of the company's mortgage bonds pledged that they would accept a ten-year 9% refunding issue of new bonds from the company in lieu of the payment of principal due on November 30, 1974, so that the risk of default would be avoided. The meeting approved the plan after some discussion and criticism, the directors present voting the controlling interest they had received from the bus line (60,000 shares) in favour of the motion for approval. At the time the hotel company's shares were trading at $1.25.

About four months later the prospects of the hotel company improved greatly with the public announcement of a major office-building development in the immediate vicinity. Zweig, a minority holder of 21,000 shares, applied for and obtained a court order authorizing him to commence action in a representative capacity for himself and all other shareholders (except those being sued) on behalf of General Wolfe Hotel Company Ltd. against Stillwell and the other directors, to require them to account to the company for their personal profits on the refinancing plan.

(a) Describe the nature of the legal argument or arguments that would be made by the plaintiffs Zweig and others.

(b) Outline the nature of the defence that could be offered by Stillwell and others.

(c) Express an opinion about the outcome of this litigation. (For reference, see: *Zwicker et al. v. Stanbury et al.* [1952] 3 D.L.R. 273; 30 M.P.R. 106; [1952] 4 D.L.R. 344; [1953] 2 S.C.R. 438; [1954] 1 D.L.R. 257.)

PART SIX
Credit Transactions

CHAPTER 30

Legal Devices for Securing Credit

TYPES OF SECURITY

The best security for a debt is the good reputation and the earning power of the debtor; such security is the basis for most loans and accounts receivable. Over and above this willingness and ability to pay back the debt, there are various devices for giving a creditor added (collateral) protection or assurance that his debt will be repaid. Most of these devices either give the creditor a *preference* over other creditors, that is, a right to repayment out of the debtor's general assets before other creditors have any right to repayment,[1] or give the creditor *collateral security,* that is, the right to take possession of and to resell specified assets of the debtor for the exclusive satisfaction of his debt. A third device we have noted is the guarantee of a third party to pay the debt if the debtor defaults. We have noted that most credit sales are unsecured. This practice makes good sense: unsecured transactions are simpler and cheaper, and thus keep down overhead costs on sales. If a seller loses only a very small proportion of credit extended through default of payment, it might well be more costly for him to seek the added protection of securing the credit.

Earlier chapters have discussed such collateral security as guarantees, the conditional assignment of accounts receivable (*book debts*), the pledge, the unpaid seller's lien, and the real estate mortgage. Among the more important forms

---

[1] Although a creditor cannot bargain for a preference over general creditors, he may be persuaded to advance credit in the knowledge that he will receive priority in payment of his debt should the debtor become insolvent. We discuss the priority of claims in the next chapter.

of security we have yet to consider are conditional sales, chattel mortgages and bills of sale, floating charges, and security under section 88 of the Bank Act.

A relatively new form of financing the acquisition of goods and equipment is by leasing. Leases are used both to acquire consumer goods (such as television sets and automobiles) and capital equipment for commerce and industry (everything from photocopying machines to large computers and heavy manufacturing equipment). A lease may be combined with an option to purchase the goods during the lease period or at its expiry, or it may be a straight lease, as with land. When a lease is coupled with an option to purchase, the transaction is considered analogous for most purposes to a conditional sale. In England, this type of transaction is called a *hire-purchase* and is used instead of a conditional sale. There is some evidence that sellers in Canada use the device in the hope of avoiding the requirements of consumer-protection statutes, some of which may apply only to "sales" and not to "leases".

Straight leases are not considered secured transactions; the lessor retains full ownership and expects to recover possession at the end of the lease period. Equipment leasing is increasingly becoming an alternative method of financing, a means of acquiring expensive capital equipment without capital investment.

Because the leasing of chattels is a relatively new business activity, there is little reported law in the area. Legal principles are likely to develop by analogy to bailment and secured transactions and, perhaps to a lesser extent, by analogy to landlord and tenant.

The reader will find it helpful at this point to review Chapter 26 on real estate mortgages, and in particular the section entitled, "The Mortgagee's Rights Compared with the Rights of Other Creditors".

CONDITIONAL SALES

The Nature of a Conditional Sale

We noted in Chapter 26 that the real estate mortgage was the most important device for obtaining credit upon the security of land; in almost every sale of land, a mortgage is an essential element. Although in contrast to sales of land, most sales of goods take place for cash or unsecured credit, secured credit transactions still occur very frequently, especially when the goods are quite expensive.

A common form of secured credit transaction for the sale of chattels is the conditional sale. All common law provinces except Manitoba[2] have statutes

---

[2] Currently Manitoba has in force only the Lien Notes Act, R.S.M. 1970, c. L140. This Act is the only Manitoba legislation concerning conditional sales and is not comparable with the Conditional Sales Acts of the other provinces. In 1973, Manitoba passed a Personal Property Security Act, St. of Man. 1973, c. 5, but only those portions with respect to registration of transactions are currently in force. The remainder of the Act will repeal the Lien Notes Act and will substantially change the statute law with respect to secured credit transactions in Manitoba, but as of August 1st, 1975 these provisions have not yet been proclaimed. For further discussion, see the final section of this chapter.

regulating many aspects of conditional sale transactions. A conditional sale is a type of agreement to sell; it is popularly known as "buying on the instalment plan". In our discussion below, it will be helpful to refer to the two parties to a conditional sale agreement as the *conditional seller* and the *conditional buyer,* particularly when we are concerned with their relationship to third parties.

The chief characteristic of a conditional sale is that the conditional buyer acquires possession and use of the article at the time of the agreement or shortly thereafter but the title or formal ownership of the article remains with the conditional seller until the buyer completes payment of the debt. While the buyer has possession, and before he makes full payment for the article, he is a bailee of it for value. Ordinarily, a bailee for value who obtains goods for his own use is under a duty to take as good care of the article as a prudent man would take of his own property (as with a bailment for hire and use). A conditional seller, however, often places the buyer under a considerably higher duty by making it a term of the agreement that the buyer be responsible for damage to the article whether caused by his fault or not — that is, the conditional sale agreement places the buyer under strict liability.

Remedies of a Conditional Seller and Buyer

A conditional sale agreement has much in common with a mortgage of land: a conditional seller retains title to the chattel much as a mortgagee obtains legal title to the land; a conditional buyer has the right to possession of the chattel so long as he meets the terms of the conditional sale agreement much as a mortgagor has a right to possession of the mortgaged land while he honours the terms of the mortgage; a conditional buyer obtains a full ownership in the chattel as soon as he makes his final payment to the seller much as a mortgagor is entitled to a re-transfer of the legal title upon repayment of the mortgage loan. The most important common characteristic, however, is that the essence of both transactions is the creation of a debt: both the conditional buyer and the mortgagor promise to pay a sum of money. Each debtor usually makes subsidiary promises as well — he must keep the property in good condition, and for large and expensive chattels like automobiles and mobile homes, keep them insured for at least the value of the debt. But his most important obligation is to repay the debt, and it is this obligation on which the debtor most often defaults.

What are a conditional seller's remedies on default by the conditional buyer? First, as a creditor, he has the ordinary contractual remedy to sue the conditional buyer for the unpaid balance of the debt. Secondly, a conditional seller invariably makes it a term of the agreement that he may retake possession of the goods on default by the buyer. *Repossession,* as it is commonly called, does not affect the ownership of the goods since the seller has retained title from the outset. A conditional seller is not entitled to use force in recovering goods by self-help. If he does, he may be sued by the buyer for trespass or assault in attempting to assert his rights without regard for the buyer's property or person. When a conditional seller encounters resistance in retaking possession, therefore, he should not persist. His proper course of action is to obtain a court order authorizing him to take the necessary steps in acquiring possession. In some provinces, in fact, a seller is not entitled to repossess goods except by court process. If the buyer resists in the face of the court order, he is then guilty of contempt of court. The consumer protection legislation of some of the provinces provides that a term in a conditional sale contract allowing the conditional seller to retake possession or resell the goods on default is generally unenforceable after a certain proportion of the purchase price (for example, two thirds) has been paid.[3]

Despite the legislation, conditional sale contracts still frequently contain terms claiming the right to repossession even after the statutory proportion has been paid. Most statutes provide no penalty for including such terms, so that from the seller's point of view the worst that happens is that the terms are ineffective. When questioned about these practices, sellers give the stock answer that their contracts are drafted for nation-wide use, including some provinces that do not provide for this aspect of consumer protection. An effective way to prevent this abuse is to put substantial penalties in the act, such as fines, or forfeiture of the right to collect the remainder of the debt if repossession is even threatened after the statutory percentage has been paid.

Except for Alberta, provincial Conditional Sales Acts give the conditional buyer the right to redeem the goods within a specified period, upon payment of: (a) the amount in arrears together with interest (in British Columbia, Nova Scotia and Prince Edward Island, upon payment of the entire balance of the contract price), and (b) the seller's actual costs and expenses of taking and keeping possession of the goods.[4] In this respect, then, a conditional buyer is again much like a mortgagor with a right to redeem. What happens after the specified period in the statute expires? If the seller simply retains possession, the answer appears to be unclear.[5] The conditional sales statutes do not provide an answer. Apparently the seller is in the position of any unpaid seller of goods who has possession of them. His rights and duties are then governed by the Sale of Goods Act as we have discussed them in Chapter 17 under "Remedies of the Seller".

After repossession, the seller has a third remedy: he may resell the goods to a third party. He may not do so, of course, until the statutory period for redemption afforded to the buyer has expired. If, without notifying the buyer, the seller resells the goods and obtains a price equal to or less than the amount of the debt

---

[3] See, for example: Consumer Protection Act, R.S.O. 1970, c. 82, s. 35. Upon special application a judge of a county or district court may still grant the right to repossess or resell. See also, R.S.M. 1970, c. C200, s. 49.

[4] See, for example: St. of B.C. 1961, c. 9, s. 14(1); R.S.O. 1970, c. 76, S. 9(1); R.S.N.S. 1967, c. 48, s. 12(1). In Alberta, the respective rights and duties of buyer and seller are somewhat more complex and are governed by the Seizures Act, R.S.A. 1970, c. 338, ss. 14 and 26-37, especially s. 30.

[5] In Alberta, a conditional seller who repossesses the goods loses his right to sue for the debt: R.S.A. 1970, c. 61, s. 19(3).

and expenses, all rights and duties under the contract are terminated.[6] The seller cannot successfully sue the buyer for any remaining deficiency. If, however, the seller complies with the terms of the statute, he may obtain judgment for a deficiency. The statute requires the seller to give the buyer notice in writing of the intention to sell, a detailed description of the goods, an itemized statement of the balance of the contract price due, a demand that the amount as stated in the notice be paid on or before the date of sale, and a statement that unless the amount is paid, the goods will be sold and the seller will look to the buyer for any deficiency.

What happens if the sale by the seller brings in more than the amount of the debt outstanding? Again, the law appears to be unclear in this area. The conditional sales statutes say nothing about the matter. The situation does not occur very frequently because, unlike land, goods usually depreciate in value rather rapidly after the conditional buyer takes possession and uses them. It seems highly probable, however, that the seller would be obligated to return any surplus to the buyer.[7] The reasoning is that the seller's primary interest is in the debt, and that the buyer is the beneficial owner subject to payment of the debt, that is, the equity is his whether the contract is a secured transaction or not. Thus, once the seller has received his full debt and any expenses incurred in the resale, any profit remaining is "equity" belonging to the buyer.

We should note that conditional sale contracts made by door-to-door sellers are subject to the new consumer protection legislation (discussed in Chapters 11 and 17) which allows buyers to rescind during a "cooling-off" period, thereby avoiding all liability under such contracts.

Registration of a Conditional Sale Agreement

All conditional sales acts make provision for the registration of conditional sale agreements. To comply with these provisions, a conditional seller must make a written memorandum of the contract and have it signed by the buyer, and he must register the agreement within the time specified by the act. The time varies considerably from province to province, from as little as ten days to as long as 40 days after the seller delivers the goods.[8] The conditional seller must file a copy of the contract in the appropriate public office in the district in which the buyer resides at the time of the conditional sale. Some provinces maintain a central registry system for all conditional sale agreements, and some have it for motor vehicles only. For a small fee, a prospective purchaser of an article may search

---

[6] The statutes do not state expressly that the contract is terminated, but they do state that if the seller does wish to sue for a deficiency, he must comply with the terms of the statute. It necessarily follows that he cannot claim for a deficiency if he fails to comply with the statute. See: St. of B.C. 1961, c. 9, s. 14(2) and (3); R.S.O. 1970, c. 76, s. 9(3) and (4); R.S.N.S. 1967, c. 48, s. 12(3) and (4).

[7] See C.C. Motor Sales Ltd. v. Chan [1926] 3 D.L.R. 712.

[8] See, for example: St. of B.C. 1961, c. 9, s. 6; R.S.O. 1970, c. 76, s. 2(1); R.S.N.S. 1967, c. 48, s. 2(2).

the records in his local office or in the central provincial office, where applicable, to ascertain that there is nothing registered to suggest that the second-hand goods he is planning to buy have not been fully paid for.

What are the consequences of registration? As between the two original parties to the contract, the conditional seller and the conditional buyer, registration is of no consequence whatever. The rights and remedies of the parties remain as discussed above. The significance of registration is with respect to the rights of third parties — creditors of, and innocent purchasers from, the conditional buyer, discussed in the sections immediately following.

Position of Creditors of a Conditional Buyer

How does registration affect third parties? We begin to answer this question by first examining the position at common law. As we have noted, a conditional seller retains title to goods delivered to his conditional buyer and they cannot be seized by creditors of the conditional buyer. But legislation such as the Bankruptcy Act and Conditional Sales Act may affect this position. Suppose a conditional buyer becomes bankrupt before he pays for the goods. Must his conditional seller have complied with the Conditional Sales Act to retain his priority in the goods against the general creditors? The provisions vary greatly from province to province, but generally speaking, the title of a seller who does not comply with the Act is void against many types of creditors,[9] except in Ontario, where the seller takes priority over creditors.[10] Registration *is* necessary in Ontario, however, to preserve a conditional seller's priority over other creditors of his conditional buyer in one instance — when the goods have been obtained by the conditional buyer for the purpose of resale by him.[11]

Position of an Innocent Third Party Who Buys from a Conditional Buyer

Since a conditional buyer does not have title to goods under the common law, he cannot transfer title to an innocent purchaser. Therefore, as far as the common law is concerned, a conditional seller can always recover the goods from a subsequent purchaser. On the other hand, the Sale of Goods Act, in referring to sales of goods generally, states:

> Where a person having bought or agreed to buy goods, obtains, with the consent of the seller, possession of the goods or documents of title to the goods, the delivery or transfer by that person . . . of the goods or documents of title, under a sale, pledge or other disposition thereof to a person receiving the same in good faith and without notice of any lien or other right of the original seller in respect of the goods, has the same effect as if the

---

[9] See Ziegel, "Uniformity of Legislation in Canada. The Conditional Sales Experience", 39 *Can. B. Rev.*, p. 165 (1961).

[10] R.S.O. 1970, c. 76, s. 2(1).

[11] *Ibid.*, s. 2(3).

person making the delivery or transfer were a mercantile agent in possession of the goods or documents of title with the consent of the owner.[12]

In other words, a conditional seller, if this statute applies to him, gives his conditional buyer the same power to transfer title as if he were a mercantile agent; the seller is prevented by the Sale of Goods Act from denying the validity of any disposition of the goods to an innocent third party.

We must now ask whether the common law rules apply to conditional sales or whether these rules have been changed by the application of the Sale of Goods Act. The question is an important one, for under the common law an innocent buyer takes possession at his peril, whereas under the Sale of Goods Act a conditional seller parts with possession at his peril.[13]

All conditional sale statutes share a common policy: they encourage conditional sellers to register their transactions under the provisions of the act, *by taking away* their common law protection against innocent purchasers if they fail to register. The Sale of Goods Act applies to unregistered conditional sales. A question remains whether even registering protects a conditional seller. Some Sale of Goods Acts make it clear that the section of the Act quoted above does not apply to a registered conditional sale, and the seller by complying with registration retains his common law protection. In other acts this protection is left to inference, that is, if the conditional seller is left unprotected by failing to register, then upon registering he would be protected. Court decisions, however, leave the matter in doubt; some suggest that the only protection a registered conditional seller receives is against the general creditors of the conditional buyer, and that the Sale of Goods Act permits the buyer to pass good title to an innocent third party. This interpretation seems unreasonable, as it would destroy one of the main purposes of registration under a conditional sales act. The better judicial position probably is that registration does permit a conditional seller to retain his common law protection even against innocent third party purchasers.

Registration provisions are useful, in any event. They do provide protection for a conditional seller against general creditors at the very least, and a prudent purchaser who does not wish to obtain a risky title from a person in possession of a valuable chattel such as an automobile may protect himself by searching the public records under the heading of conditional buyers to see whether the name of the person in possession appears there. In this respect, the conditional sales register provides a means of protection similar to that in land registry systems.

We have noted that if a conditional seller has not registered his agreement, he loses his title to an innocent purchaser from the conditional buyer. But the purchaser must be innocent: before he is entitled to keep the goods as against the

---

[12] R.S.B.C. 1960, c. 344, s. 31(2); R.S.O. 1970, c. 421, s. 25(2); R.S.N.S. 1967, c. 274, s. 27(2).

[13] For discussion of opposing points of view, see: LaForest, "Filing Under the Conditional Sales Act: Is it notice to Subsequent Purchasers?" 36 *Can. Bar Rev.*, p. 387 (1958); Joanes, "Third Party Rights in Goods Subject to Conditional Sales Agreements and Chattel Mortgages", 1 *U.B.C. Law Rev.*, p. 23 (1959).

conditional seller, he must be a bona fide purchaser who had no knowledge from any source that the goods were not fully paid for.

Illustration:

> Jones purchases a stereo tape recorder from Brown's Appliances Ltd. under a conditional sale agreement. After making a down payment, he agrees to pay the balance, including service charges of $450, in 18 equal monthly instalments. Two months later Jones wrongfully sells the tape recorder to Green without disclosing that only a small proportion of the purchase price has been paid. May Green as an innocent purchaser keep the tape recorder?
>
> (a) If Brown's Appliances Ltd. has not registered the agreement and Green has no knowledge of it then he may keep the tape recorder.
>
> (b) If Brown's Appliances Ltd. has not registered the agreement and Green has reason to believe that the recorder is not owned fully by Jones (as, for example, when Jones' brother has commented to Green that Jones has recently bought a new tape recorder "on time"), then Brown's Appliances Ltd. will be able to recover it.
>
> (c) If Brown's Appliances Ltd. has registered the conditional sales agreement in the public office in the district in which Jones resided at the time of the sale and if Green took the precaution of searching the conditional sale registry he would have notice of the agreement and could not keep the tape recorder. Indeed, he would not be an "innocent purchaser" as he would have knowledge of the title of the conditional seller.
>
> (d) If, as in (c), the conditional seller has registered the agreement but Green has not suspected the recorder was subject to a conditional sale agreement and did not search the registry, he probably would be unable to retain the tape recorder, despite his innocence. Judicial decisions suggest that the conditional seller could recover it.

Ontario no longer requires registration of conditional sales if the contract is one for certain "household furniture" or for "goods that are used or acquired for use primarily for personal, family or household purposes where the amount secured by the contract does not exceed $300."[14] Nor is registration required in Ontario or Alberta for manufactured goods which have the conditional seller's name and address affixed to them.[15] In three other provinces, registration is waived only if such goods are sold directly by their manufacturers.[16] In those provinces which have made this exemption to registration, a prospective purchaser is assumed to have the means of inquiry through the name of the seller affixed to the goods; he may inquire directly of their seller whether the goods have been fully paid for, and unless a seller answers such inquiry, he may be liable to a fine under the Conditional Sales Act. This protection for a prospective

---

[14] R.S.O. 1970, c. 76, s. 2(5)(a) and (b)(ii).

[15] *Ibid.*, s. 2(5)(b); R.S.A. 1970, c. 61, s. 11.

[16] R.S.S. 1965, c. 393, s. 5(7); R.S.N.B. 1973, c. C-15, s. 4; St. of Nfld. 1970, c. 56, s. 5.

purchaser is, however, often illusory; the seller does all that is required to protect his title if he affixes his name in a permanent fashion in a position where it may be readily seen, and it does not matter if his name later becomes obliterated.[17] Indeed, in view of the doubtful protection to sellers obtained by registration, affixing his name may give a seller greater protection than registration! Registration remains the more common practice, perhaps because a seller avoids the problem of having to prove that his name was affixed, should it later become obliterated. He also avoids a prospective buyer's objections to an unsightly label on the article.

Renewal of Registration and Late Registration

Four of the provinces require that a renewal of a conditional sale agreement be filed within three years if the agreement extends beyond that time.[18] Saskatchewan requires a renewal within four years and Nova Scotia within five years.[19] Failure to renew results in loss of the protection given a conditional seller under the Act.

If a conditional seller fails to register his conditional sale agreement or a renewal of it within the time specified by the statute, he may not lose the protection of the Act altogether if he takes steps to remedy the defect. In Saskatchewan he may register at any time, but in so doing he cannot prejudice rights already acquired by a third party.[20] Except for Nova Scotia and Prince Edward Island, which have no provisions for late filing, the remaining provinces provide procedures for appearing before a judge and explaining the cause of the failure, such as accident or ignorance of the requirement. In such circumstances, the judge may permit registration to be effective from the date of his order. If, however, any rights have accrued to a third party in the interval before the registration, these will not be prejudiced by the subsequent registration.

Effect of Wrongful Disposition by a Buyer

When a conditional buyer wrongfully disposes of goods, an innocent party is bound to be the loser as the result of his fraud. If the conditional seller has taken the necessary precautions under the statute and is able to recover the goods from the innocent third party, the third party suffers the loss. The latter may, of course, sue the conditional buyer for breach of warranty of title, though such an action will be useless unless the conditional buyer has resources sufficient to satisfy a court judgment.

---

[17] Wettlaufer v. Scott (1893) 20 O.A.R. 652, followed by Ontario Court of Appeal in McBride v. Appleton [1946] 2 D.L.R. 16.
[18] St. of B.C. 1961, c. 9, s. 8; R.S.O. 1970, c. 76, s. 5(1); R.S.N.B. 1973, c. C-15, s. 7; St. of Nfld. 1970, c. 56, s. 11.
[19] R.S.S. 1965, c. 393, s. 13; R.S.N.S. 1967, c. 48, s. 11(1).
[20] R.S.S. 1965, c. 393, s. 30.

Where the conditional seller has not complied with the Conditional Sales Act, and as a result the conditional buyer transfers a valid title to an innocent purchaser, the conditional seller may still sue the conditional buyer for the balance of the debt owing. Alternatively, he may sue for the tort of conversion since the goods disposed of were his goods. Again, however, the victim of the wrongful act of the conditional buyer can obtain sufficient compensation only if the fraudulent buyer has adequate assets to satisfy a judgment against him.

Effect of Taking Goods to Another Registration District or Another Province

A problem arises when a conditional buyer removes the goods from the district in which they are registered. A prospective purchaser in the second district will not, of course, find any record of the conditional sale in his registry office unless the seller registers again in the new district. Most provinces have district registry offices at least for chattels other than motor vehicles, and the provisions concerning the necessity of, and the time limits for, re-registration vary widely from province to province.[21] In some circumstances an innocent purchaser may retain the chattel: in others, the conditional seller may recover it from him. Confronted by these differences, a buyer's best protection is care in ascertaining the integrity of the seller and seeking prompt legal advice in case of doubt.

A conditional buyer may take the subject-matter of the sale, a car for example, from the jurisdiction in which he has purchased it to another province. The conditional sale agreement invariably makes removal of the car a breach of contract unless the seller gives his consent. Nevertheless, the question arises whether the conditional seller is protected when the buyer purports to sell the car to an innocent purchaser in another province. All the provincial statutes give the conditional seller a chance to register his agreement in the second province. The provisions vary widely, however, from province to province; the effect of decided cases in the light of these varying provisions is bewildering. Most writers agree that the state of the law is unsatisfactory at present, and the problem is difficult to resolve. Probably nothing short of a national registration system would come close to protecting both the secured party and an innocent third party.

Trade Practice

In the business world, the conditional sale serves two main functions as a security device: (1) to give the secured party a right, with or without the help of the courts, to look to the goods in satisfaction of the debtor's obligation; (2) to give the secured party priority in the goods over the interest of third parties, especially

---

[21] For a detailed comparison of the various provincial Conditional Sales Acts, see Ziegel, "Uniformity of Legislation in Canada. The Conditional Sales Experience", 39 *Can. Bar Rev.*, p. 165 (1961).

creditors. Registration relates only to the second function. It is not necessary to register in order to have the advantage of either self-help or the assistance of the court in repossession. Distinguishing these two functions helps explain the difference in trade practice between consumer and non-consumer transactions.

In consumer transactions, security devices are used primarily to give the secured party a right to repossession. In those jurisdictions (such as Alberta) where the secured party cannot help himself, but must invoke the aid of a sheriff, the purpose of security is still to enable the creditor to threaten the debtor with deprivation of the goods. This primary concern with remedies directly against the conditional buyer helps to explain why many sales-finance companies do not register secured consumer transactions, automobiles being the notable exception. In the non-consumer field, that is, in transactions between two businesses, the important purpose of security devices is to protect the secured seller in the event of his debtor's insolvency. The security is not generally taken in order to obtain the capacity to repossess in case of default, as it is in the consumer field, but rather to give the secured party preference in bankruptcy proceedings. Since registration is important in giving a security holder protection against general creditors, registration is more common in non-consumer transactions.

Many merchants who sell goods on the instalment plan do not finance their customers themselves. Instead, they sell or assign their conditional sale agreement to a finance company (which may or may not register the agreement). The finance company collects the instalments and administers the contract. A conditional seller is in this way able to realize cash quickly from his credit sales, and thus requires less capital with which to operate. In most assignments of conditional sale contracts to finance companies, however, conditional sellers remain contingently liable for payment if their conditional buyers should default.

In addition to signing the conditional sale agreement, a conditional buyer was formerly required to give his promissory note for the total price due under the contract. The conditional seller then discounted the note with a finance company, that is, endorsed it and received payment from the finance company. Before recent developments in the law, this practice improved the position of the finance company: without a promissory note, the finance company was simply an assignee of contractual rights subject to all the defences which could have been raised against the conditional seller, as for example, when there was a misrepresentation: a finance company that took a promissory note endorsed in its favour by the conditional seller had the greater rights of a holder in due course and did not need to worry about the personal defences that a conditional buyer could have raised against the conditional seller. There was widespread opinion that unscrupulous conditional sellers were abusing this system, and buyers found themselves liable to pay the full amount of their promissory notes to the finance companies as holders in due course, even when they had valid defences to raise against an action on the debt had it been brought by their conditional sellers. In some instances, conditional sellers were fly-by-night operations that had gone out of existence at the time the promissory notes were enforced.

The Supreme Court of Canada, in a 1969 case, limited the right of finance companies to sue as holders in due course, making them subject to the defences that would have been available to conditional buyers against their conditional sellers — at least in those cases where the finance company had received a copy of the conditional sale contract, and could thus be considered to have a special interest in the transaction.[22] With the growing concern for consumer protection, a 1970 amendment to the Bills of Exchange Act expressly removed the protection of a holder in due course in consumer sales.[23] As a result, trade practice appears to be changing and the use of promissory notes may be diminishing, since they no longer improve the position of assignee finance companies.

A dealer or other retail merchant may finance his purchases of stock-in-trade from a manufacturer by buying them from the manufacturer under a conditional sale contract. The manufacturer may in turn assign these contracts to a finance company. This practice is common in the automobile business. In these circumstances, financing takes place at the wholesale rather than retail level; the dealer is being financed, not the ultimate consumer. The Conditional Sales Acts provide that when delivery is made to a person for the purpose of resale by him in the course of business, a purchaser from him acquires title to the goods.[24] As a result, if a dealer were to resell goods but failed to pay his debt in respect of them, the finance company could not assert its title against the retail customer even though it had registered the conditional sale contract between the manufacturer and the dealer. Registration does, however, serve to give finance companies a priority for repayment as against outside creditors of the dealer so long as the goods remain unsold in the dealer's inventory.

CHATTEL MORTGAGES

The Nature of a Chattel Mortgage

The chattel mortgage has become increasingly important as a device for securing credit with the large-scale movement of chartered banks into the field of consumer financing in recent years. The chartered banks now dominate the field of consumer financing, and it may well be that the chattel mortgage is more common than the conditional sale agreement. A chattel mortgage is roughly equivalent to a real-estate mortgage in both its form and effect. It may arise in one of two ways: first, as a result of a sale where a seller transfers title to a buyer, who in turn gives back a chattel mortgage as security for the unpaid balance of the purchase price; secondly, where a debtor gives a chattel mortgage on goods he already owns as security for a loan from a creditor. As a device for securing credit, a chattel mortgage is the opposite of a pledge, where possession is transferred to the lender but title remains with the borrower.

---

[22] Range v. Corporation de Finance Belvédère (1969) 5 D.L.R. (3d) 257.

[23] R.S.C. 1970 (1st Supp.) c. 4.

[24] St. of B.C. 1961, c. 9, s. 18(2); R.S.O. 1970, c. 76, s. 2(4); R.S.N.S. 1967, c. 48, s. 5.

A debtor can mortgage goods which he has not yet acquired or which are not yet in a deliverable state, such as unfinished manufactured goods or growing crops. In Manitoba, a chattel mortgage on the security of a growing crop is prohibited by statute except to the extent that it is used to obtain funds for seed.[25] Alberta and Saskatchewan have similar statutory prohibitions, but in addition to seed, the Acts permit chattel mortgages for farmers' "necessaries", such as groceries and repairs to farm equipment.[26]

A chattel mortgage has an additional flexible aspect in that a person may, for example, mortgage "all office fixtures, lamps, desks, chairs, furniture and stationery". In addition, he may mortgage his stock-in-trade, which by its nature is constantly changing its composition in the course of business. Such a mortgage usually contains a provision that subsequent merchandise purchased will automatically become mortgaged as part of the stock-in-trade, and also a covenant that the mortgagor will keep the realizable value of the stock-in-trade in excess of a stated amount. A term that subsequent acquisitions of property of the same type become subject to the mortgage is called an *after-acquired property clause*.

A chattel mortgage usually provides that the mortgagor is in default if he attempts to sell or dispose of the goods or permits them to be seized to satisfy the claims of other creditors without the prior written consent of the mortgagee. In this respect, a chattel mortgage differs from a real estate mortgage, for a chattel mortgagee may prevent the sale of the mortgaged property by withholding his consent, whereas a mortgagee of real property cannot do so. A mortgagor usually covenants that he will keep the mortgaged goods insured against loss and damage by fire, and that he will pay the insurance premiums and make the insurance payable to the mortgagee.

Remedies of a Mortgagee

A chattel mortgagee's remedies are similar to those of a conditional seller. First, as a creditor he may sue on the covenant to pay the debt. Secondly, he may take possession of the goods upon default by the mortgagor. If the mortgagor refuses to give up possession voluntarily, the mortgagee may follow the same procedure as a conditional seller in repossessing goods. So long as the goods remain in the possession of the mortgagee, the mortgagor may redeem them by paying the balance of the debt with interest and costs.

A chattel mortgagee invariably reserves the right upon default to resell the goods to a third party. In exercising his right of sale, he must act reasonably and fairly to obtain a good price for them. If he fails to do so, he may be accountable to the mortgagor for the difference between the price he obtained and what would

---

[25] Bills of Sale Act, R.S.M. 1970, c. B 40, s. 29. The same statutes regulate both chattel mortgages and bills of sale. The statutes are called either Bills of Sale Acts or Bills of Sale and Chattel Mortgages Acts. Note that this statute will be repealed when the new Personal Property Security Act is proclaimed. See n. 1, *supra*.

[26] Bills of Sale Act, R.S.A. 1970, c. 29, s. 30.

have been a fair price for the goods. If on selling at a fair price, the mortgagee obtains less than the debt outstanding, he may obtain judgment against the mortgagor for the deficiency, except in Alberta,[27] but if there is any surplus he must return it to the mortgagor.

A chattel mortgagee, like a mortgagee of real property, may foreclose the interest of the mortgagor by court proceedings and thereby have the chattel declared to be his property absolutely. In contrast with a real estate mortgagee, however, a chattel mortgagee seldom resorts to this measure.

Position of an Innocent Third Party Who
Transacts Business with a Chattel Mortgagor

At common law, the position of a chattel mortgagee would be similar to that of a conditional seller: since he has obtained legal title to the goods in question, his mortgagor cannot transfer valid title to an innocent third party. Each of the common law provinces, however, has a statute governing in detail the registration of chattel mortgages. Failure to register deprives the mortgagee of his protection. He cannot assert his title in the chattels against an innocent third party who has subsequently acquired an interest in them. In addition, the chattel mortgage is void as against creditors of the mortgagor.[28] They may seize the goods which are the subject of the mortgage and sell them in order to satisfy their debts. In these circumstances, the chattel mortgagee loses his security, but he may still share as a general creditor in the moneys realized from the sale of the goods.

The requirements and effect of registration of a chattel mortgage are similar to those of a conditional sale agreement. The mortgagee must register the mortgage within a specified period after the mortgage has been entered into. Chattel mortgages are generally registered in the same office where conditional sales agreements are registered. Registration protects the mortgagee's title against subsequent attempts by the mortgagor to transfer an interest in the goods within the district where it is registered. A prospective purchaser of goods may search in the registry office in the name of the seller under the heading ''mortgagor'' to see whether he has mortgaged the goods.

Registration of a chattel mortgage in a public office must be accompanied by, among other things, an affidavit of bona fides. An *affidavit of bona fides* is a sworn declaration by the mortgagee that the document was ''executed in good faith and for the express purpose of securing the payment of money . . . and not for the purpose of protecting the goods . . . against the creditors of the said mortgagor.'' The purpose of this requirement may be readily seen: it is to prevent an insolvent debtor from giving fraudulent preference to one of his creditors, or

---

[27] The Conditional Sales Act, R.S.A. 1970, c. 61, s. 19.
[28] See, for example: St. of B.C. 1961, c. 6, s. 16; R.S.O. 1970, c. 45, s. 8; R.S.N.S. 1967, c. 23, s. 2.

to a friend or a member of his family, by mortgaging valuable goods to them and thus putting them out of the reach of his general creditors.[29]

Each of the provinces also requires that the mortgagee file a renewal of the chattel mortgage after a specified period if he wishes to continue to receive the protection of registration.[30] If he fails to file either the original chattel mortgage or its renewal within the time specified in the statute, he is subject to the same risks as a conditional seller who fails to register within the time specified. In a similar manner, he may apply to a court to register a chattel mortgage or a renewal after the specified period,[31] but he remains subject to the risk that before the subsequent registration, rights may accrue to third parties.

Re-registration When a Mortgagor Moves the Chattel to Another District or Province

A chattel mortgage always contains a term prohibiting the chattel mortgagor from removing the chattels from the district in which they are registered without the mortgagee's consent. The acts governing chattel mortgages make provisions for the re-registration of chattel mortgages in other districts. Sometimes these provisions concerning re-registration are the same as those for conditional sale agreements, and sometimes they differ considerably. Failure to comply with the requirements results in loss of the protection of the act.

All the provinces except Ontario and British Columbia provide in their statutes for the re-registration of chattel mortgages, first registered in other provinces, when the chattels are subsequently brought within their boundaries. In Ontario and British Columbia there are no provisions for re-registration; in these provinces, unless a mortgagee manages to obtain a new chattel mortgage in proper form for the province concerned and registers it (a highly unlikely event), a mortgagor may effectively give title to a chattel previously mortgaged and registered in another province to an innocent purchaser.

Sale of Mortgaged Chattels

A chattel mortgagor cannot sell mortgaged goods without the consent of his mortgagee. When the goods are stock-in-trade, however, consent to their sale in the ordinary course of business is presumed from the after-acquired property clause described above. In all other circumstances, the mortgagor must obtain specific consent of the mortgagee. If he attempts to sell without the consent of the mortgagee he is, of course, in breach of the mortgage. In addition, if he has not told the purchaser about the mortgage, he has defrauded the purchaser by securing a price for the chattels higher than the purchaser would otherwise have been willing to pay: if the mortgage is duly registered, the innocent purchaser

---

[29] St. of B.C. 1961, c. 6, s. 6; R.S.O. 1970, c. 45, s. 4(b); R.S.N.S. 1967, c. 23, s. 7.

[30] St. of B.C. 1961, c. 6, s. 12; R.S.O. 1970, c. 45, s. 25(1); R.S.N.S. 1967, c. 23, s. 10.

[31] St. of B.C. 1961, c. 6, s. 14; R.S.O. 1970, c. 45, s. 11; R.S.N.S. 1967, c. 23, s. 24.

must pay off the mortgage debt in addition to the price he has already paid, in order to keep the goods. His only recourse is to sue the mortgagor for his breach of warranty of title. If the mortgagee has not registered the mortgage, an innocent purchaser obtains good title free from the mortgage, and the mortgagee's only recourse is to sue the mortgagor for the debt.

Business Uses of a Chattel Mortgage

In business practice, the chattel mortgage is used in the sale of a business as a going concern where office equipment, machinery, or vehicles are included in the sale transaction. If the purchaser of the business does not have all the cash required, the vendor may agree to take a chattel mortgage on specific equipment or machinery, or the stock-in-trade, as security for the unpaid balance. In other words, the vendor receives his price partly in cash and partly in a promise to pay secured by a chattel mortgage.

Another common use of the chattel mortgage arises on the sale of a building with equipment. Typical examples are the sale of an apartment building in which each suite has a refrigerator and stove, a furnished office building, or a hotel. Frequently in the sale of such property, the sale price includes both real property and equipment in the building. Not only may the vendor take back a real estate mortgage for the unpaid balance of the purchase price, but he may also take back a concurrent chattel mortgage on all moveable equipment. By so doing, he obtains better security for the debt should it become necessary to foreclose or sell. In addition to preventing the mortgagor from disposing of any of the equipment, the chattel mortgage may serve to remove any problems that may arise over whether certain equipment is a fixture; a real estate mortgage would cover only fixtures, but with a concurrent chattel mortgage the question becomes irrelevant.

The chattel mortgage is not much used to finance the acquisition of new equipment by businesses. Often, a business prefers to pay cash for the equipment, and to do so it may borrow from a medium-term source of credit, such as a finance company, or it may borrow on a long-term basis in the bond market. And it may, of course, purchase equipment on credit under a conditional sale agreement. Various "business chattels" — office furniture and equipment, machinery, stock-in-trade, and vehicles — may also provide security for borrowing by the business through an issue of debentures secured by a "floating charge" as explained below.

The Bank Act empowers the chartered banks to take a chattel mortgage as additional security for an already outstanding loan. Banks are able, therefore, to buttress their security in this way when the borrower gets into difficulties or if the value of the original collateral security has declined.

BILLS OF SALE

A bill of sale is a written contract of sale of goods in which the seller acknowledges the transfer of the ownership of specified goods to the buyer for a stated price. Possession of the instrument and its registration in a public office may be important for the buyer when he leaves the goods in the possession of the seller: only by such registration may the buyer protect his title against creditors of the seller or an innocent purchaser or mortgagee should the seller fraudulently sell the goods a second time, or should he mortgage them.

A bill of sale may also in fact be used as a chattel mortgage. One may "sell" his title to goods still retaining possession and use of them as a means of providing security for the repayment of a sum of money he has borrowed. In these circumstances, the intention is not really to sell the goods at all, but simply to use the bill of sale as an instrument for securing credit; indeed the bill of sale may provide for a transfer of the title back to the original owner upon his repayment of the money. The courts regard such a bill of sale as a chattel mortgage, and the provincial statutes apply to both types of instruments.

FLOATING CHARGES

The usual method by which a limited company borrows money for a long term is by an issue to the public of mortgage bonds using its land and buildings as security. Each of the certificates issued to bondholders is evidence of an interest in a *trust deed,* an elaborate form of mortgage on the lands and buildings of the company. The parties to a trust deed are the borrowing company (as mortgagor) and a trustee for the bondholders (as mortgagee); the bondholders themselves are beneficiaries of the mortgagee's rights, and the trustee administers these rights for their benefit. Generally, a trust company acts as trustee for the bondholders.

A common feature of the issue of mortgage bonds by Canadian companies is the provision of additional security over and above the mortgage of real property by the creation of a floating charge. A *floating charge* adds the remaining assets not already mortgaged or pledged to the security available for the debt. When a trust deed includes provision for a floating charge, the trustee for the mortgage bondholders also has access to the residue of business assets, including chattels and choses in action, ahead of the unsecured creditors of the company.

The floating charge nicely complements a mortgage of real property because it provides security over the whole of the assets as a working unit. If the company defaults in the payment of its bond obligations, it is then easier to place the company in the hands of a receiver and manager who can operate it in the interest of the bondholders. A sale of the mortgaged lands and buildings on default by the company is often an ineffective remedy for the bondholders; if the buildings and fixtures are of a highly specialized nature, they will have relatively small realizable value on a forced sale. Such value as they possess is best realized through continued operation of the company. On the other hand, one of the criticisms of a floating charge is that it is too pervasive a type of security and operates to the great disadvantage of the remaining creditors; it takes precedence even over arrears of wages.

Occasionally, a company issues bonds secured only by a floating charge and without any mortgage of specific assets. Such corporation bonds are usually called *debentures,* although that term is also used to describe the bond issues of municipalities where the security is the taxing power of the municipality and not a mortgage charge against any tangible assets.

All provinces require that mortgages and floating charges contained in trust deeds be registered in the provincial office where company documents are recorded. As with conditional sales and chattel mortgages, failure to register makes the trust deed void against creditors and subsequent purchasers or mortgagees. The statutory requirements vary from province to province. Some are incorporated in corporations acts, while others are found in separate acts.[32]

ASSIGNMENT OF BOOK DEBTS

A businessman may obtain credit on the security of his accounts receivable; he does so by making a conditional assignment of book debts to his creditor. If the assignor subsequently defaults on repayment of the debt, his assignee may realize directly on the book debts owed to the assignor and in priority to the general creditors of the assignor. In this way, an assignment of book debts may seriously prejudice the position of general creditors of the assignor if he becomes insolvent. Hence, general creditors need a means of ascertaining whether an assignment has been made. The common law provinces have passed statutes rendering an assignment of book debts void as against the creditors of the assignor and as against subsequent assignees of his book debts unless his assignment is registered in a designated public office where its terms are available for public inspection.[33]

The object of the statutes is to assure present and prospective creditors of a business that unless there is a registered public notice to the contrary, the assets of that business in the form of accounts receivable will be available to meet their claims. Compliance with the statutes affords public notice that a certain category of assets — accounts receivable — is not so available. Having been given access to this information, creditors who advance credit without searching the records cannot thereafter complain if they learn that someone has an exclusive recourse against their debtor's accounts receivable. On the other hand, creditors who have not been provided with this means of information, through failure of the assignee to register, retain their recourse against the book debts as general creditors despite the assignment.

Illustration:

> Wearwell carries on business as a shoe jobber and wholesaler. To finance a spring stock of shoes from various manufacturers, he obtains a large amount of credit from the Bank of Mariposa and conditionally assigns his accounts

---

[32] See, for example: Corporations Securities Registrations Act, R.S.O. 1970, c. 88; R.S.N.S. 1967, c. 60.

[33] See, for example: Assignment of Book Accounts Act, St. of B.C. 1961, c. 4, s. 12; Assignment of Book Debts Act, R.S.O. 1970, c. 33, s. 3; R.S.N.S. 1967, c. 15, s. 3.

receivable to the bank. Through inadvertence the bank messenger neglects to register the assignment as instructed by the manager. Subsequently Wearwell becomes insolvent, and his general creditors obtain an order declaring him bankrupt. The bank cannot insist on prior payment from Wearwell's accounts receivable; it ranks only as a general creditor.

Suppose that before the creditors had obtained an order for bankruptcy, Wearwell had defaulted on the bank loan and the bank had consequently obtained payment under the assignment of book debts from several of Wearwell's customers. In these circumstances the bank would be entitled to retain the money, provided the loan had been made and the security had been given in good faith and without any intention of giving the bank a preference over the other creditors of Wearwell. Since the assignment was not registered, however, all money received from the collection of Wearwell's book debts *after* the date of his bankruptcy belongs to the trustee for the benefit of the general creditors.

The statutes apply to a *general assignment,* that is, an assignment which embraces not merely existing book debts but future book debts arising out of future business activities of the assignor. They do not apply to an assignment of book debts already due at the date of the assignment from specified debtors, or to an assignment of debts growing due under specified contracts, as when a business discounts specific book debts with a finance company or sells them to a factor. These book debts no longer form part of the assets of the business: they have been replaced by cash. Accordingly, the assignee need not register under these statutes to protect his rights as purchaser of the book debts.[34]

BANK LOANS UNDER SECTION 88 OF THE BANK ACT

History

The right to lend to primary producers against the security of their natural products has long been a distinctive feature of Canadian banking practice, and in fact antedates Confederation.[35] Early Canadian economic activity was largely in the form of production of raw materials. The typical producer — usually a small-scale farmer — required short-term financial assistance to help him defray his costs at the beginning of, and throughout, the growing season; it was in the nature of his business that he must wait several months to recoup his costs by selling his product, and that he would not have an initial invested capital to finance himself in the interim. In these circumstances, the appropriate financing is

---

[34] St. of B.C. 1961, c. 4, s. 2(f) and (g); R.S.O. 1970, c. 33, s. 2(b) and (c); R.S.N.S. 1967, c. 15, s. 2(b) and (c). See also, The Bankruptcy Act, R.S.C. 1970, c. B-3, s. 72.

[35] See Jamieson, *Chartered Banking in Canada* (rev. ed.), p. 163. Toronto: The Ryerson Press, 1962.

a short-term *self-liquidating loan* — that is, a loan for which the source of repayment must be the proceeds from the sale of the very goods whose production the loan is financing.

Types of Borrower and Security

The Bank Act has expanded somewhat the types of security as well as the types of borrower who may have the advantage of this kind of bank loan, but the underlying philosophy remains the same. Specifically, section 88 of the Bank Act[36] now empowers Canadian chartered banks to lend to the following types of borrower:

    (a) wholesale purchasers or shippers of, or dealers in, products of agriculture, the forest, quarry, mine, sea, lakes, or rivers;

    (b) manufacturers; and

    (c) farmers and fishermen.

We should note that the section does not authorize loans to assist retail businesses, or wholesalers of other than primary products.

The type of security that banks are authorized to take under this section varies with the type of borrower. At the wholesale level, a bank may take as its security primary produce while held in stock during an intermediate stage of its marketing. Thus, a grain-elevator company may borrow under section 88 to permit it to pay farmers on receipt of their grain for storage. Manufacturers may borrow under the section on the security of their inventories of raw materials, goods in process and finished goods; a significant proportion of the loans now made under section 88 is to manufacturers. When lending to farmers, a bank may accept as security their threshed grain, their future crop, their livestock or their agricultural implements. Thus, section 88 permits advances to a farmer for the purchase of seed, fertilizer or binder twine, with the future crop serving as security for the loan; the purchase of feed with the livestock as security; the purchase of agricultural equipment or the installation of a farm electric system on the security of the equipment thus acquired; or the improvement or alteration of various forms of farm equipment or buildings on the security of agricultural implements. A fisherman may obtain a loan on the security of his fishing vessels, equipment, supplies, or products of the sea.

The security taken by a bank is neither a pledge nor a chattel mortgage. It is not a pledge because the borrower does not physically transfer to the bank the property he offers as security; indeed, the security may not even be in existence when the loan is made — it may be a crop yet to be grown. Nor is the security in the form of a chattel mortgage, because the bank does not acquire title to the property offered as security: to realize the security the bank must have a power of attorney from the borrower.

---

[36] R.S.C. 1970, c. B-1, s. 88.

Rights of the Lender

A borrower under section 88 signs an agreement in which he makes the following promises: to keep the property insured and free from claims; to account to the bank for the proceeds of sales; to give the bank a right to take possession in the event of default or neglect; to grant a power of attorney to the bank; and to consent to the sale of security without notice or advertisement if the borrower defaults.[37] While the loan is in good standing the borrower must deposit separately the money realized from the sale of the goods towards a reduction of the loan. As a further assurance that the proceeds from sales are applied against the loan, a bank frequently takes a conditional assignment of the borrower's accounts receivable. If the borrower defaults and the bank takes possession of the goods in the borrower's hands and sells them, it is entitled to retain out of the proceeds whatever amount will repay the balance owing on the loan plus costs;[38] any surplus belongs to the borrower, and any deficiency represents a debt still due from him.

To protect its security against the borrower's unsecured creditors and subsequent purchasers or mortgagees in good faith, a bank must insist that the borrower file a standard form of notice expressing his intention to give this type of security. The place for filing is the local or nearest office of the Bank of Canada.[39] In order to protect the value of the security itself, it may also require borrowers other than farmers or fishermen to submit at frequent intervals a statement showing the current value and location of the goods comprising the security.

When a company has issued bonds secured by a floating charge, the floating charge has prior rights against all assets including inventories unless the trust deed contains a clause to the contrary. The advantage to a company of such a qualifying clause in a trust deed is that the company may then be able to obtain credit under section 88: a bank may extend credit because its security takes priority over the floating charge.

How effective is the security given to banks under section 88? From a bank's point of view, the security is helpful but certainly not decisive; the value of the security in the form of goods and equipment may deteriorate seriously by the time the borrower defaults. In practice, such collateral security for a bank loan is only a precaution. A bank is not likely to lend money on the strength of its protection under section 88 if it does not have confidence in the borrower.

OTHER FORMS OF COLLATERAL SECURITY FOR BANK LOANS

The Bank Act also authorizes the chartered banks to avail themselves of many of

---

[37] See Melvin, "Section 88", *The Canadian Banker,* Winter 1954, p. 26.

[38] Employees of the borrower take priority over the bank to the extent of three months' arrears of wages: Bank Act, R.S.C. 1970, c. B-1, s. 88(5).

[39] *Ibid.*, s. 88(4).

the devices for securing credit that we have considered earlier in this book. In addition to, or instead of, security under section 88 a bank may require any of the following types of security as a condition for granting credit:

(a) An assignment of a warehouse receipt, representing title to goods while held in storage, or of an order bill of lading representing title to goods while in the course of transit.[40]

(b) A pledge of stocks and bonds, accompanied by a power of attorney signed by the borrower authorizing the bank to sell these items as his agent if need be.

(c) A pledge of drafts drawn by the borrower against his customers.

(d) An assignment of book debts.

(e) An assignment of cash surrender value of a life insurance policy.

(f) A chattel mortgage.[41]

(g) A real estate mortgage up to 75 per cent of the value of the property (except where the mortgage loan is made under other statutes, such as the National Housing Act [1954], which place a different limit on the relationship between the amount of the loan and the value of the property). To the extent that such mortgage loans are made on the security of residential (as opposed to commercial) property, their aggregate amount for each bank is limited by a formula which keeps it within a maximum percentage of the deposit liabilities and debentures payable of the bank.[42]

(h) A guarantee by a third party.

While the right is not expressly granted by the Bank Act, Canadian judicial decisions show that a bank has, in addition to collateral security specifically lodged by the borrower, a right of lien on other personal property belonging to him in the bank's possession.[43] A bank may apply against a loan drafts which the borrowing business has left with it for collection.[44] It may apply in settlement of the loan any deposit balances kept with it by the borrower provided he has not previously earmarked these balances for some particular purpose.[45] A bank lien does not extend to property left with the bank for safe-keeping.[46]

NEW PERSONAL PROPERTY SECURITY LEGISLATION

The provinces of Manitoba and Ontario have enacted legislation which promises to change substantially the practice affecting legal devices for securing credit

---

[40] *Ibid.*, s. 86.

[41] S. 75(1)(c) authorizes loans on the security of both choses in action and chattels.

[42] S. 75(1)(c) and 75(3).

[43] Re Williams (1903) 7 O.L.R. 183. The Bank Act, s. 83, does give the bank a privileged lien on shares of its own capital stock held by the borrower and on any dividends payable to the borrower, and entitles the bank to refuse to permit the transfer of such shares until the loan is repaid.

[44] Merchants Bank v. Thompson (1912) 26 O.L.R. 183.

[45] Riddell v. Bank of Upper Canada (1859) 18 U.C.R. 139.

[46] Leese v. Martin (1873) L.R. 17 Eq. 224.

within those provinces.[47] The Ontario legislation, although passed in 1967, has yet to come into force, but it appears that part of the Manitoba legislation with respect to registration is already in effect. The new legislation simplifies the legal means of creating a securities interest, as it does not require security arrangements to be in a particular form. The legislation replaces the Conditional Sales Act, the Lien Notes Act and parts of the Bills of Sales and Chattel Mortgages Act, and codifies some of the common law with respect to pledges of personal property.

The legislation recognizes that a number of different security devices are really designed to serve the same function. It provides therefore, for a uniform system of registration, uniform rules concerning the secured party's remedies, and a uniform system of priorities between secured parties, third-party purchasers, subsequent secured parties, and general creditors. The legislation does not create a single system of priorities, but rather a uniform system of principles by which priorities can be ascertained.

The inherent difficulties in creating a security interest as discussed in this chapter are not removed by the legislation. The drafter of an agreement must still anticipate the kinds of problems that the drafter of one of the various security devices in use under the older legislation has to worry about. There are, however, general rules set out in the legislation in the place of various minute and specific rules so that when a problem does arise, it will be easier to find the answer to a question such as who has the prior claim.

Despite these changes, there is nothing in the legislation to prevent businessmen from continuing to use their old contracts and to keep calling them conditional sales or chattel mortgages or whatever.

The Acts authorize the establishment of a central registry system for all secured transactions. The delay in implementing the legislation in Ontario has been explained by the need to develop massive central computer facilities for storing the details of individual transactions and establishing "on-line" connections with local registry offices. It appears now, however, that the on-line connections have been abandoned in favour of a courier system of prompt delivery to local registries.

The new system also adopts a method from the land titles system in the sense that provincial governments retain a fund to reimburse losses caused by incorrectly-processed information, and a central registry office will provide a guaranteed certificate of search. Of course, a search is made under the name of an individual to learn whether some security device is registered against him rather than a search against the property itself, as in the case of the land titles system.

These statutes are modeled after Article 9 of the U.S. Uniform Commercial Code already adopted in many of the states of the U.S.A. If other Canadian provinces follow suit, a uniform system of searching for security interests may develop on a country-wide rather than a province-wide basis.

---

[47] R.S.O. 1970, c. 344; St. of Man. 1973, c. 5.

QUESTIONS FOR REVIEW

1. What devices for securing credit require registration in a public office?
2. What do we mean by collateral security?
3. If there were no statute requiring registration of a conditional sale and an innocent purchaser acquired second-hand goods from a conditional buyer, who would have title to them, the purchaser or the conditional seller?
4. If a person, without checking the public records, purchases second-hand goods already subject to a registered conditional sale, and the conditional seller repossesses them, what recourse, if any, has the purchaser?
5. Conditional sale agreements invariably contain a term prohibiting the buyer from moving the goods from the provincial jurisdiction. Why?
6. Distinguish between a chattel mortgage and a pledge.
7. To what extent does the mortgagee's control over the mortgaged property differ in a chattel mortgage and a land mortgage?
8. Why should a lender under a chattel mortgage give public notice when a lender under a pledge does not?
9. What is the advantage for the bondholders of a corporation to have a floating charge included in the trust deed?
10. Why would a province pass legislation prohibiting the mortgaging of crops yet to be grown, except to finance seed or necessaries?
11. What precaution is required by statute to ensure that a chattel mortgage transaction is not a device to defraud other creditors of the mortgagor?
12. What interest has an ordinary trade creditor in knowing the extent to which his debtor's assets have become the subject-matter of a security transaction?
13. Benson & Co. Ltd. has sold office furniture to Carson Bros. under a conditional sale agreement, but it has neither registered the agreement nor affixed its name to the furniture. Carson Bros. use the furniture in their general office. They are adjudged bankrupt. Is Benson & Co. Ltd. a secured creditor for the balance owing on the furniture? Does the location of Carson Bros.' office affect the matter?
14. For each of the following situations describe the most suitable device which may be employed for securing credit or for obtaining priority:

    (a) The proprietor of a flour mill in Windsor has purchased grain which is stored in a public elevator in Thunder Bay. The proprietor of the mill now requires money to pay for the grain purchased.

    (b) X's wife is pressing him to buy an electric ironer. X has no money in the bank but has a steady job and some life insurance (whole life, not term insurance).

    (c) A large, well-established retail store with a satisfactory earnings record requires the temporary use of an additional $10,000.

    (d) A small company, with barely adequate capital, is obliged for competitive reasons to extend 90 days' credit to customers, whereas for the purpose of paying its own accounts it requires customers' money more promptly.

(e) *Y* has heard about an extraordinarily good buy in some mining stock. He has insufficient money in the bank.

(f) A farmer wishes to make improvements to his farm buildings and has insufficient funds for the purpose.

(g) A furniture manufacturer has sold finished stock to a retail furniture dealer on credit. Before the furniture in question reaches the retail store, the manufacturer learns that the retail dealer is insolvent.

CASES FOR DISCUSSION

CASE 1

Holmes purchased a refrigerator and stove from Watts Electric Ltd. under a conditional sale agreement. Watts Electric Ltd. discounted the contract with Domestic Finance Co. Neither Watts Electric Ltd. nor Domestic Finance Co. registered the agreement.

Several months later Holmes sold the appliances to Fowler for cash without disclosing that there was an unpaid balance under a conditional sale agreement. Holmes left the province. After default by Holmes, Domestic Finance Co. discovered that Fowler had possession of the appliances. The finance company repossessed them. Fowler then brought an action against Domestic Finance Co. for wrongful seizure of the appliances.

State the arguments for the plaintiff and the defendant. What should the decision be? (See *General Motors Acceptance Corp. v. Feraday* [1952] O.W.N. 650.)

CASE 2

Carter was employed for years as a truck driver for a large road-haulage firm. He decided to go into business for himself and spent his savings to buy a new $15,000 truck. Within a few weeks he discovered that he had made a mistake buying the truck for cash; he needed capital to modernize his garage where he stored the truck and kept a small office. Ready Finance Co. lent Carter $8,000 on the security of a chattel mortgage on the truck.

Carter found that his one-man operation was not sound. He defaulted on his third payment to the finance company when the balance owing was $6,900. The company seized the truck and sold it for $6,500 and is now suing Carter for the deficiency of $400. Carter is convinced that the company has acted improperly.

What facts would be relevant to ascertain whether he is correct? If he is correct, what recourse does Carter have?

CASE 3

Arthurs purchased a second-hand Cadillac from Better Buy Motors Ltd. under a conditional sale agreement. Arthurs used the car for several months in his work as a travelling sales representative and paid his instalments regularly. After he had paid a substantial portion of the price, Crimson Motors Ltd. repossessed the car under a prior, properly-registered chattel mortgage; the chattel mortgagor had fraudulently sold the car to Better Buy Motors.

Describe the nature of Arthurs' rights, and state against whom they are available. What factors should be taken into account in assessing his loss? (For a similar problem, see *McNeill v. Associated Car Markets Ltd.* (1963) 35 D.L.R. (2d) 581.)

CASE 4

Mechanical Industries Ltd. was adjudged bankrupt on a petition of its trade creditors. As of the date of the judgment the company had assets of an estimated realizable value of $54,000 including accounts receivable of $15,000. The liabilities and capital side of its balance sheet was as follows:

Current Liabilities		
Trade creditors	$ 61,000	
Bank loan	24,000	
Note payable—shareholder	50,000	
	———	
Total current liabilities		$135,000
Shareholders' Equity		
Share capital, issued and fully		
paid 15,000 shares of no par value	100,000	
Less deficit	80,000	
	———	
		20,000
		———
		$155,000

The bank loan is a demand loan for which the security is a general assignment of accounts receivable. At the time the bank made the loan it agreed that the assignment was conditional — that it would not require the customers of Mechanical Industries Ltd. to pay their accounts to the bank unless the loan was in default.

What steps should the bank have taken to protect its security? Assuming it has taken these steps, what amount will it receive on liquidation? Assuming it failed to take these steps, what amount will it receive?

CASE 5

Oliver purchased a car from Hardy Motors Ltd. for $5,500 and paid $3,800 in cash as a down payment on the understanding that he should have 30 days in which to pay the balance. The proprietor of Hardy Motors Ltd. stated that 30-day credit was unusual for this type of purchase and that he would still have to get Oliver's signature on a conditional sale agreement "as a matter of form". The conditional sale agreement which Oliver signed included a term that Oliver should pay the balance of the purchase price over 24 months in monthly instalments of $89.50 each. Hardy told Oliver that he would hold the conditional sale agreement for 30 days so that Oliver would have that time in which to raise the balance of the purchase price.

Hardy Motors Ltd. was in financial trouble. In breach of his understanding with Oliver the proprietor at once discounted (assigned) the conditional sale contract with Vanguard Finance Co. The finance company advised Oliver of the assignment and requested payment to it of the monthly instalments specified in the conditional sale agreement. Oliver ignored this notice, and before the expiration of the 30 days he paid the balance of $1,700 directly to Hardy Motors Ltd. Shortly thereafter Hardy Motors Ltd. was adjudged bankrupt, and Hardy absconded with the cash assets of the business. Vanguard Finance Co. seized the car from Oliver. Oliver brought an action against Vanguard Finance Co. for wrongful seizure, asking for a court order for return of the car to him.

Should Oliver's action succeed? (See *Ostrikoff v. Vancouver Finance Co.* (1956) 1 D.L.R. (2d) 179.)

CASE 6

Camp purchased a prefabricated summer cottage on the instalment plan from the Green Lumber Co. The purchase price was $7,500 of which he paid $2,100 down. He then signed a conditional sale contract for $5,400 plus a finance charge of $1,980. The contract required the amount of $7,380 to be paid in equal monthly instalments of $123 over a period of five years. Camp also made a promissory note for $7,380 in favour of Green Lumber Co.

The conditional sale contract signed by Camp contained the following clause:

> Purchaser takes notice that this agreement together with Vendor's title to property in and ownership of said goods and said note are to be forthwith assigned and negotiated to Income Finance Corporation Limited and that said Corporation shall not be affected by any equities existing between Vendor and Purchaser and that all payments are to be made to said Corporation.

Income Finance Corporation Limited had recently advertised a special feature of the financing services it could provide where the money was to be devoted to home improvements or buildings. It had published an advertisement which read:

> You get automatic life insurance (arranged through Perpetual Life Insurance Company) covering the balance owing up to an amount of $5,000 — no extra cost, no physical examination. You receive a certificate containing provisions and details of the policy.

The Perpetual Life Insurance Company is a subsidiary of Income Finance Corporation Limited. The premium cost of insurance coverage on Camp's life was included in the finance charge of $1,980.

Green Lumber Co. assigned the conditional sale contract and endorsed Camp's note to the Income Finance Corporation Limited immediately following the sale. Camp died after he had paid only one of the monthly instalments. Income Finance Corporation Limited then claimed the balance owing from the executor of Camp's estate. The executor protested that the proceeds of the life insurance policy were by the conditional sale contract to be applied in liquidation of the debt in the event of Camp's death; he produced a "Life Insurance (Family Protection) Certificate" found among Camp's papers to prove his point. The finance company replied that no legal relation with respect to the contract of insurance existed either between the deceased and itself or between the deceased and Perpetual Life Insurance Company, and it brought action against Camp's estate for the balance due under the conditional sale agreement.

Discuss the merits of the finance company's argument and indicate whether its action should succeed.

CASE 7

Dowdy formed a company called Economy Cabs Limited and, as president and general manager, negotiated for the purchase of five used cars from Vintage Motors Ltd., a firm of automobile dealers. The price of the five cars was $8,350 and the purchase was financed and arranged as follows: Economy Cabs Limited gave its promissory note for $8,350 to Vintage Motors Ltd.; in a covering letter, Economy Cabs Limited undertook to repay the holder of the note by monthly instalments of $500 with the whole amount of the balance to become immediately due on default in any monthly instalment; Vintage Motors Ltd. endorsed the note and discounted it with the Bank of Southern Canada. Under a separate conditional sale contract between Vintage Motors Ltd. and Economy Cabs Limited, Vintage Motors Ltd. retained title and right to repossession and resale of the cars as security for the payment of the purchase price.

After this financing had been completed, Dowdy mailed to Vintage Motors Ltd. the following statement:

> This is to advise you that in view of the accommodation which you kindly arranged through the Bank of Southern Canada for $8,350 on behalf of Economy Cabs Limited, I give you my personal guaranty that I will see that this indebtedness is paid off according to the arrangements made.
>
> *(signed)* "U.R. Dowdy"

Economy Cabs Limited soon found that to attract adequate business it would have to purchase newer cabs to replace some of the old ones. Only six months after it had commenced operations, it traded in three of its cabs on a purchase of three newer ones from Vintage Motors Ltd. After an allowance on the cabs traded in, the net effect of this transaction was to increase its indebtedness by $5,200. At this time, its liability on the original promissory note had been reduced by $3,000 (six payments of $500) to $5,350, each part payment being acknowledged by an endorsement of the bank on the note. Economy Cabs Limited made a new note for $10,550 in favour of Vintage Motors Ltd. and that company obtained the additional portion from the Bank of Southern Canada by endorsing the new note and substituting it for the original one; the original note was cancelled by the bank and returned to Economy Cabs Limited. A new conditional sale contract was drawn up to cover the new amount of debt and the existing cabs.

In a further six months' time, Economy Cabs Limited was insolvent and unable to make any further monthly payments to the bank. Its cabs had a resale value, in total, of about $7,000. The Bank of Southern Canada demanded from Vintage Motors Ltd. an immediate settlement of the then balance of $8,050 on the strength of its endorsement on the note. In turn, Vintage Motors Ltd. sought reimbursement from Dowdy, and when he refused to pay, brought an action against him.

Describe the nature of the defences available to Dowdy and indicate to what extent, if any, he would be liable. (For reference, see *Adelaide Motors Ltd. v. Byrne* [1964] 49 M.P.R. 197.)

CHAPTER 31

Creditors' Rights

STATUTORY ARRANGEMENTS FOR PROTECTION OF CREDITORS

A debtor's financial position may become so hopeless that it is unwise or indeed impossible for him to carry on. This may happen when he becomes insolvent, that is, when he is unable to meet his debts to his creditors as they fall due or when his liabilities exceed his realizable assets. When a debtor finds himself in such an unhappy condition, at least some of his creditors must expect to share the loss with him.

A number of statutes have been passed which have as their main purpose the protection of creditors' claims. These statutes set out the rights of creditors both against their debtor and against each other. In this chapter, our main concern will be with ways in which the Bankruptcy Act, the Bulk Sales Act and the Mechanics' Lien Act assist this purpose.

THE BANKRUPTCY ACT

History and Purposes

The present Bankruptcy Act was passed in 1949, superseding an earlier act of 1919, and has been amended in important respects in recent years. Since bankruptcy is one of the matters assigned to the jurisdiction of the federal government under the British North America Act, the Bankruptcy Act is a federal statute. In the years from 1880 to 1919 there was no federal legislation on the subject of bankruptcy. During this period, the provinces passed some legislation governing procedure for "assignments" and prohibiting fraudulent conduct by debtors. There was, however, no legal machinery by which a debtor could be compelled to make an assignment for the benefit of his creditors, nor was there any means of giving an honest bankrupt a formal discharge from his obligations.

The Bankruptcy Act performs three tasks. First, it establishes uniform practice in bankruptcy proceedings throughout the country on as inexpensive a basis as possible. Secondly, it provides for an equitable distribution of the debtor's assets among creditors. Thirdly, it provides for the release of an honest but unfortunate debtor from his obligations and so permits him to resume business activities afresh.

The details of bankruptcy procedure are technical and are the province of lawyers and licensed trustees in bankruptcy. This chapter does not purport to be a manual on the subject of creditors' rights but merely outlines the nature of the problem and how, in general, the law attempts to solve it. [1]

Public Policy

It is helpful in bankruptcy law to distinguish the public interest from that of the parties to a bankruptcy proceeding. The interests of the public and creditors may in general coincide but the creditors, who must absorb the costs, may not be prepared to push an investigation to the point required by the public interest. Creditors may well be fatalistic by the time matters have deteriorated to the point of bankruptcy, and they can after all claim reasonable deductions for bad-debt expense in calculating taxable income.

The public policy justifying bankruptcy legislation is to promote an atmosphere of confidence in business relations generally, and foster the expectation that when a misfortune occurs, a debtor's remaining assets will by and large be salvaged and distributed fairly. When confidence among business people is undermined by bankruptcy frauds, the costs of doing business are increased for all (and not just for the particular creditors concerned in a specific bankruptcy). The cost of credit is increased by more extensive investigations of credit standing and possibly even by higher interest rates; investment in small and medium-sized businesses is discouraged. Ultimately, the higher cost of doing business is passed on to the consumer. Thus, there is a real social cost in bankruptcy malpractice, apart from the losses caused to the creditors themselves.

---

[1] A proposed new bankruptcy act was introduced as Bill C-60 in the House of Commons, May 5, 1975. It will introduce several sweeping changes in bankruptcy law when it finally comes into force. Since it is a very complex statute that may undergo substantial alteration in Parliament before it is passed, we can only note its introduction in a tentative way at this time.

For a detailed account of bankruptcy law and procedure see: Duncan and Honsberger, *Bankruptcy in Canada* (3rd ed.). Toronto: Canadian Legal Authors Ltd., 1961; Houlden and Morawetz, *Bankruptcy Law of Canada*. Toronto: The Carswell Company Ltd., 1960 and *Cumulative Supplement,* 1974; Canada, *Report of the Study Committee on Bankruptcy and Insolvency Legislation,* Canada, 1970. Ottawa: Information Canada, 1970.

A case can also be made for the public interest in assisting bankrupt debtors. Bankruptcy legislation provides for the discharge of an honest but unfortunate debtor so that he is not saddled forever with a burden of debts he cannot repay; he gets a fresh start. An important policy is to keep economic initiative alive and prevent it from being stifled by past misfortune. However, as business comes to be conducted more and more through corporations, this line of argument must carry less weight; the discharge of a bankrupt corporation might save its owners the expense of incorporating another company to replace it, but would probably do little to encourage economic initiative. On the other hand, although the benefits of bankruptcy law also are available to individuals not engaged in business, they appear to use it infrequently to obtain relief from a heavy burden of debt.

Government Supervision

The Act has created the position of Superintendent of Bankruptcy.[2] The Superintendent keeps a record of all bankruptcy proceedings in Canada and has power to inspect the administration affecting insolvent estates as he sees fit. He is responsible for investigating the character and qualifications of persons who apply for licences and renewals of licences to act as trustees. He has also the power to investigate situations where a bankruptcy offence may have been committed and, where the evidence so indicates, to report the matter to the Deputy Attorney-General or other appropriate provincial legal officer.[3] As a result, the trustee of a bankrupt estate is no longer burdened with the obligation of investigating irregularities.

For the purposes of administration, the Act makes each province and each of the two territories a bankruptcy district. Each district may be divided into two or more bankruptcy divisions, according to the size of the province. For each division, the Superintendent appoints one or more official receivers. The official receiver makes a report to the Superintendent of Bankruptcy of every bankruptcy originating in his division.

When a debtor is adjudged bankrupt, the court names a licensed trustee to administer his affairs. If the creditors disapprove of the trustee appointed, they may substitute another licensed trustee. The Act requires that creditors appoint a number of inspectors (not exceeding five) to instruct the licensed trustee and review and approve his accounts.[4] No one against whom the estate has a contested claim can be appointed as an inspector, nor can anyone who has a contested claim against the estate be appointed. It is only possible for an inspector to purchase or acquire property from the bankrupt estate if he has the prior approval of the court.

---

[2] The Bankruptcy Act outlines the machinery and administration under the Act in R.S.C. 1970, c. B-3, ss. 5 to 10. (Subsequent references to the Bankruptcy Act will be by section number only.)

[3] S. 6(7).

[4] S. 94.

The Bankruptcy Act designates the highest trial court in each province as the court for bankruptcy proceedings. The duties assigned to the court include hearing creditors' petitions for the bankruptcy of their debtor and considering whether the debtor should be discharged after his affairs have been wound up.

Methods of Procedure

Receiving order. A creditor is entitled to petition for the bankruptcy of his debtor if he is owed $1,000 or more, or a group of creditors may petition collectively if they are owed that amount in the aggregate.[5] To succeed, they must be able to convince the court that the debtor has committed an act of bankruptcy within the past six months. A court order issued following a successful petition by a creditor or creditors is called a *receiving order* or, sometimes, a *compulsory receiving order*. The effect of the receiving order is to authorize a transfer of all the property (estate) of the bankrupt debtor to a licensed trustee in bankruptcy for realization and distribution to the creditors.[6]

Assignment. A debtor may voluntarily institute bankruptcy proceedings by applying to the official receiver for his district to have a licensed trustee in bankruptcy appointed.[7] The trustee then proceeds in the same way as if he had been appointed under a compulsory receiving order. The expression *authorized assignment* is sometimes used for an assignment of this kind, to distinguish it from an unauthorized transfer of assets made by a debtor in order to defeat his creditors, or to give a preference to one creditor over the others; unauthorized transfers are either void or else both void and fraudulent.

The Bankruptcy Act distinguishes between a bankrupt debtor and an insolvent person. A *bankrupt* (that is, a bankrupt debtor) is a person against whom a receiving order has been made or who has made an authorized assignment. An *insolvent person* is a person who, though not bankrupt, has liabilities of at least $1,000, and is either unable to meet his obligations as they generally become due, or has ceased paying current obligations in the ordinary course of business, or whose property has a realizable value insufficient to pay all of his obligations.[8] Thus the term insolvency describes a financial condition whereas bankruptcy describes a legal condition. A person may be insolvent without having yet become bankrupt.

Anyone who satisfies the definition of an insolvent person can make an authorized assignment.[9] But what would be his motive for doing so, without waiting for his creditors to petition him into bankruptcy? A debtor may prejudice himself by continuing to trade after realizing that he is insolvent; when his creditors eventually put him into bankruptcy, the court may refuse to grant him a

---

[5] S. 25.
[6] S. 50(5).
[7] S. 31.
[8] S. 2, para. (j).
[9] A history of Canadian insolvency and bankruptcy legislation is given in Chapter 2 of *The Report of the Study Committee on Bankruptcy and Insolvency Legislation, Canada, 1970.*

discharge because of such conduct.[10] A wage-earner may also wish to make a voluntary assignment if his financial position is desperate. If he is unable to come to some arrangement with his creditors and is being harassed by them, he may have sufficient incentive to make an assignment in order to obtain a discharge from his obligations. Historically, a voluntary assignment was the only method of bankruptcy before the Act was amended; creditors were unable on their own initiative to obtain a compulsory receiving order against their debtor.[11]

Proposal. An insolvent person may also make certain proposals to his creditors with a view to avoiding bankruptcy.[12] If his proposals are accepted, the resulting *scheme of arrangement* or *composition* provides an alternative to bankruptcy proceedings. The debtor must still, however, present his proposal to his creditors through the medium of a licensed trustee in bankruptcy.

An insolvent debtor must give the trustee a statement setting out the particulars of his proposal and a statement showing his financial condition. The trustee then calls a meeting of the creditors to consider the proposal: the proposal is not accepted unless creditors whose claims aggregate three fourths of the total claims represented at the meeting approve its terms.[13] Next, the trustee presents the scheme of arrangement for approval by the court. The court will usually refuse to ratify any proposal that does not provide for the payment of at least 50 cents on the dollar to unsecured creditors, or that in the court's opinion is not calculated to benefit the general body of creditors. It may also refuse its approval where a debtor has been guilty of any of the bankruptcy offences mentioned below.

If the court grants its approval, the scheme binds all the creditors, including those who dissented or were not represented at the creditors' meeting. The Act does, however, make an exception to this rule when the approval requires creditors to contribute funds to the business of the debtor, possibly through the purchase of an issue of shares or bonds. In these circumstances, the claim of any creditor who elects not to participate in the proposal is valued by the court and must be paid in cash.

An alternative is available to an incorporated company that has issued bonds through a trustee to whom it has mortgaged its assets, and that subsequently defaults on the payment of bond interest or principal. It may choose to make a proposal to its bondholders under the Companies' Creditors Arrangement Act[14] rather than under the Bankruptcy Act.

Under the Bankruptcy Act, the right to make a proposal to creditors remains available to a debtor even when he has already been adjudged bankrupt if his estate is not yet wound up. The approval of the bankrupt's proposal by his creditors and by the court operates to transfer his assets back to him or to someone else whom the court has approved, unless the proposal indicates otherwise.[15]

---

[10] Ss. 142 and 143.
[11] See Duncan and Honsberger, *Bankruptcy in Canada*, p. 244.
[12] Ss. 32-46.
[13] S. 36 and s. 2, para. (t).
[14] R.S.C. 1970, c. C-25, as amended by St. of Can. 1970, c. 44 (1st supp.), s. 10; 1972, c. 17, s. 2(1).
[15] S. 41(9).

Persons to Whom the Act Applies

The Bankruptcy Act applies, in general, to limited companies and individuals who carry on business in Canada. When we say that the act "applies" to a class of person, we mean that all or at least some of the three methods of procedure outlined above are available should that person become insolvent or commit an act of bankruptcy.

There are some important exceptions to the application of the Act. It does not apply at all to banks or to insurance, trust, loan, or railway companies; special statutes regulating these concerns set out the procedures for winding up their affairs. Furthermore, the provisions permitting a compulsory receiving order do not apply to individuals engaged solely in farming or fishing or to employees who earn less than $2,500 a year in wages, salary, commission, or hire, and who do not on their own account carry on business;[16] these persons may, however, make a voluntary assignment or a proposal under the Act.

While a compulsory receiving order is not available against a salary or wage earner who earns less than $2,500 annually, his creditors may, as we have noted earlier in Chapter 15, apply to a court official to have his earnings garnisheed and paid by his employer to the creditor through the court. The extent to which the earnings of employees generally may be garnisheed varies from province to province, but a considerable percentage of earnings is always exempt to provide for the current sustenance of the employee and his family.[17] The earnings of some types of employees, such as the salaries of federal civil servants and of judges, are not subject to garnishment at all.[18]

Acts of Bankruptcy

We have noted that before creditors can succeed in having their debtor adjudged bankrupt and a receiving order issued, they must prove that he has committed an act of bankruptcy. The Bankruptcy Act sets out in detail the various types of conduct that constitute an act of bankruptcy by a debtor.[19] In summary they are as follows:

(*i*) *Assignment of assets to a trustee.* If a debtor makes an assignment of his property to a trustee for the benefit of his creditors, whether it is an authorized assignment or not, and the arrangement is not satisfactory to the creditors, they may cite the assignment as an act of bankruptcy and petition to have a receiving order issued. They might choose to do so, for example, when the debtor has transferred his assets to a trustee who is not acceptable to them.

---

[16] S. 30.

[17] See, for example: Attachment of Debts Act, R.S.B.C. 1960, c. 20, s. 3; Wages Act, R.S.O. 1970, c. 486 as amended by St. of Ont. 1971, c. 20, s. 7; Garnishment Act, R.S.M. 1970, c. G 20, s. 6.

[18] However, in Ontario the salary of a provincial civil servant may be garnisheed under the Public Service Act, R.S.O. 1970, c. 386, s. 26.

[19] S. 24.

(ii) A fraudulent transfer of assets to a third party other than a trustee. A transfer of property by a debtor in anticipation of bankruptcy in order to withhold assets from distribution to creditors is a fraudulent transfer. As we shall see when discussing "Powers and Duties of the Trustee", below, any attempt to deprive creditors of access to these assets by transferring them to a third person (including the debtor's spouse or child) is void if the transfer takes place within a specified period prior to bankruptcy.

(iii) A fraudulent preference. Any payment by a debtor which has the effect of settling the claim of one creditor in preference to the outstanding claims of other creditors is a fraudulent preference.

(iv) An attempt by the debtor to abscond.

(v) A failure to redeem goods seized under an execution issued against the debtor.[20] As we have seen in Chapter 15, a creditor may sue his debtor, obtain judgment, and seek to satisfy the judgment by having the debtor's assets seized. When the debtor's assets are scanty, the seizure may well benefit the judgment creditor to the disadvantage of other creditors; accordingly, if a debtor fails to take steps to prevent the sale of his property under an execution order, he commits an act which entitles his creditors to apply to the court for his bankruptcy. If they do so, all the debtor's property, including the property subject to the execution order, is put in the hands of a licensed trustee for distribution to all his creditors.[21]

(vi) Presentation at a meeting of creditors of (a) a statement of assets and liabilities disclosing the debtor's insolvency, or (b) a written admission by the debtor that he is unable to pay his debts.

(vii) An attempt to remove or hide any of his property.

(viii) Notice to any of his creditors that he is suspending payment of his debts.

(ix) Default in any proposal which he has previously persuaded his creditors to accept as a means of forestalling bankruptcy proceedings.

(x) A failure to meet liabilities generally as they become due.

The most common of these acts of bankruptcy are failing to pay debts as they become due, and failing to redeem goods seized under an execution.

---

[20] More specifically, a debtor commits an act of bankruptcy if he permits an execution to remain unsatisfied until within four days of the time fixed for the sale by the sheriff, or in a variety of other circumstances set out in section 24(1)(e).

[21] It is possible that, instead of petitioning for a receiving order, all the debtor's major creditors might choose the route of obtaining individual judgments and execution orders. In Ontario, the Creditors Relief Act, R.S.O. 1970, c. 97 provides for a scheme of rateable distribution of the proceeds of sale among execution creditors.

ADMINISTRATION AND SETTLEMENT
OF A BANKRUPT'S AFFAIRS

Powers and Duties of the Trustee

"The appointment of a trustee is the first and vital step in initiating the principle of creditor control."[22] The trustee takes possession of the assets of the bankrupt debtor and of all books and documents relating to his affairs. He becomes in effect a temporary manager of the business, subject to the supervision of the inspectors appointed by the creditors. He may carry on the business, or alternatively, sell the assets. He can do such things as employ a lawyer, borrow further money for the business by pledging or mortgaging its remaining free (unsecured) assets, and negotiate with creditors for the acceptance by them of specific assets in lieu of money settlement of their claims. He may even engage the bankrupt debtor himself to assist in the administration of the bankrupt estate. To do these things, however, he must have specific authority from the inspectors.[23]

A trustee has the power and duty to recover property that under bankruptcy law should form part of the debtor's estate and thus be available to satisfy the claims of creditors.[24] Eleven lengthy sections of the Act under the heading "Settlements and Preferences" are needed to set out the complex rules for the recovery of property.[25] In general, any transfer of property by a debtor that occurred within a year before his bankruptcy becomes void and recoverable by the trustee. It is even possible for the trustee to impeach a transfer of property made as long as five years before the bankruptcy, but the burden is then on the trustee to show that at the date of the transfer the debtor was unable to pay his debts in full without the aid of such property.[26] In realizing the assets of the debtor the trustee in bankruptcy may demand such property, or its value, from the party who received it.

Payments of money made by the debtor within six months preceding bankruptcy may also be recovered. Even if a payment were made more than six months before bankruptcy the trustee may recover it, ". . . unless the person to whom the payment . . . was made proves that . . . at the date of the payment or transfer the [debtor] was able to pay all his debts without the aid of the money so paid . . ."[27]

A payment of money or transfer of property made by a debtor who is an insolvent person and which amounts to a fraudulent preference is recoverable if made within three months preceding bankruptcy.[28] The Act contains a number of

---

[22] Duncan and Honsberger, *Bankruptcy in Canada*, p. 250.

[23] S. 14.

[24] S. 12(2), (3), and (8).

[25] Ss. 69 to 79 inclusive.

[26] St. 69(1) and (2). In practice it is almost impossible for a trustee to establish the exact financial status of a bankrupt debtor at a time as long as a year or more before the bankruptcy.

[27] S. 71(1)(b).

[28] S. 73. Under s. 74, the time limit is extended to 12 months where the preference is in favour of a person related to the insolvent person.

detailed rules that expand on the types and effect of the transactions described above. We shall deal with the concept of "reviewable transactions" in a section "Amendments to the Act", below.

These provisions are designed to nullify transactions which would otherwise defeat the legitimate claims of the creditors; but they do not invalidate bona-fide sales of stock-in-trade or other business assets made before bankruptcy in the normal course of business. Thus, a purchaser who buys goods in good faith and for valuable consideration need not fear that the goods can be recovered from him later should the vendor become bankrupt. Nor does a trustee have access to property which a debtor has acquired as a result of his marriage and which he has transferred back for the benefit of his wife and children.

A debtor may have mortgaged some of his goods prior to bankruptcy. The transfer of title to a chattel mortgagee is not void if the chattel mortgagee took the mortgage in good faith and without notice of any act of bankruptcy by the mortgagor. As we have seen in the preceding chapter, a chattel mortgagee is required to give an affidavit of bona fides when his mortgage is registered.

The trustee distributes *liquidating dividends* (payments on account) to the creditors from time to time as required by the inspectors and as realization of the debtor's assets permits. In doing so he must, of course, be careful to take account of the claims of the secured and preferred creditors.

Priority of Claims

Before making payments to other creditors, the trustee must first settle with the *secured creditors* of the bankrupt debtor. Each secured creditor must pay to the trustee any surplus if the security he holds is worth more than the debt owing to him. When the trustee and secured creditor cannot agree on the value of the security, it may be necessary to sell it and pay the secured claim out of the proceeds.[29] The bankrupt estate is entitled to any surplus for the benefit of other creditors. When the security does not have a value as great as the secured debt, the creditor is entitled to the full value of the security and in addition ranks as a general claim along with other unsecured creditors for the deficiency. When the trustee and secured creditor agree on the value of the assets that comprise the security without having to sell them, the creditor may accept the security in settlement of his account, either by paying any excess value to the trustee or by claiming against the trustee as a general creditor for the deficiency.

Out of the free assets remaining after payment or settlement of secured claims, the trustee must next pay the *preferred creditors*. Preferred creditors are defined in the Bankruptcy Act.[30] The following is a summary of these preferred claims, listed in the order of their priority:

    (a) When the bankrupt debtor is deceased, his reasonable funeral and legal expenses related to his death.

---

[29] Ss. 98 to 105.
[30] S. 107.

(b) Expenses and fees of the licensed trustee in bankruptcy and his legal costs.

(c) A levy for the purpose of defraying the expense of the supervision of the Superintendent in Bankruptcy.

(d) Three months' arrears of wages of employees of the bankrupt debtor to the extent of $500 for each employee. (The Act postpones all claims for wages by spouses, former spouses, parents, children, brothers, sisters, uncles and aunts of the debtor, until all other claims have been satisfied.[31])

(e) Municipal taxes levied within two years preceding bankruptcy.

(f) Arrears of rent due to the landlord for a period of three months preceding bankruptcy.

(g) The costs of the first execution or attachment creditor. A creditor obtains an execution order against tangibles, such as land or goods, and an *attachment* against choses in action, such as accounts receivable or bank deposits.

(h) Indebtedness of the bankrupt under the Workmen's Compensation Act, the Unemployment Insurance Act and the Income Tax Act for amounts deducted from employees' salaries.

(i) Claims for certain injuries sustained by employees.

(j) Claims of the Crown not previously mentioned.

After settling the secured and preferred claims, the trustee pays the general or unsecured creditors rateably to the extent of the funds remaining.

To rank as a claim against the bankrupt estate, all creditors must "prove" their debts. They do so by submitting declarations to the trustee outlining the details of their accounts and specifying the vouchers or other evidence by which they can substantiate these claims. The declaration states whether or not the claim is a secured or preferred claim.

Because the assets are in all probability insufficient to satisfy all the claims in full, the priority of claims is important. A trustee must act with great care in the administration and liquidation of the debtor's affairs; he may be personally liable to creditors for losses caused them by his failure to pay the claims in the proper order of priority, or for any breach of trust.

Duties of the Bankrupt Debtor

Following a receiving order or authorized assignment, the debtor must submit himself for examination by the official receiver to explain his conduct, the causes of his bankruptcy, and the disposition of his property. He must submit a sworn statement of his affairs to the trustee, together with a list of the names and addresses of his creditors and the security held by them. He must attend the first meeting of creditors and give the information they require. He must deliver up

---

[31] Ss. 108(2) and 109.

possession of his property to the trustee, co-operate with the trustee, and "aid to the utmost of his power in the realization of his property and the distribution of the proceeds among his creditors."[32]

Bankruptcy Offences

A bankrupt debtor is liable to imprisonment if he is guilty of any of the offences set out in detail in the Bankruptcy Act. These offences include failing to perform any of the duties we have considered above, making a fraudulent disposition of his property before or after bankruptcy, giving untruthful answers to questions put to him at an examination, concealing, destroying, or falsifying books or documents, and obtaining any credit or property by false representations before or after bankruptcy.[33]

Discharge of the Bankrupt Debtor

As we have noted, an important object of our bankruptcy legislation is to clear an honest but unfortunate debtor of his outstanding debts and to leave him free to resume business life. The discharge of a bankrupt debtor usually cancels the unpaid portion of his debts remaining after their reduction by the liquidating dividends, and gives the debtor a clean slate with which to start business again.[34]

The discharge of a debtor is an official act of the court. In deciding whether to grant or refuse the debtor's application for discharge, the court consults the report of the trustee.[35] One of the more important reasons why a court may refuse or suspend the debtor's discharge is that his assets have proved to be insufficient to pay his unsecured creditors at least 50 cents on the dollar; he may still obtain a discharge, however, if he can show that he cannot justly be held responsible for this circumstance. Other reasons for refusing to give a discharge are that the bankrupt debtor neglected to keep proper books; that he continued to trade after he knew he was insolvent; that he failed to account satisfactorily for any loss or deficiency of assets; that he caused the bankruptcy by rash speculation or extravagant living; that within three months preceding bankruptcy he gave an undue preference to a creditor; that he was bankrupt or made a proposal to his creditors on a previous occasion; that he is guilty of any bankruptcy offence or has failed to perform his duties, as explained above. Other related reasons are set out in the Act.[36]

Until he obtains his discharge, a bankrupt debtor is liable to fine or imprisonment if without disclosing his status he obtains credit of $500 or more for a purpose other than the supply of necessaries for himself and his family, or if he

---

[32] S. 129(k).
[33] S. 169.
[34] The Act specifies in s. 148 those types of debts that are not released by an order of discharge — for example, fines, alimony, liabilities for goods supplied as necessaries of life.
[35] Ss. 140-142.
[36] S. 143.

recommences business and fails to disclose to those with whom he deals that he is an undischarged bankrupt.[37]

ABUSES OF THE BANKRUPTCY PRIVILEGE

Inadequacies of the Bankrupt Act

Our present bankruptcy legislation has evolved slowly and with great care over the years. Although by no means perfect, it does a commendable job of carrying out its objects in the majority of insolvencies. Unfortunately, however, a bankruptcy statute can be applied more readily to natural persons than to corporate entities. As we noted in Chapter 28, the concept of corporate personality carries with it new problems. Regulations and remedies which are workable when applied to natural persons are inappropriate and ineffective when applied to corporations. For example, the sanction of refusal to discharge a bankrupt natural person is an effective instrument to ensure his co-operation in many instances; he knows that he cannot have a fresh start unless he obtains a discharge. Similarly, the threat of imprisonment for contempt of court in refusing to comply with a court order or for committing a bankruptcy offence is usually an effective sanction. Both refusal of discharge and threat of imprisonment are inappropriate against a corporation. Shareholders who have benefited from the misconduct of their corporation do not care what happens to the corporation after it is insolvent since they have no further financial interest in it. The courts cannot imprison an abstract entity. True, in some circumstances they may imprison its officers, but often it is very difficult to fix the blame with any certainty in an organization with divided responsibility.

Occasionally, a limited company may be adjudged bankrupt with considerable losses to its creditors and virtually no losses to its shareholders. The shareholders may in fact have profited greatly from their association with the company. First, the shareholders may have subscribed merely a nominal sum of money for the qualifying shares in the company: most of the capital they did provide may have been as creditors, taking a mortgage and floating charge as security. Upon insolvency they take priority over the general creditors and even over the employees of the company. Secondly, the shareholders may have redeemed a large number of preference shares or drawn excessive dividends when they foresaw that the company would soon be in difficulty. Thirdly, they may have arranged for the company to pay excessive salaries to themselves as officers or exorbitant management fees to another company which they own. Fourthly, they may have sold the company's products to an associated company at below cost or bought its wares from an associated company at excessive prices. Perhaps more likely, the controlling shareholders may have used a combination of these schemes to deplete the assets of the company before bankruptcy, leaving the general creditors to absorb the loss.

---

[37] S. 170.

Amendments to the Act

Important amendments were made to the Bankruptcy Act in 1966 with a view to controlling these abuses. The Act has adapted from income tax law the concept of a "non-arm's length transaction"; it authorizes a review of transactions between the bankrupt party and persons who are closely connected with him when the transactions have occurred within twelve months prior to bankruptcy.[38] The trustee may ask for a court judgment in favour of the creditors and against a party to such a transaction where the consideration for property or services has been conspicuously greater or less than fair market value.[39] The other party has the onus of showing that the fair market value claimed by the trustee is incorrect.

Another amendment deals with the possibility that a corporation, already insolvent but not yet declared bankrupt, may redeem its shares or pay a dividend as a method of benefiting its shareholders at the expense of its creditors. The Act provides that the trustee may take court action to recover such amounts paid out of the company during the 12 months preceding its bankruptcy. The onus is on the directors and shareholders to prove that the corporation was *not* insolvent when the dividend was paid or the shares redeemed.[40]

The Superintendent of Bankruptcy has been given extensive powers to initiate investigations on information supplied by any source: these powers include entering and searching for records and documents and examining under oath the bankrupt debtor or any person thought to have knowledge of the affairs of the bankruptcy.[41] The audit staff available to the Superintendent has been increased for this purpose. At the same time, the trustee must report directly to the Superintendent within two months of his appointment concerning the probable causes of bankruptcy, identify the persons involved, and indicate whether in his opinion the deficiency between assets and liabilities has been satisfactorily explained.[42]

In many situations, in spite of these provisions, the damage done to creditors' claims by the time of bankruptcy will be largely irreparable. Accordingly the best protection for creditors is always their own astuteness in granting credit. Before doing so, they may check the credit rating of the prospective purchaser or borrower and they may require collateral security where some risk is apparent. In the words of a former Superintendent of Bankruptcy:

---

[38] The definition of persons who are deemed not to deal with each other at arm's length is quite complex and is set out at length in s. 4 of the Act. It is noteworthy, however, that the section recognizes that a corporation may be one of the parties to a reviewable transaction where the other party is one who controls the corporation or is a member of a related group that does so; and that two corporations under a common control may also be "related persons" so that their transactions are subject to review. For a discussion of the burden of proving that a transaction is not at arm's length, see Houlden and Morawetz, 1974 Cumulative Supplement to *Bankruptcy Law of Canada*, p. 7.

[39] S. 78. See also, Baird, "Reviewable Transactions", 14 C.B.R. (N.S.) 1 (1971).

[40] S. 79(5).

[41] S. 6. See also: Tassé, "Recent Developments in Bankruptcy Law", *Can. B. Jour.*, Vol. 10, No. 4 (August, 1967).

[42] S. 141.

It must be appreciated that there is no law that can make good, a bad credit judgment. The law can help to minimize the loss once it has occurred and it ought to provide for the punishment of the offenders. But I do not believe the law can be expected to do more.[43]

To assist prospective creditors by making more information available to them, the Act now authorizes filing with the office of the Superintendent of Bankruptcy the names of bankrupt debtors, the names and addresses of directors and officers of bankrupt corporations, the names of persons who in the opinion of the trustee actively controlled the day-to-day operations of the business, or who were responsible for the greater proportion of its liabilities, plus a statement of the trustee's opinion about whether the deficiency between the assets and liabilities of the debtor business has been satisfactorily accounted for or whether there is evidence of a disappearance of property. Due notice must first be given to all the persons identified in this connection but when formalities have been observed both the trustee and the publisher are exonerated from liability in a possible libel action.[44]

An alternative remedy applicable to all insolvent companies is presented in the federal Winding-Up Act. Probably because its procedures are very cumbersome, the Winding-Up Act has been very little used despite the fact that it has been in force for many years, and before the 1966 amendments to the Bankruptcy Act seemed to offer more effective remedies. With the reforms in the Bankruptcy Act and the clear priority given to the Bankruptcy Act over the Winding-Up Act,[45] the Winding-Up Act is probably obsolete for the purpose of insolvency proceedings.[46]

OTHER METHODS OF LIQUIDATION

We have seen that the Bankruptcy Act provides a means by which insolvent limited companies, sole proprietorships, and partnership firms may be liquidated. There are, in addition, a variety of ways in which the affairs of a solvent limited company may be wound up, but the proceedings are initiated by shareholders rather than by creditors or the debtor himself.

Each of the provinces has a separate statute or a part in its corporations act to provide a means of winding up solvent companies with provincial charters.[47] This legislation may authorize the shareholders to appoint a liquidator, who may be a director, officer, or employee of the corporation, to wind up the affairs of

---

[43] Tassé, *op. cit.*, p. 314.
[44] S. 141, ss. (2) to (6).
[45] S. 184.
[46] Other possible uses of the Winding-Up Act are explained below.
[47] See, for example: Companies Act, St. of B.C. 1973, c. 18 as amended by St. of B.C. 1973 (2nd Sess.) c. 103 (Part 9, Division 3); Companies Act, R.S.M. 1970, c. C160, Part VII and s. 206; Business Corporations Act, R.S.O. 1970, c. 53, ss. 230-246; Companies Winding-Up Act, R.S.N.S. 1967, c. 47.

the company without recourse to the court, or alternatively it may authorize them to apply to the court for a winding-up order and the appointment of a liquidator.

In addition, the federal Winding-Up Act[48] outlines a procedure by which the shareholders of a solvent, federally-incorporated company may petition the court to issue a winding-up order. The court may issue a winding-up order if the capital of the company has been impaired to the extent of 25 per cent, or if a substantial proportion of the shareholders petition for winding-up because of a lack of integrity or responsibility on the part of the company management.

A company can also surrender its charter, apart from proceedings under either the Bankruptcy Act or a Winding-Up Act. For example, the Canada Business Corporations Act provides for dissolution, if a company has no property and no liabilities, by special resolution of the shareholders. ''Articles of dissolution'' are then sent to the director of the federal government office that regulates federally-incorporated companies and he issues a certificate of dissolution.[49] A company may wish to dissolve in this way when it has sold all its assets to another company and distributed the proceeds to its shareholders, and when the purchasing company has assumed all its liabilities with the consent of creditors.

PROTECTION OF CREDITORS' RIGHTS IN A BULK SALE

Unencumbered Assets as a Security for General Creditors

In general, a prospective creditor has two main sources to which he may look as an assurance of repayment of the credit he is asked to provide: the existing assets of the applicant, and the money generated from future operations of the applicant's business. The assessment of the second of these sources is primarily the subject of financial analysis which may take the form of an estimate of future cash receipts and payments, to determine whether the predicted cash flows can comfortably include the required repayment. The first of these sources of repayment more directly concerns the law. In the preceding chapter, we examined how systems of registration may assist prospective creditors to ascertain the extent to which the assets of a prospective debtor have already been encumbered. We noted that a debtor removes assets from the reach of any present or future unsecured creditor when he uses them as collateral for obtaining secured credit. It is only the remaining unencumbered assets that are available to satisfy the claims of the unsecured creditors.

The Nature of a Bulk Sale

A debtor may also remove even these assets from the reach of his creditors, directly and irrevocably, by a bulk sale. A bulk sale, as defined by the provincial

---

[48] R.S.C. 1970, c. W-10 as amended by St. of Can. 1970, c. 44 (1st Supp.), s. 10; 1972, c. 17, c. 2(2).

[49] St. of Can. 1973-74, c. 33, s. 203. Some provincial corporations statutes also provide for dissolution of companies formed under their acts. See, for example: R.S.M. 1970, c. C160, s. 206; R.S.O. 1970, c. 53, ss. 247-50.

statutes, is a sale of essentially all the stock-in-trade of a business or of the fixtures, goods, and chattels with which a person carried on business. It is a sale of such proportions as will seriously impair continued operation of the business. Often a seller makes a bulk sale incidental to the sale of the business as a going concern. On the other hand, a sale of goods in the ordinary course of business, even though a large sale, is not a bulk sale.

Bulk Sales Act

Each of the common-law provinces has enacted a Bulk Sales Act. The object of the statute is to protect the creditors of a person who makes a bulk sale. The statute proceeds on the premise that creditors are entitled to regard the assets of a debtor's business as security for the amounts owing them. If a bulk sale merely caused a change in the composition of the business assets — inventory or equipment exchanged for cash — the creditors would have no cause for concern: the business would be at least as capable of paying its debts as formerly. The danger for creditors is, however, that the proceeds of the sale may not be retained within the business. The seller, for example, may abscond with the money or apply it in ways such that the creditors cannot recover it. The solution proposed by the Act is a shrewd one. It places the onus on the buyer in a bulk sale to see that certain prescribed steps are taken to inform his seller's creditors of the proposed sale, to obtain their consent to the transaction without having their accounts paid, or, if they demand the payment of their accounts, make sure that the necessary portion of the purchase money is paid to the creditors before the balance is paid to the seller.

What sanctions does the Act impose to ensure the compliance of the buyer? It gives the creditors recourse against the buyer if he fails to fulfil the statutory requirements. The sale is voidable and the buyer becomes personally liable to the seller's creditors for the value of the goods. Creditors must act promptly, however, if they wish to attack the sale; they lose their remedies if they wait beyond the time limit set out in the Act.

A buyer can avoid any possibility of being held liable to creditors of the seller when the purchase price agreed on is greater than the outstanding claims of all the creditors. All he need do is withhold the proceeds from the seller and personally see that the creditors are paid in full out of the purchase money, before he pays the balance to the seller.

When, however, the purchase price to which the buyer is willing to agree is less than the total claims of the creditors, he cannot safely pay the price either to the seller himself, or to a trustee who has been appointed by the seller to receive the purchase price for distribution to the creditors. In these circumstances, a buyer must obtain consent to the terms of the transaction from a minimum proportion of the creditors as set out in the Bulk Sales Act.[50] Even when the

---

[50] See, for example: R.S.B.C. 1960, c. 39, s. 6(c); R.S.O. 1970, c. 52, s. 8(2); R.S.N.S. 1967, c. 28, s. 4.

required proportion of creditors consent to the bulk sale, the sale may sometimes be upset by proceedings under the Bankruptcy Act if the creditors are to be paid less than one hundred cents on the dollar. If, for example, a dissenting minority of creditors believe the sale is at an unreasonably low price, they may apply for a receiving order on the grounds that the seller's assignment to a trustee for the benefit of his creditors is an act of bankruptcy. The relation between the provincial Bulk Sales Act and the federal Bankruptcy Act is complicated and technical, and requires the advice of qualified experts in the field.

Bulk sales legislation succeeds in making it difficult for the owner of a business to dispose of his stock-in-trade without the payment or concurrence of his trade creditors. What happens, however, if he decides to mortgage his stock-in-trade instead of selling it? By executing a chattel mortgage, a debtor can deprive his trade creditors of access to an asset in the same way as if he had sold it. The Bulk Sales Act does not apply to a chattel mortgagee; he is not obliged to comply with the Act to protect his security. The only protection for creditors when a chattel mortgage is given and duly registered is in the affidavit of bona fides; as we noted in the preceding chapter, a mortgage is void unless it was made in good faith for valuable consideration. The risk remains, of course, that the mortgagor may dissipate the consideration received before his creditors can recover it.

The Ontario Act

The Bulk Sales Act of Ontario provides a good illustration of the law affecting this type of transaction: it should be helpful briefly to summarize its provisions.[51] At the outset, the Act gives a discretion to the court on the application of a seller to exempt a sale in bulk from the application of the Act if the court is satisfied that the sale is advantageous to the seller and will not impair his ability to pay his creditors in full.[52] When the seller obtains such an order, the buyer may pay him directly without risk.

The Act then states the circumstances in which a buyer may, without resort to the court, pay the purchase money directly to the seller and still be assured of obtaining a valid title to the goods and equipment. They are as follows:

(a) when the buyer obtains from his seller a detailed statement of creditors showing that the aggregate claims of the unsecured creditors as a group and the secured creditors as a group each do not exceed $2,500; or

(b) when the seller provides the buyer with an affidavit that before the sale he has paid all his creditors in full or that he has made adequate provision for giving security for payment in full after the completion of the sale.[53]

---

[51] See Catzman, "Bulk Sales in Ontario", 3 *Can. B. Jour.*, p. 28 (1960).
[52] R.S.O. 1970, c. 52, s. 3. Note however, that a creditor of the seller may still demand particulars of the sale in writing under s. 7.
[53] *Ibid.*, s. 8(1).

In either of these instances, the buyer may reasonably rely on the seller's representation if he has no knowledge to the contrary.

As a further protection for creditors, the Ontario Act requires public notice of a bulk sale — as required also by some of the other provinces. The onus is on a buyer to see that the relevant documents and prescribed statements and affidavits are filed in the office of the clerk of the county or district court in the area where the seller's stock or equipment is located within five days after completion of the sale.[54]

If a seller does not fulfil any one of the requirements set out above, then the buyer must follow the more formal requirements of the Act. He must first obtain evidence from the seller that his creditors have been advised of the details of the proposed bulk sale and have agreed to it.[55] More specifically, the buyer must obtain from the seller written consent to the sale by at least 60 per cent of the seller's unsecured creditors in number and amount of claims in excess of $50. The buyer must also obtain an affidavit from the seller that the seller has sent the following documents to his creditors at least 14 days before the sale: a copy of the proposed bulk sales contract; a statement of his affairs; a statement of all his creditors showing the amount due to each one. This advance disclosure gives the creditors an opportunity, if they so wish, to petition for a receiving order against the seller, and so avoid the bulk sale. Assuming they do not, the buyer may then pay the purchase money to a trustee appointed by the seller with the consent of a prescribed majority of his creditors, or to a trustee appointed by a judge.[56] If creditors wish to challenge a bulk sale on the grounds that the purchaser has failed to comply with the provisions of the Act, they must do so within six months.[57]

MECHANICS' LIENS

The Nature of a Mechanic's Lien

We noted in Chapter 19 that a bailee who makes repairs or improvements on goods bailed with him obtains a possessory lien on the goods for the value of his services. He may keep them in his possession until the bailor or the owner pays the amount due him. In addition, in some provinces a bailee may sell the goods to satisfy his claim. By contrast, when a person extends credit by performing work or supplying materials in the construction of a building, bridge, or other structure affixed to land, it is physically impossible for him to exercise a possessory lien. In any event, under the law of real property, when goods are affixed permanently to land they become fixtures: the supplier of the goods is not permitted to sever them from the property. In these circumstances, a creditor has no

---

[54] *Ibid.*, s. 11(1).
[55] *Ibid.*, s. 8(2).
[56] *Ibid.*, s. 9.
[57] *Ibid.*, s. 19.

recourse at common law except to sue for the debt owing and obtain judgment and an order for execution against the land — a rather cumbersome process and not practical where the debt is small.

In all provinces of Canada, persons who have extended credit in the form of goods and services to improve land now have a statutory remedy under the Mechanics' Lien Act. Although the wording of the Act varies from province to province, each Act provides substantially the same protection for creditors. Its basic purposes are to give creditors who have provided work and material for the improvement of land an interest in the land as security for payment and "to prevent multiplicity of actions for small claims, in which the cost would be enormously out of proportion to and in excess of the sums claimed . . . ."[58]

The provisions of the Mechanics' Lien Act operate in two somewhat different ways which can best be understood by an example.

Illustration:

Osborne owns a valuable piece of land zoned for an apartment building. He has an architect prepare plans for a ten-storey, 80-unit apartment block and arranges to finance the project by giving a large mortgage to the Eagle Insurance Co. Osborne then hires Arden Construction Co. Ltd. to erect the building for an agreed price. Arden in turn subcontracts the special tasks of installing the plumbing and heating systems, electrical wiring, the supply and erection of the structural steel, and the supply and installation of elevators, to various firms specializing in these trades.

Here we have two types of contracts, a master contract between the owner of the property and his main contractor and a series of sub-contracts between the main contractor and specialized trades. In respect to the master contract, Osborne is personally liable for the whole amount of the contract price as a contractual debt; Arden Construction has a mechanic's lien, that is, an interest in Osborne's land and building as it is erected, for the total value of work and materials (to the maximum of the contract price) provided by Arden Construction and its subcontractors. In turn, the subcontractors and suppliers have a right of action against Arden Construction for the value of the work and materials supplied for the project under the terms of the sub-contracts. There is, however, no privity of contract between Arden Construction's subcontractors and suppliers and Osborne. Nevertheless, the Mechanics' Lien Act also gives liens against Osborne's land to the subcontractors and suppliers. The value of these liens is limited by the Act to a specified proportion of the price due from Osborne to Arden Construction under the master contract. This proportion, called a *holdback*, varies somewhat from province to province but is generally fifteen or twenty per cent.[59]

---

[58] McPherson v. Gedge (1884) 4 O.R. 246, per Wilson C.J., at 257.

[59] See, for example: Mechanics' Lien Act, R.S.B.C. 1960, c. 238, s. 21(1); Mechanics' Lien Act, R.S.O. 1970, c. 267, s. 11(1) and (2); Mechanics' Lien Act, R.S.N.S. 1967, c. 178, s. 12(1). (Subsequent references to these particular acts in footnotes will be simply to B.C., Ont. and N.S. followed by section number.)

Where the value of the work and materials exceeds the holdback, the subcontractors and suppliers have no security in Osborne's land for the excess sum.

Osborne fully protects against liens of the subcontractors and suppliers by retaining the holdback during construction and for a specified period afterwards. If Arden Construction should become insolvent during this period, Osborne would pay the holdback into court for the benefit of the lienholders. The court would then supervise the payment of this money amongst the lienholders, and neither Osborne personally nor his land would be subject to their claims.

A mechanics' lien is available only to creditors who participate directly as workmen or who supply material for use directly in the construction work. In *Brooks-Sanford Co. v. Theodore Tieler Construction Co.*, the court said:

> While the objects and policy [of the Mechanics' Lien Act] . . . is to prevent an owner from obtaining the benefits of the labour and capital of others without compensation, it is not the intention to compel him to pay his contractor's indebtedness for that which does not go into or benefit his property.[60]

The courts have held that an architect who prepares the plans for a building comes within this definition and is entitled to a lien. Some of the provincial statutes give a lien to a lessor who *rents* equipment for use on the contract site for the price of the rental of the equipment.[61] On the other hand, a person who *sells* tools or machinery to a contractor is not entitled to a lien against a building constructed with the use of the tools or machinery he has supplied; such tools and machinery remain the property of the contractor and can be used in other projects as well.[62] Nor can suppliers obtain a lien against property where the contractor has ordered materials for the building and has had them delivered to his own premises, unless the supplier can prove that the supplies were later used in the construction of the building. Where, however, the supplier delivers the goods directly to the building site, he obtains a lien immediately, whether the materials are eventually used in the structure or not.[63] The reason for this provision is that the supplier who delivers materials to the building site reasonably assumes that they will be used there and relies upon the property as security for his claim.

Suppliers of materials may, if they choose, waive their right of lien by contract. They may find an advantage in doing so when the effect is to persuade a

---

[60] (1910) 22 O.L.R. 176, per Moss, C.J.O., at 180.

[61] This type of lien is available in Ontario, Alberta, Newfoundland and Saskatchewan: R.S.O. 1970, c. 267, s. 5(5); Builders' Lien Act, R.S.A. 1970, c. 35, as amended 1972, c. 102, s. 4(4); The Mechanics' Lien Act, R.S. Nfld. 1970, No. 24 as amended 1971, No. 47, s. 8; The Mechanics' Lien Act, R.S.S. 1965, c. 277, as amended 1971, c. 30, s. 2.

[62] Crowell Bros. v. Maritime Minerals Ltd. [1940] 2 D.L.R. 472.

[63] B.C., s. 5; Ont. s. 5(1); N.S., s. 5. Delivery of material to a place in the vicinity of the land may give rise to a lien upon delivery if the place has been designated by the owner or his agent: see Ont., s. 5(1).

mortgagee to lend additional funds for the completion of a project: the suppliers may then realize their claims out of the proceeds of a sale of the completed building.

The provincial legislatures seem to have acknowledged that the bargaining power of wage-earners (or at least of those who receive low rates of pay) may be unequal to that of the builders and contractors who employ them, and that these wage-earners may not fully understand the nature of their rights. As a result, the various provincial Mechanics' Lien Acts contain a provision that a term in a contract of employment waiving the employee's right of lien is void. However, in some provinces this provision does not apply to employees whose wages exceed a specified amount per day.[64]

The provincial acts give wage earners a priority in payment for approximately one month's arrears of wages over all other liens derived through the same contractor or subcontractor.[65] This priority is given in recognition of the fact that wages provide the sole means of existence of the wage earner, whereas a supplier of materials or lessor of equipment is probably carrying on business with several construction projects at once, and usually has larger capital funds to depend on if a single contractor or owner defaults in payment.

Procedures under the Mechanics' Lien Act

A mechanic's lien arises immediately upon work being done or materials being used in the improvement of property or (in some provinces) upon the supply of rented equipment for use on a contract site. To make his lien legally actionable, a lienholder must register it. He may register it during performance of the work or services or supply of material or within a specified period of time after completion or abandonment of the work, service or supply of material. The specified period is, for example, 31 days in British Columbia, 37 days in Ontario, 45 days in Nova Scotia.[66] The effect of not registering within the time specified is that the lien ceases to exist. The effect of registering is to provide a period of time within which the lienholder must commence a legal action. The period of time specified for this purpose is usually 90 days after the work has been completed or the materials have been placed or furnished, or after the expiry of the period of credit.[67]

The various Mechanics' Lien Acts also permit contractors and subcontractors to acquire liens against property. A contractor or subcontractor must

---

[64] In Ontario, the provision making waivers void does not apply to managers, officers or foremen or to those whose wages are more than $50 a day (Ont. s. 4.). The provinces of Nova Scotia, New Brunswick, Prince Edward Island and Saskatchewan declare all waivers by workers void (e.g., N.S., s. 5). Alberta makes all waivers by anyone void. Manitoba *allows* any lienholder to waive his rights. The other provinces, like Ontario, permit workers earning over a specified amount to waive their rights (e.g., $15 a day, B.C., s. 10).

[65] B.C., s. 7(4); Ont., s. 15; N.S., s. 15.

[66] B.C., s. 23(4); Ont., s. 21; N.S., s. 23.

[67] B.C., s. 26(1) (one year); Ont., s. 23; N.S., s. 25(1).

register his lien within a specified period of time after the completion or abandonment of the contract or subcontract. For this purpose the provinces have interpreted "completion of the contract" to mean "substantial performance of the contract".[68]

In most of the provinces, an action brought by one lien claimant is deemed to be brought on behalf of all other lien claimants, and it is unnecessary even to name other lien claimants as defendants since they must be served with notice of the trial.[69]

A lien may be registered against land in the same way and in the same place as other interests in land are registered. Registration provides public notice of a lienholder's claim and establishes his priority over unsecured creditors of the owner of the property and over subsequent mortgagees and purchasers of it. After registration, a lien expires unless the lienholder brings an action to enforce his claim within the prescribed time and registers a certificate stating that the action has been started, or unless another lienholder starts his action within this period.

A mechanic's lien does not give a lienholder the right to personally take possession of or to sell the land and buildings to realize his claim. In fact, if the lienholder is a subcontractor and if the owner pays the statutory holdback into the court, the lienholder's rights are limited to his share in this fund: he has no rights against the land and buildings of the owner. Even if the owner fails to pay the statutory holdback into court, the lienholder's claim against the land is limited to the amount the owner should have paid into court. To realize his claim against the land, a lienholder, whether a main contractor or a subcontractor, must first bring an action and obtain a court order appointing a trustee. The trustee then has the power to manage the property and to sell it for the benefit of the lienholder and other creditors. If eventually the trustee does sell the property, he must pay the proceeds to satisfy, first, the claims for municipal taxes; second, those of mortgagees who have prior registered mortgages; third, lienholders' claims for wages regardless of the order in which they filed their liens; fourth, all other lienholders' claims regardless of the order in which they filed their liens; fifth, subsequent mortgagees or other persons who have a secured interest in the land; and, finally, if there are any proceeds left, claims of the general creditors of the owner.[70] After all creditors are paid, any balance remaining belongs to the owner.

During the construction period of the building and for the specified statutory period afterwards, the owner may safely make progress payments to his contractor for all amounts except the statutory holdback.[71] However, if he receives notice from subcontractors or suppliers that liens are outstanding and unlikely to be

---

[68] B.C., s. 2; Ont., s. 1(1)(a).

[69] Ont., ss. 29(5) and 30; N.S., ss. 33(3) and 33(4).

[70] The problem of priorities, particularly those respecting lienholders as opposed to prior and subsequent mortgagees, is complex and technical. See Macklem and Bristow, *Mechanics' Liens in Canada*, pp. 233-61. Toronto: The Carswell Company Ltd., 1972.

[71] B.C., s. 21(3); Ont., s. 11(6); N.S., s. 12(4).

paid by the contractor, he should cease payments to the contractor at once and ascertain the extent of the liens. If there is some doubt whether the holdback is sufficient to satisfy the claims for liens, he should seek legal advice immediately; as soon as he has knowledge of these claims, he loses the protection of the Mechanics' Lien Act to the extent that he continues to make payments to the contractor. On the other hand, he must not make the error of wrongfully withholding payment due to a solvent contractor because of an unfounded claim for a lien.

In some jurisdictions, all money received by contractors and subcontractors on account of the contract price are deemed to be trust funds to be held for the benefit of those who have performed work or services or furnished materials. The contractor or subcontractor, accordingly, cannot divert those funds to his own use until all of these claims against him are satisfied.[72]

Once the statutory period has elapsed and no claims have been registered, the owner may pay the amount withheld to his contractor and so complete his obligations under the contract.

Practical Application of Mechanics' Liens

An owner of land usually finances a construction project by mortgaging the land to a mortgagee who advances the mortgage money as work progresses on the building. Some Mechanics' Lien Acts require a mortgagee to withhold from his mortgage advances an amount equal to the sum which the owner should withhold from his contractor. Even if the provincial Act does not have such requirements, it is sensible for a mortgagee to do so to protect his mortgagor, the owner, who is liable to subcontractors and suppliers for the amount of the holdback if the contractor does not pay his accounts.[73]

When a tenant contracts to have a building erected on his landlord's property or, perhaps more commonly, to have improvements made to existing buildings, a mechanic's lien is not enforceable against the landlord's interest in the property unless the lienholder can establish that the work was undertaken either expressly or impliedly at the request of the landlord.

We should note that the person who takes the greatest risk in the construction industry is the general contractor. Most large contracts are awarded by tender to the lowest bidder who has a sound reputation. In this highly competitive business, contractors often cut their margin both for errors and profit to a very small sum in order to obtain the contract. Bad luck in the form of unexpectedly difficult foundation work (such as striking a bed of hard rock or quicksand), extremely bad weather delaying the project, a breakdown of essential equipment, an accident seriously injuring key personnel, or occasionally a labour dispute, may leave the contractor in a deficit position. Mismanagement or inadvertence, such as making a mistake in calculating an important cost figure in the contract or underestimating the cost of subcontracts, may also bring failure to the contractor.

---

[72] Ont., s. 2.
[73] See Woodard, *Canadian Mortgages*, pp. 113 ff. Don Mills, Ontario: Collins, 1959.

Even when his contractor is in financial difficulty, an owner incurs no liability himself if he follows the procedures of the Mechanics' Lien Act. The subcontractors, on the other hand, take the risk that the holdback will not be sufficient to pay their claims. Where the subcontract is for a large sum of money, they generally protect themselves by receiving progress payments from the contractor: they do not let themselves get too far ahead in the work without being paid a proportion of the price.

Contractors often undertake to construct buildings on their own behalf on land owned by themselves. This is especially true in residential buildings — one-family houses and smaller apartment blocks. Often a builder erects such a building with a view to selling it soon after its completion. If bad luck or mismanagement should cause his insolvency, his "subcontracts" with specialized trades are really main contracts with himself as owner. Accordingly, the land is subject to liability for the total value of the liens, and the holdback provisions do not apply. Often a builder will have obtained mortgage money on the land; the mortgagee will have priority over the lienholders for the money already advanced to the builder before the liens arise.[74] When a mortgagor becomes insolvent, his mortgagee usually stops making progress payments immediately. If the lienholders and mortgagee can come to an agreement, the mortgagee may advance the rest of the money to permit the completion of the building, thus making it easier to sell and realize sufficient funds to pay off the lienholders, and perhaps to obtain a sound buyer who will manage the property successfully and honour the mortgage commitments.

LIMITATIONS OF CREDITORS' RIGHTS

The Effect of Limitations Statutes

We noted in Chapter 14 that a promisee who has a right of action for default of payment on a debt or for other breach of contract must begin his action within a prescribed period or lose his right to sue. In the common law provinces the remedy for breach of ordinary contracts is barred when six years has elapsed from the time the right of action arose.[75] The plaintiff must start his court proceedings within the six-year period or lose his right to resort to the courts. Such limitations on actions are justified as being in the public interest: the opportunity for litigation should end after a certain defined period because, first, a person who neglects to pursue his claim leaves the other party in a state of uncertainty which ought not to continue perpetually; and secondly, as the years pass, it becomes more difficult to adduce the evidence necessary to settle disputes concerning the facts of the case — memories may fade and witnesses die, and important records may be lost.

---

[74] See Macklem and Bristow, *op. cit.*, p. 60 ff.
[75] See, for example: Statute of Limitations, R.S.B.C. 1960, c. 370, s. 3; Limitations Act, R.S.O. 1970, c. 246, s. 45(1)(g); Limitations of Actions Act, R.S.N.S. 1967, c. 168, s. 2(1)(e).

It is important to ascertain when a right of action "arises" in order to calculate the limitation period. A right of action does not arise until there has been a breach or default. Thus, in a contract for the sale of goods on credit, the seller's right of action does not arise at the time of the making of the contract or even at the time of the delivery of the goods; the buyer has not yet defaulted on his promise to pay. The cause of action arises when the price falls due and the buyer fails to pay. A trade account receivable often comprises a number of charges for goods or services invoiced at different times in the past and since paid in part. A customer (debtor) is entitled to specify the particular purchases against which a payment on account is to be applied, but in the absence of such instructions his supplier (creditor) is entitled to treat each payment as discharging the oldest outstanding purchases and so to keep the debt current.

Ways by Which the Limitation Period is Extended

We noted in Chapter 24 in our discussion of adverse possession that if at any time after the statutory limitation period begins to run, a person in adverse possession acknowledges the owner's right by paying rent, he ceases to be an adverse possessor. The limitation period stops running; an entirely new limitation period begins to run if the tenant remains in possession after the period for which he has paid rent expires. In a similar manner, the limitation period for an action for breach of contract starts over again if the debtor makes a part payment or delivers a written promise to pay; the creditor has six years in which to bring his action from the time of the making of the part payment or delivery of the written promise.

An important difference exists, however, between limitation periods regarding possession of land and limitations of actions in contract. When a limitation period runs out against the owner of land, his title is extinguished — it is completely gone. When a limitation period against a contractual right of action expires, the debt is not thereby extinguished — only the remedy is barred. The statute has provided the debtor with a shield, but he may, if he chooses, throw it aside. If the debtor makes a new promise to pay the debt, he is bound by his promise and may be sued upon it. In these circumstances the creditor sues not on the original claim but on the new promise to pay. We see here a modification of the doctrine of consideration: the still existing but statute-barred debt provides good consideration for the subsequent promise of the debtor. Since the creditor's right of action is derived from the new promise, he has no greater rights than the new promise bestows upon him. Thus, if the debtor promises to pay the debt out of the proceeds of a particular transaction if it should produce a profit, or if he promises to pay only half the sum in satisfaction of the whole debt, the creditor's rights are limited to suing on these terms.[76]

The Limitations Acts required a promise to pay a statute-barred debt to be in

---

[76] See *Phillips v. Phillips* (1844) 67 E.R. 388, per Sir James Wigram, V.C., at 396. See also Weaver, *Limitations*, pp. 3-5 and 370-3. Toronto: Canadian Law List Publishing Co., 1939.

writing to be enforceable by the creditor; he could not sue on an oral promise alone. Although this requirement appeared in early Limitation Acts in England, courts of equity ignored it when the oral promise was accompanied by a part payment of the debt; they permitted the creditor to sue on the oral promise. This exception to the requirement of writing is now formally recognized in most of the limitations statutes.[77]

A debtor need not make an express promise to pay; his promise to pay may be implied from the circumstances of the part payment. Generally speaking, a presumption of a new promise to pay arises from the mere fact of making a part payment without other evidence to contradict the presumption. But if a debtor should say, "Take this — it is all you are going to get," then, of course, no such presumption arises, and his creditor has no right of action for the balance. The reasoning applies as well to a written acknowledgment of a debt. A written acknowledgment is not an express promise to pay, but usually such a promise is implied in the debtor's acknowledgment. The terms of the acknowledgment itself or the surrounding circumstances may, however, contradict such an implication — as when a debtor writes to his creditor, stating: "I know I owe you $1,000, but the debt is barred by the Limitations Act. Since I believe you overcharged on the contract price anyway, I have no intention of paying this balance." Quite clearly, no implied promise to pay arises from such a statement.

Limitations in Other Types of Actions

The limitation period for actions on negotiable instruments is the same as for ordinary contracts, six years. When a cause of action arises from breach of a promise under seal, the limitation period is considerably longer, usually 20 years, but it may vary according to the subject-matter of the promise. For example, the covenant of a mortgagor in a mortgage of land is discharged after ten years in some provinces.

Each province has a general limitations statute governing limitation periods for a number of different classes of actions. In addition, numerous other statutes, both federal and provincial, prescribe limitation periods for various rights of action under them. Some of these statutes extinguish the cause of action, as with adverse possession; others only bar recourse to the courts. The limitation periods vary from a few days to many years, according to the purposes which the statute serves. For this reason, when considering starting an action or defending one under the provisions of a statute, a lawyer first checks to see if a limitation period may affect the rights of the parties.

QUESTIONS FOR REVIEW

1. Explain each of the following terms: void assignment; receiving order; preferred creditor; lienholder; holdback; secured creditor; authorized assign-

---

[77] See, for example: R.S.B.C. 1960, c. 370, s. 12 (para. 3); R.S.O. 1970, c. 246, s. 50.

ment; licensed trustee; liquidating dividend; undischarged bankrupt; insolvent person; bulk sale.

2. What are the purposes of the present federal bankruptcy legislation? In what ways does the Bankruptcy Act attempt to accomplish these purposes?

3. Why is a creditor likely to be concerned when he learns that another creditor has obtained an execution order against the debtor?

4. What is the difference between a receiving order and an assignment under the Bankruptcy Act?

5. What steps may an insolvent person take to avoid bankruptcy?

6. Describe briefly three acts of bankruptcy. What is the legal significance for a debtor committing an act of bankruptcy?

7. What is the difference between an act of bankruptcy and a bankruptcy offence?

8. What is the value to a bankrupt debtor of obtaining a discharge from a court?

9. Upon his debtor's becoming bankrupt, when may a secured creditor retain the assets he holds as security?

10. Should a licensed trustee pay preferred creditors before he settles with secured creditors?

11. What are three duties of a bankrupt debtor?

12. What procedure should a buyer of a business follow when his seller discloses that the sale price is insufficient to pay all the seller's creditors in full?

13. Why is it important for a buyer in a bulk sale to comply with the Bulk Sales Act?

14. What is the difference in effect of a limitation period expiring against an interest in land and one expiring against the right of action for breach of contract?

15. What is the difference in the security of a supplier of materials for use in the construction of a building when (a) the building is being built by a contractor on his own account "on speculation", and (b) the building is being built by a contractor engaged by the owner?

16. To what classes of persons does the description *mechanics* apply in the term *mechanics' lien*?

17. ". . . notwithstanding the elaborate provisions designed to ensure good and effective creditor control of bankruptcy administration in Canada, creditor control, as in many countries, has failed." *Report of the Study Committee on Bankruptcy and Insolvency Legislation, Canada, 1970*, p. 152.

 Explain this quotation, referring both to the nature of the provisions made for creditor control and the reasons for their lack of effectiveness.

18. "There is no end to questions that may arise in connection with a category of legal study. The further we go the more we find that one category blends into another; and we perceive the law as a unity whose so-called categories are directly related to one another." (Zelermyer, *Introduction to Business Law: A Conceptual Approach*, p. 76.) Along the same line of reasoning one frequently encounters the observation that "the law is a seamless web."

Explain with simple illustrations how two or more branches of law (for example, contract, tort, trust, land and criminal law) may overlap when defining the issue in a legal dispute.

CASES FOR DISCUSSION

CASE 1

Smith, a contractor, laid a cement floor in Brown's garage. Brown refused to pay for the work on the grounds that the grade on the floor did not drain water properly whenever water got into the garage. Two years after the floor was built, in response to a demand for payment, Brown wrote as follows, "We have discussed this matter many times, and you should know by now that I will never pay for this work until you correct the grade of my garage floor." Smith did not do further work to change the grade. Five years after he received the letter quoted above, Smith sued Brown for the price agreed before the floor was laid, $150.

Should Smith succeed?

CASE 2

Martin's creditors obtained a receiving order against him and had a trustee appointed to realize his assets. In the course of his duties the trustee was unable to account for the disappearance of certain assets which once appeared on Martin's books. Martin disclaimed any knowledge of them. Upon further investigation the trustee discovered that two months prior to the receiving order, Martin deposited $1,000 cash in his wife's savings account and gave $3,000 worth of merchandise to a creditor, Jamieson, in settlement of a business debt of $2,700.

Discuss the consequences of this discovery for each of the following persons: (a) Mrs. Martin, (b) Jamieson, (c) Martin himself.

CASE 3

At various times between 1960 and 1968, Sands acted as Waters's lawyer, representing him in a series of real estate transactions and in the incorporation of a private company. Sands's total charges for these services came to $4,000. In an interview between them on August 5, 1969, Waters gave Sands his cheque for $2,500. The cheque was dated August 5, 1969, but at Waters' request Sands agreed not to cash it until the end of the month when Waters' salary cheque would be deposited in his account.

Sands cashed the cheque on September 4, 1969, but did nothing to collect the balance of his account. He died in June 1975. In the course of winding up his estate, Sands's executors sought to recover the balance of $1,500 from Waters. When Waters refused to pay, the executors issued a writ on August 28, 1975.

Should this action succeed? (See *Marreco v. Richardson* [1908] 2 K.B. 584.)

CASE 4

Frontenac Manufacturing Co. Ltd. engaged Acme Construction Co. Ltd. to construct a new plant. Acme estimated that it would require 60,000 bricks for the job and ordered that quantity at $71 per thousand from Mason Builders' Supplies Ltd. Mason delivered the bricks to Acme's warehouse. Subsequently Acme found that it had miscalculated and needed only 40,000 bricks for the Frontenac building; it used the remaining 20,000 bricks on another job. Acme failed to pay Mason and became insolvent. Mason registered a lien against Frontenac's new building claiming $4,260 from the holdback.

Should Mason succeed? What change in procedure in the sale of the bricks between Mason and Acme would affect the result?

CASE 5

Powell awarded a contract to Dawson Bros., building contractors, for the erection of a house on Powell's land. The price of the house was $32,000. Powell was a man of substance, whereas Dawson Bros. was a new contracting firm of no financial standing.

Dawson Bros. ordered lumber from Hill Lumber Co. to be used in the construction of the Powell house. At the time the lumber was supplied, Hill Lumber Co. wrote to Powell as follows: "We are furnishing building material to Dawson Bros. for the construction of your residence. We would ask you to see that this material is paid for before settling with Dawson Bros. in full; otherwise we will have to protect ourselves in the usual manner." Powell agreed to these terms, and Hill Lumber Co. supplied lumber to the value of $7,200.

While the house was being built, Powell made progress payments from time to time to Dawson Bros. In making these payments he withheld 15 per cent of the value of the house to its then current stage of construction, as estimated by the architect; this was the percentage specified in the Mechanics' Lien Act of the province. To keep Dawson Bros. going on with the construction work, Powell paid out of the money held back some $1,500 for the workmen's wages and electrical and plumbing services. Finally, when the house was nearly finished, Dawson Bros. abandoned the contract. By this time Powell had made progress payments totalling $26,350, and the architect's estimate of value was $31,000. It cost Powell a further $1,400 in wages to complete the building on his own.

Dawson Bros. had paid Hill Lumber Co. $2,200 on account when it abandoned the contract. Hill Lumber Co. then sought the balance of its account, $5,000, from Powell. Powell refused to pay, claiming that he was liable for only the balance of the money he had held back in making his progress payments to Dawson Bros., *viz.*, $3,150. Powell paid the $3,150 into court. Hill Lumber Co. duly registered a mechanic's lien against Powell's house and brought an action against him for $5,000, asking also for a court order that if the requested judgment for $5,000 was not satisfied by Powell, the house should be sold and the judgment satisfied out of the proceeds.

Should this action succeed? (See *Hill Ltd. v. Pozetti and Davis* [1936] O.W.N. 632.)

CASE 6

The N.S.F. Manufacturing Co. Ltd. was adjudged bankrupt on a petition of its creditors, and the trustee in bankruptcy realized the following amounts from the sale of its business assets:

Cash in bank	$ 500
Accounts receivable	3,500
Inventories	18,000
Land and buildings	26,000
	$48,000

The liabilities of the business were as follows at the time of the receiving order:

Bank loan secured under section 88	$10,000
Trade accounts payable	17,400
Municipal taxes payable	600
Wages payable (five months at $300 per month)	1,500
First mortgage on land and buildings	15,500
Second mortgage on land and buildings	12,000
	$57,000

The expenses of liquidation were $1,600. The trustee's fee was $1,800.

How many cents on the dollar did the general creditors receive? Show the order in which the trustee in bankruptcy made payments to the various types of creditors. Assume that all secured creditors had taken the necessary steps to protect their security.

CASE 7

The Canadian Goldentone Corporation Ltd., manufacturers of stereo components and television receivers, purchased substantial quantities of electrical parts from Koyle Electric Ltd. during the past four years. During this period Koyle Electric Ltd. assigned individually and for value all its accounts receivable to Ashbee, a factor, who then undertook their collection. All of the invoices of Koyle Electric to Canadian Goldentone were stamped with a notification that the sum shown as owing had been assigned to Ashbee and directed that payment be made to Ashbee.

In November last, Koyle Electric contracted to buy from Canadian Goldentone a number of stereo tuners to be used as prizes in a sales promotion contest; the total price was $4,900, payable 60 days after delivery. Canadian Goldentone delivered the tuners. At the time, it owed Koyle Electric $14,700, representing a number of individual purchases for which it had already been invoiced. In the following month Koyle Electric made an authorized assignment under the Bankruptcy Act, its management having conceded that the company had become insolvent.

Realizing that if it had to file a claim against the bankrupt estate of Koyle Electric Ltd. it would probably realize much less than the $4,900 owing to it for the stereo tuners, Canadian Goldentone proposed to set this amount off against its account payable of $14,700 and to pay the factor, Ashbee, the net amount of $9,800. Ashbee refused, however, to accept the tender of $9,800 and sued Canadian Goldentone Corporation Ltd. for the full amount of $14,700.

Should he succeed? Give reasons. (See *L.F. Dommerich & Co. Inc. v. Canadian Admiral Corporation Ltd.* (1962) 34 D.L.R. (2d) 530.)

CASE 8

Rufus Jones incorporated an Ontario corporation, Jones Cement Ltd., in 1975. On January 2, 1976, he went to a finance company, Financial Acceptance Corporation (F.A.C.) and asked for a loan on some equipment that Jones Cement Ltd. then owned. He stated that there were no *liens*, charges or *writs of execution* outstanding against Jones Cement Ltd. or against any of its assets. F.A.C. decided to grant the loan in consideration of Mr. Jones' guaranteeing payment personally. On January 10, 1976, Mr. Jones went to F.A.C.'s office and signed on behalf of Jones Cement Ltd. a *chattel mortgage* for $90,000 on the equipment. There were still no liens, charges or writs of execution against the company. Mr. Jones was also asked to sign the chattel mortgage as guarantor. This guarantee was on the same document, and was under seal: it was a personal guarantee in which Jones agreed to pay any sums not paid to F.A.C. by Jones Cement Ltd. (This is a standard business practice.) F.A.C. then proceeded *to register* the chattel mortgage in the County Clerk's office on the same day.

On May 1, 1976, everything went wrong and Jones Cement Ltd. filed an *assignment in bankruptcy*. F.A.C. claimed in the bankruptcy as a *secured creditor* relying upon its registered chattel mortgage.

The trustee in bankruptcy would not allow the claim alleging that F.A.C. had not completed the *affidavit of bona fides* and therefore had not properly registered the chattel mortgage. The Court upheld the trustee's position and F.A.C. was forced to file a proof of claim in the bankruptcy as an unsecured creditor. If F.A.C. had been a secured creditor it would have been able to recover the full amount of the loan, i.e., $90,000. However, as an unsecured creditor, F.A.C. received only $12,000.

After receiving the $12,000, F.A.C.'s solicitors wrote to Mr. Jones demanding payment of the remaining $78,000. The solicitors stated that they were relying on the guarantee signed by Mr. Jones.

Mr. Jones refused to pay the $78,000 and was subsequently sued by F.A.C. A *writ of summons* was issued out of the Supreme Court of Ontario and served on Jones at his home in Mississauga by the Sheriff of the County of Peel. Jones entered an appearance to the action and subsequently filed a statement of defence.

At the spring *assizes* the trial came on before Keensight, J. at the Brampton sittings.

Jones' defence was that he had relied on F.A.C. to register the chattel mortgage properly and that because of its neglect to do so, F.A.C. could not transfer a right to full recovery to him by way of subrogation. F.A.C.'s position was that the guarantee was a separate and distinguishable contract and did not obtain its validity from the proper or improper registration of the chattel mortgage.

After hearing all the evidence and arguments from both sides, Keensight, J. reserved his decision.

Required:

(a) There are ten terms or phrases underlined; briefly define each term, and explain its use or significance.

(b) Discuss the defences put forward by Mr. Jones and state, with reasons, whether you think the action against him would succeed or fail.

Bibliography

1. General References

Allen, C.K. *Law in the Making* (7th ed.). London: Oxford University Press, 1964.

Black, H.C. *Black's Law Dictionary* (rev. 4th ed.). St. Paul, Minn.: West Publishing Co., 1968.

Clermont, B.L. *General Introduction to Canadian Law*. Montreal: Institute of Canadian Bankers, 1968.

Fridman, G.H.L., ed. *Studies in Canadian Business Law*. Toronto: Butterworth, 1971.

Jackson, R.M. *The Machinery of Justice in England*. Cambridge: Cambridge University Press, 1972.

Lloyd, D. *The Idea of Law*. Harmondsworth: Penguin, 1964.

Plucknett, T. *A Concise History of the Common Law*. London: Butterworth, 1956.

Turner, J.W.C., ed. *Russell on Crime* (12th ed.). London: Stevens & Sons, 1964.

Zelermyer, W. *Introduction to Business Law: A Conceptual Approach* (2nd ed.). New York: Macmillan, 1971.

2. Social Context

Friedmann, W. *Law in a Changing Society*. New York: Columbia University Press, 1972.

Ganong, C.K., and R.W. Pearce. *Law and Society*. Homewood, Ill.: Irwin, 1965.

Hart, H.L.A. *The Concept of Law*. London: Oxford University Press, 1961.

Hazard, L. *Law and the Changing Environment*. San Francisco: Holden-Day, 1971.

Kempin, F.G. *Legal History: Law and Social Change*. Englewood Cliffs, N.J.: Prentice-Hall, 1963.

Lederman, W.R., ed. *The Courts and the Canadian Consti-*

tution. Toronto: McClelland and Stewart, 1964.

Lloyd, D. *Introduction to Jurisprudence*. London: Stevens & Sons, 1972.

Russell, P., ed. *Leading Constitutional Decisions* (rev. ed.). Toronto: McClelland and Stewart, 1973.

Schmeiser, D.A. *Civil Liberties in Canada*. London: Oxford University Press, 1964.

Schur, E.M. *Law and Society: A Sociological View*. New York: Random House, 1968.

Scott, F.R. *Civil Liberties and Canadian Federalism*. Toronto: University of Toronto Press, 1959.

Summers, R. *Law, Its Nature, Functions and Limits* (2nd ed.). Englewood Cliffs, N.J.: Prentice-Hall, 1972.

Tarnopolsky, W.S. *Some Civil Liberties Issues of the 70's*. Toronto: York Publications, 1975.

Weissman, J. *Law in a Business Society*. Englewood Cliffs, N.J.: Prentice-Hall, 1964.

3. Torts

Fleming, J.G. *The Law of Torts* (4th ed.). Sydney: Law Book Co. of Australasia, 1971.

———. *An Introduction to the Law of Torts*. Oxford: Clarendon Press, 1967.

Hart, H.L.A., and A.M. Honoré. *Causation in Law*. London: Oxford University Press, 1959.

Linden, A.M. *Studies in Canadian Tort Law*. Toronto: Butterworth, 1968.

Prosser, W.L. *Handbook of the Law of Torts* (4th ed.). St. Paul: West Publishing Co., 1971.

Salmond, J.W. *The Law of Torts* (16th ed.), R.F.V. Heuston, ed. London: Sweet & Maxwell, 1973.

4. Contracts

Anson, W.R. *Principles of the English Law of Contract* (23rd ed.), A.G. Guest, ed. London: Oxford University Press, 1969.

Cheshire, G.C., C.H.S. Fifoot and M.P. Furmston. *The Law of Contract* (8th ed.). London: Butterworth, 1972.

Pollock, F. *Principles of Contract* (13th ed.), P.H. Winfield, ed. London: Stevens & Sons, 1950.

Treitel, G.H. *The Law of Contract* (4th ed.). London:

Stevens & Sons, 1975.

Waddams, S.M., ed. *Milner's Cases and Materials on Contract* (2nd ed.). Toronto: University of Toronto Press, 1971.

Williston, S. *Treatise on the Law of Contract* (3rd ed.), W.H.E. Jaeger, ed. Mount Kisco, N.Y.: Baker, Voorhis & Co., 1957.

5. Special Types of Contracts

Agency Fridman, G.H.L. *The Law of Agency* (3rd ed.). London:Butterworth, 1971.

Powell, R. *The Law of Agency* (2nd ed.). London: Pitman & Sons, 1961.

Bailment Paton, G.W. *Bailment in the Common Law*. London: Stevens & Sons, 1952.

Vaines, J.C. *Personal Property* (4th ed.). London: Butterworth, 1967.

Employment Carrothers, A.W. *Collective Bargaining Law in Canada*. Toronto: Butterworth, 1965.

The Labour Relations Law Casebook Group, ed. *Labour Relations Law* (2nd ed.). Kingston: Queen's University, 1974.

Smith, C.M. *A Treatise on the Law of Master and Servant* (6th ed.), E. M. Smith, ed. London: Sweet & Maxwell, 1906.

Guarantee Stearns, A.A. *Law of Suretyship* (5th ed.), J.L. Elder, ed. Cincinnati: W. H. Anderson, 1951.

Insurance MacGillivray, E.J. *On Insurance Law Related to All Risks Other than Marine* (5th ed.), D. Browne, ed. London: Sweet & Maxwell, 1961.

Crawford, B., et al. *Cases on the Canadian Law of Insurance*. Toronto: Carswell, 1971.

Laverty, F.J. *The Insurance Law of Canada* (2nd ed.). Toronto: Carswell, 1936.

Sale of Goods Atiyah, P.S. *The Sale of Goods* (4th ed.). London: Pitman, 1971.

Chalmers, M.D.E.S. *Sale of Goods* (16th ed.), Michael Mark, ed. London: Butterworth, 1971.

Fridman, G.H.L. *Sale of Goods in Canada*. Toronto: Carswell, 1973.

6. Real Property

General Burn, E.H., ed. *Cheshire's Modern Law of Real Property*

(11th ed.). London: Butterworth, 1972.

Preston, C.H.S., and G.H. Newsom. *Restrictive Covenants Affecting Freehold Land* (5th ed.). London: Sweet & Maxwell, 1971.

Landlord and Tenant   Foà, E.C. *General Law of Landlord and Tenant* (8th ed.), H. Heathcoate-Williams, ed. Ipswich: Thames Bank Publishing, 1957.

Lamont, D.H. *Residential Tenancies.* Toronto: Carswell, 1973.

Rhodes, F.W., ed. *The Canadian Law of Landlord and Tenant* (4th ed.). Toronto: Carswell, 1973.

Woodfall, W. *Law of Landlord and Tenant* (27th ed.). London: Sweet & Maxwell, 1968.

Mortgages   Falconbridge, J.D. *The Law of Mortgages* (3rd ed.). Toronto: Canada Law Book Company, 1942.

Woodard, H. *Canadian Mortgages.* Don Mills, Ont.: Collins, 1959.

7. Forms of Business Organization

Corporations   Beck, S., and D. Johnston. *Cases and Materials on Securities Regulation.* Toronto: Osgoode Hall Law School, York University, 1973-74.

Fraser, W.K. *Fraser's Handbook on Canadian Company Law* (6th ed.), H. Sutherland and D.B. Horsley, eds. Toronto: Carswell, 1975.

Gower, L.C.B. *The Principles of Modern Company Law* (3rd ed.). London: Stevens & Sons, 1969.

Ziegel, J.S., ed. *Studies in Canadian Company Law,* Vol. I. Toronto: Butterworth, 1967.

———. *Studies in Canadian Company Law,* Vol. 2. Toronto: Butterworth, 1973.

Partnership   Drake, C.D. *Law of Partnership.* London: Sweet & Maxwell, 1972. (Based on 15th ed. of *Pollock on the Law of Partnership* by Gower.)

Underhill, A. *Principles of Law of Partnership* (9th ed.), G. Hesketh, ed. London: Butterworth, 1971.

8. Credit Transactions

Bankruptcy   Canada. *Report of the Study Committee on Bankruptcy and Insolvency Legislation, Canada 1970.* Ottawa: Information Canada, 1970.

Houlden, L.W., and C.H. Morawetz. *Bankruptcy Law of Canada*. Toronto: Carswell, 1960; and *Cumulative Supplement*, 1974.

Limitations of Actions　Weaver, E.L. *Limitations,* A.E. Laverty, ed. Toronto: Canadian Law List Publishing Co., 1939.

Mechanics' Liens　Macklem, D.N., and D.I. Bristow. *Mechanics' Liens in Canada* (3rd ed.). Toronto: Carswell, 1972.

Index

X-Y-Z